LET HISTORY JUDGE

The Origins and Consequences of Stalinism

ROY A. MEDVEDEV

LET HISTORY JUDGE

The Origins and Consequences of Stalinism

Translated by
COLLEEN TAYLOR

Edited by
DAVID JORAVSKY,
NORTHWESTERN UNIVERSITY

and by
GEORGES HAUPT,
ÉCOLE PRATIQUE DES HAUTES ÉTUDES

ALFRED A. KNOPF   NEW YORK   1971

THIS IS A BORZOI BOOK
PUBLISHED BY ALFRED A. KNOPF, INC.

Library of Congress Catalog Card Number: 72–136336
International Standard Book Number: 0–394–44645–3

Manufactured in the United States of America

FIRST EDITION

"We need complete, truthful information. And the truth should not depend on whom it is to serve."

—V. I. LENIN

"All revolutionary parties that have perished until now, perished because they became self-satisfied. They could no longer see the sources of their strength and were afraid to talk about their weaknesses. But we will not perish, because we are not afraid to talk about our weaknesses and we will learn how to overcome them."

—V. I. LENIN

"Self-criticism—ruthless, harsh self-criticism, which gets down to the root of things—that is the life-giving light and air of the proletarian movement."

—ROSA LUXEMBURG

"Achieving a greater awareness of the past, we clarify the present; digging deeper into the meaning of what has gone before, we discover the meaning of the future; looking backward, we move forward."

—A. I. HERZEN

Contents

PART THREE

THE CONSEQUENCES OF STALINISM

Editor's Introduction

UP TO NOW scholarly analyses of Stalinism have appeared only outside the Soviet Union, nearly all of them written by non-Communists. With this book, a Soviet Marxist is trying to begin the discussion at home. He submitted the work to a Soviet publisher; it was turned down; so he has authorized publication abroad. The author's motives for writing it in the first place are amply explained in his own introduction, written for the intended Soviet audience. This introduction is primarily for the benefit of outsiders, who may wish to know who the author is, how his analysis of Stalinism compares with previous interpretations, and how this translation compares with the Russian original.

The author is one of twin sons born in 1925 to a Soviet Marxist philosopher, Alexander Romanovich Medvedev, who coined names for his children that were in keeping with the times—as many believers in a revolutionary break with the past were then doing. Roy (or Roi) means "Dig" (the imperative of *ryt'*), and Reis, the original name of his twin, means "A Route." When Reis altered his name for euphonic reasons to Zhores, the brothers seemed to be named for the French Socialist Jaurès and the Indian Communist M. N. Roy, a pleasant coincidence of revolutionary tradition and linguistic innovation.

In the late thirties, when the father was teaching dialectical materialism at the Tolmachev[1] Military-Political Academy, an institution that trained commissars for the Red Army, the terror snatched him away. The sons nevertheless followed his example, both of them becoming scholars with strong social consciences. Zhores is now a distinguished biochemist who has written exposés of tyranny in Soviet intellectual life.[2] (In reprisal, the tyrants dissolved his labora-

[1] N. G. Tolmachev, a Bolshevik who died in the Civil War, not to be confused with the Tolmachev who was expelled from the Party in 1933 and killed by the terror. They may have been brothers. The Academy seems to have been renamed for Lenin when the terror struck it. See below, pp. 155 and 212.
[2] See his *Rise and Fall of T. D. Lysenko* (New York, 1969), and *The Medvedev Papers* (New York, 1971).

tory and had him dragged off to a mental institution, but the protests of fellow scientists won his release and restoration to a laboratory.) Roy, trained in philosophy at Leningrad University, went on to receive a graduate degree in education. After teaching history and serving as a principal of a secondary school, he became a research associate in the Academy of Pedagogical Sciences. He has published two books and many articles, chiefly in the field of vocational training.[3] He is, in short, a scholar with an unusual combination of *Sitzfleisch* and versatility, who has moved from philosophy to pedagogy and has now arrived at history.

The XXth Party Congress in 1956 precipitated Roy Medvedev's involvement in history. That Congress startled the world by opening a campaign against the Stalinist legacy of despotism and terror. Medvedev joined the Party and began an intensive study of Soviet history. When the XXIInd Congress in 1961 reaffirmed the call for de-Stalinization, he began to write this book. But by the time he finished, in 1968, there were growing signs of a reversal. *Kommunist,* the theoretical organ of the Party's Central Committee, published a defense of Stalin, which provoked Roy into sending a long critical letter to the editor. A common act, with very strange results. The letter sent to *Kommunist* appeared in *Posev,*[4] an anti-Soviet journal published in West Germany by an émigré organization that is widely believed to be supported by the CIA and penetrated by the KGB. The émigrés are ready to publish any dissident Soviet manuscripts they get their hands on, whether or not the authors approve, and Soviet authorities are just as ready to punish anyone whose manuscript is published by the émigrés.

This weird cooperation between anti-Soviet émigrés and Soviet vigilantes—perhaps sincerely ideological on both sides, since both genuinely dislike Communist reformers—has a very practical function. It helps to keep alive within the Soviet Union the fear of putting disapproved thoughts on paper. Post-Stalin legal officials have tried to distinguish between permissible criticism and the sort of thing that American vigilantes call subversion, but the distinction can hardly become meaningful as long as the KGB turns criticism into subversion simply by channeling it to the émigrés in West Germany. Because of the letter to *Kommunist* that wound up in *Posev*, Roy Medvedev was expelled from the Party. *Posev* strengthened the case against him by publishing another letter over his name, this one a complete fabrica-

---

[3] See his *Professional'noe obuchebie shkol'nikov na promyshlennom predpriiatii; nekotorye vyvody iz opyta raboty eksperimental'nykh shkol v RSFSR* (Moscow, 1960); translated into German (Berlin, 1962) and Bulgarian (Sofia, 1962). See also his *Voprosy organizatsii professional'nogo obucheniia shkol'nikov* (Moscow, 1963).

[4] 1969, Nos. 6–7; see also the French translation: *Faut-il réhabiliter Staline?* (Paris, 1969).

tion. His angry protest elicited a declaration of scrupulous delicacy from the editors: they refrained from checking the authenticity of names attached to the manuscripts that they printed, for fear, they said, that their inquiries might endanger the authors. Anyhow, they guessed that Medvedev's *disavowal* might be a fabrication, created with the participation of the KGB.[5] That vicious circle is the background of Roy Medvedev's decision, when news of his big manuscript began to spread in the West, to authorize untainted publication, by a Western press with an impeccable reputation in the field of historical scholarship.

The Soviet audience for which this book was written would take for granted many things that may puzzle or annoy outsiders. Stalinism itself is a term that may cause confusion, for many people in the West have only a vague notion of the difference between Stalinism and the Soviet system or Communism in general. Medvedev draws a sharp distinction. He uses Stalinism to mean personal despotism sustained by mass terror and by worship of the despot ("the cult of the personality"), precisely those features of the Soviet system that Stalin's successors repudiated, sometimes calling them crimes but usually brushing them off as "mistakes." Medvedev agrees with the official view in one sense: he regards despotism and terror and the cult as accidental deformations of a fundamentally sound system, mistakes on the part of the Party and the country as a whole. He vehemently denies that they were mistakes on Stalin's part, for Stalin deliberately engineered them. They must be listed among Stalin's crimes, not among his mistakes.

The reader who detects a scholastic odor in such reasoning, or who is simply annoyed by the author's heavy use of the term "mistakes," should bear in mind that this is not Medvedev's personal idiosyncrasy. It is standard Soviet usage, perplexing to outsiders because it tends to confuse miscalculation and misbehavior—being factually wrong and being morally wrong. Medvedev's desire to overcome that confusion is one of the reasons he labors the distinction between Stalin's mistakes and Stalin's crimes.[6] He is less aware of a more serious difficulty: implicit in the constant talk of mistakes is the dubious assumption that there is always a "correct line" in politics, and an associated confusion between two different methods for establishing it, the say-so of unimpeachable authority and the usual rules of reasoned judgment. Medvedev insists on the sovereignty of reason,

[5] The fabrication is in *Posev*, 1970, No. 1. Medvedev's disavowal is in the *New York Times*, April 26, 1970. For the oily reply by *Posev*, see *Le Monde*, May 6, 1970.
[6] See below, p. 343, for Medvedev's objection to the Stalinist tendency to fuse the "objective" and "subjective" aspects of behavior.

but he limits its rule in two important ways. He constantly appeals to Lenin's dicta as unquestionable truth. (There is one important exception: he criticizes Lenin's 1922 recommendation on extra-legal justice.) And he usually fails to consider the perfectly rational, though depressing possibility that human beings in certain situations cannot find the correct line, or, worse yet, that some problems may be insoluble. He is, in short, struggling to clarify the Bolshevik mode of thought, not to abandon it.

The strongest evidence of his difficulty is the book's underlying interpretation, or rather, the bundle of interpretations that keep him in constant tension, struggling to prove them consistent with each other. In this case, his difficulty is a spur to very considerable achievement. His tensely balanced interpretations are as fascinating to the intellect as his vivid extracts from unpublished memoirs are to the imagination. He takes for granted the Marxist rule that the development of state superstructures is determined by the development of socio-economic bases, but he seems to make Stalinism an exception: it was *not* a product of the Soviet social system. He offers brilliant analyses of the conditions, the long-run historical trends, that enabled Stalin to establish despotism, terror, and the cult, but he is anxious to prove that these enabling conditions were not determining causes. He insists that Stalin's criminal plotting was the most important determinant. Stalin created Stalinism.

At first glance this seems to be an ironic triumph of the Stalinist cult over Marxist determinism. The "personality" formerly praised for all good is now blamed for all evil; he still seems endowed with superhuman power to alter history by acts of will. Readers inclined to such criticism should give special attention to the passages, especially in Chapters X and XI, where Medvedev analyzes the historical trends that enabled Stalin to carry out his criminal plot. He argues that Stalin's will was a necessary, not a sufficient, cause of Stalinism. Such readers should also ask themselves whether they do not misunderstand the diversity of Marxist responses to the problem of determinism. Marx can be quoted against himself on this matter, which is hardly surprising, for he was dealing with a fundamental paradox of social science. Patterns of social development are affected, perhaps effected, by individual acts of will, but the converse is also true: individual acts of will are affected, perhaps effected, by patterns of social development.

This paradox raises difficult problems for the moral philosopher as well as for the social scientist, and the reader will see that Medvedev is as intensely involved in moral philosophy—in moralizing, some critics may say—as he is in social science. He is against rigid determinism, above all, because it seems to exculpate Stalin. The only way to prove Stalin guilty, he believes, is to prove that personal despotism and mass terror were caused by, could not have occurred without, Stalin's willing them. To assert that irrepressible historical trends gave rise to despotism and terror strikes Medvedev as a denial of Stalin's responsibility. This may seem a simpleminded confusion of historical causation and moral responsibility, especially to American readers, who are currently learning the intricate problems of assigning personal responsibility to the cogs of a state machine that impersonally destroys multitudes of human beings. But the charge of simpleminded moralizing is clearly inapplicable to the passages where Medvedev examines the involvement of lesser officials and ordinary citizens in the mass crimes of the Stalin era. He shows great sensitivity to the various degrees of moral responsibility of particular individuals, who may approve or oppose or try to look the other way, but cannot stop the carnage. In other words, he applies different moral standards at different levels of the political pyramid. And he is right to do so, if he is also right in his basic assumption about individual will and historical causation: the closer to the apex of the pyramid, the more nearly they are fused. The higher one goes the harder it is to argue, "Don't blame me. If I didn't, someone else would."

Aside from Medvedev's urge to find Stalin guilty, he has strong grounds in Marxist political theory for objecting to the fatalistic view that despotism, terror, and the cult were predetermined by unalterable historical forces. Such a view cuts the nerve of political action. A combination of voluntarism and determinism, the will to act on the basis of realistically appraised historical trends, has been a persistent feature of Marxism, and is one of the main reasons for its recurrent vitality despite repeated indications of imminent extinction. Extreme voluntarism can have the same enervating effect on Marxists as extreme determinism. Whether irresistible power is assigned to impersonal historical forces or to the will of great leaders, the political consequence can be the same mass torpor, a passive waiting for fate to have its way. Stalin himself, in his last years, began to perceive this self-defeating aspect of his cult, and Khrushchev campaigned against it vigorously, though with his usual erratic inconsistency. Khrushchev called for a revival of the kind of Marxism that charges everyone with responsibility to take bold action on behalf of history's inevitable goal. Perhaps that is, as critics have remarked, a secular version of Calvinism, but one should make such a remark without a sneer. The scholar who is trying to revive the grand old faith in this book, at great risk to himself, deserves unalloyed respect. Besides, if we take that historical analogy seriously, we should recall the strangely mixed potential of Calvinism for democracy as well as despotism, "for freest action form'd under the laws divine."

The Western reader who accommodates himself to an unfamiliar conceptual framework and somewhat annoying word usage will discover that Medvedev has achieved a penetrating analysis of Stalinism. To appreciate it fully, one must be aware of the explanations that have been favored by authors outside the Soviet Union. Reflection discloses six basic theories. They rarely appear in such extremely simple, separate form as I will give them here. They are frequently combined with each other in complex ways, and almost always the deterministic motif is muted by a great array of historical particulars. What I am offering is a typology, which resembles the actual theorizing of real authors as the zoologist's taxonomy resembles the essential structures and functions of real animals.

1. The oldest theory holds that despotism is inherent in socialism. Private property is alleged to be the foundation of individual liberty; if it is replaced by collective property, then everyone becomes totally subject to the small group or the individual that gets control of collective property. This argument antedates not only Stalinism but the Bolshevik Revolution. It was an early response to the first proposals for socialism, and is still widely used by defenders of capitalism, who like to hold up Stalinism as the great minatory example.

2. Another venerable theory derives Stalinism from Lenin's program for a tightly disciplined party leading a lower-class revolution. Beginning with the Mensheviks, who charged Lenin with Jacobin and Bonapartist tendencies in the early years of this century, many critics have argued that his program entails the subjection of the lower classes to the vanguard party, of the party to its higher echelons, and, ultimately, of all to a single individual. Recently, advocates of this theory have added a sociological explanation to account for the durability of the Leninist-Stalinist system: it creates a new class of officeholders with a vested interest in maintaining the rigid pyramid of power.

3. Another theory arose concomitantly with Stalinism, as part of a Marxist effort to explain the anomaly of backward Russia leading the way to socialism. The theorist may begin with Trotsky's doctrine of "permanent revolution," or with Stalin's metaphor of world imperialism breaking at its weakest links. In either case, a socialist state is assumed to be irreversibly in charge of a backward country, which must then be forced through a period of "primary accumulation." The huge peasant class must be "proletarianized," and great industrial and military power must be rapidly built up to hold off hostile capitalist powers. In short, the reversal of the sequence that Marx expected—the socialist revolution coming *before* industrialization—obliges the socialist state to

become despotic in order to do the dirty work of capitalism and to do it with special haste.

4. Recently a non-Marxist analogue to number 3 has gained popularity, as many people have noted the extreme difficulties of industrialization in the twentieth century. The prevalence of one-party states and military regimes in backward countries gives rise to the argument that Stalinism is a Communist species of a general type: the backward nation-state trying to force industrialization, while in almost hopeless competition with the nation-states that acquired industrial power in an earlier and easier time. Sometimes internal difficulties are emphasized, such as increases in peasant populations outstripping industrial growth rates; sometimes foreign difficulties, such as the tendency of international terms of trade to move against the sellers of raw materials, and the tendency of capital to flow toward advanced countries. Optimistic versions of this theory echo Herzen's prophecy of Russia moving to freedom through socialism, while the West moves to socialism through freedom. Pessimistic versions predict a widening gap between advanced and backward nations, with a consequent intensification of despotism in the backward states.

5. Extreme pessimists consider Stalinism a species of a more general type. The universal urge to industrialize, with rapidly swelling populations mobilized for nationalist conflict, is seen as a universal push toward totalitarianism. Some emphasize total war and the rise of the garrison state as the chief cause of the process; others stress such internal factors as the technological juggernaut, the population explosion, and "mass culture." In any case, the conclusion is that we are all on the way to highly regimented societies under despotic regimes. Stalinism is seen as an early, extreme, and rather inefficient variety.

6. Some have denied a universal pattern in Stalinism, interpreting it as the product of uniquely Russian traditions, or, at most, of a supposed Asiatic pattern of an amorphous society under a despotic state. This is in effect a continuation of a view that was common among earlier generations of Western observers, who contrasted tsarism, or "Asiatic despotism," with the supposed tradition of constitutional representative government in the West.

Medvedev gives brief consideration to a few versions of these theories toward the end of his book, when he criticizes "bourgeois" and "revisionist" analyses of Stalinism. However, he is not well acquainted with the Western literature on the subject. His thinking is shaped overwhelmingly by Soviet sources, including an array of interpretations that have been circulating by word of mouth. (Another invaluable service of this book is its systematic catalogue of that oral tradition.) Of course, there are unintentional similarities between Soviet and Western thinking on Stalinism. In reviving discussion of "bureaucratic degeneration"—which was a hotly debated issue among Soviet Marxists of the twenties—Medvedev is reviving a Leninist treatment of the historical tendencies that are hypostatized in theories 1, 2, and 6. His comments on the Stalinist aspects of industrialization, collectivization, and the cultural revolution will evoke familiar lines of thought among students of Western monographs on those subjects. In recalling Marx's critique of "barrack socialism" and Gorky's biting characterization of the vindictive revolutionary, Medvedev is discussing socialist reactions to the problem that theory 1 treats from an anti-socialist point of view. Except for theories 4 and 5, which postulate trends that Medvedev has entirely overlooked or ignored, many such coincidental points of correspondence can be discerned between his and Western studies of Stalinism. The most important lies in his insistence that historical trends made Stalinism possible, not inevitable; Stalin's hunger for limitless power was fed by difficulties, not fatalities. Constantly returning to this theme, Medvedev is persistently examining the interaction between individual leaders and the evolving social process, correlating political accident with socio-economic essence, a procedure that historians of all countries and schools will recognize as the fundamental method of their discipline.

Of course, there is a pronounced biographical element in this book, for Medvedev insists that Stalin's criminal character was the main cause of Stalinism. And of course some readers will cavil at the one-sided vehemence of the biography. Olympian detachment comes easily to outsiders. If it is used without Olympian arrogance, it can assist the discussion that Medvedev is trying to start. It is pointless to charge Medvedev with ignoring Stalin's good traits. He argues, with considerable effect, that the traits which have often been praised —the spartan quality of Stalin's private life, the overwhelming will to make "his" country strong, the concern for scholarship and the arts—are further evidence of a fanatical concentration on becoming god.

Useful criticism would focus on the greatest problem that Stalin presents to his biographers: his cagey reticence, which grew the more extreme as he became the man whose every word was law. It is therefore very hard, some would say impossible, to ascertain whether important changes of character accompanied his successive transformations: from Lenin's "wonderful Georgian" in 1913—whose name slipped Lenin's mind in 1915[7]—to the "gray blur" among the revolutionary leaders of 1917, to the chief of the moderates in the mid-twenties, finally, at the age of fifty, to the wild "revolutionary

[7] See below, p. 327.

from above" and the bloodthirsty despot of the thirties. Medvedev tries to get around the paucity of psychological evidence, which becomes crippling precisely during the last and most important transformation, by drawing analogies with the personalities of famous despots and scoundrels of the past. Some of the analogies are quite suggestive, but they are heaped up in such diversity that they finally confuse the issue. It is hard to conceive how Stalin's personality could have contained both Nechaev and Azev, Fouché and Napoleon, Sulla and Nero, Ivan the Terrible and Hitler, all rolled into one.

Perhaps the best way out of the tangle is to note the conspicuous omission of Peter the Great, with whom Stalin liked to be compared. Medvedev denies to Stalin the tribute customarily given to Peter, that he "accelerated the Westernization of barbarous Russia by his readiness to use barbarous methods of struggle against barbarism."[8] Medvedev insists that Stalin intensified barbarism, and critics would be well advised to concentrate on that major problem, Stalin's influence, rather than the relatively minor issue of his psychopathology. With respect to psychology, Medvedev's greatest contribution is his analysis of the upper strata of Soviet society: Party members at various levels, managers and specialists, writers and scholars, who alone might have prevented or stopped their country's descent into utter lawlessness. Instead, they submitted or cooperated, though they were the chief victims after the peasants. The most astonishing aspect of the process is their tendency to worship the man in charge of their torment. Medvedev has studied their mental processes from within, as expressed in a multitude of reminiscences, oral as well as written, self-condemnatory as well as self-justifying. He has produced the first reliable study of one of the most disturbing puzzles in social psychology.

The level of analysis in Medvedev's book is especially remarkable when one considers the background from which it emerges: the official school of thought on Soviet history. Within that school, Stalinism is brushed aside as an anti-Soviet fiction, created by bourgeois and revisionist propagandists to obscure the essential continuity of Soviet development from the Leninist beginnings to the Leninist present. The basic formula enjoined on Soviet historians might add a seventh theory to the foregoing list of six, if it were not so completely anti-intellectual. The history of Bolshevism must be viewed as the utterly admirable record of correct policies formulated by wise leaders and carried out by the virtuous people (*narod*). Anything not admirable must be brushed aside as the mistakes of leaders who proved unworthy of their posts, or ascribed to residues (*perezhitki*) of the prerevolutionary past, or to the influence of foreign enemies. The definition of the admirable and the unadmirable changes from time to time to suit the present policies of current leaders, who are always wholly admir-

[8] Lenin, *Sochineniia,* 4th edn., XXVII, p. 307.

able. Historians must elaborate and illustrate the received truth of the moment; they must not question it.

Medvedev is by no means the first Soviet scholar to challenge this rigid subordination of the historian to the politician. He repeatedly draws on the work of other critical historians, some that have managed to get into print, others as yet unpublished. But it seems fair to say that the present book is the most ambitious effort to date to start an autonomous academic discussion of the most vital issues in Soviet history. His title expresses his central appeal, and throughout the book the reader will find him continually challenging the official school, sometimes derisively, sometimes sorrowfully, always pleading that genuine patriotism requires study of the homeland's failings as well as its accomplishments. The most important failing, he insists, is the imperfect development of a socialist version of constitutional government.[9] By writing and publishing this book he has offered more than historical arguments in favor of constitutionalism. As a pledge of his faith in the triumph of constitutional principles, he has offered himself.

This translation is substantially full and faithful; it is not absolutely complete. The best way to explain that distinction is to tell how the translation was made. First, Georges Haupt and I did preliminary editing of the Russian manuscript. Our main effort was to reduce the number of excessively long quotations and repetitious passages, either by deleting them, if we thought them superfluous, or by summarizing them, if we thought them essential to the author's argument. Colleen Taylor then performed the enormous labor of translation, eliminating some redundant verbiage in the process. Finally I checked her translation against the Russian, making extensive changes as I did so, not so much to correct what I considered errors, as to eliminate still more redundance and to bend the English toward my notions of style. In many places I also altered Georges Haupt's preliminary editing—eliminating or abridging what he had let stand, or restoring what he had marked for deletion. I also checked, corrected, and completed such assertions and references as I thought dubious or incomplete, and I wrote the footnotes indicated by *Ed.* Any criticism of the translation or the editing should therefore be directed against me, the "responsible editor," as the Russians say.

Virtually no liberties were taken with the long extracts that Medvedev has culled from unpublished manuscripts and from archival materials. (He had no access to archives, yet he quotes such finds as a previously unpublished letter of Lenin's, one of Stalin's, and correspondence of the tsarist police concerning Stalin.) These original

[9] See the public letter that Medvedev, together with the physicists Sakharov and Turchin, sent to the Central Committee. An English translation appeared in *Survey*, Summer, 1970.

materials were not only translated in full; an effort was made to find English equivalents for their stylistic idiosyncrasies, prolixity included. In translating quotations from published works, I made the same effort at mimicry. Many quotations from Stalin, for example, and from other Soviet authors who absorbed his heavy, repetitious Russian, are rendered into heavy, repetitious English. When, to take a different example, I found a mixed metaphor in the purple prose of Bukharin's last letter—or in his widow's memorized version of it—I reproduced it in English.

Perhaps Colleen Taylor and I should have attempted the same mimicry in translating Medvedev's prose. We decided not to because we regard him as a contemporary scholar whose work deserves the best English we could give it. His book is not an exotic or antique source that must be translated verbatim to preserve its special flavor. I hope that it will soon be possible for him to publish it at home, so that he can either rebuke the presumptuous liberties we have taken with his style, or streamline the Russian as we have tried to do the English. In any case, the present Russian text is being published along with this translation for the benefit of specialists. They may accuse me of making the style worse rather than better, or of failing to improve it sufficiently, but I am confident that they will not accuse me of omitting or altering anything of substance.

I have corrected a few errors that seemed to me obvious slips of the pen; for example, the statement that Trotsky *began* publication of *Pravda* in 1912, when the author meant to write *ceased*. There were many other places where I felt inclined to insert an editorial note of disagreement with the author, but in almost every case I refrained. I was tempted, for example, to point out an inconsistency in the matter of alternative leadership after Lenin. At the end of Chapter II Medvedev states that the Party was in the tragic position of having no acceptable alternative to Stalin. Toward the end of the book he says that there were many alternatives. But it is not the editor's function to call attention to inconsistencies and dubious arguments; that is the job of the whole community of scholars who are summoned by Medvedev to reasoned discussion. As the editor I felt obliged to complete references that lacked publication data, page numbers, or even titles. In some cases I was able to complete the references; in some I surmised that the works were unpublished; sometimes I was completely baffled. I also made a spot check of the complete references, and corrected such errors as I found. I traced quotations from English, French, and German sources back to the originals and quoted or translated from them instead of Medvedev's Russian versions. I made an exception, however, for Marx and Engels, who are quoted from the Russian.

The editorial notes are mostly explanations and clarifications for the benefit of the reader who is not familiar with Soviet history and terminology. Some terms are used so frequently that they are explained in a separate glossary. Others raised problems by seeming to have exact English equivalents, when in fact they do not. *Administrirovanie*, for example, seems to mean "administration," and that is the way it is rendered in many translations from Soviet Russian. In fact it means something like "rule by fiat," and that is the way it is usually translated here. Using analogous logic, Colleen Taylor translated *diversant* as "subversive," which is indeed the American term that confounds the dissemination of disapproved ideas with acts of treason. In this case I perversely held out for "diversionist," hoping that the American reader will be jarred by the foreign quality of the word into realizing that even Roy Medvedev is not always aware of its ugly ambiguity. Subversive would have been calmly accepted by many Americans as a matter-of-fact description of something genuinely criminal. It is impossible to be completely consistent in such matters. *Inakomysliashchii* (literally: "one who thinks differently") has been translated as "dissident," even though the English word carries a load of historical significance that is lacking in the Russian. The protracted troubles that transformed dissidence from a crime into a right are not yet completed in the Russian-speaking community.

One could go on forever about such problems of translation. I will add only two more, of considerable importance in this history. *Vozhd'* has been translated as "chief" rather than "leader," because *vozhd'*, like chief, has the slightly florid quality of an archaism, and mainly because Soviet Russian makes a distinction between an ordinary leader (*rukovoditel'*) and a *vozhd'* such as Stalin. The single most troublesome word was probably the homely adjective *grubyi*, which Lenin used to describe Stalin when urging his dismissal from the post of General Secretary. "Rude" or "coarse," the usual translations, are too mild to carry the charge that Medvedev puts into the word, which he repeats incessantly. Colleen Taylor and I have used "nasty," "mean," "dirty," or even "vicious," the analogous terms in American political discourse.

Finally, I wish to thank Northwestern University for paying the considerable cost of typing this long book twice, first in Colleen Taylor's translation, then in my edited version. I also wish to make it known that the usual royalties are being set aside for the author in a trust fund.

DAVID JORAVSKY

Evanston, Illinois
June 18, 1971

Glossary

agitprop The Agitation and Propaganda Department of the Party's Central Committee.

aktiv Party members whose full-time occupation is Party work, as contrasted with the part-time, rank-and-file Party members.

apparat The machine, the organization of offices and officeholders; for example, the Party *apparat,* the state *apparat,* and so on. The English expression, "political machine," would be an accurate translation, except that it is pejorative, while *apparat* is not.

apparatchik Member of an *apparat.*

artel' An old form of producers' cooperative among artisans, now chiefly used to describe the contractual relationship of peasants in a collective farm.

cadres The most important members of an organization or institution, those who constitute its nuclei of leaders at various levels. By extension from the term for the skeleton organization of a military unit.

Central Committee or CC A high policy-making and administrative organization of the Communist Party, nominally elected by and responsible to the Party Congress. See Medvedev's text, pp. 43 *et passim,* for its evolving structure and functions.

Central Executive Committee Until 1936 a high policy-making and administrative organization of the Soviet government, nominally elected by and responsible to the Congress of Soviets. In 1936 its place was taken by the Presidium of the Supreme Soviet.

Cheka Acronym for the Extraordinary Committee to Combat Counter-revolution, etc.; the first agency for the administration of terror, 1917–22. Superseded by the OGPU.

Chekist An agent of the Cheka. By extension the honorific term for an agent of any of the subsequent organizations for administering terror or gathering intelligence.

collective farm (kolkhoz) An agrarian producers' cooperative, obliged to make deliveries to the state at prices fixed by the state. Each member receives a share of the net income commensurate with the share of "labor days" he contributes to the collective operations. Members also have private plots around their family homes. Not to be confused with the peasant commune, the *kommuna*, or the state farm (*sovkhoz*).

commune (mir or obshchina) The old form of peasant organization, superseded in the thirties by collective and state farms. Members received the produce of their family allotments, strips of land scattered through the communal fields. Not to be confused with collective farm, *kommuna*, or state farm.

Council of People's Commissars or (since 1946) Council of Ministers The chief administrative agency of the Soviet government.

degeneration (pererozhdenie) Defined by a Soviet dictionary (*Ozhegov*) as "the loss of one's former world view, of one's social cast of mind, through the action of an alien environment or ideology."

intelligentsia In Soviet usage the equivalent of such English terms as professional people or even white-collar workers. But the term still retains, in certain contexts, its prerevolutionary connotation of intellectuals, educated people, the class identified with *obshchestvennost'* (public opinion), a critical view of *vlast'* (the regime) and of the social order.

KGB The Committee of State Security. The chief investigative and intelligence agency of the Soviet government, which was separated from the NKVD some time before the Second World War. First known as the NKGB, then as the MGB, finally, as the KGB.

kommuna The most completely collectivized form of agricultural enterprise. All means of production are held in common and all income is distributed equally. Not to be confused with collective farm (*kolkhoz*), commune (*mir, obschina*), or state farm (*sovkhoz*).

krai A large territorial subdivision of a Soviet republic.

kraikom The Party committee, i.e., the Party's chief organization, in a *krai*.

NKVD or (since 1946) MVD The People's Commissariat or Ministry of Internal Affairs. From 1934 to 1953 the agency for the administration of terror.

oblast A major administrative subdivision of a Soviet republic, comparable to a province or state.

obkom The Party committee, i.e., the Party's chief organization, in an *oblast*.

OGPU The State Political Administration, which administered terror from 1922, when it superseded the Cheka, to 1934, when it was superseded by the NKVD.

Politburo The Political Buro of the Party's Central Committee, the chief policy-making agency.

political (noun) A political prisoner, as contrasted with a criminal. See p. 274 for information on its changing meaning.

Presidium of the Central Committee The name of the Politburo from 1952 to 1966.

Presidium of the Supreme Soviet See Central Executive Committee.

raion Administrative subdivision of an *oblast* or of a city.

raikom The Party committee, i.e., the Party's chief organization, in a *raion*.

repression (repressiia) Officially defined as punishment for crimes against the state or against the socialist order, this term has acquired in Soviet Russian the connotation of extra-legal punishment for nonexistent crimes.

RSFSR The Russian Republic of the Soviet Union.

Secretariat of the Central Committee The chief administrative agency of the Party, headed by the General or First Secretary.

state farm (sovkhoz) A farm run like a factory, paying wages to its workers. Not to be confused with collective farm, commune, or *kommuna*.

wrecker (vreditel') An epithet derived from the word for pest, a creature like a Japanese beetle or a Hessian fly; used to describe those who were allegedly trying to wreck the Soviet state and the socialist order.

Dates are given according to the Julian calendar (Old Style) until February 1 (14), 1918, when the Soviet government adopted the Gregorian calendar (New Style).

Transliteration of Russian words and proper names follows the Library of Congress rules, with the usual unavoidable inconsistencies —e.g., Tomskii but Trotsky, Kondrat'ev but Zinoviev (instead of Zinov'ev), Smolny instead of Smol'nyi. Custom is sometimes stronger than the Library of Congress rules.

Weights and measures are usually given according to the version of the metric system that makes a centner equal a hundred kilos (220 pounds). But Medvedev has the common habit of using the prerevolutionary pood (about 36 pounds) from time to time, especially when he is discussing grain production.

References to Lenin, *Sochineniia*, specify the 3rd or the 4th editions, as the case may be. References to Lenin, *Polnoe Sobranie*, do not bother to specify that this is the 5th edition.

Foreword

THIS BOOK was conceived after the XXth Congress of the Communist Party of the Soviet Union (CPSU) in 1956 and written after its XXIInd Congress in 1961. After the XXth Congress there were many who asked what was the point of stirring up the past, exposing Soviet infirmities to the world and causing our enemies to rejoice. Wasn't it better to keep Stalin's image as it had been presented to the Soviet people in the past? Wasn't it better to concentrate on current problems of Communist construction, leaving the analysis of Stalin's crimes to future historians? In other words, wouldn't it be better to forget about the "multitude of base truths" and preserve the "illusion that uplifts us"?

Even today we hear such questions. However, we now know that Stalin's crimes were so great that it would be a crime to remain silent about them. "The pharisees of the bourgeoisie," Lenin wrote, "like the saying: 'Either be silent about the dead or speak well of them.' But the proletariat needs the truth about all those involved in politics, whether alive or dead. For those who are genuine political leaders live on in politics even after their physical death."[1]

In her book on Stalin, the American journalist Anna Louise Strong makes the following appraisal of the 1930's and 1940's:

> This was one of history's great dynamic eras, perhaps its greatest. . . . It gave birth to millions of heroes and to some devils. Lesser men can look back on it now and list its crimes. But those who lived through the struggle, and even many who died of it, endured the evil as part of the cost of what was built.[2]

Such an appraisal of these tragedies is natural for an ardent follower of Mao Tse-tung, who several years ago took up permanent residence in China and in 1966 was proclaimed an "honorary Red Guard." But we cannot agree with such a judgment.

---

[1] *Sochineniia,* 4th edn., XXXVI, p. 545.
[2] A. L. Strong, *The Stalin Era* (New York, 1956), p. 9. Russian translation (Moscow, 1957), p. 6. *Ed.:* Anna Louise Strong died in Peking in 1970.

Of course, under the conditions prevailing in a backward country such as Russia, it was not only possible but even inevitable that the liquidation of the old society and the building of a new socialist one would be accompanied by petty-bourgeois and anarchistic outbursts, by the violation of revolutionary legality and the abuse of power. Still, these deviations from a correct revolutionary line could have been fewer; it was not inevitable that lawlessness and the abuse of power would become state policy for several decades of our history. What is more, the historical inevitability of petty-bourgeois and anarchistic tendencies is no reason to excuse or to justify them. The true Marxist must fight such shortcomings in his movement as resolutely as possible. He must insistently expose them, in order to avoid them in the future.

Though the crimes and faults of Stalin's era should be criticized and condemned, I have no desire to paint it only in dark colors. It was a time of great accomplishments both at home and abroad. Soviet historians have neglected neither the great dam on the Dnepr nor the metallurgical complex at Magnitogorsk, nor the battles of Stalingrad and Berlin, nor the many other heroic feats of the people. They remain a central theme of Soviet literature and history, and justifiably so. However, we see clearly now that it is impossible to understand our past and our present if we continue to ignore the completely unjustified tragedies that were so abundant in the era of Stalin's cult, if we forget how much Stalin's crimes hampered the development of the Soviet Union and the entire world Communist movement.

The significance of Stalin's cult should not be exaggerated. The history of the Party during those decades cannot be analyzed only in terms of Stalin's crimes and lawlessness. But it would be just as serious an error to ignore or to minimize their grave consequences. We must respect the memory of our fallen fathers and brothers, the hundreds of thousands and millions of people who were the victims of Stalin's lawlessness. For if we are unable to learn all the necessary lessons from this tragedy, then the destruction of an entire generation of revolutionaries and millions of other innocent people will remain nothing more than a senseless catastrophe.

The dangerous effects of Stalin's cult cannot be overcome unless they are discussed openly and honestly. Only by open and honest self-criticism, not by secret instructions through hidden channels, can the Party generate the movement, the feelings, the social indignation capable of destroying all the effects of Stalin's cult and of preventing the revival of new cults and new arbitrary rule.

At its XXth and XXIInd Congresses, the Communist Party resolutely exposed Stalin's crimes and began to restore Leninist norms.

Victims of bloody arbitrary rule were rehabilitated. An extensive critique of the cult of personality began in literature, art, and science. The political atmosphere of the USSR began to be cleansed of the filth of adventurism and despotism. Soviet people could breathe and work more easily.

Nevertheless, none of us can or should forget our past, and not only because the ashes of our tortured fathers and brothers continue to burn in our hearts. Unfortunately, in some socialist countries Communist parties are reviving the same spirit of sectarianism, dogmatism, and lawlessness that did such harm to the Communist movement in the past. Even within the Soviet Union there is a movement to rehabilitate Stalin. Since the spring of 1965, Stalin's name has appeared increasingly often in Soviet journals and newspapers, not as a criminal, but as a "great general," a "great revolutionary," an "outstanding theorist," a "wise statesman" or even a "prudent manager, who knew how to take care of state funds." His name has been mentioned even from official tribunals, and a considerable part of the audience has applauded. Some Party officials openly and proudly call themselves Stalinists, without risking expulsion from the Party. Stalinism is not yet a mere bogeyman, as one of the orators at the XXIIIrd Party Congress tried to argue.

Stalinism remains a real threat, in open as well as disguised forms. Thus it is especially important to continue the discussion that began at the XXth Congress. We must know the whole truth, and not only to prevent the return of that arbitrary rule which the Party has rejected. If we do not study our past, we will be in no condition to move forward in the necessary direction.

"Truth is revolutionary," wrote Antonio Gramsci in a fascist prison. Truth was the main weapon of Lenin and the Leninist party in their struggle for socialism. And this meant truth not only about the enemies of the Revolution but about our own shortcomings and mistakes as well.[3] Of course our enemies try to use our self-criticism to their own advantage. That is one of the more serious consequences of Stalin's cult. But it too can be overcome, not by silence but by a frank explanation of the truth.

Inevitably the study of the genesis of Stalinism creates scholarly and psychological difficulties. A serious disease has left many lesions that have not yet healed. And there are people who tell us "Why pour salt, why rub wounds, if they are still bleeding?" We should not pour salt on unhealed wounds. But it would be naïve to think that they will heal by themselves. We must heal them, and to do this we must know

[3] For Lenin's stress on the need of public discussion of our faults, see his *Sochineniia*, 4th edn., XXXII, p. 453, and XXXIII, p. 70.

the causes and the nature of the disease whose germs survive in the social organism. And pain is unavoidable when healing such deep, numerous, and neglected lesions.

Now as always, we must be responsible and careful. The abuses of the past can be criticized from various standpoints, some of which would lead to completely wrong conclusions. Some people not only in the enemy camp but even in the USSR use criticism of Stalinism to reject what cannot and should not be rejected. Opportunists of all kinds now malign socialism, trying to deny the democratic and humanist nature of the October Revolution. But our response should not be denials or silence regarding the mistakes and crimes of the past. Dogmatic, sectarian preaching will nourish opportunism. Therefore we cannot support those who appeal for caution and restraint as a pretext for stopping or at least toning down criticism and self-criticism.

To expose Stalin's cult politically is not easy. Since the Soviet people knew little about the extent of Stalin's lawlessness, disclosure gave rise to confusion, bewilderment, and disillusionment. Some were pushed into the alien camp, while with others the result was political indifference, loss of ideology, mistrust, and bitterness. Nonetheless, it would be a harmful illusion to believe that these unhealthy reactions could have been avoided by keeping the people in ignorance of the mistakes and crimes of the past.

We live in a big world, in which many political forces contend for men's minds. The truth can never be kept hidden for long; it will always find a way to people's hearts and minds. And it would be infinitely more difficult if the Soviet people learned the truth about Stalin's crimes from some other source than its own Communist Party, in which it has shown such great trust.

Stalin's cult of personality cannot be reduced to political murders and the boundless adulation of a single man. The prolonged period of terror had a great influence on the ideological life of the Party, on the country's literature and art, on the natural and social sciences, on the psychology and ethics of the Soviet people, on the methods of governing the Party and the state, on the union of the workers and the peasants, on the way that tens of millions think and behave. Therefore it is not surprising that throughout the world an intense ideological struggle has been waged concerning the problems that we call for short the "cult of personality," a term that is not very apt. And if we should now recoil from a profound and comprehensive examination of Stalin's era, "lest we delight our enemies," we would only achieve the opposite result. We would in fact be surrendering a huge, important terrain of ideological conflict without a battle, allowing bourgeois propagandists to derive further profit from our mistakes and difficulties. The longer we keep silent or vacillate, the more successfully will bourgeois propagandists use the cult of personality for their own ends. Communists cannot bury their heads in the sand, trying not to notice what was and what still is bad in their political and social life. We must soberly and dispassionately investigate these difficult problems of the Communist movement. We must say openly that Marxism-Leninism will cease to be a scientific study of society if it does not find within itself the strength and the ability not only to describe but also to explain the complex political, economic, and social processes in socialist countries. At a certain stage in the development of these countries, those processes led to the degeneration and the bureaucratization of part of the state and Party apparatus; in some cases, they wrought monstrous perversions. A genuine Marxist-Leninist should be able to analyze the faults as well as the achievements of modern socialist systems, and he should learn how to do this with the same scientific conscientiousness and boldness that Communists have applied to presocialist systems.

Some will claim that the imperialists, pinning their hopes on a split of the Communist movement into Stalinists and anti-Stalinists, support every critic of Stalin's cult of personality. But that is far from the truth. Our enemies support slanderers who use criticism of Stalin to discredit socialism, communism, and Marxism-Leninism. Our ideological opponents cannot support those Communists who criticize Stalinism in order to invigorate the Communist movement, to make the ideas of socialism and communism more attractive to the masses of the world. It is in fact the defenders of Stalin and his methods of "leadership" who are now playing into the hands of imperialist propagandists. And only resolute and honest *Communist* self-criticism, and resolute and honest correction of Stalinist perversions, will cut the ground from under bourgeois propagandists, who have long used these perversions in their fight against socialism. By identifying the Stalinist regime with socialism in general, they have long tried (and not without success) to represent socialism as a system in which there is no respect for law, where the rights and freedom of the individual are violated and suppressed. Silence and vacillation about Stalin's many crimes repel rather than attract friends abroad.

Lenin wrote that the Soviet land will further the development of the world socialist revolution largely by the successes of its economic and cultural development. But at the present time it is impossible to ignore the fact that the attention of the masses and the intelligentsia of the world is not focused only on our country's achievements in cultural and economic development. They pay much closer attention to the development of democratic tendencies in Soviet society and to the correction of the shortcomings and faults of the recent past.

"What was hurt under Stalin," asks Ilya Ehrenburg, "the idea or people? Not the idea," the writer replies. "It was not the idea that was stricken. It was people of my generation that were stricken."[4] That is not true. In reality, for millions of people the very idea of socialism was damaged. It is our job to restore the idea of socialism by undoing the results of the cult of personality. Above all, we must eliminate in ourselves the most dangerous consequence of the cult—fear of speaking the truth.

We talk a great deal about educating youth in the traditions of revolution and battle, of conscientious labor, of the fight against capitalism and resistance to bourgeois propaganda. But it is no less important to encourage implacable resistance to injustice and arbitrary rule, to lying and bureaucratism. We should encourage initiative, independence, political awareness, and responsibility. Not one of these qualities can be developed if the truth is hushed up. If we dodge the questions asked by the young, we will inevitably alienate them. Of course many of our students will manage to find their own way to the truth even without our help. But hypocrisy, political indifference, and cynicism are spreading among other sections of our young people. Thus we have every reason to declare that the Leninist revolutionary spirit will be fostered in our youth by books that reveal certain ugly pictures of our past truthfully, and from correct Party positions, much more than by books that deliberately conceal our difficulties or errors.

In recent years the Chinese and Albanian press has repeatedly demanded that our Party restore the political "reputation" of Stalin. In 1963 the Peking *People's Daily* wrote that the attitude toward Stalin was the "demarcation line" between true Marxist-Leninists and contemporary revisionists. When it refused to participate in the XXIIIrd Congress of the CPSU, the Chinese Communist Party, in its letter of March 22, 1966, again asserted that our Party, by attacking Stalin, was attacking Marxism-Leninism, the Soviet Union, China, Communist parties, and Marxist-Leninists of all countries. Admittedly, at the beginning of the cultural revolution the Chinese press changed some of its former pronouncements on this "demarcation line." In an article of July 11, 1966, *People's Daily* declared that "the ideas of Mao Tse-tung are the apogee of Marxism-Leninism of our time"; support of Mao or opposition to him is "the dividing line between Marxism-Leninism and revisionism, between the revolution and the counter-revolution." Even today, however, the Chinese press, while heaping boundless praise on the ideas of Mao Tse-tung, continues to praise the "services" of Stalin also. That is another reason this book was written. Let the facts show who are genuine Marxist-Leninists, those who are openly the defenders and heirs of Stalin's cult or those who wish to eliminate the cult and its aftereffects once and for all.

Some who have been kind enough to review this work have said that it examines Stalin's activity in a partisan spirit, solely from a

[4] *Novyi mir*, 1962, No. 5, p. 154.

negative standpoint. We recognize the justice of this opinion. This work is indeed one-sided, and not only because what is negative in Stalin's deeds far outweighs what is positive. This book is not a history of a certain period in the life of our country or Party. It could be called the "history of a disease," to be precise the history of that serious and prolonged disease which has been termed the "cult of personality" after one of its symptoms (by no means the chief one). Naturally we will be concerned only with facts related to the origins and the course of this disease. This does not mean that we wish to depreciate other facts and other phenomena. All the same, one cannot help observing that hundreds and thousands of books have been written about those other facts, about the positive aspects of our history. Many of those books are undoubtedly of value. But historical scholarship cannot examine the past only from the bright side. In this discipline there is also room for works that analyze the darker pages of the past. Unfortunately, as Victor Hugo remarked, history does not have a wastebasket.

It is also natural that the author's attention should be focused on Stalin. But this book is not a biography of Stalin; it was not written about him alone. Although his rise to power was not inevitable, it did reflect certain tendencies that existed in our country and our Party before the period of terror and then flourished because of Stalin. However great the role of Stalin himself may have been in the tragic events we describe, one cannot help seeing that he relied on certain people and on certain historically determined political and economic conditions.

Socialist revolutions can develop along various paths. It is mistaken to imagine that Stalin knew how to lead his people to socialism by a road that was difficult, even bloody, but nevertheless very short. By his crimes Stalin did not help, he hindered, he did not accelerate, he slowed the people's movement to socialism and communism in the Soviet Union and in the whole world. In some respects Stalin even turned this movement backward.

The world Communist movement still contains a variety of possibilities and tendencies. Many forces are pushing that movement onto a wrong road full of new tragedies, new dangerous gambles, adventures, new cults of personality. The road to disaster can be by-passed only if the dogmatists and sectarians can be confronted with the united will of the Communists of all countries, a will guided by a clear understanding of the enormous damage done to the world Communist movement by the arbitrary rule and the crimes of the cult of personality.

The problem of sources is critical. Not all the documents in Soviet archives are accessible for unclassified historical research. Moreover, many documents on the history of the Party, including those connected with Stalin's activities, have been destroyed. According to S. M. Dubrovskii, as early as 1924 Stalin ordered his assistant I. P. Tovstukha to go through the archives of the Central Committee and destroy all "useless" (*nenuzhnyi*) material. In the thirties when leaders were arrested their personal papers were usually destroyed. Even many of Lenin's letters vanished in this way. Numerous documents vanished from the archives of Gorky, Krupskaia, Ordzhonikidze, and other prominent leaders. Some documents disappeared from the archives of the Central Committee and from Stalin's personal archives just after his death, when these and other archives were still controlled by the Minister of State Security—that is, by Lavrentii P. Beria. Besides, it is now known that throughout the period of Stalin's cult, historical documents were deliberately falsified.

After the XXth Party Congress in 1956, the Central Committee ordered a careful investigation of Kirov's murder, which precipitated the mass repression of the late thirties. The findings of the special commission created for this purpose have not yet been made public. At the same time, all the materials relating to the political trials of 1935–38 were re-examined, proving that most of the accusations were false. Nevertheless, apart from a short notice to that effect at the All-Union Conference of Historians in 1962,[5] nothing new has been published about those trials. Neither have the court records in the cases of Beria (1953) and his chief henchmen—Abakumov *et al.* in Leningrad, Rukhadze *et al.* in Tbilisi, Bagirov *et al.* in Baku. All this naturally makes the historian's job very difficult.

Of course there is a considerable historical and political literature about Stalin and his era; indeed, it was already massive during his lifetime. But this literature is uneven in quality. For example, all the apologetics about Stalin and his "labors," which appeared in huge quantities during the years of the cult, have practically no scholarly value. And foreign bourgeois literature about Stalin and the history of the CPSU has little value. For all their show of objectivity, bourgeois historians analyze Stalin's crimes from plainly anti-Soviet viewpoints. They use the crimes not so much to discredit Stalin as to defame the ideas of socialism and communism. And many foreign publications mix invention and rumors, factual inaccuracies and distortions, in their accounts of Stalin's real crimes and mistakes. I am not even speaking here of the writings of White émigrés; most of them are filled with such blind malice against everything Soviet that they are incapable of a scholarly analysis of our reality. Tendentiousness and one-

---

[5] *Ed.*: For the record of the conference, see *Vsesoiuznoe soveshchanie o merakh uluchsheniia podgotovki nauchno-pedagogicheskikh, kadrov po istoricheskim naukam, 18–21 dekabria 1962 g.* (Moscow, 1964). Hereafter referred to as *Vsesoiuznoe soveshchanie istorikov.*

sidedness are also characteristic of émigré Trotskyite writings about Stalin and his time.

This work is based on the numerous Soviet publications that have followed the policy of the XXth and XXIInd Party Congresses in examining Stalin's cult honestly and truthfully. I have also used many unpublished manuscripts—documents, memoirs, and eyewitness accounts—belonging for the most part to older Party members who survived the lawlessness of the 1930's and 1940's. These sources are especially important because many of Stalin's illegal orders and actions were not recorded in any documents during his lifetime. Some of the manuscripts I have used report deathbed testimony passed on to Party comrades in Stalinist camps and prisons. In the tortuous journey of such testimony, sometimes measured in decades, distortions and inaccuracies were inevitable. But it would be irreverence to the dead to cast aside their testimony as unreliable or unobjective, instead of carefully compiling and comparing their various accounts.

I would like to thank the following old Bolsheviks who placed valuable historical documents and memoirs at my disposal: I. P. Gavrilov, S. O. Gazarian, L. M. Portnov, E. P. Frolov, A. M. Durmashkin, S. I. Berdichevskaia, D. Iu. Zorina, P. I. Shabalkin, A. V. Snegov, A. E. Evstaf'ev, Ia. I. Drobinskii, A. I. Todorskii, B. I. Ivanov, S. B. Brichkina. I also wish to express gratitude to the following people, who, along with many other comrades, helped me with their documents and comments: I. G. Ehrenburg, V. A. Kaverin, M. P. Iakubovich, L. P. Petrovskii, Iu. Kariakin, D. I. Lev, I. Nikolaev.

Naturally I also made use of the many materials on Party history published before the period of Stalin's cult, and also of the stenographic records of Party congresses and conferences and of plenary meetings of the Central Committee. The study that resulted is to a certain extent private research. I am not an historian by profession and have never worked in research institutions that study historical or political problems. I have not used the materials of any state or Party archives, of any "special collection" or other limited-access depositories. Although over the past six years I have repeatedly informed many official agencies of the nature and content of this work, I have received neither help nor instructions from these or from any other organizations or institutions. By the same token, I have not encountered any obstructions or difficulties on the part of official agencies during the course of the research.

The first drafts of this book were called *Before the Court of History (Pered sudom istorii)*. This title was criticized as being too pretentious. Historical scholarship is only beginning a genuine study of the period of Stalin's cult. I was told that I am still too subjective, that I am judging Stalin in a party court rather than in the tribunal of history, which will give its evaluation in the future, not only of individual personalities but also of all the parties and movements of our time. Therefore I have decided to call the book *Let History Judge,* or *Toward the Court of History* (*K sudu istorii*). I hope that future historians will not overlook the material I have collected and the judgments I have made. However inadequate historical scholarship may be when directed to the recent past, the available facts are enough to obtain a basically correct understanding of the origins of Stalinism, to show the historical conditions and political mistakes that made for all these deviations from the correct Marxist-Leninist revolutionary line.

In conclusion, the author wants to emphasize once again that it is Communists who should be the strictest judges of their own history. Otherwise it will be impossible to restore the unity, moral purity, and strength of this great movement. And that has been the prime motive of my work, which in all respects has been far from easy.

ROY A. MEDVEDEV

Moscow, 1968

Part One

STALIN'S

USURPATION

OF POWER

I

Stalin as Party Chief

1

AFTER THE XXth and XXIInd Party Congresses, Soviet historians put an end to the legend that Stalin was the best and most talented of Lenin's pupils, his favorite comrade in arms, who never deviated or vacillated from Lenin's general line. Of course, Stalin cannot be denied some credit for services to the Party both in the prerevolutionary period and afterward. From his earliest participation in the revolutionary movement, Stalin displayed such great energy, organizational ability, and single-minded will that he was soon given an important position. But other pages of Stalin's political biography are not so splendid.

The impression should not be created that Stalin's activity consisted only of crimes and mistakes. It was Stalin who perfected the art of classifying his opponents' mistakes in such a way as to ignore their services and to stress not only their real mistakes but also imaginary ones, until it became difficult to understand how such people could have been among Lenin's closest colleagues in the Party leadership. In the pre-Stalin period of the Party's development, the truth was almost always determined by means of argument. Disagreements were overcome by discussion and controversy—that was not the exception but the rule. So when I discuss the many disagreements between Lenin and Stalin, it is not to condemn Stalin for them. I only want to show that many of Stalin's negative traits had already appeared, such as boorishness and self-importance, pathological conceit and callousness, mistrust and stealth, an inability to take the criticism of his comrades, and a craving for influence and power.

Those defects were no secret to many members and leaders of the Party. Even today, among old Bolsheviks of Georgia and Azerbaijan, stories are told of young Dzhugashvili's nastiness toward his Party comrades, his mother, his family, and his acquaintances. When on the Batum Committee of the Party, Stalin was capable not only of cursing a fellow committeeman but even of throwing a stool at him. When he was arrested and exiled to eastern Siberia in 1903, Stalin cursed a fellow exile simply because the other man had become upset upon receiving bad news from home.

During the Revolution of 1905, Stalin was a "practical" leader. He organized a number of demonstrations, strikes, and underground presses, and took part in several armed expropriations. However, he also devoted attention to theoretical problems, as can be seen from his articles in Georgian Bolshevik newspapers. Later, in the foreword to his collected works, Stalin himself pointed out a number of serious errors he made during this time. He took an incorrect position on the agrarian question when he opposed Lenin's program of land national-ization. He also believed at that time that the victory of socialism was impossible in countries where the proletariat did not constitute a majority of the population. Stalin writes indulgently about these mis-takes, attributing them to "a young Marxist who had not yet acquired the final shape of a Marxist-Leninist."[1] The clear implication of this statement is that subsequently he made no more mistakes, which is of course far from the truth.

After the Revolution of 1905, Stalin assumed a conciliatory atti-tude toward attacks on the philosophy of Marxism and vacillated in the struggle against *otzovism* and liquidationism.[2] Before the Prague Conference in 1912, he sneered at Lenin's agitation against these devi-ations: "What is the source of this tempest in a teapot?" he wrote to Mikha Tskhakaia. ". . . 'Philosophical' disagreements? Tactical dis-agreements? Questions of organizational policy (relationships with the left Mensheviks, etc.)? The self-esteem of various 'egos'? . . . Our Party is not a religious sect, it cannot divide into groups on the basis of philosophical tendencies."[3]

In 1909, following the arrest of S. G. Shaumian, Stalin persuaded the Baku Party Committee to adopt a special resolution on the dis-agreements within the editorial board of the main Bolshevik news-paper, which was then the central political organization led by Lenin. Though supporting the ideological position of the Leninist majority on

---

[1] Stalin, *Sochineniia,* I, p. xi.
[2] *Ed.: Otzovism* was the view that the Bolsheviks should recall (*otozvat'*) their deputies in the newly created national legislature (the Duma) and concentrate solely on underground preparation for a new revolution. Liquidationism was the opposite belief of moderate Marxists, who wanted to liquidate all underground organizations and concentrate on legal forms of political activity.
[3] See S. Shaumian, *Sochineniia,* I, p. 267; I. Dubinskii-Mukhadze, *Ordzhonikidze* (Moscow, 1964), pp. 92–93.

the editorial board, the Baku Committee's resolution, which was written by Stalin himself, sharply opposed Lenin's organizational policy: "The Baku Committee protests against any 'ejection from our midst' of those who support the minority of the editorial board."[4] The newspaper replied with a special article, written by Lenin, in which he rebutted the charge that his organizational policy was "splitting" the Party.[5]

Stalin clearly did not understand the essence of the decisions that the Prague Conference adopted on the liquidationists; he stubbornly called for greater concessions to them. Stalin also sharply deviated in editing *Pravda*. Though Lenin demanded that the workers be given an honest and straightforward exposé of liquidationist demagogy, Stalin, in his first article as editor of *Pravda*, called for unity "at all costs," a unity of Bolsheviks and liquidationists "without distinction as to factions."[6] In further defiance of Lenin, Stalin endorsed a proposed boycott of the 1912 elections to the Duma. He called the Bolshevik rejection of the boycott an "accidental deviation from the old Bolshevism." "But does it follow," Stalin wrote in a letter, "that we must 'go the limit' in these accidental deviations, making a mountain out of a molehill? . . . Lenin somewhat overestimates the importance of such [legal] organizations" as the Duma.[7]

Stalin's lack of restraint and good manners, his nastiness, were frequently displayed during his exile in Turukhanka. For example, R. G. Zakharova (*née* Rose Brontman), the wife of the Bolshevik Philip Zakharov, who was in Turukhanka from 1903 to 1913, recalls her husband's account of Stalin's arrival in 1912:

> It was an unwritten law that each new arrival would report on the situation in Russia. And whom would you expect to give a more interesting and profound elucidation of what was happening in far-off Russia, left so long ago, than a member of the Bolshevik Central Committee? A group of exiles, among them Ia. M. Sverdlov and Philip, were at that time working on construction [of a home] in the village of Monastyrskoe. . . . Stalin was to arrive there soon. Dubrovinskii was no longer alive. Philip, who was not inclined by nature to set up idols for himself and who, moreover, had heard Dubrovinskii's unbiased evaluation of the leading revolutionary activists of the time, was not especially delighted over Stalin's impending arrival. Sverdlov, on the contrary, . . . tried to do everything possible under the conditions to give Stalin a grand welcome. They prepared a separate room for him, saved up some food for him from their

[4] See Stalin, *Sochineniia*, II, p. 168.
[5] *Proletarii*, Oct. 3 (16) 1909, No. 49. *Ed.*: The chief point in dispute was whether those who disagreed with Lenin's ideology should be driven out of the Bolshevik Party.
[6] See V. T. Loginov, *Lenin i "Pravda," 1912–1914 godov* (Moscow, 1962).
[7] *Voprosy istorii KPSS*, 1965, No. 2, p. 39.

very scanty provisions. He arrived! He entered the room prepared
for him and . . . didn't show his face again! Nor did he deliver a
report on the situation in Russia. Sverdlov was very upset. . . . Stalin
was sent to his assigned village, and soon it transpired that he had
seized for himself all of Dubrovinskii's books. But before his arrival,
the exiles had reached a general understanding that Dubrovinskii's
library would in his memory be considered the property of everyone,
a sort of circulating library. What right had one man to take it?
Hot-tempered Philip went to get an explanation. Stalin "received"
him more or less as a tsarist general would receive an ordinary
soldier who dared to appear before him with a demand. Philip was
indignant (as was everyone!), and the impression of that conversation stayed with him for the rest of his life. He never changed his
unflattering opinion of Stalin.[8]

Stalin behaved no better at the town of Kureika, where he was
sent to finish his term of exile. Here he quarreled with almost all the
exiled Bolsheviks, including Sverdlov. "There are two of us," wrote
Sverdlov at the beginning of his exile when he was still in Turukhanka.
"With me is the Georgian Dzhugashvili, an old acquaintance. He's a
good guy, but too much of an egoist in everyday life."[9] However, after
he had lived with Stalin for some time, Sverdlov began to refer to him
in harsher terms. "A comrade is with me," Sverdlov wrote of Stalin
in May, 1914, when they were in Kureika. "We know each other quite
well. Nevertheless, saddest of all, in conditions of exile, of prison, a
man is stripped and all his little parts are revealed. . . . Now my comrade and I are living in different apartments, and rarely see each
other."[10]

Stalin's conflict with Sverdlov and other Bolsheviks continued also
after Stalin had been transferred to the village of Monastyrskoe and
even when many exiles, including Stalin himself, had received notices
of military induction. The old Bolshevik B. I. Ivanov, who was then
living in exile at Turukhanka, recalls the episode in his memoirs:

> The departure of the twelve wagons [of draftees] was a great event
> for Monastyrskoe. Departure for the army should have made
> Dzhugashvili and A. A. Maslennikov reasonable, made them see the
> need to revive comradely relations with the majority of the colony
> of political exiles. This was necessary also from the point of view of
> Party organization. But neither Dzhugashvili nor Maslennikov tried
> to do this, and there was no one else on their side. Spandarian died
> in the Krasnoiarsk hospital in September, and after his death Vera
> Schweitzer evidently lived in Krasnoiarsk, so that Maslennikov and

[8] The reminiscences of R. G. Zakharova were published in part in Iu. Trifonov,
Otblesk kostra (Moscow, 1966), pp. 47–48.
[9] K. T. Sverdlova, *Ia. M. Sverdlov* (Moscow, 1960), p. 199. *Ed.*: The Russian word
for individualist, a pejorative in Sverdlov's usage, has been translated "egoist."
[10] Ia. M. Sverdlov, *Izbrannye proizvedeniia*, I (1957), pp. 276–77.

Dzhugashvili represented a tiny minority of the exile community, if you don't count the anarchists, members of the Polish Socialist Party, and the Menshevik Toponogov, who inclined toward their side. When Dzhugashvili arrived at Monastyrskoe from Kureika, he stayed with Maslennikov and as before kept aloof from all the other political exiles. He did not resume Party ties with the two members of the Russian Buro of the Central Committee who were there, Sverdlov and [F.] Goloshchekin, or with the leading members of the Party underground. . . . The necessary reconciliation did not take place. Dzhugashvili remained as proud as ever, as locked up in himself, in his own thoughts and plans. . . . As before, he was hostile to Sverdlov, and would not move toward reconciliation, although Sverdlov was prepared to extend the hand of friendship, and was willing to discuss problems of the workers' movement in the company of the three members of the Russian Buro of the Party's Central Committee.

Stalin's behavior in exile at Turukhanka was indirectly censured in the Russian Buro of the Central Committee, which maintained general leadership of Party work up to Lenin's return to Russia. On March 12, 1917, Stalin, M. K. Muranov, and L. B. Kamenev returned from exile to Petrograd. On the same day a meeting of the Buro was held. The minutes of that meeting contain the following item:

> Next the question of comrades Muranov, Stalin, and Kamenev was decided. The first was invited by a unanimous vote [to join the Buro]. Concerning Stalin, it was reported that he had been an agent of the Central Committee in 1912, and therefore it would be advisable to have him as a member of the Buro of the Central Committee. However, in view of certain personal characteristics, the Buro decided to give him only a consulting vote. As for Kamenev, in view of his behavior at the trial [that is, the trial of the Bolshevik deputies of the Duma described below, p. 42] and in view of the resolutions passed in Siberia and in Russia, it was decided to add him to the staff of *Pravda* if he offers his services, but to demand from him an explanation of his behavior. His articles are to be accepted for *Pravda,* but he is not to get a by-line.[11]

However, on the following day Stalin was made a member of the Buro. On the same day the Buro named the editorial board of *Pravda*: M. S. Ol'minskii, Stalin, K. S. Eremeev, M. I. Kalinin, and M. I. Ul'ianova. Once he was on the board, Stalin in fact seized control of the paper. On March 15 *Pravda* was already listing Stalin, Kamenev, and Muranov as editors. The other members of the editorial board, who had been named by the Buro, were not even mentioned. As a result of Stalin's activity, the Buro on March 17, 1917, adopted

[11] Central Party Achive, Institute of Marxism-Leninism (*F.* 17, *op.* I., *ed. khr.* 385, *l.* 11).

another resolution, proposed by Ol'minskii: "The Buro of the Central Committee and the Petrograd Committee, while protesting the annexationist procedure by which Comrade Kamenev was placed on the editorial board, postpone the question of his behavior and his participation in the editorial board of *Pravda* until the next Party conference."[12]

Once they had taken over *Pravda,* Stalin and Kamenev began to publish articles and other material that did not reflect Lenin's line on the basic problems of the revolution but actually contradicted that line. The arbitrary rule of Stalin and Kamenev reached the point where they refused to print three of Lenin's four "Letters from Afar." The one they did publish appeared in a distorted and abridged form.[13] In fact, during the second half of March and the beginning of April, *Pravda* under Stalin and Kamenev took a semi-Menshevik position on many important questions. The paper then came out in favor of putting "pressure" on the Provisional Government rather than overthrowing it, and of uniting with the Mensheviks. Stalin declared outright that the "petty" differences with the Mensheviks could be overcome within a single Party. Moreover, in his speech at the All-Russian Conference of Party Officials, which met in Petrograd from March 27 to April 2, 1917, Stalin made a clearly incorrect evaluation of the "dual power" (the simultaneous existence of the Provisional Government and the Soviets). Not only did he fail to urge complete Bolshevik mistrust of the Provisional Government; he even called for support of the Provisional Government "as long as it aids the progress of the revolution."[14] Even after Lenin's return to Russia, Stalin and Kamenev continued for some time to oppose his celebrated April theses. The theses were published in *Pravda* on April 7, and on April 8 the paper carried an article by Kamenev that, with Stalin's complete support, harshly and dogmatically criticized Lenin's brilliant ideas. When Lenin reached Petrograd, he was obliged to make decisive changes in the line that Stalin and Kamenev had established for *Pravda.*

Before the VIth Party Congress in July, 1917, Stalin committed a number of errors in evaluating the current situation and even tried to conceal important theses of Lenin's from the Party activists. (Lenin, outlawed by the Provisional Government, was hiding in Finland.) Party officials in Petrograd knew of the existence of Lenin's theses. On July 16, 1917, when Stalin spoke to the Second Petrograd Conference of Bolsheviks, a group of dissatisfied delegates demanded that

[12] *Ibid., l.* 26.
[13] See N. Krutikova, *Na krutom povorote* (Moscow, 1965).
[14] *Voprosy istorii KPSS,* 1962, No. 5, p. 112 and *passim; Voprosy istorii,* 1966, No. 2, p. 67 and *passim.*

Lenin's theses be read into the record. In reply to this demand, according to the minutes of the Conference, "Stalin reported that he did not have these theses with him, but that they could be summed up in three propositions: 1) the counterrevolution was victorious, 2) . . . [RM: illegible], 3) 'All power to the Soviet' is, under present circumstances a quixotic slogan; power must be transferred to classes, not to institutions."[15] So it was with Stalin's active participation that the Conference practically rejected the theses that Lenin had prepared for the forthcoming VIth Congress.

Stalin also made a number of errors in his report to the VIth Party Congress. He declared that during the July days[16] the Bolsheviks had been isolated; that, were it not for the war, it would be utopian to raise the question of a socialist revolution in Russia; and that Lenin's slogan "All power to the Soviets" meant a bloc ranging from Social Revolutionaries to Bolsheviks. Stalin did not take a correct position on the Provisional Government's order that Lenin appear before a court for trial. Stalin thought it possible for Lenin and the other indicted leaders to appear before the court of the counterrevolutionary bourgeoisie, if guarantees of safety were given, and if the authorities would have "some honor." Stalin's proposal met with resolute opposition from most delegates at the VIth Congress. "The resolution Stalin put forward," said N. A. Skrypnik, "includes a condition by which our comrades could end up in a republican prison—after all, prison is a guarantee of safety. I think that the resolution should be based on a different proposition: we will not surrender our comrades to the class-oriented, prejudiced court of the counterrevolutionary band." M. M. Volodarskii concurred: "One point of Stalin's resolution is unacceptable—an honorable bourgeois court." As a result of this opposition, Stalin's proposal was rejected. By an overwhelming majority and then unanimously, the Congress adopted the resolution that N. I. Bukharin proposed on this issue.

The problem of Stalin's behavior and political position in the decisive days and weeks of October, 1917, is not yet sufficiently clear. During the years of the cult, historical analyses of the October Revolution invariably asserted that, while Kamenev and Zinoviev opposed the armed insurrection and Trotsky wavered badly, Stalin was virtually the main practical leader, Lenin's closest aide, the second supreme chief and demiurge.

[15] As quoted by Dr. A. L. Fraiman, at the All-Union Scholarly Conference on the History of the October Revolution (Nov. 13–16, 1962, in Leningrad). See *Lenin i Oktiabr'skoe vooruzhennoe vosstanie v Petrograde* (Moscow, 1964), p. 44.

[16] *Ed.*: A few weeks before the VIth Congress, armed supporters of the Provisional Government dispersed an armed demonstration of Bolsheviks.

Original documents and the memoirs of participants do not support this tale. The sources show that during the decisive days of September and October, 1917, when Lenin was urging immediate preparation for an insurrection, *Pravda,* edited by Stalin, did not carry some of Lenin's articles or else cut entire paragraphs from them. This behavior on the part of *Pravda,* along with a certain "moderation" in the upper echelons of the Party, provoked sharp protests from Lenin; he even began to communicate with Party organizations over the head of the Central Committee. In October, 1917, Lenin wrote to the Central Committee, the Petrograd Committee, the Moscow Committee, and to Bolshevik members of the Petrograd and Moscow Soviets, insisting that it would be a crime to postpone the insurrection until the Second Congress of Soviets might approve it, that undue respect for parliamentarianism was inconsistent with revolution, and that his protests on this crucial matter were being covered up. He finally felt obliged to submit his resignation from the Central Committee in order to get the freedom to agitate among the lower ranks of the party.[17]

On October 10, 1917, the Central Committee, following a speech by Lenin, resolved to prepare for an armed insurrection without delay. Only Kamenev and Zinoviev voted against this resolution. On October 11, Lenin's resolution was adopted by the citywide Conference of Petrograd Bolsheviks. On October 16 it was endorsed by an expanded meeting of the Central Committee. Kamenev and Zinoviev, opposing Lenin's line on an armed insurrection, took an unprecedented step: they published in the semi-Menshevik paper *Novaia Zhizn'* a declaration of their disagreement with the resolution of the Central Committee. By that action they handed the Bolsheviks' plans to the enemy. Lenin sharply condemned this "strikebreaking" and demanded that Kamenev and Zinoviev be expelled from the Party. Stalin acted in a completely different way. Without the approval of the Central Committee, he published a statement by Zinoviev attempting to refute Lenin's accusations. Stalin added a comment "from the editorial board," which defended Kamenev and Zinoviev. "We in our turn," wrote Stalin, "express the hope that, with Comrade Zinoviev's statement (and also Comrade Kamenev's statement in the Soviet), the matter can be considered closed. The harsh tone of Comrade Lenin's article does not alter the fact that essentially we remain of one mind."[18] This comment, published without the knowledge of the other members of the editorial board, in the newspaper that was the central organ of the Party, shocked many members of the Central Committee. At a Central Committee meeting held on the same day, Sverdlov read Lenin's letters demanding the expulsion of Kamenev and Zinoviev.

[17] Lenin, *Polnoe sobranie,* XXXIV, pp. 280–83, 340–41, and *passim.*
[18] *Rabochii put',* 1917, No. 41.

The only one who spoke against this demand was Stalin.[19] When he was criticized he offered his resignation, which the Central Committee did not accept.

On the morning of October 24, the Central Committee gathered for another meeting, to assign tasks in the leadership of the insurrection. Stalin did not attend this meeting and no mission was assigned to him. In the middle of the day, the paper he edited came out with a lead article by him that said:

> Workers, soldiers, peasants, Cossacks, all toilers! Do you want the present government of landowners and capitalists to be replaced by a new government of workers and peasants? . . . If you do, then rally all your forces, arise all together as one man, hold meetings, elect delegates and send your demands with them to the Congress of Soviets, which opens tomorrow at Smolny.[20]

It is difficult to find here any difference from the views of Trotsky, who wanted to put off the insurrection until the opening of the Congress of Soviets.

It may have been just after this issue of the Party paper, along with other information about moods in the Central Committee, reached Lenin that he wrote his famous "Letter to the Members of the Central Committee":

> I am writing these lines on the evening of the 24th. The situation is utterly critical. It is clearer than clear that now, already, putting off the insurrection is equivalent to its death. With all my strength I wish to convince my comrades that now everything is hanging by a hair, that on the agenda now are questions that are decided not by conferences, not by congresses (not even congresses of soviets), but exclusively by populations, by the mass, by the struggle of armed masses. . . . No matter what may happen, this very evening, this very night, the government must be arrested, the junior officers guarding them must be disarmed (or beaten, if they resist), and so on . . . History will not forgive revolutionaries for delay, when they can win today (and probably will win today), but risk losing a great deal tomorrow, risk losing everything.[21]

Lenin sent this letter with M. V. Fofanova to the Vyborg District Committee of the Party but was unable to wait until she returned.

---

[19] It is significant that after the victory of the October Revolution, Lenin was reluctant to recall the behavior of Kamenev and Zinoviev, since these leaders had admitted their mistakes and were doing useful work in the Party. Stalin behaved completely differently. He, who had tried to defend Zinoviev and Kamenev in 1917, a few years later began to raise a hue and cry about their treacherous behavior during the October days, and attempted, in his struggle for power, to take advantage of mistakes that they themselves had already condemned. This episode will be discussed in more detail below.

[20] *Sochineniia,* III, p. 389.

[21] Lenin, *Sochineniia,* 4th edn., XXVI, pp. 203–204.

With the help of Eino Rakh'ia and at the risk of his life, Lenin on the evening of the twenty-fourth went to Smolny and took command of the insurrection, which began a day before the opening of the Congress of Soviets. By the morning of the twenty-fifth, the Provisional Government was overthrown and power passed to the Military-Revolutionary Committee of the Petrograd Soviet.

Even when the armed insurrection had become a fact, Stalin's role was modest. An analysis of the documents and source materials of the "ten days that shook the world" shows that the real organizer of the October Revolution was Lenin. An important role in its practical success was played by the Military-Revolutionary Committee of the Petrograd Soviet, then headed by Leon Trotsky. His services in organizing the October insurrection were acknowledged by Stalin himself, in an article written in 1918. (Until the early 1930's, this article was always included in collections of Stalin's writings.) Other Bolsheviks who played crucial roles during the armed insurrection and during the first days of the Soviet regime were N. V. Krylenko, P. E. Dybenko, V. A. Antonov-Ovseenko, A. S. Bubnov, F. E. Dzerzhinskii, N. A. Miliutin, and Sverdlov. As for Stalin, we barely see him during those days, whether among the armed workers and sailors or at meetings of soldiers and workers. It is not surprising that the American Communist John Reed, an eyewitness, did not give Stalin a single line in his remarkable book on the October Revolution.[22]

Stalin also made a number of mistakes in the first months and years after the October Revolution. For example, he vacillated when the peace of Brest-Litovsk was discussed in the Central Committee. Later, in the summer of 1918, he was sent to Tsaritsyn as extraordinary commissar for food supply. In fact he took over all power in the Tsaritsyn region, squeezing out and subordinating to himself all local, Soviet, Party, and military organs. Undoubtedly Stalin did accomplish much in Tsaritsyn, supplying the industrial centers of Soviet Russia with food. But even then his main technique for running things in the city and at the front was mass terror. He not only ordered dozens of real enemies shot; he also destroyed many people who were only suspected of having connections with the White Guards.[23]

Contrary to Lenin's instructions and the decrees of the Central Committee, Stalin began to vilify military specialists indiscriminately, to remove them from their jobs, and even to shoot some of them. In one of his telegrams from the Southern Front, Stalin demanded from

[22] In a foreword to *Ten Days That Shook the World,* Lenin expressed a very high opinion of it and recommended publication in millions of copies in every language. But Stalin banned it. During the years of the cult it was removed from libraries, and was reprinted only after the XXth Party Congress. In 1937–38 Party members were sent to prisons and camps for "keeping John Reed's book."

[23] See K. E. Voroshilov's account in *Izvestiia,* Jan. 3, 1935.

the Central Committee nothing less than re-examination of the whole "question of the military specialists [who have been recruited] from the ranks of nonparty counterrevolutionaries." Dogmatic and sectarian, Stalin did not want to consider the great role that nonparty military specialists were called upon to play in building the Red Army. He was hostile and distrustful, in particular toward the military leader of the North Caucasus, A. E. Snesarev.[24] A general of the old tsarist army and also an outstanding orientalist, Snesarev was one of the first to volunteer for the Red Army; he devoted his knowledge and experience to defense of the young Soviet republic. His energetic leadership helped to beat the enemy back from Tsaritsyn. Nevertheless, just at this time Stalin sent a telegram to Moscow accusing the general of sabotage. "Military leader Snesarev," Stalin wrote, "in my opinion is very skillfully sabotaging the operation." Stalin demanded that Snesarev be recalled, because he allegedly could not and would not make war against counterrevolution. Stalin declared Snesarev's strategy for the defense of the city to be a "wrecker's" plan on the grounds that it was "defensist" rather than aggressive. In mid-July, 1918, when the position at Tsaritsyn had just been stabilized, Stalin arbitrarily removed almost the entire military staff of the district and had them arrested and placed on a barge on the Volga. This prison barge then unexpectedly sank with all on board. An inspection committee of the Supreme Military Soviet, headed by A. I. Okulovyi, went to Tsaritsyn in the summer of 1918 to investigate these arbitrary actions. Snesarev was set free and on September 11 appointed the chief of defense of the western region. Later he worked as director of the Academy of the General Staff of the Red Army—until he was arrested again in 1930.

The same hostility was shown to another leading military specialist, N. N. Sytin, appointed commander of the Southern Front in the fall of 1918. On Stalin's suggestion, the Revolutionary-Military Soviet of the Southern Front changed Sytin's first orders of operation and then removed him from his command. Stalin was thereby defying the instructions of the Revolutionary-Military Soviet of the Republic, the demands of the Central Executive Committee, even the orders of the Party's Central Committee, not to interfere in the orders of a front commander. As a result of these arbitrary and completely unjustified actions, Stalin was finally removed from the Revolutionary-Military Soviet of the Southern Front, while Sytin remained commander of that same front.[25]

It must also be noted that Stalin and Voroshilov were hardly ideal leaders of the military operations at Tsaritsyn, the city later named

[24] See *Voenno-istoricheskii zhurnal*, 1955, No. 1.
[25] Later Sytin worked in the Revolutionary-Military Soviet of the Republic. See *Voenno-istoricheskii zhurnal*, 1962, No. 2.

for Stalin (Stalingrad) and renamed once again after his death (Volgograd). Although Tsaritsyn managed to hold out in 1918, the army suffered enormous losses there. In a speech to the VIIIth Party Congress (March, 1919), which has not been published,[26] Lenin sharply criticized the Revolutionary-Military Soviet of the Tenth Army, which was in charge of the Tsaritsyn operation. Participants in the VIIIth Congress recall Lenin's condemnation of the anarchistic behavior of many of the Red Army units at Tsaritsyn, their refusal to follow the orders of military specialists and their enthusiasm for guerrilla tactics. Lenin declared that the military specialists

> will be in charge, though we will place our own people alongside them. And we know from experience that this will lead to successful results. [I. A.] Akulov carried out the line of the Central Committee, yet they are saying that he destroyed the army. Akulov informed us that the Third Army indulged in guerrilla tactics even at Tsaritsyn. Akulov proved this by objective facts. It is permissible to sacrifice 60,000 men, but from the standpoint of our general line, can we simply throw away 60,000 men?
>
> I am fully aware that you have killed many of the enemy. But we would not have had to throw away 60,000 men if the specialists had been there, if it had been a regular army. We must not do this again.
>
> The absence of a commanding staff at the front means that soldiers do not go into battle but into a slaughterhouse.
>
> A regular army can exist only on condition that the most rational use is made of the work of specialists.[27]

This issue was part of the clash between Lenin and the "military opposition," which was explicitly supported by Voroshilov and indirectly by Stalin as well. The problem of this "military opposition" has not been properly studied by our historians. It is known that the following were open adherents: A. Z. Kamenskii, Voroshilov, E. M. Iaroslavskii, G. I. Safarov, F. I. Goloshchekin, and S. Milin. But behind them stood Stalin, clearly sympathizing with this opposition and trying to create the impression that Lenin and the Central Committee did not understand military affairs, which they entrusted to Trotsky. The basic point of disagreement was the recruiting of military specialists for the Red Army; the "military opposition" resisted that

---

[26] *Ed.:* See *Vos'moi s'ezd RKP(b): protokoly* (Moscow, 1959), p. vii: the closed session of the VIIIth Congress, devoted to military problems, is omitted from this record "because the Secretary's notes are utterly crude."

[27] See S. A. Fediukin, *Sovetskaia vlast' i burzhuaznye spetsialisty* (Moscow, 1965), pp. 63–64; S. I. Aralov, *Lenin vel nas k pobede* (Moscow, 1962), pp. 102–103; and *Vos'moi s'ezd . . .*, pp. 412–23 and 538–40. *Ed.:* None of these citations contains the actual words that Medvedev quotes from Lenin's unpublished speech. Neither does the little biography, A. S. Blinov, *Ivan Akulov* (Moscow, 1967). Apparently Medvedev was able to consult the unpublished minutes of the closed session.

recruitment. Later Stalin issued an order "not to consider the military opposition as an opposition." He tried in every possible way to emphasize that it was an opposition not against Lenin and the Central Committee but against Trotsky. But the facts show a different picture. The VIIIth Party Congress reprimanded Kamenskii, and a resolution of the Central Committee explained that there was no military policy of Trotsky's but a policy of the Central Committee, which Trotsky was carrying out.[28] It must be noted that Stalin, while continually agitating against Lenin, never took part in one of the open and "official" opposition groups. At the decisive moment he always withdrew his objections and invariably appeared among the majority. It is difficult to believe this was due only to the persuasiveness of Lenin's arguments.

Stalin behaved badly not only with the military specialists but also with many Communists who were his subordinates. Even at that period he demanded from his subordinates unquestioning obedience. He removed people he found objectionable and chose workers who were capable of acting only according to the principle of "Pay attention; do what you're told; report when you're through." His cruelty and lack of self-restraint were clearly shown in the letter he sent from Tsaritsyn to Stepan Shaumian in May, 1918: "With respect to the Dagestanian and other bands who are obstructing the movement of trains from the North Caucasus, you must be absolutely ruthless. A number of their villages should be set on fire and burned to the ground, to teach them not to make raids on trains."[29] Twenty years later, the experience of terror that Stalin acquired in Tsaritsyn was applied to the entire country.

In 1920, when Stalin was a member of the Military Council of the Southwest Front, he refused to submit to a decision of the Politburo concerning his area of operations and sent a letter to Lenin which contained harsh and nasty expressions. Stalin's arbitrary behavior delayed the transfer of the First Cavalry Army and other units to the Western Front, and was one of the reasons for the failure of the Soviet advance on Warsaw.

One cannot help asking how Stalin got away with such abuses of power and arbitrary actions. It is not easy to answer this question, but certain factors do stand out. Stalin was already powerful in the years of the Civil War. He had many supporters and knew how to stick up for himself. Under the conditions of the savage Civil War, when the Soviet regime was often placed in a critical situation, Lenin had to make use of every available force that supported the revolution.

[28] One of the older Communists, D. Iu. Zorina, several years ago wrote an interesting article, still not published, "On the Problem of the Military Opposition."

[29] *Pravda,* Sept. 20, 1963.

In the young Soviet republic, hemmed in on all sides by military fronts, the struggle of the two principles or tendencies that may be called Leninism and Stalinism had not yet developed, and could not develop in sufficient depth and force to be a major issue. Moreover, not only Stalin but many other Central Committee representatives at the fronts behaved with excessive severity at times. Many such complaints against Trotsky came to the Central Committee, because both commanders and commissars of certain units were the victims of his swift and by no means always just punishment.

Stalin's performance as Commissar of Nationalities was also characterized by many excessive actions. Following the formation of a Soviet government in the Ukraine, Lenin on April 3, 1918, sent greetings in which he expressed "enthusiastic sympathy for the heroic struggle of the laboring and exploited masses of the Ukraine, who are at present one of the advanced detachments of the world socialist revolution." But Stalin on April 4 sent the following telegram to the Soviet government of the Ukraine: "Enough playing at a government and a republic. It's time to drop that game; enough is enough." In reply to this missive, which was intolerable both in tone and content, N. A. Skrypnik, the leader of the Soviet Ukrainian government, sent the following telegram to Moscow on April 6:

> We must protest in the strongest possible way against the statement of Commissar Stalin. We must declare that the Central Executive Committee of the Ukrainian Soviet base their actions, not on the attitude of any Commissar of the Russian Federation, but on the will of the toiling masses of the Ukraine, as expressed in the decree of the Second All-Ukrainian Congress of Soviets. Declarations like that of Commissar Stalin would destroy the Soviet regime in the Ukraine. . . . They are direct assistance to the enemies of the Ukrainian toiling masses.[30]

2

AT THE END of December, 1921, Lenin became seriously ill. On December 31 the Politburo granted him a six-week leave, which was subsequently extended to the beginning of the XIth Party Congress in March, 1922. During those months Lenin continued to write articles and letters, to give instructions by telephone, and to have talks with various comrades. On March 27, 1922, he gave the main speech to the XIth Party Congress. He also participated in the plenary meeting of

[30] See the speech of A. V. Snegov at the conference in the Institute of Marxism-Leninism, June 26–28, 1966. *Ed.:* This seems to be an unpublished manuscript.

the Central Committee, which, on April 3, 1922, set up a new post, General Secretary of the Central Committee, and elected Stalin to it.

At that time the General Secretary was not considered the main official in the Party. The Secretariat was only one of the organs of the Central Committee that were subordinated to the Politburo. The secretaries of the Central Committee, who were in charge of the current work of the Party *apparat,* were not members of the Politburo, which was one of the reasons for the inadequate authority and the poor work of the Secretariat. In order to improve the work of the Secretariat, the decision was made to name a Politburo member General Secretary of the Central Committee.

In 1922 Stalin was the least prominent figure in the Politburo. Not only Lenin but also Trotsky, Zinoviev, Kamenev, Bukharin, and A. I. Rykov were much more popular among the broad masses of the Party than Stalin. Closemouthed and reserved in everyday affairs, Stalin was also a poor public speaker. He spoke in a low voice with a strong Caucasian accent, and found it difficult to speak without a prepared text. It is not surprising that, during the stormy years of revolution and civil war, with their ceaseless meetings, rallies, and demonstrations, the revolutionary masses saw or heard little of Stalin. He was generally to be found somewhere behind the scenes. But within the Party *apparat* Stalin was a fairly prominent official, well known for his organizational abilities and his harsh manners. Evidently it was assumed that appointing a man such as Stalin to the post of General Secretary would bring some order into the working organs of the Party, which, to judge from many of Lenin's letters and remarks, were not operating very efficiently in 1921–22.

Thus there was nothing unexpected in Stalin's appointment to the new post. It was accepted by the Party as routine. "It was one of a number of such events to which no one ascribed any special significance," writes E. Ia. Drabkina in her memoirs, "and even in Party circles no one paid any attention to it."[31] In April, 1922, Lenin was still at the head of the Party and the government; he was the universally recognized chief of the revolutionary masses. Therefore Stalin's election in 1922 to the post of General Secretary was not, despite the legends that were created later on, the promotion of a new Party chief; it was not Lenin's designation of his successor.

Although the post of General Secretary was not the most important office in 1922, some people have reproached Lenin for entrusting it to Stalin, whose shortcomings were well known to the majority of Party leaders. But there is no proof that Lenin proposed the creation

[31] E. Ia. Drabkina, *Zimnii pereval. Ed.:* Medvedev gives no place or date of publication. Neither does the French translation: Drabkina, *Solstice d'hiver. Le dernier combat de Lénine* (Paris, 1970). I have been unable to locate the Russian original.

of the new post, or that he nominated Stalin for it. The plenary meeting of the Central Committee that convened immediately after the XIth Party Congress was presided over by Kamenev at its opening session. It was Kamenev, according to eyewitness reports, who proposed that Stalin be chosen as General Secretary. Furthermore, even before the beginning of the Plenum, pressure was applied to the newly elected Central Committee. According to Snegov, a member of the Elections Committee of the XIth Party Congress, during the election of the Central Committee some delegates wrote "General Secretary" on their ballots after Stalin's name. This angered Skrypnik, chairman of the Elections Committee, who demanded that these ballots be declared invalid. Kamenev had to explain to the Congress that it was not the Congress but the Plenum of the Central Committee that elected the Secretariat of the CC. Thus it may be argued that the election of Stalin as General Secretary was presented to Lenin as a *fait accompli*. Furthermore—and this is the most important aspect of the matter— Lenin never had (or sought) the plenitude of power that Stalin subsequently possessed. Thus Lenin could not by himself decide important questions of policy, or even questions of appointments. He was often obliged to give in to his comrades on the Central Committee, and it would appear that this was the case with Stalin, who was actively supported by such prominent members of the Politburo as Zinoviev and Kamenev, to say nothing of influential members of the Central Committee, including Ordzhonikidze and Voroshilov.

Many letters and memoranda, a large part of which have been published only in the last few years, reveal Lenin's sometimes difficult position during 1921 and 1922. Some of Lenin's letters, although they do not have a direct bearing on Stalin's appointment, show how hard it was for Lenin to obtain any appointment he desired during that period or to prevent one. In the spring of 1921, the old Bolshevik G. L. Shklovskii, whom Lenin had known well in émigré days, asked for a job in one of the trade delegations of the USSR abroad. Lenin supported his request. However, the Orgburo of the Central Committee turned down Lenin's proposal. Lenin took this rather unimportant matter to the Politburo and won his point. Even then the Commissariat of Foreign Trade, or more likely some of its leading officials, did not want to implement the Politburo's decree. Shklovskii sent a letter to Lenin, asking for his assistance. Lenin immediately wrote to V. M. Molotov, who at that time was in charge of the Central Committee Secretariat. In this note he accused Iu. Kh. Lutovinov and B. S. Stomoniakov of sabotaging the Politburo's decision to appoint Shklovskii. Anyone who really believed that Skhlovskii did not deserve the appointment, Lenin wrote, should make an open appeal to the Central Committee and stop whispering about "Lenin's favoritism."[32]

[32] *Polnoe sobranie*, LII, pp. 249–50.

At the same time, Lenin sent a note to Shklovskii:

June 4, 1921

Comrade Shklovskii:

I received your long letter after sending you my note. You are completely right: to accuse me of "favoritism" in this case is utterly outrageous and disgusting. I repeat, there is a complicated intrigue here. They are taking advantage of the deaths of Sverdlov, Zagorskii and others.

You will have to start from scratch. There is both prejudice and stubborn opposition and deep distrust of me in this problem. I am extremely pained by this. But it's a fact. I don't blame you for your letter. I understand that things are very difficult for you. I have seen other such examples in our Party nowadays. New men have come in and don't know the old men. You recommend and they don't trust you. You repeat your recommendation—their distrust is redoubled, and they begin to get stubborn. "But we don't want it! ! !"

Nothing else remains but this: starting from scratch, by struggle, we must *win* the *new* youth to our side.

Greetings,
LENIN[33]

Shklovskii's problem was settled a month or so later, according to a note that Lenin sent in the middle of July:

Comrade Shklovskii:

I spoke with Stomoniakov and [L. B.] Krasin, and am enclosing Krasin's note. He promised to see you. Lutovinov gave me his "word of honor" that he will treat you in "an unbiased manner." I did all I could. I repeat what I said to you personally: in Berlin you must "start from scratch" and win yourself a position by your performance. This has happened to several old Party members since 1917. Best wishes to you and all your family.

LENIN[34]

And there were not a few such cases. "You are mistaken," wrote Lenin to the Soviet diplomat A. A. Ioffe,

to repeat continually: "the Central Committee—that's me" [*TsK, eto ia*]. This could have been written only in a state of great nervous tension and exhaustion. The old Central Committee (1919–1920) beat me on one of the immensely important questions, as you know from discussions. On organizational and personnel questions, there is no counting the times when I was in the minority. You yourself saw examples of this many times, when you were a member of the CC. Why then do you get so nervous that you write the *COM-*

---

[33] Unfortunately, this note of Lenin's, extremely interesting both as an historical document and from a psychological point of view, has not yet been published even in his "complete" collected works (*Polnoe sobranie sochinenii*).

[34] *Polnoe sobranie*, LIII, pp. 30–31. In 1937, Shklovskii, for whom Lenin went to so much trouble, was shot as an "enemy of the people."

PLETELY IMPOSSIBLE, COMPLETELY IMPOSSIBLE phrase,
"the CC—that's me?"[35]

During 1922, Lenin's illness continued to develop. In May his
health took a sharp turn for the worse. From sclerosis of the brain,
the movement of his right arm and leg weakened and he developed a
speech disorder. Although these symptoms passed several weeks later,
it was not until October that Lenin was able to return to Moscow and
get back to work. And although from then through December Lenin
worked almost with his old intensity, he could not help thinking
about his successors in case he should be put out of action for a
prolonged period or even die.

From letters published in the last few years it can be seen that
toward the end of 1922 political and personal relations between Lenin
and Trotsky, which had seriously deteriorated during the trade-union
debate (see below, pp. 31–38, began to mend. Lenin showed great
confidence in Kamenev as well. Although Lenin, as chairman of the
Council of Commissars, had two good deputies, A. D. Tsiuriupa and
Rykov, he proposed that a "first" deputy be appointed, and suggested
Kamenev for that post. It was Kamenev who chaired the meetings of
the Council of Commissars and the Politburo during Lenin's illness
in 1923. Despite his serious shortcomings and mistakes, Kamenev
was an outstanding leader, a man with great authority in Party circles.
Lenin did not, of course, forget how Zinoviev and Kamenev had
behaved during the October Revolution, but this did not prevent him
from showing respect for Kamenev in the years that followed.

Gorky in his memoirs recounts a little episode that stuck in his
mind.

> With respect and amazement he [Lenin] said, as he accompanied
> one of his "executive" comrades from his office: "Have you known
> him long? He would have been at the head of the cabinet of any
> European country." And, rubbing his hands and smiling, he added:
> "Europe is poorer than we are in talented men."[36]

Even in the notes to the collected works of Gorky, it is not indicated
that Lenin in this case was speaking of Kamenev.

Besides ignoring Stalin as a possible successor, during 1922 and
1923 Lenin referred to his activity in an increasingly negative way.
There were good reasons for this. Stalin made a number of crude
political mistakes in 1922. For example, he supported Bukharin and
G. Ia. Sokol'nikov in their attempts to abolish the state monopoly of
foreign trade. Only the decisive intervention of Lenin saved the Party
from this dangerous act. In 1922 Stalin made a very serious mistake

[35] *Ibid.*, LII, pp. 99–100.
[36] M. Gorky, *V. I. Lenin* (Moscow, 1959), p. 50.

in the national question. During Lenin's illness, in September, 1922, Stalin persuaded a commission of the Central Committee to endorse his proposal for "autonomization," that is, for unifying the republics of non-Russian nationalities by incorporating them in the Russian Republic with rights of autonomy. According to Stalin, what was needed was not a Union of Soviet Socialist Republics but a Russian Soviet Socialist Republic, which would include all the other nationalities. Thus Stalin did not take into consideration the Leninist view of federation, which had been formulated at the Xth Party Congress in 1921. He was in fact proposing to liquidate the independence of the union republics. Lenin sharply criticized Stalin's position in a letter of September 27, 1922, and proposed a completely different solution: the creation of a new kind of state, the Union of Soviet Socialist Republics, based on the complete equality of these republics. This solution was accepted by the Party.

Nor did Stalin take a correct position in the conflict that broke out in 1922 between G. K. (Sergo) Ordzhonikidze and the leadership of the Central Committee of the Communist Party of Georgia. Lenin was deeply disturbed by this conflict, which prompted him to dictate his memorandum "On the Nationality Question" at the very end of 1922. In it he expressed great alarm at Ordzhonikidze's readiness to use force against the local leaders in Georgia:

> I think that a fatal role was played here by Stalin's impatience and his infatuation with administrative fiat, and also by his hostility towards notorious "social nationalism." . . . But hostility generally plays the worst kind of role in politics. . . . In this case, our relations with the Georgian nation, we have a typical example of the need for extreme carefulness, a conciliatory and permissive spirit, if we are to handle this matter in a truly proletarian manner.

Later, with Stalin foremost in his mind, Lenin wrote:

> That Georgian who takes such a scornful attitude toward this aspect of the matter, who scornfully hurls accusations of social nationalism (while he himself is a real genuine "social nationalist," and even a crude Great Russian Derzhimorda [a policeman in Gogol's *Inspector General*])—that Georgian is in reality violating the interests of proletarian class solidarity. . . . It is Stalin and Dzerzhinskii who must be held politically responsible for this entire Great Russian nationalist campaign.[37]

A month later, Lenin returned to the conflict of Ordzhonikidze, Stalin, and Dzerzhinskii with the leadership of the Central Committee of the Georgian Communist Party. In the "Diary of the Office Secretaries of V. I. Lenin"[38] there is the following note made by L. A.

[37] *Polnoe sobranie,* XLV, pp. 356–60.
[38] *Voprosy istorii KPSS,* 1963, No. 2, p. 80.

Fotieva on January 30, 1923:

> On January 24, Lenin called Fotieva and instructed her to ask
> Dzerzhinskii or Stalin for the materials of the commission on the
> Georgian question and to study them in detail. . . . He said, "On
> the eve of my illness Dzerzhinskii told me of the work of the com-
> mission and of the 'incident,' and this had a very depressing effect
> on me."
>   On Thursday, January 25, he asked whether the materials had
> been received. I replied that Dzerzhinskii would be arriving only on
> Saturday so that I had been unable to ask him.
>   On Saturday, I asked Dzerzhinskii, who replied that Stalin had
> the materials. I sent a letter to Stalin but he was not in Moscow.
> Yesterday, on January 29, Stalin phoned to say that he couldn't give
> the materials without the Politburo's permission. . . . Today (Janu-
> ary 30), Vladimir Il'ich called to find out the answer and said that
> he would fight to have the materials handed over.

Clearly Stalin was discourteous in his refusal to send the materials
Lenin requested. Reference to Lenin's illness in this case could only
be an excuse, since refusal to send the documents upset Lenin far
more than receiving them would have done.

Five weeks later, on March 5, 1923, Lenin again returned to the
Georgian affair, as the following letter to Trotsky shows.

> Respected Comrade Trotsky:
>   I would like to ask you to take upon yourself the defense of the
> Georgian affair in the Central Committee. This matter is now being
> "prosecuted" by Stalin and Dzerzhinskii, and I cannot rely on their
> impartiality. Indeed, quite the opposite. If you would agree to take
> on its defense, I would have some peace of mind. If for some reason
> you do not wish to do so, then return the whole matter to me. I will
> consider that a sign of your refusal.
>
>   With best comradely greetings,
>   LENIN[39]

Even when Lenin was ill, he followed Stalin's activities in the post
of General Secretary closely and with uneasiness. It is not surprising
that in 1922, Stalin, with his characteristic callousness and meanness,
and against the advice of some of Lenin's physicians, tried to isolate
Lenin, to deprive him of all information about current Party business
and disagreements, on the pretext of concern for Lenin's health. Stalin
even tried to get control of conversations between Lenin and his wife,
N. K. Krupskaia, and in the process treated Krupskaia with his usual
rudeness. This is especially evident in the following letter, written by
Krupskaia on December 23, 1922, to Kamenev in the Politburo:

[39] *Sochineniia,* 4th edn., XLV, p. 535.

Lev Borisovich:

Yesterday, in connection with a short letter that I wrote under Vladimir Il'ich's dictation, with the doctor's permission, Stalin behaved towards me in a very nasty way. I didn't join the Party yesterday. For all the thirty years that I have been a member I have never heard a single nasty word from a comrade. The interests of the Party and of Il'ich [Lenin] are not less dear to me than to Stalin. Now I need a maximum of self-control. I know better than any doctor what can and what cannot be discussed with Il'ich, because I know what upsets him and what doesn't, and in any case, I know better than Stalin. I am appealing to you and to Grigorii [Zinoviev] as Vladimir Il'ich's closest comrades to protect me from this nasty interference in my personal life, from these undeserved insults and threats. I don't doubt the unanimous decision of the control commission that Stalin permits himself to threaten me with, but I have neither the time nor the strength to waste on this stupid squabble. I am also a live being, and my nerves are stretched to the breaking point.

N. KRUPSKAIA[40]

Lenin learned of the conflict between Stalin and Krupskaia only at the beginning of March, 1923, probably from Kamenev. Outraged by Stalin's meanness, Lenin called his secretary, and despite the fact that more than two months had passed from the time of the conflict, dictated the following letter:

Respected Comrade Stalin:

You had the effrontery to call my wife to the telephone and to swear at her. Although she has expressed to you her willingness to forget what was said, she nonetheless made this fact known to Zinoviev and Kamenev. I do not intend to forget so easily what is done against me, and it goes without saying that what is done against my wife I consider done against myself. Therefore I ask you to consider carefully whether you will agree to take back what you said and to apologize, or whether you would prefer to break off all relations between us.

Respectfully,
LENIN
March 5, 1923[41]

The two letters that Lenin wrote on March 5, 1923, one to Trotsky, the other to Stalin, were his last written documents. On March 6 his health took a new turn for the worse, and on March 10 he suffered another stroke, which caused loss of speech and intensified paralysis of the right arm and leg. It is hardly possible to doubt that the deterioration of Lenin's condition was accelerated by his irritation at Stalin's behavior.

[40] *Ed.:* This letter was quoted in Khrushchev's speech to the XXth Party Congress.
[41] *Polnoe sobranie,* LIV, pp. 329–30.

To be sure, Stalin did not decide to break off relations with Lenin in 1923. He made apologies to Krupskaia, but they were, as his subsequent treatment of her would show, insincere and purely formal. It is also impossible to overlook the fact that during the summer and fall of 1923, when Lenin's condition improved and he began to receive people at his home in the hills near Moscow and to go for walks—once he even visited Moscow—he saw and spoke with a number of leading Party and state officials but not once with Stalin.

3

STALIN'S ARBITRARY WAYS and Trotsky's many personal and political faults created a real danger of a split in the Party by the end of 1922. Lenin, with his customary foresight, clearly saw the growing peril and felt increasingly worried by it. A considerable part of his letters in 1922 are devoted to a single question: how to unite the Party's core of leaders and to ward off the danger of a split. With this goal in mind, Lenin proposed a reorganization of the system of supervision (*kontrol'*) over the work of Party and state agencies. He also proposed an increase in the number of members in the Central Committee, and personnel changes in that body. And he proposed that Stalin be removed from the post of General Secretary.

By Lenin's "Testament" I mean those letters, articles, and memoranda that he dictated at the end of 1922 and the beginning of 1923. In a more restricted sense, however, Lenin's "Testament" often refers only to a few letters, in which Lenin speaks of the work of the Central Committee and gives characterizations of its leading members.[42] In one memorandum, for example, Lenin proposed a great increase in the size of the Central Committee, hoping thereby to reduce the significance of personal conflicts among the leaders. In a continuation of this memorandum written the next day, Lenin singled out the conflict between Stalin and Trotsky as the most serious:

> Comrade Stalin, on becoming General Secretary, concentrated enormous power in his hands, and I am not sure he always knows how to use this power carefully enough. On the other hand, Comrade Trotsky is distinguished not only by outstanding abilities. . . . Personally, he is, I daresay, the most capable member of the present Central Committee, but he is possessed by excessive self-confidence and by excessive infatuation for the purely administrative side of things.
>
> These two qualities of the two outstanding chiefs of the present Central Committee may result in a split, and if our Party does not

[42] These documents were published in full in *Polnoe sobranie,* LIV.

take measures to prevent this, then the split could come about quite unexpectedly.

In other memoranda, Lenin repeated at length his hope that an expansion of the Central Committee would reduce the danger of conflicts among its leading personalities, and went on to urge Stalin's removal from the office of General Secretary:

> Stalin is too coarse, and this fault, though quite tolerable in relations among us Communists, becomes intolerable in the office of General Secretary. Therefore I suggest to the comrades that they think of a way of transferring Stalin from this position and assigning another man to it who differs from Comrade Stalin only in one superiority: more tolerant, more loyal, more polite and more considerate of his comrades, less capricious, and so on. This situation may seem an insignificant trifle. But I think, from the viewpoint of preventing a split and from the viewpoint of what I wrote above concerning the mutual relations of Trotsky and Stalin, this is no trifle, or rather, it is a trifle which may acquire decisive importance.

Lenin's letter of December 23–26, and the addendum written on January 4, were addressed in the XIIth Party Congress, which was to be held in the spring of 1923. This is obvious from the letter's content. For it was to the approaching XIIth Congress that Lenin recommended increasing the Central Committee to from fifty to a hundred members and giving legislative force to the decisions of the State Planning Commission (Gosplan). It was for the delegates to the XIIth Congress that Lenin gave his characterization of the most prominent members of the Central Committee and recommended that Stalin be replaced as General Secretary.

This "Letter to the Congress," at Lenin's request, was typed in five copies: one for himself, three for Krupskaia, and one for Lenin's secretarial staff. He asked that all this material be kept in envelopes sealed with stamped wax, with a note to the effect that only Lenin could open them, and, after his death, Krupskaia. However, the secretary on duty, M. A. Volodicheva, for some reason did not inscribe the words "and after his death" on the envelopes.

Some aspects of the further history of Lenin's letters are not clear. His secretaries kept a "Registration Book of the Letters, Memoranda, and Directives of V. I. Lenin." According to this record, the first part of the "Letter to the Congress" was sent to Stalin on the same day that Lenin dictated it. Probably the secretaries on duty did not consider the letter secret. Only on the following day, after the first dictation, did Lenin make a point of warning Volodicheva that "What was dictated yesterday (December 23) and today (December 24) is *absolutely* secret." He repeated and stressed this. We must therefore assume that the second part of the "Letter to the Congress," and the supplement written on January 4, 1923, were not communicated to Stalin or to any other member of the Central Committee.

The second half of Lenin's letter was not brought to the attention of the delegates to the XIIth Congress, which met in April, 1923. The delegates were familiar with many other of Lenin's letters and articles, some of which were published in the press. The Congress carried out the wish expressed in the first part of Lenin's letter, giving Gosplan certain legislative functions. The membership of the Central Committee was also enlarged. To be sure, the Central Committee was by no means enlarged in the way that Lenin had proposed—by the addition "of workers who stand below the stratum of Soviet civil servants, which has risen in the past five years." Among the seventeen new members of the Central Committee there was not one worker or one peasant.[43] Nor were there any among the thirteen candidate members of the Central Committee who were elected at the XIIth Congress.

Why did this happen? The most likely explanation is that the delegates did not know of Lenin's memorandum of December 26, 1922, in which he explained that the membership of the Central Committee should be increased by adding representatives of the toilers, who "stand closer to rank-and-file workers and peasants." This memorandum was made public only at the XIIIth Party Congress, in May, 1924. However, one cannot but notice that the XIIIth Party Congress did not follow Lenin's advice either. In fact, among the fifteen new members of the Central Committee elected at the XIIIth Congress, we find such leading officials as N. K. Antipov (secretary of the Moscow Committee), A. I. Dogadov (secretary of the Central Trade Union Council), N. N. Kolotilov (secretary of the Ivano-Voznesensk Committee), S. V. Kosior (secretary of the Siberian Buro of the CC), L. B. Krasin (Commissar of Foreign Trade), G. M. Krzhizhanovskii (chairman of Gosplan), and so on. The XIIIth Congress also elected twenty-four new candidate members of the Central Committee, and here too there were only commissars, secretaries of district committees (gubkomy), secretaries of the Komsomol Central Committee, leaders of the Supreme Economic Council—in short, prime representatives of the stratum that had risen to the upper echelons of the Party and government. This is not to deny the great merits of these people, many of whom deserved to be members of the Central Committee. Still, we cannot ignore the fact that the expansion of the Central Committee in 1923–24 was not accomplished as Lenin had advised.

An essential part of Lenin's "Testament," including his personal characterizations of members of the Central Committee, was not made public at the XIIth Congress. Nor did the Congress discuss the transfer

---

[43] Ed.: Medvedev lists the newly elected members of the Central Committee, indicating the high governmental and Party posts they occupied.

of Stalin from the post of General Secretary.[44] We must not assume that this was the result of some evil plot. Only Lenin himself could have opened the sealed letters, and he lay paralyzed and unable to speak. Krupskaia was to open those letters only after Lenin's death; but he was still alive, although critically ill, and those close to him had not lost hope for his recovery. Thus a confused situation developed, which Lenin had not foreseen in making the arrangements concerning his documents.

Krupskaia opened the envelopes containing Lenin's letters after his death. A few days before the XIIIth Party Congress in May, 1924, and clearly without having made any kind of agreement with Stalin, Krupskaia handed Lenin's "Letter to the Congress" over to the Central Committee. "Vladimir Il'ich," she wrote on this occasion, "expressed a strong desire that after his death this memorandum should be communicated to the next Party Congress."[45]

Lenin's suggestion about Stalin's transfer immediately became the subject of many unofficial discussions in the Central Committee. When Stalin learned of Lenin's proposal, he made a show of handing in his resignation, which Zinoviev and Kamenev, who at that time played a leading role in the Central Committee, "persuaded" him to take back. A rather strange procedure was worked out for informing the Congress of Lenin's "Testament." In spite of Lenin's wishes, his letter was not officially read out at the Congress and discussed by the delegates, nor was it included among the documents of the XIIIth Congress. It was read only to separate delegations as they arrived, which naturally allowed those who were Stalin's defenders to reject Lenin's recommendations.

Zinoviev, helped by Kamenev, put up a fight to retain Stalin as General Secretary. They called meetings for this purpose among the most important delegations. Evidently, before the XIIIth Congress some kind of "agreement" was struck between Zinoviev and Stalin. Stalin approved Zinoviev's designation as the principal speaker to the XIIIth Congress, and thus seemed to be promoting Zinoviev, an ambitious and rather unprincipled man, to the role of Party leader. Zinoviev, with the help of Kamenev, who was then under his influence, was obliged to defend the post of General Secretary for Stalin.

We do not know whether any comrades made speeches in favor of Stalin's removal when the matter was discussed in the delegations. However, we do know that the overwhelming majority of delegates

[44] Did Stalin know the contents of the second part of Lenin's "Testament"? Some historians have suggested that he could have found out about it from Fotieva or Volodicheva, or even from his wife, Nadezhda Allilueva, who worked in Lenin's secretarial staff and was in charge of his archives. I consider such an assumption unlikely.

[45] *Polnoe sobranie*, XLV, p. 594.

gave way to the pressure of authoritative members of the Central
Committee and voted to keep Stalin as General Secretary. In 1924,
among Party officials who were less farsighted than Lenin, Stalin did
not seem dangerous. During that period he could not ignore the
opinions and the influence of the other leaders of the Central Committee, so that it was impossible to conceive of one-man rule or of
Stalin's personal dictatorship. On the contrary, in 1924 Stalin was the
spokesman of "collective leadership." Together with other members of
the Politburo he accused Trotsky of striving for one-man leadership
and defended Zinoviev and Kamenev, whom Trotsky had attacked in
his book *The Lessons of October*. At a time when a considerable part
of the Central Committee supported Trotsky, and many Party activists
saw Trotskyism as the greatest danger, Stalin's personal faults really
did seem trifling, since he was actively opposing Trotsky. The Central
Committee believed Stalin's protestations when he acknowledged
Lenin's criticism, and left him in the post of General Secretary. This
was an inexcusable mistake; as Lenin had foreseen, what seemed to
many of Stalin's comrades to be a trifle in 1924 later acquired decisive
significance for the country and the Party.

The further history of Lenin's "Testament" is interesting. In 1926,
Boris Souvarine in France and Max Eastman in the USA published the
"Testament," which was evidently sent abroad by one of the oppositionists. At first the Soviet press declared it to be apocryphal slander.
However, in 1927 the question of the "Testament" was repeatedly
raised within the Central Committee, and Stalin was obliged to
comment: "Yes, I am coarse, comrades, in dealing with those who
coarsely and treacherously destroy and splinter the Party. I have not
concealed this and do not conceal it." As L. S. Shaumian points out,
Stalin was unscrupulously twisting the meaning of the document, for
Lenin accused Stalin of coarseness not toward the Party's enemies and
destroyers but toward comrades who had performed great services for
the Party.[46]

Lenin's "Testament" was also discussed at the XVth Party Congress. A participant describes what happened:

> On opening the thirteenth morning session, on December 9, 1927,
> Chairman G. I. Petrovskii said: "We forgot to vote on Comrade
> Ordzhonikidze's motion to honor the request of the United Plenum
> of the Central Committee and the Central Control Commission in
> July 1926, to publish Lenin's letter in the *Leninskie sborniki*
> [*Leninist Miscellanies*], the one that is often called his "Testa-
> ment," which the XIIIth Party Congress decided not to publish.
> The question is open for voting." The following speaker, Rykov,

---

[46] *Filosofskaia entsiklopediia*, III, p. 114.

proposed publication not only of the letter called the "Testament" but also of other unpublished letters by Lenin dealing with intraparty problems; the so-called "Testament," he said, should be appended to the minutes. The Congress supported his motion and unanimously decided to publish both the "Testament" and the letters on intraparty problems.[47]

However, the "Testament" did not appear in the minutes of the Congress, which were published in 1928, or in the *Leninskie sborniki*. Many other letters of Lenin were also not published. But the delegates of the XVth Congress (1,669 strong) could read the "Testament" in the *Bulletins* printed during the Congress "only for members of the All-Russian Communist Party."[48] These *Bulletins* were printed, according to the information on the title page, in an edition of 13,500 copies. How the 11,831 surplus copies were distributed is unknown; in any case, the *Bulletins* did not reach the Party organizations.

Thus, after the XVth Congress of 1927 Lenin's "Testament" became somewhat more widely known among the Party *aktiv*. But in the 1930's all talk about the "Testament" was suppressed. First it became a secret document, which young Party members knew nothing about. With the beginning of mass repression, Lenin's "Testament" was declared to be a fabrication. Those who owned copies of the *Bulletins* of the XVth Congress were, with few exceptions, among the repressed, and many of those who escaped arrest preferred to destroy the "criminal" document. According to some old Bolsheviks who were imprisoned during the years of Stalin's cult, in the prisons and camps there were Communists condemned to long terms and even to execution for possession of "a counterrevolutionary document, the so-called Testament of Lenin."

[47] From the personal papers of E. P. Frolov.
[48] See Appendix I to *Bulletin* No. 30, pp. 35–37.

II

Stalin's Struggle
with the Opposition

1

THE RISE OF STALINISM cannot be understood without examining, if only briefly, the struggle within the Party during the middle and late 1920's. Many episodes connected with that struggle need to be reconsidered in light of the tragic events of the 1930's. No problem of Party history was so blatantly falsified for twenty to thirty years as the fight with the oppositions. Even a superficial acquaintance with the most readily available source materials—the records of Party congresses and conferences, the speeches, platforms, and forecasts of the quarreling groups—makes it clear that many episodes, and indeed the trend of the struggle as a whole, were already presented in a subjective and tendentious way in the publications of the 1920's. From the start the intraparty struggle was bitter, with each side trying to portray its opponents in the most unattractive light. Often statements were distorted beyond recognition and mistakes were exaggerated out of all proportion. Viciousness and disloyalty were stimulated on both sides. And after the defeat of the successive oppositions, the interpretations of the events of the twenties that appeared in official publications and in émigré Trotskyite literature grew even more unobjective and tendentious—culminating in *The History of the CPSU (Short Course)*,[1] which depicts the opposition leaders as masked traitors and imperialist spies, who were recruited by foreign intelligence services in the earliest years of the Soviet regime. Unfortunately, many recent

[1] *Ed.*: Published in 1938, without any authors listed on the title page, this book was quickly established as the most authoritative text for the world Communist movement, and remained so for fifteen years. See below, pp. 499 *ff*.

works on the intraparty struggle of the twenties are not free from bias.[2] Although these works do not accuse the opposition leaders of espionage or premeditated betrayal, they do not correct many other inaccuracies. Stalin is hardly mentioned as the leader of the struggle with the oppositions, nor do the names of Molotov, L. M. Kaganovich, and Stalin's other aides appear. This makes the history of the intraparty struggle incomprehensible to the uninitiated reader.

Almost all those who took an active part in the opposition movements of the twenties perished in the mass repression of the thirties. Only a few of the rank-and-file participants returned to their families after the XXth Party Congress in 1956. Some are now trying to vindicate certain opposition leaders, on the grounds that they were correct and bold, though unsuccessful, in their criticism of Stalin. Their point of view is understandable but not accurate. Because Stalin, after winning the fight with the opposition, usurped all power in the country and then wiped out most of his former opponents and allies, it does not follow that Stalin was completely wrong in his struggle with the opposition or that his opponents were completely right. It would also be wrong to imitate bourgeois historians who depict the fight between the different groups as only an unprincipled struggle for power, masked by theoretical arguments to deceive the workers. In the twenties there was not only a struggle for power within the Party; there were also serious theoretical and practical disagreements and a contest of ideas, especially over the methods and possibilities of building socialism in the Soviet Union, which at that time was the only socialist country in the world.

It is impossible to trace all the complicated twists and turns of this conflict, but certain episodes must be examined here.

There have been ideological and political struggles within the Party at practically every period of its development. In the post-October period alone, Lenin had to fight the so-called "left" Communists, the "military" opposition, the "workers'" opposition and the "democratic centralist" group, while in 1920–21 a heated discussion arose within the Party on the problem of the trade unions. Lenin was always at the center of the struggle. But however embittered the polemics may have become, Lenin never brought into the ideological battles among *Party members* the methods that were used against the Party's enemies, its ideological and political opponents.

[2] See, for example, the following: A. Ia. Viatkin, *Razgrom Kommunisticheskoi partiei trotskizma i drugikh antileninskikh grupp* (Leningrad, 1966); V. M. Ivanov, *Iz istorii bor'by partii protiv "levogo opportunizma"* (Leningrad, 1965); B. I. Makarov, *Kritika trotskizma po voprosu o stroitel'stve sotsializma v SSSR* (Moscow, 1965); Iu. V. Voskresenskii, *Razgrom Kommunisticheskoi partiei trotskistsko-men'shevistskoi "novoi" oppozitsii* (Moscow, 1962). See also numerous articles in the journal *Voprosy istorii KPSS*.

As long as fundamentals of Party theory and policy were not in dispute, Lenin treated his opponents as Party comrades. He patiently persuaded them, explained their mistakes, and tried to unite everyone who could be united around correct slogans. As a rule, Lenin tried to prevent expulsions, seeking to keep blundering comrades within the Party. In 1920, for example, in the heated battle with the "workers' " opposition, Lenin nominated its leader, A. G. Shliapnikov, for membership in the Central Committee. "When a comrade from the workers' opposition is included in the CC," Lenin said, "that is an expression of his comrades' confidence."[3] It is also enlightening to note Lenin's treatment of the mistakes of T. Ryskulov, chairman of the Turkestan Central Executive Committee.[4] An honest and selfless official, who actively fought for Soviet power in Central Asia, Ryskulov made serious mistakes of a nationalist nature in 1920. In particular he insisted on the creation of a separate "Turkic Party" and a separate "Turkic Republic." In May, 1920, Lenin proposed that Ryskulov's report be rejected and summoned him to Moscow. But Lenin, who always handled Party cadres with care, opposed the use of repressive measures, and Ryskulov quickly recognized his errors. In 1921–22 he worked as Deputy Commissar for Nationalities and in 1922 the Party made him chairman of the Council of Commissars of the Turkestan Republic.

In October, 1920, Lenin wrote to the Politburo, recommending that the Control Commission apply

> careful, individual treatment, even a kind of therapy to members of the so-called opposition, who have suffered a psychological crisis in connection with failures in their Party careers. We should try to calm them, to explain things to them in a comradely manner, find them work suitable for their psychological idiosyncrasies (without issuing orders), and offer them the advice and suggestions of the Orgburo.[5]

Of course, when disagreements went too far, when even prominent Party leaders violated Party discipline, Lenin did not hesitate to break with former comrades. For example, in October, 1917, when Zinoviev and Kamenev not only opposed an armed insurrection but even published their objections in a semi-Menshevik paper, thereby informing the enemy of the CC's secret decision, Lenin angrily condemned this strikebreaking behavior and demanded their expulsion. "I would consider it a personal disgrace," Lenin wrote to the CC,

> if, because I was once close to these former comrades, I began to waver about condemning them. I say plainly that I no longer con-

[3] *Sochineniia*, 4th edn., XXXII, p. 236.
[4] *Ed.:* Turkestan is the area in Central Asia that was subsequently divided into four republics of the Soviet Union. In most of them the languages are varieties of the Turkic family.
[5] *Polnoe sobranie*, XLI, p. 394.

sider them my comrades, and I will fight with all my strength, in the CC and at the Congress, to have them expelled from the Party.[6]

But Lenin was congenitally incapable of the thought of revenge; he never persecuted people who recognized their errors, never demanded public confessions from them. His treatment of Zinoviev and Kamenev shows this quite clearly. Soon after October, 1917, Zinoviev and Kamenev admitted their error in opposing the insurrection and immediately were assigned to important positions in the Soviet regime. Kamenev was chairman of the Second Congress of Soviets at the very moment of the insurrection and was elected chairman of the Central Executive Committee. It is true that for several days Kamenev tried to achieve "unity" with the Mensheviks and Social Revolutionaries, hoping to create a coalition government of all "socialist" parties. When the CC of the Bolshevik Party objected, Kamenev together with seven commissars handed in their resignations. But then they admitted their error, and Lenin again drew them into responsible work. In a letter to Italian Communists in 1921, Lenin described such experiences as a norm of Party life.

To be sure, Lenin noted in his "Testament" that the October episode was not accidental for Zinoviev and Kamenev. But in no way did he question the right of these two prominent Bolsheviks to be leaders of the Party. Even in his relations with Mensheviks, Lenin showed no sectarian narrow-mindedness or blind distrust. "Comrades," he declared at the VIIth Congress of Soviets in December, 1919,

> I have followed the activities of the Mensheviks, I daresay, more closely than anyone. On the basis of this fifteen-year period of observation, I maintain: . . . The development of the Mensheviks, especially at such a great moment as has begun in the history of the Russian Revolution, shows the greatest vacillations among them. On the whole they have reached the point where, against their will, with the greatest difficulty, they are beginning to leave the bourgeoisie and its prejudices. Although they resisted many times, they are beginning [1919] to draw nearer to the dictatorship of the proletariat, and in a year will have come a few steps closer—of this I am completely sure.[7]

Lenin was not a liberal. When necessary he was tough on his opponents, including Party members. But Lenin's toughness did not strike at people's self-respect or insult them.[8] Stalin treated his opponents and critics in a completely different manner. Even in the period from 1918 to 1923, when Lenin was still alive, Stalin distinguished himself by his unpleasantness and harshness toward those

---

[6] *Sochineniia*, 4th edn., XXVI, p. 186.

[7] *Sochineniia*, 4th edn., XXX, pp. 210–11.

[8] Lenin's sister gave a good description of his ability to criticize without offending. See M. I. Ul'anova, *Iz vospominanii o Lenine* (Moscow, 1928).

who made ideological or practical mistakes. Stalin was not in the least concerned with changing his opponents' minds or drawing them into the common work. He only sought to break them, to bend them to his will; if this failed, he rudely threw them aside. Unlike Lenin, who could perceive the fine distinction between an erring comrade and an enemy, Stalin saw every opponent as his personal enemy, to be dealt with by any methods that could humiliate and degrade him.

A good illustration of this difference is the contrast between the speeches of Lenin and of Stalin to the Communist caucus of the IVth All-Russian Congress of Trade Unions on May 18, 1921. At that meeting D. B. Riazanov sharply criticized the CC and supported the independence of the trade unions from the Party. He introduced a motion that contradicted the line of the CC, including a demagogic proposal for the payment of wages in goods, which caused great excitement among the delegates. It was attractive because of the sharp drop in the purchasing power of money. A majority of the Communist caucus unexpectedly voted for Riazanov's motion rather than the resolution prepared by the Party's Central Committee. Stalin, who was present, tried to get the motion repealed. But his speech lacked convincing arguments; he spoke in a harsh, irritated tone, and made personal attacks on M. P. Tomskii, Riazanov, and the whole caucus. He provoked shouts of protest, yells, and general alarm in the hall. When Riazanov had replied, Stalin, instead of criticizing his argument, shouted: "Shut up, you clown!" Riazanov jumped up and answered in the same way. Tension mounted; even delegates who had voted against Riazanov's resolution condemned Stalin's speech.

Lenin was obliged to interfere in the conflict between the Communist delegates and the Central Committee. His speech went to the heart of the issues and it was persuasive. Although the parts directed against Riazanov and Tomskii were sharply polemical and uncompromising, Lenin refrained from making any personal attacks and insults. Instead, he won by the unshakable force of his logic. The caucus that had just voted against the resolution of the Central Committee by an overwhelming majority now rescinded Riazanov's motion and approved that of the CC. "This speech," writes a witness, "has remained in my memory as a good example of Lenin's ability to talk with people and to persuade them."[9]

2

AFTER LENIN HAD LEFT the Party leadership, the first to come out with his own platform—and with a poorly disguised ambition to lead

[9] A. M. Durmashkin, in *O V. I. Lenine; vospominaniia* (Moscow, 1963), pp. 528–32.

the Party—was Leon Trotsky, who had a considerable following at that time. Since we shall frequently come across Trotsky and Trotsky-ism in these pages, something should be said here about this complex and contradictory political figure.

Trotsky joined the Social Democratic Party when its first organizations were being formed. He was arrested and sent to Siberia when he was only nineteen, and escaped abroad in 1902. At the IInd Party Congress in 1903, he sided with the Mensheviks. In the 1905 Revolution he became chairman of the Petersburg Soviet, where he made a number of political and theoretical mistakes. Still, it is impossible to deny the important revolutionary activity performed by the Petersburg Soviet and its chairman in 1905. When the Soviet was arrested, Trotsky was again sent to Siberia but escaped en route, and in 1907 attended the Vth London Congress of the Party.

In 1912, Trotsky, who was based in Vienna, organized the "August Bloc" and ceased to publish *Pravda*.[10] The prime goal he set himself was to reconcile all the Social Democratic groups, especially the Bolsheviks and Mensheviks. Thus he fought mainly against the Leninist Bolsheviks, who did not want to reach an agreement with the liquidationists and the *otzovists*. Obviously Lenin gave as much as he got. It was in 1912–13 that he expressed those extremely derogatory opinions of Trotsky which were constantly quoted during the 1920's and subsequent years. Lenin accused Trotsky of deliberately misleading the workers by concealing the truth about the liquidationists. He referred to Trotsky as a "vile careerist," an "adventurist," an "intriguer," and so on. That was when Lenin used the expression "Little Judas" (*Iudushka*), comparing Trotsky's efforts at peacemaking with the hypocritical attempts of Iudushka Golovlev, in M. E. Saltykov-Shchedrin's novel *The Golovlevs*, to reconcile his family.

In the twenties, historians and politicians assiduously collected these derogatory comments, many of which were expressed in private memoranda and letters not intended for publication. Lenin was often harsh and merciless in polemics. But it would be unreasonable if words said in anger or in the heat of argument, not only to political opponents but even to close friends and family, were attached to them as lifelong nicknames or labels. And Lenin above all never intended such a thing.

After the February Revolution of 1917, Trotsky returned to Russia and sided with the internationalist group called the *mezhraiontsy*, who were drawing close to Lenin's outlook. Thus it was not accidental that the *mezhraiontsy* were admitted into the Party at the VIth Congress in August, 1917, and Trotsky was elected to the CC. After the Bolshe-

[10] *Ed.*: Trotsky had founded *Pravda* in 1908. In 1912 the Bolsheviks began to publish a newspaper with the same name, edited by Stalin, and Trotsky's paper lapsed.

viks won a majority in the Petrograd Soviet, Trotsky became its chairman once again.

Like Stalin, Trotsky also made many mistakes during that period. However, whatever one may think of Trotsky's subsequent political career, one cannot overlook the eminently useful work he did in the decisive months before the October Revolution. "Generally speaking," writes the old Bolshevik A. P. Spunde,[11]

> Trotsky displayed his best qualities in 1917. He was the idol of mass meetings in Petrograd; his political line aroused a great feeling for him. In his actions one sensed a 1917 version of Danton. Determination and boldness showed in everything he did. No one then noticed that he lacked Lenin's depth and Lenin's ability to subordinate all his human feelings to the victory of socialism. . . . Trotsky was one of the best orators of the Revolution. He always spoke with amazing brilliance and had the ability to popularize even difficult ideas, though the foundation of principles was often incommensurate with the oratorical skill.

Another such testimonial occurs in a speech that Lenin made in October, 1917, to the Petrograd conference of Bolsheviks on the choice of candidates for the Constituent Assembly. "No one would argue against a candidate such as Trotsky," Lenin declared, and continued:

> Firstly, because right after his arrival he took the position of an internationalist; secondly, because he campaigned among the *mezhraiontsy* for a fusion [with the Bolsheviks]; and thirdly, because he rose to the occasion, during the difficult July days, as a devoted supporter of the Party of the revolutionary proletariat.[12]

There are many legends about Trotsky's role in the organization of the insurrection in Petrograd. (Trotsky himself was the author of some of these legends.) But just because there is a tendency to exaggerate his importance,[13] it should not be underrated. Trotsky was, after all, the leader of the Military-Revolutionary Committee of the Petrograd Soviet, to which all power passed in the first day after the overthrow of the Provisional Government. There are many eyewitness reports of the great role he played in the revolutionary events. Suffice

---

[11] Spunde was Deputy Commissar of Finance in the first Soviet government. Later he was a member of the Council of Labor and Defense and the Central Executive Committee of the USSR, deputy chairman of the State Bank, and director of the foreign-currency division. He was not arrested in 1937–38 but was expelled from the Party, and worked as bookkeeper, cashier, and accountant in the Moscow Trading Company. After the XXth Party Congress he was completely rehabilitated. Spunde wrote his memoirs of the revolution in 1947–49. They remain among his family's papers.

[12] *Polnoe sobranie*, XXXIV, p. 345.

[13] For example, in Professor I. K. Dashkovskii's letter to the editor of *Voprosy istorii KPSS. Ed.:* This seems to be an unpublished manuscript.

it to recall John Reed's *Ten Days That Shook the World*,[14] and the testimonial of Stalin himself:

> The revolution was guided from beginning to end by the Party CC, headed by Comrade Lenin. Vladimir Il'ich was then hiding on the Vyborg side of Petrograd, in a secret apartment. On the evening of the 24th he was summoned to Smolny to lead the movement. The whole job of the practical organization of the insurrection was under the direct leadership of the Chairman of the Petrograd Soviet, Comrade Trotsky. We can say with certainty that, for the rapid movement of the proletariat to the side of the Soviets and for the skillful, constant work of the Military-Revolutionary Committee, the Party is obligated first and foremost to Trotsky. Comrades Antonov-Ovseenko and [N. I.] Podvoiskii were his chief assistants.[15]

Trotsky's behavior during the negotiations with Germany at Brest-Litovsk was wrong. But it is clear to every objective historian that there was not a trace of intentional "betrayal," "capitulation," or "treason" in his words and deeds during those critical days. These terms entered historical writing during the cult of personality, when an effort was made to forget that right after the Treaty of Brest-Litovsk was concluded (March 3, 1918), Lenin entrusted to Trotsky a job of exceptional importance—the formation of the Red Army. Trotsky was appointed Commissar of Military and Naval Affairs and chairman of the Revolutionary Military Council.

Trotsky's actions during the Civil War are also the subject of many legends. Some have tried to represent him as the chief creator of the Red Army, the organizer of victory. On the other hand, utterly different appraisals have been given, not only in historical retrospect but even during the course of the war.[16] The truth lies somewhere in between. Lenin, who was well acquainted with the negative opinions that many military men expressed about Trotsky, always valued his military performance highly and never raised the question of finding a different Commissar of Military and Naval Affairs.[17]

To be sure, Lenin did speak of Trotsky's non-Bolshevism. But he also acknowledged that Trotsky was the most able member of the

[14] John Reed, *10 dnei kotorye potriasli mir* (Moscow, 1959), pp. 76, 78, 128 and *passim*.
[15] Stalin, "Oktiabr'skii perevorot," *Pravda*, Nov. 6–7, 1918.
[16] See, for example, the letter quoted by Iu. Trifonov, *Otblesk kostra* (Moscow, 1966), pp. 151–52, and the well-known letter that Ordzhonikidze sent to Lenin from the Southern Front. *Ed.:* The letter, dated Oct. 15, 1919, was first published in 1936. For a convenient reprint, see Ordzhonikidze, *Stat'i i rechi*, I (1956), pp. 101–102.
[17] See Gorky's reminiscence of Lenin's comment on Trotsky, variously reported in the 1924 (p. 37) and the 1930 (or 1959, p. 52) editions of Gorky, *V. I. Lenin*. Whichever version is more nearly accurate, it is clearly wrong to say that Trotsky "fought Lenin continuously," as R. Palme Dutt does in his book, *The Internationale* (London, 1964), p. 183. Medvedev quotes the Russian translation, *Internatsional* (Moscow, 1966), p. 188.

Politburo. Thus it is understandable that many of Trotsky's supporters considered him the most likely and the most desirable successor to Lenin as leader of the Party and the government. Their expectations were based not only on Trotsky's ambition but also on his great popularity among sections of the Party intelligentsia, the army, and the youth. Trotsky and his group cloaked their attacks on other members of the Politburo—especially Zinoviev, Kamenev, Stalin, and Bukharin—with the slogan of democracy. "The most dangerous of all dangers," Trotsky wrote, "is the regime within the Party." In his book *The Lessons of October,* Trotsky exaggerated his services to the revolution, thereby distorting the position and role of Lenin. Trotsky's main targets were Zinoviev and Kamenev, whom Lenin in 1917 had called strikebreakers of the revolution. Trotsky also sharply criticized Zinoviev for his leadership of the Comintern, insisting that the 1923 insurrection in Germany would have succeeded if the Comintern and the German Communists had been bolder.

This concern for democracy smelled of demagogy. Even many of Trotsky's supporters called him "the lord" (*barin*), for his arrogance and conceit were famous. Trotsky's scorn for Party discipline and the preemptory, bureaucratic style of his work were obvious during Lenin's lifetime. It was Trotsky who coined the slogans "shake up" (the trade unions) and "tighten the screws." At that time he was starting, among his supporters, a cult of his own personality.

Trotsky's famous theory of permanent revolution was also wrong; it resembled Marx's and Lenin's theories of uninterrupted revolution in name only. This theory, which Trotsky tried to defend for the rest of his life, was associated with one of his major errors: underestimation of the revolutionary potential of the peasantry, as the main ally of the proletariat not only in the bourgeois democratic period of the Russian Revolution but also, in the case of the poorer peasants, during the socialist period. Since he did not see the possibilities for building socialism in the countryside and did not understand Lenin's cooperative plan, he accused the Party of a "kulak deviation." He pinned his hopes largely on the speedy victory of the world proletarian revolution. He demanded that the work of Soviet Russia be subordinated to this goal, and did not care if the peasantry was sacrificed in the process. Thus in 1922 Trotsky wrote:

> After seizing power the proletariat will conflict not only with the bourgeois groups that supported it in the early stages of the revolutionary struggle, but also with the broad masses of the peasantry which helped it come to power. The contradictions in the situation of a workers' government in a backward country, with an overwhelming peasant majority, can be solved only . . . in the arena of the world proletarian revolution.[18]

[18] Trotsky, *1905* (Moscow, 1922), pp. 4–5.

Some Trotskyites expressed themselves even more strongly. For example, E. A. Preobrazhenskii wrote that socialist accumulation had to be based on the proletariat's *exploitation* of presocialist forms of economy.[19] Such statements were incorrect. The state did have to take part of the gains of peasants, artisans, and especially nepmen, by means of taxes and the price system, in order to meet the needs of industrialization. But this was not exploitation, because industrialization benefited all the people, not only the proletariat. Besides, the proletarians themselves gave up a large part of the surplus product they created to meet the needs of expanded reproduction, that is, capital accumulation.

Many Trotskyites thought that the transition to large-scale socialist industry would be accomplished not by the transformation of petty commodity production through the growth of cooperatives but by the destruction and ruin of the petty producers. "The socialist and the private-enterprise systems are opposed," wrote Preobrazhenskii, "one must devour the other." Exaggerating economic difficulties and the shortcomings of the economic leadership, in 1923 the Trotskyites predicted complete paralysis of the Soviet Union's external activity, a general economic crisis, and a collapse of the state's viability.

Trotsky was tendentious in his appraisal of the Soviet situation in 1924–25, which was difficult, though hardly as bad as he made it seem. "The cuckoo has cuckooed its final hour," he said on one occasion. He was demagogic also in his appeal to the student youth, as the truest "barometer of the Party." The Trotskyites opposed currency reform, which was absolutely necessary in 1923–24, protesting against the "dictatorship of the Commissariat of Finance." The Party did not follow Trotsky, and his opposition was checked with relative ease. Although he remained in the Politburo, he was relieved of his post as Commissar of Military and Naval Affairs and given comparatively minor positions.

Should the system of views that formed around Trotsky in 1923–24 be called Trotskyism? Opinions differ. Professor I. K. Dashkovskii of Kharkov maintains that Trotskyism as a well-defined ideological trend has never existed. At various stages of the revolution, Dashkovskii writes, Trotsky attracted varying groups of supporters "whenever disagreements on concrete problems of Party politics arose. But these groups rose along with the rise of the disputed problems and dissolved as the problems were solved. They never formed a coherent trend or 'ism.'" On the other hand, some historians exaggerate the significance of Trotskyism, arguing that it has always been a well-developed anti-Leninist system of views. "Trotskyism as a political trend," writes S. P. Trapeznikov, "has been extremely harmful at every stage of the Russian Revolution. Cut off from the proletariat, Trotskyism has

[19] *Vestnik Kommunisticheskoi akademii*, No. 8.

represented a very motley crew of dabblers in politics, recruited from
the urban petty bourgeoisie and a section of the intelligentsia.[20] At
times Trotskyism is turned into a kind of universal devil, and even
the current perversions of Marxism-Leninism in China are called "contemporary Trotskyism." In my opinion, both Dashkovskii and Trapeznikov are wrong.

The erroneousness of most of Trotsky's assertions and demands
in 1923–24 is obvious today, as it was then. Nevertheless, although
the motives of the Trotskyite opposition were a far cry from a pure
interest in democracy, some of their criticisms contained a considerable
measure of truth. And although the logic of the struggle within the
Party pushed Trotsky to a number of overstatements, many of the
dangers connected with the bureaucratization of the Party's upper
echelons really did exist. "Bureaucratization," according to Trotsky,
was developing because "the Party *apparat,* ignoring the ideological
growth of the Party, has stubbornly persisted in doing the thinking
and deciding for the Party."[21] "Does bureaucratization contain the
danger of degeneration or not?" Trotsky asked.

> It would be blindness to rule out such a danger. Protracted bureau-
> cratization threatens to isolate us from the masses, to make us
> concentrate all our attention on problems of administration, of
> appointments and transfers, to narrow our field of vision, to weaken
> our revolutionary sense. In short, it does threaten a more or less
> opportunistic degeneration of the older generation, or at least a
> significant part of it.[22]

"We have" said the Trotskyite I. N. Stukov at a meeting of the Moscow Party activists,

> a certain system of Party government, which has taken shape over
> the years. This system is one of bureaucratic centralism. . . . The
> regime has received its practical training in the system of bureau-
> cratic government, and a certain type of Party official has appeared,
> who is used to setting himself off from the backward Party masses
> at every step in everyday work, is used to regarding himself as the
> guardian, the leader, while the Party mass, which he is called upon
> to govern, is obliged to obey him.[23]

These statements can be interpreted as political exaggeration, especially when it is remembered that they refer to the conditions of
1923–24. But it is impossible to deny that many of these warnings
were justified by later events. And if there was demagogy in some of

[20] Trapeznikov, *Leninizm i agrarno-krest'ianskii vopros* (Moscow, 1967), II, p. 45.
[21] *Novyi kurs,* pp. 10–11.
[22] *Ibid.,* 13.
[23] See *Partiia i oppozitsiia po dokumentam; materialy k XV s'ezdu partii, vypusk* I
     (Moscow, 1927), p. 17.

Trotsky's assertions, then it should be noted that many of the assertions of Stalin, Zinoviev, Kamenev, and Bukharin, to the effect that
the Party had completely preserved a Leninist and democratic regime,
were also demagogy.

3

THE FEATURES of an unprincipled political quarrel can also be found
in the attacks on Stalin by the "new" or "Leningrad" opposition,
which was headed by Zinoviev and Kamenev. For years Zinoviev had
been one of the Party's main leaders. He joined the Bolsheviks before
the Revolution of 1905, when he was twenty, and rose relatively fast.
He was elected to the Central Committee at the Vth Congress in 1907,
and was then given a place on the editorial board of the chief Bolshevik newspapers, *Proletarian* and *Social Democrat.* Zinoviev was with
Lenin in exile and returned to Russia by the same route after the
February Revolution. He took a leading part in the work of the Party,
and after the July days was forced to hide with Lenin in the famous
hut at Razliv.

Long personal association did not keep Lenin from sharply condemning Zinoviev's and Kamenev's behavior in October, 1917. After
the October Revolution, Zinoviev supported a coalition "socialist"
government and resigned from the CC as a token of protest. However,
he submitted to Party discipline and returned to responsible positions
in the Party and government. During the Civil War, Zinoviev was the
real leader of the Bolshevik organization in Petrograd, pursuing severe
policies that were not always justified. Even the chairman of the
Petrograd Cheka, M. S. Uritskii, was regarded by Zinoviev as too
soft for his job. During General Iudenich's advance on Leningrad,
Zinoviev lost his head and began to prepare the city for evacuation,
which provoked strong objections from Lenin. Some believe it was at
this time that a bitter quarrel occurred between Zinoviev and Trotsky,
which made them personal enemies. (The Central Committee sent
Stalin as well as Trotsky to Petrograd in 1919 to help organize the
city's defenses.)

When the Third International was organized, on Lenin's recommendation Zinoviev was elected chairman of the Executive Committee. He also remained chairman of the Petrograd Soviet (after 1924,
the Leningrad Soviet). It would be wrong to deny the services of
Zinoviev, for he occupied several responsible posts following the
October Revolution. But many people who knew Zinoviev have remarked not only on his extensive activity but also on his unscrupulous
methods and his vanity and egotism.

Kamenev also sided with the Bolsheviks after the IInd Party Congress, when he too was twenty. Later he took part in the IIIrd and IVth congresses, and was given an editorial position on *Proletarian.* During the revolutionary upsurge of 1912–14, Kamenev was sent to Russia to lead the Bolshevik faction in the Duma. He was the editor of *Pravda* until the beginning of the First World War. In 1914 Kamenev made his first serious political mistake. Taken to court in the treason trial of the Bolshevik faction, he behaved disgracefully. He declared that he disagreed with Lenin's slogan about the "defeat of our imperialist government." This behavior was sharply condemned by the Bolsheviks, including the exiles in Turukhanka, where Kamenev was sent after the trial.

Still, it was Kamenev who was the chairman of the April 1917 Conference of Bolsheviks and was elected to the CC on a motion by Lenin. Lenin defended this motion by saying that his dispute with Kamenev had allowed him to clear up the mistaken views some Bolsheviks held and thus to develop more convincing arguments to unite the Party around correct slogans. In 1918, Kamenev was the Chairman of the Moscow Soviet and a member of the CC. Here too his work was not free of errors. But his overall activity in the post-October period was steadily appraised by Lenin in a positive way. For example, in his last public speech in 1922 to an expanded meeting of the Moscow Soviet, Lenin called Kamenev an "exceptional horse" who was pulling two carts at once: in the Moscow Soviet and in the Council of Commissars, where Kamenev, on Lenin's recommendation, had been appointed first deputy chairman in 1922. As M. P. Iakubovich wrote in his memoirs, Kamenev was

> undoubtedly a man of high talents, broadly educated, devoted to the idea of the socialist revolution, and able to orient himself quickly in a complex political situation. He also had an outstanding literary talent, . . . and was a master of analysis. No one could formulate the conclusions of a discussion as clearly and precisely, or state them as objectively, as Kamenev.

But Iakubovich also noted that Kamenev had a dogmatic, formalist outlook on the Russian Revolution; he lacked Lenin's sensitivity and mastery of revolutionary theory.

In 1923–24 Kamenev chaired the meetings of the Politburo and the Council of Commissars. According to those who knew him well, he was not an ambitious man. He was a compliant leader, unreservedly under the influence of his political friend Zinoviev. It was obvious that in the political bloc of Zinoviev and Kamenev, Zinoviev played the leading role. After Lenin had stepped down from the Party leadership, Zinoviev—and Kamenev along with him—sought to fill the role of Party leader, to become the main theorist and interpreter of Leninism. Zinoviev saw the main threat to himself coming not from Stalin but from Trotsky. Stalin was not well educated in theory and was not popular in the Party. Both Zinoviev and Kamenev depicted themselves as veterans of the Bolshevik Party and constantly emphasized that Trotsky had joined the Bolsheviks only in 1917. In response, Trotsky would bring up their capitulatory behavior during that year. Concurrently, Trotsky's supporters were creating an aura around him as the leader of the October armed insurrection and the organizer of the Red Army's victories in the Civil War. That is why Zinoviev and Kamenev brought Stalin to the forefront, since he too had taken an active part in the preparations for the October insurrection and in the Civil War. Zinoviev, aware of the mutual dislike between Stalin and Trotsky, assumed that Stalin would be able to check Trotsky and open the way for his own rise to power. Thus Zinoviev and Kamenev actively opposed implementation of Lenin's proposal—in his "Testament"—to remove Stalin from the post of General Secretary.

Stalin turned out to be much craftier than Zinoviev. In a short time, Stalin managed to see the advantages of his position and to make use of them. Although the Secretariat was formally subordinate to the Politburo, the actual relations between these two organs of the Central Committee were quite different. Whereas the Politburo in 1924 met only about once a week, the Secretariat was the working organ of the Central Committee. It coordinated the various services of the CC, directed all Party organizations in the *oblasti* and the big cities, and appointed and transferred many state and Party officials. These roles gave the Secretariat a great opportunity to exercise the actual leadership of the Party. The Secretariat also prepared questions for the Politburo and thereby often predetermined their solution.

Lenin was simultaneously leader of the government's Council of Commissars and of the Party's Central Committee. The greater part of his time was devoted to the Council of Commissars; from it and from the Council for Labor and Defense, basic directives went out to the provinces signed by Lenin. This procedure greatly increased the importance of Soviet, that is, governmental institutions. After Lenin had withdrawn from the Party and state leadership, the functions were divided: the leader of the Party CC and the chairman of the Council of Commissars were different people. But the real leader of the CC turned out to be not the man who presided at meetings of the Politburo, Kamenev, but the General Secretary—and that was Stalin. Since the Communist Party was the only ruling party, the role of Party leader became dominant after the division of functions between the leaders of the government's Council of Commissars and the Party's Central Committee. Thus the post of General Secretary of the Party became the most important office in the Soviet state, although at first few people were aware of the process. At the same time the Party organs in the provinces enjoyed an upsurge in their importance, while many Soviet organs suffered a commensurate decline.

Stalin took clever advantage of these changes. Relying on the many "fighters" and "practical" people in the Party, steadily encouraging their resentment against the preponderant "theorists," Stalin also formed a bloc with the Bukharin-Rykov group in the Politburo. Thus, when Trotsky's opposition was defeated in 1923–24, it was not Zinoviev but, rather surprisingly, Stalin who acquired decisive influence in the CC. Another element in this turn of events was the fact that Rykov, Stalin's ally, became chairman of the Council of Commissars after Lenin's death. Kamenev, who had been the real leader of the Council during Lenin's illness, was denied the formal title on the pretext of his Jewish origins. "We must," Stalin is supposed to have said, "consider the peasant character of Russia." As for Bukharin, it was in this period that he was raised to the rank of chief theorist, and it was his economic platform that Stalin endorsed in 1924–25.

Thus, by the first half of 1925 Stalin had driven Zinoviev out of the Party leadership. Furthermore, he tried everything possible to bring Zinoviev's and Kamenev's actions under his control. The end of the "friendship" of Stalin with Zinoviev and Kamenev was to a large extent the origin of the protests of the "left" against Stalin's leadership. Of course such personal motives were not the only cause; a large and often crucial role was played by differences over economic and political platforms.

After the October Revolution in Russia, Lenin and all the other Party leaders expected that socialist revolutions would break out in the countries of Western Europe. They thought that Russia would begin the socialist revolution and Europe would continue it. The November, 1918 revolution in Germany and the 1919 outbreak in Hungary seemed to confirm these expectations. Although events in Germany did not progress beyond a bourgeois-democratic revolution and the Hungarian Soviet Republic was suppressed by foreign intervention, still the creation of the Comintern, the rise of the Communist movement throughout the world, and the new revolutionary upsurge in Europe, which lasted until 1923, generated hopes for a rapid development of world revolution. But by 1924 the revolutionary movement in Europe had obviously declined and the period of the so-called stabilization of capitalism had begun. This gave rise to disillusionment and depression among some revolutionaries, and the Party did not escape such moods. Party members and leaders were confronted with the problem of how to build socialism in an economically backward country encircled by capitalism.

Until that time the opinion in the Party had been that backward

Russia could begin the socialist revolution, but could not continue it—
not to speak of achieving a complete socialist society—without the
aid and support of a socialist Europe. Trotsky was not alone in this
belief. In the early years of the revolution this opinion was shared by
Lenin. For example, on March 12, 1919, Lenin told the Petrograd
Soviet:

> Only by appraising the role of the Soviets on a world scale can we
> achieve a correct understanding of the details of our internal life
> and a proper regulation of them. *The job of construction is com-*
> *pletely dependent on how soon the revolution will succeed in the*
> *more important European countries. Only after it succeeds there can*
> *we seriously get down to the job of construction.*[24]

On November 6, 1920, Lenin said to the Moscow Soviet:

> If we take a look at international relations at this time—and we
> have always emphasized that we look at things from an international
> point of view, *and that in a single country it is impossible to com-*
> *plete such a thing as a socialist revolution*—and if we look at the
> history of the wars waged against Soviet Russia, then we will
> see. . . .[25]

In 1921–22, when it became clear that the socialist revolution in
Europe would be delayed and the New Economic Policy (NEP) was
beginning in the USSR, Lenin re-examined his position on building a
socialist society. Analysis of his last works makes this clear, especially
the articles "On Cooperation" and "On Our Revolution." But many
Party leaders did not pay proper attention to Lenin's new approach
to this problem, and continued as before to assert that it was impossible to build a socialist society in a single country, and a backward
one at that. Stalin was a leader of this type. In the first versions of
his *On the Foundations of Leninism,* Stalin wrote that for "the organization of socialist production, the efforts of one country, especially a
peasant country like Russia, are not enough. For this, the efforts of
the proletariat of several developed countries are needed."[26] Later, in
1925, Stalin reconsidered his point of view, and made certain changes
in editing this work. But Zinoviev and Kamenev still clung to confused and for the most part incorrect views on this question.

[24] *Severnaia Kommuna,* No. 58, Mar. 14, 1919. In the third edition of Lenin's collected
works, a footnote informs us that this speech is printed according to the text of the
newspaper *Severnaia Kommuna.* But the two sentences italicized here have been
omitted.
[25] *Stenograficheskie otchety Moskovskogo Soveta rabochikh, krest'ianskikh i krasnoar-*
meiskikh deputatov, Biulleten', No. 15. (In the second and third editions of Lenin's
collected works, this speech was printed exactly according to the text of the
Bulletin. But in the fourth and fifth editions, the part we have italicized is missing,
although the reference to *Bulletin* No. 15 is preserved.)
[26] See *XIV s'ezd VKP(b),* p. 429. *Ed.:* See E. H. Carr, *The Interregnum* (New York,
1954), p. 359, for full bibliographical information on this passage.

Zinoviev and Kamenev also made incorrect statements and proposals on a number of concrete problems of economic development. For example, Kamenev proposed not only that taxation of the prosperous sections of the peasantry be raised—he suggested that the agricultural tax be increased from 300 million to 400 or 500 million rubles—but also that an additional billion rubles be extracted from the countryside for the needs of industrialization. The opposition believed that this was the only way to maintain the dictatorship of the proletariat in the country until the socialist revolution triumphed in the West. Zinoviev's main theoretical work, *Leninism,* which came out in 1925 before the XIVth Party Congress, contained several theoretical errors and misguided recommendations. He was wrong in arguing that the Soviet economy and many industrial enterprises were state-capitalist. Zinoviev saw the New Economic Policy largely as a retreat. The leaders of the "new opposition" exaggerated the influence of the kulak in the postrevolutionary countryside. Zinoviev failed to appreciate the difference between the 1921 and the 1923 views of Lenin on the prospects of peasant cooperation. The list of such mistakes and "sins" could be extended—and complicated by the fact that the leaders of the "new" opposition differed among themselves on many important theoretical questions.[27]

In 1925 the Party rejected Zinoviev and Kamenev's bid for leadership of the Central Committee, as it had just rejected Trotsky's. In retrospect, it can be seen that the "new" opposition made not only mistakes but also many statements and demands which were justified. The justice of their warnings about the danger of the growing cult of certain leaders, especially the cult of Stalin, must be acknowledged.[28] And the criticism of Stalin's and Bukharin's agricultural policies that Zinoviev and Kamenev made in 1925 was not without foundation. The opposition pointed out that the policy of restricting the kulaks was not being applied consistently, and that the development of cooperatives was slow. While Kamenev suggested an increase in the agricultural tax, Stalin and Bukharin proposed and put into effect a major decrease and also lowered wholesale prices on many manufactured goods sold in the countryside. Bukharin's slogan for the peasants, "Get rich," was not untypical of him in 1925. And although this slogan was condemned in the CC, the condemnation was very mild and did not touch on his basic economic proposals. The adoption of these proposals, in the conditions of the goods shortage in 1925, led to an increase in the money held by the kulaks and a decrease in the state revenues available for the needs of industrialization.

[27] See their speeches to the XIVth Party Congress.
[28] See especially the remarks on this subject that Kamenev and G. Ia. Sokol'nikov made to the XIVth Party Congress.

The opposition was also justified in its criticism of the growing harshness of the intraparty regime under the slogan of Party unity. As L. S. Shaumian has pointed out, Stalin was incapable of persuading his opponents, of subordinating them to the Party's ideological influence, of resolving disagreements by democratic methods, as Lenin had done. Resorting to administrative decrees, Stalin used the intra-party struggle to strengthen his personal position and power.[29] Under such conditions a normal struggle of ideas within the Party became impossible. Many who sympathized with the views of the opposition leaders were obliged to conceal their opinions and to vote with the majority more from fear of reprisals than from conviction. On the other hand, some Party leaders and members (evidently including Krupskaia) found themselves for a while in the opposition camp not so much because of sympathy for the opposition's views as in protest against Stalin's mean and imperious ways. Thus Krupskaia spoke at the XIVth Party Congress against suppression of intraparty democracy, against the removal of opposition members from important Party posts, against the demand that opposition members not only carry out the decisions of the majority but also immediately and publicly renounce their own views, a demand Lenin never made of his opponents.

Stalin hastened to consolidate his victory over the "new" opposition by organizational measures. Although Zinoviev and Kamenev remained members of the Politburo, Zinoviev was removed from the the post of chairman of the Executive Committee of the Comintern. That post was simply abolished in 1926, and Bukharin was named head of the secretariat of the Comintern's Executive Committee. Zinoviev was also removed as chairman of the Leningrad City Soviet, and the leadership of the Leningrad *oblast* Party Committee was taken from his supporters. S. M. Kirov was made first secretary of the Leningrad *obkom*. Kamenev was removed as chairman of the Council of Labor and Defense—Rykov replaced him—and as deputy chairman of the Council of Commissars.

4

STALIN'S PERSONAL POWER and influence were also increased by the sudden deaths of two of the oldest and most respected Bolsheviks with key positions in the Soviet government, M. V. Frunze and F. E. Dzerzhinskii.

The first to die was Frunze, an outstanding Civil War general who held a leading position in the Red Army. In March, 1924, Frunze replaced E. M. Sklianskii as deputy chairman of the Revolutionary-

---

[29] Shaumian, "Kul't lichnosti," *Filosofskaia entsiklopediia,* III (1964), p. 114.

Military Soviet, and at the same time was appointed Chief of Staff of the Red Army. In January, 1925, Frunze replaced Trotsky as Commissar of Military and Naval Affairs and as chairman of the Revolutionary-Military Soviet.

An able, determined, and intelligent man, Frunze enjoyed considerable influence in the Party as well as the army. (It has been suggested that Lenin had Frunze or Ia. E. Rudzutak in mind when he suggested the replacement of Stalin as General Secretary.)

Frunze suffered from a stomach ulcer that at times incapacitated him. But a stomach ulcer is not malignant; it does not threaten the patient's life, and the prognosis is generally good. Even in 1925 an experienced doctor knew that a special diet should be tried, and only if this was unsuccessful would there be need of surgery.

The evidence suggests that Frunze did not want an operation, for he was improving without it. On October 26, 1925, the day before entering the hospital, he wrote to his wife:

> I am feeling absolutely healthy and it is somehow ridiculous not only to go to the hospital, but even to think about an operation. Nevertheless both consultations brought the decision to operate. [My italics.—R.M.] I am personally satisfied with this decision. Let them once and for all take a good look at what's there and try to decide on a real cure. In my own mind the thought constantly recurs that there is nothing seriously wrong with me, since, if the opposite is true, it is difficult to explain my speedy recovery after rest and treatment.[30]

There is reason to doubt that Frunze was really satisfied with the decision to operate, which had been discussed in the Politburo with Stalin and Voroshilov insisting that it be done. Frunze was a soldier and did not want to appear cowardly, but he spoke freely to an old friend, who writes:

> Not long before the operation, I went to see him. He was upset and said he did not want to lie down on the operating table. . . . The premonition of some trouble, of something irreversible, oppressed him. . . . I tried to persuade Mikhail Vasilievich to refuse the operation, since the thought of it depressed him. But he shook his head: "Stalin insists on the operation," he said, "to get rid of my ulcers for good. So I decided to go under the knife."[31]

Chloroform was used, although ether was known to be a better anesthetic for the purpose. Worse yet, Frunze was given more than a normal dose of chloroform, which was clearly dangerous for his heart. No stomach ulcer was found, only a little scar tissue at the site of a

[30] See S. Sirotinskii, "Poslednie dni," *Krasnaia zvezda*, Oct. 31, 1930.
[31] I. K. Gamburg, *Tak eto bylo* (Moscow, 1962).

healed ulcer. Very soon after the operation, Stalin and A. I. Mikoian came to the hospital but were not admitted to the patient's room. Stalin sent Frunze a note: "Dear Friend: Today at 5.00 P.M. Mikoian and I saw Comrade [Doctor] Rozanov. We wanted to visit you, but he wouldn't let us—ulcer. We were obliged to give in. Don't worry, old buddy. Greetings. We'll come again, we'll come again . . . Koba."[32]

Neither Stalin nor Mikoian was obliged to see Frunze alive. Thirty hours after the operation, his heart stopped. The autopsy and other medical reports published in *Pravda* (November 1, 1925) were confused, inconsistent, and evasive. On November 3, 1925, *Pravda* carried several articles dedicated to Frunze's memory. ("Can we reproach his poor heart," wrote Mikhail Kol'tsov, for example, "for giving way to sixty grams of chloroform after it had endured two years of a death sentence, with the hangman's noose around its neck?") An official article was included—"On the History of Comrade Frunze's Disease." "In view of the interest that the question of the history of Frunze's disease has for his comrades," the introduction said, "and the associated question of his operation, the editors consider it appropriate to print the following document." Then came the records of the two consultations at Frunze's bedside and the concluding report about the operation. The records asserted that an operation was required because Frunze's life was endangered by recurrent hemorrhaging from a bleeding ulcer. Yet the concluding report of the operation spoke only of "a little scar . . . evidently on the site of a healed ulcer."

On November 3, *Izvestiia* published an interview with one of the surgeons, Professor Grekov. His account, which pictured Frunze as smiling joyfully at the news of Stalin's visit, was inconsistent with the other medical reports, and gave no evidence to support the final declaration: "All the changes revealed by the operation undoubtedly support the view that, without the operation, Comrade Frunze was incurable, and was threatened by inevitable and possibly sudden death." The circumstances surrounding Frunze's death were so unclear and contradictory that at the end of 1925, the Communists of Ivanovo-Voznesensk—with which Frunze's revolutionary activity had been closely connected—demanded the creation of a special commission to examine the causes of his death. In *Novyi Mir*, No. 5, 1926, the writer Boris Pilnyak published a story, "The Tale of the Unextinguished Moon," in which he unambiguously accused Stalin of the death of Frunze.[33] The entire issue of the journal with Pilnyak's story was quickly confiscated. A few subscribers received the journal, but some hours later the postmen took back the copies they had delivered.

---

[32] See Sirotinskii, *op. cit.*
[33] *Ed.*: For an English translation see Boris Pilnyak, *Mother Earth and Other Stories* (Garden City, N.Y., 1968), pp. 181–211.

Frunze was succeeded as Commissar of Military and Naval Affairs by Voroshilov, who could claim certain services to the Party and the revolution, but utterly lacked Frunze's intellect and was heavily under Stalin's influence.

July, 1926, saw the sudden death of F. E. Dzerzhinskii, the "knight of the revolution," chief of the punitive organs of the young Soviet state. He succeeded Trotsky as Commissar for Communications, and from 1924 was chairman of the Supreme Council of the National Economy. At the same time he remained the chairman of the Cheka, and later of the OGPU. Many books have been written about this outstanding revolutionary and we will not give here any facts from his biography. "Dzerzhinskii," said V. R. Menzhinskii, "had his own special talent, which sets him apart. That was a moral talent, a talent for unwavering revolutionary action and for creativity that was not stopped by any obstacles, and was not guided by any goals except one —the triumph of the proletarian revolution."[34] Dzerzhinskii's enemies hated him, but in the Party he was not only respected but loved. According to some reports, in 1925, before the XIVth Party Congress, a semilegal meeting of some CC members was held at the apartment of G. I. Petrovskii, to discuss the need to remove Stalin from the position of General Secretary. Dzerzhinskii was suggested for the position. Ordzhonikidze spoke against the change, claiming that the Party would interpret it as a concession to Trotsky. The bitterness of the intraparty conflict upset Dzerzhinskii very much and hastened his end.

For a short while the death of Dzerzhinskii united all the groups of the Party. According to the evidence of M. P. Iakubovich, his coffin was carried to Red Square by Trotsky, Zinoviev, Kamenev, Stalin, Bukharin, and Rykov. But that was a last demonstration of Party solidarity over the grave of a Party favorite and hero. For it was in that same summer of 1926 that the intraparty struggle flared up with new force. The position of chairman of OGPU was filled by Menzhinskii, one of Dzerzhinskii's leading colleagues. For all his good points, Menzhinskii could not really replace Dzerzhinskii in that responsible post. Besides, he was often ill and could devote little time to OGPU business. Thus an ever greater role was played by the deputy chairmen of OGPU, one of whom soon came to the fore—Iagoda, who enjoyed Stalin's protection.

5

AT THE XIVth Party Congress in December, 1925, Trotsky took no part in the conflict between the majority and the "new" opposition.

[34] *Pravda*, May 11, 1934.

Most of Trotsky's active supporters voted against the platform of Zinoviev and Kamenev. Only two years earlier, Zinoviev and Kamenev had been Trotsky's strongest opponents. Zinoviev had demanded that the victory over the Trotskyites be consolidated by organizational measures, that Trotsky be expelled from the Politburo. Zinoviev had dismissed as slander Trotsky's warnings about the danger of degeneration and bureaucratization of the Party *apparat*. In his speech summing up the XIIIth Congress in May, 1924, Zinoviev had declared:

> When they say here that the Party lives on two stories—upstairs they decide, downstairs they only learn of the decisions—I ask: Can you imagine a more poisonous weapon against the Party? . . . Can a more serious accusation be hurled at the Party? Comrade Trotsky continues . . . the same thing for half a page: "bureaucratic mistrust," "the arrogance of the *apparat*," "suppression," "artificial selection," "intimidation," "maneuvers," "temporary concessions," "diplomatic methods." . . . What worse things could be said against the Party? . . . What more can a man say, if he is consciously trying to compromise its leading cadres?[35]

Zinoviev had also declared that Trotskyism had nothing in common with Leninism: "Whoever wants to build the Party in alliance with Trotsky, in collaboration with Trotskyism, which openly opposes Bolshevism, such a person is abandoning the fundamentals of Leninism."[36] Zinoviev was echoed by Kamenev. "Our Party," he told the Vth Krasnopresnenskaia Conference, "is united by its wish to stay on the Leninist road; we will allow no one, not even Comrade Trotsky, to change Leninism or to add to Leninism a single drop of Trotskyism or Menshevism."

In 1923–24, Zinoviev and Kamenev spoke out strongly not only against Trotsky's faction but against all factions, groups, and trends within the Party. Even in 1925, when they had organized their own faction, Zinoviev and Kamenev continued to oppose Trotsky and also accused the CC majority of being soft on Trotskyism. Speaking in Leningrad just before the XIVth Party Congress, Zinoviev's supporters called the CC "semi-Trotskyite." But when Zinoviev and Kamenev found themselves in a minority at the XIVth Congress, they radically changed their line. Embittered by defeat, Zinoviev proposed to Trotsky in the summer of 1926 that they form a union against Stalin and create the "united" opposition under Trotsky's leadership. Trotsky agreed. The union was accompanied by a mutual remission of sins. For example, Zinoviev said:

> There was an unfortunate time when we, two groups of genuine proletarian revolutionaries, were at each other's throats, instead of

[35] See *XIII s'ezd VKP(b); stenograficheskii otchet* (Moscow, 1924).
[36] G. Zinoviev, *O neobkhodimosti trekh perestrakhovok* (Moscow, 1925).

joining forces against backsliding Stalin and his friends. We regret this very much, and hope it will never happen again.[37]

And Trotsky returned the favor:

> In *Lessons of October* I associated the names of Comrades Zinoviev and Kamenev with political opportunism. As the ideological struggle within the CC has shown, that was a nasty mistake. It can be explained by the fact that I was unable to follow the ideological struggle within the septemvirate, to determine in time that it was the group headed by Stalin which was starting opportunistic maneuvers against Comrades Zinoviev and Kamenev.[38]

The unexpected alliance of Zinoviev, Kamenev, and Trotsky intensified the struggle within the Party. But it did not improve the chances of the opposition. Everyone could still remember the bitter struggle between the Trotskyites and the Zinovievites, during which the leaders were not sparing in their opinions of each other. The reversal of the leaders was too sharp, and their mutual amnesty led to the defection of many rank-and-file members. The "united" opposition turned out to be weaker than any of the previous groups, and many of the supporters of both Trotsky and Zinoviev considered its formation a major political mistake.

A comparison of Trotsky's platform of 1923–24 with that of Zinoviev and Kamenev in 1925 reveals several points in common, which formed the basis of the platform of the "united" opposition. Without analyzing this platform in any detail, it should be noted that some of its criticisms were justified. As subsequent events would show, it was correct to demand that the theory of "social fascism"[39] be condemned. This theory helped the right-wing leaders of the Social Democrats, and hindered the formation of a united front of all the democratic forces against fascism. Nor can one disagree with the opposition's protests against the increasingly rigid control over Party members, who were steadily being trained to shut up and stand at attention.

There was also justice in the opposition's criticism of aspects of the economic policies of Stalin, Bukharin, and Rykov. Although industrial production increased at a fast pace in 1925–26—by about a third—some dangerous disproportions could be detected in the national economy. Despite the growth of industrial production, the shortage of manufactured goods became more acute, mainly because of a rapid increase of effective demand in the cities and especially in

---

[37] G. Zinoviev, *Rech' na prezidiume Ts.K.K.* 26/VI, p. 62.

[38] L. Trotsky, "Zaiavlenie po lichnomy voprosu." *Ob'edinennyi plenum Ts.K. i Ts.K.K., 14–23 iiulia 1926 g., vypusk* 4, p. 103.

[39] *Ed.:* Stalin applied this label to the Social Democratic parties of Western Europe, until the triumph of Nazism in Germany caused him to turn about and seek a united front.

the countryside. The shortage of goods put a strain on the economy. It impeded the flow of peasant grain surpluses to the market. Exports were appreciably curtailed, largely at the expense of grain, and imports had to be cut back. Of course the cuts were not made in imports of industrial equipment, but in raw materials such as cotton. That made trouble in the textile industry; there was partial unemployment in the factories, and the quality of many products deteriorated. The supply of foreign currency grew extremely short, and from month to month foreign trade became more and more passive. The Soviet Union's debt to foreign firms rose by hundreds of millions of rubles. Exceptional measures had to be taken: the delivery of goods purchased abroad had to be put off on various pretexts; gold had to be sent abroad to support Soviet credit; special commissions on foreign currency had to be formed. At the Third Plenum of the Moscow Party Committee (February, 1926), it was reported that the Soviet Union had bought and imported a large number of tractors but was obliged to exclude from the import plan the implements designed to be attached to them, without which the tractors could not be used.[40]

The Central Committee and the Council of Commissars did devise measures to keep the temporary difficulties from developing into a general economic crisis. But not all of these measures were well conceived or effective. This is especially true of the CC's price policy in 1926–27, which was harshly attacked by the opposition. The great increase in effective demand and the simultaneous decrease in goods available inevitably led to an increase in wholesale and retail prices. Obviously the process had to be regulated somehow, so that prices would not rise too quickly with wages following. A real decrease in prices could be effected only by swift growth in the production of deficit goods, by raising the productivity of labor, and by lowering trade costs. But the CC tried to lower prices by a series of decrees. For example, a CC Plenum in February, 1927, noting that previous orders for price reduction had been without effect, simply reasserted the orders more strenuously. A 10 per cent reduction in retail prices was to be achieved in less than six months, by "mobilizing all the forces of Party organization and the broad masses of the toiling people."[41] We know of no serious contemporary research on this matter, but analysis of some decrees that Party and state agencies issued in 1927–28 shows that the decree of the 1927 February Plenum, especially with respect to retail prices, could not be implemented.

Kamenev's and Zinoviev's warnings in the summer and fall of 1926 about an impending crisis in the state procurement of grain were also correct. In the fall of 1926, Stalin and many of his cohorts scoffed

---

[40] *Tretii plenum MK VKP (b). Doklady i rezoliutsii* (Moscow, 1926).
[41] *Rezoliutsii Plenuma TsK VKP (b)* (Moscow, 1927), pp. 29–30.

at the opposition's "prophecies" of a possible breakdown in grain procurements. *Bol'shevik,* the theoretical journal of the CC, carried an article at the end of 1926 sneering at Kamenev's dire warnings and declaring that the campaign that fall had brought in more grain at lower prices than in the previous year.[42] But very soon after this article appeared, the crisis in grain procurement became a reality. The government was unable to influence the grain market by any maneuvers. In December, 1927, and at the beginning of 1928, Stalin explained the crisis in grain procurement, which had come as a complete surprise to most of the Party, by citing almost the same causes that Kamenev had talked about much earlier.

In the summer of 1926, Kamenev had called not only for a change in price policy, but also for an increase in the agricultural tax. These proposals were rejected at the XVth Party Conference in October, 1926. "The opposition has been howling," wrote E. Goldenberg,

> about the need for a sharp increase in the tax. But at whose expense? At the expense of the poor peasants, who are exempt from the tax? That is out of the question. At the expense of the middle peasants? But that would mean forcing the process of stratification, weakening the stability of the middle peasants, making them less capable of struggling with the kulaks. At the expense of the kulaks? But who doesn't know that increasing the tax to more than 25 per cent of their income would mean going beyond a tax to virtual dekulakization, a return to the methods of war communism? Everything the opposition has said and written on this subject is nothing but empty and irresponsible demagogy.[43]

Several months later, Stalin himself was forced to implement a policy of exceptional measures in the countryside—a policy that went much further than anything Kamenev had proposed. This will be discussed in more detail in the following chapter.

Despite some correct criticism and proposals, the platform of the "united" opposition was wrong. Just as it had been for Trotsky, so also for Zinoviev and Kamenev the starting point was the impossibility of building a socialist society in a single country like Russia. According to most of the opposition leaders, the nation was in no position to overtake the capitalist countries without state aid from the Western proletariat, which could not be expected until they won power. This was stated in a declaration of fourteen leading oppositionists on June 2, 1927:

> The technological backwardness of our country and the resulting low productivity of labor are enormous obstacles to the building of a socialist society. Because of this backwardness, the transition to a

[42] E. Goldenberg, "Khoziaistvennyi vopros na XV Konferentsii," *Bol'shevik,* 1926, No. 21–22, pp. 14–15.
[43] *Ibid.,* p. 17.

truly socialist organization of production (in which the workers are transformed from instruments into masters of production, and the commodity character of production is eliminated) is impossible without aid from advanced countries, without a world socialist revolution.[44]

Moreover, the opposition leaders in the heat of polemics exaggerated the country's shortcomings, which provoked the Party cadres to protest. They depicted tendencies as well-developed processes, unripe fruit as completely ripened. At a time when only a small part of the Party leadership was touched by degeneration, the opposition was speaking of the degeneration of the entire Party or at least of a majority of the CC. While the opposition's criticism of the Party regime was not without basis, its call for a "revolution in the Party regime" seemed to the majority of the Party cadres to be dangerous pseudoleftism. Denying genuine achievements, the opposition tried to represent the Party's course as an uninterrupted retreat. From the increase of kulaks and the nepman bourgeoisie—completely natural under NEP—the opposition drew the conclusion that Stalin and Bukharin were reviving capitalism. As an opposition platform put it:

> There are two mutually exclusive positions. One is the position of the proletariat building socialism, the other the position of the bourgeoisie trying to switch our development onto the rails of capitalism. . . . Between these two positions, but moving closer all the time to the second, lies the Stalinist line [read: the line of the CC], which consists of brief zigzags to the left, and extended ones to the right.[45]

Other false claims of the opposition were that the private sector was accumulating capital more quickly than the social sector, and that the bourgeois intelligentsia had more control over industry and finance than the Bolshevik party. " 'Ambassadors' of Ustrialov—yes, and of Miliukov[46] too—" Zinoviev told a meeting of the Central Control Commission in 1926,

> are in Moscow. They are in fact directing work in the Commissariat of Finance, the Commissariat of Agriculture, the State Planning Commission; they are directing more than we and Kalinin are. In words, these "Changing Landmarks" professors are merely working for us, but in fact they are making the decisions.[47]

[44] *Oppozitsionnyi neomen'shevizm* (Moscow, 1927), p. 4.
[45] *Bol'shevik*, 1927, No. 19–20, p. 13.
[46] *Ed.:* N. V. Ustrialov, an émigré professor, was the leading spokesman of the trend known as "Changing Landmarks" (*Smena vekh*), after its chief publication, which called on the intelligentsia within the Soviet Union to work with the Bolshevik regime in the expectation that it would evolve into a parliamentary democracy. Paul Miliukov, head of the Constitutional Democratic Party (Cadets) before the Bolsheviks suppressed it, was then an émigré in France.
[47] *Partiia i oppozitsiia po dokumentam, vypusk* I (1927), p. 57.

Zinoviev's thesis about Miliukov's "ambassadors" in the economic
apparat served Stalin well a few years later, when he tried to throw
all the blame for the faults of his own economic leadership onto the
"wreckers" among the specialists. "The ruling circles," declared
Trotsky,

> are increasingly growing together with the upper strata of Soviet-
> nepman society. Two strata are being created, two life styles, two
> types of attitudes, two types of relationships, or, to put it more
> strongly, the elements of a dual power[48] in everyday life are being
> created. Further development may transform it into a political dual
> power, and a political dual power would be a direct threat to the
> dictatorship of the proletariat. . . . The proletariat must understand
> that in a certain period of history, if its policy goes wrong, the
> Soviet state could become an apparatus through which power could
> be moved from its proletarian base and put into the hands of the
> bourgeoisie, which would then kick aside the Soviet "footstool"
> and convert its power into a Bonapartist system.[49]

It goes without saying that the upper echelons of Party and state were
not growing together with the upper levels of the nepman bourgeoisie
in 1926. The degeneration of a section of the Party was far more
complex and concealed.

The opposition leaders were right to criticize the policy of lowering
retail and wholesale prices when there was a shortage of goods, but
some of them suggested that prices on industrial goods be raised by
30 per cent, which was incorrect. It was typical of them to denounce
the seven-hour working day, which was introduced in celebration of
the tenth anniversary of the October Revolution. The desire of the
workers to mark this occasion by some major social reform was entirely
natural. Of course one might claim, in view of the economic difficulties
of 1926–27, that the seven-hour day was premature. But Zinoviev
was exaggerating when he said, "I maintain that there has never yet
been a more demagogical and reckless proposal in the history of our
Party than this proposal for a seven-hour day." And some of the most
"left-wing" oppositionists reported to the XVth Party Congress that
the CC had already taken the road toward overturning the state and
liquidating the Party.

The opposition resorted to exaggeration to discredit the CC majority and remove Stalin from the Party leadership. This might have
been a worthy goal, in view of the harm Stalin later did the Party.
But Stalin's political opponents were too hasty with their attack, striking at Stalin in conditions unfavorable to themselves. The problem
was that the real shortcomings, faults, and potential effects of Stalin's

[48] *Ed.:* A reference to the dual power of the Provisional Government and the Soviets in
the period between March and November, 1917.
[49] *Ibid.,* p. 58.

leadership were not yet completely evident; not only the rank and file but the majority of Party leaders had not yet recognized his true character. Stalin's opponents in the CC did not adequately appreciate another complication: in a one-party system, in the complex setting of the mid-1920's, an opposition group within the Party would attract certain antiparty and anti-Soviet forces. The opposition should have taken this into consideration when choosing forms and methods of intraparty struggle, but it did not always do so.

Stalin craftily took advantage of a situation unfavorable to the "united" opposition. He accused its leaders of being unprincipled, by quoting the harsh remarks that the opposition leaders had recently made about each other. Moreover, Stalin lumped together the past mistakes of Trotsky, Zinoviev, and Kamenev. At the same time Stalin was careful not to emphasize the diverse, complex problems of economic policy, for here his arguments were not very convincing and the economic difficulties were only too evident. He stressed Party unity; he accused the opposition of fomenting factional conflict. At a time when the building of socialism was only beginning, and the question of "who will win" (*Kto kogo?*) was still far from decided, the Party masses felt a powerful urge for unity, which allowed Stalin to rally round himself an overwhelming majority of the Party.

Practically speaking, by the fall of 1926—that is, only a few months after the creation of the "united" opposition—it had become clear that this opposition was foundering. When its leaders realized this, they gave the signal for retreat. In *Pravda* for October 17, 1926, a declaration by Zinoviev, Kamenev, Sokol'nikov, Trotsky, G. L. Piatakov, and G. E. Evdokimov briefly reaffirmed their views on "a series of fundamental issues" but acknowledged at length their sins against the Leninist rules of Party organization. They had formed factions to support their views. Now they called upon their followers to dissolve all factional groups and to confine further advocacy of their views to "the forms provided by the Party statute and by the decisions of the Congresses and the CC." On this basis they hoped that recently expelled oppositionists would earn readmission to the Party, where they could join the struggle against any slackening of Party discipline.

However, the oppositionist leaders could not live up to such declarations. They could not help displaying their dissatisfaction with Stalin and the CC majority. While continuing to defend their views in "the forms provided by the Party statute"—newspaper and magazine articles, petitions, and declarations—in many instances they were forced by the logic of struggle to overstep the limits of the Party statute, which provoked immediate repression by Stalin and the Central Committee majority. For Stalin vigilantly followed the activity of the leaders of the opposition. He openly rejected a truce with Trotsky and Zinoviev. Realizing his advantage, Stalin sought to smash his political rivals completely and to establish one-man rule over the Party. Not only the opposition but Stalin as well frequently committed very serious violations of Leninist norms in Party life. He did everything possible to obstruct Party discussions of theoretical and practical problems. While exhorting the opposition to be sincere and condemning its hypocrisy, he was himself a hypocrite who deceived the Party and concealed his true goals. By first supporting Zinoviev and Kamenev against Trotsky, then Bukharin, Rykov, and Tomskii against Zinoviev and Kamenev, Stalin did not unite the Party. He split it; he intensified existing disagreements, pushing toward the suppression and expulsion of those who disagreed with him.

Stalin, Molotov, Kaganovich, E. M. Iaroslavskii, and some of their supporters made the intraparty struggle of the twenties dirtier and harsher than it had been previously—and so, for that matter, did Trotsky, Zinoviev, Kamenev, and some of their supporters. The clash of ideas was increasingly replaced by organizational conflict; the least mistake or vacillation was blown up to huge proportions and many statements were willfully distorted and misinterpreted. The slightest disagreement with the Central Committee majority was immediately turned into "an enemy outburst," or "subversion of the proletarian dictatorship and the Soviet regime," and the opposition was declared to be an "active counterrevolutionary force." Such criticism was not designed to win over the oppositionists or to draw them back to united work in the Party. It was primarily intended to terrorize opposition members and the "conciliators" who sympathized with them. This kind of fight among the Party leaders, who enjoyed great prestige in foreign Communist parties, weakened the Comintern and caused some leaders of Western Communist parties to protest. Antonio Gramsci, for example, tried to send a letter from a fascist prison to the Soviet Central Committee, expressing his dismay at the intraparty struggle in the Soviet Union.

It is not surprising that a "truce" would not last for long. And, in fact, in 1927 just before the XVth Congress, the intraparty struggle was taken to the streets. There was a demonstration when I. T. Smilga was banished from Moscow for factional activity. When the train for Siberia left the Iaroslav Station, about a thousand people gathered to protest the policy of banishment. The opposition leaders, constantly obstructed in their efforts to bring their program to the Party's notice, secretly mimeographed their documents and Lenin's "Testament," and even tried by conspiratorial methods to gain control of a Moscow publishing house. This enabled Stalin to bring the GPU as well as the Party machine into the fight against the opposition. GPU agents infiltrated the ranks of the opposition without much difficulty, and one of them became an operator of an illegal Trotskyite printing press—

obviously engaged in more than simple observation of the opposition's activity. In the fall of 1927, the first arrests of oppositionists were made.

The opposition's semilegal and occasionally illegal activities were the main issue at the joint meeting of the Central Committee and the Central Control Commission at the end of October, 1927. Trotsky's speech at this meeting, the last he ever gave before the Central Committee,[50] shows clearly how unrealistic the opposition was. A program criticizing the leaders in an extremely sharp manner, indeed with elements of demagogy, could hardly win support among the leaders, or even among the rank and file, of a party *in power*. The program did win some sympathy in opposition circles outside the Party, among Western Social Democrats, and among a small section of the Party youth and intelligentsia. On the other hand, the ugly speeches of Trotsky's opponents, such as Skrypnik, Goloshchekin, I. S. Unshlikht, V. Ia. Chubar, and G. I. Lomov, make a very bad impression, especially on the reader who knows that only ten years later they would be destroyed by Stalin.

The Plenum decided that Trotsky and Zinoviev had broken their promise to cease factional activity. They were expelled from the Central Committee, and the forthcoming XVth Congress was directed to review the whole issue of factions and groups. The opposition responded by attempting to stage an independent demonstration on the tenth anniversary of the October Revolution. But this demonstration— the opposition leaders spoke from the balcony of a building on what is today Gorky Street—was a demonstration of weakness rather than strength. There were almost no workers in attendance; student youth and office workers predominated. In comparison with the official parade, the opposition demonstration made a pathetic impression. An attempt to organize an opposition demonstration in Leningrad was even more unsuccessful. Zinoviev, who greatly overestimated his influence in that city, was almost beaten up in the official parade.

A peculiar opposition demonstration occurred at the funeral of A. A. Ioffe, who committed suicide in 1927. Ioffe, a prominent diplomat who had served the Party well, especially in negotiating the Treaty of Brest-Litovsk, was one of Trotsky's closest supporters. An eyewitness to the funeral, M. P. Iakubovich, describes it in his memoirs:

> The coffin containing Ioffe's body was standing in the building of the Commissariat of Foreign Affairs on Lubianka Square, waiting to be taken to the Novodevichi Cemetery. A huge crowd filled all the streets around the building and blocked traffic. Trotsky made his way through the crowd with difficulty, accompanied by [K. B.] Radek and [N. I.] Muralov. . . . (Among those who followed the

[50] *Pravda,* 1927, No. 251, Nov. 2. Discussion sheet No. 2 for the XVth Congress.

coffin, incidentally, was Nadezhda Allilueva, Stalin's wife.) A lot of
people followed the coffin—for the most part Komsomol student
youth who had Trotskyite leanings. There were quite a few former
military and military-political officials who had worked under
Trotsky in the past. The procession sang songs of the Civil War,
mentioning Trotsky's name, some with the refrain "Long live
Trotsky—the leader of the Red Army." . . . At the cemetery, after
the official funeral speech delivered by Chicherin, on behalf of the
Central Committee, Trotsky, Zinoviev, and Kamenev spoke.
Trotsky's speech was largely an appeal for the restoration of Party
unity . . .; it contained no harsh thrusts, the name of Stalin was not
mentioned at all. But Zinoviev spoke in a vehement, aggressive tone;
he spoke of the crimes of Stalin, who had betrayed the Party's interests, violated its members' rights, misrepresented the Party's wishes.
When the participants were leaving the gates of the Novodevichi
Monastery after the funeral, a military unit stood nearby in formation, probably sent to fire the funeral salute. A young man in the
group around Trotsky broke away, ran up to the unit, and shouted:
"Red Army comrades! Give a cheer for the leader of the Red Army,
Comrade Trotsky!" A critical minute followed. No one moved in
the formation. Dead silence reigned. Trotsky stood some distance
away, also silent, and looked at the ground. Then he turned and
went to a car, followed by Zinoviev and Kamenev. It must have
been obvious for those watching this scene that Trotsky's cause was
hopelessly lost. The new generation of Red Army soldiers did not
know him, had not taken part in the Civil War, were raised in a
new spirit. The name of Trotsky meant little or nothing to them.
The composition of the funeral demonstration also made one stop
and think, for there were no workers in it. The united opposition
had no proletarian support.

These demonstrations did not help the opposition; on the contrary,
they gave Stalin the pretext he wanted for final reprisals against its
leaders. In November, 1927, Trotsky and Zinoviev were expelled from
the Party. Other members of the opposition were expelled from the
Central Committee and the Central Control Commission. Then, in
December, 1927, the XVth Congress confirmed the expulsion of
Trotsky and Zinoviev and resolved to expel seventy-five additional
members of the opposition, including Kamenev, Piatakov, Radek,
Smilga, G. I. Safarov, I. N. Smirnov, Khristian Rakovskii, and M. M.
Lashevich. The Congress also urged all Party organizations to purge
their ranks "of all clearly incorrigible elements of the Trotskyite oppo-
sition." Trotsky was exiled first to Alma Ata and then abroad.

   In the years following, almost all the leaders of the united opposition except Trotsky and some of his closest supporters were readmitted
to the Party. But their will to fight had been broken. And although, at
the end of the twenties and the beginning of the thirties, Stalin was

guilty of many crude mistakes, miscalculations, and crimes, neither Kamenev, Zinoviev, Radek, nor Piatakov spoke out against him. He was increasingly slipping into adventurism and arbitrary rule, but Trotsky alone tried to continue the struggle. Trotsky wrote an enormous amount—abroad. He tried to create his own opposition press and to send its publications to the Soviet Union. But his supporters were few, and his *Bulletin of the Opposition* had no influence on the political life of our country. Trotsky remained a supporter of the proletarian revolution and not a fascist counterrevolutionary, as Stalin soon labeled him. However, because of his dogmatism, his inadequate information, and his bitterness, Trotsky's analysis of the complicated processes going on in the USSR and in the world Communist movement in the thirties was one-sided and tendentious. Consequently, he could not formulate an alternative Marxist program. In Trotsky's writings of the thirties, justified criticism is constantly mixed up with conscious and unconscious distortions. His writings on the October Revolution, the Civil War, and the early years of reconstruction contain crude misrepresentation and self-advertisement. In place of the Stalinist legend, Trotsky tried to create his own, which also was far from historical truth.

Soon after Trotsky was exiled from the Soviet Union, he began to negotiate with left-wing Social Democrats for the creation of a new international. After the negotiations failed, he called upon Trotskyites to join Social Democratic parties. Then he considered the creation of an independent Trotskyite international organization. Although Trotskyite groups were created in many countries, almost nowhere did they manage to attract any significant number of supporters. Thus Trotsky's Fourth International, though it exists even now, has always been a sect, not an influential organization. For all practical purposes Trotsky was a has-been, and despite his feverish activity, neither the left Social Democrats nor the "right" or "left" Communists followed him. It is also worth noting that Trotsky established authoritarian, militaristic methods in his organizations, demanding unquestioning execution of the "leader's" will. According to the Polish Marxist Andrzej Stawar, who opposed both Stalin and Trotsky in the 1930's: "If Stalin was the infallible pope of the Comintern, then the Trotskyites created a cult of the anti-pope, a pretender to the throne of the pope—Trotsky."

6

THE NOISY BATTLE with the "united left" opposition had hardly died down when a fight began with the so-called "right" deviation. In

December, 1927, and January, 1928, to overcome the acute shortage of grain, the Central Committee resolved on extraordinary measures against the kulaks, that is, the confiscation of grain. These measures hurt the prosperous middle peasants as well as the kulaks. Such a drastic change in the Party's agrarian policy came as a complete surprise to most of the rural cadres, with the unsurprising result that some officials in the Party *apparat* and the economic agencies began to criticize the new policy.

One of the first to criticize was the Deputy Commissar of Finance and Commissar of Foreign Trade, M. I. Frumkin. On June 15, 1928, he sent a long letter to the Central Committee, to which Stalin quickly and harshly replied.[51] By October, 1928, speaking to the Plenum of the Moscow Party Committee and Control Commission, Stalin was referring to a "danger from the right." He mentioned no names, for he located the right-wing danger in the lower party organizations, on the *volost* and village level, and said that the Central Committee contained only "very insignificant elements which are conciliatory toward the right-wing danger." As for the Politburo, Stalin declared that there were no "right-wingers" or "left-wingers" or conciliators in it. Barely a month later, in a speech to the Central Committee, Stalin decried a "right deviation in the Party," naming Frumkin as an agent of it, and Uglanov, the first secretary of the Moscow Committee, as one of the "conciliators." But once again he declared, "We are all united in the Politburo."[52]

However, in the winter of 1928–29 the situation in the countryside became much worse. The collection of grain was going badly, and the question of applying extraordinary measures again arose. Three members of the Politburo—Bukharin, Rykov, and M. P. Tomskii—spoke against a continuation of grain confiscations. A conflict ensued, as a result of which the three submitted their resignations. Rykov soon withdrew his, but Bukharin and Tomskii, despite the request of the majority of the Politburo, refused to return to their positions. (Rykov at that time was chairman of the Council of People's Commissars; Bukharin was secretary of the Central Executive Committee of the Comintern and editor in chief of *Pravda;* Tomskii was chairman of the Trade Union Council.)

It was impossible to hide this bitter conflict from the Party. In April, 1929, at a Plenum of the Central Committee and the Central Control Commission, Stalin made a detailed and largely biased criticism of the "group of Bukharin, Rykov, and Tomskii." Stalin called Tomskii a "trade-union politician." Bukharin, he said, "sings in harmony with the Miliukov[53] crowd and tags along behind the enemies of

[51] Stalin, *Sochineniia,* XI, pp. 116–26.
[52] *Ibid.,* p. 290.
[53] *Ed.:* See above, *n.* 46.

the people." Bukharin "was only recently one of Trotsky's pupils," a man with a "swollen sense of his own importance," whose theories were "nonsense," whose statement was "barefaced, slanderous mudslinging," and so on. The efforts of Bukharin, Tomskii, and N. A. Uglanov to neutralize these statements by recalling their recent friendship with Stalin were summarily rejected as "whining and wailing."[54]

The April Plenum condemned Bukharin's views, declaring them incompatible with the Party line. The Plenum decreed the removal of Bukharin and Tomskii from their positions in the Comintern, *Pravda*, and the Trade Union Council. But it left them and Rykov in the Politburo. Rykov also remained in his post as Chairman of the Council of People's Commissars.

What was the background of the leaders of this "right" opposition? N. I. Bukharin joined the Bolsheviks in 1906, when he was only eighteen. Thus he belonged to the younger pleiad of Party leaders. From the beginning he showed great interest in Marxist theory and wrote articles and pamphlets on theoretical questions. These works were not free from errors and were criticized by Lenin, but Bukharin did not persist in his incorrect assertions. Returning from emigration in 1917, he joined Lenin, became a member of the Moscow Party Committee and *oblast* Buro, and though only twenty-nine years old, was elected to the Central Committee at the VIth Party Congress in July, 1917. In 1918 he headed the faction of "left Communists," who opposed the Treaty of Brest-Litovsk.[55] Lenin called them "revolutionaries of the phrase," but it must be noted that the "left Communists" included at one time or another Frunze, Dzerzhinskii, G. I. Lomov, Bubnov, Uritskii, M. N. Pokrovskii, N. N. Krestinskii, V. V. Kuibyshev, and many other Party leaders. All of them subsequently admitted that Lenin was right, and by the end of 1918 the question of "left Communists" lost all practical significance.

During the trade-union controversy, Bukharin was the author of the so-called "buffer platform," and in 1920 could not understand the economic perspectives of the young Soviet state. Lenin's "Testament" neatly states the basic reasons for Bukharin's theoretical errors: there was something scholastic about Bukharin, because he never studied and, "I think, never fully understood dialectics." But in the same place Lenin also declared Bukharin to be the Party's most eminent and most valuable theorist, who "is rightly considered the favorite of the entire Party." And Lenin's attitude, in the last years of his life, was very friendly to Bukharin.

[54] Stalin, *Sochineniia*, XII, pp. 1–107.
[55] *Ed.:* Rather than cede the territories demanded by the Germans, the "left Communists" hoped to rouse the country to a war of revolutionary defense. Lenin insisted that the hope was futile.

After Lenin's death Bukharin, as one of the highest Party leaders, took an active part in the fight against the Trotskyite, the Zinovievite, and finally the united oppositions. In fact it was Bukharin who was responsible for most of the theoretical struggle with these oppositions. Bukharin played a great if not decisive role in formulating the economic policy, and also the Comintern policy, that the Central Committee followed from 1925 to 1927. This policy was not, as we have seen, free from error. Bukharin's intellectual scholasticism was in particular evidence here. If we analyze Bukharin's theoretical work in economics, politics, the world Communist movement, philosophy, and literary criticism—there can be no doubt about Bukharin's enormous erudition—we can see at once a schematic quality in almost all of his theoretical constructs. For him the first and most important step was to find some kind of scheme or formula, even though such schemes and formulas sometimes missed the most essential aspects of the matter at hand. However, Stalin, as F. F. Raskol'nikov later wrote, was far more schematic and scholastic than Bukharin.

In the period following Lenin's death, Stalin openly courted Bukharin and took advantage of his many abilities. Most of the Party cadres continued to regard Bukharin as a special favorite; among the Komsomol youth his authority was enormous. It suffices to examine the record of the XIVth Congress in December, 1925, when Zinoviev and Kamenev attacked Bukharin for telling the peasants to get rich. Ordzhonikidze evoked prolonged applause by dwelling on Lenin's admiration for Bukharin, and by emphasizing Bukharin's courage both in voicing his opinions and in admitting his mistakes.[56] Molotov praised Bukharin's leadership in the struggle against the opposition.[57] And Kalinin, A. A. Zhdanov, and Stalin defended Bukharin in the same spirit.

A. I. Rykov was another outstanding Party leader. He came from a proletarian background, became a Bolshevik, and actively participated in the underground fight against tsarism. Exiled several times, he was in Narym when the February Revolution broke out. After the October Revolution he was the first Soviet Commissar of Internal Affairs. Along with Kamenev, V. P. Nogin, and other Bolsheviks, Rykov insisted for a while on a coalition government of all socialists, and resigned from the Council of People's Commissars. But soon he recognized his error and rejoined the government. During the Civil War he headed the Supreme Council of the National Economy, and then became deputy chairman of the Council of People's Commissars and of the Council of Labor and Defense. From 1924 he was chairman of the Council of People's Commissars, a position that only Lenin had

[56] *Stenograficheskii otchet XIV s'ezda* (Moscow, 1926), p. 223.
[57] *Ibid.*, pp. 471–72.

held before him, a great honor for the forty-three-year-old Bolshevik and a sign of the Party's trust in him. As chairman Rykov bore an enormous load of work during those years.

M. P. Tomskii was also of proletarian origin, a lithographer by trade. He joined the Bolsheviks during the Revolution of 1905, and took an active part in the illegal work of the Party in St. Petersburg and Moscow. He was arrested and sentenced to five years of hard labor. The February Revolution freed Tomskii from penal servitude, and in 1917 he worked for the Party in Petrograd and Moscow. Soon after the October Revolution Tomskii became the leader of the trade unions, and remained so to the end of the 1920's.

The April Plenum of 1929 did not put an end to the fight with the "right" opposition, for Bukharin's group continued to defend its views. We will not consider here all the twists and turns of this struggle. Suffice it to recall that Bukharin's and Rykov's economic policies—which were supported in 1925–27 by Stalin and the majority of the Central Committee—were partly to blame for the grain crisis and the resulting confiscations in 1927–28. Bukharin's understanding of NEP was debatable, to say the least. He did not have a clear concept of the kulak as an active opponent of the construction of socialism. In 1924–27 Bukharin and Rykov considered it possible to make greater concessions to capitalist and petty-bourgeois elements, both rural and urban, than the Party could or should have made at that time.

Today some historians try to picture the agricultural policies of Bukharin's group as the only correct ones, in contrast with the incorrect policies of Stalin. I would not like to take such a stand. While Stalin's agricultural policies were far from Lenin's plan for developing peasant cooperatives, Bukharin's proposals were not irreproachable either, though perhaps, in the conditions of 1929–33, they represented less of a threat to the union of the working class and the peasants than the adventuristic extremes of Stalin. The experience of the European socialist countries in recent decades has shown that it is possible to have the most varied combinations of socialist industry in the cities with cooperative and small peasant agriculture in the countryside. Communist parties may take various approaches to the peasants while preserving a general socialist perspective, without raising any question of "capitulation" or "betrayal."

In Bukharin's writings there is no clear, precise answer to the question how to move the peasant village toward socialism. For example, he saw a sharp contrast between buyers' and sellers' cooperatives on the one hand and producers' cooperatives on the other. He maintained that socialism could be reached through the process of buying and selling, not through the process of production. In explaining this thesis, Bukharin gave the following forecast for the development of cooperatives:

> What elements will there be in the countryside? The cooperatives of poor peasants will be collective farms (*kolkhozy*).[58] The cooperatives of middle peasants will be buyers', sellers', and credit co-ops. In some places there will even be kulak cooperatives. This whole ladder of co-ops will be attached to the system of our [state] banks.[59]

Such confused and scholastic discussions of the "growth" of the kulak into socialism were mistaken.

Still, when we look back at the disagreements of the past, we cannot help noticing that many of the "right" opposition's critical comments were justified. At the end of 1927 its leaders supported the application of extraordinary measures against the kulaks—that is, the confiscation of grain—but then they justifiably opposed the transformation of these measures into Party policy. The rightists protested against the policy of forced and hasty collectivization, which was not, from an economic point of view, adequately prepared for. The rightists also had good reason to oppose "gigantomania" in industrial construction and excessive capital expenditures, which frequently lacked economic sense. Their proposals for a change in the prices that the state paid the peasants for grain were also reasonable. The grain prices in 1927 were very low, lower than the cost of production, which obviously gave the peasants no economic incentive to increase the amount of grain they sold to the state.

As we shall see, Stalin, who had previously shared Bukharin's views, made a sudden sharp turn to the "left" at the end of the twenties. He proclaimed a policy of extraordinary measures in dealing with the kulaks that far surpassed the most radical proposals of Zinoviev and Kamenev. He suddenly appropriated Trotskyite conceptions of "primary socialist accumulation" and significantly extended them. What is more, Stalin brought in several prominent Trotskyites to apply these conceptions. His turnabout produced a split among the Trotskyites in the spring of 1929, when some of them (Smilga and Radek, for example) decided to support Stalin on the grounds that he was adopting their program of an offensive against the kulaks and a swift rate of industrialization. Trotsky himself strongly opposed Stalin's new policies, declaring that they had nothing in common with the earlier proposals of his own group. Indeed, although Stalin in 1929 did appropriate some of Trotsky's former slogans, his violence against the peasants, bureaucratic caprice, and arbitrary rule, both in the countryside and in the city, diverged from Leninism far more than any of the

[58] *Ed.*: See Glossary for explanation.
[59] *Stenogr. otchet XVI konferentsii VKP/b* (Moscow, 1962), pp. 305, 352.

opposition groups had ever proposed. Small wonder that many Communists who justifiably opposed Stalin's abrupt turn were unjustifiably branded as "rightists."

Stalin also criticized Bukharin's leadership of the Comintern from an "ultra-left," sectarian, dogmatic standpoint. He insisted that the Comintern mount a sharp attack against the left wing of Social Democratic parties.[60] Instead of maintaining a united front with the left Social Democrats against fascism, monopolies, and the right Social Democratic leaders, Stalin called upon Communists to concentrate their attacks on leftist tendencies in Social Democracy, which at that time were closely connected with the mass of the working classes. Many honorable Communists, both in the Soviet Union and in the West, were labeled "rightists" or "conciliators" without justification, simply because they opposed such an incorrect policy.

Indeed, in the attack on Bukharin, Rykov, and Tomskii, Stalin pinned the label of "right deviation" on many other tendencies and groups that had no organizational or ideological connection with Bukharin's faction. This lumping together of the most diverse political groups, which had nothing in common except some disagreement with the basic Stalinist line, greatly facilitated Stalin's attack on Bukharin and his sympathizers. He heaped on them many accusations which had no bearing on their real views. The simple fact is that in spite of their mistakes, they remained loyal members of the Party. Unfortunately, these Stalinist judgments are preserved to this day in some historical works. For example, S. P. Trapeznikov writes:

> The Bukharin-Rykov group opposed the Party in 1928, at the very time that a grain crisis was developing, when the grain supply was being sabotaged by the kulaks, who hoarded grain and would not hand it over to the state at the fixed prices. In this extremely critical situation, *the Bukharin-Rykov group openly took the side of the kulaks and all the reactionary forces in the country.* The anti-Party group of Bukharin, Rykov, and Tomskii, rallying *all the dissatisfied, politically unstable elements*, openly attacked the Party's policy of industrialization and collectivization.[61]

It would not be surprising to find such an appraisal in 1937, but it is strange to see it in 1967.

Bukharin, Rykov, and Tomskii never created a clear-cut faction within the Party, as Stalin himself admitted. "Do the right deviationists have a faction?" Stalin asked in one speech. "I think not. Can it be said that they do not submit to Party decisions? I think we have as yet no basis to accuse them of this. Can we assert that the right

[60] *Sochineniia,* XI, pp. 21–22.
[61] S. P. Trapeznikov, *Leninizm i agrarno-krest'ianskii vopros* (Moscow, 1967), II, pp. 187–88. Italics added.

deviationists will for certain organize their own faction? I doubt it."[62]
Thus the "rightists" did not formally violate the well-known resolution
on Party unity adopted by the Xth Congress. By using repressive measures against them, by pitting the organization against them, declaring
the defense of "rightist" views to be incompatible with Party membership, Stalin was in fact violating every member's right to discuss freely
problems of Party policy, a right guaranteed by the Party statute.

Although talk about the "right" danger continued into the 1930's,
Stalin's actual fight with the "right" opposition lasted only about a
year. As early as the November Plenum of the Central Committee in
1929, Rykov read a declaration by Bukharin, Tomskii, and himself,
which said that there was a single general Party line but that the
troika had stood and still stood for a different method of implementation than the one supported by the majority of the Central Committee.
The *troika* went on to admit that "the actual method of implementing
the Party's general line has achieved, on the whole, great, positive
results." Therefore, acknowledging "the Party's indisputable success,"
the three authors declared: "We believe that the disagreements between us and the majority of the Central Committee have been
eliminated."[63]

But this statement was not considered satisfactory. Stalin demanded
complete capitulation, without any reservations. The November
Plenum of 1929 therefore expelled Bukharin, Rykov, and Tomskii
from the Politburo, after a drumfire of criticism from nearly every
speaker. Right after the Plenum, these three leaders of the opposition
submitted a statement to the Politburo admitting their mistakes. Their
will to fight was broken. There is a story that on New Year's Eve in
1930, while Stalin was having a lively party with friends, Bukharin,
Rykov, and Tomskii arrived uninvited to ask for a reconciliation. And
there was a show of reconciliation, but none of the "rightist" leaders
regained his former position in the Party. In 1931 Rykov was appointed Commissar of Posts and Telegraphs. Bukharin became the
main editor of *Izvestiia* and the director of the planning section of
scientific research within the Supreme Council of National Economy.
Tomskii was appointed director of the State Publishing House. The
XVIth Party Congress in July, 1930, elected all three to the Central
Committee, but the XVIIth Congress in February, 1934, demoted
them to the rank of candidate membership.

Never again did the former leaders of the "right" speak against
Stalin, although there were subsequently many occasions for them to
do so. There was forced collectivization at the beginning of 1930,

[62] *Sochineniia,* XI, p. 287.
[63] *Bol'shevik,* 1930, No. 2, p. 8.

followed by the mass exodus of peasants from the collective farms. There was the liquidation of the kulaks as a class, which ravaged a considerable portion of the middle peasants as well. Entire villages and Cossack *stanitsy* were transported to the north. Neither Bukharin, Rykov, nor Tomskii voiced any protest against these perversions. Stalin also made many mistakes in "superindustrialization." For example, in 1930 he and Molotov, who had never before attended meetings of the Council of People's Commissars, suddenly appeared and proposed an adventuristic plan to double the optimal variant of the Five-Year Plan for metals, motor vehicles, and other crucial branches of industry. Rykov, who was still chairman of the Council of People's Commissars, contributed his vote to the unanimous approval of this proposal, which was, of course, not fulfilled.

Although, at the beginning of the thirties, grain production decreased, bread was in short supply, and millions of peasants were starving, Stalin insisted on exporting great quantities of grain. In 1928 less than 1 million centners were exported; in 1929 13 million, in 1930 48.3 million, in 1931 51.8 million, and in 1932 18.1 million.[64] Moreover, Soviet grain was sold for next to nothing, because of the economic crisis in the West. The most galling aspect of the sacrifices that the people suffered—the peasants most of all—is that they were unnecessary, in spite of certain historians' assertions. The scale of capital investment in industry, which Stalin forced in the early 1930's, was too much for the economy to bear. Many construction projects— in some branches of industry more than half—had to be suspended midway, which immobilized enormous amounts of capital. Neither Rykov nor Tomskii nor Bukharin uttered any protest.

Despite their submission, the press poured unceasing abuse on the former "rightists" throughout the first Five-Year Plan. Even in 1935 the journal *Bol'shevik* continued to call Bukharin a "right capitulationist," who proposed nothing less than the rejection of industrialization and collectivization and a grant of unlimited freedom of trade to capitalistic elements. The "kulak essence" of Bukharin's program was —need we add?—"unmasked by the Party under the leadership of Stalin." It was typical of Stalin to intensify attacks on opponents after they had been crushed.

Stalin's destruction of all opposition groups was not, as some dogmatic historians claim, a "great victory." After all the oppositions had capitulated, the situation in the Party deteriorated. It was precisely in this period of "unprecedented unity" that Stalin adopted a policy of mass crimes, which damaged the Party so badly that it has not yet fully recovered. Thus Stalin's victory over the opposition

[64] *Sel'skoe khoziaistvo SSSR. Ezhegodnik 1935*, p. 222.

groups was by no means a victory for Leninism. And the opposition itself shares a good deal of the responsibility. The tragedy of the Party was not only that a man like Stalin led the Central Committee in the twenties but also that the opposition was led by men such as Trotsky, Zinoviev, and Bukharin, who could not offer an acceptable alternative to Stalin's leadership.

III

Some of Stalin's Serious Mistakes During Collectivization and Industrialization

1

LENIN REPEATEDLY CALLED attention to the tremendous difficulty of building a socialist society in a country like Russia, and to the inevitability of mistakes and miscalculations in the process. "It is certain that we have done and will do a lot of stupid things," Lenin told the Fourth Congress of the Comintern in 1922.

> No one knows this better than I. Why do we do stupid things? In the first place, because we are a backward country. Secondly, education in our country is minimal. Thirdly, we are getting no help. Not one civilized state is helping us. On the contrary, they are all working against us. Fourthly, our state *apparat* is to blame. We took over the old state *apparat* and that was our misfortune. . . . We now have enormous masses of civil servants, but we don't have sufficiently educated people to make really good use of them.[1]

Lenin also repeatedly called attention to another reason for Soviet mistakes and stupidities: the proletariat of the former Russian Empire was the first in the history of mankind to start building a socialist society. No nation had any practical experience for the Party to use.

This should be kept in mind when we analyze collectivization and industrialization, especially their beginnings. Mistakes were inevitable, but that fact does not excuse us from serious study of the mistakes.

[1] *Sochineniia,* 4th edn., XXXIII, pp. 390–91.

And Stalin, who had greatly increased his power toward the end of the twenties, did not help to avoid or correct these mistakes. On the contrary, his inclination toward administrative fiat, toward coercion instead of convincing, his oversimplified and mechanistic approach to complex political problems, his crude pragmatism and inability to foresee the consequences of alternative actions, his vicious nature and unparalleled ambition—all these qualities of Stalin seriously complicated the solution of problems that were overwhelming to begin with.

2

IN THE SECOND HALF of the twenties a striking imbalance emerged in the development of industry and agriculture. The beginning of industrialization, the growth of cities, and the revival of foreign trade required the availability of a large amount of grain for the market. But the state's procurement of grain increased much more slowly than other agricultural indices. By 1927 the value of gross agricultural output was 21 per cent greater than it had been in 1913, the best year of the prerevolutionary period, but this increase was mostly ascribable to livestock and industrial crops. Indeed, grain production fell far short of the prerevolutionary level both in acreage of cultivation and in gross output. An especially sharp decline occurred in the production of grain for the market. Between 1909 and 1913 the amount of marketed grain (within the pre-1939 boundaries) averaged more than a billion poods a year (the pood is 36.113 pounds); between 1923 and 1927 the average was 514 million.[2]

This situation can be attributed to many factors. The prices that the government paid for grain were low, giving the peasant no incentive to develop grain farming. In 1926–27 the price index for livestock products (using 1913 as the base year) was 178 per cent; for industrial crops such as flax and sugar beet it was 146 per cent; for grain it was only 89 per cent.[3] But low government prices were not the only problem. An increase in prices paid for grain—the basic product of our agriculture—required a major rise in the production of consumer goods and agricultural machinery needed by the peasants; banknotes alone were of no use to them. But industry was not able to end the shortage of goods either in the cities or in the countryside. A rapid increase in marketed grain was also hindered by the new structure of agriculture that issued from the October Revolution. The gentry's estates, which had been the basic source of marketed grain, were liquidated. Then the years of the Civil War significantly diminished

[2] *Narodnoe khozistvo SSSR v 1958. Statisticheskii ezhegodnik.* (Moscow, 1959), p. 351.
[3] S. P. Trapeznikov, *Leninizm i agrarno-krest'ianskii vopros*, II, p. 55.

the kulaks' farms both in size and in number, and they never regained their prerevolutionary level despite the introduction of the New Economic Policy. According to the calculations of the eminent agricultural statistician V. S. Nemchinov,[4] in 1927 the kulaks supplied one-fifth of all the grain on the market (around 130 million poods). Collective farms, *kommuny*,[5] and state farms marketed about 40 million poods, which was a large percentage of the grain they produced, but hardly a significant contribution to the country's grain supply. Thus the main producers of grain, including the crucial portion that was marketed, were the small farms of the poor and middle peasants. These farms produced 4 billion poods of grain toward the end of the twenties, as against the 2.5 billion that they produced before the Revolution. But these farms put little of their grain on the market—around 440 million poods, or 11 per cent of the grain they produced. And that was the main reason for the enormous difficulties on the grain front.

All these problems could have been foreseen at the very beginning of NEP. Lenin at any rate clearly perceived the probability of such difficulties, and explained how to overcome them. Lenin said it was necessary to give all possible help to the poor and middle peasants, since their potentialities for growth were by no means exhausted. This was the main agrarian goal of the first stage of NEP. But the kulak farms could not be ignored. The development of kulak production in the early years of NEP was no threat to the dictatorship of the proletariat. The alarmist declarations on the rise of the kulaks, made by the "new" and then by the "united" opposition, were largely unfounded. In the years following the October Revolution, as Lenin repeatedly pointed out, the countryside suffered not so much from capitalism as from an insufficient development of capitalism. The main problem was to increase agricultural production, and Lenin proposed means of encouraging all the peasants who showed enterprise and initiative. Since grain was in short supply and producers' cooperatives were in their infancy, an increase in grain marketings had to be

[4] Nemchinov's calculations were repeatedly cited by Stalin. However, some historians and economists dispute these figures, as the "united" opposition did. In the mid-twenties Trotsky's and Zinoviev's supporters in the Central Statistical Administration produced figures allegedly showing that the kulaks provided up to 50 per cent of all grain marketed. In a recently published work Trapeznikov also tried to show that the "basic mass" of grain surpluses was acquired by the kulaks, who obtained grain grown by the poor and middle peasants by renting out land and hiring laborers, by usury, by processing agricultural goods, and so on. Trapeznikov's arguments (see his *Leninizm i agrarno-krest'ianskii vopros*, II, pp. 58–60), like those of the "united" opposition, look convincing. No doubt careful research is needed on this matter. It is our opinion that Stalin and Nemchinov did underestimate the potential of the kulaks. One cannot deny that much of the grain attributed by Nemchinov to the poor and middle peasants actually came to the state's storage bins from the better-off stratum of middle peasants, many of whom sided with the kulaks in their grain-selling policies.

[5] *Ed.*: See explanation in the Glossary.

promoted not only among the poor and middle peasants but also among the kulaks. Lenin even proposed to give prizes to kulaks for increased production.[6]

Such a policy, while completely correct in the first part of NEP, could not become the basic policy of the dictatorship of the proletariat for a prolonged period. It would have been wrong to base the long-run development of Soviet agriculture on kulak production. The kulak was clearly an enemy of socialism and the Soviet regime, and a compromise with this last exploiting class was only a temporary phenomenon. The main agrarian job of the Communist Party was to develop all sorts of cooperatives, including producers'. Within the context of proletarian dictatorship, the growth of cooperatives would mean the triumph of socialism.[7]

However, Lenin understood how complicated the collectivization of agriculture would be in what was formerly tsarist Russia, and his plan for cooperatives involved not a brief campaign but many years of intense labor to develop literacy and general culture among the peasants, to teach them to work together, and to produce agricultural machinery and tractors. In one of his last memoranda in 1923 Lenin was quite clear on this point:

> To achieve through NEP the participation of the entire population in the cooperative movement requires an entire historical epoch. We may get through this epoch successfully in one or two decades. But in any case, this will be a special historical epoch, and without this epoch, *without universal literacy, without a sufficient degree of explaining, of teaching the population how to use books, and without a material basis for all this, without a certain guarantee, if only, let us say, against crop failure, against famine,* and so on—without that we shall not attain our goal.[8]

Lenin's cooperative plan was not worked out in detail with a precise description of the time schedule and forms of cooperation. He set out only general principles for the reorganization of agriculture. The rest of the plan would have to be the result of studying the actual experience of socialist construction. The same thing must be said about the Leninist general line of the Party. As Stalin used this concept, it acquired the same meaning that T. D. Lysenko later gave to the concept of Michurinist biology, that is, whatever the boss wishes. Lenin never tried to project some strictly defined line, the least deviation from which would be considered a "left" or "right" opportunistic deviation. H. G. Wells, after his meeting with Lenin, put it this way:

[6] *Istoriia SSSR,* 1965, No. 2, p. 18.
[7] See, e.g., Lenin, *Sochineniia,* 4th edn., XXXII, p. 264.
[8] *Polnoe Sobranie,* XLV, p. 372. Italics R.M.'s.

Lenin, . . . whose frankness must at times leave his disciples breath-
less, has recently stripped off the last pretence that the Russian revolution is anything more than the inauguration of an age of limitless
experiment. "Those who are engaged in the formidable task of overcoming capitalism," he has recently written, "must be prepared to
try method after method until they find the one which answers their
purpose best."[9]

In conditions of unbelievable desolation and backwardness, with
an economy ruined by two wars, the Party decided to begin with the
restoration of agriculture. Trotsky called for the "dictatorship of
industry," but the XIIth Party Congress in April, 1923, singled out
agriculture as the crucial sector. At that time there were formidable
difficulties in the development of agriculture. The peasant farms had
almost no stock of capital and almost no surplus produce to sell. On
the other hand, both the cost of production and the price of manufactured goods were high. Thus, despite the weakness of industry, a crisis
of oversupply arose, a glut of manufactured goods that caused some
industrial enterprises to shut down and others to suspend wage payments, with strikes resulting. To avert a general economic crisis, the
condition of the peasantry had to be improved. Thus prices were
lowered on many items that the village needed, while the prices of
agricultural products were raised. A system of easy credit was introduced in the villages, especially for the poor and middle peasants.
Finally, in 1925, following a proposal of the XIVth Party Conference,
a law was passed enlarging the right to hire agricultural labor and to
lease land from the state and from fellow peasants. This law was used
extensively by the better-off peasants, but to a degree it was also
advantageous to the poor peasants, since it legalized the hiring of day
laborers, which had been fairly widespread even before 1925, and
established supervision of the conditions of hire.

The glut of manufactured goods was eliminated by these measures,
and a certain equilibrium was achieved between the development of
industry and of agriculture. But it was very brief. New disproportions
emerged in 1925–26—of the opposite kind. Measures had to be found
that would adjust the development of agriculture to the needs and
potentialities of the economy as a whole. Unfortunately, a rational
adjustment was not maintained in the mid-twenties. From 1925 to
1927, although the Central Committee continued a basically correct
policy—and no one can doubt the leading role of Stalin, Bukharin,
and Rykov in working out this policy—some measures were taken
that, though they remained within the framework of NEP, proved to
be ill advised. For example, the XIVth Party Conference in April,

[9] Wells, *Russia in the Shadows* (London, 1921), p. 133.

1925, resolved to lower the single agricultural tax and to turn over a large portion of its yield to local government units.[10] In the fiscal years 1925–26, this tax was lowered from approximately 313 million rubles to 245 million. Admittedly, the levy on the kulaks was lowered only slightly—by one million rubles. The middle peasants benefited most—their tax payments dropped by 60 million rubles.[11] Still, in view of the large harvests of 1926–27, the tax cut favored not only the middle peasants but the kulaks as well, whose agricultural surpluses increased considerably. What is more, this tax cut was made at a time when the purchasing power of the peasants was rising rapidly. In 1923–24, their purchasing power was estimated to be 1.6 billion gold rubles; in 1925–26 it had reached 2.6 billion. In 1923–24, 16.8 per cent of the peasants' purchasing power was withdrawn by the agricultural tax, and in 1925–26 only 10.8 per cent was withdrawn in this way.[12] This trend would have been all to the good, if only the swift rise in peasant purchasing power had been matched by a corresponding increase in the manufactured goods that the peasants needed.

At this critical juncture both wholesale and retail prices on manufactured goods were significantly lowered, when there was not a surplus but a growing shortage of manufactured goods. As a result the decreed cut in retail prices was widely ignored and did not reach the peasant consumer. At the same time, the reduction of wholesale prices lowered the profits of industrial enterprises. With goods in short supply, the lowering of wholesale prices unavoidably widened the gap between wholesale and retail prices, thereby enriching private merchants, who still controlled at least 40 per cent of retail trade in 1927.[13] While they were getting increased profits, socialist industry was not receiving the capital it needed—a need that was sharply increasing, since 1925–26 marked the turn from the restoration of old industrial enterprises to the construction of new ones.

To some extent the cut in retail prices did reach the peasant consumer cooperatives. But this reduction increased demand in the countryside, which the government lacked the goods to meet. There was some growth in the delivery of manufactured products to the countryside, but it did not produce the desired effect; the supply of goods "grew in volume but, because of the lowering of prices, did not grow in value (*ne vyroslo po svoemu tsennostnomu vyrazheniiu*)."[14] At the end of 1927 the manufacture of goods for general consumption

[10] *KPSS v rezoliutsiiakh*, II (1953), p. 39.
[11] *Istoriia SSSR*, 1963, No. 4, p. 199.
[12] *Bol'shevik*, 1926, No. 19–20, p. 52.
[13] *KPSS v rezoliutsiiakh*, II (1953), p. 355.
[14] *Ibid.*, p. 373. From a resolution of the Central Committee in April, 1928. *Ed.:* The Russian is included because of the distinction between *tsennost'* and *stoimost'*, both of which are translated as "value."

was only 1 to 2 per cent above the previous year, while the total wage bill in state industry was up by 16 per cent, and the earnings of peasants—counting only receipts for grain sold to the state, minus taxes—were up by 31 per cent. All in all, the purchasing fund of the cities and the countryside had risen by more than 20 per cent in a single year.[15]

Thus, as a result of the shortsighted policies of Stalin, Bukharin, and Rykov, the peasants, especially the kulaks and prosperous middle peasants, accumulated much currency with which it was impossible to buy the goods they needed. In such circumstances it is not surprising that prosperous peasants were in no hurry to sell their grain to the state. The principal possessor of grain surpluses, the kulak, had no acute financial need, nor even an immediate interest in selling his grain. The relatively low agricultural tax could be paid by the receipts from the sale of secondary products and industrial crops, for which the state paid fairly high prices. And, in fact, more flax, sunflower seeds, hemp, beets, cotton, butter, eggs, hides, wool, and meat were bought by the state in the fall of 1927 than in the previous fall. But the state's purchase of grain at the end of 1927 was a completely different story.

3

THE ECONOMIC MISCALCULATIONS of Stalin, Bukharin, and Rykov and the kulaks' sabotage of grain procurement brought the USSR at the end of 1927 to the verge of a grain crisis. Although there was a bumper crop, grain procurements were much lower than in previous years. The kulaks and prosperous middle peasants tried to keep their grain until the spring, when they could sell it at higher prices. By January, 1928, the government had acquired barely 300 million poods—in sharp contrast with the figure of 428 million in January, 1927. The supply of bread to the cities and the army was seriously endangered.

Various proposals were made. The Trotskyite-Zinovievite opposition, for example, thought the time had come for the decisive assault on the kulaks. They proposed that at least 150 million poods of grain be taken from the kulaks and the prosperous middle peasants by force. But the majority of the Party objected, and the plenary meeting of the Central Committee on August 9, 1927 rejected these proposals "as absurd and demagogical, calculated to create additional difficulties in the development of the national economy."[16] The proposals that the

[15] *XV s'ezd VKP(b)*, II (Moscow, 1962), p. 857.
[16] *KPSS v rezoliutsiiakh*, II (1953), pp. 160–61.

opposition made at the XVth Party Congress in December, 1927, when the grain crisis was in full effect, were also unhesitatingly rejected. Stalin's report to the Congress carefully evaded the underlying difficulties, but he did speak plainly on the Party's policy toward the kulaks:

> Those comrades are wrong who think that we can and should do away with the kulaks by administrative fiat, by the GPU: write the decree, seal it, period. That's an easy method, but it won't work. The kulak must be taken by economic measures, in accordance with Soviet legality. And Soviet legality is not an empty phrase. Of course, this does not rule out the application of some administrative measures against the kulaks. But administrative measures must not replace economic ones.[17]

Many of Stalin's supporters spoke in much stronger terms. For example, in a special speech on the Party's agrarian policy, Molotov declared that those who proposed a "forced loan" from the peasantry were enemies of the alliance between the workers and peasants; they were proposing "the destruction of the Soviet Union." At that point Stalin called out, "Correct!"[18] G. Ia. Sokol'nikov, who had quit the opposition in 1922 and joined the Party majority, stated that the peasants had reserves of a billion poods of grain, but that, he said, was not excessive.

> We must not think that the peasants' grain reserves are a sign of some kind of kulak war against the proletarian economic system, and that we should launch a crusade to take them away. If we do this, we will only be returning to *prodrazverstka* [the policy of forced requisition practiced during the Civil War].[19]

A. I. Mikoian discussed the problem of grain procurement in greater detail. He argued that the imbalance of prices on manufactured and agricultural products was the main reason for peasant reluctance to sell grain. He urged a determined effort to bring large supplies of low-priced manufactured products into the village, even at the expense of temporary shortages in the cities. Only in this way could the peasants be persuaded to part with their grain.[20] Mikoian virtually admitted that the shortages in grain procurement were due to the oversights and mistakes of the government. He proposed economic measures as the least painful way out of the mess, and the XVth Party Congress incorporated his proposals in its resolutions.

The delegates, however, had barely got back to their home districts when completely different instructions came flying after them from

---

[17] *Sochineniia,* X, pp. 311–12.
[18] *XV s'ezd VKP (b),* II (Moscow, 1962), p. 1222.
[19] *Ibid.,* p. 1134.
[20] *Ibid.,* pp. 1094–95.

Moscow. A few days after the end of the Congress, which had expelled the leaders of the Zinoviev-Trotsky opposition from the Party and even refused to hear a statement by Kamenev, Stalin made a sudden sharp turn "to the left" in agricultural policy. He began to put into effect the forced requisition of grain that the entire Party had just rejected. On December 14 and 24, 1927, Stalin sent out instructions for the application of extraordinary measures against the kulaks. Local Party officials, who had just heard and read the speeches mentioned above, must have been thunderstruck. Then, on January 6, 1928, Stalin issued a third directive unique both in tone and in content, which ended with threats against local Party leaders if they failed to achieve a decisive break in grain procurements within the shortest possible time.

The "extraordinary measures" of the winter of 1927–28 included not only the confiscation of the kulaks' grain surpluses but also the use of force on a mass scale. The result was a significant increase in grain procurements, but only briefly. In the spring of 1928 the sale of grain to the state dropped off sharply once again, and Stalin explained the reason why:

> If we were able to collect almost 300 million poods of grain from January to March, it was because we were dealing with the peasants' reserves that had been saved for *bargaining*. From April to May we could not collect even 100 million poods because we had to touch the peasants' *insurance* reserves, in conditions when the outlook for the harvest was still unclear. Well, the grain still had to be collected. So we fell once again into extraordinary measures, administrative willfulness, the violation of revolutionary legality, going around to farms, making illegal searches, and so on, which have caused the political situation in the country to deteriorate, threatening the alliance of the workers and peasants.[21]

And, in fact, the political situation in the countryside had become extremely tense in the summer of 1928.

Today it is not easy to say how much justification there was for extraordinary measures in the winter and spring of 1927–28. Although the economic mistakes made by Stalin and his advisers in the preceding years did not leave much room for political and economic maneuvering, there were still some possibilities for the use of economic rather than administrative measures, that is, for the methods of NEP rather than War Communism. "Grand" policy, that is, the management of the state and the Party, has its own laws, its own logic. If the state gets off one road, it often proves impossible to get back onto it. That was the case with the use of extraordinary measures against the kulaks.

[21] *Sochineniia*, XI, p. 206.

When Stalin issued his directives in December and January of 1927–28, he evidently did not plan to make them the basis of agrarian policy for years to come. The kulaks would inevitably react to extraordinary measures by curtailing their production, and since there were very few state and collective farms at the time, the result would be famine. Stalin, it seems, only wanted to frighten the kulaks into submission, to make them more compliant in selling grain to the state. Such an intention is indicated by the new directives that went out to the rural areas in the spring and summer of 1928: use no more extraordinary measures, raise grain prices by 15 to 20 per cent, increase the supply of manufactured goods in the countryside. In July, 1928, Stalin, speaking to the Leningrad Party organization, stressed the necessity of avoiding further searches and seizures of grain, of reestablishing strict legality in dealing with the peasants and of relying on economic incentives to obtain grain.[22] In the same spirit, the July Plenum of the Central Committee adopted a special resolution forbidding extraordinary measures, calling for increased grain prices, sending a flow of goods to the countryside, and so on. Likewise the Party press in the second half of 1928 carried many assertions that extraordinary measures must now be absolutely ruled out.

But Stalin was unable to carry out this new reversal. For in effect the extraordinary measures in the winter of 1927–28 had been a declaration of war against the kulaks, the end of NEP in the countryside. And although, several months later, Stalin ordered the termination of military operations against the kulaks and even moved toward substantial concessions to the affluent strata of the countryside, it was impossible to return to the former methods of procuring grain. The kulaks and the prosperous middle peasants had already countered the use of extraordinary measures by sowing less grain. Many kulaks "liquidated themselves"—they sold their basic means of production and hid their money and valuables. Thus in the fall of 1928 the grain-procurement plan was once again in danger, despite the good harvest and the economic concessions of the summer.

In November, 1928, the Central Committee noted that "the planned quotas . . . in agriculture are underfulfilled and the underfulfillment is especially severe in grain." The result was an "extremely tight situation in the country's supply of food and raw materials," "violation of the plan for exports," and "stoppages in the textile industry and disorganization in a number of fields." It is hardly surprising that Stalin, in the winter of 1928–29, forgot his recent conciliatory orders. On the contrary, during these months new directives went out to the rural areas, calling for more extraordinary measures against the kulaks.

[22] *Sochineniia*, XI, p. 211.

In the winter of 1927–28, Bukharin, Rykov, and Tomskii had given their consent to such measures; Rykov had even helped Stalin draw up special instructions on grain procurement in December, 1927.

However, at the end of 1928 they opposed a repetition of them. Stalin flatly rejected their protests. In his April, 1929, speech, "On the Right Deviation," he said that the lower strata of the countryside had to be mobilized for struggle against the kulaks. Only thus, he declared, could the necessary amount of grain be collected. He sneered at "the comical wailing of Bukharin and Rykov," who were pleading for "a bourgeois liberal policy, not a Marxist policy" in dealing with the kulaks.[23]

The renewal of extraordinary measures in the winter of 1928–29 increased grain procurements for some months. But in February and March there were again great difficulties, and less grain was collected by April, 1929, than in the same period of the preceding year. The sale of bread was often interrupted even in Moscow, and the gap widened between market and government prices of grain. Various kinds of black-market operations began. The new pressure on the kulaks also caused a new decrease in the amount of land sown and a new wave of "self-liquidation." Efforts were made to increase the amount of land sown by poor and middle peasants, but this could not produce a noticeable increase in the amount of grain marketings. In 1929, despite a relatively good harvest, rationing of grain and many other agricultural products had to be introduced in the cities.

Thus a very dangerous situation was taking shape in the middle of 1929. An undeclared war with the kulaks was going on, in conditions unfavorable to the dictatorship of the proletariat. The country was threatened with complete disorganization of the whole national economy, and with famine. Something had to be done at once, but the incorrect policies of Stalin had left even less room for political or economic maneuvering than in 1927–28. Only two choices were left. One was to admit that mistakes had been made and to undertake major concessions to the kulaks. But that was an extremely difficult course to follow. The more prosperous peasants had lost faith in the policies of NEP; for the situation to be stabilized, substantial concessions would have had to be made to these strata. The Party could not adopt such a policy even to correct its own mistakes. The other possibility was to speed up the collective-farm movement, in order to limit and ultimately to destroy the kulaks' monopoly on grain marketings. The Party chose this second course, which was also extremely difficult. In the conditions that had taken shape in 1929 this was the correct

[23] *Sochineniia*, XII, pp. 88–90.

choice. Unfortunately Stalin was unable to carry out this new reversal
of the Party's agrarian policy—the fourth in two years—without once
again making the most serious and unforgivable mistakes.

4

THE COLLECTIVIZATION of agriculture in the Soviet Union was the
major revolution, the great economic and political crisis, that determined the victory of socialism. The epic of collectivization abounds
in great achievements by thousands of Party members. Thus it is very
bitter for the historian to recall that this revolution, which would have
been complex and unusually difficult in any case, was made extremely
difficult by Stalin's incompetent and adventuristic leadership.

First of all, one must bear in mind the slow development of producers' cooperatives until the end of the twenties. The main emphasis
fell on the development of purchasing and marketing cooperatives.
Even in mid-1928, less than 2 per cent of all peasant households belonged to collective farms, the main type of producers' cooperative.
Although the XVth Party Congress in December, 1927, resolved to
speed up collectivization, the resolution cautioned that "the privately
owned farm will continue to be the basic unit of the entire economy
for a significant time to come."[24] In 1928, the July Plenum of the
Central Committee again pointed out the need to "encourage an increase in the productivity of the individual small and medium-size
peasant farm, which will continue to be the country's basic unit of
grain production for a significant time."[25] And Stalin said in July,
1928:

> There are people who think that individual peasant farming is fin-
> ished, that it is not worth supporting. This is not true, comrades.
> Such people have nothing in common with our Party line. . . . We
> need neither belittlers nor boosters of the individual farm. We need
> sober politicians who know how to get the maximum of what can
> be got from the individual peasant farm, and know at the same
> time how to switch the individual farm onto the rails of collec-
> tivism.[26]

The XVIth Party Conference in April, 1929, also stressed that
most of the increase in agricultural production in the years ahead
would come from "the individual farm of the poor and middle peasants," and that "the small farm was and is still far from the end of
its potentialities."[27] According to the optimal variant of the first Five-

[24] KPSS v rezoliutsiiakh, II (1953), p. 352.
[25] Ibid., p. 393.
[26] Sochineniia, XI, p. 208.
[27] KPSS v rezoliutsiiakh, II (1953), p. 459.

Year Plan, adopted by the same Conference, 23 per cent of the peasant farms were to be collectivized in the next five years, thereby putting into the socialized sector 17.5 per cent of the total cultivated area and 43 per cent of grain production for the market. At the same time plans for the first year of the Five-Year Plan (July, 1928–July, 1929) were very modest: the level of collectivization was to be raised merely from 1.7 to 2.2 per cent.

Probably all these plans would have been correct and realistic in 1928. But they were no longer suitable in the tense situation of 1929. For the third straight year there was no relaxation in the now chronic grain crisis, and the state's shortage of grain threatened the export program and the industrialization of the country. Thus the Central Committee's first directives to speed up the development of collective farms were accepted by all Communists. The progress of collectivization began to be visible in the middle of 1929: by July 1, more than a million peasant households had joined collective farms instead of the projected 564,200. This was still a very modest increase; only 4 per cent of all households had joined collective farms.

The material and technical base of agriculture was still backward. In 1929 less than 10 per cent of the cultivated area was worked by tractors, while harvester combines were still counted in hundreds.[28] The collective farms had almost no cattle sheds or silos.

However, Stalin could not appraise correctly the situation taking shape in the countryside. At the first signs of progress, he embarked on a characteristically adventurous course. Apparently he wanted to compensate for years of failures and miscalculations in agricultural policy, and to astonish the world with a picture of great success in the socialist transformation of agriculture. So at the end of 1929, he sharply turned the bulky ship of agriculture, without checking for reefs and shoals. Stalin, Molotov, Kaganovich, and several other leaders pushed for excessively high rates of collectivization, driving the local organizations in every possible way, ignoring the subjective and objective difficulties.

At the beginning of November, 1929, there were around 70,000 collective farms, but most of these were small cooperatives that had amalgamated 1,919,400 peasant households, or 7.6 per cent of the total. The overwhelming majority of collective farmers were poor peasants; only in a few villages and *raiony* had sizable numbers of middle peasants joined the collective farms. But Stalin hastily generalized these scattered facts, interpreting them as the beginning of a crucial breakthrough. "What is new about the present collective-farm

[28] *Osnovnye voprosy sploshnoi kollektivizatsii; discussiia v Komakademii* (Moscow, 1930), pp. 5, 9.

movement?" Stalin asked in his article, "The Year of the Great Break," published on November 3, 1929.

> What is new and decisive in the present collective-farm movement is the fact that peasants are joining collective farms not in separate groups as before, but in entire villages, *volosti, raiony,* even *okrugi.* And what does this mean? This means that the middle peasant has joined the collective farms. This is the basis of the radical break in the development of agriculture, which has been a major achievement of the Soviet regime in the past year.[29]

On this hasty and ill-founded generalization Stalin based his call, in the fall of 1929, for total collectivization. Most of the middle peasants were still wavering, while the kulaks were not yet neutralized and isolated from middle peasants, especially the more prosperous ones. In such a situation the call for total collectivization unavoidably led to perversions in the collective-farm movement, to administrative pressure on the peasants, to the use of force against the middle peasant.

Recently there have been attempts to dispute the facts, established by historical research after the XXth and XXIInd Party Congresses, which reveal Stalin's adventurism in collectivization. For example, F. Vaganov writes:

> The second half of 1929 was marked by a rapid upsurge in the collective-farm movement. . . . The major feature of this period was the influx of middle peasants into the collective farms, which made that section of the peasantry active participants in socialist construction. Collective farms in the country numbered 67.4 thousand. They held 3.6 per cent of the cultivated land and produced 4.9 per cent of the agricultural marketings. All this shows that the necessary material, technical, and political preconditions had been created for total collectivization.[30]

Vaganov deliberately withholds the data on the percentage of collectivized households. Even a simple juxtaposition of the figures—7.6 per cent of the peasant households but only 3.6 per cent of the cultivated land—shows clearly that the middle peasant had not yet joined the collective farms. It is also obvious that 3.6 per cent of the cultivated area and 4.9 per cent of marketings simply cannot be construed to prove that the material, technical, and political preconditions for immediate total collectivization had been created.

Stalin's negative role in collectivization becomes obvious upon analysis of the work of the special commission of the Central Committee set up at the end of 1929 to draft the decree "On the tempo of collectivization and measures to help the organization of collective

[29] *Sochineniia,* XII, p. 132.
[30] "Preobrazovanie sel'skogo khoziaistva," *Kommunist,* 1966, No. 3, p. 95.

farms." Many members of the Central Committee, though agreeing that collectivization must be speeded up, protested against an excessive and unnecessary speed-up, for which neither the subjective nor the objective preconditions existed. The Commission took these views into consideration. But Stalin severely criticized the Commission's draft decree. At his insistence, the draft was stripped of rules indicating what portion of livestock and farm implements should be collectivized, and what procedure should be followed in the creation of indivisible funds and circulating capital. The following important provision was omitted:

> The Central Committee will judge the success of collectivization not only on the basis of the increase in the number of households joining the collectives but above all on this basis: to what extent does collective organization enable a given *raion* to make a real expansion in its cultivated area, to achieve a real increase in yields, and a real improvement in stockbreeding.

In the final version the period of collectivization in the North Caucasus and the Middle Volga was reduced to one or two years, and rules were omitted concerning socialization of instruments of production. In other words, the peasants' right to keep small livestock, implements, and poultry was omitted. Also deleted were guidelines for liquidating the kulaks, including a proposal that the kulaks be used as a labor force if they would submit and voluntarily carry out all the duties of collective-farm members. In the final version collectivization was to be completed in the major grain-producing *raiony* by the fall of 1930, or in any case by the spring of 1931. In other *raiony* it had to be completed by the fall of 1931 or the spring of 1932. For many *raiony* no target dates were set, which encouraged an unnecessary race to complete collectivization ahead of other *raiony*.[31]

On January 5, 1930, the Central Committee adopted the decree as altered by Stalin. Going beyond this decree, many *oblasti* and republic Party organizations set themselves an even more impossible task: to finish collectivization by the spring of 1930. In support, the newspapers in January and February of 1930 demanded that the resistance of opportunists be crushed and that collectivization be speeded up.

Total collectivization had not been envisaged by the first Five-Year Plan. Thus the material and financial resources needed to organize hundreds of thousands of collective farms had not been set aside. The decree of January 5 did call for a speed-up in the construction of factories for tractors, harvester combines, and other agricultural machinery. Some machine and tractor stations were switched

---

[31] See N. I. Nemakov, *Kommunisticheskaia partiia—organizator massovogo kolkhoznogo dvizheniia* (Moscow, 1966), pp. 98–102.

entirely to servicing the collective farms. The state assumed the expenses of reorganizing the land in setting up collective farms, which were also given credits of 500 million rubles for the following year. However, all these supplementary provisions were still directed toward collectivization in one or two years, not in one or two months. Most of the local Party, Soviet, and economic organs, to say nothing of the peasants themselves, were not prepared for total collectivization in such a short time. In order to carry out the orders that came from above, not only in written but often in *oral* form, almost all Party and Soviet organs were forced to put administrative pressure on the peasants and also on the lower officials. In short, an emergency situation was created in the countryside, and with it an increase in the role of the GPU.

Such methods absolutely contradicted the basic principles of Marxism-Leninism. The proletarian state, according to Marx, should adopt such measures in relation to the peasants "as would in embryo ease the transition from private ownership of land to collective ownership, so that the peasant would come to this economic path on his own."[32] Lenin often expressed the same ideas. His principle that the union of peasants into collective farms must be voluntary was endorsed by a special resolution of the VIIIth Party Congress in 1919:

> The only worthwhile unions are those which the peasants form themselves on their own free initiative, and the advantages of which they confirm by practice. Excessive haste in this matter is dangerous, for it will only intensify the middle peasants' prejudices against innovations. Representatives of the Soviet regime who allow themselves to use direct or even indirect force to bring peasants into *kommuny* must be called to the strictest accounting and removed from work in the countryside.[33]

Moreover, Stalin's own speeches contain many valid comments on the gradual and voluntary principles of collectivization. "We plan," he said in a 1927 conversation with some foreign delegations,

> to achieve collectivism in agriculture gradually, by measures of an economic, financial, and cultural-political nature. . . . Complete collectivization will come about only when peasant farming is reorganized on a new technical base by mechanization and electrification, when most of the toiling peasants are members of cooperative organizations, when most of the countryside is covered with agricultural associations of a collective nature. Things will eventually reach this point, but have not as yet, and will not in the near future. Why not? Because, among other reasons, this requires enormous financial resources which our state does not yet have, but which will be certainly accumulated in the course of time.[34]

[32] K. Marx, F. Engels, *Sochineniia*, XVIII, p. 612.
[33] *KPSS v rezoliutsiiakh*, I (1953), p. 448.
[34] *Sochineniia*, X, pp. 221, 225.

But only two years later, when the economic situation was not very different from that of 1927, Stalin spoke differently. He issued a call for massive and rapid total collectivization, which could be accomplished at that time only by administrative fiat and pressure. "To get the small peasant village to follow the socialist city," Stalin said in December, 1929,

> it is necessary . . . to *implant* in the village large socialist farms, collective and state farms, as bases of socialism, which, with the socialist city in the vanguard, can drag along the masses of peasants. . . . The socialist city can drag along the small peasant village in no other way than by *implanting* in the village collective and state farms and by reshaping the village on new socialist lines.[35]

And in fact, at the end of 1929 and the beginning of 1930, Lenin's principle of voluntary collectivization was violated almost everywhere, under pressure from Stalin and his closest aides. Organizational and explanatory work among the peasants was replaced by crude administrative fiat and force directed against the middle peasants and even some of the poor peasants. They were forced to join collective farms under threat of "dekulakization." In many *oblasti* the rule was quite simple: "Whoever does not join collective farms is an enemy of the Soviet regime." Along with force many local organs tried all kinds of fantastic promises. They promised the peasants tractors and considerable credit. "Everything will be supplied—join the collective farms." In many *raiony* an attempt was made to create not collective farms but *kommuny,* which meant that the peasants were forced to put all their livestock, poultry, and household gardens into the collective pool. Instead of offering financial and material aid, the authorities in some *oblasti* started "months of mobilizing resources," forcing individual peasants, before joining a collective farm, to pay up for the farm's credit fund, the seed supply, and membership dues.

Such perversions aroused great dissatisfaction among the peasants, especially the middle peasants. Influenced by kulak agitation, many peasants, before joining the collective farms, began to slaughter their livestock: cows, sheep, pigs, even poultry. Just in February and March, 1930 around 14 million head of cattle were destroyed; also one-third of all pigs and one-fourth of all sheep and goats. Although the percentages of collectivization rose rapidly—in January and February around 10 million peasant households joined the collective farms—tension also increased. In many *raiony,* enemies of the collective farms succeeded in provoking anti-Soviet outbursts among the peasantry.

The situation began to ease up only in March, 1930, following the publication of Stalin's article "Dizzy with Success," which he wrote at the demand of the Central Committee. In his article Stalin con-

[35] *Ibid.,* XII, p. 149. Stalin's italics.

demned violation of the principle that joining collective farms must be voluntary. He criticized the leap from the *artel'* to the *kommuna*.[36]

However, he shifted the responsibility for these mistakes onto local officials. Stalin's typical insincerity threw them into complete confusion. For it was precisely Stalin himself, Molotov, Kaganovich, and other leaders of the Central Committee who had pushed and prodded local agencies in collectivization. Special reports had been sent regularly, every seven to ten days, to all members of the Politburo. It was Stalin who had endorsed, at the end of 1929 and the beginning of 1930, the proposal made by some of his colleagues for the collectivization of farm implements, small livestock, milch cows, and so on.[37] Moreover, the newspapers of the time had been filled with the pledges of this, that, and the other *raion* to speed up total collectivization, and with appeals to speed the creation of collective farms all over. It is hard to believe that Stalin did not read any papers or magazines during this time. His attempt to blame the local agencies for all the mistakes of collectivization was obviously dishonest.

"Comrade Stalin," wrote Comrade Belik, a worker from Dnepropetrovsk:

> I, a rank-and-file worker and a reader of *Pravda*, have all this time been following the newspapers closely. Is the person to blame who could not but hear the uproar about collectivization, about who should lead collective farms? All of us, the lower ranks and the press, messed up that crucial question of collective-farm leadership, while Comrade Stalin, it seems, at that time was sleeping like a god, hearing nothing, his eyes closed to our mistakes. Therefore you too should be reprimanded. But now Comrade Stalin throws all the blame on the local authorities, and defends himself and the top people.[38]

A similar protest against Stalin's insincerity was made by Krupskaia in the summer of 1930, in a speech to the Party Conference of Bauman *raion*. Among the delegates were S. I. Berdichevskaia, a Party member since 1919, and M. Tsilales, who have described the scene. Krupskaia declared that collectivization was not being carried out in a Leninist manner. She said that the methods being used had nothing in common with Lenin's plan for developing cooperatives. In pushing collectivization the leaders of the Central Committee had sought advice from no one, neither the Party nor the lower ranks nor the people. And it made no sense, said Krupskaia, to accuse local officials of the mistakes made by the Central Committee itself. Kaganovich immediately took the

[36] *Ed.:* See the Glossary for an explanation of these terms.
[37] See *Voprosy istorii*, 1965, No. 3, p. 12.
[38] See *Istoricheskii arkhiv*, 1962, No. 2, p. 197.

floor and gave Krupskaia a scolding. In addition to repudiating her criticism, he declared that, as a member of the Central Committee, she did not have the right to criticize the Central Committee's line. "Krupskaia should not think," Kaganovich said, "that just because she was Lenin's wife, she has a monopoly on Leninism." A. S. Bubnov also sharply criticized her speech. "Krupskaia," said Bubnov, "is a beacon who does not guide our Party toward the good."

Stalin did not stop at blaming local officials; in the spring of 1930, in many *oblasti*, there were mass repressions of local officials, and in many *raiony* there were trials of "left deviationists." Many of the defendants did deserve punishment for violating revolutionary legality in the countryside. Bewilderment and resentment were aroused, however, by the fact that most of the bigger officials, whose instructions had been carried out by the *raion* leadership, were not brought to justice.

Even today some historians try to whitewash Stalin by reviving his notion that local agencies were responsible for the perversions in collectivization. For example, S. P. Trapeznikov asserts that the switch to total collectivization was determined not by the willful decision of particular individuals, as "bourgeois falsifiers" imagine, but objectively, by conditions. "Life has shown," Trapeznikov writes, "that the Party did not miscalculate in this political step."[39] Trapeznikov works out a peculiar approach to the errors made during collectivization. The Central Committee's directives were correct, he asserts, but local and central agencies made serious errors in carrying them out. The same interpretation is offered by F. Vaganov, who denounces as "bourgeois," "Trotskyite," or "right opportunist" the argument that the policy of the highest authorities was responsible for the force and violence of collectivization. Instead, he places the blame on the unforeseen complexities of a great innovation.[40]

What can be said about this interpretation? In the first place, violations of the peasant's freedom of choice and the use of administrative fiat occurred not in just a number of cases; they were universal. Secondly, the scale and speed of the movement were not spontaneous but were determined by the central leadership. Collectivization was not some sort of uncontrollable process, as the events following the publication of Stalin's "Dizzy with Success" showed. Thus assertions of Stalin's responsibility are by no means "speculative"; they are based primarily on the fact that he was the head of the Party in 1929–30, that he was the one who sent the basic directives to local officials, orally as well as in writing. Local officials, unprepared for

[39] *Istoricheskii opyt KPSS v osushchestvlenii leninskogo kooperativnogo plana* (Moscow, 1965), p. 197.
[40] See Vaganov's articles in *Kommunist*, 1966, No. 3, and in *Voprosy istorii KPSS*, February, 1968.

such rapid and wholesale collectivization, did many stupid things. But it was the job of leaders, in approaching the problem, to take into consideration the abilities and preparation of the officials who had to apply the solution. Stalin, at the end of 1929, did not consider either the objective or the subjective factors. That is why the mistakes which are inevitable in any great new undertaking were so far-reaching, so profound, so massive. And only unbelievable exertions by the Party, the working class, and the peasantry managed, in spite of Stalin, to save Soviet agriculture, if not from enormous losses, at least from catastrophe.

Soon after the publication of Stalin's article, the Central Committee adopted a resolution, "On the struggle against distortions of the Party line in the collective-farm movement," which proposed to stop the use of force and to allow peasants to leave the collective farms if they so wished. This resolution led to a mass exodus of peasants from the collective farms. (In the southern *oblasti* where spring sowing had already begun, the exodus and the resulting confusion did serious damage.) By July 1, 1930, less than six million peasant households were left in the collectives, that is, less than one-fourth of all poor and middle peasants. In a number of *oblasti* almost all the collective farms were dissolved. In many cases the difficult work of collectivization had to start from scratch again.

The collectivization of agriculture was designed to achieve a rapid increase in total output and simultaneously in marketings, the share of total output that was sold. Thus the first Five-Year Plan forecast an increase of gross agricultural output from 16.6 billion rubles in 1927–28 to 25.8 billion rubles in 1932–33; that is, an increase of more than 50 per cent. These calculations were correct and well founded. But the gross errors made during collectivization upset these calculations and ruined plans for a well-balanced, rapid development of agricultural production. Instead of expanding as planned, gross agricultural output declined throughout the first Five-Year Plan. If we take 1928 agricultural output, by all categories of farms, as 100 per cent, in 1929 it was 98 per cent, in 1930 94.4 per cent, in 1931 92 per cent, in 1932 86.0 per cent, and in 1933 81.5 per cent. There was an especially sharp drop in livestock production, which in 1933 stood at 65 per cent of the 1913 level. The total number of cattle dropped from 60.1 million head to 33.5 million. The number of goats, sheep, and pigs decreased to less than half its prewar level. The number of draft animals, especially horses, declined by more than half. This decline was so great that it could not be offset by the massive delivery of tractors, which began in the early 1930's. Only in 1935 did the total draft power in agriculture—including animals and tractors—surpass the 1928 level.[41] With the fall in livestock, supplies of organic fertilizer also declined sharply, which caused a further drop in yields. The consequences of this fall, unprecedented in peacetime, continued to be felt even during the second and third Five-Year Plans.[42]

Vaganov has tried by clever manipulation of figures to minimize the serious effects of Stalin's adventuristic leadership. He writes that as a result of collectivization, the gross output of tillage was 50 per cent greater in 1937 than in 1913. These figures are correct. But if the figure for livestock as well as for crops is included, then the overall increase of agricultural output between 1913 and 1937 is not 50 per cent but 34 per cent. Besides, it would be more valid to compare 1937 not with 1913 but with 1928. In that case, the increase in gross output is not 34 per cent but 8 per cent—not impressive for a whole decade. It should also be noted that 1937 was an especially good year. In 1938 and 1939, despite a significant increase in area under cultivation, agricultural output was below the level of 1928. Indeed, it slightly exceeded the 1928–29 level only in two of the prewar years—in 1937 and 1940. Moreover, even if we do compare the second half of the thirties not with the second half of the twenties, but with 1913, the increase in gross agricultural output was basically due to a rise in the cultivation of high-priced industrial crops and some secondary products. With respect to basic agricultural production, no growth can be detected. For example, the annual production of grain averaged 4.56 billion poods from 1933 to 1940, whereas in 1913 (within the boundaries of September 17, 1939) 4.67 billion poods were produced. The production of meat dropped more significantly, especially if we exclude from the comparison the livestock raised by industrial and white-collar workers in small cities and suburbs.

The decline of agricultural output during the first Five-Year Plan affected fulfillment of the plan for the procurement of agricultural products. As industry continued its rapid development, the urban population increased by more than 2 million people each year. Consequently, despite the rise of collective farms, the disproportion between the needs of industry and the volume of agricultural production became constantly greater.

Stalin saw only one way out of this situation: coercion, the forced extraction of agricultural surpluses, and not only surpluses. The following figures show what happened. If the average yearly output of agricultural products from 1926 to 1929 is taken as the basic index figure of 100, then during the following ten years, 1930–39, the average yearly figure is 95. During the same decade, the state's pro-

---

[41] *Istoriia SSSR,* 1964, No. 5, p. 6.
[42] The data are taken from the yearbooks of *Ts. S. U.,* the Central Statistical Administration.

curement of agricultural products grew considerably larger than it had been in the second half of the twenties. In grain, for example, the state's acquisitions almost doubled. In 1932 the collective farms delivered to the state a little more than a quarter of all the grain they harvested; in 1933–34 more than a third; in 1935 almost 40 per cent. Moreover, the prices set for obligatory deliveries were several times lower than the cost of production of grain and some other basic agricultural products even for specialized state farms. In collective farms the cost of production was not calculated, but it was higher than in the specialized state farms.

Stalin constantly exaggerated the danger of raising procurement prices, declaring that if they were raised, it would be necessary to boost retail prices in the cities. In fact there was no special danger here, for the gap between procurement and retail prices was excessive. In 1933–34 the procurement price paid for wheat in grain-growing *raiony* was 8.2 to 9.4 kopecks per kilogram (in the prices of those years). At the same time the retail price of one kilogram of rationed wheat flour was 35 to 60 kopecks, and in nonrationed stores it was 4 to 5 rubles. The single state retail price of flour was 3.4 rubles per kilogram, that is, 40 times greater than the procurement price. For potatoes the procurement price was 3 to 4 kopecks per kilo; the rationed retail price, 20 to 30 kopecks; the nonrationed retail price, 1.2 to 2 rubles; the single state retail price, 24 to 35 kopecks. Beef was bought from the collective farms at 21 to 55 kopecks per kilogram, then sold in rationed stores at 3 to 4 rubles and in nonrationed stores at 10 to 12 rubles. The single state price for a kilogram of beef in the central *raiony* was 7.6 rubles per kilo.[43] Thus, from the very first years of the collective farms, Stalin introduced the practice of obliterating the farmers' personal, material incentives by forcing them to sell grain at arbitrary prices. Many collective farms were even forced to sell the grain they needed for fodder and for food.

In the collective farms these policies caused a collapse of labor discipline and mass theft of grain. Although most of the kulaks had been exiled, rural agitation against the Soviet regime increased. In a number of *raiony*, particularly in the Kuban, the Don, and the Ukraine, grain strikes broke out; not only individual peasants but collective farmers cut back their acreage, refused to surrender grain to the state, and buried it in the ground. But instead of correcting his errors, Stalin intensified the use of force. Draconian measures were taken against the theft of grain in the collective farms. Many peasants, convicted of stealing products they themselves had raised, were sentenced to long terms of imprisonment or were even shot.

[43] See the article by I. E. Zelenin in *Istoriia SSSR*, 1964, No. 5, pp. 19–20.

In some *raiony,* in 1932–33, a policy of mass terror was introduced. Goods were not delivered to *raiony* that did not fulfill their quota of grain procurement; state and cooperative stores were closed down. Local officials were fired en masse, expelled from the Party, brought to trial. In some cases, whole villages were resettled in the far northern *raiony.* For example, in the fall of 1932 a commission headed by Kaganovich, and granted virtually unlimited power, was sent to the Northern Caucasus to investigate the difficulties in grain procurement. In November, 1932, the buro of the North Caucasus Party organization, with Kaganovich taking part, resolved to smash all the saboteurs and counterrevolutionaries responsible for the failure of the grain collection and the fall sowing.[44] As a result, sixteen villages of the North Caucasus, including Poltavskaia, Medvedovskaia, Urupskaia, and Bagaevskaia, were moved to the far north. Mass repressions were also carried out, under the leadership of Molotov and Kaganovich, in the Ukraine and Belorussia (the resettlement of the so-called *chernodosochnye raiony*).

There is a revealing letter from Mikhail Sholokhov to Stalin on the outrageous actions of the grain procurers in Veshenskaia and other *raiony* of the Don. On April 16, 1933, Sholokhov wrote that "disgusting methods" were being used to collect grain, including cursing, beating, and torture. "These examples," the letter said,

> can be multiplied endlessly. They are not isolated cases of deviation; they are the "method" of procuring grain that has been decreed for the whole *raion.* I have heard these facts either from Communists or from the collective farmers themselves, who have personally experienced these "methods," and afterwards have come asking me to write about it in the newspaper. Do you remember, Joseph Vissarionovich, Korolenko's story "In a Pacified Village?" Here the "disappearing act" has been performed, not on three peasants suspected of stealing from a kulak, but on tens of thousands of collective farmers. And, as you can see, it's been done with a richer application of technical methods and more sophistication.

Sholokhov asked Stalin to look into what was happening on the Don, and to investigate not only the people who used intolerable methods against collective farmers but also the higher-ups who directed them.[45]

But Stalin remained deaf to such appeals. He even tried to give this antipeasant terror his own kind of "theoretical foundation." "What is the collective-farm peasantry?" asked Stalin, at a meeting on November 27, 1932.

[44] See the newspaper *Molot,* Nov. 5, 1932.
[45] *Ed:* Medvedev is using material that Khrushchev drew from the archives. See *Pravda,* March 10, 1963. For Korolenko's "In a Pacified Village," a 1911 account of brutal mistreatment of peasants, see V. G. Korolenko, *Sobranie sochinenii,* V (Moscow, 1953), pp. 392–402.

The collective-farm peasantry is the ally of the working classes. The vast majority of these peasants support the Soviet regime in the countryside. But this does not mean that, among the collective farmers, there cannot be individual groups who are against the Soviet regime and support the sabotage of grain procurements. It would be stupid if Communists, merely because collective farms are a socialist form of enterprise, did not counter the blows of these individual collective farmers and farms with crushing blows of their own.[46]

The newly formed state farms also experienced repression. As a typical example, there was the decree, "On the work of livestock state farms," published in the spring of 1932:

The Council of People's Commissars, the Central Committee of the Party, and the People's Commissariat of Agriculture consider it intolerable and dangerous that certain officials in livestock state farms try to gloss over shortcomings resulting from their poor leadership by references to the fact that livestock state farms are in the early stages of construction.

The names of thirty-four directors followed, with the suggestion that they be fired and brought to trial, and the names of ninety-two other directors, who were only to be fired. The decree was signed by Stalin, Molotov, and the Commissar of Agriculture, Ia. A. Iakovlev.

Stalin also brushed aside reports of famine, which appeared in many areas in 1932–33, as a result of crop failures and forced grain collections. Tens of thousands of peasants died of starvation, and hundreds of thousands, perhaps even millions, left their homes and fled to the cities. In 1932 R. Terekhov, a secretary of the Ukrainian Communist Party's Central Committee, reported to Stalin on the terrible situation developing in the villages of Kharkov *oblast* as a result of the crop failures. He asked Stalin to send some grain to the *oblast*. Stalin's reaction was strange. Sharply cutting off the speaker, Stalin said:

We have been told that you, Comrade Terekhov, are a good speaker; it seems that you are a good storyteller, you've made up such a fable about famine, thinking to frighten us, but it won't work. Wouldn't it be better for you to leave the post of *obkom* secretary and the Ukrainian Central Committee and join the Writers' Union? Then you can write your fables and fools will read them.[47]

However, in the thirties it was impossible to read any "fables" about the famine of 1932–34. Only nowadays a few writers specializing in rural problems (*derevenshchiki*) have touched on this formerly banned theme. In *Bread Is a Noun* Mikhail Alekseev writes:

[46] *Bol'shevik,* 1933, No. 1–2, p. 19.
[47] *Pravda,* May 26, 1964.

After the kulak the middle peasant left the village, but voluntarily. In accordance with one order or another, all the grain and all the fodder were taken away. Horses began to die en masse, and in 1933 there was a terrible famine. Whole families died, houses fell apart, village streets grew empty, more and more windows became blind—sightless—those who went to the city boarded them up.[48]

"In Petrakovskaia," writes V. Tendriakov in his recently published novel *Death,*

cattle died for lack of fodder, people ate bread made from nettles, biscuits made from one weed, porridge made from another. And not only in Petrakovskaia. A year of hunger moved through the country, nineteen hundred and thirty-three. In Vokhrovo, the *raion* capital, in the little park by the station, dekulakized peasants expelled from the Ukraine lay down and died. You got used to seeing corpses there in the morning; a wagon would pull up and the hospital stable hand, Abram, would pile in the bodies. Not all died; many wandered through the dusty mean little streets, dragging bloodless blue legs, swollen from dropsy, feeling out each passer-by with doglike begging eyes. In Vokhrovo they got nothing; the residents themselves, to get bread on their ration cards, queued up the night before the store opened. Thirty-three.[49]

"It was frightening to walk through villages in 1933–34," writes A. E. Kosterin in his memoirs.

And I had the occasion to go through dozens of villages in Stavropol, on the Don, Kuban, and Terek, and in Saratov, Orenburg, and Kalinin *oblasti*. . . . Houses with boarded-up windows, empty barnyards, abandoned equipment in the fields. And terrifying mortality, especially among children. . . .

On the deserted road to Stavropol I met a peasant with a knapsack. We stopped, greeted each other, had a smoke. I asked him, "Where are you tramping, comrade?"

"To prison."

Astonishment kept me from saying or asking anything. I only looked my amazement at the old man. He was about forty, had the usual peasant beard and mustache. (At that time, this was called the Kalinin style of shave.) He smoked calmly and quite unexcitedly told me his story. He was a middle peasant who had been sentenced to ten years on the basis of Article 58, Point 10 (Agitation and Propaganda), for refusing to join a collective farm and for speaking against the plenipotentiary in the village meeting. The village policeman lacked the time or the inclination to escort him to Stavropol, so he was going alone.

On the surface the man was indifferent to his fate, but he also had his muzhik shrewdness: in prison he would be saved from

[48] *Zvezda,* 1964, No. 1, p. 37.
[49] *Moskva,* 1968, No. 3, p. 37.

starvation. Famine, in early 1933, was striking down hundreds of people in the villages.

And all this unjustified deprivation and suffering were primarily the result of the inept and adventuristic leadership of the man who had been criticized by the "left" opposition for a peasant deviation, who had even been called the "god of the peasants."

5

BEFORE THE REVOLUTION, the kulaks were a major force in the Russian countryside. Just after the October Revolution, they even improved their position as a result of the expropriation of the noble landowners' estates. At that time up to 20 per cent of all peasants were kulaks, who owned more than 40 per cent of the land. In the summer of 1918 they came out against the Soviet regime; a wave of kulak uprisings swept over Russia. It was the kulaks who opposed the government monopoly of the grain trade and the forced requisition of grain, which were necessary measures in the conditions of the Civil War. The Party countered the kulaks' sabotage by creating food detachments and committees of poor peasants.[50] In that period Lenin insisted on the fiercest struggle against the kulaks. "There can be no doubt at all," he wrote in August, 1918,

> that the kulaks are rabid enemies of the Soviet regime. Either the kulaks will cut down an infinite number of workers, or the workers will mercilessly put down the risings of the robbing kulak minority against the regime of the toilers. There can be no middle way.[51]

Although Lenin called for the ruthless suppression of kulak risings, he never demanded the complete expropriation of the entire kulak population, much less the physical annihilation or banishment of the kulaks and their families. Even noble landlords, Lenin argued, should be permitted to join a *kommuna* if the peasants were willing to accept them. Lenin wanted to use their managerial skills if possible. As for the kulaks, he insisted repeatedly that they were not to be stripped of their property like the landlords and capitalists. Part of what they had was the fruit of their own labor on the land. If they rebelled they should be put down, but they should not be expropriated.[52]

When planning NEP as an entire historical period of economic competition between socialism and private capital, Lenin thought of squeezing out the kulaks by economic measures. "If you can give the

[50] *Ed:* Food detachments, recruited from the urban proletariat, went through the countryside requisitioning food. Committees of poor peasants were authorized to equalize landholding by seizing kulak property.

[51] *Sochineniia*, 4th edn., XXVIII, p. 39.

[52] See, e.g., *ibid.*, XXIX, pp. 123 *ff*.

peasants machines," he wrote, "you will raise them up, and when you give them machines or electrification, tens or hundreds of thousands of petty kulaks will be crushed."[53]

In the mid-twenties it was the Trotskyites who urged the intensification of class struggle in the countryside. Sometimes directly but usually in a veiled way, many followers of Trotsky and Zinoviev came out for a "third revolution"[54] in the countryside. The well-known Party official and economist Iu. Larin declared: "In time the inviolability of kulak farms will come to an end, and their accumulated livestock and equipment will form the material basis of collective farms organized by appropriate groups of day laborers."[55] This statement was sharply criticized by the Party press. "What does this mean?" asked D. Maretskii in the journal *Bol'shevik*:

> "In time the inviolability of kulak farms will come to an end?"
> . . . The "expropriation of the expropriators" in the countryside, the "third revolution" in the flesh—that is the inevitable conclusion one draws from all of Larin's premises.
>
> There would be nothing wrong with a third revolution if there were no middle peasants. But once the middle peasant is the central figure in the countryside, the third revolution is not only unnecessary, it would be a disaster, since it would at once alienate the middle peasants from us, thereby striking a fatal blow at the alliance of workers and peasants, the foundation of the Soviet state.[56]

Even after the XVth Party Congress, in December, 1927, when the cooperative movement was beginning to catch on, the Party leaders looked for the least painful way of solving the kulak problem. Under certain conditions, some of the kulaks were thought fit to join cooperatives. Even in the middle of 1929, in a decree "On the organization of agricultural cooperatives," the Central Committee did not advocate the expulsion of former kulaks from the cooperatives. In the second half of 1929, Party leaders who were by no means supporters of the so-called right deviation—for example, M. I. Kalinin—urged a less painful solution to the kulak problem than mass repression. But by the end of 1929, it became clear that mass repression could hardly be avoided. In early December, 1929, a special commission of the Politburo concluded that it would be necessary to liquidate the class of kulaks. The commission proposed that kulaks' farms be divided into three categories:

[53] *Ibid.*, XXXII, p. 202.
[54] *Ed.:* The February Revolution of 1917 may have been considered the first, the October Revolution the second. Or 1905 may have been the first, and 1917 the second.
[55] See Iu. Larin, *Sovetskaia derevnia* (Moscow, 1925).
[56] *Bol'shevik*, 1925, No. 19–20, pp. 41–42. D. Maretskii was one of Bukharin's disciples. In 1925 he expressed the point of view shared by the majority of the Central Committee headed by Stalin.

(1) Kulaks who actively opposed the organization of collective farms and carried on counterrevolutionary subversive activities. These should be arrested or exiled to remote regions.

(2) Kulaks who less actively opposed the measures designed to bring about total collectivization. These were to be banished from their own *oblast* or *krai*.

(3) Kulaks who were prepared to submit to steps toward collectivization and to behave loyally toward the Soviet regime. The commission thought it possible to accept such kulaks as members of collective farms, but without the right to vote for three to five years.

Following Stalin's amendments, the commission decided not to let the third category join collective farms. Therefore, in the instructions issued by the Central Executive Committee and the Council of People's Commissars on February 4, 1930, the kulaks were categorized in a different way. For example, the first category was to consist of active counterrevolutionary kulaks who organized terror and insurrections. They were to be isolated at once, by incarceration in prisons and corrective labor camps, and there was to be no hesitation in applying the most extreme measure of punishment—shooting—against them. All members of their families were to be banished to distant regions. It was proposed that more than 50,000 households be assigned to this category.

The second category included the rest of the politically active richest kulaks. The commission proposed that they and their families be banished to remote regions of the country or to remote localities of their own *krai*. It was indicated that there would be about 112,000 of these households.

In the third category were less powerful kulak households. It was proposed that they be left in their own *raion* but that they be resettled outside the collectivized villages with new allotments of land apart from the collective-farm fields. These kulaks, according to the instructions, were to be assigned production goals and duties. It was proposed that the majority of kulak households be assigned to this category. There was no word, in these instructions and decrees, of "subkulaks" or of prosperous middle peasants.

Even these severe recommendations were exceeded in most *oblasti*. Because of the intensification of class struggle in the countryside, many more kulaks than the number planned at the beginning of 1930 were banished to remote, usually northern *raiony,* sent to corrective labor camps, or shot. According to data presented to the January Plenum of the Central Committee in 1933, 240,757 kulak families (about 1 to 1.5 million people) were banished to remote *raiony.* There is good reason to believe that these figures are greatly understated.

Soviet historical literature usually places the responsibility for the intensification of the class struggle on the kulaks alone. But much of the blame must be placed on the Party and Soviet organizations that fell into grave excesses and perversions in setting up collective farms. From the start of collectivization, it was obvious that this fundamental transformation was directed against the interests of the kulaks and that the kulaks would oppose it. Therefore, the main job of Party and Soviet agencies was to win the middle peasants over to their side and to isolate the kulaks. If the kulaks had been isolated, their resistance to collectivization would have been greatly weakened and they would have been obliged to submit to the measures of the Soviet regime. Without hope of success, without the support of the middle peasants, the majority of the kulaks would not have decided to try counter-revolutionary terror, the organization of anti-Soviet uprisings, the creation of robber bands. Unfortunately, in many *oblasti* and *raiony* the kulaks were not isolated and neutralized.

Because of the mistakes discussed above, a significant portion of the middle peasants began to oppose the creation of collective farms, and the peasant masses became receptive to the kulaks' anti-Soviet propaganda. Sensing their strength, the kulaks intensified their opposition to collectivization. This led in turn to an intensification of repressive measures, not only against all kulaks without exception but also against the considerable number of middle peasants who were temporarily influenced by kulak agitation or simply hesitated to join the collective farms. The many well-to-do middle peasants, those who had occasionally hired labor, were hit especially hard.

Often the mere fact of having once hired a laborer was sufficient pretext for dekulakization, although middle peasants and even occasional poor peasants, unable for some reason to work their own land, had done so from time to time. In 1927, during the struggle with the "left" opposition, which exaggerated the strength of the kulaks, Agitprop had issued a pamphlet making the facts clear:

A significant share in the hiring of laborers falls to the lot of middle-peasant households, which use hired labor as an auxiliary force. A significant amount of hired labor is used by big-peasant households of the exploitative type, but this amount is far less than that used by the middle-peasant category.[57]

But barely three years later, many of the peasants earlier categorized as middle peasants were put down as kulaks and subjected to "dekulakization." Many lower-middle peasants, poor peasants, and even some day laborers, who had never hired labor but were momentarily influenced by kulak agitation, were given the senseless label of "sub-

[57] *Fakty i tsifry protiv demagogii i izmyshlenii oppozitsii* (Moscow, 1927), p. 75.

kulaks" and were banished. In some *raiony* up to 20 per cent of the peasants were banished; for each kulak evicted, three or four middle or poor peasants had to be arrested.[58]

In 1930–31 the Party press published much about abuses during dekulakization. For example, in many *raiony* dekulakization preceded collectivization, when there were no grounds for such action and neither the poor nor middle peasants were ready for it. Dekulakization was therefore carried out suddenly, by the *apparat,* and produced negative results. In 1930, *Bol'shevik,* the organ of the Central Committee, reported that levying a special tax on peasants who would not join a collective farm was widely regarded as a preliminary to deprivation of the franchise, which in turn was a preliminary to dekulakization. *Bol'shevik* reported cases of middle peasants being subjected to dekulakization because they had once sold a dozen scythes, some grain, a cow, shoe soles, or hay. In some places groups of poor peasants explicitly decreed the expropriation of middle peasants, ordering the confiscation of such luxuries as sewing machines, mirrors, and beds. In one *raion,* investigation revealed that only three of thirty-four households subjected to dekulakization were actually kulak.[59] There were thousands and thousands of such cases.

Some *raiony* declared martial law (*osadnoe polozhenie*) during the liquidation of the kulaks, and did not leave the banished kulaks even the statutory minimum of equipment and supplies. Hundreds of kulak special settlements (*spetsposeleniia*) were created at the beginning of the thirties in uninhabited regions of Siberia and the East. The settlers were deprived of most rights and privileges for a long time, including freedom of movement. Contrary to instructions, even those kulaks were banished who had family members who had served in the Red Army. And these excesses were not sporadic incidents; they took place on a mass scale.

Indeed, there can be no justification for many actions that conformed to instructions, such as the arrest of an entire family along with a kulak or "subkulak," including young children. In unheated railway cars hundreds of thousands of peasants, with their wives and children, went east, to the Urals, Kazakhstan, Siberia. Many thousands died en route from hunger and cold and disease. E. M. Landau met a group of these transportees in Siberia in 1930. In winter, during a severe frost, a large group of kulaks with their families were being taken in wagons three hundred kilometers into the *oblast.* One of the muzhiks, unable to endure the crying of a baby sucking its mother's empty breast, grabbed the child from his wife's arms and dashed its head against a tree.

[58] *Istoriia KPSS* (Moscow, 1960), p. 423.
[59] See A. Angarov in *Bol'shevik,* 1930, No. 6, p. 20.

It must be remembered that Stalin raised the slogan of kulak liquidation suddenly, causing confusion among many Party organizations. Even in terms of form, this decision was a clear violation of the collective principle (*kollegial'nost*) in the leadership of the Party.

It must also be borne in mind that, after the Second World War, the new socialist countries moved toward the liquidation of the kulaks *as a class,* but they did so by restricting and squeezing out the kulaks, not by totally expropriating them. In Czechoslovakia, Rumania, Bulgaria, Hungary, and the German Democratic Republic, kulaks were allowed to join collective farms and prove their transformation by honest labor.[60] One author attributes this development to the consolidation of the world socialist system and the strength of the regimes in the peoples' democracies. But such an explanation is incomplete. The main difference is that the transformation of agriculture in the people's democracies was not accomplished with so many mistakes as in the USSR.

6

THE SERIOUS MISTAKES and the misuse of power in collectivization have often been criticized in Soviet historical, political, and artistic literature.[61] Much less study has been made of the industrialization of the USSR in the late twenties and early thirties. It is widely believed that the situation was different in the cities during this period; that Stalin, though he made many mistakes in agriculture, achieved successful industrialization with his firm leadership. This view is wrong.

No one will deny, of course, the successes achieved by the people under the leadership of the Party in building modern industry. Colossal work was accomplished by the working class, by the intelligentsia, by all Party organizations. During the first Five-Year Plan alone, approximately 1,500 big enterprises were built, including Dneproges, the Magnitogorsk and Kuznetsk metallurgical complexes, the Ural machine factory, the Rostov agricultural-machinery plant, tractor factories at Cheliabinsk, Stalingrad, and Kharkov, automobile factories in Moscow and Sormovo, the Ural chemical works, the Kramator factory of heavy machinery, and so on. New sectors of industry were established, which

[60] See L. I. Krylov, *Voprosy istorii KPSS*, 1966, No. 1, p. 8.
[61] Among artistic works of recent years, S. Zalygin's interesting and profound story "On the Irtysh" is especially worthy of note. The most significant historical work is undoubtedly *The Collectivization of Agriculture in the USSR, 1927–32,* a monograph written by a group of scholars in the Institute of History of the Academy of Sciences, with V. P. Danilov as editor. This work was endorsed by the Institute's scholarly council (*uchenyi sovet*) and accepted (*podpisana k pechati*) by the publishing house Mysl' in 1964. But publication has been held up since October, 1964, for political reasons that have nothing to do with scholarship.

had not existed in tsarist Russia—machine-tool production, automobile and tractor manufacturing, a chemical industry, motor works, airplane factories, the production of powerful turbines and generators, of high-grade steel, of ferrous alloys, of synthetic rubber, artificial fibers, nitrogen, and so on. Construction was begun of thousands of kilometers of new railroads and canals. Major centers of heavy industry were created in the territories of the non-Russian minorities, the former borderlands of tsarist Russia—in Belorussia, the Ukraine, Transcaucasus, Central Asia, Kazakhstan and Tartary, in the North Caucasus and in Buriat-Mongolia. The eastern part of the country became the second metallurgical and oil center of industry. Hundreds of new cities and workers' settlements were founded. A firm basis was laid for the further development of industry and the strengthening of the USSR's defense capacity.

Great contributions in solving the complex problems of industrial development were made by F. E. Dzerzhinskii, S. M. Kirov, V. V. Kuibyshev, G. K. Ordzhonikidze, Ia. E. Rudzutak, V. Ia. Chubar', I. D. Kabakov, G. L. Piatakov, and other Party leaders. Stalin also made contributions. But here too, as in collectivization, Stalin often acted not as a wise statesman but as a voluntarist, a promoter of unrealizable schemes (*prozhektor i voliuntarist*). Thus Stalinist leadership frequently created unnecessary difficulties instead of triumphs.

Let us examine Stalin's industrial policy during the first Five-Year Plan, basing the analysis primarily on materials published in recent years.

Gosplan drew up the first Five-Year Plan of 1928/29–1932/33 in two variants: the base-line (*otpravnoi*) and the optimum, the first setting goals about 20 per cent below the second. The optimal variant assumed: (a) the absence of a major crop failure during the five years of the plan, (b) a significant expansion of connections with the world economy, both as a result of greater exports and especially as a result of greater long-term credits for equipment and technical aid, and (c) a quick steep climb in qualitative indices. Hence many elements of the plan were contingent. All sorts of factors that could not be foreseen in 1928–29—such as total collectivization—could complicate implementation. Thus it was not only sensible but necessary to have two variants, with the base-line (*otpravnoi*) as the fundamental one. However, in the discussion of the draft plan, most of the base-line goals were called a concession to the "right deviation." In fact, the Central Committee directed all Party organizations to consider the optimal goals as control figures. It was even proposed to fulfill the Five-Year Plan in four years.

After the XVIth Party Conference, in April, 1929, and when the Vth Congress of Soviets had finally ratified the optimal variant, the entire country began the tremendous task of carrying it out. With great enthusiasm the Soviet people overcame many difficulties and deprivations, built new factories, mines and electrical power stations, oil wells and railways. But in the first two years of the Five-Year Plan, it became obvious that some of the major conditions for fulfilling the optimal variant had not materialized. There was no great increase in credits from the capitalist countries for equipment and technical aid, nor did the Soviet Union's capacity to export show dramatic growth. On the contrary, the industrial and agricultural crisis that hit the major capitalist countries in 1929–30 created unforeseen difficulties for the USSR. World prices of raw materials dropped sharply, and for each machine imported it was necessary to export more than twice the amount that the plan had provided for. Nor was there a steep rise in the qualitative indices of economic development. On top of that, the gross output of agricultural products in 1929 and 1930 fell below the 1928 level.

Thus, despite the broad scope (*razmakh*) and great enthusiasm of socialist construction, the first Five-Year Plan did not get off to a successful start in all sectors. For example, the production of pig iron and steel increased by only 600,000 to 800,000 tons in 1929, barely surpassing the 1913–14 level. Only 3,300 tractors were produced in 1929. The output of food processing and light industry rose slowly. And in the crucial area of transportation, the railways worked especially poorly.

Under these conditions, fulfillment of the optimal variant was threatened. Either some of its goals had to be lowered or the Party and economic organizations had to be reoriented toward the base-line variant. Neither of these actions was taken. Instead, Stalin and Molotov suddenly appeared at a meeting of the Council of Commissars—previously Stalin had hardly ever attended its meetings—and proposed that the control figures of the plan be increased almost twofold. These proposals were completely unrealistic, but Stalin insisted that they be adopted and the former "right opportunist" Rykov did not object. At the XVIth Party Congress in June, 1930, Stalin announced sharp increases in the goals—for pig iron, from 10 million to 17 million tons by the last year of the plan; for tractors, from 55,000 to 170,000; for other agricultural machinery and trucks, an increase of more than 100 per cent; and so on. He dismissed as "hopelessly bureaucratic" the argument that such arbitrary increases undermined the whole principle of planning.[62]

Stalin's proposals were seriously questioned not only by many of the nonparty specialists working in the economic organs and in Gosplan but also by eminent Bolshevik executives. Stalin accused the

[62] *Sochineniia*, XII, pp. 345–47.

former group of "wrecking," and rudely brushed aside the Communist critics as well. When the chief director of the Central Board of Nonferrous Metals, A. S. Shakmuradov, gave a convincing critique of the fantastic new targets in nonferrous metallurgy, he was demoted and later repressed. Of course repression and threats of repression did not speed up the development of industry. For example, in 1930 Stalin predicted an increase in industrial output of 31 to 32 per cent.[63] The actual increase, according to the yearbooks of the Central Statistical Administration, was 22 per cent. For 1931 a new target was adopted: an increase of 45 per cent.[64] The actual increase in 1931 was 20 per cent. In 1932 it dropped to 15 per cent, and in 1933 to 5 per cent. In 1932 the XVIIth Party Conference was forced to drop the slogan "17 million tons of pig iron" and many other unrealistic goals in metallurgy and in machine production.

In January, 1933, Stalin reported that the first Five-Year Plan had been fulfilled in four years and three months, that industrial output in 1932 had reached the goals set by the optimal variant for 1932–33. He told the January Plenum that the Plan as a whole had been fulfilled at the end of 1932 by 93.7 per cent, and in Group A (heavy industry) by 103.4 per cent. A noisy propaganda campaign was launched on the occasion. Many of the participants rejoiced at the successes achieved, but for Stalin the campaign had a major political purpose. The years 1932 and 1933 were a time of crisis for the national economy. Agricultural production had reached its lowest point, famine was beginning in many rural areas, and the industrial working class had also suffered a sharp deterioration in its standard of living. All this forced Stalin to declare the premature fulfillment of the plan, in order somehow to get the people to see some justification for the sacrifices forced on them by collectivization and industrialization, which were not so much due to the actual needs of the economy as to the poor leadership of Stalin and his aides.

Industry made great strides forward during the first Five-Year Plan. Production of all types increased both absolutely and relatively, the productivity of labor increased, and managerial personnel improved and acquired experience. But the leap ahead was nowhere near as great as Stalin reported to the January Plenum in 1933. His figures on the increase in gross output were not precise. The Supreme Council of the National Economy had planned that gross industrial output would increase by 2.8 times from 1927–28 to 1932–33, with heavy industry increasing by 3.3 times. In fact, by 1932 gross industrial output a little better than doubled and heavy industry increased by 2.7 times, considerably short of the planned targets. According to the

[63] *Ibid.*, XIII, p. 30.
[64] *Ibid.*, p. 29.

plan, the output of consumer goods was to rise by a factor of 2.4; the actual increase was 56 per cent.[65]

But these figures on gross output do not tell the whole story. Nowadays we are aware how deceptive and inadequate they can be if they are not supplemented by other economic indices. Suppose, for example, that the automobile industry spends 500 million rubles to produce, not 100,000 cars at a unit value (*stoimost'*) of 5,000 rubles, as specified in the plan, but only 25,000 cars at a unit value of 20,000 rubles. Has this branch of industry met its assignment, just because the total value of cars produced seems to agree with the planned objective? It must also be borne in mind that the intensive growth of industrial specialization during the first Five-Year Plan caused gross output to rise in many sectors without any real increase in goods actually produced. This happened because the value of a half-finished product was now counted twice: first in evaluating the performance of the enterprise turning out the half-finished product, then in evaluating the work of the enterprise making a finished product out of the half-finished one.

What do we find if we analyze fulfillment of the first Five-Year Plan not only on the basis of gross output but also on the basis of physical indices of goods produced? The results were much more modest than the propaganda claimed. Despite the massive resources invested in the development of industry, despite the exertions of the people, almost none of the optimal goals, as expressed in physical units, was reached. Even further from fulfillment were the unrealistic goals that Stalin spoke of at the XVIth Party Congress. Here are some of the relevant figures.[66]

Ten million tons of pig iron were planned for the last year of the Five-Year Plan, and Stalin in 1930 declared this goal raised to 17 million tons. In 1932, 6.16 million tons were poured. On the eve of the war, in 1940, 15 million tons of pig iron were poured and only in 1950 did the figure pass 17 million. Other indices of ferrous metallurgy tell the same story. Instead of the 10.4 million tons of steel planned for 1932 by the optimal variant, around 6 million tons were poured, and the output of the rolling mills was 4.43 million tons in 1932 instead of the planned 8 million. The XVIth Party Congress endorsed a control figure of 22 million kilowatt-hours to be generated in the last year of the plan; in fact 13.5 million kilowatt-hours were generated in 1932. The production of coal and peat that year fell short

[65] See *Promyshlennost' SSSR*, pp. 12, 13; and *Kratkii kurs istorii SSSR*, II (Moscow, 1964), p. 234.
[66] The plan goals are taken from the works of Gosplan published in three volumes in 1928–29, and from the materials of the XVIth Party Congress. The facts on plan fulfillment are taken from the yearbooks published by the Central Statistical Administration in the last ten years.

of the target by 10 to 15 per cent. Petroleum output was somewhat better: already in 1931, 22.4 million tons were extracted, more than planned for 1932–33. In the next two years, however, petroleum production dropped, in 1932 to 21.4 million tons and in 1933 to 21.5.

The optimal goals in the production of building materials were not met. Instead of the 9.3 billion bricks planned, 4.9 billion were produced in 1932. It was even worse with mineral fertilizers. The plan called for 8–8.5 million tons in 1932, but only 920,000 were produced in 1932 and 1,030,000 in 1933.

Many of the more important goals in the machine industry were not reached, including the production of agricultural machinery. According to the plan, 100,000 automobiles and trucks were to be produced in the last year of the plan, and in 1930 Stalin declared this goal doubled. In fact, 23,879 were manufactured in 1932 and 49,710 in 1933. Not until 1936 did automobile manufacture pass the 100,000 mark. In 1932, 48,900 tractors were produced, as against the 55,000 planned. As for Stalin's declared figure of 170,000 tractors, it was reached neither before the war nor during the first postwar decade. Nor was Stalin's unrealistic goal of 40,000 harvester combines attained by 1932. The same is true for the production of horse and tractor plows, seed drills, and other farm machinery.

As for light industry and food processing, many important branches showed no growth at all during the first Five-Year Plan. In cotton cloth, for example, 2.678 billion meters were manufactured in 1928 and 2.694 billion in 1932, whereas the plan called for 4.588 billion. Woolen cloth: 86.8 million meters were manufactured in 1928 and 88.7 million meters in 1932, when the Plan called for 270–300 million meters. Linen cloth: 174.4 million meters in 1928 and 133.6 million meters in 1932, in comparison with the planned 500 million meters. The production of sugar was to have increased twofold; in reality it stood 30 per cent lower in 1932 than in 1928. A similar decline occurred in the production of meat and milk. And there were many other important sectors of the economy where the optimal targets were not reached: paper, rubber footwear, railway tonnage, and so on and on.

Despite the nonfulfillment of the plan's physical indices, the working-class population grew much faster than planned. The number of workers increased not by just a third, as the plan had forecast; it nearly doubled.[67] This was due to a number of unforeseen circumstances: extended delays in completing many big industrial projects, the mass exodus of peasants to the cities because of the bad situation in the countryside, and failure to achieve the planned increase in the productivity of labor. The immoderate growth of the urban popula-

[67] See *Voprosy istorii KPSS*, 1967, No. 2, p. 58.

tion created a multitude of disproportions. While the production of grain dropped in 1930–32, the number of people supplied by centralized grain distribution rose from 26 million in 1930 to 33.2 million in 1931 and to 40.3 million in 1932.[68] The transfer to the cities of millions of peasants, most of them poor, was accompanied by an improvement in their standard of living. And of course the material position of the former unemployed was improved; now they all had work. But the standard of living of the regular workers grew worse, even though, as ratified by the XVIth Party Conference, the Plan forecast a steady increase in the prosperity of the working class and in the purchasing power of the ruble. As early as 1926 the XVth Party Conference had warned against any attempt to "effect savings at the expense of the vital interests of the working class." Any such attempt was to be opposed as a distortion of Party policy.[69] The XVth Party Congress adopted a similar resolution:

> A correct solution of the central problems of the Five-Year Plan will bring the kind of increase in national income and its distribution that will guarantee a rise in the prosperity of the working class. . . . Any further increase in wages must be in real wages, not just in monetary units.[70]

These important directives were not carried out, either in the countryside or the city. At the very beginning of the first Five-Year Plan the purchasing power of the ruble fell and prices on the open market rose severalfold. In 1929 rationing was introduced for all the basic foodstuffs and also many industrial goods. "Commercial," i.e., unrationed, stores appeared, where scarce goods could be bought at high prices. All this led to a considerable decrease in real wages, both for blue-collar and for white-collar workers. The historian O. I. Shkaratan, studying data for Leningrad, has shown that in 1930 the real wages of factory workers in all sectors were lower than their 1927–28 level. Beginning in 1931, price indices for food and manufactured goods were no longer published. But the drop in the volume of consumption of these products shows that the decline in real wages continued in 1931–32. Only during the second Five-Year Plan did real wages begin to rise anew, reaching the 1928 level only in 1940. During the same period, the productivity of labor increased severalfold.[71]

The failure to achieve most of the goals of the first Five-Year Plan, as stated in physical indices, was due to many causes, particu-

[68] *Ibid.*
[69] *KPSS v rezoliutsiiakh,* II, (1953), pp. 195–96.
[70] See *Stenograficheskii otchet XV s'ezda VKP/b,* II, p. 1450.
[71] See *Istoriia SSSR,* 1964, No. 3, pp. 34–38.

larly the still inadequate level of planning. There were also certain objective factors which could hardly have been taken into account when the plan was being drawn up. However, a big role must be assigned to Stalin's approach to the complex problems of economic development. To set a great number of excessively high and clearly unrealizable goals for industry was inevitably to create disproportions in the national economy, to squander still meager material and human resources, and in the final analysis not to speed up industrial development but to slow it down. Suffering from gigantomania, Stalin encouraged the creation of huge, inviable collective and state farms and of immense industrial enterprises, even though there was not enough accumulated capital at the time of the first Five-Year Plan. As a result, the building of enterprises dragged on for many years, and great material resources were immobilized for long periods. Often construction projects were begun and then suspended because there were not enough resources to finish them.

Stalin introduced the "willful" (*volevoi*) method of planning into Soviet economic life, and there are many cases that prove how wrong it was. It will suffice to recall the development of synthetic rubber.[72] The first batch of experimental synthetic rubber was produced in January, 1931. Immediately the construction of one or two large factories was proposed. All the leading engineers, including Academician S. V. Lebedev, whose process had been used to produce the synthetic rubber, doubted the practicality of such a program. Nonetheless, striving for a rapid development of the Soviet chemical industry, the participants in the discussion endorsed a plan to build one or two factories. The specialists were astonished to learn that the government had decided, on Stalin's proposal, to build *ten* big synthetic rubber factories during the first Five-Year Plan. Lebedev himself categorically opposed such a grandiose project in an area of production that still had many unsolved problems. Opposition was also expressed by Ia. E. Rudzutak, Chairman of the Committee on Chemical Production. But Stalin brushed aside these well-founded objections. The search for construction sites and building materials began. Such resources as were available were now spread out over ten units. Finally, in 1932–33, starts were made on only three factories; the rest were not built either in the first or in the second Five-Year Plan.

There were many similar examples of Stalin's incompetence and adventurism, which greatly complicated the already complex job of industrialization. Stalin's poor leadership was one of the reasons that industrial development at the end of the twenties and the beginning of the thirties cost much more than it would have with more rational

[72] See *Voprosy istorii*, 1964, No. 8, pp. 38–39.

planning and leadership. And if the extreme exertions and sacrifices which the people made for the sake of industrialization are compared with the results, the conclusion cannot be avoided: the results would have been far greater without Stalin.

The article "Socialist Industrialization in the USSR" in the *Soviet Historical Encyclopedia,* makes a just appraisal:

> Stalin and his entourage often did not give due consideration to real possibilities; to an excessive degree they intensified tempos of industrial construction that were high to begin with. As a result, resources were overtaxed, and a number of plan announcements turned out to be unreal and detrimental.[73]

This comment has been sharply criticized by three historians, who claim that the encyclopedia article contradicts itself. First it says that "industrialization was carried out in conditions of capitalist encirclement," and then it supposedly forgets about encirclement and argues against excessive speed-up of industrialization. The country, say these critics, was faced with a choice, which the encyclopedia article ignores: between heroic sacrifice and submission to the forces of reaction.[74] It is easy to see that these critics are unscrupulous and tendentious; they do not even bother to offer any proof of their assertions. They deliberately ignore the fact that the author of the encyclopedia article does not object to forcing the rates of industrialization but only to *excessive* forcing of "rates that were high to begin with," which caused in painful fact not a speed-up in industrial construction but a slowdown, a prolongation of industrialization.

---

[73] *Sovetskaia istoricheskaia entsiklopediia,* VI, p. 31.
[74] A. Gukovskii, A. Ugriumov, and V. Kul'bakin, in *Kommunist,* 1968, No. 4.

IV

The Beginning of Stalin's Cult:
Stalin's Crimes and Provocations
in the Early Thirties

1

THE SERIOUS MISTAKES made during collectivization and industrialization lowered the workers' standard of living, disrupted the supply of food and manufactured goods, and weakened the alliance between the city and the country. Strict rationing had to be reintroduced in the cities. Discontent grew. It was hard to ascribe all these shortcomings only to kulaks and "subkulaks." Another scapegoat had to be found for Stalin's faults. And such a scapegoat was found: the specialists, the intelligentsia, who had been tainted before the Revolution.

Many of these so-called bourgeois specialists, who derived from the old intelligentsia and from the classes overthrown by the October Revolution, were working in the Soviet economic *apparat,* in industrial enterprises, in scientific and educational institutions, in agricultural agencies, in Gosplan, and in the statistical offices. Lenin had written that communism could be built only by people trained with bourgeois psychology:

> This is one of the difficulties of building a Communist society, but it is also a guarantee of its success. Marxism is distinguished from the old utopian socialism precisely by the fact that the latter wanted to build a new society not out of the masses of human material created by bloody, dirty, moneygrubbing, rapacious capitalism, but out of especially virtuous people raised in special greenhouses and hothouses.[1]

[1] *Sochineniia,* 4th edn., XLV, pp. 97–98.

Lenin therefore commended efforts, which began as early as 1918, to use the technical skills of the bourgeoisie.

> We are only doing half the job if we strike the exploiters on their hands, neutralize, and harass them. Here in Moscow ninety out of a hundred responsible officials think that this is the whole job, that is, to harass, to neutralize, to strike on the hands. But it is half the job. Even in 1918 . . . it was half the job, and today [in 1922] it is even less than a quarter of the job.[2]

Stalin was one of those officials who thought the entire job was "to harass, to neutralize, to strike on the hands." This shortcoming had a marked effect on the forms and methods of class struggle in the late twenties and early thirties, in the city as well as the countryside. The Party's attack on capitalist elements and the decline in the population's standard of living led to a revival of counterrevolutionary activity by various anti-Soviet organizations abroad, and also by underground groups within the Soviet Union. Various types of monarchist and bourgeois Cadet[3] organizations, and also Menshevik and Social Revolutionary centers abroad, had some underground committees in the USSR. These anti-Soviet organizations enjoyed some support not only among kulaks and nepmen but also among the bourgeois intelligentsia and specialists, who had jobs in Soviet institutions. In such conditions it was, of course, necessary to suppress any kind of counterrevolutionary activity. But at the same time it was necessary to keep the loyalty that many of the old intelligentsia and specialists felt toward the Soviet regime. Their know-how and experience were essential to the job of socialist construction. Unfortunately, Stalin went much further in his repression than reason or necessity required. Trying to blame "bourgeois specialists" for the mistakes of industrialization, Stalin and some of his closest aides began vilifying and breaking up the cadres of nonparty specialists as a matter of policy. Stalin masked this policy with arguments about the need to attract the bourgeois intelligentsia to serve the Soviet regime, about converting members of that intelligentsia, and so on. But the true nature of the new policy was manifested in the political trials staged at the end of the twenties and in the early thirties.

2

As EARLY AS 1928 in Moscow, with A. Ia. Vyshinskii presiding, there was an open trial dealing with "the Shakhty Affair." The accused were engineers working in the coal industry. They were charged with

---

[2] *Ibid.*
[3] *Ed.: Cadet* is an abbreviation for the Constitutional Democratic Party, the chief liberal organization in Russia between 1905 and 1917.

organizing accidents in the mines, wrecking, maintaining criminal ties with the former mineowners, and buying unnecessary imported equipment. According to the indictment, the activity of these wreckers was financed by White Guard centers abroad. At the trial some of the defendants confessed their guilt, but many denied it or confessed to only a part of the accusations. The court acquitted four of the fifty-three defendants, gave suspended sentences to four, and prison terms of one to three years to ten. Most of the defendants were given four to ten years. Eleven were condemned to be shot, and five of them were executed in July, 1928. The other six were granted clemency by the All-Union Central Executive Committee.

According to S. O. Gazarian, an old Chekist, there was such a thing as wrecking. But this form of anti-Soviet struggle was comparatively insignificant. Wrecking as a conscious policy, pursued by the entire stratum of bourgeois specialists, never existed. In fact, the émigré N. V. Ustrialov, one of the most famous ideologists of the bourgeois intelligentsia, reacted to forced industrialization by calling on his followers within the Soviet Union to support it. He urged them to shun not only wrecking—even Miliukov did that—but even passive neutrality; active loyal work for the country's upbuilding was the patriot's only course.[4]

Gazarian, who was head of the economic section of the NKVD in Transcaucasia and thus had a good picture of the economic side of the class struggle, said there really was criminal mismanagement in the Donbas in 1928, which was the cause of many serious accidents (flooded mines, explosions, and so on). Both central and local management were still understaffed; there was a lot of casual help and unconscientious people; in a number of Soviet and economic organizations, bribery, thieving, and disregard for the interest of the workers flourished. These crimes should obviously have been punished with the full severity of Soviet law. There may have also been individual cases of wrecking in the Donbas in 1928. But all sorts of accusations of wrecking and of connections with foreign counterrevolutionary organizations were added to various criminal accusations—thieving, bribery, mismanagement—in the course of the investigation. This was intended "to mobilize the masses," "to arouse their wrath against the imperialists," "to intensify vigilance."

Some prosecutors indulged in such faking for "ideological" reasons. A. M. Durmashkin, an old Bolshevik, met in a camp an NKVD executive, sentenced in 1937 to fifteen years, who told him that many of the accusations in the Shakhty trial were fake. The writer V. T. Shalamov met in prison two specialists, Boiaryshnikov and Miller,

[4] See N. V. Ustrialov, *Na novom etape* (Harbin, 1930), as quoted in *Bol'shevik*, 1930, No. 10, pp. 183–84.

who had been through the Shakhty affair. They told Shalamov that in 1928 investigators used such methods as the "conveyor" (*konveier* or *vystoika*)—uninterrupted interrogation, allowing the accused no sleep—as well as solitary confinement and cells with hot or cold floors.

Stalin of course did not look into these "fine points" of the Shakhty trial. He was eager to "generalize" its lessons; he called on Party members to seek out "Shakhtyites" in every link of the Soviet and Party *apparat*. "The so-called Shakhty affair must not be considered an accident," Stalin told the Central Committee in April, 1929.

> "Shakhtyites" are now ensconced in every branch of our industry. Many of them have been caught, but by no means all have been caught. Wrecking by the bourgeois intelligentsia is one of the most dangerous forms of opposition to developing socialism. Wrecking is all the more dangerous in that it is connected with international capital. Bourgeois wrecking is a sure sign that the capitalist elements have by no means laid down their arms, that they are massing their forces for new attacks on the Soviet regime.[5]

After such instructions, it is not surprising that the terror against the so-called bourgeois specialists sharply increased. In the Ukraine in 1929 there was an open political trial concerning the SVU, the Union for Liberating the Ukraine. The leaders of this organization were declared to be the famous historian M. S. Hrushevskii, who was not, however, arrested, and the vice-president of the Ukrainian Academy of Sciences, S. A. Efremov. They were charged with forming a secret alliance with Poland in order to separate the Ukraine from Russia. According to the old Bolshevik A. V. Snegov, who was then working in the Ukraine, there were many dubious elements about the whole affair. Although nationalist feelings among a certain part of the Ukrainian intelligentsia were quite strong, it was ridiculous to accuse these people of a secret alliance with Poland.

In 1930 the discovery of a new counterrevolutionary organization was announced: the so-called Toiling Peasant Party (TKP). The supposed leaders were Professor N. D. Kondrat'ev, an economist who had been a colleague of the Minister of Food in the Provisional Government, the economists L. N. Iurovskii and A. V. Chaianov, and the prominent agronomist A. G. Doiarenko. The TKP was accused of having nine major underground groups in Moscow—in the system of agricultural cooperatives and agricultural credit, in the Commissariats of Agriculture and Finance, in the newspaper *Bednota* ("The Poor Peasantry"), in research institutes of agricultural economics, and in the Timiriazev Agricultural Academy. The TKP also, according to the OGPU, headed a considerable number of underground groups in the provinces, especially in agricultural agencies and among former

[5] *Sochineniia*, XII, p. 14.

kulaks and Social Revolutionaries. Membership in this underground party was estimated at 100,000 to 200,000. The OGPU began to organize a great open trial. The necessary testimony was prepared, and a large number of people were supposed to be summoned for investigation, mostly agronomists and organizers of cooperatives. The trial was almost completely rehearsed, but for some reason Stalin changed his mind about having an open political trial. The arrested "members and leaders of the TKP" were condemned in a closed court. The press concentrated not so much on the concrete deeds of TKP members as the theoretical pronouncements and writings of the Moscow professors who were supposed to head the party.

In the fall of 1930 it was announced that the OGPU had uncovered a sabotage and espionage organization in the food-supply system, especially in meat, fish, and vegetables. According to the OGPU, this organization was headed by the former landowner and professor A. V. Riazantsev, the former landowner and general E. S. Karatygin, and other former noblemen, industrialists, Cadets, and Mensheviks, who had wormed their way into responsible positions in the Supreme Economic Council, the Commissariat of Trade, the Meat, Fish, Vegetable, and Fruit Agencies (*Soiuzmiaso*, etc.), and other such institutions. The press reported that these men had succeeded in disorganizing the supply of food products to many cities, and in creating famine in a number of *raiony*. They were also responsible for the increase in prices on meat and for the distribution of poor-quality canned goods. All forty-six who were brought to closed trial were sentenced to be shot.

From November 25 to December 7, 1930, a new political trial was held in Moscow, this time an open one. A group of prominent technical specialists were accused of wrecking and counterrevolutionary activities, as members of the *Prompartiia* (the Industrial Party).[6] The eight defendants were accused of being the executive committee, whose aims were to organize wrecking and subversion, espionage and

---

[6] The presiding judge was A. Ia. Vyshinskii; the associate judges were V. P. Antonov-Saratovskii, V. L. L'vov, P. A. Ivanov; the state prosecutors were N. V. Krylenko and V. I. Fridberg. The role of defense attorneys was played by I. D. Braude and M. A. Otsep.

Eight men were accused of wrecking and espionage activities: L. K. Ramzin, director of the Institute of Heat Engineering, the leading specialist in heat engineering and boiler construction; V. A. Larichev, chairman of the Fuel Section of Gosplan; I. A. Kalinnikov, deputy chairman of the Production Section of Gosplan and professor at the Air Force Academy; Professor N. F. Charnovskii, chairman of the Scientific and Technical Council of the Supreme Council of the National Economy; Professor A. A. Fedotov, chairman of the collegium of the Scientific Research Institute on Textiles; S. V. Kupriianov, technical director of the Textile Organization of the Supreme Council of the National Economy; V. I. Ochkin, head of the Department of Scientific Research of the Supreme Council of the National Economy; and K. V. Sitnin, an engineer.

sabotage, to prepare for the intervention of imperialist states and the armed overthrow of the Soviet regime. Around two thousand people were supposed to be members of the Industrial Party, most of them highly qualified technical specialists.

At the trial the defendants confessed their guilt and willingly gave the most improbable detailed testimony about their wrecking and spying, their connections with foreign embassies in Moscow, even with Raymond Poincaré, the President of France. A wave of meetings swept the country, with the speakers demanding that the leaders of the Industrial Party be shot. The court obligingly sentenced most of them to be shot, but a decree of the Central Executive Committee granted clemency, changing the sentences to various terms of imprisonment. During and after the trial the Western bourgeois press waged a great anti-Soviet campaign. Poincaré himself published a special declaration:

> I do not know whether Professor Ramzin and the other members of the "Industrial Party" organized a conspiracy against the government of their country. I am not their confessor. . . . But in any case —and I affirm this once again—if there really was such a conspiracy, no one in France was involved in it. There must be rather gullible people in Moscow, if some actually believe or believed these fairy tales. . . . If by chance there are still judges in Moscow, they would do well to unmask the accusers and the accused, who are acting against their own interests in this strange affair and are participating in the dissemination of falsehood. In any case, I must repeat that neither Briand nor I nor the French general staff ever had any knowledge of the real or imaginary plans of an "Industrial Party," whether in 1928 or before or after, and therefore we did not approve and did not encourage such plans.

If, Poincaré continued, he had known of such adventures, he would have condemned them as dangerous folly. He asked to be informed

> in what secret room the Russian conspirators conversed with my double, and by what authorization he gave them an audience. Above all, I would like them to send me the supposed plans of the French general staff and to inform me where, when, and under what conditions the supposed attack was to take place.[7]

In March, 1931, a few months after the trial of the "Industrial Party," another open political trial was held in Moscow, the trial of the so-called Union Bureau of the Central Committee of the Menshevik

---

[7] The complete text of Poincaré's declaration was published in *Pravda*, Dec. 3, 1930, translated from the French publication *Excelsior*, and entered in the court record. Evidently this was done to show the court's objectivity. Since public confidence in Soviet courts was only slightly shaken in 1930, the bulk of Soviet citizens regarded Poincaré's declaration as proof of a real plot.

Party.[8] Most of the accused had left the Menshevik Party between 1920 and 1922, and held responsible posts in economic and planning agencies. They were accused of secretly rejoining the Mensheviks at the end of the twenties, of organizing a center for that Party within the USSR. The "Union Bureau" was accused of wrecking, especially in drawing up plans for economic development. If the indictment is to be believed, the accused systematically lowered all the draft plans, trying thereby to slow down the development of industry and agriculture.

We are also told that the Mensheviks had formed a secret bloc with the "Industrial Party" and the "Toiling Peasant Party" to prepare for armed intervention from without and an insurrection within. Each contracting party was assigned a certain function: The "Industrial Party" was to conduct preliminary negotiations with representatives of the countries who were supposed to inspire or take part in armed intervention, to organize flying brigades of engineers for subversive and terrorist activities, to arrange for military conspiracies with individuals in the high command of the Red Army. The "Toiling Peasant Party" was to organize peasant insurrections and disorders, to supply the insurrectionists with weapons and munitions, and to demoralize the Red Army units sent to suppress the disorders. The "Union Bureau" of the Mensheviks was to prepare a citizens' guard in the cities, which could seize government institutions and provide the initial support for a new counterrevolutionary government.

The indictment, and the press reports of the trial, contained clear hints of connections between the Mensheviks and the former opposition groups within the Bolshevik Party, primarily the Trotskyites and the rightists. Some of the testimony was openly directed against D. B. Riazanov, the director of the Marx-Engels-Lenin Institute. At the trial all the defendants confessed, giving the most detailed accounts of their wrecking. At one session the prosecutor, N. V. Krylenko, tried to demonstrate the objectivity of the court by reading a special declaration of the Menshevik Party's émigré leadership. They categorically denied any connection between the Menshevik Party and the defendants, who had quit the Party in the early twenties. The émigré center declared that it had sent genuine Mensheviks into the Soviet Union to try and keep the organization alive, despite the ban that the Bolsheviks had placed on all parties but their own. But the

[8] The defendants were: V. G. Groman, a member of the Presidium of Gosplan; V. V. Sher, a member of the board of the State Bank: N. N. Sukhanov, a writer; A. M. Ginzburg, an economist; M. P. Iakubovich, deputy director of the Division of Supply of the Commissariat of Trade; V. K. Ikov, a writer; I. I. Rubin, professor of economics; A. Iu. Finn-Enotaevskii, A. L. Sokolovskii, and five others.

The presiding judge was N. M. Shvernik; the associate judges were V. P. Antonov-Saratovskii and M. K. Muranov. The state prosecutors were N. V. Krylenko and G. K. Roginskii; attorneys for the defense were I. D. Braude and N. V. Kommodov.

Menshevik emissaries never tried to organize wrecking or prepare for armed intervention. In any case, none of the accused had ever been in touch with the emissaries of the Menshevik Party. After this declaration had been read, the accused, at the suggestion of the presiding judge, refuted it and reaffirmed their guilt. A few days later the court sentenced all fourteen defendants to terms of imprisonment ranging from five to ten years.

3

EVEN SINCE THE XXth and XXIInd Party Congresses many historians have continued to treat the political trials of 1928–31 in the same way as the press did four decades ago. For example, a supposedly authoritative textbook contains a simple, uncritical recapitulation of the accusations and the "severe and just" verdicts, which "rallied workers, collective peasants, and the intelligentsia still more closely around the Communist Party and raised still higher their activism in work and in politics."[9] S. A. Fediukin's *The Soviet Regime and the Bourgeois Specialists* has the same viewpoint. His substantial and interesting analysis of Lenin's policies toward the bourgeois specialists, in the first part of the book, is strangely contradicted in the second part, where a large number of the bourgeois specialists are suddenly converted to counterrevolution and wrecking at the end of the twenties.[10]

Even now one finds historians who assert that the "Industrial Party," the "Toiling Peasant Party," and the "Union Bureau of the Mensheviks" were real organizations. For example, D. L. Golinkov repeats the old accusations as self-evident truths, noting that several copies of an émigré Menshevik journal were found in a conspirator's apartment and that one of the accused confessed that he had written a number of articles for the journal, in which he had given a slanderous picture of the Soviet economy.[11] Golinkov forgets that many documents are drawn up not to establish the truth but to distort and falsify it. Trial records of the "Industrial Party" and the "Union Bureau" are documents of this type.[12] One has only to read them to perceive that a large part of these materials is fraudulent.

[9] B. M. Ponomarev, ed., *Istoriia KPSS* (Moscow, 1959), p. 435.

[10] Fediukin, *Sovetskaia vlast' i burzhuaznye spetsialisty* (Moscow, 1965).

[11] See *Voprosy istorii*, 1968, No. 2, pp. 150–51.

[12] See, e.g., the following: *Protsess Prompartii* (Moscow, 1931); *Protsess kontrrevoliutsionnoi organizatsii men'shevikov* (Moscow, 1931); *Sotsial-interventy pered sudom proletarskoi diktatury* (Moscow, 1931); *Vrediteli piatiletki* (Moscow, 1931); *Vrediteli rabochego snabzheniia* (Moscow, 1930); A. A. Sadovskii, *Zavershim razgrom kondrat'evshchiny* (Moscow–Leningrad, 1931); *Shpiony i vrediteli pered proletarskim sudom* (Moscow–Leningrad, 1930); *Ekonomicheskaia kontrrevoliutsiia v Donbasse* (Moscow, 1928).

In the case of the "Industrial Party," the discrepancies begin with the indictment, especially with the explanation of the defendants' motives for establishing counterrevolutionary organizations. Before the Revolution almost all the ringleaders were alleged to have been big industrialists and capitalists, or to have held the highest-paying managerial posts under them. But it became clear during the trial that not one of the eight defendants had ever been a capitalist or even the son of a capitalist. They came from families of artisans, peasants, civil servants, or middling landlords. Only three had worked in private industry before the war, one of them for only three years.

"One of the prime reasons for the creation of the counterrevolutionary organization," the indictment also said, "is the political convictions of the old engineers, which usually range from Cadet to right-wing monarchist." This assertion was not proved at the trial. Of the eight defendants, only Fedotov had clearly expressed Cadet views. The rest had little interest in politics, and some had been Russian Social Democrats. Even the prosecutor, N. V. Krylenko, was obliged to characterize some of the accused as people without a political ideology, for whom "political questions do not play any role."

The indictment also stated that the political feelings of the accused were "reinforced by the difference in the professional and material position of engineers before and after the Revolution, and by the Soviet regime's natural mistrust of engineers." However, the trial materials make it clear that all the defendants held major posts before their arrest, so that it is difficult to see any mistrust in the government's treatment of them. Their material position was, for the most part, better at the time of their arrest than before the Revolution. In general, the motives behind the "wrecking activity" of the "Industrial Party" were left unclear at the end of the trial.

Krylenko wiped out everything he had said earlier when he declared in his summation:

> They had and have no ideas or even inner convictions, nor could they have any, for you have seen the price for which everything was done. . . . Lacking any ideological support, they leaped into the camp of outright counterrevolution and began to work for money, like mercenaries, renouncing any pretensions of ideological and political commitment. . . . Ramzin is not one of those people who work selflessly for an idea. It is nonsense to say he did not receive any money for this.

Even Ramzin, who had supported almost every accusation, felt obliged to retort to Krylenko in his final speech.

> Was it possible that I risked my neck, became a traitor and a saboteur, out of purely financial considerations, for the sake of a

10–20–30 per cent addition to my salary? I doubt whether anyone will believe that. . . . What could I hope to gain from a change of the regime? Nothing better, in any case, than what I had, because rarely could a foreign scientist even dream of having what I have had in the Soviet Union, in terms of standard of living and favorable conditions for research.

A great many absurdities and inconsistencies can be found in the defendants' testimony about their counterrevolutionary activity. Ramzin, for example, the supposed leader of the "Industrial Party," gave extremely dubious testimony. During his trip to Paris, he allegedly asked the White Guard organizations to prove the existence of serious plans for French intervention, whereupon a meeting was arranged with some eminent officials of the French general staff. Besides informing Ramzin about the French government's decision for intervention in the near future, they handed over to him the detailed operational plans of the French high command, including the direction of the main attacks by the French expeditionary force and by its allies, the debarkation points and the time schedules. Ramzin made a clean breast of this at the trial. But it is obvious that no general staff would let a man such as Ramzin into their plans, even on the recommendation of prominent White Guardists.

The very possibility of organizing, on Soviet territory, entire underground parties with thousands of members, central committees sending instructions to the provinces and maintaining close contacts with foreign centers, embassies, and so on, is to be doubted. The investigative agencies frankly informed the court that they could not produce any material evidence or documents proving the existence of underground parties. There was much talk about instructions and directives, appeals to members, circular letters, resolutions, and records of plenary meetings, but not one of these documents was presented to the court and the press. The defendants were said to have destroyed all such documents before their arrest. "Let us analyze this problem further," said Krylenko in his summation.

> What evidence can there be? Are there, let us say, any documents? I inquired about that. It seems that where documents existed, they were destroyed. . . . But, I asked, perhaps one of them has accidentally survived? It would be futile to hope for that.[13]

Krylenko tried to prove that "sincere" confessions made any material evidence unnecessary. But then he could not explain what motivated the accused to make "sincere" confessions in the complete absence of any material evidence. After all, these were supposed to be class enemies, spies, diversionists, murderers. Krylenko himself

[13] *Proletarskii prigovor nad vrediteliami-interventami* (Moscow, 1930), p. 32.

declared in his opening speech: "I cannot take Citizen Ramzin and the others at their word, I cannot believe them, despite their declarations of sincere repentance." The mix-up concerning the Riabushinskiis—a well-known family of big capitalists—was typical. According to the indictment, P. P. Riabushinskii was slated to be Minister of Trade and Industry in the future Russian government. Further on the indictment said that "In October, 1928, two members of the Central Committee of the 'Industrial Party,' Ramzin and Larichev, got in touch with P. P. Riabushinskii." And P. I. Pal'chinskii and A. A. Fedotov, two other members of the Central Committee, were also said to have had close connections with Riabushinskii. But as soon as the indictment was published in the newspapers, almost all the foreign papers reported that the head of the Riabushinskii family had died before 1928 and only his sons were living abroad. A clumsy switch had to be made in mid-course.

"As for Riabushinskii," Fedotov declared in his testimony,

> things are rather unclear. I didn't understand which Riabushinskii was named here, because the prominent public figure Pavel Riabushinskii was already dead at that time. Vladimir Riabushinskii was the man. And in general, the reports about Vladimir Riabushinskii were unimportant. He was said to be an unintelligent man who could not be of any use.

Ramzin also had to do some re-explaining, since he had said earlier that he had met P. P. Riabushinskii in Paris. "I am not completely sure," he now declared, "about the first name of the Riabushinskii with whom I spoke in Paris. It may have been Peter [why not Pavel?] or Vladimir. . . . I can describe his appearance, if that would help." Krylenko: "It is important to establish that it was evidently Vladimir." Ramzin: "That is most likely."

A similar mix-up occurred concerning a well-known Soviet historian, Academician E. V. Tarlé. The indictment said that he was to have been Minister of Foreign Affairs in the White Guard government. Naturally he was immediately arrested and expelled from the Academy of Sciences. But soon afterward Tarlé was quietly freed and reinstated in the Academy. There was a multitude of inconsistencies in the testimony on other matters, too: on the composition of the Central Committee of the "Industrial Party" and the distribution of assignments; on the composition of the future government; on the amount of money received from abroad and what had happened to it; and so on. Confusion marked the testimony on concrete acts of wrecking. It was said, for example, that the defendants who took part in drawing up the Five-Year Plan regarded the "base-line" variant as the real one and the "optimal" variant as unrealistic wrecking. However, the defendants declared, as a result of the heroic labor of the Soviet people, the "optimal" plan turned out to be feasible. "We regarded the maximum plans and tempos," said Larichev, "as impossible, but this has been refuted by life."

Sometimes the president of the court had to prompt the accused openly. There was, for example, this curious dialogue between Vyshinskii and Fedotov:

> VYSHINSKII: Was there a directive to build new factories while existing factories were insufficiently used?
> FEDOTOV: No, there was no such directive.
> VYSHINSKII: There wasn't?
> FEDOTOV: Excuse me, there was a directive to build factories although factories already existed.
> VYSHINSKII: No, there is no wrecking in that. Factories must be built.

And Vyshinskii went on, leading Fedotov to say that "the directive was to build factories while existing factories were not working at full capacity." And Fedotov was brought to agree that

> if it had not been for wrecking, fewer factories would have been built. Not, it is true, much fewer, maybe one or two, but still some foreign currency would have been saved. The intensification of construction was enthusiastically welcomed by executives who were Party members.

Insufficient contact between scientific research institutions and industry was also declared to be wrecking, along with many other shortcomings that are often discussed in the press to the present day. Even draining swamps in border areas was declared to be wrecking, since it allegedly facilitated imperialist intervention in the USSR.

Just as many absurdities and inconsistencies can be found in the trial of the Menshevik "Union Bureau" in 1931. The most vulnerable point of the indictment was the connection of the "Union Bureau" with the "Industrial Party," a connection that was discussed in considerable detail. An utterly improbable secret "agreement" was introduced, supposedly concluded between the "Industrial Party" and the Menshevik Party. It specified that the Mensheviks, though participating as much as possible in general wrecking, did not consider it possible to take part in diversionary acts, and that the Mensheviks would not personally receive any payment for their services in wrecking.[14]

Ramzin, summoned to the trial of the "Union Bureau," declared:

> To be perfectly clear, we must recall what was established at the trial of the Industrial Party—the necessity of forming a tight-knit bloc and establishing connections between the Industrial Party, the

[14] M. Charnyi, *Sud istoricheskii i neizbezhnyi* (Moscow, 1931), p. 30.

Toiling Peasant Party, and the Menshevik organization. That was the directive we received from abroad.

In fact the "Union Bureau" had not been mentioned at the trial of the "Industrial Party"; no reference had been made to any connections or individuals, even though, at the time of the "Industrial Party" trial (December, 1930), all the leading figures of the "Union Bureau" had already been arrested: V. G. Groman on July 13, N. N. Sukhanov on July 20, V. V. Sher on September 13, L. B. Zalkind on August 20. To explain this discrepancy, it was said that "frank confessions" had been obtained from the members of the "Union Bureau" only toward the end of December, 1930. But the truth was that Stalin and his aides had got the idea of organizing the "Union Bureau" trial only after the "success" of the "Industrial Party" trial, and then began to prepare the appropriate legends.

Several annoying discrepancies arose. For example, the indictment said that collusion between the "Union Bureau" and the "Industrial Party" was discussed at the third plenum of the "Bureau," which allegedly met in April, 1930. But according to the testimony of the preceding trial, the "Industrial Party" had been broken up by April, 1930, and the Mensheviks could have had no connections with it. Therefore Sher, in his testimony, introduced a correction: The bloc with the "Industrial Party" was discussed not at the third but at the second plenum of the "Union Bureau," in 1929. The indictment quoted Sukhanov's deposition of January 25, 1931:

> We began to talk with Ramzin directly. . . . Two days later I called Ramzin, who arranged for a meeting with me, again in his apartment. The meeting was very short. . . . In the same way, after making preliminary arrangements by telephone, I received 15,000 rubles from him in October, 1929, and the last 15,000 rubles in March, 1930.

But at the trial, Ramzin declared that he had never negotiated personally with Sukhanov, and that in general he didn't know Sukhanov, had never met him. Sukhanov was obliged to confirm this. Further questioning "cleared up" the matter: it was not Sukhanov but Groman who had received money from the "Industrial Party," and it was not Ramzin but Larichev who had handed it over.

The membership of the so-called "Union Bureau" also remained unclear at the trial. During the questioning it became apparent that most of the accused had not had any connections with the Menshevik Party for a long time, while some had never been Mensheviks until, as they put it, they entered that Party in 1927–28. How then did they so quickly become its leaders in the Soviet Union? A. Iu. Finn-Enotaevskii's testimony on this score was incoherent, including his answers to the questions of the defense lawyer. Great confusion also marked the defendants' testimony on the program committee of the "Union Bureau" (it was not even made clear whether this committee ever met), on the subjects of discussion at various meetings of the "Union Bureau," and about meetings with R. A. Abramovich, one of the leaders of the émigré Mensheviks, who was alleged to have come illegally to the USSR to give instructions.

The examples of wrecking activity were completely unbelievable. This is how A. L. Sokolovskii described one of his acts of "wrecking":

> In the control figures for 1929–1930, the Presidium of the Supreme Council of the National Economy set the task of lowering costs of production by 10 per cent. I put down only 9.5 per cent and began to insist on this figure, arguing with genuine facts. During that entire period, with the exception of 1927–28, the actual decline of production costs was lower than the planned figure, and in 1925–26 costs did not drop, as you may recall, but rose. I even think that the figure of 9.5 per cent was also not achieved, as you know. So that, in this respect, you can say that in the field of cost reduction, even my minimal projections always turned out to be high. But I repeat that, *in a manner of speaking,* they were nevertheless incorrect.

While the members of the "Industrial Party" had confessed that they had inflated many goals of the plan for the purposes of wrecking, the members of the "Union Bureau" were accused of *deflating* goals. Various speeches were quoted, in which the accused, at Gosplan meetings, had objected to excessively high control figures in the Five-Year Plan. Since Stalin and Molotov, in 1930, had demanded a considerable increase in the control figures, it is not surprising that almost all the earlier targets set by Gosplan, including 10 million tons of pig iron and 100,000 cars, were declared to be "wrecking." Now that we know that most of the goals in physical units were not actually achieved, it is difficult to agree with such accusations. Many of the speeches made by the defendants at Gosplan meetings, which were quoted at the trial, were rational warnings by specialists against the adventurism and unrealistic schemes of some Party leaders.

A person attending the trials of 1930–31 might have thought that the first Five-Year Plan had not been discussed in detail at the XVIth Party Conference in April, 1929, and had not been ratified at all levels of the Party and state. Similarly, anyone hearing the defendants' testimony about their deliberate disruption of the food supply, about their organization of famine in some rural areas, about the deliberate spoiling of millions of tons of vegetables, meat, fish, and grain, about the slowing down of coal and peat production, about the organization of a crisis in the supply of electricity, might have thought the people's commissariats were not headed by Communists, that wreckers were in complete control of the economic and state machinery.

The testimony on the activity of the Second International was also obviously staged. There is no doubt, of course, that this International was hostile to the dictatorship of the proletariat. But it was doubtful that the leaders of the Second International were organizing wrecking in the USSR, that foreign Social Democratic parties, the German one especially, were financing preparations for armed insurrections in the Soviet Union. These charges meshed with Stalin's current theory of "social fascism" but hardly with the facts of life. The charges against the mythical "Toiling Peasant Party" were equally ridiculous. For example, the "Kondratevites" in this party were accused not only of defending kulak interests but also of "defending the necessity of taking into account the laws of commodity-monetary relations, which supposedly operate in a special form even in the USSR." In Siberia the label of wrecking was pinned on some agronomists for advocating *parotravopol'e,* a version of R. V. Williams' scheme of crop rotation. In some other regions, opposition to Williams' system was declared to be wrecking "of the Kondratevite type."[15] The outstanding agronomist A. G. Doiarenko, who was arbitrarily assigned to the Central Committee of the "Toiling Peasant Party," was freed a few years later and subsequently rehabilitated. Nowadays all published comment on Doiarenko attributes his conviction to slander.[16]

The variegated fate of the accused was also strange. All forty-six "wreckers of the food supply" were shot, although their organization was pictured in the indictment as merely an affiliate of the "Industrial Party." But the top leader of the "Party," L. K. Ramzin, "the candidate for dictator," "spy," and "organizer of diversions and murders," was for some reason pardoned. And not only pardoned; in prison he was allowed to do research on boiler construction. Barely five years after his trial, he was freed and even given the Order of Lenin. He died, according to the *Great Soviet Encyclopedia,* in 1948, holding the same post, Director of the Moscow Institute of Heat Engineering, which he held before the trial of the "Industrial Party."

How can so much fakery be explained? For what purpose did the OGPU fabricate these stories about organizations of wreckers and counterrevolutionaries in almost all the economic institutions, collaborating with imperialist circles to provoke armed insurrection within the country and intervention from without?

An indirect answer has been given in an editorial on Mao Tsetung.[17] "We are dealing," *Pravda* writes,

---

[15] See, *inter alia,* the pamphlets *Kondrat'evshchina v Kazakhstane* (Alma-Ata, 1931); *Kondrat'evshchina i vreditel'stvo* (Sverdlovsk–Moscow, 1930).

[16] See, for example, O. Pisarzhevskii, *Prianishnikov* (Moscow, 1963), p. 182.

[17] "Ob antisovetskoi politike Mao i ego gruppy," *Pravda,* Feb. 16, 1967.

with an old worn-out method of all unprincipled political hacks when they are at a dead end. If things are going from bad to worse, if one political action after another is a disaster, then people of this kind see only one solution: throw all the blame for all the troubles onto "enemies," both internal and especially "external."

And, in fact, Stalin's conscious premeditated purpose in organizing these trials was to cover up his own multitudinous mistakes and miscalculations. On top of that, Stalin desired to win credit for thwarting foreign intervention. He wanted to accumulate political capital, fictive, to be sure, but crucial for him in that period. He was deliberately forcing tension in the country, to silence his critics and once again to cast the shadow of suspicion on the leaders of all the former opposition groups.

As for the confessions of the defendants, in different cases they can be explained by different causes. A natural disaster does not, as a rule, destroy everyone in its path. The storm of "wreckermania" at the end of the twenties and the beginning of the thirties destroyed hundreds and thousands of people. But some escaped destruction to tell us what really happened. Despite the hardship of twenty-four years in prisons and camps and a long stay in a home for invalids in Karaganda, M. P. Iakubovich, one of the main defendants at the trial of the "Union Bureau," is still alive. According to people who were in camp with him, he displayed the finest human qualities during his imprisonment. In the summer of 1966, Iakubovich came to Moscow from Karaganda, and in conversation with the author told how the organs of the OGPU set up the trials of the early thirties. In May, 1967, he sent a special deposition on this matter to the Procurator of the Soviet Union, which is given here almost in full.

IAKUBOVICH'S DEPOSITION

To the General Procurator of the USSR:

In connection with your office's re-examination of the case in which I was convicted in 1931, I present the following explanation:

No "Union Bureau of Mensheviks" ever existed in reality. Not all the defendants knew each other, nor had they all belonged to the Menshevik Party in the past. Thus, A. Iu. Finn-Enotaevskii . . . had been a Bolshevik since the Second Party Congress in 1903, and although he left the Party during the Imperialist War of 1914-1917, he never had any connection with the Mensheviks. A. L. Sokolovskii had belonged in the past to the Zionist socialists but was never a Menshevik. Most of the defendants, however, had been connected to some degree with the Menshevik Party, some very accidentally and slightly, others belonging to the main leadership cadres. . . . But both the former and the latter had long since broken with the Mensheviks under various circumstances and for various reasons. The only participant in the trial who really had maintained a connection with a Menshevik center, as I learned from him later on in the Verkhneural'sk *politizoliator* [a prison for politicals only], who had even been the chairman or secretary of a Menshevik Bureau, was V. K. Ikov. But he never breathed a word about these activities during the investigation or the trial, and the very existence of the "Moscow Bureau" remained undiscovered during the investigation and the trial.

. . . The OGPU investigators did not make the least effort to discover the real political connections and views of Ikov or of any other defendant. They had a ready-made scheme of a "wrecker" organization that could have been constructed only with the participation of big, influential officials; real underground Mensheviks, who did not hold such offices, were unsuitable for such a scheme. Evidently this scheme was suggested to OGPU officials by the leading figures in trials of the "Industrial Party" and the "Toiling Peasant Party," Ramzin and Kondrat'ev, who subsequently testified for the prosecution at the trial of the "Union Bureau." For the sake of balance, to round out the political picture, they had to add a third politico-wrecking organization—a Social Democratic one. This was the explanation given to me by Professor L. N. Iurovskii, who confessed to being the Minister of Finance in Kondrat'ev's "shadow cabinet." He was planted in my cell for several days, evidently to explain the nature of the investigation to me.

Kondrat'ev's idea was taken over wholeheartedly by his personal friend V. G. Groman, who was found in Kondrat'ev's apartment when the OGPU came to arrest Kondrat'ev, and on this ground was himself subjected to investigation. He was promised restoration of his job and complete pardon if he cooperated in the trial of the Menshevik wreckers. Subsequently, when the people convicted in the trial of the "Union Bureau" were brought to the Verkhneural'sk *politizoliator*, Groman, who was in the prison "station," shouted out loud, in despair and indignation, "They tricked me!" Groman's willingness to cooperate was reinforced by his alcoholism. The interrogators would make him drunk and get all the evidence they wanted. Once, during the trial, while I was being sent back to the inner OGPU prison, I found myself in the same car as Groman, where I heard a conversation between him and the investigators. "Well, Vladimir Gustavovich," they said to him, "should we fortify ourselves with a little cognac?" "Hee hee," laughed Groman, "of course, as always." His active helper, in making up the story of the wrecking Menshevik organization, was the defendant Petun, an unintelligent man who had joined the Menshevik Party after the February Revolution and left it after the October victory of the Bolsheviks. According to his account, told afterwards in Verkhneural'sk, he "calculated" that he would gain the most, given his arrest, by actively cooperating in setting up the wrecking trial. For this he would receive a reward from OGPU, that is, the restoration of freedom and a job. If he didn't cooperate, he could get a long term in prison or even die. It was Petun who got the idea of creating the "Union Bureau" on the principle of departmental representation: two people from the Supreme Economic Council, two from the Commissariat of Trade, two from the State Bank, one from the Central Trade Union Council, and one from Gosplan. The "departmental representatives" he named were leading officials in appropriate departments, of whom he had heard it said that they were former Mensheviks. Not knowing precisely, however, the political past of the people he named, he made such mistakes as including in his list the Zionist Sokolovskii as a "representative" of the Supreme Economic Council. Such an "inaccuracy" did not bother the investigators; they had to get "confessions" out of the victims, and did not care whether they were really Mensheviks.

Then came the extraction of "confessions." Some, like Groman and Petun, yielded to the promise of future benefits. Others, who tried to resist, were "made to see reason" by physical methods. They were beaten—on the face and head, on the sexual organs; they were thrown to the floor and kicked, choked until no blood flowed to the face, and so on. They were kept on the *konveier* without sleep, put in the *"kartser"* (half dressed and barefoot in a cold cell, or in an unbearably hot and stuffy cell without windows), and so on. For some, the mere threat of such methods, with an appropriate demonstration, was enough. For others, application of the methods was necessary to some degree, on a strictly individual basis, depending on the man's resistance. The most stubborn were A. M. Ginzburg and myself. We knew nothing of each other and sat in different prisons, I in the northern tower of Butyrskaia, Ginzburg in the Inner Prison of the OGPU. But we came to the same conclusion: we could not endure the methods used; we would be better off dead. We opened our veins. But we did not succeed in dying.

After my attempt at suicide, they no longer beat me, but for a long time they did not let me sleep. My nerves reached such a state of exhaustion that nothing on earth seemed to matter—any shame, any slander of myself and others, if only I could sleep. In such a psychological condition, I agreed to any testimony. I was still restrained by the thought that I alone had fallen into such cowardice, and I was ashamed of my weakness. But I was confronted with my old comrade V. V. Sher, a man who had joined the workers' movement long before the victory of the Revolution, though he came from a rich bourgeois family, that is, a man unconditionally committed to ideas. When I heard from Sher's own lips that he had confessed to being a participant in the Menshevik wrecking organization, the "Union Bureau," and had named me as one of its members, I surrendered right there at the confrontation. I no longer resisted, and wrote any testimony I was told to write by the investigators: D. Z. Apresian, A. A. Nasedkin, D. M. Dmitriev. During the investigation some of the accused, myself included, were taken to Suzdal for more intensive methods of physical coercion. There we were kept in an old monastery prison used in tsarist times for the incarceration of so-called heretics. Once, when told to write some improbable confession, I said to investigator Nasedkin: "But you understand that never happened and could not have happened." Nasedkin, a very nervous man, who never took part in torture, replied: "I know it didn't happen, but Moscow demands it."

Was there any wrecking in the Commissariat of Trade, in the planning for the utilization of industrial goods? That is what L. B. Zalkind and I were charged with. Not only was there none; none was possible. The plans for the "supply of industrial goods" throughout the economic *raiony* were drawn up by me and the Board of Industrial Goods, which I directed. These plans were reported by me to meetings of the Collegium of the Commissariat of Trade, with a detailed explanation and justification of each point. The meetings of the Collegium were attended by responsible and experienced Party officials and experts from various departments— from the Supreme Economic Council, the Commissariat of Finance, and from big economic aggregates such as the textile syndicate. A. I. Mikoian presided over the Collegium, and he critically, even hypercritically, examined each figure before agreeing to endorse it. What kind of wrecking could have occurred under such conditions? Was everyone blind except me? Such an absurd supposition cannot be made. Yes, I enjoyed the confidence of the Collegium, of the Commissariat, and of all responsible officials who knew me. But this confidence was earned by the substantial and persuasive quality of my reports, by many years of work in the Soviet state apparatus, beginning with its very first organization, and finally by the "Soviet political line" that I followed, first in the ranks of the Menshevik Party and afterward, when I had broken with it because I became convinced that I could not turn it onto the "Soviet path." In the record of the investigation there is a deposition written in my hand, in which wrecking documents are listed with their file numbers in the Commissariat of Trade. But I did not see a single document in prison, and no one ever showed me any. Those numbers were taken out of thin air, in the expectation that no one would ever check them.

. . . When the "Union Bureau" had been "formed" on an "international basis," additional members joined, as the investigators directed. Among these, to the surprise of the main "participants," was V. K. Ikov. How this addition was made can be seen from the example of M. I. Teitelbaum. The composition of the "Union Bureau" had already been determined and agreed upon by the investigators and the accused when investigator Apresian summoned me from my cell. In his office I found Teitelbaum, whom none of the accused had named in their depositions. I had known Teitelbaum for years as a Party official, a Social Democrat. Originally a Bolshevik, he had gone over to the Mensheviks during the First World

War; in 1917 he was the secretary of the Moscow Committee of Mensheviks, but after the October Revolution he broke with the Mensheviks and worked abroad for the Commissariat of Foreign Trade. When I entered, Apresian got up and went out, leaving us two alone. Teitelbaum said to me: "I've been in prison for a long time. They beat me, demanding a confession that I took bribes abroad from capitalist trading firms. I couldn't stand the torture and 'confessed.' It's terrible, terrible to live and die with such shame. Investigator Apresian suddenly said to me, 'Perhaps you want to change your testimony, to confess participation in the counterrevolutionary Menshevik Union Bureau? Then you would not be a common criminal but a political.' 'Yes, I want that,' I replied; 'how do I do it?' Apresian said, 'I will call Iakubovich in now. Do you know him?' 'Yes.' So he called you. Comrade Iakubovich, I beg you —take me into the Union Bureau. I would rather die as a counterrevolutionary than a rotten crook." At this point Apresian came into the room. "Well, have you reached an agreement?" he asked me with a mocking grin. I was silent. Teitelbaum begged me silently with despairing eyes. "I agree," I said. "I confirm the participation of Teitelbaum in the Union Bureau." "Well, good enough," said Apresian. "Write a deposition, and the others will sign it after you. And you, Teitelbaum, rewrite all your depositions, and I will destroy the old ones." That is how the "Union Bureau" was formed.

Several days before the beginning of the trial, the first "organizational meeting" of the "Union Bureau" was held in the office of the senior investigator, D. M. Dmitriev, who presided. In addition to the fourteen accused, the investigators Apresian, Nasedkin, and Radishchev took part in this "meeting." The accused got acquainted with each other, agreed upon their behavior at the trial, and rehearsed it. This work was not finished at the first "meeting," so it was repeated.

I was beside myself. How should I behave at the trial? Deny the depositions I had made during the investigation? Try to disrupt the trial? Create a worldwide scandal? Whom would that help? Wouldn't it be a stab in the back for the Soviet regime and the Communist Party? I had not joined the Communist Party when I quit the Mensheviks in 1920, but politically and morally I was with it and remain with it. Whatever crimes were committed by the OGPU *apparat,* I felt I ought not betray the Party and the state. I won't hide the fact that I had something else in mind. If I repudiated my earlier depositions at the trial, what would the investigators, the torturers, do to me? It was terrible just to think of it. If it were only death. I wanted death. I sought it, I tried to die. But they wouldn't let me die; they would slowly torture me, torture for an infinitely long time. They wouldn't let me sleep until death came. And if it came from lack of sleep? Probably madness would come first. How could I bring myself to that? In the name of what? If I had been an enemy of the Communist Party and the Soviet state, I would per-

haps have found moral support for my courage in hatred. But I
wasn't an enemy. What could have roused me to such desperate
behavior at the trial?

With such thoughts and in such a state of mind I was summoned
from my cell and taken to the office of N. V. Krylenko, who had
been named state prosecutor for our trial. I had known him for a
long time, from prerevolutionary days. I knew him intimately. In
1920, when I was Commissar of Supplies for the Smolensk Guberniia, he came to Smolensk as a plenipotentiary of the Party Central
Committee and the Soviet Central Executive Committee to observe
and direct the collection of grain. He lived in my apartment for
some time; we slept in the same room. That year the Smolensk
Guberniia was the first in the RSFSR to fulfill its quota of forced
grain requisitions, earning approval and praise from Lenin himself.
In short, Krylenko and I knew each other quite well.

Offering me a seat, Krylenko said: "I have no doubt that you personally are not guilty of anything. We are both performing our duty
to the Party—I have considered and consider you a Communist. I
will be the prosecutor at the trial, you will confirm the testimony
given during the investigation. This is our duty to the Party, yours
and mine. Unforeseen complications may arise at the trial. I will
count on you. If the need should arise, I will ask the presiding
judge to call on you. And you will find the right words." I was
silent. "Have we agreed?" Krylenko asked. I mumbled something
indistinctly, but to the effect that I promised to do my duty. I think
there were tears in my eyes. Krylenko made a gesture of approval.
I left.

At the trial a complication did in fact arise, as Krylenko had
foreseen. The so-called "Foreign Delegation" of the Menshevik
Party sent the court a lengthy telegram that disproved the depositions before the court. Krylenko read the telegram to the court, and,
when he had finished, asked N. M. Shvernik, the presiding judge,
to call on defendant Iakubovich for a reply. My position would
have been very difficult if the telegram of the "Foreign Delegation,"
which honestly refuted the fabrications about wrecking done on its
orders, had also expressed sympathy for the accused, obliged by
force to give false testimony. What could I have replied to such a
statement? But the "Foreign Delegation" itself made my job easy.
Though refuting the prosecutor's case, it also declared that the
defendants did not have and had never had any relations with the
Social Democratic Menshevik Party, that they were nothing but
provocateurs hired by the Soviet government. On this point I could
speak truthfully and honestly, accusing the "Foreign Delegation"
of lies and hypocrisy, recalling the role and service of a number of
the defendants in the history of the Menshevik Party, and charging
the Menshevik leaders with betraying the Revolution, the interests
of socialism and the working class. I spoke emotionally, with the
strength of conviction. That was one of my best political speeches.
It made a great impression on the audience in the packed Hall of

Columns. (I could sense this from my experience as a speaker.) It was, if I may say so, the culminating point of the trial and assured its political success. My promise to Krylenko had been kept.

The next day A. Iu. Finn-Enotaevskii began his testimony by saying that he was in complete agreement with everything I had said about the "Foreign Delegation," and added that in this matter I spoke for all the defendants.

The trial ran smoothly, and from the outside had the look of truth, despite the crude errors made by the investigators in its staging. The story of an illegal visit to the Soviet Union by the Menshevik leader R. A. Rein-Abramovich was especially clumsy. You had to know Abramovich, as I knew him, to understand the utter absurdity of this story. In the whole "Foreign Delegation" there was no one less capable of such a risk than he. Both during the investigation and during the court interrogation in court, I managed to avoid corroborating my meeting with him. But Groman and some other defendants vied with each other in telling about their meetings with him. I later heard that Abramovich published in the West irrefutable proof of his alibi.

In his concluding speech, Krylenko demanded the supreme measure of social defense against five defendants, including myself. He did not humiliate me in his speech; he said that he did not doubt my personal integrity and disinterestedness, called me an "old revolutionary," but characterized me as a fanatic for my ideas and called my ideas counterrevolutionary. That is why he demanded that I be shot. I was grateful to him for his characterization of me, for not degrading me before my death; he didn't drag me in the mud. In my "defense" speech I said that the crimes I had confessed deserved the supreme penalty, that the state prosecutor had not demanded excessive punishment, that I was not asking the Supreme Court to spare my life. I wanted to die. After giving false testimony in the investigation and the trial, I wanted nothing but death. I did not want to live in shame. When I returned to my place on the defendants' bench after my speech, Groman, sitting next to me, grabbed my hand and whispered, in anger and despair, "You're out of your mind! You'll destroy us all! You had no right, with respect to your comrades, to speak that way!"

But we were not condemned to death.

After the sentencing, when they were taking us out of the hall, I bumped into Finn-Enotaevskii at the door. He was older than all the other defendants, twenty years older than I. He said to me, "I will not live to see the day when the truth about our trial can be told. You are the youngest; you will have more chance than all the others to see that day. My bequest to you is to tell the truth."

In fulfillment of this bequest of my older comrade, I am writing this statement, and have also given oral depositions in the office of the Procurator of the USSR.

MIKHAIL IAKUBOVICH
May 5, 1967

Iakubovich's statement is not the only document revealing the mechanics of the political trials in 1930–31. Recently another has come into our hands, "B. I. Rubina's Memoir," concerning her brother I. I. Rubin, who was also a participant in the trial of the "Union Bureau." Rubin, a professor of economics, had taken part in the revolutionary movement since 1905. He first belonged to one of the Bund[18] organizations, and later joined the Mensheviks. In 1924 he abandoned political activity and worked at Marxist economics. In 1926 he became a research associate in the Marx-Engels Institute, where he enjoyed the confidence of the Institute's director, D. B. Riazanov. It is obvious that Rubin was included in the "Union Bureau" primarily to compromise Riazanov, whom Stalin hated. Immediately after Rubin's "depositions" had been obtained and even before the trial of the "Union Bureau" had begun, Riazanov was removed from his job at the Institute he had founded and was expelled from the Party, "for treason to the Party and direct aid to the Menshevik interventionists."

After the trial, Rubin spent three years in solitary confinement; then his sentence was commuted and he was exiled to the town of Aktiubinsk. His wife joined him here, and later his sister, to whom he described the circumstances which compelled him to give false testimony about himself and Riazanov.

B. I. RUBINA'S MEMOIR

This is what I learned from my brother. When he was arrested on December 23, 1930, he was charged with being a member of the "Union Bureau of Mensheviks." This accusation seemed so ridiculous that he immediately submitted a written exposition of his views, which he thought would prove the impossibility of such an accusation. When the investigator read this statement, he tore it up right there. A confrontation was arranged between my brother and Iakubovich, who had been arrested earlier and had confessed to being a member of the "Union Bureau." My brother did not even know Iakubovich. At the confrontation, when Iakubovich said to my brother, "Isaac Il'ich, we were together at a session of the Union Bureau," my brother immediately asked, "And where was this meeting held?" This question caused such a disruption in the examination that the investigator interrupted the examination right there, saying, "What are you, a lawyer, Isaac Il'ich?"

My brother in fact was a lawyer, had worked in that field for many years. After that confrontation, the charge that Rubin was a member of the "Union Bureau" was dropped. Soon after, my brother was transferred to Suzdal. The circumstances of that transfer were so unusual that they were bound to inspire alarm and fear. On the station platform there was not a single person; in an empty

[18] *Ed.:* The Jewish Socialist Party of prerevolutionary Russia.

railroad car he was met by an important GPU official, Gai. To all of
Gai's attempts at persuasion, my brother replied with what was
really true: that he had no connections with the Mensheviks. Then
Gai declared that he would give him forty-eight hours to think it
over. Rubin replied that he didn't need forty-eight minutes.

. . . The examination at Suzdal also failed to give the investigators the results they wanted. Then they put Rubin for days in the
kartser, the punishment cell. My brother at forty-five was a man
with a diseased heart and diseased joints. The *kartser* was a stone
hole the size of a man; you couldn't move in it, you could only
stand or sit on the stone floor. But my brother endured this torture
too, and left the *kartser* with a feeling of inner confidence in himself, in his moral strength. . . . Then he was put in the *kartser* for
a second time, which also produced no results. At that time Rubin
was sharing a cell with Iakubovich and Sher. When he came back
from the *kartser* his cellmates received him with great concern and
attention; right there they made tea for him, gave him sugar and
other things, and tried in every way to show him their sympathy.
Telling about this, Rubin said that he was so amazed: these same
people told lies about him, and at the same time treated him so
warmly.

Soon Rubin was put into solitary confinement; in those circumstances he was subjected to every kind of tormenting humiliation.
He was deprived of all the personal things he had brought with him,
even handkerchiefs. At that time he had the flu, and walked about
with a swollen nose, with ulcers, filthy. The prison authorities often
inspected his cell, and as soon as they found any violation of the
rule for maintaining the cell they sent him to clean the latrines.
Everything was done to break his will. . . . They told him his wife
was very sick, to which he replied: "I can't help her in any way,
I can't even help myself." At times the investigators would turn
friendly, and say: "Isaac Il'ich, this is necessary for the Party." At
the same time they gave him nighttime interrogations, at which a
man is not allowed to fall asleep for a minute. They would wake
him up, wear him out with all sorts of interrogations, jeer at his
spiritual strength, call him the "Menshevik Jesus."

This went on until January 28, 1931. On the night of January
28–29, they took him down to a cellar, where there were various
prison officials and a prisoner, someone named Vasil'evskii, . . . to
whom they said, in the presence of my brother: "We are going to
shoot you now, if Rubin does not confess." Vasil'evskii on his knees
begged my brother: "Isaac Il'ich, what does it cost you to confess?"
But my brother remained firm and calm, even when they shot
Vasil'evskii right there. His feeling of inner rightness was so strong
that it helped him to endure that frightful ordeal. The next night,
January 29–30, they took my brother to the cellar again. This time
a young man who looked like a student was there. My brother
didn't know him. When they turned to the student with the words,

"You will be shot because Rubin will not confess," the student tore
open his shirt at the breast and said, "Fascists, gendarmes, shoot!"
They shot him right there; the name of this student was Dorodnov.

The shooting of Dorodnov made a shattering impression on my
brother. Returning to his cell, he began to think. What's to be
done? My brother decided to start negotiations with the investigator; these negotiations lasted from February 2 to 21, 1931. The
charge that Rubin belonged to the "Union Bureau" had already
been dropped in Moscow, after the confrontation with Iakubovich.
Now they agreed that my brother would consent to confess himself
a member of a program commission connected with the "Union
Bureau," and that he, Rubin, had kept documents of the Menshevik
Center in his office at the Institute, and when he was fired from the
Institute, he had handed them over in a sealed envelope to [D. B.]
Riazanov, as materials on the history of the Social Democratic
movement. Rubin had supposedly asked Riazanov to keep these
documents for a short time. In these negotiations every word, every
formulation was fought over. Repeatedly the "confession" written
by Rubin was crossed out and corrected by the investigator. When
Rubin went to trial on March 1, 1931, in the side pocket of his
jacket was his "confession," corrected with the investigator's red
ink.

Rubin's position was tragic. He had to confess to what had never
existed, and nothing had: neither his former views; nor his connections with the other defendants, most of whom he didn't even
know, while others he knew only by chance; nor any documents
that had supposedly been entrusted to his safekeeping; nor that
sealed package of documents which he was supposed to have
handed over to Riazanov.

In the course of the interrogation and negotiations with the
investigator, it became clear to Rubin that the name of Riazanov
would figure in the whole affair, if not in Rubin's testimony, then
in the testimony of someone else. And Rubin agreed to tell the
whole story about the mythical package. My brother told me that
speaking against Riazanov was just like speaking against his own
father. That was the hardest part for him, and he decided to make it
look as if he had fooled Riazanov, who had trusted him implicitly.
My brother stubbornly kept to this position in all his depositions:
Riazanov had trusted him personally and he, Rubin, had fooled
trustful Riazanov. No one and nothing could shake him from this
position. His deposition of February 21 concerning this matter was
printed in the indictment and signed by Krylenko on February 23,
1931. The deposition said that Rubin handed Riazanov the documents in a *sealed* envelope, and asked him to keep them for a while
at the Institute. My brother stressed this position in all his statements before and during the trial. At the trial he gave a number of
examples which were supposed to explain why Riazanov trusted
him so much. . . .

Putting the problem in such a way ruined the prosecutor's plan. He asked Rubin point-blank: "Didn't you establish any organizational connection?" Rubin replied, "No, there was no organizational connection, there was only his great personal trust in me." Then Krylenko asked for a recess. When he and the other defendants got to another room, Krylenko said to Rubin: "You did not say what you should have said. After the recess I will call you back to the stand, and you will correct your reply." Rubin answered sharply: "Do not call me any more. I will again repeat what I said." The result of this conflict was that, instead of the agreed three years in prison, Rubin was given five, and in his concluding speech Krylenko gave a devastating characterization of Rubin like that of no one else. Everyone interested in the case could not understand why there was so much spite and venom in this characterization.

Rubin set himself the goal of doing everything in his power to "shield" Riazanov. . . . At the trial the possibility of defining in this way his position with respect to Riazanov gave Rubin a certain moral satisfaction. But these legal subtleties made little sense to anyone else. Politically Riazanov was compromised, and Rubin was stricken from the list of people who have the right to a life worthy of man. Rubin himself, in his own consciousness, struck himself from the list of such people as soon as he began to give his "testimony." It is interesting what my brother felt when they took him back to Moscow from Suzdal. When, sick and tortured, he was put into the sleigh, he remembered, in his words, how self-assured and internally strong he had been when he came to Suzdal, and how he was leaving morally broken, destroyed, degraded to a state of complete hopelessness. Rubin understood perfectly well that by his "confession" he had put an end to his life as an honorable, uncorrupted worker and achiever in his chosen field of scholarship.

But that was not the main thing; the main thing was that he was destroyed as a man. Rubin understood perfectly well what repercussions his confession would have. Why had Rubin borne false witness against himself? Why had he also named Riazanov? Why had he violated the most elementary, most primitive concepts of human behavior? Everyone knew with what mutual respect these two men were connected, Rubin and Riazanov. Riazanov, who was considerably older than Rubin, saw in him a talented Marxist scholar who had devoted his life to the study and popularization of Marxism. Riazanov had trusted him unreservedly; he himself was bewildered by what had happened. Here I want to recount an episode, a very painful one, the confrontation between Rubin and Riazanov. The confrontation took place in the presence of an investigator. Rubin, pale and tormented, turned to Riazanov, saying, "David Borisovich, you remember I handed you a package." Whether Riazanov said anything, and precisely what, I don't remember for sure. My brother right then was taken to his cell; in his cell he began to beat his head against the wall. Anyone who knew how calm and self-controlled Rubin was can understand what a state he had been brought to. According to rumors, Riazanov used to say that he could not understand what had happened to Isaac Il'ich.

The defendants in the case of the "Union Bureau" were sentenced to various terms of imprisonment, and all fourteen men were transferred to the political prison in the town of Verkhneural'sk. Rubin, sentenced to five years, was subjected to solitary confinement. The others, who received terms of ten, eight, and five years, were placed several men to a cell. Rubin remained in solitary confinement throughout his imprisonment. During his confinement he continued his scholarly work. Rubin became sick in prison, and lip cancer was suspected. In connection with this sickness, in January, 1933, he was taken to Moscow, to the hospital in Butyrskaia Prison. While in the hospital Rubin was visited twice by GPU officials who offered to make his situation easier, to free him, to enable him to do research. But both times Rubin refused, understanding the price that is paid for such favors. After spending six to eight weeks in the prison hospital, he was taken back to the political prison in Verkhneural'sk. . . . A year later, in 1934, Rubin was released on a commuted sentence, and exiled to the town of Turgai, then an almost unpopulated settlement in the desert. Aside from Rubin there were no other exiles there.

After several months at Turgai, Rubin was permitted to settle in the town of Aktiubinsk. . . . He got work in a consumer cooperative, as a plan economist. In addition he continued to do his own scholarly work. In the summer of 1935, his wife became seriously sick. My brother sent a telegram asking me to come. I went right away to Aktiubinsk; my brother's wife lay in the hospital, and he himself was in a very bad condition. A month later, when his wife had recovered, I went home to Moscow. . . . My brother told me that he did not want to return to Moscow, he did not want to meet his former circle of acquaintances. That showed how deeply he was spiritually shaken by all that he had been through. Only his great optimism that was characteristic of him and his deep scholarly interests gave him the strength to live.

In the fall of 1937, during the mass arrests of that time, my brother was again arrested. The prison in Aktiubinsk was overcrowded, the living conditions of the prisoners were terrifying. After a short stay in the prison, he was transferred somewhere outside of Aktiubinsk. We could find out nothing more about him.

The tragic fate of N. N. Sukhanov, the author of *Notes on the Revolution,* also deserves recording. Broken by the preliminary investigation, Sukhanov did not let down his investigators at the trial. But later on he found strength to protest, and after several hunger strikes he was released. Then in 1937 he was arrested again and shot. As for V. Ikov,

Iakubovich's testimony has been contradicted by B———, who asserted, in a conversation with the writer, that the Moscow Menshevik underground was completely destroyed by 1925–27, and that Ikov was virtually the only Menshevik who remained at liberty until 1930. Thus he could not give any information about an underground Menshevik organization in Moscow, since such an organization did not exist. B——— obtained his information from the Mensheviks he met in camps in the years of Stalin's arbitrary rule.

4

THE POLITICAL TRIALS of the late twenties and early thirties produced a chain reaction of repression, directed primarily against the old technical intelligentsia, against former Cadets who had not emigrated when they could have, and against former members of the Social Revolutionary, Menshevik, and nationalist parties. The press explained that the specialists' wrecking had penetrated everyhere, that the trials had exposed only the leaders of the wrecking organizations, not the broad membership.[19] The word went out that "90 to 95 per cent of the old engineers absolutely must be considered as counterrevolutionary in their mood."[20]

Not all the repression of those years was unjustified. Still, a great many of the arrests, made with the knowledge and sometimes on the direct orders of Stalin, were completely unwarranted. A significant fraction of the specialists who were arrested or exiled (for example, Academician P. P. Lazarev) had not done any wrecking or counterrevolutionary work. These individuals were of course not Marxists, but they were sufficiently loyal to the Soviet regime and served the nation with their knowledge and experience.[21] Repression struck not only the technical intelligentsia but also many "adjacent" areas. Many military specialists were arrested in 1930, on a trumped-up accusation of creating a monarchist counterrevolutionary organization in various military districts. Most of them were loyal commanders, including such prominent men as N. E. Kakurin and A. E. Snesarev, the former head of the General Staff Academy, to whom the Central Executive Committee had just given the Hero of Labor award.[22] This was also the time when the case of the Slavicists was fabricated. Some prominent linguists, including Academician V. V. Vinogradov, were accused of

---

[19] See, e.g., *Vyvody i uroki iz protsessa "Prompartii"* (Moscow, 1931), p. 3.
[20] See the pamphlet, *Klassovaia bor'ba putem vreditel'stva* (Moscow and Leningrad, 1930), p. 9.
[21] See S. A. Fediukin, *Sovetskaia vlast' i burzhuaznye spetsialisty* (Moscow, 1965).
[22] Both Kakurin and Snesarev have been completely rehabilitated. See *Voenno-istoricheskii zhurnal*, 1965, No. 11.

active struggle against the Soviet regime, and were arrested. Among agronomists and biologists there were mass arrests. The great plant breeder V. V. Talanov, one of the founders of the varietal testing system in the Soviet Union, was imprisoned from 1931 to 1935. In Leningrad, Professor B. E. Raikov, a major specialist in the teaching and history of science, was arrested, along with some of his students.

There would have been many more arrests had it not been for the protests of many important Party leaders, whose opinions still had to be taken into consideration by Stalin and the OGPU. The intercession of Army Commander I. E. Iakir and of the prominent Chekist G. E. Evdokimov won the release of many loyal military specialists. Iakir and Evdokimov persuaded the Politburo to discuss the "case of the military specialists" and to review the sentences given by the OGPU. Lunacharskii protested against excessive purges in institutions of higher education, while G. K. (Sergo) Ordzhonikidze of the Supreme Economic Council argued against the arrest of valuable technical specialists.

Many high Party leaders had no illusions concerning the kind of "wreckers" who were in prisons and camps in the early thirties. "I've heard that you need specialists," said Ordzhonikidze to A. V. Snegov, who was the Party organizer for Military *Kombinat* No. 9. "I'll give you three outstanding specialists—'wreckers.' They'll do good work for you, if you treat them well and don't bring up the past." And in fact, three specialists were soon brought under guard to the *Kombinat,* where they helped to get production going. But a significant fraction of those who suffered in those years were rehabilitated only after the XXth Party Congress in 1956.

The economic difficulties that developed in 1929–30, the introduction of rationing, the regression to forced grain requisitions and the policies of war communism, all this made it difficult to continue NEP, although economically and politically its possibilities were still far from exhausted. But Stalin by this time was not planning to continue NEP. From the beginning of the first Five-Year Plan, many small private enterprises were forced to close down, and private businessmen were compelled to curtail their activity by an increasingly severe tax policy. Stalin began a policy of persecution, even terror, against the petty nepmen entrepreneurs.

The "gold" campaign was especially memorable; many private businessmen were required to turn in all their gold to the state. Those who were slow in complying with this demand were arrested by the OGPU and held as hostages until their relatives produced the gold. The repressive campaign was an abuse of power, hardly disguised by invoking such concepts as socialist construction and the dictatorship of the proletariat. Much of the gold extracted in this way had only recently been sold to the nepmen on the free market by disguised agents of the OGPU. The idea was to strengthen the declining value of the ruble and to decrease the quantity of paper money in circulation. Needless to say, there was a glaring contradiction between ends and means. In general, Stalin was not fussy about methods for bringing more gold and foreign currency into the treasury. He decided, for example, to sell some national treasures, and sent abroad paintings by Titian, Raphael, Velázquez, Rembrandt, Rubens, and Watteau, taken from the Hermitage Museum. One must also note the loss caused by the persecution of specialists; many outstanding members of the technical intelligentsia fled abroad.

Some historians place the end of NEP in 1937, on the argument that a significant part of the peasantry had not yet been collectivized in the first half of the thirties. We think this dating is wrong. As a clearly defined policy toward the peasants, private industry, and private trade, NEP actually came to an end in 1929–30. The entire first Five-Year Plan was already beyond the limits of NEP. But NEP was terminated without proper economic justification, with the result that industrial development was not speeded up but slowed down. In any case this question stands in need of additional and profound investigation.

5

THE PREVIOUS CHAPTERS have shown that long before 1937, in the repression of nonproletarian elements, Stalin was preparing the weapon he would later use against the Bolshevik Party itself. But even in this earlier period, many Communists were persecuted by Stalin. Throughout the first Five-Year Plan, the intraparty regime became increasingly ferocious, as Stalin began to turn from bossing the Party to ruling it by terror. Soon after the trial of the "Union Bureau," D. B. Riazanov, the founder of the Marx-Engels Institute, who had done much to discover and publish the manuscripts of valuable Marxist classics, was expelled from the Party and then arrested. Riazanov had long treated Stalin sarcastically, and it was not accidental that his name came up in the fabricated depositions at the trial of the "Union Bureau."

Many Trotskyites were arrested in the early thirties. Trotsky had been expelled from the Soviet Union in 1929, and most of his supporters were broken, both in an ideological and an organizational sense. They bowed down before Stalin and severed their connections with Trotsky. But some maintained or sought such relations, and this was used as a pretext for repression. Thus in 1932–33, hundreds of Trotskyites were arrested, some for a real but many for an imaginary connection with Trotsky. Among them was I. N. Smirnov, who had earlier been an eminent Party official.

The fate of the former left Social Revolutionary Bliumkin requires clarification also. In 1918, on his Party's orders, he had assassinated the German Ambassador Mirbach. Arrested by the Cheka, Bliumkin was pardoned by Dzerzhinskii with Lenin's approval. Later he began to work for the Cheka. In the early thirties he made a secret visit to Trotsky abroad. When he returned to the Soviet Union, he was arrested and shot. According to one interpretation, Bliumkin was shot for his connection with Trotsky; according to another (heard from the Latvian old Bolshevik I. I. Sandler, later imprisoned in Vorkuta), Bliumkin was given the job of winning Trotsky's confidence and then of killing him. He did win Trotsky's confidence but could not bring himself to kill him, and was shot for this on his return to Moscow.[23]

At the beginning of the thirties a fair-sized campaign was also launched against "nationalist deviations." It would be incorrect to deny the existence of nationalist currents in the Union Republics, which in some cases were encouraged from abroad. But in the guise of struggle against nationalism Stalin began a systematic restriction of the rights of the Union Republics, a violation of the nationality policy that had been worked out under Lenin. This caused many Party members to protest, whereupon these internationalists were arbitrarily reviled as nationalists. Moreover, Stalin frequently exaggerated the mistakes of inconvenient comrades in the Union Republics. Unjustified criticism of this sort was heaped on N. A. Skrypnik, one of the leaders of the Ukrainian Bolsheviks and a member of the Executive Committee of the Communist International.

Friction between Stalin and Skrypnik began at the VIth Party Congress in August, 1917, when Skrypnik criticized Stalin for taking an unclear and indecisive stand on the question whether Lenin should appear before a court of the Provisional Government. In 1918 Skrypnik had sharply criticized the way that Stalin, as Commissar for Nationality Affairs, was treating the Ukraine. At the Xth Party Congress in March, 1921, Skrypnik had criticized Stalin's inane, abstract speech on the nationality question. "The nationality problem," said

[23] At the very beginning of the thirties, Trotsky's articles did not call for the overthrow of Stalin. On the contrary, he wrote that under existing conditions the overthrow of the Stalinist bureaucratic *apparat* would inevitably lead to the triumph of the counterrevolution. Thus he recommended that his supporters limit themselves to ideological propaganda. But in the mid-thirties, that is, when mass repression began, Trotsky and some of his closest advisers apparently came to the conclusion that it was necessary to destroy Stalin as a tyrant. It was then that Stalin directed the NKVD to arrange Trotsky's assassination.

Skrypnik, "is important, critical. Not the slightest solution was proposed in Comrade Stalin's speech this morning."[24] Skrypnik's own pronouncements on the nationality question were not always correct. The process of "Ukrainization," which he directed, was not free of errors and excesses; bourgeois nationalist elements sometimes got involved. But instead of criticizing Skrypnik's mistakes in a comradely manner, instead of an open discussion of the difficult problems of nationality policy in the Ukraine, Stalin and Postyshev launched a political campaign against Skrypnik, virtually accusing him of conscious support for class enemies on the cultural front.

The fraudulent trial of the "Union for the Liberation of the Ukraine" was used for this purpose. This trial, said P. P. Postyshev in one of his speeches, "has shown . . . that the strongest nuclei of the nationalistic counterrevolution have existed in higher education and in vocational schools, in the [Ukrainian] Academy of Sciences, in publishing houses, in writers' organizations." But "did the Ukrainian Communist Party draw the necessary conclusions from this trial? No, it did not." As a result of this "weakening, and even, in some cases, this loss of Bolshevik vigilance," Postyshev felt obliged to state, in 1933, that

> the sector which Comrade Skrypnik has directed until recently—I have in mind the Commissariat of Education and the entire educational system of the Ukraine—has been completely infested with wrecking, counterrevolutionary, nationalistic elements. It is in these very institutions that wrecking elements were given completely free rein, placing their people in the most responsible, the leading, sectors of the ideological front.[25]

Many valuable cadres of the Ukrainian national intelligentsia were discredited, and some were subjected to various kinds of repression, ranging from loss of jobs to arrest. And Skrypnik, as a result of the slanderous campaign against him, committed suicide in 1933.[26]

In Armenia in the early thirties, on a charge of "nationalism," the distinguished Leninist N. Stepanian was dismissed from his post as Commissar of Education. The outstanding Armenian poet E. Charents was slandered, and his *Book of the Road* was banned. Many Armenian intellectuals protested, including Academician A. Tamanian and People's Artist M. Sar'ian. The writer Aksel' Bakunts was also subjected to persecution.[27]

Mass repression also occurred, in 1931–32, among the lower Party organizations in rural areas.

[24] *X-yi s'ezd RKP (b)* (Moscow, 1963), p. 210.
[25] P. Postyshev, *Ot XVI do XVII s'ezda. Stat'i i rechi.* (Moscow, 1934), pp. 59, 203.
[26] See *Izvestiia,* Jan. 25, 1962.
[27] See the pamphlet of Ts. Agaian, *N. Stepanian* (Erevan, 1967), pp. 44–47.

As we have seen, all the former opposition groups had been broken by the early thirties and no longer opposed Stalin's policies. But dissatisfaction with these policies still existed within the Party. One person who expressed discontent was V. V. Lominadze, first secretary of the Party's Transcaucasian Committee (*kraikom*). Lominadze spoke out against neglect of the workers' and peasants' needs, against fakery, against the feudal and seignorial behavior of some Party officials in Transcaucasia. On the last issue, Lominadze and his assistant N. Chaplin prevailed upon the *kraikom* to adopt a special resolution. Dissatisfaction with Stalin's policies was also expressed by the talented official S. I. Syrtsov, a candidate member of the Politburo and Chairman of the Council of People's Commissars for the RSFSR. He and his sympathizers protested against excessive expansion of capital construction. He called attention to the serious situation in the countryside, especially in stockbreeding, declaring that it was too early to speak of the victory of socialism in the countryside or the imminent completion of the foundations for a socialist society in the USSR.

In 1930 Lominadze visited Syrtsov in Moscow, and for several hours they had a conversation about Party and state affairs. Stalin learned about the conversation, and that was enough to create a story about the formation of a "rightist-leftist" bloc by Lominadze and Syrtsov. The press began to attack this nonexistent bloc and its alleged members, including the ideologist L. Shatskin. In December, 1930, Syrtsov and Lominadze were removed from the Central Committee. This action was taken at a meeting of the Politburo and the Presidium of the Central Control Commission, without calling a plenary session of the Central Committee and the Control Commission, in violation of the Party statute. Syrtsov was demoted from Chairman of the RSFSR Council of People's Commissars to director of a factory producing phonograph records. Lominadze was transferred from the Transcaucasian *kraikom* to work in the Commissariat of Trade, and then was sent to Magnitogorsk as secretary of the city's Party committee.

A real anti-Stalinist opposition that did arise in the early thirties was the Riutin group. M. N. Riutin worked in the Central Committee *apparat* in 1930 and then was head of one of the Moscow *raion* committees. Disturbed by failures in collectivization and industrialization, and by increasing ferocity within the Party, Riutin and P. A. Galkin organized an opposition group in Moscow, drawing in some of Bukharin's students (including D. Maretskii and A. Slepkov) and some supporters of Zinoviev and Kamenev. The philosopher Ia. E. Sten and such once prominent Party officials as P. G. Petrovskii and N. A. Uglanov also joined this group. The Riutin group was essentially conspiratorial in nature. Its main goal was to remove Stalin and to change Party policies in the direction of greater democratization, greater consideration for the interests of workers and peasants, and an end to repression within the Party. Zinoviev and Kamenev were familiar with the documents and the platform of this organization. Stalin found out about the group through the OGPU and struck swiftly. Demagogically accusing Riutin and like-minded people of a counterrevolutionary plot, of creating a "kulak organization" and attempting to restore capitalism, Stalin not only insisted on the arrest of most of the participants in the group but demanded that its leaders be shot. The Politburo, however, did not agree with Stalin. It decided to expel the participants from the Party, and to exile most of them to remote cities and *raiony*.

An abnormal situation was also created in the social sciences at the beginning of the thirties. The first wave of repression among Marxist historians was precipitated by Stalin's famous letter to the editor of *Proletarian Revolution*, laying down extremely fallible views on the history of Bolshevism in an extremely nasty manner. Many historians were fired, and some were even expelled from the Party without cause. At the end of 1931 the Institute of History reported to the Presidium of the Communist Academy that it had carried out Stalin's instructions by firing people who did not write the history of Bolshevism in the prescribed way. In particular, I. M. Al'ter and A. G. Slutskii were fired from the Institute, and Slutskii's candidate membership in the Party was subsequently canceled. N. El'vov and G. Vaks, contributors to the multivolume *History of the CPSU,* were expelled from the Party, while the editor, Emilian Iaroslavskii, was severely criticized.[28]

Repression also hit many other disciplines. The Leningrad Branch of the Communist Academy reported in 1933 that it had rooted out "Trotskyism, Luxemburgism, and Menshevism, not only on the historical but also on the economic, agrarian, literary, and other fronts.[29] Under Kaganovich's leadership and with Stalin's support, a savage campaign was launched against the prominent Party official M. N. Pokrovskii, whose mistakes as an historian were enormously exaggerated. Even today there are people who try to dismiss Pokrovskii's work with the declaration that he was not a Marxist-Leninist. They point to the scholarly and political mistakes that Pokrovskii did in fact make in his long development as a scholar and Party activist, ignoring the fact that Lenin repeatedly referred to Pokrovskii as a Marxist and a Bolshevik.

There were also intolerable excesses in the struggle on the philosophical "front." Of course mistakes can be found in the philosophical works produced by Deborin's group or by Timiriazev's and Sarab'ia-

---

[28] See the article by V. A. Dunaevskii in *Evropa v novoe i noveishee vremia* (Moscow, 1966), pp. 508–10.

[29] *Ibid.,* p. 509.

nov's.[30] But it must be noted that discussion of philosophical questions became unusually harsh following Stalin's talk, on December 9, 1930, with the Party Buro of the Institute of Red Professors. Philosophical disagreements among various Marxist trends were made to look like fights against the enemies of socialism. As a result many prominent and talented Soviet philosophers were discredited and in many cases dismissed. It was in those years that such people as M. B. Mitin, P. F. Iudin, and F. V. Konstantinov were pushed to the top in philosophy, people whose long years of activity have contributed no fruitful ideas to the discipline. For more than two decades, Soviet philosophical literature was dominated by a stereotyped, superficial mechanism draped with mere phrases about dialectics.

Many pseudoscientific struggles erupted at the beginning of the thirties. There were fights against "Menshevizing counterrevolutionary Rubinism" in economics, against "the Bogdanovian mechanistic theories of Bukharin" in social theory, against "Raikovism" in the methods of teaching biology, against "Voronskyism" and "Pereverzevism" in literary criticism, against "Menshevizing idealism" and the "mechanistic revision of Marxism" in philosophy, against the theory of the "withering away of the school" in pedagogy, and so on and on. In almost every case, insignificant differences in phraseology were elevated "to principled heights." In the tiniest phraseological inaccuracies someone would try to find enemy influences; in the guise of "revolutionary vigilance," narrow-minded sectarians cultivated intolerance and viciousness. Here, for example, is the reasonable advice given to journalists in an article:

> Fellow newspapermen, the reader begs you not to admonish him, not to teach, not to exhort, not to goad, but to give him clear and understandable exposition, to analyze, to explain what, where, and how. Lessons and exhortations will emerge from such writing by themselves.

And here is what was said about that reasonable advice in a special resolution adopted by the Communist Institute of Journalism: "These are very harmful [*vredneishie,* which is close to wrecking, *vreditel'skie*] bourgeois theories; they reject the organizing role of the Bolshevik press, and should be destroyed once and for all." Such talk is scarcely distinguishable from the wall posters of the Red Guards in China.

In 1930–33 T. D. Lysenko and other less famous adventurists

[30] *Ed.:* During the twenties there was vigorous philosophical argument among Soviet Marxists. The main schools were the admirers of Hegel, led by A. M. Deborin, and the admirers of natural science, who were called mechanists. A. K. Timiriazev and V. M. Sarab'ianov were prominent mechanists. Both schools were condemned in 1930.

began their meteoric careers in science. An intolerable situation also developed in literature. By the end of the twenties Maxim Gorky was protesting against the development of self-serving groups and internecine strife among Soviet writers. "The fights and quarrels among the circles," he wrote to A. B. Khalatov, "are word-chopping, inspired by self-conceit, by personal grudges and by every kind of egoism." To A. D. Kamegulov, Gorky wrote that

> your "disagreements," in my view, are quite petty and extremely harmful, . . . especially in the tone of expression. Maybe I'm mistaken, but it seems to me that personal relations among you, Party members, show that you are very poorly educated politically. And if Vladimir Il'ich were alive, he would, believe me, cut down these endless discussions by 50 per cent. At least.[31]

Not long ago the writer V. A. Kaverin described his astonishment on leafing through a notorious journal of the late twenties, *On Literary Guard*. He found literature sharply divided into two camps, enemy and friendly. Though the dividing line shifted constantly and weirdly, at any given moment enemies and friends were clearly set apart, the one for hatred and poorly concealed envy, the other for love—and a lust for a share in power, a lust so obvious that at times it seemed rather ludicrous to Kaverin.[32]

At the beginning of the thirties the situation in literature got even worse. Demian Bedny, a leading proletarian intellectual and poet of the October Revolution, was given a rough going-over. Stalin had some justifiable criticism of some poems by Bedny (*"Slezai s pechki," "Bez poshchady,"* etc.), but he also indulged in intolerable vilification of him as a man and a Bolshevik. For several years Stalin would not see this leading Soviet poet. Bedny was evicted from the Kremlin apartment that had been given to him at Lenin's request in 1918. As a result of such campaigns, the Soviet intelligentsia was divided into factions. Quarreling, slander, informing, and defamation became a way of life in most research institutes, in institutions of higher education, and in writers' and artists' organizations. And this abnormal way of life was justified with talk about the intensification of the class struggle in the USSR.

A serious situation also developed in foreign Communist parties in the early thirties, as bitter struggles were waged against "rightists" and "leftists," with methods borrowed from the Soviet Party to beat down dissent. In a few cases, ferocious varieties of repression were also used. As early as the end of the twenties, Stalin and Kaganovich exaggerated some mistakes made by the Communist Party of the

---

[31] *Novyi mir,* 1964, No. 11, p. 228. *Ed.:* Kamegulov was a literary critic and leader of the aggressive Russian Association of Proletarian Writers (RAPP).

[32] *Novyi mir,* 1966, No. 11, pp. 141–42.

Western Ukraine. Then, in the early thirties, that Party was unjustly accused of nationalism and betrayal, culminating in its liquidation. Many of its leaders, including M. T. Zaiachkovskii and G. V. Ivanenko, became victims of lawless repression.[33] In 1933 the same treatment was given to the Communist Party of West Belorussia. P. P. Voloshin, F. I. Volynets, I. E. Gavrilik—former deputies in the Polish Sejm—and other Communists who, after long prison terms in bourgeois Poland, had been released in a prisoner exchange with the Soviet government and given political asylum in the USSR, were falsely accused of counterrevolutionary and anti-Soviet activity and arrested. Along with them some other leaders of the West Belorussian Party went to jail; among them Ia. Bobrovich, A. G. Kaputskii, P. A. Klintsevich, and L. I. Rodzevich.[34]

6

THE EARLY THIRTIES was also the time when Stalin was identified with socialism and the Party. This cult did not spring up overnight. Even at the beginning of the twenties one can detect certain abnormal cultist phenomena. Party organizations became self-contained, the dividing line between Party members and nonparty people was more sharply drawn, and within the Party elements of militarization and rule by command began to spread. Although a cult of individual personalities had not yet appeared, there was the inception of a religious, cultist attitude toward such concepts as the Party, the Soviet state, the Revolution, and the proletariat. Party members were inculcated with the conviction that the Party as a whole could not make mistakes, that the Party knew everything. There could be no secrets from the Party, even of the most intimate nature; everything had to be revealed to it, as to God at confession. For the sake of the Party and the state a Communist had to do anything; the Revolution justified any cruelty.

Gradually this cult of the Party was transferred to its leaders, in the first place to members of the Politburo. Their names were affixed to streets, factories, collective farms (the Rykov plant, the Bukharin streetcar depot, etc.), and to cities as well. In 1924–25, with the approval of the Politburo, not only Leningrad and Stalingrad but cities such as Trotsk and Zinovievsk appeared on the map. By the end of the twenties almost every *oblast* and republic had its own cult of a local leader. Extravagant tributes to Stalin were combined in the local press with equally extravagant tributes to Kaganovich, Postyshev, Kirov, B. P. Sheboldaev, R. I. Eikhe, M. O. Razumov, Akmal' Ikra-

[33] See the newspaper *Pravda Ukrainy*, Oct. 11 and Nov. 18, 1963.
[34] See *Kommunist*, 1963, No. 10.

mov, and others. Tributes to Stalin became more and more immoderate as a hierarchy of cults emerged with the main cult of Stalin at the top.

In December, 1929, when Stalin's fiftieth birthday was celebrated with a pomposity that was unusual at that time, the press bestowed on him, as chief and teacher, such epithets as "great," "remarkable," and even "genius." The State Publishing House issued a special anthology, *Stalin,* with contributions by Kalinin, Kuibyshev, Kaganovich, Voroshilov, Ordzhonikidze, and other leaders. Exaggerations and distortions abounded, especially one that was insistently repeated:

> During Lenin's lifetime, Comrade Stalin, though he was one of Lenin's pupils, was however *his single most reliable aide,* who differed from the others by never faltering, by always moving hand in hand with Vladimir Il'ich at all the crucial stages of the Revolution, at all the sharp drastic turns through which Lenin took the Party.[35]

Some contributors also tried to prove that Stalin was not just a practical leader but also a major theorist of Marxism-Leninism. Voroshilov's "Stalin and the Red Army" contained an unusually large number of distortions, especially on the defeat of Denikin in the Civil War. Voroshilov assigned to Stalin the main role in planning his defeat, although his role was actually modest.

There were other efforts to fabricate Stalinist legends at the end of the twenties and the early thirties. In 1929 the book *L'vov-Warsaw* appeared, not without Stalin's knowledge, altering the facts to blame the mistakes in the Polish campaign of 1920 on Generals S. S. Kamenev and M. N. Tukhachevskii. This book even denied that the advance on Warsaw was the main strategic move in the war with Poland. By 1931 V. V. Adoratskii was writing, in the preface to the six-volume collection of Lenin's works, that Stalin's works were the indispensable guide to Lenin's. At the same time, A. S. Bubnov, E. Iaroslavskii, and other historians were bringing out cultist revisions of their books on Party history. After the Central Committee Plenum in January, 1933, there was an extraordinary intensification of Stalin worship.

There was not a little sincerity in this flood of praise for Stalin. But there was far more carefully encouraged fawning. The simple fact that members of the Politburo (especially Molotov and Kaganovich) were the first to extol Stalin immediately bestowed on such praise the character of official policy, and as such it had to be endorsed even by those who had not previously considered Stalin an infallible genius.

Even former oppositionists joined the general chorus of praise;

[35] *Stalin* (Moscow, 1929), p. 161. Italics added.

indeed, their voices often sounded louder than the rest. One after the other Zinoviev, Kamenev, Bukharin, and other opposition leaders published articles confessing again that they had erred while the "great chief of toilers throughout the whole world," Comrade Stalin, had always been right. The first issue of *Pravda* for 1934 carried a huge two-page article by Radek, heaping orgiastic praise on Stalin. The former Trotskyite, who had led active opposition to Stalin for many years, now called him "Lenin's best pupil, the model of the Leninist Party, bone of its bone, blood of its blood." Stalin was distinguished by "the greatest vigilance against opportunism" combined with "adamantine composure"; he "personifies the entire historical experience of the Party"; "more than any other pupil of Lenin, he has fused with the Party, with its basic cadres." He "is as farsighted as Lenin," and so on and on. This seems to have been the first large article in the press specifically devoted to adulation of Stalin, and it was quickly reissued as a pamphlet in 225,000 copies, an enormous figure for the time. To his former associates in the opposition Radek offered the following explanation of the praise he had lavished on Stalin: "We should be grateful to Stalin. If we, that is, the opposition, had lived at the time of the French Revolution, we would long ago have been shorter by a head." Events soon showed how little Radek knew Stalin.

After Radek's article, tributes to Stalin became grotesquely hypertrophied. Genius and more than genius, great and the greatest, wisest of the wise, all-knowing and all-seeing—these are but a few of the epithets that accompanied almost every reference to Stalin. The businesslike speeches of the delegates to the XVIth Party Congress in 1930 had not included any praise of Stalin. Most of the delegates, when speaking about the Party's achievements, did not even mention Stalin's name. The XVIIth Party Congress in 1934 was quite different. Nearly every speaker dwelt on Stalin's greatness and genius. At times it seemed that the Congress was convened to celebrate Stalin, that the nation owed all its achievements to Stalin alone. For the first time in the Party's history, a congress did not adopt a detailed resolution in accordance with the report of the Central Committee, but instead directed all Party organizations simply "to be guided in their work by the theses and objectives set forth in Comrade Stalin's speech."[36]

For some time now, Soviet publications on the cult of Stalin's personality have offered the following explanation: the Party's successes during the first Five-Year Plan engendered great love for the Party's leader, with the people and the Party somehow transferring to Stalin the enthusiastic joy inspired by the successful building of socialism. But this explanation must be revised. As we have seen, the beginning of the thirties was a very difficult time for the Soviet Union.

[36] *KPSS v rezoliutsiiakh,* II (1953), p. 744.

There was famine in many *raiony,* agricultural output decreased, food was rationed. Serious difficulties were also apparent in industry. An objective analysis would have had to conclude that "Stalinist leadership" in the building of socialist industry and socialist agriculture was unsatisfactory. For that reason Stalin and his sympathizers cast aside any objectivity, replacing it with boundless glorification of Stalin, eradicating any criticism before it could start. Thus, extravagant tributes to Stalin originated not so much from successes as from the need to cover up the miscalculations, the mistakes, and the crimes that Stalin had committed, was committing, and was preparing to commit. Stalin was placed in a unique position, free of control by the Central Committee, inaccessibly high above the Party, completely isolated from any criticism.

Through the Comintern, Stalin's cult began to be implanted in all other Communist parties. The example of the CPSU encouraged many parties to create cults of their own leaders and to pervert democratic principles of party life.

There was no precedent in the history of the movement. Marx and Engels were hostile to adulation. Marx wrote to Wilhelm Blos:

> Out of hatred for any cult of personality, I never allowed publication of the laudatory messages with which I was pestered from various countries during the life of the International. I never even sent answers, except for a few rebukes.[37]

"Both Marx and I," wrote Engels in response to a proposed reception in their honor,

> have always been against any public demonstrations in honor of individuals, except when it is for some important purpose. We have especially opposed such demonstrations for ourselves during our lifetimes.[38]

Lenin felt the same way. He reacted with disapproval to the tribute that was spontaneously paid to him at the closing session of the IXth Party Congress in 1920. He walked out of the meeting to protest against this relatively modest attempt on the part of the delegates to show their affection and respect. Lunacharskii recalls how, in 1918, soon after he was seriously wounded, Lenin called in V. D. Bonch-Bruevich and some other people and said:

> I've noticed with great displeasure that my personality is beginning to be extolled. This is annoying and harmful. We all know that our cause is not in a personality. I myself would find it awkward to forbid any such phenomenon. That would be somewhat ridiculous

[37] Marx-Engels, *Sochineniia,* 2nd edn., XXXIV, p. 241.
[38] Marx-Engels, *Sochineniia,* 1st edn., XXVIII, p. 385.

and pretentious. But we must gradually put the brakes on this whole business.[39]

Lenin was also quite upset by Gorky's tributes—the article "V. I. Lenin" and the public letter to H. G. Wells—which were permeated with the spirit of the cult of personality. As soon as Lenin read them, he wrote the following draft for a Politburo resolution:

> The Politburo considers the publication of Gorky's articles in *Kommunistcheskii Internatsional*, No. 12 [1920], to be extremely inappropriate, especially as the feature piece, for there is nothing Communist in these articles but much that is anti-Communist. Henceforth in no case shall such articles be published in *Kommunisticheskii Internatsional*.[40]

But how did Stalin react to the growing cult of his personality? The facts show that he not only accepted the praise calmly and as his due, which was improper enough for a Marxist-Leninist, but that it was Stalin himself who directed and encouraged this praise. The facts show that he reacted hostilely not to praise but to insufficient praise, to belittling of his "great services." Far from checking his servile flatterers, he supported and promoted them.

In a 1937 interview with Lion Feuchtwanger, Stalin made a show of mild disapproval of the praise being showered on him. Feuchtwanger raised the subject of tasteless and immoderate tributes, whereupon Stalin

> shrugged his shoulders. He apologized for his workers and peasants, who are too busy with other things to cultivate good taste. He joked a little about hundreds of thousands of portraits of a man with a mustache, blown up to monstrous size, which flit before his eyes at demonstrations. I pointed out that even people who obviously had taste put up busts and portraits of him—and what busts and portraits!—in utterly inappropriate places, for example at a Rembrandt exhibition. At this point he became serious. He suggested that these are people who have accepted the existing regime rather late, and now are trying to prove their loyalty with doubled zeal. Yes, he considers it possible that this could be a plot of wreckers to discredit him. "A timeserving fool," said Stalin angrily, "does more harm than a hundred enemies." He tolerates all this ballyhoo, he declared, only because he knows what naïve joy the festive hubbub gives to its organizers, and he knows that all this relates to him not as an individual person, but as the representative of the trend which believes that the building of a socialist economy in the USSR was more important than permanent revolution.[41]

[39] *Leninskie stranitsy* (Moscow, 1960), p. 100.
[40] *Polnoe sobranie*, LIV, p. 429.
[41] Lion Feuchtwanger, *Moskva 1937* (Moscow, 1937), pp. 51–52. *Ed.:* There are versions in other languages, including English, *Moscow, 1937; My Visit Described for My Friends* (N.Y., 1937).

According to Feuchtwanger, the Party committees of Moscow and Leningrad had already adopted resolutions strongly condemning the "false practice of unnecessary and senseless tributes to Party leaders," and ecstatically congratulatory telegrams had disappeared from the newspapers. We do not know whether there actually were such resolutions or whether they were even made public. We do know that the press continued in the mid-thirties to praise Stalin with greater and greater ecstasy.

As we mentioned earlier, though Stalin denounced oppositionists in words, in practice he put into effect many of their ideas. In this case too, by encouraging the cult of his own personality, Stalin was actually putting into effect some ideas of very early opportunists, such as the "god-builders," who sought to make a god of "the collective power of humanity," who preached a new "socialist" religion "without a god." This school of religious philosophy, which emerged from the ideological disarray that followed the defeat of the 1905 Revolution, urged that scientific socialism be declared the most religious of all religions. Adapting themselves to the most backward part of the popular masses, they presented socialism in a religious form. Lenin severely castigated this fideism, calling any belief in any god necrophilia (*trupolozhestvo*).[42] But Stalin ignored Lenin's fight against god-building. He put all its basic ideas into effect and went much further, seeking to create a "socialist religion" *with* a god. And the all-powerful, all-knowing, all-holy god of the new religion was himself, Stalin.

The Party as a whole shared some responsibility for the creation of the cult of Stalin's personality. "Now, thirty to forty years after the event," the old Bolshevik A. M. Durmashkin has written in his memoirs,

> it would be a mistake to hold to the same view we had then, in the heat of struggle. Of course, the Party was fully justified in its basic line: insisting that socialism could be built in one country, unaided by proletarian revolution elsewhere; striving to industrialize the country, to secure its independence of capitalist countries; striving for collectivization, to ensure the socialist transformation of the countryside. These policies derived from Lenin's doctrine, and were fully justified in practice. But it is our Party's duty to make a critical analysis of the actual ways and means of carrying out Lenin's legacy. This obligation derives especially from the fact that the Party permitted the rise of Stalin's cult, fell into the grave error of such adulation that his every action was automatically assumed to be necessary and just, his every slogan a directive. And all of us, the old generation of Communists, are responsible for this state of affairs in the Party.

[42] *Lenin, Sochineniia,* 4th edn., XXXV, p. 89.

V

The Assassination of Kirov

1

I HAVE TOLD of Stalin's many mistakes and crimes in the first decade following Lenin's death. I have told of the decline in the workers' standard of living, of the increase in arbitrary rule and repression, of the extravagant adulation of Stalin. Whether we like it or not, the question arises: how could the Party have allowed Stalin to remain as its leader?

Of course, Stalin's personal power was already very great in the early thirties. After the main opposition groups had been smashed, Stalin had become a dictator wielding almost unlimited power. Not only did he have virtually complete control over the growing Party machine but also, through Voroshilov, over the Red Army and, through G. G. Iagoda, over the security organs. It would therefore have been very difficult to remove Stalin from the post of General Secretary at the beginning of the thirties. In any case, practically no legal democratic possibility of performing such an operation remained. But that was not the only problem.

Nowadays, when we analyze Stalin's mistakes and crimes, we are abstracting them from a huge and complex flow of events. The Party directly or indirectly participated in these events, and for many of its members it was hard to abstract Stalin's crimes and mistakes from the general flow. Moreover, many of the miscalculations and crimes that Stalin committed before 1934 were fully revealed only later, some after his death. In the early thirties they were carefully concealed or even, in many cases, propagandized as Stalin's great achievements.

It is a general rule that the full significance of a given man's deeds, whether positive or negative, is rarely understood by his contemporaries. The world's rulers did not understand the danger, for them, of Karl Marx, a German political émigré living modestly in

London. Marx was known as a socialist and a communist, but to many capitalist leaders his activity seemed much less dangerous than that of petty-bourgeois revolutionaries who have since fallen into oblivion. Unfortunately, revolutionary classes and parties sometimes share this inability to discern the long-run significance of individuals and their actions. After the victory of the October Revolution, Lenin simply walked out of Smolny[1] and took a streetcar to a fellow Bolshevik's apartment to rest. This episode reveals not only Lenin's modesty but also his friends' and colleagues' failure to appreciate the tremendous value of his life, the importance of guarding him against any accidents.

On the other hand, the danger of Stalin was not perceived by the Party in time. This was not due merely to the difficulties of long-run forecasts, or to insufficient public information. Nor was it only because Stalin had established his influence over Lenin's leading colleagues, whom he impressed with his silent determination, his seeming archrevolutionary firmness. It is also important to bear in mind the complexity of the situation in the early thirties. Faced with unprecedented difficulties, many Party leaders thought it impossible to begin any kind of struggle within the Party, lest the situation become even worse. No one dreamed that Stalin would go as far as he did a few years later. Moreover, by 1934 many Party leaders had greatly changed. Stalin succeeded not only in subjecting but also in corrupting a significant portion of the Party cadres. Many of the Party's leaders actively participated in the mistakes and crimes of the late twenties and early thirties, and these people could hardly become energetic critics of Stalin.

Nevertheless, a certain estrangement did emerge in the early thirties between Stalin and a significant part of the old Bolsheviks. They were not former leaders of the opposition; they belonged to the basic nucleus of Party leadership that took shape in the struggle against the oppositions.

Stalin expressed his hostility and contempt toward a number of old Bolsheviks as early as 1925 in a private letter:

> We in Russia have also experienced the withering away of many old leading theorists, propagandists, and political chiefs. This process has intensified in periods of revolutionary crisis, it has slowed down in periods of consolidation, but it has always gone on. The Lunacharskiis, Pokrovskiis, Rozhkovs, Goldenbergs, Bogdanovs, Krasins, etc.—these are the first that come to mind as examples of onetime Bolshevik chiefs who have sunk to secondary roles.[2]

[1] *Ed.:* The headquarters of the victorious Bolsheviks was a former girls' school called the Smolny Institute.

[2] Stalin, *Sochineniia,* VII, p. 43. *Ed.:* First published in this 1950 volume under the heading "Letter to Comrade M——," it was actually written to A. Maslow, the German Communist leader.

By lumping together colleagues of Lenin, who were still alive and holding important posts in 1925, with people who had fought Lenin, Stalin was trying to denigrate Lenin's colleagues, to run down their role in the Party.

From the beginning of the thirties Stalin relied more and more on young Party officials, hand-picked by himself, and slighted many veterans of the Revolution, who, as he saw it, had played out their roles. At this time, on Stalin's suggestion, the Society of Old Bolsheviks was disbanded. A revealing conversation occurred between G. I. Petrovskii, the president of the Ukrainian branch of the Society, and S. V. Kosior, concerning the publication of memoirs by participants in the October Revolution and the Civil War.

> "The veterans should be helped," suggested Kosior.
> "No, Stanislav Vikent'evich," replied Petrovskii, "we won't be able to. It's not that we don't want to, it's a matter of policy."
> "Whose policy?"
> Petrovskii faltered but he had known Kosior for a long time and still felt friendly, so he did not dissemble.
> "Stalin's policy. For some reason he has taken a dislike to old Bolsheviks; he's out to get them. Just after M. S. Ol'minskii died, I asked the Politburo to publish a biography of him. Stalin cut me off sharply and opposed the project, saying, "Let future historians worry about that."[3]

For their part some old Bolsheviks became increasingly disillusioned with Stalin, disturbed by the growth of his arbitrary rule. Stalin's unchanging nastiness and increasing unwillingness to consider any opinion but his own brought some Party leaders to protest, although Stalin cut such objections short. Even I. P. Tovstukha, who had once been Stalin's personal secretary, began to express dissatisfaction. Once, for example, when Tovstukha was away, Stalin reorganized the section of the Central Committee that Tovstukha headed, firing some people and transferring others. When Tovstukha learned of this, he sent in a strong protest against such arbitrary rule. Stalin disposed of the protest with this notation: "Ha, ha, ha. Here's a real bantam."[4]

When it became apparent that ferrous metallurgy could not reach the fantastic targets dictated by Stalin, he cursed Sergo Ordzhonikidze and ordered that all the officials in the Main Administration of the Metallurgical Industry be sent out to factories. Ordzhonikidze requested an exception only for his deputy, A. I. Gurevich, because he was needed in Moscow and also because he had a bad heart. But Stalin said, poking his finger toward Gurevich, "With a mug like that,

[3] As quoted in A. Mel'chin, *Stanislav Kosior* (Moscow, 1964), p. 71.
[4] *Kommunist,* 1962, No. 18, p. 37.

and sick too! No matter, let him go." On his return to Moscow, Gurevich wrote a lengthy report for Stalin and the Central Committee on the causes of backwardness in ferrous metallurgy, which he blamed in part on the poor nutrition of the workers. Stalin threw the report aside and said to Ordzhonikidze, "Look what a wise guy you've got— he demands more bread for the workers."[5] Such meanness was bound to produce dissatisfaction with Stalin in certain Party circles.

In this connection it is worth examining the case of the "Riutin-Slepkov anti-Party group" and the group of N. B. Eismont, G. G. Tolmachev, and A. P. Smirnov, which was discussed at the meeting of the Central Committee and the Central Control Commission in January, 1933. A resolution was adopted condemning the creation of an underground factional group, allegedly dedicated to the disruption of industrialization and collectivization and the restoration of capitalism, the kulaks in particular. It was therefore resolved to expel Eismont and Tolmachev from the Party, while Smirnov was removed from the Central Committee with a warning that expulsion from the Party would follow if his future work did not merit trust. Tomskii, Rykov, and V. V. Shmidt were publicly warned that they would be subjected to "severe measures of Party punishment" unless they ceased their alleged support of right-wing antiparty elements.[6] Today we know that the chief sin of Smirnov, Eismont, and Tolmachev was a little discussion, among a few people, about replacing Stalin as General Secretary. "Only enemies," Stalin told the Central Committee meeting, "can say that you can remove Stalin and nothing will happen."[7] A few years later, Smirnov, Party member since 1896, onetime Commissar of Agriculture, deputy chairman of the RSFSR Council of People's Commissars, and secretary of the Central Committee, was shot. So was Tolmachev. Eismont had died earlier as the result of an accident.

What happened at the XVIIth Party Congress early in 1934 thus acquires special significance. Officially this Congress was a demonstration of love and devotion to Stalin. But if we put together the scanty reports of old Bolsheviks, the conclusion can be drawn that a considerable number of leading Party members formed an illegal bloc at this Congress, consisting basically of secretaries of *oblast* committees and secretaries of the non-Russian central committees, people who knew the shortcomings of Stalin's policies better than anyone else. The reports say that one of the leaders of this bloc was I. M. Vareikis, and that S. M. Kirov was proposed as General Secretary. At the very beginning of the Congress, or before it, a group of Party officials,

[5] E. G. Veller-Gurevich, "Vospominaniia o Sergo i Gureviche," unpublished manuscript.
[6] *KPSS v rezoliutsiiakh*, II (1953), p. 742.
[7] Quoted in *Vsesoiuznoe soveshchanie istorikov* (Moscow, 1964), p. 291.

including M. D. Orakhelashvili, G. I. Petrovskii, Ordzhonikidze, and Mikoian, had a talk with Kirov, touching on the need to replace Stalin. But Kirov would not agree either to get rid of Stalin or to be elected General Secretary himself. The reports also say that Stalin somehow found out about this discussion.

Dissatisfaction with Stalin was also expressed in the election of the Central Committee by the XVIIth Congress. Stalin received fewer votes than any other candidate. Only three votes were cast against Kirov, while 270 delegates voted against Stalin, who was elected only because there were exactly as many candidates as there were members to be elected. According to V. M. Verkhovykh, who was deputy chairman of the Elections Commission at the XVIIth Congress, the Commission was embarrassed and decided not to announce the results of the voting. The chairman of the Elections Commission, V. P. Zatonskii, called in L. M. Kaganovich, who ran the organizational side of the Congress. Kaganovich ordered the destruction of many ballots on which Stalin's name was crossed out. The Congress was told that only three votes had been cast against Stalin, the same as against Kirov. But Stalin must have known the actual results.

There is a slight reference to these events in *History of the CPSU*, a textbook published in 1962:

> The abnormal situation developing in the Party alarmed some Communists, especially the old Leninist cadres. Many delegates at the Congress, especially those who were familiar with Lenin's testament, thought that the time had come to transfer Stalin from the post of General Secretary to some other job.

It must be noted, however, that Stalin's position was strengthened by a significant change in the membership of the Central Committee. The XVIIth Congress removed many people who were unsuitable to Stalin, and, on the other hand, some top officials of the NKVD (V. A. Balitskii, E. G. Evdokimov) were for the first time elected to the Central Committee. L. Z. Mekhlis was also elected, although he had not even been a delegate at the previous Congress. N. I. Ezhov became a member of the Central Committee and G. G. Iagoda was promoted from candidate to full membership.[8]

Complicated processes continued within the Party leadership after the XVIIth Congress. In 1934 a new type of official, men like Ezhov and Mekhlis, continued to be promoted to key posts. According to M. I. Romm, it was in this period that Kaganovich remarked to a circle of his friends that there would soon be a mass replacement of the leading Party cadres. Stalin also demanded that Kirov, whom the Congress had elected secretary of the Central Committee, move from

[8] *Ed.:* Mekhlis, Ezhov, and Iagoda were notorious administrators of mass terror in the late thirties.

Leningrad to Moscow. Kirov, however, did not want to leave Leningrad, and to support his position a delegation of Leningrad Bolsheviks went to see Stalin, who gave them a very cold reception.

According to Durmashkin, who knew Kirov well, a barely perceptible estrangement between Stalin and Kirov could be sensed in 1934. That summer there was a conference of *obkom* secretaries to discuss the fate of the political sections of the Machine Tractor Stations. Kirov spoke strongly at this conference, proposing the revival of Soviet power in the countryside.[9] Stalin ignored this speech and said nothing about it in his concluding remarks. More than once Durmashkin heard in Leningrad Party circles that Kirov had repeatedly opposed Stalin at Politburo meetings when the latter demanded severe repression of Trotskyites or other former oppositionists. (Stalin allegedly demanded the death penalty for Riutin.) Often Kirov was supported by V. V. Kuibyshev and Ordzhonikidze.

These are fragments of information, but they allow us to conclude that in 1934 the relations between Stalin and the Party's basic cadres were undergoing certain changes. Stalin's usefulness as the Party's leader had long since passed, but some of the eminent members of the Central Committee realized this only toward 1934. Stalin himself must have perceived these changes in the mood of the top leaders, for he had the finest possible sensitivity concerning any decline in his influence.

If it is true that there is no essential difference between Stalin before 1934 and Stalin after 1934, it is also true that this year was in many respects critical in the history of the country and Party, as the tragic events of December, 1934, proved.

2

ON DECEMBER 1, in Smolny, a shot in the back killed S. M. Kirov, a member of the Politburo, and Secretary of the Central Committee, the First Secretary of the Leningrad *oblast* committee. The murder aroused profound grief and anger among the Soviet people. Everyone demanded that the culprits be caught and severely punished. The report of the assassination said that the shot was fired by a young Party member, Leonid Nikolaev, who had been caught while trying to escape. It would seem that this would have made possible a careful investigation. In fact the investigation was carried out in complete violation of the law, of common sense, of the desire to find and punish the real culprits.

[9] *Ed.:* Party organizations, such as the political sections of the MTS, completely dominated organizations such as the village Soviets, the supposed units of state power.

Kirov's assassination was obviously not the work of Nikolaev alone. Peter Chagin, a prominent Party official and close comrade of Kirov, has told the author that several attempts were made on Kirov's life in 1934. It was a real manhunt, directed by a strong hand. For example, there was an attempt during Kirov's trip to Kazakhstan in the summer of 1934.

As for Nikolaev, at first he acted on his own initiative. Psychologically unbalanced, he imagined himself a new Zheliabov,[10] and planned the murder of Kirov as an important political act. (The story that Nikolaev acted from envy was spread around later on, apparently to compromise Kirov or for some other reason.) Kirov liked to walk around Leningrad, and Nikolaev carefully studied the route of these walks. Of course Kirov was carefully guarded; his guards, headed by the NKVD official Borisov, walked before and after him in civilian clothes.

Once the guard's suspicions were aroused by a passerby who tried to get too close. He was detained. This was Nikolaev. His briefcase had a slit in the back, through which a revolver could be taken without opening the briefcase. And a revolver was there, loaded, along with a map of Kirov's route. Nikolaev was at once sent to Leningrad NKVD headquarters, where he was questioned by Deputy Director I. Zaporozhets. (It was subsequently explained that Zaporozhets and other officials of the Leningrad NKVD were active participants in the plot. But the director, F. D. Med'ved', apparently did not take part in the planning of Kirov's assassination.) After questioning Nikolaev, Zaporozhets phoned Moscow and reported everything to Iagoda, then Commissar of Internal Affairs and one of the people Stalin most trusted. A few hours later, Iagoda instructed Zaporozhets to let Nikolaev go. With whom had Iagoda consulted in the meantime? During the trial of the so-called "Right-Trotskyite bloc" in 1938, the defendant Iagoda confirmed the facts given above, but claimed that he got his instructions in 1934 from Avel' Enukidze and Rykov. Nowadays this story is not believed by anyone: Iagoda had far more influential patrons.

When Nikolaev was released, he acted in a very clumsy way, and a few days later, on a bridge, he was again arrested by Kirov's guard. For a second time the same loaded revolver was taken from him. The strange liberalism of the Leningrad NKVD officials, who again let Nikolaev go, aroused serious suspicions among Kirov's guards. Some tried to protest, but they were told at the NKVD that it wasn't their business. Individual guards had their Party cards temporarily taken away and were threatened with expulsion. All this was so

---

[10] Ed.: Zheliabov was one of the populists who assassinated Alexander II in 1881.

suspicious that Borisov decided to tell Kirov that someone was after him and that the armed terrorist Nikolaev, who had been arrested twice by the bodyguards, had once more been released. We do not know what steps Kirov took after the conversation with Borisov. In any case, the conspirators quickly learned of Kirov's conversation with Borisov, and that soon decided Borisov's fate.

In spite of all this, it was Nikolaev who killed Kirov in Smolny on December 1. On the same day, Stalin, Molotov, Voroshilov, Ezhov, Iagoda, Zhdanov, A. V. Kosarev, Ia. D. Agranov, and L. M. Zakovskii came to Leningrad from Moscow. When Med'ved', the head of the Leningrad NKVD, went to welcome Stalin at the Moscow Station in Leningrad, Stalin, without removing his gloves, struck Med'ved' in the face. Right after his arrival, Stalin took complete charge of the investigation, and Nikolaev was brought to him for questioning. What happened can be pieced together from three reports.[11]

Behind a table in a large room sat Stalin, Molotov, Voroshilov, Zhdanov, Kosarev, and several others. In back of them stood a group of Leningrad Party officials and, separately, a group of Chekists. (On the day of Kirov's murder, Zaporozhets was vacationing in the south and could hardly have returned to Leningrad by the following day.) Nikolaev was brought in, held under the arms on both sides. Stalin asked him why he shot Kirov. Falling on his knees and pointing at the group of Chekists standing behind Stalin, Nikolaev shouted, "But they forced me to do it!" Then some Chekists ran to Nikolaev and began to beat him with their pistol butts. Covered with blood and unconscious, he was carried out of the room. Some of those present, including Chudov, believed that Nikolaev was killed at the interrogation; they thought that another person was substituted for Nikolaev in the trial at the end of December. Chudov later told this to Sh——. But Nikolaev was not killed at the interrogation. He was taken to the prison hospital and revived with difficulty, by alternating hot and cold baths.

Borisov was to be interrogated after Nikolaev. Although the arrested men came to the interrogation in automobiles, for some reason Borisov was brought in a closed truck with several Chekists carrying crowbars. One sat beside the driver. On Voinov Street, as the truck was passing the blind wall of a warehouse, the Chekist suddenly jerked the wheel. The driver nevertheless managed to avoid hitting the wall head-on; the truck struck it a glancing blow and then managed to reach the place of the interrogation. But Borisov was dead, killed by the crowbars. The autopsy report drew the false con-

---

[11] They are by Zhdanov's assistant, I. M. Kulagin, who was present at the interrogation of Nikolaev, the above-mentioned P. Chagin, and V. Sh——, a friend of M. S. Chudov, who was the second secretary of the Leningrad *obkom*.

clusion that he had died in the truck accident. Some of the doctors who signed this report were alive after the XXth Party Congress in 1956, and they said that the autopsy report was of course forced, and that Borisov had died from the blows of heavy metal objects on his head.

The strange story of Borisov's death, following his repeated efforts to prevent the assassination of Kirov, was told to the XXIInd Party Congress in 1961 by Khrushchev. He added that the men who killed Borisov were themselves shot, and he promised a careful investigation. Following this revelation and others at the XXth Congress, hundreds of people wrote to the Central Committee, expressing their doubts about the official account of Kirov's assassination, and providing much testimony that sheds new light on the crime. For example, I. P. Aleksakhin, an old Party member, told about his meeting at the Linkovyi mine with Comrade Duboshin, a fellow prisoner who had earlier been head of the Petropavlovsk NKVD. Duboshin told Aleksakhin how, when he was living in the Hotel Selent in Moscow in 1934, an NKVD executive closely connected with the central leadership dropped in on him and said: "A terrible assassination is being planned in Leningrad." At the time Duboshin did not attach any importance to these words, but after Kirov's assassination he said to the same executive: "It appears that some of you knew about the plans for the attempt on Kirov's life." But the other man could give no convincing explanation.

E. P. Frolov, a Party member since 1919, who in 1934 was head of the Machine Building Sector of the Central Committee's Industrial Section, submitted this report: On the morning of December 1, 1934, Ezhov, who was then head of the Industrial Section and was also charged by Stalin with checking up on NKVD activity, went to Stalin's office and spent a good part of the day there. That was unusual; there had not previously been an occasion for Ezhov to spend so many hours with Stalin. Ezhov did not return to the Industrial Section until 7 P.M., when he called one of his assistants, V. Tsesarskii, and ordered him to get ready for an immediate trip to Leningrad.

I. M. Kulagin, Zhdanov's assistant in the Leningrad *obkom*, sent in this report: Several months after Kirov's assassination, Borisov's wife came to the Party headquaters in Smolny. She said that she had been put by force into a madhouse but had managed to escape, and she asked to be taken into custody since "they" wanted to poison her. She also told Kulagin that the NKVD had interrogated her, trying to find out whether her husband had told her anything before Kirov's assassination. She was willing to be transferred into any ordinary hospital. At that time Kulagin could not do this without notifying the Leningrad NKVD. He phoned the Deputy Director and got permission for the woman to be admitted to the city hospital. Some time later Kulagin learned that the woman died in the hospital with indications of poisoning.

M. Smorodina, the daughter of P. I. Smorodin, one of Kirov's chief aides, reported that when Med'ved', the head of the Leningrad NKVD, heard of Kirov's murder, he rushed to Smolny without hat and coat in the middle of the winter. But he was stopped at the entrance by unknown Chekists from the Moscow NKVD, who had somehow appeared at the entrance before him. According to S. N. Osmolovskaia, the wife of Kirov's close friend P. P. Petrovskii, a few days before Kirov's assassination an attempt was made on Petrovskii's life. Two strangers came up to him on the boulevard and began to beat him with iron objects, but he managed to cover his head and escape. When he learned of Kirov's assassination, he immediately declared that it was Stalin's work.

Moreover, soon after Kirov's assassination, Med'ved' and his deputy Zaporozhets were fired from their jobs as heads of the Leningrad NKVD, on the charge of criminal negligence. But they were given light punishment at first; they were sent to work for the NKVD in the Far East. Only in 1937 were they shot. "It is possible," as Khrushchev told the XXth Party Congress, "that they were later shot to cover up all the traces of the organizers of Kirov's assassination."

The following sequence of events is also noteworthy. On the evening of December 1, 1934, at Stalin's suggestion and without the approval of the Politburo—that was formally established by a referendum only two days later—the secretary of the Presidium of the USSR's Central Executive Committee, Enukidze, signed the decree that would serve as the basis for a great deal of repression:

(1) Investigating authorities are to speed up their work on cases of those accused of preparing or carrying out terrorist acts.

(2) Judicial authorities are not to postpone the execution of sentences of capital punishment because of appeals for clemency by criminals of this category, since the Presidium of the USSR's Central Executive Committee does not consider it possible to consider such appeals.

(3) The agencies of the NKVD are to execute sentences of capital punishment on criminals of the above-mentioned category immediately after such sentences have been issued.[12]

This decree, unprecedented in peacetime, specified that the entire investigation of such cases be concluded in not more than ten days, and that the indictment be handed over to the accused only one day before the trial. Moreover, the trial was to be conducted without con-

[12] *Ed.:* Khrushchev quoted this decree in his speech to the XXth Congress.

testing parties, that is, without defense lawyers. Thus any decision of
the court was immediately regarded as correct and was not subject to
any kind of review. The decree gave the widest scope to lawlessness,
since any "political case" could be represented as preparation for a
terrorist act. Also, the ten-day limit encouraged superficial examination
and outright fabrications. It obstructed the determination of the guilt
or the innocence of suspects as well as the discovery of all those really
involved in a crime.

On the basis of this decree, dozens of cases of counterrevolutionary crimes, which were in no way connected with Kirov's murder
but happened to be at various stages of investigation on December 1,
were quickly transferred to the Military Collegium of the Supreme
Court and just as quickly decided there. On December 5, in closed
session, the Military Collegium sentenced almost all the accused to be
shot. They were shot at once. This was reported the following day,
which was the day of Kirov's funeral. In Leningrad thirty-nine people
were shot this way, in Moscow twenty-nine. During the next few days
twelve people were reported arrested in Minsk, nine of whom were
shot, and thirty-seven in Kiev, twenty-eight of whom were shot. It
was also reported that the Military Collegium remanded some cases
for further investigation, which demonstrates the juridical absurdity of
the order to speed up investigations.[13]

The investigation of Kirov's assassination was also carried out with
unusual haste. On December 22 a report said that Nikolaev belonged
to an underground terrorist organization set up by members of the
former Zinovievite opposition, who killed Kirov on the order of the
"Leningrad Opposition Center" in revenge for Kirov's struggle against
the opposition. The same report named the members of the "Leningrad Center" who were arrested by the NKVD. Most of them had
been members of the Zinovievite opposition. On December 27, the
indictment of the "Leningrad Center" was published, signed by the
Procurator of the USSR, A. Ia. Vyshinskii, and by the investigator for
especially important cases, L. Sheinin. The indictment asserted that
Kirov's murder was part of a long-range plan for the murder of Stalin
and other Party leaders. Two conspiratorial terrorist groups had
allegedly been discovered: one led by Shatskii, the other by I. I.
Kotolnyov, who ordered Nikolaev to kill Kirov. The murderer was
said to have received five thousand rubles from a foreign consul, who

---

[13] Among those arrested in the Ukraine were A. V. Krushelenitskii and his two sons,
Ivan and Taras. The sons were shot. The father was no counterrevolutionary but a
progressive Ukrainian writer, who died in prison in November, 1941, and was
rehabilitated after the XXth Party Congress. (See *Kratkaia literaturnaia entsiklo-
pedia*, III.) In the same list of Kievan counterrevolutionaries was the name of the
Ukrainian writer V. A. Masyk, whose unhappy fate is told in *Literaturnaia gazeta*,
1967, No. 33.

connected the conspirators with Trotsky. (At the end of 1934, the Consul General of Latvia, George Bissenieks, was expelled from the USSR, though the Latvian government categorically denied his participation in the assassination of Kirov.)

It is obvious from the indictment that only Nikolaev and two of his friends, who had not been Zinovievites, had confessed to Kirov's murder. The rest of the accused confessed only to participation in a Zinovievite group. Not one of them named Nikolaev as a member of the Zinovievite "Center." The only proof that the Zinovievites were involved in Kirov's assassination, and that Nikolaev was a member of their group, was the deposition of Nikolaev himself, which contradicted the other defendants' testimony and all the other evidence as well. The material evidence—addresses, various notes, Nikolaev's diary—did not confirm the existence of the "Leningrad Center." But this fact was brushed aside; the indictment declared that all the papers and notes found on Nikolaev were fabrications designed for "camouflage."

This indictment, riddled with contradictions, was the only document published in the case. Neither the text of the verdict, nor the depositions of the accused, nor their final speeches were ever published. There were no speeches for the prosecution or for the defense, because the case was tried without prosecuting and defense attorneys and also without the right to appeal or the right to petition for clemency. According to the military jurist A. B———, who attended the trial, Nikolaev behaved quite differently than during his interrogation by Stalin. He confessed to premeditated murder of Kirov on instructions from the "Leningrad Center," and named the members of the "Center." But most of the other defendants did not confess, and many claimed they had never seen Nikolaev before. All received the death sentence and were shot immediately. The papers reported the executions on December 30.

There is also important testimony of Katsafa, a former NKVD agent, who was one of the constant guards in Nikolaev's cell (it was feared that he might commit suicide). Nikolaev told Katsafa how the assassination had been arranged, and how he had been promised his life if he implicated the Leningrad Zinovievites. He asked Katsafa whether he would be deceived. When his sentence was read out, he began to shout and struggled with the guards.

At the very beginning of the investigation, Stalin asked the Leningrad NKVD for a thorough report on the former Zinovievites. There was in fact a small illegal group of Zinovievites in the city. The NKVD knew the members and had even asked Kirov to authorize their arrest. But Kirov had refused, since he believed that former oppositionists should not be repressed but won over ideologically. The list of the Leningrad Zinovievites, together with Kirov's decision, had been put in NKVD files. Now the list was brought to Stalin. From it, and from a list of Moscow Zinovievites, Stalin himself put together the "Moscow Center" and the "Leningrad Center." The roll, written in Stalin's own hand, is still preserved in his papers. (At least it was there in the years immediately following the XXth Party Congress, when a photocopy was made and submitted to handwriting experts.) Stalin shuffled some of the names from the "Moscow Center" to the "Leningrad Center," and vice versa. Everyone on his list was arrested.

The section of the decree in which the Central Executive Committee ordered a speed-up of investigations was a dead letter following the Kirov case; in most subsequent "political cases" the investigation dragged on for months. But in the Kirov case it was important for Stalin to achieve the swiftest judicial vengeance, in order to hide all the inconvenient evidence. The other points in the "Law of December," however, were actively used by the authorities. The charge of terrorist activity was a favorite in 1937–38, since it permitted all legal restrictions to be disregarded in the investigation and trial.

Immediately after the assassination, meetings were held in every enterprise and office throughout the country. In Moscow, Zinoviev, then a member of the administration of the Central Trade Union Council, spoke at the Council meeting that denounced the vicious murder. On the evening of December 1, the head of the Central Milk Board, G. E. Evdokimov, spoke at the meeting of his organization. But a few days later Zinoviev, Evdokimov, Kamenev, and many other leaders of the former Zinovievite opposition were arrested. In January, 1935, following a brief investigation, the first political trial of former opposition leaders was held. On the bench for the accused sat G. E. Zinoviev, L. B. Kamenev, G. E. Evdokimov, A. M. Gertik, I. P. Bakaev, A. S. Kuklin, Ia. V. Sharov, B. L. Bravo, S. M. Gessen, and ten others, nineteen people in all. During the unusually brief trial, meetings were held throughout the country, demanding that all the accused be shot. But the investigators in this case apparently had not used "unlawful methods"—torture, in plain English—and thus were not able to "prove" the direct responsibility of the "Moscow Center" in the assassination of Kirov. To quote the verdict of the court: "The investigation did not establish facts that would provide a basis for describing the crimes of the Zinovievites as instigation of the assassination of S. M. Kirov." Therefore Zinoviev's sentence was "only" ten years in prison, and Kamenev's five. The other defendants received similar punishment.

At the same time a special assembly in the NKVD (*Osoboe soveshchanie pri NKVD*), without any legal judicial proceedings, sentenced a large group of once prominent Party members to two to five years for belonging to the Leningrad and Moscow "Centers." These included I. K. Naumov, P. A. Zalutskii, I. V. Vardin-Mgeladze, A. P. Kostina, V. S. Bulakh, A. I. Aleksandrov, and I. I. Zelikson. On January 18, 1935, a confidential letter from the Central Committee was sent to all Party organizations, demanding the mobilization of all forces to destroy enemy elements and to root out counterrevolutionary nests of enemies of the Party and the people. Every *oblast,* Leningrad especially, was swept by the first wave of mass arrests, which was later called the "Kirov flood" in the camps. Simultaneously former noblemen and their families were deported en masse from Leningrad, although the vast majority of them had not carried on any underground anti-Soviet activity.

Zinoviev and the Zinovievites are no longer accused of the murder of Kirov. The 1962 textbook of Party history had this to say:

> The murderer, arrested at the scene of the crime, was filled with enmity and hatred for the Party and its leaders. . . . An embittered outcast who had earlier got himself expelled from the Party, he hid behind a Party card and committed this vicious crime. This was a premeditated crime, the circumstances of which, as N. S. Khrushchev reported to the XXIInd Party Congress, are still being clarified.

No mention is made of any underground Leningrad and Moscow "Centers," or of the murder of Kirov, in the short biographies of Zinoviev and Kamenev that have appeared in the new edition of Lenin's works, although all their major oppositional activity is described in considerable detail.

In 1934, however, Stalin's story that Zinoviev and his supporters were the organizers of Kirov's murder seemed plausible. Everyone knew that in 1926 Kirov had succeeded the Zinovievite G. E. Evdokimov as leader of the Leningrad Party organization. It is therefore not surprising that right after the murder the thoughts of many people turned towards the former "Leningrad" or "new" opposition. But it is just this obvious plausibility that obliges us to have doubts about Stalin's story. The Zinovievite opposition would have gained no political benefit from the murder of the man who was at that time the most popular Party leader after Stalin. On the contrary, the character of the investigation directed by Stalin and the chain of subsequent events makes it plausible to assume that Kirov was killed with Stalin's knowledge. Kirov had been Stalin's friend a long time, but personal friendship meant little to Stalin when his political goals were involved.

The portrait of Kirov should not be gilded. He had many characteristics of Stalin's entourage, and many reprehensible events of the late twenties could not have occurred without his participation. Still, as an individual, Kirov was in many ways different from Stalin. His simplicity and accessibility, his closeness to the masses, his tremendous energy, his oratorical talent, and excellent theoretical training —all this made Kirov a Party favorite. His influence was steadily growing, and in 1934 his authority in the Party was without doubt second only to Stalin's. When the question arose that year, in connection with Stalin's illness, of his possible successor as General Secretary, the Politburo expressed its support of Kirov.

Nasty, suspicious, cruel, and power-hungry, Stalin could not abide brilliant and independent people around him. Kirov's growing popularity and influence could not fail to arouse Stalin's envy and suspicion. Kirov's great authority among Communists and his reluctance to go along with Stalin unquestioningly served to impede the realization of Stalin's ambitious plans. It can therefore be said with assurance that Stalin had no regrets at Kirov's death. Moreover, it gave him a desired pretext for reprisals against everyone obstructing his road to power. Kirov's assassination was an important link in the chain of events leading to Stalin's usurpation of all power in the country. That is why Stalin's guilt in the assassination, which would have seemed improbable in 1934–35, nowadays appears plausible and, logically and politically, almost proved. On the other hand, Zinoviev's and Kamenev's guilt, which seemed reasonable in 1934–35, today appears quite unlikely.

3

POLITICAL TENSION steadily increased after the trial of the former Zinovievites. In every Party organization there was a campaign for "confessions" and "repentance." "Big, packed halls were turned into confessionals," wrote E. S. Ginzburg in her memoirs.

> Although the remission of sins was granted very stingily (on the contrary the confessions were most often judged "inadequate"), the flood of "repentance" spread every day. Every meeting had its soupe du jour. People repented for incorrect understanding of the theory of permanent revolution and for abstention in the vote on the opposition platform of 1923; for an "eruption" of great-power chauvinism and for undervaluation of the second Five-Year Plan; for acquaintance with certain "sinners" and for infatuation with Meyerhold's theater.

In every *oblast,* during 1935 and the first half of 1936, hundreds of people were arrested, both former oppositionists and Communists who had never belonged to any opposition. At the same time, many people were expelled from the Party "for a connection with hostile elements" or "for lack of vigilance." But these arrests and expulsions as a rule still had a "selective" rather than a mass character. Most of the former oppositionists remained free and even held responsible positions in the commissariats, in publishing, and in educational institutions. Articles by Radek, Piatakov, Bukharin, and others appeared almost daily in the central papers and magazines. The higher circles were as yet scarcely touched by repression. But some middle-level Party officials were arrested, such as P. I. Shabalkin, a member of the Buro of the Far Eastern *kraikom,* and V. V. D'iakov, a leader of the Volga-Don enterprise. At the beginning of 1935, V. I. Nevskii was arrested. A prominent historian of the Party, who had once been a leader of the Central Committee's Military Organization, he was the director of the Lenin Library at the time of his arrest. M. A. Solntseva testifies that he refused to discard a significant part of the Library's holdings in political literature, despite a written order from Stalin. "I am not running a baggage room," Nevskii declared. "The Party directed me to preserve all this."

Only one member of the Central Committee seems to have suffered: Avel' Enukidze, the secretary of the Central Executive Committee of the USSR. He was expelled from the Party but was not arrested at that time. Formerly one of Stalin's closest friends, he was accused of loss of vigilance and of moral corruption (these charges have now been rescinded). Although several people spoke against him at the Central Committee meeting that examined his case, Enukidze neither repented nor argued back. Slanderous attacks on V. V. Lominadze, then secretary of the Party Committee in Magnitogorsk, resulted in his death. Stalin had begun to circulate copies of NKVD interrogations to all Politburo members and other important Party officials. One of them contained Kamenev's testimony about a conversation he had had with Lominadze during a summer vacation. This decided the man's fate. At a reception for metalworkers in the Kremlin, Stalin acted as if he did not recognize Lominadze. Soon after his return to Magnitogorsk, Lominadze was summoned to Cheliabinsk. He shot himself in an automobile on the way.

In 1936, the right to carry weapons was taken away from Communist Party members. Preparing for mass terror against the Party, Stalin feared some kind of active response.

The intensification of arbitrary rule and repression was accompanied by the intensification of the Stalin cult. Newspapers and magazines carried pictures of Stalin, greetings to Stalin, articles dedicated to Stalin, and speeches addressed to him. Everyone seemed in competition to say the most glowing things about the merits of the "great chief," and to avow their love and devotion to him.

The progress of socialist construction in 1935–36 was in fact considerable, and the economic situation improved noticeably. In

1934 gross industrial output rose by 19 per cent, in 1935 by 23 per cent, and in 1936 by 29 per cent. After several years of stagnation, agricultural production also began to increase: in 1935 gross agricultural output was 18 per cent higher than in 1933. Rationing was ended, and collective farms were permitted to sell grain on the open market, which stimulated the farmers' interest in increasing grain production. (The system of grain procurements did not create such a stimulus because of the low procurement prices.) Prices began to drop. The acute food crisis of the early thirties was apparently over. The standard of living, both urban and rural, rose appreciably. Life really did become "more joyful,"[14] and this atmosphere engendered a certain enthusiasm. But the way this enthusiasm poured out, as perverted adulation of Stalin, reveals political calculation. Stalin himself assiduously promoted his own cult, as did the politicians closest to him.

The repression of 1935–36 met with no significant opposition. Although Communists were greatly disturbed, there was no organized protest. Stalin's hands were untied once and for all, and in 1936 he proceeded to the next stage of his plans for the usurpation of power—new provocations, directed against his former political and personal opponents and against the Party as a whole.

4

ON AUGUST 25, 1936, the newspapers published a report by the Procurator of the USSR concerning a new investigation into the Kirov assassination.[15] Many of the accused were going on trial for the second time. The report said that the accused had fully confessed not only to Kirov's murder but also to the organization of terrorist acts against Stalin, Voroshilov, Zhdanov, Kosior, Ordzhonikidze, and Postyshev, and to the creation in 1932 of a "Trotskyite-Zinovievite United Center."

In the new court proceedings of August, 1936, there were no more denials of guilt. On the contrary, Zinoviev, Kamenev, and the other defendants willingly and smoothly told about their roles in the assassination of Kirov and about their plans to kill Stalin, Molotov, Chubar', Postyshev, Kosior, and Eikhe. (As things turned out, the last four were murdered without any help from the Zinovievites; they were shot two years later on Stalin's orders.) Zinoviev said that Stalin was to have been killed during the VIIth Congress of the Comintern,

[14] *Ed.:* Medvedev is quoting a famous slogan of the time.
[15] The following people were accused of responsibility: Zinoviev, Kamenev, Evdokimov, I. N. Smirnov, I. P. Bakaev, V. A. Ter-Vaganian, S. D. Mrachkovskii, E. A. Dreitser, E. S. Gol'tsman, I. I. Reingol'd, and a number of other ex-oppositionists.

in order to move Communists throughout the world to support Trotsky, and to shake up the Central Committee of the CPSU so badly that it would have to start negotiations with Trotsky, Zinoviev, and Kamenev and invite them to take over the leadership. Only one of the accused, I. N. Smirnov, the alleged leader of all the Trotskyites in the Soviet Union, tried to refute the charges. He was, however, "exposed" by the testimony of other defendants—Mrachkovskii, Ter-Vaganian, Evdokimov, Kamenev.

The trial of the "United Center" was open but violated the most elementary rules of judicial procedure. No material evidence or documentary proof of the guilt of the accused was presented to the court. The entire case rested on the contradictory "depositions" and "confessions" of the accused. Moreover, they were deprived of the right to defense counsel; a number of foreign lawyers offered to defend them but were rejected. The trial was brief, the testimony of the accused uniform. Basically it consisted of the enumeration of various monstrous crimes or, more often, the plans for such crimes, prepared both by the "Center" and by its individual members.

Today the falsity of such "depositions" is quite blatant. It is easy to imagine what sort of methods were used to make the defendants deliver such accusations against themselves. But in 1936 the Party and the people still trusted Stalin, the NKVD, and the Soviet courts. So the vast majority of the Soviet people believed the testimony of the accused and approved the sentences they received. It is hard to imagine that many former oppositionists who were still at large could share this faith in the truth of Zinoviev's and Kamenev's testimony. But these people were terrified by the avalanche of anger that was sweeping over the country, intensified by mass propaganda; they rushed into print with disavowals of Zinoviev and Kamenev and renewed confessions of their former errors.

A letter in *Pravda,* under the title "There Should Be No Mercy," is typical. Its author was Khristian Rakovskii, formerly one of Trotsky's leading supporters, who had defended Trotsky and his program even when most of the Trotskyites had abandoned their former leader. Rakovskii had repented and confessed his "mistakes" only after the XVIIth Party Congress in 1934. Now he wrote that a feeling of limitless, ardent sympathy for the leader and teacher of the masses, Comrade Stalin, and a feeling of burning shame for his past association with the opposition, led him to demand that these rotten agents of the German Gestapo be shot.[16] This letter did not save Rakovskii; he was soon arrested and in 1938 appeared in the same kind of "open trial."

The press carried dozens of such letters in August, 1936. Out on

[16] *Pravda,* Aug. 21, 1936.

the Pacific Coast Movsevov, who had signed the "Declaration of the
83" in 1927 but had since broken with the Trotskyites and was now
in charge of a construction project, wrote to his local journal:

> As the legitimate son of my Party, though expelled from it, and a
> devoted son of my socialist native land, I not only join my voice to
> the massed millions of our socialist fatherland calling for physical
> vengeance on the Zinovievite-Trotskyite gang; I declare my Bol-
> shevik readiness to be the person who executes the sentence of the
> Military Tribunal. I assure you, comrades, that I am made of impla-
> cable Leninist-Stalinist stuff.[17]

The trial, and the shooting of the accused, engendered a new wave
of repression throughout the country. First to be arrested were former
Trotskyites and Zinovievites, and also many people whom the NKVD
suspected of connections with these "enemies of the people." The
papers were crammed with exposés of concealed Trotskyites, although
many of them had never dreamed of hiding themselves or their past.
Hundreds of articles appeared with such headlines as: "A Secret
Trotskyite," "Protectors of Trotskyites," "Trotskyites on the Ideological Front," "Trotskyite Subversion in Scholarship," "The Trotskyite
Salon of the Writer Serebriakova," "Clues to Trotskyites in the
Uzbekistan Commissariat of Agriculture."

Some of the defendants in the trial of the "Trotskyite-Zinovievite
United Center" unexpectedly, in addition to their pretrial depositions,
began to talk about their "criminal" connections with Bukharin,
Rykov, and Tomskii, and also with Radek, Piatakov, Sokol'nikov,
L. P. Serebriakov, Uglanov, Shliapnikov, and other ex-oppositionists
who had not yet been arrested. On August 21, 1936, the newspapers
carried an order from Procurator Vyshinskii starting a new investigation into the counterrevolutionary conspiracy of the people mentioned.
In offices and factories throughout the country, meetings demanded a
full investigation of "the connections of Bukharin, Rykov, Tomskii,
and others with the despicable terrorists." The same issue of *Izvestiia*
that included this demand in its lead article listed Bukharin as its
editor in chief on the last page.

Radek, who had published an article against Zinoviev and Kamenev on the first day of their trial, was soon arrested, along with
Serebriakov, Sokol'nikov, and many others. Tomskii, according to a
newspaper report, committed suicide. But Bukharin, Rykov, and the
majority of the former "right" oppositionists were still free at the end
of 1936. Moreover, on September 10, the Procurator published his
report: "The investigation has not established a juridical basis for
legal proceedings against N. I. Bukharin and A. I. Rykov, as a result
of which the present case is discontinued." But this was only a respite.

[17] *Tikhookeanskaia Zvezda*, August, 1936.

The discontinuance had of course been sanctioned by Stalin. It was only a maneuver designed to make the best possible preparations for the next stage of repression. Not only did Stalin temporarily "rehabilitate" Bukharin; for some reason he even found it useful to make a false show of favor to him. According to Bukharin's wife, A. M. Larina, on November 7, 1936, Bukharin decided to celebrate the holiday on Red Square; not, as usual, from the top of Lenin's tomb, but in the stands with his wife. He had a pass from *Izvestiia,* which, Larina recalls,

> was for the stands nearest to the tomb. From the tomb Stalin noticed Bukharin, and suddenly I saw a guard making his way through the crowd toward Bukharin. I decided he would tell Nikolai Ivanovich to leave or that he was coming to arrest him, but the guard saluted and said: "Comrade Bukharin, Comrade Stalin asked me to inform you that you are not in the right place and he begs you to go up on the tomb."

The wave of repression that began in the summer of 1936 abated somewhat in the autumn and early winter. An orgy of terror was apparently checked by the nationwide discussion on the new constitution, which guaranteed—in words—the inviolability of the individual and many other democratic rights. Even more important was the mass turnover of personnel in the security organs. Iagoda was no longer useful to Stalin, who suddenly demanded the replacement of this faithful servant, accusing him of insufficient speed in "exposing" enemies of the people. On September 25, 1936, Stalin and Zhdanov sent a telegram from Sochi to Kaganovich, Molotov, and other Politburo members:

> We consider it absolutely necessary and urgent to appoint Comrade Ezhov Commissar of Internal Affairs [NKVD]. Iagoda has obviously proved unequal to the task of exposing the Trotskyite-Zinovievite bloc. *The OGPU was four years late in this matter.* All Party officials and most of the NKVD agents in the *oblasti* are talking about this.

The next day Iagoda was removed from the NKVD and appointed Commissar of Communications. Soon he was removed from that post, too, and arrested.

N. I. Ezhov, the new Commissar of Internal Affairs, was fated to play one of the most shameful and frightful roles in the history of the country, indeed in the history of the world. He had risen relatively quickly as a favorite of Stalin's. At the end of the twenties he was still a little-known *obkom* secretary in Kazakhstan. In 1929 he became Deputy Commissar of Agriculture of the USSR; at the XVIth Party Congress in 1930 he was only a delegate with a consulting vote. That same year he was transferred to work in the Party *apparat* and became chief of the Central Committee's Sections of Assignments and Cadres. Thus he acquired influence in Party circles, by his power to make important assignments and transfers. During this period he won Stalin's favor by unconditional devotion and obedience to the "chief," along with zeal, cruelty, and a mediocre intellect. After the XVIIth Party Congress in 1934, at which Ezhov was elected to the Central Committee for the first time, he moved rapidly to the top. He became a member of the Organizational Buro, deputy chairman of the Commission of Party Control, and head of the Industrial Section of the Central Committee. For unknown services to the international Communist movement he was elected to the Executive Committee of the Comintern. Even during this period Ezhov checked the activity of the NKVD for the Central Committee, taking an active part in the first arrests of Communists. Thus his appointment as Commissar of Internal Affairs was no surprise.

Together with Iagoda, many leading officials of the NKVD were fired and later arrested. But many of Iagoda's protégés continued to serve under Ezhov, who still had a poor grasp of the mechanics of the punitive organs. He was helped to master them by such men as L. M. Zakovskii, S. Redens, and Mikhail Frinovskii.

1937 began with a big political trial.[18] Most of the accused had been prominent activists from prerevolutionary days through the October Revolution and the Civil War. In the mid-twenties almost all of them supported Trotsky, for which they were expelled from the Party. But in the early thirties they had all broken with Trotsky, were readmitted to the Party and given important posts in the commissariats, in publishing, and the like. Now they were accused of belonging to the so-called "Parallel Center," of plotting terrorist acts (including once again the murder of Kirov), of espionage, of trying to provoke a war with fascist Germany and Japan and to bring about a Soviet defeat in this war. They were also accused of trying to restore capitalism in the USSR and, to secure help in this undertaking, of promising the Amur and Pacific Coast regions to Japan, Belorussia to Poland, and the Ukraine to Germany.

The "Trotskyite-Zinovievite United Center" had been tried without defense counsel, but this time some rules of judicial procedure were observed. There were state-appointed defense lawyers, none of whom really tried to defend their clients or even to take an active part in the court proceedings, much less to challenge the findings of the investigating organs. None of the defense lawyers met with their cli-

---

[18] The Military Collegium of the Supreme Court tried Iu. L. Piatakov, K. B. Radek, G. Ia. Sokol'nikov, L. P. Serebriakov, Ia. A. Livshits, N. I. Muralov, Ia. N. Drobnis, M. S. Boguslavskii, I. A. Kniazev, S. A. Rataichek, B. O. Norkin, A. A. Shestov, and others, seventeen people in all.

ents in conditions where the clients were free of pressure, and none gave speeches for the defense that could be distinguished from the speeches for the prosecution. Convinced of the efficiency of the "investigating" machine, the NKVD invited many foreign correspondents and diplomats to the trial. But once again no documents or material evidence were produced. As soon as the procurator declared that certain documents of "the G——n intelligence service" were to be presented to the court, the open session was closed. In plain fact, the only evidence offered at the trial was the depositions of the accused.

What then made the prisoners confess? The indictment tells us that they had long ago lost all shame and conscience, had become hired assassins and diversionists and could hope for no mercy. Almost all of them declared that they had not been tortured or coerced. Procurator Vyshinskii turned to these "murderers, wreckers, traitors, and spies," and prodded them to explain what motivated their sincere confessions. He asked Muralov why, after repeatedly denying his guilt, he had finally decided "to put all his cards on the table." Muralov replied that three motives had made him hold back in the beginning: his hot temper, his attachment to Trotsky, and, "you know, in every cause there are extremists." But then he realized to his horror that he would become the symbol of counterrevolutionaries, of people who opposed what he had fought for in three revolutions. "For me that was decisive, and I said: O.K., I'll go and tell the whole truth."[19]

At this trial, explicit accusations were made against Bukharin and Rykov. Radek, for example, in his first statement said that friendship had long prevented him from implicating Bukharin. He had wanted very much to give his friend the chance to disarm himself by volunteering honest testimony. But when his own trial was about to begin, Radek said, he decided that he could not enter the court still hiding another terrorist organization.[20] He and others offered detailed stories about their counterrevolutionary "connections" with the Bukharin-Rykov group. For some reason neither Radek nor Piatakov nor Muralov was so frank about their "connections" with the military. They said nothing about Tukhachevskii and his colleagues, though later investigations would "establish" that such "connections" were very close. The probable explanation of this discrepancy is that at the beginning of 1937, Stalin had not yet planned Tukhachevskii's arrest.

The testimony of Radek and other members of the "Parallel Center" decided the fate of the former "right" opposition. On January 17, 1937, *Izvestiia* appeared without the signature of its editor in chief, Bukharin. Rykov too was removed from his post. But Stalin still put off arresting them, although they were being universally pro-

[19] *Pravda,* Jan. 27, 1937.
[20] *Izvestiia.* Jan. 30, 1937.

claimed "enemies of the people." Almost every day the testimony of other "rightists," who had been arrested and worked over by the NKVD, were delivered to Bukharin's and Rykov's apartments. This was a sort of psychic torture. According to his relatives, Radek wanted to commit suicide at this time, but his family talked him out of it, arguing that it would be taken as an admission of his guilt. Bukharin protested against the charges made against him by going on a hunger strike in his Kremlin apartment.

The question of Bukharin and Radek was discussed at the February-March meeting of the Central Committee, at which specially selected depositions against them were distributed to the participants. Stalin even invited Bukharin and Radek to attend. Bukharin, still on his hunger strike, came to the first session. Stalin came up to Bukharin and said: "Whom is your hunger strike directed against? The Party's Central Committee? Take a look at yourself, Nikolai; you look completely emaciated. Ask the Plenum's pardon for your hunger strike." "Why should I?" Bukharin replied. "You're getting ready to expel me from the Party in any case." "No one will expel you from the Party," Stalin answered.

Stalin let his closest aides, especially Molotov, take the initiative in the denunciation of Bukharin. When Bukharin declared, "I am not Zinoviev or Kamenev, and I will not tell lies against myself," Molotov replied: "If you don't confess, that will prove you're a fascist hireling. Their press is saying that our trials are provocations. We'll arrest you and you'll confess!" "What a trap!" exclaimed Bukharin, returning home.[21]

Bukharin tried to defend himself by reading to the Central Committee a joint statement in which he and Rykov declared all the depositions against themselves to be slanderous. Such depositions, they argued, proved once again that something was wrong in the NKVD, and that a commission must be appointed to investigate its activities. "Well, we'll send you there, and you can take a look for yourself!" Stalin exclaimed.

The Plenum set up a commission, with A. I. Mikoian as chairman, to decide the fate of Bukharin and Rykov. When the commission met and polled its members alphabetically, everyone up to the letter S —Andreev, Voroshilov,[22] Kaganovich, Kosarev, and many others— responded tersely: "Arrest, try, shoot." When it was Stalin's turn, he said, "Let the NKVD handle the case," and several other people then repeated this formula, which in 1937 meant about the same as the first one. It is worth noting that Mikoian, who called the roll, did not express his own opinion, and it is not recorded in the minutes.

After the commission's decision was reported to the Plenum,

[21] From the memoirs of A. M. Larina, Bukharin's wife.
[22] *Ed.:* V follows B in the Cyrillic alphabet.

Bukharin and Rykov were arrested, in late February, 1937. Stalin, who only a few days before had told Bukharin he would not be expelled from the Party, then gave a speech demanding intensified struggle against "enemies of the people" whatever flag they might fly, Trotskyite or Bukharinite.

The investigation of the "rightists" dragged on for more than a year. The trial, the last open and big political trial of "enemies of the people," did not begin until March, 1938.[23] The accused were an ill-assorted lot. Besides the erstwhile leaders of the "right" deviation, there were men who had never taken part in any opposition and were arbitrarily put into the "rightist" group by Stalin himself following their arrests. There were also former leftists. So it was called the trial of the "Right-Trotskyite Center." In addition to the charges made at the 1936 and 1937 trials, which were now repeated (Kirov's murder, preparations for Stalin's murder, etc.), Bukharin, Rykov, and the others[24] were accused of murdering Gorky, Kuibyshev, and V. R. Menzhinskii, of attempting to kill Lenin in 1918, and of trying to give away not only the Ukraine, Belorussia, and the Far East but also Central Asia and Transcaucasia. The British imperialists were the intended recipients, for the accused had had an espionage connection with them since 1921–22.

At the first session of the court, V. V. Ul'rikh, the presiding judge, read the indictment and asked each of the accused, "Do you admit your guilt?" Bukharin, Rykov, and Iagoda replied, "Yes, I admit it." But when it was Krestinskii's turn, he unexpectedly answered:

> I do not admit my guilt. I am not a Trotskyite. I never took part in the "Right-Trotskyite Bloc," and wasn't aware of its existence. I never committed a single one of the crimes imputed to me, and in particular I do not confess myself guilty of contacts with German intelligence.

Shaken, Ul'rikh repeated the question but received the same firm answer. Then he questioned the other prisoners, who confessed their guilt. After that, a twenty-minute recess was called.

What happened during that recess? The schedule of questioning was certainly changed. It was decided to question Sergei Bessonov first, so that he could expose Krestinskii.[25] But when Vyshinskii asked Krestinskii to confirm some of Bessonov's assertions, Krestinskii again

[23] The Military Collegium of the Supreme Court consisted of V. V. Ul'rikh, president, I. O. Matulevich and B. I. Ievlev, associate judges, and A. A. Batner, secretary. The state prosecutor was A. Ia. Vyshinskii. Defense lawyers were I. D. Braude and N. V. Kommodov.

[24] N. N. Krestinskii, M. A. Chernov, I. A. Zelenskii, G. F. Grin'ko, A. P. Rozengol'ts, Kh. G. Rakovskii, V. I. Ivanov, G. G. Iagoda, Faizul Khodzhaev, Akmal' Ikramov, P. P. Kriuchkov, V. F. Sharangovich, and others.

[25] *Ed.*: Bessonov, as a diplomat in Berlin, was supposed to have been the link with Trotsky.

repudiated the depositions he had made and signed during the preliminary investigation. Vyshinskii made an extended effort to break down this disavowal. Krestinskii stood firm but would not say why he had given false testimony before the trial. He said that he had severed all relations with Trotsky in a letter of November 27, 1927, and he asked that this letter be placed on record. Vyshinskii denied that such a letter existed, and returned to the question why Krestinskii had changed his testimony between the investigation and the trial. Krestinskii said that he was convinced that his protestation of innocence would not reach "the leaders of the Party and the government" unless he saved it for the trial, "if there should be such a trial." Vyshinskii returned to questioning Bessonov and then declared a two-hour recess. The foreign correspondents rushed to telephone their papers the news about Krestinskii's behavior.

At the evening session of March 2, Grin'ko and Chernov were questioned. When they testified about their connections with the fascists, supposedly established through Krestinskii, Vyshinskii again turned to Krestinskii, who again denied any connections with the fascists. At the morning session of March 3, Vyshinskii questioned Ivanov, Bukharin, Zubarev, and Vasil'ev. No questions were directed to Krestinskii. But at the evening session, during the interrogation of Rakovskii, Vyshinskii again turned to Krestinskii and at this point he caved in. He agreed with Rakovskii's accusations against himself and reaffirmed his pretrial depositions.

Why, then, asked Vyshinskii, did you engage in that Trotskyite provocation at yesterday's session? Krestinskii answered that he had been ashamed to tell the truth, and had denied his guilt "mechanically" (*mashinal'no*).

> VYSHINSKII: Mechanically?
> KRESTINSKII: I didn't have the strength to tell world public opinion the truth, that I have all this time been carrying out Trotskyite work against the Soviet regime. I ask the court to record my declaration that I wholly and completely confess myself guilty of all the serious accusations made against me, and I confess myself completely responsible for the betrayal and treason done by me.
> VYSHINSKII: At present I have no more questions for the defendant Krestinskii.[26]

Bukharin's testimony also deserves analysis. He confessed that he: (1) had belonged to the counterrevolutionary "Right-Trotskyite Bloc," (2) had belonged to the counterrevolutionary organization of

[26] See the complete court record: *Sudebnyi otchet po delu antisovetskogo "Pravo-trotskistskogo bloka"* (Moscow, 1938), pp. 49–146. It is significant that the abridged record and the newspapers omitted a good part of the interrogation of Krestinskii. The complete court record was published only in a small edition.

rightists, and (3) had been one of the main leaders of this "Right-Trotskyite Bloc." When questioned about the goals of this organization, Bukharin declared:

Its basic goal, speaking of its essence—although, so to speak, perhaps it was not fully aware of it, did not dot all the i's—was to restore capitalism in the USSR ... by taking advantage of the difficulties that confront the Soviet regime, in particular by taking advantage of the war that was expected.[27]

However, when Vyshinskii and Ul'rikh questioned Bukharin about concrete charges, Bukharin tried to repudiate many of them, though not as sharply as Krestinskii had done. He denied direct participation in any espionage, or in the murders of Kirov, Menzhinskii, Kuibyshev, Gorky, and Maxim Peshkov. He denied that in 1918 the "left Communists" planned to murder Lenin, Stalin, and President Sverdlov.

> VYSHINSKII: That's what you claim, but Iakovleva says just the opposite. Does that mean she is telling a lie?
> BUKHARIN: I don't agree with her, and I say that she is telling a lie.
> VYSHINSKII: And is Mantsev also lying?
> BUKHARIN: Yes, he too is lying. I am telling what I know, and it is up to them, their conscience, to tell what they know.
> VYSHINSKII: But how do you explain the fact that three of your former accomplices are speaking against you?
> BUKHARIN: See here, I don't have enough facts, either material or psychological, to shed light on that question.
> VYSHINSKII: You cannot explain it.
> BUKHARIN: It is not that I cannot, but simply that I refuse to explain it.[28]

In his final words, Bukharin gave a juridical appraisal of the trial. "Confessions of the accused," he said, "are not essential. Confessions of the accused are a medieval juridical principle." And this was said at a trial entirely based upon confessions of the accused. It is not surprising that the "judges" were annoyed with Bukharin. At one point Ul'rikh said to him: "So far you've been beating around the bush, saying nothing about the crimes."[29] Vyshinskii also took note of Bukharin's tactics:

You are obviously using certain tactics and do not want to tell the truth. You are hiding in a stream of words, in pettifoggery, sidetracking into politics, philosophy, theory, and so on. You should forget about these things once and for all. You are accused of

[27] *Ibid.*, p. 332.
[28] *Ibid.*, p. 427.
[29] *Ibid.*, p. 348.

espionage and are obviously, according to all the data of the investigation, a spy for a foreign intelligence agency. So stop the pettifoggery.[30]

The newspapers also referred to Bukharin's special tactics: "He has a system, a tactic," wrote *Izvestiia*; ". . . his aim is to deflect all concrete charges from himself by wholesale declarations of his responsibility for everything.[31]

Today some researchers (e.g., I. A. R——) believe that Bukharin deliberately sought to show the illegality and falsehood of the trial, without coming into open conflict with the procurator. Brigadier Fitzroy Maclean, a British attaché who was a spectator at the trial, expressed the same point of view in his book.[32]

Many Western political leaders could not grasp the true nature of the political repression in 1937–38. For example, the American ambassador to the Soviet Union, Joseph E. Davies, wrote to his daughter that the political trials in the USSR revealed the threads of a conspiracy to overthrow the Soviet regime. Winston Churchill, though a well-informed man, took approximately the same view, because he believed the false information spread in the West by the NKVD. "Through the Soviet Embassy in Prague," Churchill wrote,

> communications were passing between important personages in Russia and the German Government. This was a part of the so-called military and Old-Guard Communist conspiracy to overthrow Stalin and introduce a regime based on a pro-German policy. President Benes lost no time in communicating all he could find out to Stalin. Thereafter there followed the merciless, but perhaps not needless, military and political purge in Soviet Russia, and the series of trials in January, 1937, in which Vyshinskii, the Public Prosecutor, played so masterful a part.[33]

Most of the defendants in the trials of the "Parallel Center" and the "Right-Trotskyite Bloc" were shot. Only a few were given prison terms (Pletnev, Rakovskii, Bessonov, Radek, Arnold, and others), but they too were subsequently killed in one way or another. For example, Bessonov, Sokol'nikov, and N. Osinskii were transferred to Orlov Prison in 1941, after the war had begun, and there, without any trial, they were shot. Not one of the people convicted at the Moscow political trials of 1936–38 was ever freed.

Trotsky was also condemned to death, *in absentia*. A special group was set up within the NKVD to get him. Several attempts were made

---

[30] *Ibid.*, p. 377.

[31] "Shef shpionov," *Izvestiia*, Mar. 9, 1938.

[32] *Ed.:* See Fitzroy Maclean, *Eastern Approaches* (London, 1949).

[33] Winston Churchill, *The Second World War*, I (1948), pp. 288–89. Medvedev quotes the Soviet edition: Churchill, *Vtoraia mirovaia voina*, I, p. 226.

on his life, with some members of foreign Communist parties taking part. Sedov, Trotsky's son, was killed, and so was one of his secretaries. On August 20, 1940, Trotsky himself was murdered in his carefully guarded house near Mexico City. His assassin was a young Spanish Communist and NKVD agent, Ramón Mercader, who won the confidence of Trotsky's guards and associates. Mercader struck Trotsky on the head with a mountain climber's pickax. The murderer was caught and was sentenced by a Mexican court to twenty years in prison, which he served. On Stalin's order, he was awarded the title Hero of the Soviet Union, and his mother, who helped set up the murder, was given the Order of Lenin. The manager of the whole "operation," the NKVD executive Eitingen, was also given the Order of Lenin.

5

THE BRITISH COMMUNIST R. Palme Dutt, in a book published after the XXIInd Congress of the CPSU, writes that "the final verdict on the trials, whose validity is disputed by many living, will rest with future historians."[34] The truth is that all these trials were completely fraudulent. They were a monstrous theatrical presentation that had to be rehearsed many times before it could be shown to spectators.

Only a small part of the testimony of the accused, for example concerning aspects of their past oppositional activity, corresponded to the truth. It is also obvious that Iagoda, the former Commissar for Internal Affairs, did have a definite relationship to the assassination of Kirov, which was not, however, committed on the instructions of Trotsky, Zinoviev, or Bukharin. There is also some truth in the testimony of Krestinskii and Bessonov about their contacts with the German Army. But these contacts did not involve any espionage or treason. Both men had in fact met with representatives of the German Army in 1921—with Lenin's knowledge, in connection with the secret part of the Rapallo agreement between the Soviet and German governments. Stalin, as a Politburo member, must have known about those meetings. In the early twenties the Soviet government was anxious to end its diplomatic and economic isolation. Thus certain agreements with defeated Germany, even on military matters, were advantageous to the USSR. But it was ridiculous, seventeen years later, to represent these international agreements as the work of Krestinskii, Bessonov, and Trotsky. One other charge may have had some basis in fact. According to I. S. Shkapa, Gorky's son Max was murdered ("doctored

[34] Dutt, *The Internationale* (London, 1964), p. 246. Medvedev quotes the Soviet translation: Dutt, *Internatsional* (Moscow, 1966), p. 251.

to death") with the participation of Iagoda, who was acting in this case with certain personal motives.

Most of the depositions were outright lies, deliberately fabricated in the torture chambers of the NKVD and put into the mouths of the accused by sadistic investigators. Today no one charges the former opposition leaders with the murders of Kirov, Gorky, V. V. Kuibyshev, and V. R. Menzhinskii. The complete and unconditional rehabilitation of M. N. Tukhachevskii, I. E. Iakir, Ian Gamarnik, I. P. Uborevich, and other Soviet military leaders reveals the falsity of most of the charges made at the trial of the "Right-Trotskyite Bloc." A basic theme of the testimony at this trial was the defendants' "criminal connection" with the military leaders. Some of the accused "sincerely and frankly" confessed that Iakir in collusion with the "rightists" ordered one of the terrorists to murder Ezhov, while Gamarnik ordered another to kill Stalin. The "rightists" also testified that in 1934 Tukhachevskii and Gamarnik had worked out plans to seize the Kremlin, kill the members of the Central Committee, and arrest the delegates to the XVIIth Party Congress.

V. F. Sharangovich "sincerely" confessed that the leaders of the Belorussian Bolsheviks, Goloded and Cherviakov, were spies for Poland, and that not a single important appointment in Belorussia could be made without the approval of the Polish secret police. Both Goloded and Cherviakov have been completely rehabilitated, along with A. Ikramov, the Party's first secretary in Uzbekistan, and F. Khodzhaev, the Soviet Chairman of Commissars in Uzbekistan, who were trying to hand over Central Asia to the British, if the trial of 1938 can be believed. At the same trial the "rightists" repeatedly named the Bolshevik Ia. E. Rudzutak as their accomplice; he has been posthumously rehabilitated. So has Enukidze, who, Rykov testified, attended the underground meeting of the "Trotskyite-Bukharinite Center" that decided to kill Kirov.

A 1934 attempt on Molotov's life in the town of Prokop'evsk loomed large in the trial of the "Parallel Center." Many of the accused spoke at length about the organization of this attempt and told who had insisted on killing Molotov. We know now, from N. M. Shvernik's speech to the XXIInd Party Congress, that no such attempt ever took place; Molotov made up the whole story for the sake of provocation. A plot to kill Ezhov was a major theme in the trial of the "Right-Trotskyite Center." In his speech of March 11, 1938, Vyshinskii accused the conspirators of planning to poison the air in Ezhov's office by a mixture of mercury and acid. After Ezhov was killed, as an enemy of the people, this fantastic story vanished from all publications, which continued to describe the crimes of the "Right-Trotskyite Bloc."

Vyshinskii's accusation of this crime was simply removed from subsequent printings of his speeches.

After Krestinskii's attempt to repudiate his confession, the newspapers heaped special abuse on him. In 1963 Academician I. M. Maiskii gives us a completely different portrait of Krestinskii: a leading statesman who, together with M. M. Litvinov, G. V. Chicherin, and L. B. Krasin, laid the foundations of a Leninist foreign policy.[35] He receives equally high praise in the *Historical Encyclopedia*.[36] *Pravda,* in 1964, includes the Commissar of Finance, G. F. Grin'ko, and the chairman of the Trade Union Council, I. A. Zelenskii, among the Bolsheviks who directed the great upbuilding during the first Five-Year Plan. In 1938 they were shot for espionage and wrecking, by sentence of the Supreme Court. At his trial Zelenskii was also alleged to have been an agent of the tsarist secret police from 1911. Another such agent—from the time he was in the eighth grade—was V. I. Ivanov, Commissar of Forestry; he too has been fully rehabilitated.[37] So have Gorky's personal secretary P. P. Kriuchkov, accused of murdering Gorky and his son,[38] and V. A. Iakovleva, who read a fraudulent deposition at the trial of the "rightists," written for her by the investigators. According to Party member R. G. Ginzburg, Iakovleva, who had been a Party member since 1904, made a special request to her cellmates before she was shot: let them pass the word, if they should ever escape from confinement, that her depositions were lies that the investigators had forced her to sign. The list of such examples, proving the fraudulence of the political trials of the thirties, could be greatly extended.

By 1968 all the defendants in the Moscow political trials had been rehabilitated as citizens, and seventeen had also been posthumously restored to Party membership. In this way both the indictments and the verdicts in all the trials—the "Trotskyite-Zinovievite," the "Parallel," and the "Right-Trotskyite"—can be considered for all practical purposes quashed.[39] But there has not yet been a formal and public annulment of the verdicts.

Not one of the books on Party history that appeared after the XXth Party Congress mentioned the trials of the thirties. Neither do the 1960 and 1961 textbooks on Party history. The 1962 textbook has two lines on the subject: "The repression of the thirties was begun against former ideological opponents, who were represented as agents

---

[35] "Diplomat leninskoi shkoly," *Izvestiia,* Sept. 27, 1963.

[36] *Sovetskaia istoricheskaia entsiklopediia,* VIII (1966), p. 76.

[37] See the newspaper *Pravda Vostoka,* July 20, 1963.

[38] In the recently published book by I. S. Shkapa, *Sem' let s Gor'kim,* many lines are devoted to Kriuchkov.

[39] See *Vsesoiuznoe soveshchanie istorikov* (Moscow, 1964), p. 298.

of imperialism and foreign intelligence services." A more detailed though rather cautious appraisal was made in 1964 in the preliminary version of the ninth volume of the *History of the USSR,* prepared by the Institute of History of the Academy of Sciences, and circulated among historians for discussion:

> After the murder of Kirov, there were four trials of former members of opposition groups: in January 1935, August 1936, January 1937, and March 1938. Three of these followed open juridical procedure. All the defendants were accused of treason, espionage, diversions, wrecking, preparation of terrorist acts against Stalin and Molotov, the murder of Gorky and others. Analysis of the sources shows that the examination of the matter seriously violated legal norms, even in the open trials. The accusations were based on the confessions of the accused, which is in direct contradiction with the principle of the presumption of innocence. K. B. Radek declared during the trial that the entire trial rested on the depositions of two people— himself and Piatakov—and he asked Vyshinskii ironically how their depositions could be regarded as proof, if they were bandits and spies. "On what can you base your confidence," he asked Vyshin-skii, "that what we have said is the truth, the unshakable truth?" At present it has been established beyond all doubt that most of the testimony given by the Trotskyites and the right deviationists during the trials was unfounded. This raises doubts about the reliability of their testimony as a whole. General Procurator A. Ia. Vyshinskii conducted the trials in crude violation of procedural norms. Thus, when N. N. Krestinskii refused to plead guilty to the charges made against him, Vyshinskii called a recess and renewed the questioning only on the following day. When the questioning was renewed, Krestinskii said that he had mechanically answered "No, not guilty," instead of saying "Yes, guilty." N. I. Bukharin asserted that he had not participated in preparations for murders and diversions, and that the court had no proof for these accusations against him. "What proofs do you have?" he asked, "apart from the depositions of Sharangovich, whose existence I had not even heard of before the indictment?" Touching on this question in his summation, Vyshinskii cynically declared that proof of all the crimes was not required to make an accusation. All the circumstances cited above impel one to draw the conclusion that legality was crudely violated at the time of the trials.[40]

But why, despite such evidence, has there not been a formal annulment of the trials? And why have many of the accused, who were Party members at the time of arrest, not been reinstated? There is no justification for this.

A few days before his arrest, Bukharin wrote a letter "To a

[40] "Istoriia SSSR s drevneishikh vremen," IX, pp. 137 *ff.* Unpublished *maket* (preliminary version, model).

Future Generation of Party Leaders." He asked his wife, A. M. Larina, to memorize this letter. When she returned from confinement, she put it in writing, and in March, 1961, when Bukharin's rehabilitation was being arranged, she sent it to the Committee of Party Control.

I am leaving life. I am lowering my head not before the proletarian ax, which must be merciless but also virginal. I feel my helplessness before a hellish machine, which, probably by the use of medieval methods, has acquired gigantic power, fabricates organized slander, acts boldly and confidently.

Dzerzhinskii is gone; the remarkable traditions of the Cheka have gradually faded into the past, when the revolutionary idea guided all its actions, justified cruelty to enemies, guarded the state against any kind of counterrevolution. That is how the Cheka earned special confidence, special respect, authority and esteem. At present, most of the so-called organs of the NKVD are a degenerate organization of bureaucrats, without ideas, rotten, well-paid, who use the Cheka's bygone authority to cater to Stalin's morbid suspiciousness (I fear to say more) in a scramble for rank and fame, concocting their slimy cases, not realizing that they are at the same time destroying themselves—history does not put up with witnesses of foul deeds.

Any member of the Central Committee, any member of the Party can be rubbed out, turned into a traitor, terrorist, diversionist, spy, by these "wonder-working organs." If Stalin should ever get any doubts about himself, confirmation would instantly follow.

Storm clouds have risen over the Party. My one head, guilty of nothing, will drag down thousands of guiltless heads. For an organization must be created, a Bukharinite organization, which is in reality not only nonexistent now, the seventh year that I have had not a shadow of disagreement with the Party, but was also nonexistent then, in the years of the right opposition. About the secret organizations of Riutin and Uglanov, I knew nothing. I expounded my views, together with Rykov and Tomskii, openly.

I have been in the Party since I was eighteen, and the purpose of my life has always been to fight for the interests of the working class, for the victory of socialism. These days the paper with the sacred name *Pravda* prints the filthiest lie, that I, Nikolai Bukharin, have wished to destroy the triumphs of October, to restore capitalism. That is unexampled insolence, that is a lie that could be equaled in insolence, in irresponsibility to the people, only by such a lie as this: it has been discovered that Nikolai Romanov devoted his whole life to the struggle against capitalism and monarchy, to the struggle for the achievement of a proletarian revolution. If, more than once, I was mistaken about the methods of building socialism, let posterity judge me no more harshly than Vladimir Il'ich did. We were moving toward a single goal for the first time, on a still unblazed trail. Other times, other customs. *Pravda* carried a discussion page, everyone argued, searched for ways and means, quarreled and made up and moved on together.

I appeal to you, a future generation of Party leaders, whose historical mission will include the obligation to take apart the monstrous cloud of crimes that is growing ever huger in these frightful times, taking fire like a flame and suffocating the Party.

I appeal to all Party members! In these days, perhaps the last of my life, I am confident that sooner or later the filter of history will inevitably sweep the filth from my head. I was never a traitor; without hesitation I would have given my life for Lenin's, I loved Kirov, started nothing against Stalin. I ask a new young and honest generation of Party leaders to read my letter at a Party Plenum, to exonerate me, and to reinstate me in the Party.

Know, comrades, that on that banner, which you will be carrying in the victorious march to communism, is also my drop of blood.

                                                    N. BUKHARIN

This letter reveals not only Bukharin's personal tragedy but also his failure, to the very end, to comprehend the frightful meaning of events. Bukharin defends only himself in his letter; he writes nothing about Zinoviev, Kamenev, Piatakov, and the other Party leaders who had already been arrested and shot. He writes that he knew nothing about the existence of Riutin's and Uglanov's secret organizations, but he does not question their existence. Above all, he stresses that he "started nothing against Stalin." But in any case this letter, which has received international publicity, cannot remain unanswered any longer.

After the XXIInd Party Congress, four old Party activists[41] sent the following letter to the Politburo:

Dear Comrades, Members of the Presidium of the Central Committee [i.e., the Politburo]:

We appeal to you on an important matter. The path of the Bolshevik revolutionary N. I. Bukharin, stretching over thirty years, was complex. On that path he committed serious mistakes of a theoretical and political order, for which he caught it from Lenin more than once. But Lenin's criticism of Bukharin's mistakes never questioned his devotion to the Party and the Revolution; that was criticism and arguments with *a man who shared his views on the basic problems of Bolshevism.*

N. Bukharin was noted for his ability to admit his mistakes and correct them without false pride. For that very reason in Lenin's time he was not put out of the Party for his mistakes; he was a member of the Politburo and for twelve years the editor of the central organ, *Pravda.*

In his Testament, giving as it were final characterizations of some Party officials, a stocktaking of the entire past, Lenin called Bu-

[41] E. Stasova, Party member since 1898; V. Karpinskii, member since 1898; P. Katanian, member since 1903; and A. Rudenko, member since 1905.

kharin *the biggest and the most valuable theorist in the Party.*

Bukharin was expelled from the Party and removed from the Central Committee only in 1937, on the basis of testimony given during the "investigation" of his alleged espionage and terrorist activity, the absurdity of which is now clear to everyone. P. Pospelov, a member of the Central Committee, at the All-Union Conference of Historians in December, 1962, declared unequivocally (and this was published in the press) that Bukharin was no terrorist or spy. How then, after such a definite declaration at a gathering of two thousand people and in the press, can one preserve the verdict of the court and the expulsion from the Party in the absence of a corpus delicti?

This discredits the court. And he was condemned and expelled from the Party not for mistakes on the problems of Brest[42] or for disagreements over collectivization.

Annulment of the illegal verdict and reinstatement of Bukharin in the Party will not only be acts to restore justice personally in relation to one of our Party's outstanding leaders of the Leninist period; they will also play a big role in the further elaboration of the Party's history during the relevant periods, which is extremely hampered just now by the forbidden position of Bukharin's name: only bad things can be written about him now, which leads to distortion of these sections of history in general.

We think that restoration of the truth and annulment of decisions based on false documents will raise still higher our Party's authority and our country's prestige.

We, who knew Bukharin personally at many stages of our glorious history, with his shortcomings and his merits as a Bolshevik revolutionary, fully understand and share such warm words of Lenin, spoken by him in the last minutes of his life, as a sort of farewell to the Party, such words about Nikolai Bukharin as the *Testament* does not have concerning any one else: *the rightful favorite of the Party.*

Those words are a great obligation on all of us, and that forces us to turn to you, members of the Party Presidium, with the request not to let the name of a man who was so appreciated by Lenin remain in the camp of traitors, and to rehabilitate Bukharin from the charges made in 1937, by annulling the verdict and reinstating him in the Party.

A man whom Lenin called *the rightful favorite of the Party* cannot remain in the list of traitors and outcasts from the Party.

All four of the old Bolsheviks who signed this letter have died, and their appeal remains unanswered.

It is *ridiculous* for Soviet historical scholarship to keep its notorious mask of silence, to pretend that there were no political trials in

---

[42] *Ed.:* A reference to the Treaty of Brest-Litovsk in 1918, which Bukharin opposed.

the mid-thirties; that Trotsky, Bukharin, Rykov, Tomskii, Piatakov, Kamenev, and Zinoviev were not outstanding leaders; that they never worked under Lenin; that they did not, despite their mistakes, do great and useful work in our Party. It is ridiculous that their names are not to be found even in encyclopedias and handbooks published today, or, if they must be included in the index to Lenin's works or the record of a Party congress, they are followed by a careful list of only sins, blunders, and mistakes.

Another crucial question arises: What methods did Ezhov and Iagoda use to get "depositions" and "confessions" from the prisoners, many of whom had formerly been tough revolutionaries? It has been said that Bukharin, Kamenev, Rakovskii, and the others did not really appear in court; skillfully made-up and specially trained NKVD agents supposedly took their place. But some who attended the trials, including E. A. Gnedin and I. G. Ehrenburg, have rejected this supposition.

Ilya Ehrenburg, who was present at the trial of the "rightists," expressed his confidence, in a conversation with the author, that it really was Bukharin, Rykov, Krestinskii, Rozengol'ts, and Rakovskii who sat on the defendants' bench. Ehrenburg did notice, however, their general inertia and sluggishness. They gave their testimony in a kind of mechanical language, without the intonation and temperament peculiar to each of them. Although each one used some of his stylistic peculiarities, for the most part they used the language of an average office clerk, with turns of speech that they had never employed previously. At the same time they did not give the impression of people who had been recently subjected to prolonged torture. Ehrenburg said that he thought many of the prisoners had been given some kind of drug that takes away one's will (*obezvolivaiushchii preparat*). The suggestion merits consideration. There are medicines that can temporarily transform an energetic and resolute man into an obedient puppet.

S. I. Berdichevskaia, a Party member since 1919, relates the testimony of a woman doctor from the Lefortovskaia Prison. She had known her during the Civil War, and met her again at a transit prison during her years of confinement. On the second day of the rightists' trial this doctor had seen N. N. Krestinskii in Lefortovskaia Prison savagely beaten and covered with blood. Berdichevskaia therefore suggests that Krestinskii himself appeared in court for the first session, but that in subsequent sessions a double took his place. E. A. Gnedin, who worked for the Commissariat of Foreign Affairs at the same trial, considers such a conjecture quite possible. And K. Ikramov tells of a man he met in camp who knew Krestinskii quite well before 1937 and then saw him at the trial. He told Ikramov: "You know, Kamil, they must have done something awful to Krestinskii, because I simply didn't recognize him on the second day. Even his voice was somehow different." Today some comrades say the investigators may have used hypnosis and suggestion, and it is worth noting that a well-known hypnotist, Arnoldo, disappeared in the mid-thirties.

Some foreign authors have suggested that effective ideological and psychological techniques were used on the defendants before the trials. For example, the historian François Fejto argues that the accused in such trials cooperate in their own destruction, because of their abiding faith in Stalinism as a form of Marxism-Leninism. They agree that the cause must be subject to strict discipline, in other words to the will of the leaders. Thus, in a time of savage class struggle, the very fact that the leaders accuse them proves that "objectively" (or subconsciously, as people say in the West) they have indeed become allies of enemy forces. The only service they can still do for the cause is to strengthen the Party's unity by condemning themselves.[43] Arthur Koestler gives the same interpretation in his novel *Darkness at Noon*.

There is evidently some portion of truth in each of the above conjectures. Various methods of "working over" the accused were used in preparation for the trials of 1936–38, as in 1930–31. However, we have evidence that the main instrument of the investigators was the most refined torture, which broke the prisoners' wills and made them sign any story of their "crimes" prepared beforehand by the investigators. N. K. Iliukhov tells how in 1938 he shared a cell in Butyrskaia Prison with Bessonov, who had received a long prison term in the trial of the "rightists." Bessonov told Iliukhov, who had been his colleague at the Institute of Red Professorship, how he had been subjected to long and painful torture before his trial. To begin with he was kept on the "conveyor" for seventeen days without food or sleep. He would fall down and pass out, but they would bring him to and force him again and again to stand up. Then he was methodically beaten, especially on the kidneys, until this once healthy and strong man became emaciated.

Some of the accused were subjected to even more vicious torture. It is said that Bukharin began to "testify" only after the investigators threatened to kill his wife and newborn son, while Krestinskii signed the record of the investigation when his wife and daughter were similarly threatened. The defendants were warned that the tortures would be continued even after the trial if they did not give the necessary testimony. Many were promised their lives, and assignment to Party or Soviet work in the North or the Far East. They were persuaded that their testimony was needed at the time in connection with the complex international situation, and that they would be rehabili-

---

[43] Medvedev quotes Fejto, *La tragédie hongroise* (Paris, 1956), p. 90, from the Russian translation: *Vengerskaia tragediia* (Moscow, 1957), p. 55.

tated later. Ia. N. Drobnis's wife states that such a promise was made to her husband during the preparations for the trial of the "Parallel Center." He managed to send word of this promise to his family, asking them "not to worry." Some people say that Radek gave in to such promises, and voluntarily cooperated with the interrogators in preparing the basic story of the indictment. None of these promises was kept.

6

ON MARCH 5, 1937, Stalin told the Central Committee that only active Trotskyites still loyal to their exiled leader had to be repressed. "Among our comrades," he said, "are a certain number of former Trotskyites, who abandoned Trotskyism a long time ago and are fighting against it. It would be stupid to defame these comrades." Following the publication of this speech, some local NKVD agencies began to scale down the repression. But soon they received appropriate explanations of Stalin's speech, and mass repression revived with new intensity. In fact, by the end of 1937 almost all the ex-oppositionists had been arrested, regardless of the views they held at the time.

The fate of V. A. Antonov-Ovseenko is revealing. As a member of the Military-Revolutionary Committee and leader in storming the Winter Palace, he had arrested the Provisional Government. Later this legendary hero of the October Revolution commanded armies and entire fronts in the Civil War. In 1923–27 he belonged to the Trotsky-ite opposition, but then he completely broke with Trotsky. He was given responsible military and political work once again, winding up in Spain in 1936–37. In August, 1937, he was recalled to Moscow and for a month was without a job. In September, Stalin summoned him to the Kremlin for a talk about Spanish affairs.[44] After this conversation Antonov-Ovseenko was appointed Commissar of Justice of the RSFSR; that is, he was put in charge of law enforcement. Only a few weeks later, he was suddenly arrested and quickly shot.[45]

A similar fate befell the revolutionary E. Eshba, who had actively participated in the Revolution and Civil War in the Caucasus, leading the uprising in Abkhazia in 1921. In 1926 he belonged to the Trotsky-ite opposition, but soon left it and, having admitted his mistakes, was readmitted to the Party. Later, at responsible posts in the Commissariats of Foreign Trade and of Heavy Industry, he did much for the construction of socialism. But in 1937 Eshba was arrested on the

[44] See the pamphlet of A. V. Rakitin, *Imenem revoliutsii* (Moscow, 1965).
[45] Iu. Tomskii has described the courageous behavior of this hero of October during the interrogation and before his execution. See *Novyi mir,* November, 1964.

charge of Trotskyite activity and perished.[46] Both Antonov-Ovseenko and Eshba have been rehabilitated, as has the popular literary critic A. K. Voronskii. One of the old-time Leninists, Voronskii belonged to the Trotskyite opposition from 1925 to 1928 but then broke with it.

The man who held Party card Number 1 in Petersburg, G. F. Fedorov, suffered the same fate. A self-taught worker who was elected to the Central Committee at the April Conference of 1917 and took an active part in the October insurrection, he had become in the mid-thirties director of the All-Union Cartographic Trust. In 1967 *Izvestiia* devoted a large article to Fedorov, which failed to note that he was shot in 1937.[47]

The NKVD also struck at former members of earlier and smaller oppositions, for example, the short-lived "Democratic Centralist" group of 1920–21. N. Osinskii, director of the Central Statistical Agency, I. Stukov, and I. K. Dashkovskii were among its former adherents arrested in 1937. The "Workers' Opposition" of 1920–22 contributed its share of victims, including E. Ignatov, A. G. Shliapnikov, and A. S. Kiselev. Kiselev had been a Party member since 1898; from 1924 to 1938 he was the secretary of the Soviet government's Central Executive Committee. This long record could not atone for his brief adherence to the "Workers' Opposition" in the early twenties; he was arrested and shot. The same fatal flaw was in the record of N. A. Kubiak, secretary of the Party's Central Committee, Commissar of Agriculture, and chairman of the Central Executive Committee's Council on City Management. Most of the "Syrtsov-Lominadze" group also perished. In the union republics there was mass repression of Party members who had at some time been accused of "national deviationism," the Georgian Budu Mdivani, for example. Many thousands of Party members who had long ago ceased opposition activity were suddenly arrested and destroyed. (In emphasizing their cessation of political opposition, we have of course no wish to imply that oppositional activity is a criminal offense.)

At the same time that the NKVD was arresting and destroying former members of opposition groups within the Bolshevik Party, it was doing no less to the Party's defunct rivals. Socialist Revolutionaries, Mensheviks, Bundists, anarchists, and Cadets who had chosen to quit their parties and stay in the Soviet Union were now punished for their choice. These former opponents of the Bolsheviks had varied records. Some, arrested during the Civil War and subsequently released, had completely abandoned all political activity—for example. B. Kamkov, A. Gots, and M. A. Spiridonova. Many had broken with their parties during the Civil War to fight on the Soviet side, and some

---

[46] See the newspaper *Zaria Vostoka*, Mar. 20, 1968, *inter alia*.
[47] L. Shinkarev, "Mandat Revoliutsii," *Izvestiia*, Apr. 6, 1967.

of these subsequently held important posts in the Soviet state and the Bolshevik Party—for example B. F. Malkin, G. Zaks, A. P. Kolegaev, F. Iu. Svetlov, E. Iarchuk, G. B. Sandomirskii, and V. Shatov. Many, less political and less eminent, worked in Soviet and economic agencies and taught in the schools. The majority, in any case, did not engage in anti-Soviet or counterrevolutionary activity. These people were destroyed without open political trials; indeed their arrests were hardly mentioned in the press. Apparently their criminality was considered too obvious to need publicity, since former members of defunct intraparty oppositions had become "enemies of the people."

7

THERE CAN BE NO DOUBT that Stalin personally ordered the arrests of the former oppositionists. But what moved him to the physical destruction of former ideological opponents in the mid-thirties, when they represented no serious threat to his power? This is part of a larger problem that will be treated later on. Only a few comments are in order now.

It is obvious that Stalin's extermination of former oppositionists was not accidental; it was a premeditated, planned political act. In January, 1933, Stalin declared that the desperate resistance of defeated classes—*byvshie liudi* he called them at one point, the Russian equivalent of *les ci-devants*—would increase as the Soviet state approached the final victory of socialism. They would, he predicted, use every dirty trick to mobilize backward elements against the Soviet regime, and he went on to make a further prediction that would often be cited in 1937–38:

> Defeated groups of the old counterrevolutionary parties, the S.R.'s, the Mensheviks, the bourgeois nationalists of the center and the borderlands, may revive and stir; fragments of the counterrevolutionary elements of the Trotskyites and right deviationists may revive and stir. This, of course, is not frightening. But all this must be kept in mind, if we want to get rid of these elements quickly and without special sacrifices.[48]

Stalin thus left no doubt about his desire to get rid of "these elements," although they had not yet stirred and only might stir.

Did Stalin believe in the inevitability of an antisocialist outburst, and therefore decide to take "preventive measures," using Kirov's murder as a pretext? Although Stalin may have told this story to some of his retinue, it is doubtful that such considerations played any significant role in his actions.

[48] Stalin, *Sochineniia,* XIII, p. 212.

Did Stalin, striving to set up a personal dictatorship, fear the formation of a new opposition by Zinoviev, Kamenev, Bukharin, and the rest, which would have been much more dangerous than the earlier oppositions, since it was Stalin now who was taking a path leading away from Marxism-Leninism? Again, it is doubtful that such considerations played any significant role in Stalin's actions.

Revenge was the primary motive, Stalin's revenge on his former political opponents, who had sometimes made unrestrained comments. In the twenties Stalin was not powerful enough to take physical vengeance on them. He waited for his chance. Many opposition leaders capitulated, were formally forgiven, readmitted to the Party, and even given important assignments, especially in the Soviet and economic *apparat*. But Stalin's "forgiveness" was not sincere. It was a political maneuver. Stalin was the one who tricked the Party, who hypocritically said one thing and planned another. And as soon as he felt strong enough, he destroyed the activists of the former oppositions.

Of course, Stalin's resentment and vindictiveness were not the only cause. By organizing political trials of former oppositionists, people who were already discredited, defenseless, powerless, Stalin sought to terrorize the Party and the people, to create an emergency situation, allowing himself, the "warrior" and "savior" of the state, to concentrate more power in his own hands. Another important motive was undoubtedly his desire to blame the "enemies of the people" for the political and economic difficulties that still existed in the country. Every despot building the cult of his own person needs a scapegoat. In 1928–32 it was the "wreckers" among the bourgeois intelligentsia; in the mid-thirties it was the former members of various oppositions.

But Stalin could not and would not limit himself to the destruction of former oppositionists. The logic of the struggle for power and the logic of crime led Stalin further, until finally he had decimated the main cadres of Party and state personnel.

VI

The Assault on Party
and State Cadres, 1937-38

ALL THE FORMER MEMBERS of the various defunct opposition groups
numbered no more than twenty to thirty thousand people, and most
of them had been jailed or shot by the beginning of 1937. That was
a painful loss to the Party, but it was only the beginning. Throughout
1937 and 1938 the flood of repression rose, carrying away the basic
core of Party leadership. This well-planned, pitiless destruction of the
people who had done the main work of the Revolution from the days
of the underground struggle, through the insurrection and the Civil
War, the restoration of the shattered economy and the great upbuilding
of the early thirties, was the most frightful act in the tragedy of the
thirties.

1

FIRST OF ALL, the Central Committee was attacked. By the beginning
of 1939, 110 of the 139 members and candidate members elected at
the XVIIth Party Congress in 1934 had been arrested. Dozens of
outstanding leaders perished, including:

> V. Ia. Chubar', Politburo member and deputy chairman of the Council
> of Commissars, posted to Solikamsk, then arrested and shot. S. V.
> Kosior, first secretary of the Ukrainian Central Committee; in January,
> 1938, accused of insufficient vigilance, transferred to high posts in
> Moscow, but arrested anyhow and, on February 26, 1939, at age 50,
> shot. P. P. Postyshev, demoted from the Politburo and the Ukrainian
> Central Committee to a provincial post, then arrested and shot. R. I.
> Eikhe, first secretary of the West Siberian Party Committee and candi-

date member of the Politburo, demoted to Commissar of Agriculture, then arrested and shot. Ia. E. Rudzutak, deputy chairman of the Council of Commissars, formerly secretary of the Central Committee and candidate member of the Politburo. K. Ia. Bauman, former secretary of the Orgburo of the Central Committee, then head of the Science Section of the Central Committee. Ia. A. Iakovlev, former Commissar of Agriculture, then head of the Agricultural Section of the Central Committee. B. M. Tal', head of the Press and Publications Section of the Central Committee. A. I. Stetskii, head of the Agitation and Propaganda Section of the Central Committee. A. M. Nazaretian, appointed Stalin's assistant in 1922 on the recommendation of Lenin, Ordzhonikidze, Kirov, and Kuibyshev, and later given many important posts; in 1937 arrested and shot.

The Commission of Party Control was also devastated; most of the people elected to it at the XVIIth Party Congress, including S. Saltanov and A. Shokhin, were arrested. And not only leaders but also most of the subordinate personnel of the central Party *apparat,* such as the "instructors" and the technical people, were arrested.

On February 19, 1937, a special government bulletin reported the death, by heart attack, of one of the Party's most popular leaders, Sergo Ordzhonikidze. Famous from the time of the October Revolution and the Civil War, he was in 1937 a member of the Politburo and Commissar of Heavy Industry. The papers carried a detailed medical report, signed by G. Kaminskii, the Commissar of Health, and by three doctors. Only nineteen years later, at the XXth Party Congress, was it officially announced that Ordzhonikidze had died by his own hand. And it was Stalin who drove Ordzhonikidze to this act.

Ordzhonikidze was not only popular but also a true Leninist, who hindered the crimes of Stalin, Ezhov, Beria, Molotov, and Kaganovich. Stalin decided to avoid direct charges in this case, preferring to compromise and demoralize Ordzhonikidze. An older brother, Papuliia, was arrested and shot after terrible tortures, and a falsified record of the interrogation was sent to Ordzhonikidze. Some of Ordzhonikidze's closest friends and associates were shot, while many executives in heavy industry, appointed by Ordzhonikidze, were arrested. Stalin sent him the false depositions extracted from the prisoners by torture, with the comment "Comrade Sergo, look what they're writing about you."

Ordzhonikidze protested these arrests: he refused to give his approval of some, and ordered officials of his commissariat to check the grounds that the NKVD gave for others. Stalin and Ezhov ignored Ordzhonikidze's protests, and Stalin directed him to give the report on wrecking in industry at the February-March Plenum. Stalin and Ezhov even ordered a search of his Kremlin apartment. Ordzhonikidze, humiliated and enraged by this provocation, tried all night to phone Stalin.

Toward morning he got through to Stalin and received the reply: "The NKVD can even search my apartment. There's nothing strange about that. . . ." There was a conversation with Stalin the morning of the seventeenth. Eyeball to eyeball for several hours. A second conversation after Sergo returned home was uncontrollably angry, full of mutual insults and Russian and Georgian swearing. No more love or trust. Everything destroyed. . . . Sergo could not begin to share responsibility for what he had no power to prevent. He would not become a corrupt timeserver; that would mean wiping out his whole past life. . . . All he could do was leave.[1]

Today some old Bolsheviks say that Ordzhonikidze was murdered, pointing out that the day before he died he worked in the Commissariat and even issued a number of orders and made some appointments for the following day. E. P. Frolov writes in his memoirs that the circumstances surrounding Ordzhonikidze's death were not investigated in 1937; even the bullet hole was not examined. All the doctors who signed the medical report were subsequently arrested. Right after Ordzhonikidze's death, his chief bodyguard, V. N. Efimov, and his personal secretary, Semushkin, were arrested. A. Cherkasskii, who was at that time a driver in the Kremlin motor pool, says that Ordzhonikidze's entire bodyguard was arrested, and a bodyguard can hardly be responsible for a suicide. Almost everyone who worked for Ordzhonikidze was arrested, even the watchman at his country house. His former deputy Vannikov testified that a few days after the death he was summoned to Ezhov's office and told to write a report on the "wrecking" directives issued by Ordzhonikidze. According to Frolov, many of Ordzhonikidze's papers were removed and later transmitted— for "study"—to Beria, who was a personal enemy of Ordzhonikidze. In 1941 Ordzhonikidze's brothers Konstantin and Vano were arrested, along with many other relatives. This entire chain of events raises many questions, but there are not sufficient grounds to dispute the version of suicide.

Ordzhonikidze's wife, Zinaida Gavrilovna, testified that on the morning of February 18, the day before the Central Committee Plenum was scheduled to meet (this meeting was subsequently put off for ten days), Sergo did not get out of bed, did not begin to dress, and refused breakfast. All day he wrote something. His friend Gvakhariia came over, but Sergo would not see him, only ordered that he be fed in the dining room. Sergo himself refused the afternoon meal. His wife was extremely worried and phoned her sister, Vera Gavrilovna, asking her to come over. February days are short, and it began to grow dark after five. Zinaida Gavrilovna decided to go into her husband's room, but while she was on her way, turning on the light in the living room,

[1] I. Dubinskii-Mukhadze, *Ordzhonikidze* (Moscow, 1963), pp. 6–7.

a shot exploded in Sergo's bedroom. Running in, she saw her husband lying on the bed, dead, the bedclothes stained with blood.

According to Zinaida Gavrilovna the apartment had a side entrance, which everyone used, and a main entrance that was always closed because there were bookshelves in the hall. Moreover, the main entrance led into the living room, where Zinaida Gavrilovna was at the moment the shot was fired; so it could not have been used by an assassin.

Sergo's wife immediately phoned Stalin. Although his apartment was just opposite Ordzhonikidze's building, he did not come at once to see his former friend. First Stalin sent for all the Politburo members. Ordzhonikidze's sister-in-law Vera ran in before Stalin. Entering the bedroom, she saw some sheets of paper on the desk, covered with Ordzhonikidze's tiny handwriting. She automatically picked them up and clutched them in her hand, but she did not manage to read them. When Stalin and the other Politburo members finally arrived, Stalin somehow saw the papers and almost tore them out of Vera Gavrilovna's hand. Sobbing, Ordzhonikidze's wife shouted at Stalin, "You didn't protect Sergo for me or for the Party." "Shut up, you idiot," Stalin replied.

Sergo Ordzhonikidze's younger brother Konstantin survived seventeen years of confinement to set down his reminiscences of that tragic day.

> I will tell a few details connected with the death of my dear brother Sergo, who committed suicide on February 18, 1937, at 5:30 P.M.
>
> That evening, after skating in Sokolniki Park, I went as usual to see my brother in the Kremlin. At the entrance Sergo's chauffeur, N. I. Volkov, said to me, "Hurry up!"
>
> I did not understand anything. When my wife and I reached the second floor, we went to the dining room, but were stopped at the door by an NKVD agent. Then we were let into Sergo's office, where I saw G. Gvakhariia. "Our Sergo is no more," he said.
>
> I ran to the bedroom but my way was barred, and I was not allowed to see the body. I returned to the office, stunned, not understanding what had happened.
>
> Then Stalin, Molotov, and Zhdanov arrived. First they went to the dining room. Zhdanov had a black bandage on his forehead [*sic; eye?*]. Suddenly Gvakhariia was led out of Sergo's office (for some reason through the bathroom). After that Stalin, Molotov, and Zhdanov went from the dining room into the bedroom, where they stood a while beside the body, then returned to the dining room. The words of Zinaida Gavrilovna reached me from the dining room. "This must be reported in the press." Stalin answered, "We will say that he died from a heart attack." "No one will believe that," retorted Zinaida Gavrilovna, and added: "Sergo loved the truth;

the truth must be printed." "Why won't they believe it? Everyone knew he had a bad heart, and everyone will believe it." Thus Stalin put an end to that dialogue.

The doors to the bedroom were shut. Opening them slightly, I saw Ezhov and Kaganovich sitting on chairs at the feet of the deceased. They were discussing something. I closed the door immediately to avoid unnecessary reproach.

Sometime later the Politburo members and a number of other high-placed persons gathered in the dining room. Beria also appeared. In the presence of Stalin, Molotov, Zhdanov, and the rest, Zinaida Gavrilovna called Beria a rat [negodiai]. She went toward him and tried to slap him. Beria disappeared right after that and did not come to Sergo's apartment again.

The body was taken from the bedroom to the office, where Molotov's brother photographed the deceased together with Stalin, Molotov, Zhdanov, Postyshev, Ezhov, other members of the government and leaders of the Party, and Zinaida Gavrilovna. All this time I stood by the wall and didn't think that maybe I had to go somewhere else. Then the well-known sculptor S. D. Merkulov came and made a mask of Sergo's face.

Zinaida Gavrilovna asked Ezhov and Pauker to notify Sergo's relatives in Georgia so that they could come to the funeral. She also wanted our older brother Papuliia to attend. Ezhov replied to that: "Papuliia Ordzhonikidze is in confinement and we consider him an enemy of the people. Let him serve out his punishment; you may help him by sending warm clothing and food. We will inform the rest of the family; just give us their addresses." I gave them the addresses of brother Ivan and sister Julia, and also Papuliia's wife Nina.

Late that evening Emilian Iaroslavskii arrived. When he saw the deceased, he fainted. With difficulty we laid him on the couch. When Iaroslavskii came to, he was driven home. Then Semushkin arrived. It was his day off, and he had been resting at his cottage in Tarasovka. When Semushkin saw the awful scene, he began to rave and had to be sent home almost tied down.

Sergo's secretary, Makhover, overwhelmed by what he saw, uttered words that stick in my memory: "They killed him, the rats [merzavtsy]!"

. . . On the night before February 20, 1937, the body was cremated. The funeral was held the next day, the twentieth. Brother Ivan and his wife, and sister Julia and her husband, were late in getting to Moscow.

After some time, intensified arrests began. M. D. Orakhelashvili and his wife were arrested. Semushkin and his wife were arrested, and so were many officials in the Commissariat of Heavy Industry who were close to Sergo.

Ordzhonikidzes were arrested: the wife of our older brother Papuliia, and another relative, G. A. Ordzhonikidze.

And finally, on May 6, 1941, they arrested me too.

In 1937–38 the central government and economic agencies were decimated. Many members of the USSR Central Executive Committee and most of the commissars of the USSR and the RSFSR were arrested and shot. Here too the Party has not accounted for thousands of its most outstanding members. One of the most prominent victims was Avel' Enukidze, permanent secretary of the Central Executive Committee, who was a close friend of Sverdlov, Dzerzhinskii, Kirov, S. G. Shaumian, and for a long time of Stalin himself. But he got in Stalin's way, so in 1935 he was expelled from the Party, and two years later he was arrested and shot.

Stalin sanctioned the arrests of many former personal friends, and also the relatives of his first wife, née Svanidze, and of his second wife, Nadezhda Allilueva, who killed herself in 1932. Stalin's daughter, Svetlana Allilueva, in a book published abroad in 1967, has tried to blame the persecution of the Svandize and Alliluev families on Beria's intrigues. She claims he subjected Stalin to his influence. But that is a deliberate lie.

Gosplan was devastated. Arrested and shot were:

B. I. Mezhlauk, long-time Chairman. G. I. Smirnov, his successor, aged thirty-four. E. I. Kviring, Deputy Chairman. G. I. Lomov (Oppokov), a participant in the October Revolution, who had held many executive posts in the All-Union Economic Council as well as in Gosplan.

The Council of People's Commissars had its share of victims; for example:

V. Shmidt and N. K. Antipov, Deputy Chairmen of the USSR Council. D. E. Sulimov, Chairman of the RSFSR Council, and his deputies D. Z. Lebed' and T. Ryskulov. M. L. Rukhimovich, Commissar of Defense Industry. I. E. Liubimov, Commissar of Light Industry. S. S. Lobov, USSR Commissar of Forest Industry and then RSFSR Commissar of Food Industry. I. Ia. Veitser, Commissar of Domestic Trade. G. N. Kaminskii, Commissar of Health. I. A. Khalepskii, Commissar of Communications. M. I. Kalmanovich and N. N. Demchenko, Commissars of Grain and Livestock State Farms. K. V. Ukhanov, RSFSR Commissar of Local Industry. N. I. Pakhomov, Commissar of Water Transport. A. Bruskin, Commissar of Machine Building. S. L. Lukashin, Chairman of the Committee on Construction in the Council of Commissars. L. E. Mar'iasin, Chairman of the Board of the State Bank. N. Popov, Commissar of Agricultural Procurements, one of the youngest members of the Soviet government, not yet thirty-five. B. Z. Shumiatskii, head of the Committee on Cinematography. N. V. Krylenko, Commissar of Justice. A. S. Bubnov, from 1929 to 1937 RSFSR Commissar of Education. Under the tsars Bubnov was arrested and exiled thirteen times, but always managed to escape. In 1937 he was arrested for the fourteenth time, and shot.

Most of these governmental and economic leaders were also members or candidate members of the Party's Central Committee.

Of course, commissars were not arrested by themselves in 1937–38; the commissariats they headed were decimated. For example, the NKVD cooked up a story about a "gang of spies and wreckers" in the Commissariat of Heavy Industry, headed by Ordzhonikidze's deputy Piatakov. The leading officials in this commissariat were arrested even before Ordzhonikidze's death; afterwards all the major departments were ravaged. The victims included:

> A. P. Serebrovskii, A. I. Gurevich, and O. P. Osipov-Shmidt, deputy commissars. K. A. Neiman, A. F. Tolokontsev, I. V. Kosior, A. I. Zykov, Iu. P. Figatner, S. S. Dybets, E. L. Brodov, directors of various departments and sections and members of the Commissariat collegium.

The same fate befell all the other commissariats of the USSR and the RSFSR. Among many thousands of talented executives who perished were:

> Sh. Z. Zliava, N. P. Briukhanov, A. M. Lezhava, A. B. Khalatov, Paul Oras, V. P. Miliutin, K. P. Soms, V. I. Polonskii, M. V. Barinov, I. I. Todorskii, V. A. Kangelari, S. S. Odintsov, V. A. Trofimov, I. I. Radchenko, M. M. Maiorov, G. I. Blagonravov, Ia. L. Bobis, K. Danishevskii, G. Dzhabiev.

The Commissariat of Foreign Affairs was savagely purged in 1937–38. Among the victims:

> Levon Karakhan, deputy commissar. K. Iurenev, ambassador to Japan. Davtian, ambassador to Poland. M. A. Karskii, ambassador to Turkey. V. Kh. Tairov, ambassador to Mongolia. Bogomolov, ambassador to China. Ostrovskii, ambassador to Rumania. Iakubovich, ambassador to Norway. Asmus, ambassador to Finland. A. V. Sabinin, Neiman, Tsukkerman, and Fekhner, heads of departments, F. F. Raskol'nikov, ambassador to Bulgaria. A. G. Barmin, ambassador to Greece.

Of all those who were ordered to return from abroad, only the last two refused to return to certain death in Moscow.

Lenin's widow, N. N. Krupskaia, also met tragedy. In 1925 she had spoken out against Stalin's methods of resolving disagreements within the Party. At the XIVth Party Congress she supported Zinoviev and Kamenev, although she did not entirely agree with their platform. Evidently she regarded their leadership as a lesser evil. Although she soon abandoned the opposition, she was nonetheless subjected to various forms of obloquy. When she spoke out against the distortions of Lenin's plan for agricultural cooperatives, at the Bauman *raion* Party conference in 1930, she was viciously attacked and forced to "confess" her "error" before the Central Committee. When her *Reminiscences of Lenin* were published in 1934, Stalin himself phoned to congratulate her on a good and useful work. But only a few days later a harsh and unfair review appeared in *Pravda*. The reviewer, a young historian named P. Pospelov, charged that there were mistakes in her portrayal of Lenin and her treatment of certain problems of Party history. Obviously this was not done without Stalin's knowledge.[2]

When mass arrests began in 1936, Krupskaia repeatedly tried to protect many Party leaders whom she knew well. For example, at the June Plenum of 1937 she spoke against the arrest of I. Piatnitskii, who had been labeled a provocateur for the tsarist secret police. Krupskaia said that he had been a responsible official in the Bolshevik underground; he had been in charge of communications between Russia and the émigré leaders, and he had never once deviated from the Party line. But almost all these protests were ignored. Only in a few cases did she win the release of some loyal Party members. For example, I. D. Chugurin, who had issued a Party card to Lenin on April 3, 1917, was released as a result of Krupskaia's intervention.[3]

However, Stalin and the NKVD soon began to ignore her protests completely. At a meeting honoring Lenin in January, 1937, when Krupskaia asked Ezhov about the fate of some comrades, Ezhov simply turned and walked away. Krupskaia was disregarded even in the field of education, where she had done so much. Though she remained a Deputy Commissar of Education of the RSFSR to the end of her life, she was discredited and deprived of normal working conditions by a campaign against the educational leadership. In 1937 almost all the major educationists were arrested, including many who were close to Krupskaia. When she died at the beginning of 1939, Stalin was among the leaders who carried her ashes at the funeral. But the very next day her apartment was searched and many of her papers were seized. And very soon the publishing house of the Commissariat of Education received an order: "Don't print one word about Krupskaia."[4] Her name was consigned to oblivion. Under various pretexts her books were taken off library shelves, and even an exhibition devoted to the newspaper *Iskra* contained not one word about her work for it.[5]

Some other old Bolsheviks who had worked many years with Lenin escaped arrest in 1936–39, including:

> G. M. Krzhizhanovskii, F. Ia. Kon, P. A. Krasikov, M. A. Bonch-Bruevich, N. I. Podvoiskii, A. N. Badaev, D. Z. Manuil'skii, M. K. Muranov, F. I. Samoilov, N. A. Semashko, I. I. Shvartz, and A. M. Kollontai.

[2] See *Sovetskaia istoricheskaia entsiklopediia,* VIII (1966), p. 192.
[3] See *Pravda,* Dec. 22, 1963. But Chugurin was not readmitted to the Party, and to the end of his days worked as a roofer. Similarly, A. P. Spunde, an underground Bolshevik before the Revolution and a member of the first Soviet government, who subsequently became vice-president of the State Bank and head of the foreign-currency division in the Commissariat of Finance, worked as a cashier following his expulsion from the Party in 1938.
[4] *Vsesoiuznoe soveshchanie istorikov* (Moscow, 1964), p. 260.
[5] See *Pravda,* Feb. 26, 1964.

But all these people were pushed out of the leadership, terrorized, and deprived of any influence. Stalin treated them with undisguised contempt, calling them *intelligenty* (members of the intelligentsia), incapable of leading the proletariat under the new conditions.

G. I. Petrovskii, who had been a close comrade of Lenin, deputy to the Duma before the Revolution, and chairman of the Ukrainian Central Executive Committee in the Soviet period, was deeply shaken by the arrest of such close friends and colleagues as Chubar', Kosior, K. V. Sukhomlin. His older son, Peter, a hero of the Civil War and subsequently an editor of *Leningradskaia Pravda,* was arrested. His younger son, Leonid, also a Civil War hero and one of the first Komsomol organizers, was expelled from the Party and fired from his job as commander of the Moscow proletarian division. Petrovskii's son-in-law, S. A. Zager, chairman of the Chernigov Executive Committee, was arrested and shot. At the end of 1938, Petrovskii himself was suddenly called to Moscow. After a short but painful meeting with Stalin, this old Bolshevik, whose sixtieth birthday had recently been given nationwide observance, was dismissed as chairman of the Presidium of the Ukrainian Supreme Soviet and removed from the Ukrainian Politburo. The NKVD began to frame a "political case" against him, accusing him of connections with "enemies of the people." At the XVIIIth Party Congress of 1939 he was not re-elected to the Central Committee, and for a year he had no work at all. Just before the war he became Deputy Director of the Museum of the Revolution, in charge of the agricultural section.

Demian Bedny, Bolshevik poet and close comrade of Lenin, also suffered, as he did in the early thirties. In 1935 Stalin tried to resume relations with Bedny, inviting him to his country house; at another time he went himself to bring Bedny home as a guest. On New Year's Eve, 1936, Bedny was again a guest of Stalin's in a small company of intimates. But that same year his work was again raked over the coals. The musical play *Heroes,* with lyrics by Bedny, was banned, and Stalin refused to speak to him. In 1938, when Bedny wrote a pamphlet about fascism under the title "Hell," Stalin not only prohibited publication but wrote on the manuscript, "Tell this latter-day Dante that he can stop writing."[6] In August, 1938, Bedny was expelled from the Party and then from the Union of Writers. Until the war began, newspapers and journals were closed to him.

Many of Lenin's most trusted associates were also arrested. As early as 1935 this happened to N. A. Emel'ianov, the Petrograd worker who had hidden Lenin in the hut at Razliv, helping to save him from arrest in the summer of 1917. In 1921 Lenin wrote in a letter:

[6] *Vospominaniia o Dem'iane Bednom* (Moscow, 1965), pp. 220–22.

Please show *the most complete confidence,* and give all possible assistance, to Comrade N. A. Emel'ianov, whom I've known from before the October Revolution, an old Party activist and one of the leaders of the working-class vanguard of St. Petersburg.[7]

But Emel'ianov was arrested. A. V. Snegov tells how Krupskaia tearfully begged Stalin to spare Emel'ianov's life. He remained in confinement until Stalin's death, and his whole family was also arrested: his wife, and his sons Kondratii, Nikolai, and Alexander, who as little boys had helped to hide Lenin at Razliv.

Another old Bolshevik victim was A. V. Shotman, the leader of the famous Obukhov defense in 1903. In the summer of 1917, when Lenin went underground, Shotman was given the job of guarding Lenin's life and of arranging his journey from Razliv to Finland. In 1918 Lenin wrote: "Shotman is an old Party comrade, whom I know quite well. He deserves absolute trust." But Shotman was arrested and perished in 1939.[8]

The terror also killed Fritz Platten, a well-known Swiss left Socialist, later a Communist and a leader of the Third International. In 1917 he arranged the passage of Lenin and his comrades through Germany to Russia. In fact Platten went with them and took an active part in the Russian Revolution. On January 1, 1918, he saved Lenin's life from a counterrevolutionary attempt to assassinate him on the Simeonovskii Bridge over the Fontanka; Platten suffered an arm wound. Subsequently he brought his family to live in the USSR, only to be arrested along with his wife, a prominent Comintern official.[9] Platten had been in the prisons of tsarist Russia and landlord Rumania, in the torture chambers of Petliura in the Ukraine and the Kovno jail, in the Moabit of Berlin and the prisons of Switzerland. But he died in Kargopol'lag, a camp for invalids, making shingles and weaving baskets.[10]

In September, 1937, another of Lenin's comrades was shot: Ia. S. Ganetskii, a leader of the Polish workers' movement whom Lenin had personally recommended for membership in the Russian Party. In August, 1914, Ganetskii obtained the release of Lenin, who had been arrested by the Austrian authorities as a Russian spy. In 1917 he helped arrange Lenin's return to Russia, meeting him in Sweden and securing his journey to revolutionary Petrograd. After the October Revolution Ganetskii held important diplomatic and economic posts

[7] *Polnoe sobranie,* LIV, p. 24.
[8] See T. Bondarevskaia, *A. Shotman* (Moscow, 1963).
[9] The NKVD and Stalin made no distinction between men and women. Hundreds of thousands of women who had worked in the Party, trade unions, government, and Komsomol, in scientific institutions, the educational system, and publishing houses, were arrested and subjected to the same tortures as the men.
[10] See *Leningradskaia Pravda,* Oct. 1, 1964.

in the Soviet Union, eventually becoming director of the Museum of the Revolution in Moscow.[11]

Even old Bolsheviks who had retired because of age or illness were arrested. N. F. Dobrokhotov, who held many important posts until a serious disease forced him to retire in 1929, was arrested and perished.[12] Stalin did not even spare the dead; some old Bolsheviks were posthumously declared enemies of the people, others were consigned to oblivion. P. I. Stuchka, Commissar of Justice in Lenin's first government and, at the end of 1918, head of the short-lived Latvian Soviet Republic, died in 1932 and was buried in Red Square. But in 1937–38 he was declared a propagator of harmful ideology and virtually a deliberate wrecker in the field of jurisprudence.[13] Similarly, S. I. Gusev, a colleague of Lenin and outstanding leader of the Revolution and the Civil War, was buried with military honors in Red Square in 1933 but was subsequently expunged from the history of the Party. Many of his friends and relatives were arrested.[14] The name of the legendary underground Bolshevik Kamo was also suppressed. The small monument on his grave in Tbilisi was destroyed, and his sister was arrested. Ia. M. Sverdlov's brother, Veniamin M. Sverdlov, a member of the collegium of the Commissariat of Education, was killed. And such famous Bolsheviks as Krasin, Nogin, Chicherin, and Lunacharskii were erased from the pages of history.

2

THE WAVE OF REPRESSION that hit the central Party organs also swept through every *oblast* and republic. In the RSFSR around 90 per cent of all *obkomy* (*oblast* Party committees) and the majority of city, *okrug*, and *raion* committees were ravaged. In some *oblasti* several successive Party committees were arrested. In the RSFSR the following *obkom* secretaries were arrested and perished:

> L. I. Kartvelishvili, I. M. Vareikis, I. P. Nosov, N. N. Kolotilov, A. I. Krinitskii, A. I. Ugarov, F. G. Leonov, V. V. Ptukha, I. D. Kabakov, K. V. Ryndin, D. A. Bulatov, P. I. Smorodin, Shubrikov, B. P. Sheboldaev, E. K. Pramnek, M. Razumnov, I. V. Slinkin, I. Rumiantsev, M. S. Chudov, M. E. Mikhailov, L. I. Lavrent'ev, P. A. Irklis, A. S. Kalygina, Ia. G. Soifer, G. Baituni, and others.

Chairmen of *krai* and *oblast* executive committees who were destroyed included

---

[11] See *Voprosy istoril KPSS,* 1964, No. 3, pp. 96–100.
[12] See *Soldaty revoliutsii* (Iaroslavl', 1963), p. 102.
[13] See *Sovetskaia Latviia,* July 28, 1960.
[14] See G. Kramarov, *Soldat revoliutsii* (Moscow, 1963).

G. M. Krutov, N. I. Pakhomov, P. I. Struppe, Ian Poluian, I. F. Kodat-skii, chairman of the Leningrad Soviet, and many others.

The arrest of the *obkom* secretary and the chairman of the *oblast* executive committee usually meant that all the leading cadres in that *oblast* would be ravaged. For example, in Moscow *oblast* the following Party secretaries were arrested, and most of them shot:

A. N. Bogomolov, T. A. Bratanovskii, E. S. Kogan, N. V. Margolin, N. I. Dedikov, Vas. Egorov, Kul'kov, Korytnyi; N. A. Filatov, Chairman of the Moscow *oblast* Executive Committee, his deputies Fedotov and Guberman, Secretary Bidinskii, and many other officials of the Moscow Soviet.[15]

By the middle of 1939, only seven of 136 *raikom* secretaries in Moscow and the Moscow *oblast* were still at their posts. Almost all the rest had been arrested and shot, including

Tarkhanov, Volovik, Margevich, Savin, Treivas, and Gorbul'skii.

Many heads of departments in the Party's *oblast* and City Committee were destroyed, including

M. D. Krymskii, Voroshilov, Kurenkov, Verklov, and Barleben.

Some prominent Moscow Bolsheviks, Furer, for example, committed suicide. The majority of Party instructors were also arrested.

In Gorky during 1937–38, a special block of the city prison held the entire city Party Committee, with Secretary Pugachevskii, and the entire city soviet, with Chairman Grachevskii. Here too were nine of the city's *raikom* secretaries, including Velikorechin, Shumilov, and Mel'nikov, together with hundreds of city and *oblast* officials. In 1938 the head of the local NKVD, Lavrushin, told the VIth Party Conference of Gorky *oblast* that "hordes of counterrevolutionaries have been devastated."[16] In all the other major cities of the RSFSR there were analogous assaults on the local leaders, in Leningrad a continuous assault over a four-year period.

Virtually none of the autonomous republics of the RSFSR escaped. In Karelia Gustav Rovio, First Secretary of the *obkom,* the "red policemen" of Helsingfors who had helped to hide Lenin in 1917, was destroyed. So were the Chairman of the Council of Commissars, E. Giulling, and the Chairman of the Central Executive Committee, N. V. Arkhipov.

M. N. Erbanov, one of the founders of the Soviet regime in Buriat-Mongolia, was among the leaders shot there.

[15] See *Ocherki po istorii Moskovskoi organizatsii KPSS* (Moscow, 1967).
[16] *Ocherkii istorii Gor'kovskoi organizatsii KPSS* (Gorky, 1966), II, p. 32.

In the Tartar Republic, A. K. Lepa, *obkom* Secretary, G. G. Bai-
churin, chairman of the Central Executive Committee, K. A. Abramov
and A. M. Novoselov, Chairmen of the Council of Commissars, and
dozens of lesser officials were arrested and executed. S. Sand-Galiev
also perished, the First Chairman of the Council of Commissars. He
had once criticized Stalin, then Commissar of Nationalities, for lack
of principle in relation to petty-bourgeois Tartar nationalists.[17]

Betal Kalmykov, the popular First Secretary of the Kabardino-
Balkarskii *obkom,* died in confinement. He was a personal enemy of
Beria but a great friend of Ordzhonikidze and many other Party
leaders. So an elaborate provocation preceded his destruction. His
wife had formerly been married to a White Guard officer who was
living in Paris. She had a son by him, who was studying in Moscow.
Under some pretext the boy was lured to Belorussia, arrested at a
border station, and accused of trying to flee to his father in Paris.
Kalmykov was then framed for participation in a "conspiracy" against
the Soviet regime.

In Ossetia and Checheno-Ingushetia, in Bashkiria and Dagestan,
in Chuvashia and Mordovia, in Udmurtia and the Mariiskaia Republic,
the Party suffered enormous losses. In Northern Ossetia, for example,
nine out of eleven members of the *obkom* bureau were arrested. In
two years four *obkom* secretaries were removed, including S. A.
Takoev and K. S. Butaev. A large part of the Ossetian intelligentsia
was also wiped out.[18] Even in such a small, out-of-the-way republic as
Komi, a fourth of all Communists, starting with *obkom* secretaries
A. A. Semichev and F. I. Bulyshev, were arrested.[19]

We have already mentioned the destruction of Chubar', Postyshev, and
Kosior, former leaders of the Ukrainian Party. Along with them almost
all leading officials of the Republic were arrested, including

> V. P. Zatonskii, I. E. Klimenko, K. V. Sukhomlin, M. M. Khataevich,
> V. I. Cherniavskii, E. I. Veger, F. I. Golub, S. Kudriavtsev, O. V.
> Pilatskaia, A. V. Osipov, N. I. Golub, and G. I. Staryi.

Of all these leaders only Osipov and Pilatskaia were allowed to
live. A. P. Liubchenko, Chairman of the Ukrainian Council of Commissars, fearing that his family would be arrested after his death, shot
his wife and son and then himself. Almost all of the famous revolutionary Zaporozhets family were arrested: Viktor and Anton, Mariia
Kuz'minichna, and her husband Taranenko. Iurii Kotsiubinskii, Bolshevik son of the famous Ukrainian revolutionary democrat, perished.

[17] *Ocherki po istorii partiinoi organizatsii Tatarii* (Kazan, 1962).
[18] *Istoriia Severo-Osetinskoi ASSR* (Ordzhonikidze, 1966), p. 247.
[19] *Istoriia kommunisticheskoi partiinoi organizatsii Komi ASSR* (Syktyvkar, 1964).

Repression reduced the membership of the Ukrainian Party from 453,500 in 1934 to 285,800 in 1938.[20]

In Belorussia, where mass repression began much earlier than in the other republics, Party membership dropped by more than a half. By 1937 there was actually no one to work in the Central Committee. Party officials were rapidly transferred from the *oblasti* to Minsk, but there in the capital they too fell into the gigantic meat grinder. Almost all the leading Belorussian Bolsheviks perished, including:

> A. G. Cherviakov, who, the newspapers reported, killed himself "for family reasons." N. F. Gikalo, a famous hero of the Civil War and later a Party leader in the North Caucasus, Uzbekistan, and Belorussia. N. M. Goloded, M. O. Stakun, S. D. Kamenshtein, D. I. Volkovich, Ia. I. Zavodnik, A. I. Khatskevich, Grisevich, and Liubovich.

In the Transcaucasus, repression in Azerbaijan was directed by Stalin's protégé Bagirov. Among the victims were:

> G. M. Musabekov, former Chairman of the Council of Commissars of Transcaucasia, and a chairman of the USSR Central Executive Committee. Gusein Rakhmanov, secretary of the Central Committee and chairman of the Council of Ministers of Azerbaijan. S. M. Efendiev, chairman of the Central Executive Committee of Azerbaijan. M. D. Guseinov, A. P. Akopov, R. Akhundov, D. Buniatzade, M. Tserafibekov, A. G. Karaev, M. Kuliev, M. Narimanov, G. Sultanov, A. Sultanova.[21]

The Georgian Party organization also suffered heavy losses in 1937–38:

> Mikha Kakhiani, Levan Gogoberidze, Iason Mamuliia, Soso Buachidze, Peter and Levan Agniashvili, and Ivan Bolkvadze were killed or died in confinement. Mamiia Orakhelashvili, one of the founders of the Bolshevik organizations in Transcaucasia and long first secretary in that *krai,* perished. So did his wife, Maria, a Party member since 1906 and a leader of the women's movement. Successive chairmen of the Georgian Council of Commissars, G. Mgaloblishvili and L. Sukhishvili, were arrested, along with most of the commissars. The Georgian NKVD, under Beria and Kabulov, put together a "case" against Filipp Makharadze, in order to terrorize that old Bolshevik. The Abkhazian leader N. A. Lakoba, a close friend of Ordzhonikidze, Kirov, and Kalinin, was shot, and so was the *obkom* first secretary, A. S. Agrba.

The scale of repression in Georgia is revealed by this figure: of the 644 delegates to the Xth Georgian Party Congress, which met in May, 1937, 425, or 66 per cent, were soon after arrested, exiled, or shot.[22]

In Armenia mass repression began very early. The Armenian

---

[20] *Ocherki po istorii kommunisticheskoi partii Ukrainy* (Kiev, 1964).
[21] See *Ocherki po istorii kommunisticheskoi organizatsii Azerbaidzhana* (Baku, 1963).
[22] *Ocherki po istorii kommunisticheskoi partii Gruzii* (Tbilisi, 1963), pp. 158–60.

leadership was displeased when Beria became first secretary of Transcaucasia, and Beria knew it. Moreover, Beria's wretched little book
on the history of Bolshevism in Transcaucasia was condemned by local
Party leaders, such as the Armenian commissar of education, Nersik
Stepanian, for its falsehoods. Beria responded with a shrill article,
"Destroy the Enemies of Socialism," slandering Stepanian and de-
manding his physical annihilation. The terror against the Armenian
Party actually began in 1935, when the NKVD fabricated cases against
some leading officials and writers. The goal was to compromise the
first secretary, A. Khandzhian. On July 9, 1936, the Transcaucasian
Control Commission heard an NKVD report "On the Discovery of a
Counterrevolutionary Terrorist Group in Georgia, Azerbaijan, and
Armenia." Khandzhian was accused of lack of vigilance. That very
evening he was dead. Some say he killed himself;[23] others say, more
plausibly, that he was shot by Beria personally.[24] One book says
simply that Khandzhian was a victim of arbitrary rule.[25] After his
death G. Amatuni and S. Akopov, Beria's creatures, became the new
leaders of Armenia, and started to terrorize honest Party and state
cadres on the pretext of fighting nationalism and Dashnak counterrevolution. The victims included:

> G. Alikhanian, Secretary of the Armenian Central Committee. S.
> Srapionian (Lukashin), A. Ioannisian, G. Ovsepian, A. Kostanian, S.
> Ter-Gabrielian, S. Martikian, S. Kas'ian, D. Shaverdian, A. Melikian,
> N. Stepanian, A. Erzinkian, V. Eremian, A. Esaian, A. Egiazarian.[26]

Of all these, only Ioannisian was allowed to live.

In Central Asia, Kazakhstan experienced extreme repression. In 1937
every single member of the Central Committee buro elected at the
Republic's first Party Congress was arrested and shot. Among the
victims were

> L. I. Mirzoian, S. Nurpeisov, U. D. Isaev, and I. Iu. Kabulov.

At the same time most Central Committee members and Party secretaries at all levels were arrested, including such founders of the Soviet
regime in Kazakhstan as

> U. K. Dzhandosov, Iu. Babaev, A. Rozybakiev, and A. M. Asylbekov.

Today these Communists have been completely rehabilitated.[27]

---

[23] See Ts. Agaian, *N. Stepanian* (Erevan, 1967).
[24] A. Shelepin, S. O. Gazarian, A. Ivanova, and others tell this story.
[25] *Ocherki istorii kommunisticheskoi partii Armenii* (Erevan, 1964).
[26] *Ibid.*
[27] See *Ocherki po istorii kommunisticheskoi partii Kazakhstana* (Alma-Ata, 1963).

Tadzhikistan lost

A. Rakhimbaev, the president of its Council of Commissars, who had been elected to the All-Union Central Committee on Lenin's recommendation; Sh. Shotemor, secretary of the Tadzhik Central Committee; and such other Party leaders as S. Anvarov, B. Dodobaev, K. Tashev, and A. T. Redin.[28]

Kirghiz victims of terror included

Ammosov, the First Secretary of the Central Committee, and the Second Secretary, M. Belotskii.[29]

Turkmenia lost

A. Mukhamedov, Ia. A. Popok, K. Atabaev, N. Aitakov, Ch. Vellekov, Kh. Sakhatmuradov, O. Tashiazarov, D. Mamedov, B. Ataev, and Kurban Sakhatov.

For several months there was not even a Central Committee Buro in Turkmenia.[30]

The Communist Party of Uzbekistan also suffered heavy losses. I have already told how its First Secretary, Akmal' Ikramov, was arrested on Stalin's personal orders and put into the "Right Trotskyite Bloc." Stalin had not forgotten his speech to the XVIIth Party Congress, in which Ikramov warned against self-conceit. I also told about Faizul Khodzhaev, chairman of the Uzbek Council of Commissars, who were arrested and died along with hundreds of other leaders, such as

D. Tiurabekov, D. Rizaev, D. I. Manzhar, N. Israilov, and R. Islamov.[31]

Nationalism was one of the main charges against these non-Russian Communist leaders. The accusation was not only false, it was self-defeating. By destroying tens of thousands of good Communists among the minority nationalities, the charge of nationalism helped to revive many nationalistic moods and prejudices.

3

IN 1937–38 MANY TRADE-UNION OFFICIALS were falsely accused and arrested: E. N. Egorova, Secretary of the All-Union Council of Trade Unions, was repressed. In 1917 she had been the secretary of the Vyborg *raikom* in Petrograd, who filled out a Party card for

---

[28] See *Ocherki po istorii kommunisticheskoi partii Tadzhikistana* (Dushanbe, 1965).
　　Ed.: The date of publication may be in error. I have found editions of 1964 and 1968.
[29] *Ocherki po istorii kommunisticheskoi partii Kirgizii* (Frunze, 1966).
[30] *Ocherki istorii kommunisticheskoi partii Turkmenii* (Ashkhabad, 1965).
[31] *Ocherki istorii kommunisticheskoi partii Uzbekistana* (Tashkent, 1964).

Lenin. In July, 1917, she helped to hide Lenin. This old friend of
Krupskaia was accused of anti-Soviet activity and killed.[32] Many other
trade-union leaders, including A. A. Korostelev, perished. But a large
part of the secretariat of the Trade Union Council, headed by N. M.
Shvernik, was not touched by repression.

The Komsomol leaders had a more tragic fate, including many
who had moved on to other jobs but preserved a connection with the
youth organization. Among these were:

> Oskar Ryvkin, who had been elected chairman of the Komsomol at its
> first congress in 1918, was the Party secretary of Krasnodar in 1937
> when he was arrested. Lazar Shatskin, who had been First Secretary of
> the Komsomol in 1920–21, was working in the Comintern when he was
> taken away. Peter Smorodin, First Secretary of the Komsomol from
> 1921 to 1924, who spoke for the organization at Lenin's funeral, had
> become a secretary of the Leningrad Party committee and a candidate
> member of the Central Committee in 1937, when he was arrested and
> shot. Nikolai Chaplin, General Secretary of the Komsomol from 1924
> to 1928, was head of the Southeastern Railway when he perished.
> Alexander Mil'chakov, who was General Secretary from 1928 to 1929,
> was also arrested.

In short, Stalin and the NKVD would have us believe that every chief
of the Komsomol from 1918 to 1929 was an "enemy of the people."

Some Komsomol leaders of the new generation were also arrested,
but not as many as Stalin wished. According to A. Mil'chakov, V.
Pikina, and A. Dimentman, in June, 1937, A. V. Kosarev and the
other secretaries of the Komsomol CC were summoned to Stalin's office. Ezhov was there. Stalin began to reprimand Kosarev for the failure
of the Komsomol Central Committee to help the NKVD in discovering
"enemies of the people." None of Kosarev's explanations helped. For
an hour and a half Stalin hammered at one point: the Komsomol CC
must help expose "enemies." Analogous charges against Kosarev were
included in the resolutions of the IVth Plenum of the Komsomol CC,
which met in closed session in 1937 under the direction of Malenkov
and Kaganovich.[33]

Repression of Komsomol officials increased considerably following
this meeting. Among those arrested were:

> P. S. Gorshenin and Fainberg, secretaries of the CC. Vasilii Chemo-
> danov, D. Luk'ianov, G. Lebedev, and A. Kurylev, members of the
> CC. Bubekin, editor of Komsomol'skaia Pravda. S. Andreev, secretary
> of the Ukrainian CC. K. Taishitov, secretary of the Kazakhstan CC. I.
> Artykov, secretary of the Uzbekistan CC. V. A. Aleksandrov, secretary
> of the Moscow obkom.

[32] Sovetskaia Latviia, Mar. 22, 1964.
[33] Stenogramma sobraniia v Muzee revoliutsii, posviashchennogo 60-letiiu so dnia
     rozhdeniia A. Kosareva, p. 16. Ed.: This may be an unpublished manuscript; I
     have been unable to find it in US libraries.

At the end of 1938 it was Kosarev's turn. On November 19–22 there was a Plenum of the Komsomol CC, chaired by A. A. Andreev, with Stalin, Molotov, and Malenkov in attendance. With slander supplied by Mishakova, a Komsomol *apparatchik,* Stalin turned the Plenum into an attack on the Komsomol leadership. Kosarev and most of the other leaders were removed from their posts and soon after arrested. *Komsomol'skaia Pravda* attacked Kosarev for obstructing the war on enemies by arguing that the Komsomol was less infested by them than other groups. This despicable effort to demobilize the vigilantes was defeated, the paper said, by the direct intervention of the Central Committee and by Stalin personally. The war on enemies could now proceed: "There is no doubt that the enemies and politically corrupt people who have led the Komsomol have managed to implant their 'cadres' in many sectors. This political scum is still far from destroyed."[34] And this was published only a few weeks after the twentieth anniversary of the Komsomol had been celebrated with stories of its glorious path and great triumphs.

Many of Kosarev's friends and colleagues were arrested, including Valentina Pikina, Bogachev, and Vershkov. A. Mil'chakov, one of the few who survived many years of confinement, recalls the following names among those arrested:

> Oskar Tarkhanov, Rimma Iurovskaia, Vladimir Faigin, Andrei Shokhin, Dmitrii Matveev, Georgii Ivanov, Gusein Rakhmanov, Ignatii Sharav'ev, and Sergi Saltanov.[35]

Only a few of these people had reached thirty-five. The life of most resembled that of Nikolai Ostrovskii and his autobiographical hero, Pavel Korchagin. Indeed, many of the Komsomol leaders who perished were personal friends of Ostrovskii, who did not live to see what happened to them.[36] And these energetic young people, who had already done much for their country but still had more to do, were declared enemies of the people. Most of them died in the camps or were shot on Stalin's orders.

4

IN 1937–38 THE SOVIET UNION was preparing for an unavoidable war with the fascist countries, which had already begun their aggression in Spain, Abyssinia, and China. Sparing neither energy nor goods, the Soviet people strengthened the defenses of their country, nourish-

---

[34] *Komsomol'skaia Pravda,* Nov. 24, 1938.

[35] A. Mil'chakov, *Pervoe desiatiletie* (Moscow, 1965).

[36] *Ed.:* Ostrovskii's *How the Steel Was Tempered*—also translated as *The Making of a Hero*—is a very popular book in the Soviet Union. Dying of an incurable disease, the young author-hero reviews with pride his service to the Communist cause.

ing the Red Army like a favored child. And precisely in that perilous time Stalin and NKVD struck at the best cadres of the Red Army; in the course of two years they destroyed tens of thousands of loyal commanders and commissars.

The first arrests were made in the second half of 1936 and the beginning of 1937, snatching such heroes as

> I. I. Garkavyi, I. Turovskoi, G. D. Gai, Iu. V. Sablin, D. M. Shmidt, B. Kuz'michev, and Ia. Okhotnikov.

They were accused of connections with Trotskyites and Zinovievites. In June, 1937, the papers announced the arrest, trial, and hasty execution of the most important generals:

> M. V. Tukhachevskii, Russia's greatest military strategist after Frunze, a brilliant organizer with a special interest in the technical modernization of the armed forces.[37] I. E. Iakir, hero of the Civil War, member of the Central Committee, internationally recognized for his military talent. I. P. Uborevich, victor over Denikin and liberator of Vladivostok; V. M. Primakov, famous commander of the "red cossacks" in the Civil War; R. P. Eideman, hero of Kakhovka, head of the Civil Defense Organization, and also a poet, one of the founders of Soviet Latvian literature. Also condemned and shot were B. M. Fel'dman, A. I. Kork, and V. K. Putna.

At the same time the papers announced the suicide of another "enemy of the people":

> Ia. B. Gamarnik, Chief of the Army's Political Division and Deputy Commissar of Defense.

However serious the loss of Tukhachevskii, Iakir, and their comrades, it was only the beginning. Speaking in August, 1937, to a meeting of the Army's political officials, Stalin called for the extirpation of "enemies of the people" who were hiding in the Army. After this speech the Commissar of Defense, Voroshilov, and the Commissar of Internal Affairs, Ezhov, issued an order to the armed forces, which said that there was a far-reaching network of spies in the Army. It was ordered that everyone who had any contact with spies must confess, and everyone who knew or suspected anything about spying activity should report it.

The NKVD then proceeded, in the second half of 1937 and in 1938, to assault the core of the military command: the central *apparat* of the Commissariat of Defense, the Political Administration of the Army, the Revolutionary-Military Council of the USSR, the military districts (*okrugi*), the Navy, and most of the corps, regiments, and divisions. Almost all the most outstanding Red Army commanders who had risen to prominence during the Civil War perished. Marshal

[37] *Voenno-istoricheskii zhurnal*, 1963, No. 4, p. 65.

V. K. Bliukher, commander of the Special Far Eastern Army, a legendary hero of the Civil War, was shot. In the summer of 1938 he directed the rout of the Japanese at Lake Khasan, but his name did not appear in the long lists of those who were decorated for heroism in that battle. On August 18 he was called to Moscow, and on November 9, on Stalin's orders, he was shot. Stalin did not openly make any charges against Bliukher or even announce his death. For a long time the nation did not realize that Bliukher, who was tremendously popular, was dead. Rumors circulated that he was fighting in China under a different name.

Other victims included:

Marshal A. I. Egorov, chief of the General Staff, who had routed Denikin in 1919, died in confinement. I. F. Fed'ko, hero of the Civil War, appointed Deputy Commissar of Defense just before his arrest. V. M. Ordov and Ia. I. Alksnis, Deputy Commissars of Defense; in charge of naval affairs. A. I. Sediakin, E. F. Appog, G. Bokis, N. N. Petin, Ia. M. Fishman, and R. V. Longva, heads of departments in the Commissariat of Defense. I. E. Slavin, commissar. G. A. Osepian and A. S. Bulin, deputy chiefs of the Army's Political Administration. G. D. Bazilevich, Secretary of the Committee of Defense in the USSR Council of Commissars.

Almost all the commanders of the country's military districts (*okrugi*) and fleets were arrested and shot, including such heroes as:

N. V. Kuibyshev, brother of V. V. Kuibyshev, commander of the Transcaucasian military district. S. E. Gribov and N. D. Kashirin, commanders of the North Caucasian military district. M. D. Velikanov, commander of the Transbaikal military district. I. P. Belov, commander of the Belorussian military district. I. K. Griaznov, commander of a district. Ia. P. Gailit, commander of the Siberian military district. I. I. Dubovoi, commander of the Kharkov military district. A. N. Borisenko, commander of the mechanized corps. M. K. Levandovskii, commander of the Primorskaia group of the Far Eastern Army. V. V. Khripin, commander of the Special Aviation Army. A. Ia. Lapin, commander of air forces in the Far East—who had commanded the Amur Army during the Civil War.

Today all these heroes have been completely rehabilitated.

More victims:

E. I. Kovtiukh, the hero of the Taman campaign described by Serafimovich in his novel *The Iron Flood;* I. I. Vatsetis, former commander of the Lettish Rifle Division, and commander in chief of the RSFSR armed forces; I. S. Kutiakov, who at the age of twenty-two replaced V. I. Chapaev as commander of the famous 25th Division, and helped to produce the film *Chapaev;* D. F. Serdich, I. Ia. Strod, and B. S. Gorbachev, Civil War heroes. G. Kh. Eikhe, former commander of the Fifth Army of the Eastern Front, which defeated Kolchak in Irkutsk; one of the few army commanders to survive many years of imprisonment.

Many naval officers were arrested, including:

M. V. Viktorov, commander of the Pacific Fleet. I. K. Kozhanov, commander of the Black Sea Fleet. K. I. Dushenov, commander of the Northern Fleet. A. K. Vekman, head of the naval forces in the Baltic Sea. Admirals and Vice Admirals A. S. Grishin, D. S. Duplitskii, G. P. Kireev, I. M. Ludri, R. A. Muklevich, G. S. Okunev, V. M. Smirnov, E. S. Pantserzhanskii, and S. P. Stavitskii; arrested and shot.

Almost all the military academies were devastated. Among the victims were:

S. A. Pugachev, head of the Military Transport Academy. B. M. Ippo, head of the Military Political Academy. M. Ia. Germanovich, head of the Military Academy of Motorization and Mechanization. D. A. Kuchinskii, head of the General Staff Academy. A. I. Todorskii, a talented journalist and military leader, head of the Air Force Academy and of the administration of higher schools within the Commissariat of Defense; arrested but managed to survive.[38]

Hundreds of teachers and students in these academies also perished, including such outstanding military scientists as

P. I. Vakulich, A. I. Verkhovskii, A. V. Pavlov, and A. A. Svechin.

The Lenin Military-Political Academy was especially hard hit in 1937–38. To justify senseless arrests of the Army's political officials, Stalin brought up the "Belorussian-Tolmachev opposition." In 1928 some political officials of the Belorussian military district and the Academy, which was then named N. G. Tolmachev, had criticized the introduction of one-man control (*edinonachalie*).[39] By 1937 this "opposition" had been forgotten—except by those who started arresting and shooting members of the military councils and directors of the political departments in almost every military district. Most of the victims—such men as M. P. Amelin, L. N. Aronshtam, G. I. Veklichev, G. D. Khakhaniants, A. M. Bitte, and A. I. Mezis—had never had any connection with this "opposition." What is more, in 1937 Stalin himself revived the institution of political commissars in the Army, thereby restricting one-man control. In 1940 one-man control was reestablished, but in 1941 political commissars were reintroduced, only to be abolished in 1942, this time for good. The crucial fact was Stalin's repression of the Army's best commanders *and* commissars; he encouraged distrust of command *and* of political cadres, and thereby undermined discipline in the army.

[38] His tragic fate and courageous behavior were described in B. D'iakov's story "*Iz perezhitogo.*"

[39] *Ed.:* Edinonachalie is the principle that a single individual has ultimate authority and responsibility within an organization, whether a, military unit, a factory, or a governmental agency. In conflict with the revolutionary goal of popular participation and with the notion of collective leadership, *edinonachalie* occasioned disputes in many areas of Soviet life during the twenties.

Many former military leaders who had moved to civilian posts were also arrested, including

I. S. Unshlikht, director of the main administration of the Air Force, candidate member of the Central Committee, from 1935 secretary of the USSR Central Executive Committee. R. I. Berzin, commander of armies on the Eastern and Southern Fronts during the Civil War; later worked in war industry and the Commissariat of Agriculture. D. P. Zhloba, a Civil War hero who subsequently did economic work in the Kuban.

Nor did Stalin spare retired officers. V. I. Shorin, to take a notable example, was shot at the age of sixty-eight. A commander of armies and fronts during the Civil War, he had retired for reasons of health in 1925. The Revolutionary-Military Council of the USSR had issued an order granting him lifetime membership in the Red Army, in recognition of his colossal labors in its creation, his talented leadership throughout the Civil War, and his personal heroism. This was the first time in the Army's history that a man was so honored, but Stalin struck his name from the Army rolls and had him shot.

Stalin vented his enmity even on dead military leaders, consigning to oblivion such well-known soldiers as

V. Triandofilov, K. Kalinovskii, Ia. Fabritsius, S. Kamenev, and V. Vostretsov.

The Army suffered not only from the arrest but also from the demotion and discharge of thousands of talented commanders and commissars, who were expelled from the Party "for loss of vigilance." Even if this type of casualty is ignored, the total losses of the Army and the Navy were enormous. A. I. Todorskii has calculated the number of arrests in the years just before the war against Hitler: 3 of the 5 marshals, 3 of the 4 first-rank army commanders, all 12 of the second-rank army commanders, 60 of the 67 corps commanders, 136 of 199 division commanders, and 221 of 397 brigade commanders; both first-rank fleet admirals (*flagman*), both second-rank fleet admirals, all 6 first-rank admirals, 9 of the 15 second-rank admirals, both first-rank army commissars, all 15 second-rank army commissars, 25 of the 28 corps commissars, 79 of the 97 division commissars, and 34 of the 36 brigade commissars.[40] There were also huge losses among the field-grade and junior officers. The shocking truth can be stated quite simply: never did the officer staff of any army suffer such great losses in any war as the Soviet Army suffered in this time of peace.

[40] Todorskii's figures are apparently incomplete. According to the *Short History of the Great War of the Fatherland* [*Kratkaia istoriia Velikoi Otechestvennoi voiny* (Moscow, 1965), pp. 39–40], all the corps commanders, almost all division and brigade commanders, around half of the regimental commanders, most of the commissars of corps, divisions, and brigades, and a third of the regimental commissars were arrested.

Years of training cadres came to nothing. The Party stratum in the Army was drastically reduced. In 1940 the autumn report of the Inspector General of Infantry showed that, of 225 regimental commanders on active duty that summer, not one had been educated in a military academy, 25 had finished a military school, and the remaining 200 had only completed the courses for junior lieutenants.[41] At the beginning of 1940 more than 70 per cent of the division commanders, about 70 per cent of regimental commanders, and 60 per cent of military commissars and heads of political divisions had occupied these positions for a year only. And all this happened just before the worst war in history.

The destruction of the best officers of the Red Army caused great rejoicing among the Germans. It was a major consideration in Hitler's plans for an attack on the USSR. At the Nürnberg trial, Marshal Keitel testified that many German generals had warned Hitler against attacking the USSR, arguing that the Red Army was a strong opponent. But Hitler rejected their misgivings. "The first-class high-ranking officers," he told Keitel, "were wiped out by Stalin in 1937, and the new generation cannot yet provide the brains they need." On January 9, 1941, Hitler told a meeting of Nazi generals planning the attack on the USSR: "They do not have good commanders."[42]

5

STALIN RELIED on the punitive organs of the state to carry out his mass repression. But an important part, a precondition, was the physical destruction of thousands of officials in the punitive organs themselves. This ruthless "purge," in 1936–37, was a complex process. The officials in these organs could hardly be described as good Chekists. Most officials in the NKVD, the courts, and the Procurator's office had taken part in the eviction of millions of kulaks and middle peasants in 1930–33, the repression of "bourgeois specialists," the "gold campaign" of 1930–31, and the illegal repression of former oppositionists in 1935–36. In the process a sort of selection was at work, giving first place to people like Iagoda, Zaporozhets, Ul'rikh, and Vyshinskii. Many leading officials degenerated, losing the qualities that F. E. Dzerzhinskii had tried to inculcate in his assistants. But this degenerative process was not rapid enough to suit Stalin. NKVD officials who had readily consented to provocation and fraud against people of alien classes or ex-oppositionists were not so ready to turn the same weapons against the basic cadres of the Party and the Soviet state. Not all the

[41] V. A. Anfilov, *Nachalo Velikoi Otechestvennoi voiny* (Moscow, 1962), p. 28.
[42] A. I. Poltorak, *Niurnbergskii epilog* (Moscow, 1965), pp. 324–26.

officials in the punitive organs approved of the "new" methods of investigation and trial. So Stalin decided, toward the end of 1936, to "renovate" these organs en masse. Not the least factor in this decision was his desire to get rid of witnesses and participants in his former crimes, a concern that would prove to be self-perpetuating.

Earlier I mentioned the arrest and shooting of Commissar Iagoda, along with Deputies V. A. Balitskii and Ia. D. Agranov. In 1937 T. D. Deribas was arrested and shot. He had managed the NKVD in the Far East, and some Party officials from that region, notably P. I. Shabalkin, say that Deribas opposed the repression of Party and government cadres. E. G. Evdokimov, the first Chekist to receive four Orders of the Red Banner, was also arrested. He had helped to organize the trial of the "Industrial Party," and, transferring to Party work in 1936, he exerted himself to "purge" his *oblast* of ex-oppositionists. But in 1937 Evdokimov himself was arrested and shot. Also shot was Iagoda's faithful protégé, L. G. Mironov, head of the Economic Division of the NKVD.

In 1936–37 many well-known Chekists were arrested and shot, including

S. Arshakuni, A. Kh. Artuzov, A. Pilliar, V. R. Dombrovskii, M. V. Slonimskii, N. G. Krapivianskii, G. E. Prokof'ev, A. A. Slutskii, and L. B. Zalin.

According to S. O. Gazarian, M. V. Ostragradskii, and M. M. Ishov, most of these people were well-meaning Communists who did not want to take part in the destruction of Party and state cadres. Other victims included:

V. N. Mantsev, a personal friend of Dzerzhinskii; shot. I. M. Leplevskii, Belorussian Commissar of Internal Affairs, who refused to apply the "new methods"; shot. F. T. Fomin, one of Dzerzhinskii's cohorts; arrested but survived.[43] M. S. Pogrebinskii, organizer of many communes for delinquent and abandoned children, the inspiration of the excellent film *Putevka v zhizn'* (*Road to Life*). Appointed director of the NKVD in Gorky *oblast*, Pogrebinskii killed himself to avoid participation in lawlessness, as his suicide letter reveals.

The head of one of the Ukrainian NKVD agencies, Kozel'skii, also committed suicide. Indeed, a wave of suicides swept through the NKVD in 1937, taking away not only honorable officials but also some who had already traveled pretty far on the road of crime. Kurskii, for example, who had recently received the Order of Lenin for his "successful" preparation of the trial of the "Parallel Center," shot himself.

Other victims included:

[43] See Fomin's *Zapiski starogo chekista*, published in 1964.

E. P. Berzin, head of Dal'stroi, organizer of the first camps in the Kolyma region, former secretary to Dzerzhinskii and former commander of the Lettish Rifle Division, arrested in 1937 and shot in 1938. I. D. Kashirin, second of the Kashirin brothers to perish, member of the NKVD collegium. G. I. Bokii, member of the NKVD collegium, Party member since 1900, survivor of eleven terms in the Peter-Paul Fortress. Ia. Kh. Peters, a Chekist of the Dzerzhinskii school.

In his unpublished book "It Must Not Happen Again" ("Eto ne dolzhno povtorit'sia"), S. Gazarian, an old Chekist of Dzerzhinskii's school, gives a good description of the terror that arose within the NKVD itself. He headed the Economic Section of the NKVD in Georgia and Transcaucasia in 1937, when he was arrested. He survived all sorts of torture and prolonged confinement to tell how dozens of honorable NKVD officials in Georgia were seized and placed in hastily built prisons by their former friends and subordinates. Many Chekists, faced with the choice between criminal actions and arrest, committed suicide. On the other hand, it was in just those years that Beria's creatures won swift promotion, first in the Georgian, then in the USSR NKVD—men like Kobulov and Khazan, Krimian and Savitskii, Dekanozov and Merkulov, Goglidze and Mil'shtein.

Soviet intelligence was also decimated, both the NKVD branch and the branch within the Commissariat of Defense. Soon after Slutskii was done away with, his successor, Shpigel'glas, was arrested and shot. Many foreign agents were recalled to Moscow, sent to sanatoria, and then, after a "rest," arrested and shot. Among the victims were Nikolai Smirnov (Glinskii), NKVD resident in France, and L'vovich of the military intelligence. However, quite a few refused to return to certain death. To get even with these people, with diplomats who would not return, and with other people who were inconvenient to Stalin, Ezhov set up a special task force to work abroad. After long manhunts, many people were killed, including:

Ignatii Reis, tracked down and killed in Switzerland. V. G. Krivitskii, NKVD resident in Holland, who was tracked down and killed in the United States. Agabekov, former NKVD resident in Turkey, who had quit Soviet intelligence in 1929 and was tracked down and killed in Belgium.

The founder and director of Soviet military intelligence, Ia. K. Berzin, who in 1937 was named chief adviser to the Spanish Republican government, was recalled and shot.[44] Twice Berzin had been sentenced to death by tsarist courts for revolutionary activity in the Baltic region. But it was the sentence of a Soviet court that secured the death of this outstanding leader, who trained hundreds of fighters on the secret front, including Richard Sorge, Hero of the Soviet

[44] See *Komsomol'skaia Pravda*, Nov. 13, 1964.

Union.[45] Sorge's comrade Karl Ramm was recalled from Shanghai and shot. There are reports that Sorge himself was called to Moscow for the same treatment but refused to return. His wife, Ekaterina Maksimova, who was in Moscow, was arrested and perished. S. P. Uritskii, who replaced Berzin as head of military intelligence, was shot. His uncle, M. S. Uritskii, had been killed in 1918, when he was head of the Petrograd Cheka—by White Guardists.

The judicial and procuratorial organs were also savagely purged in 1936–38. In addition to N. Krylenko, the Commissar of Justice whose fate has already been described, I. A. Akulov, Procurator General of the USSR, was dismissed and then arrested. One of the oldest Bolshevik activists, he had organized the famous demonstration of 60,000 Petrograd workers in 1912. In the thirties Akulov tried to fight Iagoda's abuse of power, but Iagoda together with Vyshinskii— and of course with Stalin's support—got rid of Akulov.[46] Many other leading judicial officials were arrested and done to death, including:

A. V. Medvedev, a member of the Supreme Court. V. A. Degot', Procurator of the RSFSR. N. M. Nemtsov, member of the Supreme Court and chairman of the Moscow city court. R. P. Katanian and M. V. Ostrogorskii, high officials in the procuracy. N. N. Gomerov, Iu. A. Dzervit, and Kuznetsov, officials of the military procuracy.

In 1938, without any explanation, P. A. Krasikov, who had been one of Lenin's oldest comrades and vice-president of the IInd Party Congress in 1903, was dismissed from his seat on the Supreme Court.

Iu. Trifonov has told the tragic story of Aron Sol'ts, famous in his time as the "conscience of the Party." Working in the procurator's office, he was one of the few to demand evidence of "enemy" charges. He did so when B. Trifonov, the author's father, was caught up in such a case. Vyshinskii told him:

"If the NKVD has arrested him, it means he is an enemy." Sol'ts grew red and shouted: "You're lying! I've known Trifonov for thirty-four years as a true Bolshevik, but I know you as a Menshevik," and he threw down his briefcase and left. . . .

Sol'ts began to be taken off cases. He did not give in. In October, 1937, at the height of the repression, Sol'ts suddenly began to criticize Vyshinskii at a Party conference in Sverdlovsk. He demanded the creation of a special commission to investigate Vyshinskii's activity as Procurator General. He still believed that the methods introduced when Lenin was alive had some force. . . . Some of the

[45] *Ed.:* Sorge was a German who worked for Soviet intelligence in Japan. He was discovered and executed by the Japanese in 1944. He was made a Hero of the Soviet Union twenty years later.

[46] See the stenographic record of the meeting in the Museum of the Revolution commemorating Akulov. *Ed.:* This seems to be an unpublished manuscript. It is not cited in A. S. Blinov, *Ivan Akulov* (Moscow, 1967).

audience froze with terror, but most began to shout, "Down with
him! Get off the platform! A wolf in sheep's clothing!" Sol'ts kept
on speaking. Some enraged vigilantes ran up to the old man and
dragged him off the stand. It's hard to say why Stalin did not get
even with Sol'ts the simple way, by arresting him. . . . In February,
1938, Sol'ts was finally dismissed from the procurator's office. He
tried to get an appointment with Stalin. He had worked together
with Stalin in the Petersburg underground in 1912–13, even sharing
a bunk with him, but Stalin would not see him.

   Sol'ts still did not give in; he announced a hunger strike. Then
they stuck him in a psychiatric hospital. Two hefty orderlies came
to his house on Serafimovich Street, grabbed the little man with the
big head of gray hair, bound him, and carried him down to the
ambulance. Later he was released, but he was broken.[47]

Ostrogorskii says that Sol'ts announced his hunger strike after
Vyshinskii tried blackmail, showing him some depositions that denounced Sol'ts. In his letters to Stalin Sol'ts continued to use *ty*, the
familiar form of "you," and to call Stalin "Koba." When every meeting began the ridiculous practice of electing an "honorary presidium"
of Politburo members, who were not even present, Sol'ts, according
to A. V. Snegov, refused to stand and applaud during this religious
rite. But that was the protest of one man. Sol'ts' death, during the
war, was briefly noted only in the wall newspaper of the procurator's
office.

   Hundreds of Soviet legal officials shared Sol'ts' fate. They were
pushed aside in favor of unprincipled, cruel people, such as Vyshinskii,
Ul'rikh, Matulevich, Dmitriev, G. P. Lipov, and S. Ia. Ul'ianova.

6

IN THE MID-THIRTIES most non-Soviet parties were underground. To
preserve the leading core of these parties, many of their Central Committee members lived in Moscow, which was the center of the Comintern, the Communist Youth International, the Peasant International,
the Trade Union International, and so on. There were also several
special schools, where young Communists from abroad were trained
for underground work. In this way the Soviet Union served as the
base and center of the world Communist movement. And so the fraternal Communist parties could be and were seriously hurt by the
campaign of terror in the USSR.

   First of all, many Soviet officials of international Communist organizations were arrested and perished, among them:

[47] Iurii Trifonov, *Otblesk kostra* (Moscow, 1966), pp. 26–27.

I. Piatnitskii, secretary of the Comintern's Executive Committee, who had been leader of the Moscow insurrection and was greatly esteemed by Lenin. Rafael Khitarov, for many years head of the Communist Youth International, transferred to Party work in Cheliabinsk *oblast* before he was arrested and shot. Pavel Mif, rector of Sun Yat-sen University; K. I. Smolianskii, G. Safarov, B. A. Vasil'ev, Magyar, Kraevskii, and Ali-khanov, leading officials in the Comintern *apparat*.

M. A. Trilisser, who had been a Deputy Chairman of the OGPU, became director of a special section of the Comintern in the mid-thirties. According to V. S——, one of the jobs assigned to Trilisser was to purge the Comintern of "enemies of the people." Soon Trilisser himself fell victim to that savage purge.

Along with Soviet officials, many foreign Communists were killed. Béla Kun, the leader of the short-lived Hungarian Soviet Republic in 1919, was arrested and shot. Other leaders of the Hungarian Party perished, including F. Karikás, Bokányi, and Farkas Gábor.

The Polish Communist Party was especially hard hit. Victims included:

> Juljan Leszczynski-Lenski, general secretary of the Party's CC. A. Warski, one of the founders of the Social Democratic and then of the Communist Party of Poland, arrested and shot at the age of seventy. Wera Kostrzewa (Maria Koszucka), who had given more than forty years of her life to the Polish workers' movement.

Dozens of other leading Polish Communists were also arrested, and most of them perished, together with the leaders of the Western Ukrainian and West Belorussian Parties:

> R. D. Vol'f, E. A. Idel', I. K. Loginovich, M. S. Maiskii, N. P. Maslov-skii, A. S. Slavinskii.

In the summer of 1938 these two parties were wholly dissolved along with the Polish Communist Party, just when they were showing progress in the creation of an antifascist front. This blow at the Polish revolutionary movement seriously hampered the repulsion of German aggression and the development of the national liberation movement.

Many Polish Communists were in Polish prisons when the news reached them. Marian Naszkowski recalls the impact in his memoirs:

> A little item buried in the columns of the *Kurjer Codzienny* [*Daily Express*] reported the dissolution of the Polish Communist Party. We were stunned.
>
> At first we thought this report was a base provocation. . . . But the next days' papers had more detailed reports, and however we tried to suppress our anxiety, they continued to reveal the sorry truth. Finally, someone who had just been arrested brought official confirmation.
>
> An oppressive silence fell over the prison.

How could anyone believe such terrible accusations? How could we reconcile the monstrous crimes imputed to these people with the splendid image that we had formed of them?

Lenski, Warski, Wera Kostrzewa, Henrykowski, Pruchniak, Rwal, Bronkowski—such heroic individuals, such coryphaei of our movement. . . . People tried to figure out the causes by digging up the old history of factional struggle between the "majority" and the "minority." . . . But none of the pieces fitted, the whole thing seemed very implausible.

After all, the "liquidated agents," as the Comintern report called them, included people from the "majority" as well as the "minority." . . .

However, even if in the final analysis we accepted the news that the entire leadership of our Party was consumed by provocation, then we had to face the most important question:

What would happen to the movement?

Who were we now?

Could it be that our glorious militant Party, which we took such pride in, which had raised us, for which each of us would give his life, could it be an agency of the Pilsudskyites?

And we all answered, No, a thousand times no.

A Party that had done so much to awaken the revolutionary spirit of the masses, a Party that had led mighty working-class brigades to war with capitalism, with fascism, could not be a fraud.

. . . Shaken to the depths of our souls, accepting, with pain, with bitterness, the "truth" about our leaders' treachery, not for a moment did we doubt our idea or the rightness of our movement, our Party. That gave thousands of Communists the strength to live through the difficult times that had arrived. That was the basis for the resurrection of the Party later on.[48]

The slanderous accusations made against the Communist parties of Poland, the West Ukraine, and West Belorussia were retracted only after the XXth Party Congress in 1956. The parties of the Soviet Union, Finland, Bulgaria, and Italy joined the Polish United Workers' Party in issuing a special declaration on this subject. The Polish Communist leaders who perished in the years of Stalin's cult were completely rehabilitated.

Serious losses were also suffered by the Communist parties of Latvia, Lithuania, and Estonia, many of whose leaders lived in the Soviet Union. The innocent victims included:

Hans Pögelman and Jan Anvelt, Estonian Communists and Comintern officials. Berzin-Ziemelis, Ia. Lentsmanis, Jan Krumins-Pilat, and E. Apine, Latvian Communists. Rudolf Ia. Endrup, E. Tautkaite, N. Janson, F. Deglav, R. Mirring, O. Riastas, I. Kiaspart, R. Vakman, E.

[48] M. Naszkowski, *Nespokoinye dni. Vospominaniia o tridtsatykh godakh,* trans. from Polish (Moscow, 1962), pp. 209–10.

Zandreiter, F. Pauzer, O. Dzenis, and a great many other Baltic Communists.

As a result of this repression the Central Committees of these parties either ceased to function or struggled on in isolation from the Comintern.[49]

Many Bessarabian Communists living in the Soviet Union were arrested, including

S. Bubnovskii, K. Syrbu, S. Bantke and I. Fortuna.[50]

The Iranian Communist leader A. Sultan-Zade, who had emigrated to the Soviet Union in 1932, perished. The Mexican Communist leader Gómez was arrested but managed to survive.

The leadership of the Yugoslav Party was decimated. Among the victims were:

Filip Filipović (Valija Boskovićš), one of the Party's founders. Vlada Čopić, Secretary of the CC, who returned from Spain, where he commanded the 18th International Lincoln Brigade. S. Cvijić, D. Cvijić, Horvatin, and Novaković.

Tito discloses that the dissolution of the Yugoslav Party was even discussed, since all its leaders living in the Soviet Union had been arrested. "I was alone," Tito writes.

The Bulgarian Party suffered heavy losses, including Popov and Tanev. Together with Georgi Dimitrov at the famous Leipzig trial they had obliged a fascist court to acquit them, and the USSR had given them Soviet citizenship. But a few years later Popov and Tanev were arrested, and this time a Soviet court condemned them. (Popov survived and is today working in Bulgaria.) The NKVD also put together a special file against the leader of the Comintern, Dimitrov, for the purpose of provocation.

Many Chinese Communists were arrested, including Go Shao-tan, their Party's representative in the Comintern. The entire Korean section of the Comintern was arrested. Mukherjee, Chattopadhyaya, Luhani, and other leaders of the Indian Party were destroyed.

The arrests of German Communists require special mention. Theirs was the largest colony of foreign Communists and antifascists, since they had fled to the Soviet Union—or, on Party orders, had moved—to save themselves from Hitlerite terror. But an even crueler terror was waiting for many of them in the USSR. The NKVD tried to give an "ideological basis" to the mass arrests of German antifascists. For example, the *Journal de Moscou* declared: "It is no exaggeration to

---

[49] See *Ocherki po istorii kompartii Estonii* (Tallin, 1963), II. *Ocherki istorii kommunisticheskoi partii Latvii* (Riga, 1966), II.
[50] *Ocherki po istorii kommunisticheskoi partii Moldavii* (Kishinev, 1964).

say that every Japanese living abroad is a spy, or that every German citizen living abroad is an agent of the Gestapo."[51] Toward the end of April, 1938, the arrest of 842 German antifascists had been recorded by the German representative to the Executive Committee of the Comintern. The actual number was considerably greater. Many Germans were arrested right in the House of Political Emigrés, in Moscow. Among the arrested were:

> Hugo Eberlein, a participant in the first Comintern Congress, Secretary of the German Central Committee and its representative to the Comintern's Executive Committee. Werner Hirsch, secretary and friend of Ernst Thälmann. Leo Flieg, Secretary of the German CC. Hermann Remmele, Politburo member.[52] Heinz Neumann and Hermann Schubert, CC members. Kippenberger, the leader of the illegal *apparat* of the German CC. Heinrich Susskind, the chief editor of *Rote Fahne*.

Willi Münzenberg, one of the best Comintern officials, was expelled from the Party for refusing to leave Paris for Moscow and certain death.

The family of Karl Liebknecht,[53] which had received asylum in the Soviet Union, was persecuted. His son was expelled from the Party and his nephew Kurt was arrested. (After his rehabilitation, Kurt Liebknecht went to the German Democratic Republic, where he was given a responsible position.) S. Gazarian tells about a large group of German Communists confined in the Solovetskaia prison. When they were being transferred to a camp, they organized obstructive actions to protest the inhuman conditions of transportation. N. P. Smirnova says that a large group of German Communists was kept in the prisons of Vladivostok. When Evgeniia Ginzburg was in the Butyrskaia Prison, she talked to a German woman Communist whose body showed terrible scars of torture, first by the Gestapo and then by the NKVD. After the friendship pact with Germany was signed, in September, 1939, Stalin committed yet another crime without precedent in our country's history: a large group of German antifascists and Jews, who had fled from the Gestapo to the USSR, were handed over to Nazi Germany. Henceforth the Soviet borders were closed to refugees from enslaved Europe.

Many Italian, Finnish, Austrian, Spanish, Czechoslovakian, French, Rumanian, Dutch, and even American and Brazilian Communists were arrested and died. It is a terrible paradox that the West European Communist leaders and activists who lived in the USSR perished,

---

[51] *Journal de Moscou,* Apr. 12, 1938 (No. 19).

[52] In the early thirties the Neumann-Remmele group had opposed a united-front policy, thereby carrying out Stalin's line. Their arrest permitted all the past mistakes of the KPD and of Stalin himself to be blamed on them.

[53] *Ed.:* A founder of the Spartacist League, which became the German Communist Party. He was murdered by German rightists in 1919.

while most of those who were in prison in their native lands in 1937–38 survived.

The repression of fraternal Communists, of revolutionaries who had taken political asylum in our country, was doubly criminal. It is strange that the present Chinese leaders somehow forget about this "contribution" of Stalin to the international Communist movement.

7

SOVIET SCIENCE could not escape the tragic situation that took shape in the mid-thirties. Thousands of scientists, engineers, and business managers died, both as a result of Stalin's direct interference and because various kinds of careerists and adventurers took advantage of the spy- and wrecker-phobia. Many disputes that began in the pages of scientific journals ended in the torture chambers of the NKVD. Senseless, savage repression caused exceptionally great losses in many fields.

In history, for example, tendentious criticism of M. N. Pokrovskii's mistakes turned into a political pogrom. Many of his students and followers were labeled Trotskyites, wreckers, and terrorists, and then were arrested. "It is not accidental," runs a directive of the time,

> that the so-called school of Pokrovskii became a base for wrecking, as the NKVD has discovered; a base for enemies of the people, for Trotskyite-Bukharinite hirelings of fascism, for wreckers, spies, and terrorists, who cleverly disguised themselves with the harmful anti-Leninist concepts of M. N. Pokrovskii. Only unforgivable, idiotic carelessness and loss of vigilance by people on the historical front can explain the fact that this shameless gang of enemies of Leninism long and safely carried on their wrecking work in the field of history.[54]

Victims of Stalinist terror included:

> Iu. M. Steklov, a leading historian and revolutionary, one of the first editors of *Izvestiia*. V. G. Sorin, one of the first biographers of Lenin, editor of the first collections of Lenin's works, Deputy Director of Marx-Engels-Lenin Institute. V. G. Knorin, director of the Institute of Party History within the Institute of Red Professorship, member of the Party's Central Committee. N. M. Lukin, director of the Institute of History within the Academy of Sciences. N. N. Popov, secretary of the Ukrainian CC. N. N. Vanag, Piontkovskii, S. Bantke, G. S. Fridliand, E. Veis, Iu. T. Tevosian, who perished. S. Lotte, S. M. Dubrovskii, and P. F. Preobrazhenskii, who lived to see their rehabilitation.

Monstrous forms of struggle appeared on the philosophical "front" too. Fundamental arguments between different groups had ended in

---

[54] *Protiv istoricheskoi kontseptsii M. N. Pokrovskogo* (Moscow, 1939), I, p. 5.

1930–32, and many participants in the discussions that raged at that time had moved to constructive economic and cultural work all over the country. But some philosophers did not forget. When the struggle against "enemies of the people" began, they tried to settle old scores with the help of the punitive organs. In the pages of *Pod znamenem marksizma*[55] accusations of philosophical mistakes—mechanism, idealism, agnosticism, subjectivism, Machism, sophistry—quickly turned into various kinds of political accusations, and then to fashionable and highly effective charges of hostile and even terrorist activity. As a result of this pogrom, organized by such people as M. B. Mitin, P. Iudin, F. Konstantinov, and P. Chagin, dozens of Soviet philosophers were arrested, not only former "mechanists" or "Menshevizing idealists," but fully orthodox dialecticians and materialists. The victims included

S. Varjas, I. K. Luppol, N. A. Miliutin, I. Razumovskii, N. Karev, L. Rudas, S. Pichugin, G. S. Tymianskii, A. R. Medvedev, M. Furshchik, and G. F. Dmitriev.

Most of them died in confinement.

The outstanding philosopher and Party official Jan Sten is remembered by his friend E. P. Frolov:

Hardly anyone knew Stalin better than Sten. Stalin, as we know, received no systematic education. Without success Stalin struggled to understand philosophical questions. And then, in 1925, he called in Jan Sten, one of the leading Marxist philosophers of that time, to direct his study of Hegelian dialectics. Sten drew up a program of study for Stalin and conscientiously, twice a week, dinned Hegelian wisdom into his illustrious pupil. (In those years dialectics was studied by a system that M. N. Pokrovskii[56] worked out in the Institute of Red Professorship, a parallel study of Marx's *Capital* and Hegel's *Phenomenology of Mind*.) Often he told me in confidence about these lessons, about the difficulties he, as the teacher, was having because of his student's inability to master the material of Hegelian dialectics. Jan often dropped in to see me after a lesson with Stalin, in a depressed and gloomy state, and despite his naturally cheerful disposition, he found it difficult to regain his equilibrium. Sten was not only a leading philosopher but also an active politician, an outstanding member of the Leninist cohort of old Bolsheviks. The meetings with Stalin, the conversations with him on philosophical matters, during which Jan would always bring up contemporary political problems, opened his eyes more and more to Stalin's true nature, his striving for one-man rule, his crafty schemes and methods for putting them into effect. . . . As early as 1928, in a small circle of his personal friends, Sten said: "Koba will do

[55] *Ed.: Under the Banner of Marxism,* the chief journal of Soviet philosophy from 1922 to 1944.
[56] *Ed.:* In fact the philosopher A. M. Deborin originated this system.

things that will put the trials of Dreyfus and of Beilis in the shade." This was his answer to his comrades' request for a prognosis of Stalin's leadership over ten years' time. Thus, Sten was not wrong either in his characterization of Stalin's rule or in the time schedule for the realization of his bloody schemes.

Sten's lessons with Stalin ended in 1928. Several years later he was expelled from the Party for a year and exiled to Akmolinsk. In 1937 he was seized on the direct order of Stalin, who declared him one of the chiefs of the Menshevizing idealists.[57] At the time the printer had just finished a volume of the *Great Soviet Encyclopedia* that contained a major article by Sten, "Dialectical Materialism." The ordinary solution—and such problems were ordinary in those years—was to destroy the entire printing. But in this case the publishers of the *Encyclopedia* found a cheaper solution. Only one page of the whole printing was changed, the one with the signature of Jan Sten. "Dialectical Materialism" appeared over the name of M. B. Mitin, the future academician and editor in chief of *Voprosy filosofii,* thus adding to his list the one publication that is really interesting. On June 19, 1937, Sten was put to death in Lefortovskaia Prison.

A similar pogrom was organized in jurisprudence by Vyshinskii, acting as Stalin's mouthpiece. Many prominent jurists died, most notably E. B. Pashukanis.

Education was also engulfed in tragedy. Many outstanding educational administrators and theorists perished, including:

> M. S. Epshtein, Deputy Commissar of Education of the RSFSR. M. A. Aleksinskii, a member of the collegium of the Commissariat, who had received the Red Banner during the Civil War for ending illiteracy in the Ninth Army. A. P. Pinkevich, S. M. Kamenev, A. P. Shokhin, M. M. Pistrak, S. A. Gaisinovich, and M. V. Krupenina.

In almost every autonomous and union republic the commissariat of education was decimated. Not only administrators but tens of thousands of ordinary teachers perished. One of the most gifted victims was Alexei Gastev, who had been a professional revolutionary, organizing workers' brigades under the name Lavrentii. He was also a poet, author of the book *Poetry of the Workers' Attack.* After the Revolution, he applied all his energy to a new branch of science, time and motion study, and to the study of professional training. After he and many of his assistants were arrested, the Central Institute of Labor, which he directed, was closed, and all serious research in the field of time and motion study and industrial psychology was stopped. Of course, there were some mistakes in his own and his Institute's work, but on the whole it was work of great importance, which Lenin had endorsed.

[57] *Ed.:* For an explanation, see above, pp. 143–44.

Soviet linguistics also suffered considerable losses. N. M. Siiak, director of the Linguistics Institute in Kiev, died; in 1919 his application for Party membership had been endorsed by Lenin. Arrest and death were also the lot of N. A. Nevskii, the brilliant orientalist who deciphered Tangut[58] hieroglyphics. His great scholarly work, *Tangut Philology,* preserved in the archives of the Academy of Sciences, won a Lenin Prize in 1962.

Among many other talented scholars lost to science:

N. P. Gorbunov, secretary of the Academy of Sciences, former secretary of Lenin, and administrative chief of the Council of People's Commissars. N. F. Bogdanov, secretary of the All-Union Geographical Society. G. I. Krumin, economist, a director of the *Great Soviet Encyclopedia.* I. N. Barkhanov, economist. I. F. Iushkevich, chemist. I. A. Teodorovich, a leading agrarian economist and old Bolshevik, head of the Society of Political Prisoners and Deportees, which was of course dissolved.

"Intensified class battles," to quote the journal *Sovetskaia Nauka (Soviet Science)*, raged in all the natural sciences. Almost all the best physicists of our country—I. E. Tamm and V. A. Fok, for example— were attacked by the press as "idealists" and "smugglers of enemy ideas." Many were arrested, including

A. I. Berg, L. D. Landau, P. I. Lukirskii, and Iu. B. Rumer; they managed to survive. M. P. Bronshtein, a brilliant theoretical physicist; shot in 1938 at the age of thirty-two. V. K. Frederiks, a well-known theoretical physicist. Iu. A. Krutkov, a specialist in mechanics and mathematical physics. S. P. Shubin, a young theorist, one of Tamm's best students. A. A. Vitt, a founder of the Soviet school of nonlinear oscillations. I. N. Shpil'rein, who, like the previous four, never returned.

Even mathematics experienced "heightened class struggle." In the summer of 1936 *Pravda* attacked the great mathematician N. N. Luzin, one of the founders of the Moscow mathematical school. *Pravda* called him a "*chernosotenets,*"[59] "counterrevolutionary," and "wrecker on the mathematical front." The entire Moscow mathematical school, including such outstanding mathematicians as A. N. Kolmogorov. M. V. Keldysh, and S. L. Sobolev, was declared reactionary and bourgeois. Academician Luzin, however, escaped arrest; the Presidium of the Academy of Sciences merely gave him a warning.

Some scientists, fearing repression, refused to return from trips abroad. Among these "nonreturners" (*nevozvrashchentsy*) were A. E. Chichibabin and N. N. Ipat'ev, outstanding chemists, and N. V. Timofeev-Resovskii, geneticist. It is hardly surprising that in the sec-

[58] *Ed.:* Tangut was a Tibetan kingdom in the 11th to 13th centuries.
[59] *Ed.:* A member of the Black Hundreds, prerevolutionary gangs that used violence against radicals and Jews.

ond half of the thirties, Stalin cut down foreign trips to the barest minimum.

The years of terror brought special tragedy to biology and the agricultural sciences. As early as 1936 some leading biologists were arrested on false charges of Trotskyism, espionage, and wrecking activity, including

I. I. Agol, geneticist, secretary of the Ukrainian Academy of Sciences. S. G. Levit, director of the Institute of Medical Genetics, the leading Soviet specialist on the subject (the Institute was closed). Ia. M. Uranovskii, distinguished Darwinist and historian of science.

The young agronomist T. D. Lysenko took advantage of these early arrests to mount a noisy campaign of slander against many leaders of biology and the agricultural sciences. Lacking any serious knowledge of world science, he and his aide, I. I. Prezent, made up for their ignorance by unrestrained demagogy, including unfounded political accusations against their scientific opponents. As a result arrests were especially extensive among biologists and agricultural specialists. Institutes of cotton, stockbreeding, agrochemistry, and plant protection saw their leaders decimated. We have space for only a small list:

A. I. Muralov, president of the Lenin Academy of Agricultural Sciences, arrested and shot. G. K. Meister, a major plant breeder, awarded the Order of Lenin shortly before he perished. N. K. Kol'tsov, another of the country's leading biologists, was defamed and fired and soon died.

The arrest and death of these scientists did not stop the discussion in biology. The discussion went on in the same intolerable manner, still accompanied by arrests:

N. I. Vavilov, a great plant breeder, geneticist, geographer, administrator of science; founder and first President of the Lenin Academy of Agricultural Sciences. Arrested in 1940 and died in prison in 1943. G. K. Karpechenko, G. A. Levitskii, L. I. Govorov, and N. V. Kovalev. They were pupils of Vavilov, of whom only Kovalev survived arrest.

In that period Lysenko and Prezent worked mainly in the biological sciences, closely cooperating, however, with V. R. Williams[60] and a group of his supporters, who mounted an assault on agronomy. Research agronomists who disagreed with Williams' grassland (*travopol'naia*) system of crop rotation were falsely accused of wrecking and arrested. Many crop specialists in the Commissariat of Agriculture, in Gosplan, and in the All-Union Institute of Fertilizers shared their fate. Academician N. M. Tulaikov, a Communist scientist, was

---

[60] *Ed.:* The Russian son of an American engineer who helped build the first major railroad in Russia.

sent to die in a concentration camp. Sh. R. Tsintsadze, one of the best products of Prianishnikov's school of agricultural chemistry, also perished.

Not only the fields mentioned but all branches of biological science suffered great losses. For example:

P. F. Zdradovskii, V. A. Barykin, O. O. Gartokh, I. L. Krichevskii, M. I. Shtutser, L. A. Zil'ber, A. D. Sheboldaeva, G. I. Safonova—microbiologists, many of whom died in confinement. G. A. Nadson, brother of the poet, microbiologist, age seventy-three when arrested, died in an Arctic camp; K. A. Mekhonshin, who fought in the Civil War, director in the 1930's of the Institute of Oceanography and Fish Industry. A. A. Mikheev, botanist, beaten to death by a guard in the Kolyma region. I. N. Filip'ev, botanist, and A. V. Znamenskii and N. N. Troitskii, entomologists.

Neither did medical science escape. V. S. Khol'tsman, director of the Central Tuberculosis Institute and world-renowned specialist, perished. K. Kh. Kokh, a distinguished surgeon, was shot in the Kolyma region for failing to fulfill his quota in the gold mines. Not all the arrested doctors worked in gold mines; some hospitals in the Kolyma region equaled many in Moscow in their number of eminent physicians.

Repression struck at thousands of the technical intelligentsia, including leading inventors, designers, directors, engineers, even shop superintendents. The Soviet aviation industry was hard hit:

N. M. Kharlamov, chief of the Central Aviation Institute, arrested along with a large group of his colleagues. A. N. Tupolev, V. M. Petliakov, V. M. Miasishchev, and Kovalev, the major airplane designers. Beliaikin, the head of the aviation industry, Usachev, the director of an experimental factory, and Tomashevich, designer, all charged with sabotage after Chkalov's[61] fatal crash. M. Leitenzen, founder of the Society for Interplanetary Travel at the Zhukovskii Academy. S. M. Dansker, whose arrest and the subsequent closing down of his experimental centers interrupted development of an airplane with a rotating wing for a long time.

Many designers in the armaments industry were destroyed, including:

V. I. Bekauri, creator of various weapons. V. I. Zaslavskii, tank designer. L. Kurchevskii, inventor of the best recoilless cannon. I. T. Kleimenov and G. E. Langemak, rocket experts, inventors of the famous Katiusha rocket. S. P. Korolev, one of the great rocket experts of the century, spent several years in a camp at hard labor, until he was transferred to a special institute where he worked on rockets, but still as a prisoner (zek), plagued by serious illnesses that began in the camps.

[61] Ed.: V. P. Chkalov, 1904–38, was acclaimed for his 1936 flight across the North Pole, from Moscow to Portland, Oregon.

Repression in the Agency for Anti-Aircraft Defense had serious consequences. The theory of radiolocation was worked out in the Soviet Union at the beginning of the thirties, and in 1934 the first stations for spotting planes were built. Similar developments took place in the United States and in Great Britain only in 1935. At the end of 1934 the Commissariat of Defense made the first contract with a Leningrad factory to build five experimental radar stations; in the U.S. the first such contract was concluded only five years later. But in August, 1937, the leading radar engineer within the Agency for Anti-Aircraft Defense, P. K. Oshchepkov, was arrested. So was N. Smirnov, director of the radar program, along with many other people in the Agency. As a result, the Army entered the Second World War without radar. The first radar stations used against German aircraft were bought from England and the USA at the end of 1941.[62]

Thousands of executives, chief engineers, plant managers, and the like were arrested and perished, including such prominent figures as:

I. Ter-Astvatsatrian and V. Chichinadze, hydroelectric experts. S. M. Frankfurt, head of Kuznetsstroi. V. M. Mikhailov, chief of construction at Dneproges. I. P. Bondarenko, director of the Kharkov Tractor Factory. Chingiz Il'drym, chief of construction at the Magnitogorsk Metallurgical Complex. V. E. Tsifrinovich, director of the Solikamsk Potash Trust. M. Lur'e, director of the Zaporozhskii Metallurgical Complex. G. V. Gvakhariia, director of Makeevskii Metallurgical Factory. D'iakonov, director of the Gorky Auto Factory. V. I. Mikhailov-Ivanov, director of the Stalingrad Tractor Factory. K. M. Ots, director of the Kirov (former Putilov) Factory. Glebov-Avilov, director of the Rostov Agricultural Machinery Plant. G. P. Butenko, director of Kuznetsk Metallurgical Complex. Ia. S. Gugel', director of Azov Steel. I. P. Khrenov, director of Kramatorsk Metallurgical Factory. M. M. Tsarevskii and Surkov, directors of the Sormovo Factory. I. I. Svistun, director of the Kharkov Tractor Factory. P. G. Arutiuniants and L. T. Strezh, directors of large chemical enterprises. G. K. Kavtaradze, head of the Riazan-Ural Railway. Z. Ia. Prokof'ev, head of the Tashkent Railway. L. R. Milkh, head of the Odessa Railway.

The management of the Amur Railway and of almost all other railways was entirely destroyed. When Vladimirskii, head of the Belorussian Railway, heard of the arrest of Kaganovich's deputy Ia. Livshits, he shot his wife, his son, and then himself. Only his younger son escaped.

The extent of repression in industry can be judged by the case of metallurgy, where practically all the executives in the Central Administration and even the majority of plant directors and shop superintendents were arrested. Experienced officials were generally replaced by inexperienced people, many of whom then provided

[62] P. K. Oshchepkov, *Zhizn' i mechta* (Moscow, 1965).

the NKVD with new victims. In 1940, of 151 directors of large enterprises in the Commissariat of Ferrous Metallurgy, 62 had worked less than a year, 55 from one to two years; of 140 chief engineers, 56 had worked for less than a year. For the sake of comparison, we should note 1935, when only five directors in the entire system under the Commissariat of Heavy Industry were replaced, and only one chief engineer in Ferrous Metallurgy.[63] At the end of 1935, *Bol'shevik* boasted that the 200 biggest machine-building plants were directed almost entirely by Party members, 73 per cent of whom had joined the Party before 1920, most of them manual workers by origin. By 1939 almost all these directors had been arrested, despite their proletarian background, and many were no longer alive. Repression on the same mass scale struck the electrical and chemical industries and many other branches of the economy in 1937–38. The result was a serious slowdown in industrial development, as we shall see later.

8

IN THE FIERCE STRUGGLE among literary groups in the twenties and early thirties, RAPP—the Russian Association of Proletarian Writers —was especially vicious, sectarian, and dogmatic. Many writers hoped that the liquidation of RAPP and the formation of an all-inclusive Union of Soviet Writers would put an end to persecution and to sectarian restrictions in literature. These great expectations were expressed by nearly all the speakers at the First All-Union Congress of Soviet Writers in 1934. But they were doomed to disappointment. The rise of Stalin's cult and the increase in bureaucratic centralism turned the Union of Soviet Writers into an agency for bureaucratic control. And factional fights, far from abating, were intensified. By 1935, literary discussions were turning into purges, attempts to banish from literature—though not yet from life—those who disagreed with the sectarians and dogmatists. "At meetings of theater people," Ilya Ehrenburg recalls,

> Tairov and Meyerhold were vilified. . . . Film people went after Dovzhenko and Eisenstein. The literary critics first attacked Pasternak, Zabolotskii, Aseev, Kirsanov and Olesha, but, as the French say, the appetite grew with the eating, and soon Kataev, Fedin, Leonov, Vs. Ivanov, Lidin, and Ehrenburg were found guilty of "formalist stumbling." Finally they got to Tikhonov, Babel, the Kukryniksy.[64]

[63] See *Voprosy istorii KPSS,* 1964, No. 11, pp. 72–73.
[64] *Novyi mir,* 1962, No. 4, p. 60.

In 1936, following the trial of the "Trotskyite-Zinovievite United Center," arrests began. The well-known writer Boris Pilnyak—Stalin had old scores to settle with him—and the young writer Galina Sere-briakova were declared "enemies of the people." "In our midst," V. Stavskii, Secretary of the Writers' Union, told a meeting of Moscow writers,

> we have had Serebriakova, a sworn enemy. We accepted her as a comrade and did not recognize the enemy in her. The loss of vigi-lance among certain comrades reached the point where many eve-nings were devoted to discussion of Serebriakova's works. We served the enemy with our own hands. . . . Now we have expelled people such as Serebriakova. But who can guarantee that there are no more sworn enemies of the working class in our midst?[65]

No one could guarantee it; writers continued to be arrested on an ever-widening scale. It is impossible to list all the writers arrested and destroyed in 1936–39. Some calculations put the number in excess of 600, almost one-third of the Union's total membership, including:

> Isaac E. Babel, died in confinement in 1941. Bruno Jasienski, also died in confinement. Osip Mandelshtam, the outstanding poet, arrested a second time in 1938 and shortly after died of hunger in Magadan. Pavel Vasil'ev, talented poet, shot at twenty-six. A. Ia. Arosev, a par-ticipant in the Moscow insurrection of 1917. Mikhail Kol'tsov, arrested in December, 1938, after his return from Spain, and shot. Artem Veselyi, V. I. Norbut, S. Tret'iakov, A. Zorich, I. Kataev, I. Bespalov, B. Kornilov, G. Nikiforov, Viktor Kin, Tarasov-Rodionov, Wolf Erlich, M. Gerasimov, V. Kirillov, R. Vasil'eva, V. M. Kirshon, and L. L. Averbach—all perished. A. K. Lebedenko, A. Kosterin, A. S. Gorelov, S. Spasskii, N. Zabolotskii, I. Gronskii, V. T. Shalamov—these sur-vived many years of confinement. O. Berggol'ts, the famous poetess, spent two years in prison.

The writers' organizations in the non-Russian republics suffered great losses.

> In the Ukraine, I. K. Mikitenko, a major writer, and Epin, secretary of the Ukrainian Union of Writers, perished. In Belorussia, the poets Z. Astapenko and Iu. Taubin and the writer Platon Golovach were arrested. In Armenia, the great revolutionary poet E. Charents perished. So did the Communist writer Aksel' Bakunts. Gurgen Maari, Vaan Totovents, Alazan, V. Norents, and Mkrtych Armen were arrested but survived. In Georgia, the great writer Titsian Tabidze perished. After several summonses to the NKVD, the poet Paolo Iashvili shot himself. Prose writers M. Dzhavakhishvili and N. Mitsishvili and the critic P. Kikodze perished. The critic Buachidze was put to death at thirty-two. In Azerbaijan, T. Shakhbazy, V. Khuluflu, Husein Dzhavid, and Seid Husein were among the arrested. In Kazakhstan, Saken Seifulin, one of the founders of Soviet Kazakh literature, I. Dzhansugurov, and V.

---

[65] *Literaturnaia gazeta,* Aug. 27, 1936.

Mailin perished. The outstanding Tartar writer G. Ibrahimov was widely honored in 1967. In *Izvestiia* the First Secretary of the Tartar *obkom* described him as "a bright star in the history of Soviet culture."[66] But the secretary somehow neglected to mention that G. Ibrahimov was shot by the NKVD at the end of the thirties. K. Tinchurin, K. Nadzhmi, and other Tartar writers perished with him. Antal Hidas, a leading Hungarian writer, was arrested in the Soviet Union but survived seventeen years of confinement.

The writers who suffered under Stalin varied in talent and attitude toward Soviet reality. Some were Communists, some "fellow travelers," and some were members of the old intelligentsia who took a wait-and-see or even a critical attitude toward the Soviet regime. Many made serious mistakes, underwent ideological vacillations, and suffered creative or personal breakdowns. But in all these shortcomings a "corpus delicti" was entirely lacking, to quote the Supreme Court decisions rehabilitating these writers. Most of their books have been reprinted, but no one can ever publish the books they had in mind— and most of them were under forty when they were arrested. Even much of what they had written can never be published, for their manuscripts were usually confiscated and destroyed by the NKVD.

This tragedy, terrible in its senselessness, was expressed with great force in a poem that Bruno Jasienski[67] wrote in prison in 1938:

> Over the world rages the desert wind of war,
> Alarming my country with its nasal howl,
> But I, locked in a stone shroud,
> Am not among her sons at this moment.
>
> . . .
>
> I hear the beating of the hearts of Dneproges
> Through threadlike steel wires,
> I hear the trucks of Magnitka sing,
> Rumbling, of new progress in smelting.
>
> . . .
>
> A herald of Communism's deathless ideas,
> Who celebrates the magnificence of our days,
> I lie behind bars, like an enemy and a criminal,
> Can there be a more absurd situation?!
> But I do not reproach you, Nativeland-mother.
> I know that only by losing faith in your sons
> Could you put faith in such a heresy,
> And break my song like a sword.
>
> . . .

[66] See F. Tabeev, *Izvestiia,* Mar. 16, 1967.

[67] *Ed.:* A well-known Polish poet, 1901–41, who emigrated to the Soviet Union in 1929. The present translation makes no effort to convey his meter and rhyme.

March on, my song, in the banner formation.
Don't cry cause we lived together for such a short time.
Our lot is dishonorable, but sooner or later
The fatherland will see its mistake.[68]

Every kind of creative person and organization was struck by repression—painters, actors, musicians, architects, and film people. In Moscow, for example, Elena Sokolovskaia was arrested. The legendary head of the Odessa underground during the Civil War, she had become the artistic director of Mosfilm in the thirties. In the Leningrad film company, A. I. Piotrovskii, head of the script department, was apprehended. So was A. F. Dorn, who had made a film chronicle of the October Revolution.

The death of the great director V. E. Meyerhold was an enormous loss. A Party member since 1918, he had devoted his life to creating a theater "in tune with the epoch." The persecution of Meyerhold began early; a pejorative was coined for the purpose: "Meyerholdism" (*meierkhol'dovshchina*). By 1936 the campaign was in full swing, but Meyerhold would not repent. At a 1936 meeting, where artistic formalism was condemned and Meyerhold was excoriated, he spoke out strongly against a narrow understanding of realism. He opposed the establishment of any rigid model for theatrical art, such as the Moscow Art Theater. He opposed "prophylactic control," saying: "The theater is a living creative thing, where passions boil. We must be given freedom—yes, freedom."[69] But the persecution continued. On orders "from above," a general meeting of theatrical workers attacked Meyerhold and his creative theater. The meeting "decisively" resolved that "the Soviet audience does not need such a theater."[70] In January, 1938, it was closed. A year later, this remarkable man, who had been, like Mayakovsky, a favorite of youth, was arrested and killed, it has been reported, after especially severe and refined torture.

Among other victims from the theatrical world were:

Les' Kurbas, the "Ukrainian Meyerhold." The directors and actors Sandro Akhmetelli, Igor Terent'ev, K. Eggert, I. Pravov, L. Verpakhovskii, Mikhail Rafal'skii, Natalia Sats, Liadov, and Evgenii Mikeladze.

At the end of the thirties, the actor Aleksei Dikoi was arrested, but he was released in 1941 and later played the part of Stalin "without an accent."[71]

The painter V. I. Shukhaev, returning to the Soviet Union from abroad, was arrested. The Leningrad painter Sharapov was also arrested, after he had been called to Moscow to paint the "chief's"

[68] "Slovo o Iakube Shele," *Poemy i stikhotvoreniia* (Moscow, 1962).
[69] *Literaturnaia gazeta,* Mar. 15, 1936.
[70] From the materials of the cultural historian L. M. Zak.
[71] *Ed.:* Stalin was notorious for speaking Russian with a Georgian accent.

portrait. Two sittings sealed his fate. Stalin probably disliked the
sketches, which showed his deformed arm. (Stalin assiduously hid
this defect throughout his life.)

9

ABOUT SEVEN HUNDRED VICTIMS have been named here, chiefly the
best-known officials, military commanders, writers, artists, and scholars.
But repression was not limited to the higher strata. It struck a vast
number of officials at the middle and lower levels; it touched all
strata of the population.

Numerically, the chief victims were hundreds of thousands of
rank-and-file Party members. The result was a marked depletion of
the Party. At the time of the XVIIth Congress in 1934 there were
2,809,000 members and candidate members. More than 900,000 of
them were candidate members, almost all whom would normally have
become full members before the XVIIIth Congress in 1939. But there
was no admission to the Party in 1935–36; it was resumed only in
November, 1936. From then until the spring of 1939 slightly more
than a million people were accepted as candidate members, of whom
at least a third should have become full members before the XVIIIth
Congress. We can assume a natural loss over a five-year period—from
1934 to 1939—of approximately 300,000 to 400,000 people. Even
with such a clearly inflated estimate, we would expect by 1939 no
fewer than 3.5 million members and candidate members, including
at least 2.6 million full members. But the XVIIIth Congress counted
2,478,000 members, of whom only 1,590,000 were full members.
This huge deficit can be explained only by the mass repression.

In short, the NKVD arrested and killed, within two years, more
Communists than had been lost in all the years of the underground
struggle, the three revolutions, and the Civil War. The oldest mem-
bers were special victims, as the composition of the Congresses shows.
At the XVIth and XVIIth Congresses, 80 per cent of the delegates had
joined the Party before 1920; the figure was only 19 per cent at the
XVIIIth Congress. The losses among the young intelligentsia, the
Party's hope for the future, were also enormous.

A still greater number of victims was claimed among nonparty
people—ordinary workers, peasants, and office personnel. For example,
at the Electric Factory in Moscow, according to L. M. Portnov, more
than a thousand people were victims of repression, including not only
the executives but also many rank-and-file office workers and shock-
brigade workers. The Kirov Factory in Leningrad was short every
week of shop superintendents, engineers, Stakhanovites, and office

workers.[72] Dozens of executives and hundreds of workers, both manual and white-collar, in the construction of the Moscow subway were arrested. There was the same senseless destruction of people in thousands of other enterprises. In the process the NKVD arrested above all those workers, engineers, and white-collar personnel who had gone to American and German factories for practical training.

The farms also suffered great losses. A. I. Todorskii met in confinement one of the lesser officials of the grain-procurement system of the Northern Caucasus. He told Todorskii that two hundred Party activists in his *raion* were arrested the same night as he, and kept temporarily in the *raion* political prison. Many ordinary peasants were also arrested. Evgeniia Ginzburg tells about an old woman from a *kolkhoz* who was accused of being a Trotskyite (*trotskistka*). The old woman thought they were talking about a tractor driver (*traktoristka*), and argued that in her village old people were not put on tractors. A Belorussian Party official, Ia. I. Drobinskii, tells in his unpublished memoirs about an old man from a *kolkhoz* who sat in the corner of his cell.

> He had grown terribly thin. At every meal he put aside a piece for his son, who was a witness for the prosecution. A healthy young peasant who could not bear the beating and abuse or for some other reason, he had testified that his father had talked him into killing the chairman of the *kolkhoz*. The old man denied it; his conscience would not let him lie. No beatings or tortures could shake him. He went to the confrontation with his son with the firm intention to stick to the truth. But when he saw his tortured son, with marks of beatings on him, something snapped in the old man's spirit, and turning to the interrogator and his son, he said: "It's true; I confirm it. Don't worry, Iliushka, I confirm everything you said." And right then he signed the record of the confrontation.
>
> . . . Preparing to meet his son in court, the old man put aside a part of his food every day, and when he was taken out, he broke away from his guard for a second and handed it to Iliushka. Then Iliushka could not stand it; he fell on his knees in front of the old man and tearing his shirt, howling and groaning, he shouted: "Forgive me, Pa, forgive me, I lied about you, forgive me!" The old man babbled something, caressed him on the head, on the back. . . . The guard was embarrassed, upset. Even the judges of the tribunal were shaken when they saw the sight. They refused to try the old man and his son. But the case was not closed. The old man remained in prison. Specialists in our cell thought that the case had gone to the Special Assembly [*Osoboe soveshchanie*]. The old man was almost always silent, and continued to put aside part of his starvation rations for his "meeting with Iliushka."

Such tragedies occurred by tens and hundreds of thousands.

[72] *Istoriia Kirovskogo zavoda* (Moscow, 1966), pp. 535–42.

A wave of "open" trials swept over the country in 1937–38. This term usually refers to the big Moscow trials of former opposition leaders. They were show trials attended not only by Soviet public figures but also by dozens of foreign correspondents. The trial record was widely printed and discussed both at home and abroad. But not many people know that "open" trials were held elsewhere. Almost every republic, *oblast,* even *raion,* had its own "open" trial. These trials of local importance were not as a rule reported in the central newspapers, but the regional press gave them full coverage. There were also various types of "closed" trials in the provinces. Some were not reported in the press, but others were given fairly detailed local coverage, which is to say that the indictments and verdicts were published. Most of the arrests and verdicts were carried out without any respect for legal procedure.

In the second half of 1937, in hundreds of *raiony,* the accused were *kolkhoz* members, officials of the *raion* Party organization. Almost all of the trials had some sort of a label. It might be "the trial of the anti-Soviet wrecking group of rightists in . . . *raion,*" or "the trial of right-Trotskyite wreckers in the *kolkhoz* stock farming of . . . *raion,*" or "the trial of right-Trotskyite violators of socialist legality in . . . *raion.*" As a rule, the trial was conducted by a special collegium of the *oblast* court, with the *oblast* procurator in attendance, and documents were printed in the local papers.

Usually the same ranks of officials were put on trial everywhere, indicating a uniform scheme worked out at the center. For example, "anti-Soviet wrecking activity" was charged against the *raikom* Party secretary, the chairman of the *raion* executive committee, the head of the *raizo,* the director of the Machine Tractor Station, one or two *kolkhoz* chairmen, a senior agronomist or the *raizo* agronomist, and a senior supervisor of land use (*zemleustroitel'*). Trials for wrecking in stock farming brought in the same group, with the *raion* livestock specialist and a senior veterinary substituted for the MTS director and the agronomists. A trial for violation of socialist legality would replace such specialists by the plenipotentiary for state procurements, the tax inspector, and one or two chairmen of village Soviets. As a rule the "open" trials were held in *raiony* where *kolkhoz* output was lower than the *oblast* average. The indictment was written to a uniform formula: the *raikom* Party secretary, recruited by some leading *oblast* official, was forming a counterrevolutionary wrecking group in his *raion.* All the faults of the collective and state farms—late harvesting, poor cultivation of the land, loss of cattle, lack of fodder—were this group's doing, bent on arousing dissatisfaction with the Soviet regime among *kolkhoz* and *sovkhoz* workers.

A typical trial occurred at the end of 1937 in the Red Guard *raion* of Leningrad *oblast.* A special collegium of the *oblast* court, with the participation of the *oblast* procurator, B. P. Pozern, tried *raikom* Party secretary I. V. Vasil'ev, chairman of the *raion* executive committee A. I. Dmitrichenko, head of *raizo* F. I. Manninen, MTS director S. A. Semenov, senior land supervisor A. I. Portnov, and some other officials. The charges ran as follows: (1) For purposes of wrecking they had brought the *kolkhozy* to such a state that the farmers generally received nothing for their labor days;[73] in a few farms the members had received twenty kopecks for each labor day. (2) The majority of the *kolkhozy* had not fulfilled their obligation to supply the state with all varieties of agricultural products. Both types of malfeasance were committed to restore capitalism in the USSR.

Raikom Party secretary Vasil'ev admitted that the *kolkhozy* were in a bad way but categorically denied any deliberate wrecking or participation in any anti-Soviet organization. The other defendants, however, made full "confessions" of their counterrevolutionary activity. After the procurator's speech, completely reaffirming the charges, the defendants were all sentenced to be shot.

In many *oblasti,* besides these "typical" trials, three or four *raiony* had more "specialized" trials, for example of officials in *Zagotzerno,* the grain-procurement agency. In this case the head of the receiving point, the technical specialist, and two or three storage officials were brought to court. Sometimes these trials were held on an *oblast* or republic level. Thus in Minsk, in 1937, "wreckers" of *Zagotzerno* were tried at the food workers' club. In the North Ossetian Autonomous Republic, from October 23 to 28, 1937, leaders and collective farmers of the village of Dargavs were tried. Certain misdeeds of the leaders were presented as diversionary acts by "sworn enemies of the people." A special collegium of the Supreme Court of the Republic found the defendants guilty of "hostility towards the Soviet regime, the Communist Party, the collective farms," and even of participation in an imaginary "counterrevolutionary kulak insurrectionary organization." Six of the thirteen defendants were sentenced to be shot.[74] Similar trials were held in Kuibyshev, Voronezh, Yaroslavl, and other cities.

In many *oblasti* and republics there were show trials of "wrecking" officials in the field of trade. The usual defendants were the head of the *oblast* trade department, the leading officials of competitive bidding, the head of the *obkom* Party trade section or his deputy. They were charged with premeditated organization of stoppages in the supply of staple goods, designed to foment discontent among the workers. Similar trials were held for officials in other branches of the economy,

---

[73] *Ed.:* At the end of the agricultural year, after all the obligations of a collective farm have been met, residual money and goods are distributed among the members of the farm according to the number of labor days that each member has contributed to the farm.

[74] *Istoriia Severo-Osetinskoi ASSR* (Ordzhonikidze, 1966).

especially in the railways. For example, on May 9, 1937, the case of the "Trotskyite espionage terrorist group" on the Amur Railway was taken up by the Military Collegium of the USSR Supreme Court on circuit in the town of Svobodny. Forty-six persons were sentenced to be shot. On June 4, 1937, a second trial was held in the same town, and 28 people were shot. On July 4 there was a third trial, with 60 people sentenced to death, and on October 9, a fourth trial, with 24 executed. Thus, in Svobodny alone, counting only the sentences reported in the local press, 158 officials of the Amur railway were shot in six months. Similarly, on circuit in Khabarovsk and Vladivostok the Military Collegium tried officials of the Far Eastern Railway, and more than a hundred people were sentenced to be shot.

In some *oblasti,* NKVD officials accused children of counterrevolutionary activity. In Leninsk-Kuznetsk, sixty children between the ages of ten and twelve were arrested on a charge of forming a "terrorist counterrevolutionary group." The NKVD chief in the city, A. T. Lun'kov; the divisional chief, A. M. Savkin; the operational plenipotentiary, A. I. Belousov; and the acting city procurator, R. M. Klipp, were in charge of this case. The children were kept in the city prison for eight months, while the investigators put more than a hundred children through interrogation. The workers of the city were so outraged that *oblast* organizations interfered. The children were released and "rehabilitated," and the NKVD officials were themselves brought to trial.[75]

The clergy of various faiths were also severely repressed. In the late twenties and early thirties the Soviet state had attacked the churches, especially the Russian Orthodox Church, which took an anti-Soviet position. However, the state's punitive organs went much further than the state's interest required. Hundreds of churches and temples were simply torn down, dozens of monasteries were dissolved, and the OGPU even rounded up hermits and put them in camps. In many cities precious monuments of church architecture were destroyed —the Church of Christ the Savior and the Spasskii Monastery in Moscow, for example. In 1937–38 this repression was continued without any necessity. Many ordinary priests and bishops were arrested. The Catholicos of Armenia, Khoren I. Muradbekian, a popular leader, was killed in 1937 in his residence.

The great number of prisons built under the tsars proved to be too small for the millions of people arrested, even though several prisoners were put into cells built for one while up to a hundred were packed into cells built for twenty. Dozens of new prisons were hastily built, and former monasteries, churches, hotels, and even bathhouses and stables were converted into prisons. Some of the most famous tsarist

[75] See the newspaper *Sovetskaia Sibir',* February, 1939, Nos. 39–45.

prisons, including Lefortovskaia, had been converted into museums, with wax figures in the cells. But when the mass repression began, the wax figures were thrown out, and the jail, filled once again with living people, was modernized and expanded. A small prison for especially important prisoners was even built in the Kremlin at the end of the thirties. New concentration camps were put up all over the country, especially in the Far East, the Northern Urals, Siberia, Kazakhstan, and Karelia.

Between 1936 and 1938 Stalin broke all records for political terror. The proscriptions of Cornelius Sulla killed several thousand Romans. Tens of thousands perished in the reigns of tyrannical emperors like Tiberius, Caligula, and Nero. The cruelest of all the inquisitors, Tomás de Torquemada, is said to have burned 10,220 living people and 6,860 pictures of absent or dead heretics, and sentenced 97,321 people to such punishment as life imprisonment, confiscation of property, and wearing the garment of shame called *sanbenito*.[76] The *oprichnina* of Ivan the Terrible killed some tens of thousands; at its height ten to twenty people were killed daily in Moscow. In the Jacobin terror, according to the calculations of an American historian,[77] 17,000 people were sent to the guillotine by revolutionary tribunals. Approximately the same number were condemned without a trial or died in prison. Exactly how many "suspects" were imprisoned by the Jacobins is not known; the best estimate is 70,000.[78] In nineteenth-century Russia several dozen were executed for political reasons and several hundred, or at most several thousand, "politicals" died in prison and exile.

The scale of the Stalinist terror was immeasurably greater. In 1936–39, on the most cautious estimates, four to five million people were subjected to repression for political reasons. At least four to five hundred thousand of them—above all the high officials—were summarily shot; the rest were given long terms of confinement. In 1937–38 there were days when up to a thousand people were shot in Moscow alone. These were not streams, these were rivers of blood, the blood of honest Soviet people. The simple truth must be stated: not one of the tyrants and despots of the past persecuted and destroyed so many of his compatriots.

[76] Kh. A. L'orente, *Kriticheskaia istoriia ispanskoi inkvizitsii* (Moscow, 1936), I, p. 200. *Ed.:* The original, Juan Antonio Llorente, *Histoire critique de l'inquisition d'Espagne* (Paris, 1817–18), 4 vols., has been translated into several languages.
[77] See Donald Greer, *The Incidence of Terror During the French Revolution* (Cambridge, Mass., 1935).
[78] See Louis Jacob, *Robespierre vu par ses contemporains* (Paris, 1938).

VII

Rehabilitation and
Repression, 1939-41

1

THE SCALE OF REPRESSION began to affect the economy as well as the political situation. There was scarcely a family that was not to some degree hurt by repression. Moreover, the prisons and camps were filled to overflowing, and the available NKVD personnel could not cope with the interrogation and guarding of so many prisoners. Some changes were needed, and Stalin, a master technician of the political lightning rod, knew it.

On November 13, 1938, the Party's Central Committee and the government's Council of People's Commissars endorsed a secret decree "On arrests, procuratorial supervision, and the conduct of investigation." This decree ordered "regulation" of the punitive organs. On December 8, 1938, in the back pages of the Moscow newspapers, a short notice appeared: N. E. Ezhov had, at his own request, been released from his duties as Commissar of Internal Affairs; he would be Commissar of Water Transportation. For several weeks thereafter Ezhov remained at liberty; he appeared alongside Stalin in the Bol'shoi Theater on January 21, 1939. But shortly afterward Ezhov disappeared. The man that *Pravda* had called "the nation's favorite," who possessed "the greatest vigilance, a will of iron, a fine proletarian sensitivity, enormous organizational talent, and exceptional intelligence," was not mentioned again in any newspaper.

Ezhov, we know now, was arrested at the beginning of 1939 and accused of trying to kill Stalin in order to usurp all power. The old Bolshevik P. I. Shabalkin, who died in 1965, gave the author the following account of Ezhov's fate:

When they took me from the Solovetski Islands back to Butyrskaia Prison for reinterrogation, I found myself in a cell with D. Bulatov, a well-known Party official. Bulatov was refusing to testify and demanding interrogation by Ezhov himself. (A few years earlier Bulatov and Ezhov, when they were in charge of CC departments, had lived next to each other and often visited each other.) In the fall of 1938, Bulatov was taken to interrogation a fifth time. Suddenly a door in the wall opened and Ezhov entered the investigator's office. "Well," he said, "is Bulatov testifying?" "Not at all, Comrade General Commissar," replied the investigator. "Then lay it on him good," said Ezhov, and left by the same door. . . . After that Bulatov was beaten several times, but then they seemed to forget about him. However, a few months later, in 1939, Bulatov was again taken to interrogation and for more than a day did not return to the cell. When he came back, he fell on his bunk and began to sob. Only two days later Bulatov told Shabalkin that they had taken him to some other prison and into an investigator's office, where he saw Ezhov, now arrested and held in confinement. This was a confrontation. In a monotonous and indifferent voice Ezhov began to tell how he had been preparing to get rid of Stalin and seize power, and how Bulatov had been one of the members of his organization, whom, for "better protection," they had decided to keep in Butyrskaia Prison. Bulatov naturally denied this slander, but Ezhov kept to his story. After several hours of interrogation, they took Ezhov away and put Bulatov in a car, took him to Lefortovskaia prison, forced him to strip naked, and took him down to the basement. There he saw another naked man, whom he recognized as the head of one of the departments of the Moscow NKVD. "What are they getting ready to do with us?" Bulatov asked him. "Probably shoot us," replied Ezhov's former colleague, who was very familiar with such matters. But a few hours later they took Bulatov upstairs, gave him his clothes, and took him back to Butyrskaia Prison. Bulatov was killed later on, but Ezhov was shot earlier.

According to A. V. Snegov, Ezhov was shot in the summer of 1940. Rumors circulated that Ezhov had gone mad and was in a lunatic asylum. It is likely these rumors were spread deliberately, to give an apparent explanation of the mass repression and thus to serve as a political lightning rod.

The new Commissar of Internal Affairs, L. P. Beria, was a worthy heir and continuer of the "Ezhov tradition." Beria had never been a Marxist or a revolutionary. Right from the start he was an unprincipled careerist, capable of any crime. He began as an inconspicuous inspector of housing for the Baku city Soviet. During the Civil War the adventurer Bagirov gave Beria a job in the Cheka. At that time the Soviet regime was not firmly established in the Caucasus and Beria naturally tried to ensure himself against all eventualities. His trial in

1953 established that, as early as 1919, he had connections with the
Musawat intelligence service of Azerbaijan, and in 1920 with the
security division of the Menshevik government of Georgia.[1] In 1921 M.
Kedrov, head of a special division of OGPU checking up on the work
of the Azerbaijan Cheka, whose chairman was Bagirov and whose
vice-chairman was Beria, established that Beria had released enemies
of the Soviet regime and condemned innocent people. Suspecting
treason, Kedrov reported this to Dzerzhinskii in Moscow, and suggested that Beria be removed from his post as untrustworthy. For
reasons unknown, his letter produced no results at that time.[2]

In the second half of the twenties Beria transferred to the GPU of
Georgia. By intrigues and crimes he advanced himself to the head of
the GPU of Georgia and then of all Transcaucasia. Stalin did not
know Beria personally before 1931, although he must have heard of
him. He must also have known that Beria was an enemy of the Party's
First Secretary in Transcaucasia, L. Kartvelishvili, and that Bagirov
was Beria's protector. Stalin might also have heard negative opinions
of Beria from Kirov and Ordzhonikidze. According to A. V. Snegov,
then the head of the organizational section of the Transcaucasian
Party Committee, Stalin and Beria met under the following circumstances.

In the summer of 1931 the Transcaucasian Party Committee suddenly received a special decree from the Politburo about a rest cure
for Stalin. The Transcaucasian Committee was to make all the arrangements. Tskhaltubo was chosen as the place, with Beria as chief of
security. In an impressive flurry, he sent a multitude of OGPU agents
to Tskhaltubo and took personal command of Stalin's bodyguard for
a month and a half. In these weeks, repeatedly talking with Beria,
Stalin could see that he was a "useful" man.

In late September or early October Stalin returned to Moscow, but
he did not forget Beria. Soon the Tbilisi officials received an order to
prepare a report for the Politburo, on a subject not specified. All the
members of the Transcaucasian Party Buro and of the three republics'
Central Committees went to Moscow. Kaganovich presided at the
Politburo meeting. Of course Stalin was also there, clearly in a bad
mood. First Lavrentii Kartvelishvili spoke, then G. Davdariani for the
Georgian Central Committee, V. Polonskii for the Azerbaijan CC,
and A. Khandzhian for the Armenian CC. For some reason Ordzhonikidze was absent. Snegov asked his neighbor why, and received the
reply: "Why should Sergo attend the coronation of Beria? He's known
that crook for a long time."

---

[1] Ed.: During the Civil War independent republics were established by the Musawat
Party in Azerbaijan and by the Menshevik Party in Georgia.
[2] I. Viktorov, Podpol'shchik. Voin. Chekist (Moscow, 1968), pp. 71–73.

After the officials from Transcaucasia had finished, Stalin delivered a long speech. He spoke of nationality policy in Transcaucasia, of the production of cotton, of oil. Turning to organizational matters at the end of his speech, he suddenly proposed the promotion of Beria to be Second Secretary of the Transcaucasian Party Committee, that is, Kartvelishvili's deputy. Many people were stunned and Kartvelishvili said loudly, "I will not work with that charlatan." Not everyone, to be sure, supported Kartvelishvili; Vladimir Polonskii in particular was beginning to play some game with Beria. Still, the majority of the Transcaucasian Buro objected to Stalin's proposal because of Beria's bad reputation in the Georgian Party organization. Stalin, red with fury, said, "Well, so what, we'll settle this question the routine way." The meeting ended.

The members of the Transcaucasian Buro went straight from the meeting to Ordzhonikidze's apartment. They found him extremely depressed. Everyone began to ask him why he agreed to Beria's promotion. How could they return to Tbilisi? Sergo tried to change the subject but then, unable to contain himself, said: "For a long time I've been telling Stalin that Beria is a crook, but Stalin won't listen to me, and no one can make him change his mind."

The very next day, in "the routine way," the composition of the Transcaucasian leadership was settled. Kartvelishvili was sent to West Siberia as *kraikom* Second Secretary; A. I. Iakovlev, the Second Secretary of the Transcaucasian Party Committee, was appointed Director of the Eastern Gold Trust; G. Davdariani was sent to study in the Institute of Red Professorship; A. V. Snegov was sent to a Party job in Irkutsk. Mamiia Orakhelashvili became First Secretary of the Transcaucasian Party Committee; Beria, the Second Secretary. Within two or three months Beria became First Secretary of the Georgian CC, and soon of the entire Transcaucasian Federation. Orakhelashvili was called to Moscow as Deputy Director of the Marx-Engels-Lenin Institute. In Georgia a mass turnover of Party cadres began. Thirty-two directors of *raion* NKVD agencies became the first secretaries of the *raion* Party committees.

Beria remembered who had opposed his promotion to the "leadership" of the Transcaucasian Party organization. In 1936–38 he sought revenge. Some former Caucasian leaders (Kartvelishvili, Orakhelashvili, E. Asribekov) were brought to Tiflis not only from Moscow but even from the Far East, and were subjected to especially refined tortures under Beria's direct supervision. Even earlier, in 1932–35, Beria terrorized the Transcaucasian Party organization, getting rid of unsuitable people, replacing them with dishonest, unconscientious, but suitable officials. Scorning any rule of law, without any scruples, Beria was already a criminal. He was also a drunk and a lecher.

Stalin knew these qualities of the future Commissar of Internal Affairs. He was repeatedly warned by many Party leaders, such as Ordzhonikidze and Orakhelashvili. G. N. Kaminskii even gave a negative sketch of Beria in a speech to the CC Plenum of February-March, 1937. In Transcaucasia rumors circulated about Beria's former connections with Musawat people. E. D. Gogoberidze says that Levan Gogoberidze and Lakoba discussed this subject as early as 1933. Among the Transcaucasian Party intelligentsia, Beria's ignorance was legendary; they said he had not read a single book "since the time of Gutenberg." Letters and reports about Beria's crimes and moral corruption reached Stalin from many Party members in Transcaucasia. But Stalin, for all his suspiciousness, favored Beria, and put the punitive organs of the entire country under a man who had long ago lost any trace of conscience or honor.

However, in 1938–39 not many people knew Beria for what he really was, so the replacement of Ezhov by Beria was received as a hopeful sign. And in fact, right after Ezhov's replacement, mass repression was discontinued for a while. Hundreds of thousands of cases then being prepared by the NKVD were temporarily put aside. A special commission was even appointed to investigate NKVD activity. A. A. Andreev was made chairman of the commission, because he had been very active, during 1937–38, in the assault on "enemies of the people."

As could have been expected, right after Ezhov's replacement by Beria, the NKVD was hit by the usual wave of dismissals and arrests. Almost all of Ezhov's close associates and dozens of leading NKVD officials were arrested and shot. Among those arrested were:

> Zakovskii, who had long directed repression in Moscow and Leningrad. Mal'tsev, "chief executioner" of Novosibirsk *oblast*. Berman, the sadistic head of the Belorussian NKVD. Lavrushin, head of the Gorky NKVD, and his deputies Kaminskii and Listengurt.

Most wardens got a taste of their own prison discipline, including Butyrskaia's Popov, Vainshtok of Yaroslavl, and the warden of Solovetskaia. Many of the torturers were themselves tortured. Even Redens, whose wife was the sister of Stalin's second wife, N. Allilueva, was arrested. In 1937 he had directed the mass repression in Moscow. Then, as NKVD chief in Kazakhstan, he decimated the Party and government *apparat* of that republic. And then he was arrested and shot.

The panic that shook the NKVD following Ezhov's arrest is revealed in the case of Liushkov.[3] In the early thirties he had been in

---

[3] The facts are supplied by the former assistant procurator of Rostov *oblast*, M. P. Batorgin, and by Party members P. I. Shabalkin and A. V. Snegov.

charge of a special NKVD group for fighting Trotskyites, which made extensive use of provocation. It was Liushkov who headed the investigation of Zinoviev and Evdokimov in 1935. In 1937 he became NKVD chief in the Rostov *oblast,* where he decimated Party and government cadres. Then he became chief in the Far East, where he repeated his performance. When he learned of Ezhov's arrest, Liushkov fled to Manchuria, taking foreign currency, documents, and seals from the NKVD. He revealed to the leaders of Japan's Kwantung Army the distribution of Soviet troops in the Far East, and "exposed" Stalin's crimes, in which he himself had been an active participant.

2

INNOCENT PRISONERS and their millions of relatives, who lived on hope of rehabilitation, were doomed to disappointment. There was much talk at the XVIIIth Party Congress in 1939 about rehabilitating the unjustly condemned—A. A. Zhdanov's speech especially aroused such hope—but the actual rehabilitation affected only a few thousand people. Indeed there could not have been a mass rehabilitation in Stalin's lifetime, for hundreds of thousands of people had already been shot, and their rehabilitation would have meant that Stalin was admitting his monstrous crimes.

Some Red Army commanders were rehabilitated. The extreme shortage of officers became apparent in 1939–40, as the troubled international situation and the Soviet-Finnish War occasioned the first mobilizations. Generally it was middle-rank officers who were rehabilitated, up to the level of divisional commanders. The rehabilitated included many future heroes of the Great Fatherland War, such as:

K. Rokossovskii, future marshal; K. A. Meretskov, future marshal; A. V. Gorbatov, future Army general. Bogdanov, future commander of the Second Tank Army; G. N. Kholostiakov, future vice-admiral; S. V. Rudnev, future commissar of partisan units in the Ukraine—all of whom would be named Heroes of the Soviet Union. N. Iu. Ozerianskii, hero of the defense of Leningrad, awarded two Orders of Lenin and three Orders of the Red Banner. L. G. Petrovskii, the younger son of G. I. Petrovskii, appointed commander of the 63rd Rifle Corps, who died a hero's death on the Dnepr in August, 1941.[4]

But many equally talented officers and commissars remained in labor camps and prisons throughout the war, although most of them begged to be sent to the front. After the death of his younger son, Leonid, G. I. Petrovskii wrote to Stalin asking that his older son, Peter, and his son-in-law, S. A. Zager, be released and sent to the front. "At the beginning of the war with the fascists," he wrote,

[4] See the article "Kontrudar geroicheskogo korpusa," *Krasnaia zvezda,* Aug. 17, 1966.

I sent the CC a letter, addressed to you, asking that my son Peter be freed from prison, so that he, like Leonid, would fearlessly fight in the war against the fascists. I received no reply. . . . In the fight against the fascists every patriotic individual will relieve the nation's strain. "Everything depends on people."[5] I have lost everything that was near and dear to me, but it is better to lose it in the war against the fascists than the devil knows where. Once again I appeal to the CC to release Peter Petrovskii and Zager from prison, to give them a chance at the front or in the rear to work for the Red Army.

Stalin did not answer this letter either. Peter Petrovskii, Civil War hero, leader of the defense of Uralsk, was shot in 1942.[6]

Some scientists and technologists were rehabilitated, for example the physicist Landau and the airplane designers Tupolev and Petliakov. Frightened by the threat of epidemics, Stalin released the microbiologist P. F. Zdradovskii, one of the country's leading epidemiologists. Fewer rehabilitations were granted to Party, government, and Komsomol officials. Only two can be named: F. M. Ziavkin, a CC *apparatchik*, and Vera Khoruzha, the future heroine of the Belorussian people. For Stalin and the NKVD, these rehabilitations were only a distracting maneuver. Stalin sought to pacify public opinion, which was disturbed by the mass terror, and to explain the destruction of Ezhov. Stalin thought a small number of rehabilitations would underscore the justice of the mass repression.

3

ARRESTS OF NKVD officials and partial rehabilitations were not, of course, the main job of the new NKVD leaders. Soon Beria and his men resumed the repression. Admittedly, the mass scale of 1937–38 was not approached. But Stalin had begun to use terror, and he could not stop; arrests and shooting accompanied him to the last days of his life.

In 1939–40 thousands of cases begun under Ezhov ground on to sentencing and shooting. Reconsideration was not even granted to Communists accused of plots against Ezhov and other people who had been declared "enemies of the people." Among the victims was an old Bolshevik and OGPU official, M. S. Kedrov, who had tried to unmask Beria as early as 1921. In 1939 Kedrov was already retired. One of his sons, Igor, an investigator in the central NKVD from the time of Iagoda and Ezhov, made heavy use of illegal methods of investigation. What

[5] *Ed.:* A famous quotation from Stalin.
[6] From the papers of the Petrovskii family.

M. S. Kedrov felt about the activities of his son, of Iagoda, and of Ezhov is not known. But when he learned of Beria's appointment as Commissar of Internal Affairs, he and his son sent Stalin a number of letters exposing Beria. That was in February and March of 1939. The first reply to these letters was the arrest and shooting of Igor Kedrov. In April, 1939, M. S. Kedrov was arrested too.

He then sent a well-known letter—it was read at the XXth Congress in 1956—to CC Secretary A. A. Andreev, a man who played no small role in Stalin's machine of mass terror.

> From a gloomy cell in Lefortovskaia Prison, I appeal to you for help, Hear my cry of horror, don't pass on by, intercede, help to destroy a nightmare of interrogations, to discover the mistake. . . . I am an innocent victim. Believe me. Time will show. I am not an agent-provocateur of the tsarist secret police, not a spy, not a member of an anti-Soviet organization, as I am accused on the basis of slanderous declarations. And I have committed no other crimes against the Party or the homeland. I am a stainless old Bolshevik; for almost forty years I have fought honorably in the Party ranks for the good and happiness of the people. . . . Now the investigators are threatening me, an old man of sixty-two, with measures of physical coercion even more severe, cruel, and humiliating. They are in no condition to recognize their mistakes and admit the illegal and intolerable nature of their behavior in relation to me. They seek to justify it by picturing me as a vile enemy who refuses to disarm, and by intensifying repression. But let the Party know that I am innocent, and that no measures will succeed in turning a true son of the Party, devoted to it to the grave, into an enemy. . . . To everything, however, there is a limit. I am utterly worn out. My health has been undermined, my strength and energy have dried up, the end approaches. To die in a Soviet prison branded as a contemptible traitor and betrayer of my native land—what can be more terrible for an honorable man? What a horror! Boundless pain and sorrow press and convulse my heart. No, no! This will not happen, this must not happen, I shout. Neither the Party nor the Soviet government will allow such a cruel and irremediable injustice to be committed. I am convinced that calm, dispassionate investigation, without disgusting abuse, without spite, without terrible degradation, will easily establish the groundlessness of the charges. I deeply believe that truth and justice will triumph. I believe, I believe.

Kedrov's innocence was so obvious that even the Military Collegium of the Supreme Court completely exonerated him. In spite of this decision, Beria did not permit his release, and in October, 1941, Kedrov was shot. A new, back-dated verdict was drawn up after the shooting.

Also arrested and shot was F. I. Goloshchekin, elected to the CC at the Prague Conference of 1912, and, in the late thirties, chief of

Arbitration in the Council of Commissars. After the dismissal of M. M. Litvinov as Commissar of Foreign Affairs, there were new arrests of Soviet diplomats. Reverses in the Soviet-Finnish War resulted in new arrests of army officers. The chief of staff of the Leningrad Military District, N. E. Varfolomeev, disappeared without a trace. Mass arrests of officers who took part in the Spanish Civil War began in 1937–38, as has been noted. In 1938 the Soviet military attaché, V. E. Gorev, the real organizer of the defense of Madrid—the Spanish general José Miaja played almost no role—was recalled to Moscow and shot.

G. M. Shtern, a Central Committee member, returned from Spain to replace Bliukher as commander of the Far Eastern Theater, where he directed military operations at Khalkin-Gol[7] and pressed for the enlargement of the Far Eastern Army. (In December, 1941, the large, well-equipped regular army in the East would play a significant role in the relief of Moscow, sending divisions west when needed.) In 1940 Shtern was suddenly called to Moscow and given a post in the Commissariat of Defense. Shortly thereafter he shared Bliukher's fate —arrested and shot.

Just before the war against Germany, another large group of Spanish War veterans were arrested, including twenty-two Heroes of the Soviet Union, some of whom had twice earned the decoration. Among them were:

> Ia. V. Smushkevich, who commanded the air force in Spain in 1937–38, and on his return was put in command of the Soviet Air Force. P. Rychagov, E. S. Ptukhin, I. I. Proskurov, E. Shakht, and Pumpur.

In all probability Stalin shot many more Soviet participants in the Spanish Civil War than the number killed by fascist bullets in Spain.

Not long before the war against Hitler, A. D. Laktionov, candidate member of the CC and commander of the Baltic military district, was arrested and killed. For several months in this prewar period, it is true, only the Commissar of Armaments, CC member B. L. Vannikov, was arrested. But this case shows that Stalin had no scruples in dealing with the new CC members elected at the XVIIIth Party Congress of 1939.

A large number of illegal arrests in 1939–41 occurred in Bessarabia, the Western Ukraine, West Belorussia, and the Baltic territories.[8] Besides a few real enemies of the proletariat—agents of the tsarist secret police, reactionary politicians, members of fascist and semifascist organizations—thousands of completely innocent people were repressed. In some of these areas Stalin and the NKVD carried

---

[7] *Ed.*: The Khalka River, scene of a border clash between Soviet and Japanese forces in 1939.

[8] *Ed.*: These areas were newly acquired by the Soviet Union in the period indicated.

out a criminal deportation: tens of thousands of local people were arbitrarily sent east. This action caused widespread dissatisfaction among the local inhabitants, which led in turn to worse repression. Just before the war, all the prisons of Lvov, Kishinev, Tallin, and Riga were filled to overflowing. In the turmoil of the first days of the war, the NKVD in some cities (Lvov and Tartu, for example), unable to move prisoners, simply ordered them to be shot. The bodies were not even removed, and in Lvov, before the appearance of the Germans, the population came to the prison to identify the dead. This crime caused an outburst of indignation in the western areas, and was very useful to fascist propagandists and the followers of Bandera.[9] The criminal actions of the NKVD were largely to blame for the slow development of the resistance movement against the fascist occupation in the western regions. The partisans were much weaker here than in the other occupied areas.

4

SOVIET HISTORIANS have devoted much study to the international significance of the October Revolution and the Soviet victory in World War II. But they never examine the great influence that the criminal activities identified with Stalin's name had on the international revolutionary movement. Even in the twenties the bourgeois and Social Democratic press used such crimes for anti-Communist and anti-Soviet propaganda. Such "excesses" as the wave of rural violence in the late twenties and early thirties, the "gold campaign," and the terrorization of technical specialists seriously weakened the revolutionary movement in the West. Why did the unexampled crisis of capitalism in 1929–32 lead almost nowhere to a revolutionary situation, and why did it bring very little strength to the Communist movement? Why, in the years of crisis, did the petty bourgeoisie, the peasantry, and even part of the working class swing not to the left but to the right, producing mass support for fascism in some countries, particularly Germany? Undoubtedly this trend was strengthened by the news coming out of the Soviet Union, which was skillfully used for anti-Communist propaganda.

In the second half of the thirties, anti-Communists made the same use of news about repression in the USSR, especially the "open" political trials of 1936–38. Although many details and the inner mechanism of these trials were unknown, Western journalists and politicians could easily see that most of the testimony was pure fraud. The Western press pointed out the many inconsistencies and contradictions, the

[9] *Ed.:* A Ukrainian collaborator with the Nazis.

incorrect interpretation of certain facts, and the factual impossibility of many assertions. For example, at the first "open" trial Gol'tsman stated that in 1932 in Berlin he had arranged with Sedov, Trotsky's son, to meet Trotsky at the Bristol Hotel in Copenhagen, and did meet him there. But six days after the trial ended, the Danish Social Democratic paper reported that the Bristol Hotel had been torn down in 1917. Moreover, a commission headed by an American scholar proved that Gol'tsman had not met with Trotsky, and that Sedov had not gone to Copenhagen on the days indicated. At the second "open" trial Piatakov "confessed" that on the night of December 25, 1935, he flew to Oslo for a meeting with Trotsky. Two days after this testimony, a Norwegian paper reported that not a single plane had landed at this airport in December, 1935. Later another Norwegian paper published a statement by the airport director that not a single foreign plane had landed there in December, 1935.

To be sure, some Western intellectuals tried to defend the judicial practice of Stalin and Vyshinskii in 1936–38. Lion Feuchtwanger, who came to interview Stalin in 1937, described him as a "simple, good-natured man," who "appreciated humor and was not offended by criticism of himself." In *Moscow, 1937,* Feuchtwanger told how he was converted from skepticism to faith in Stalin's justice. During the trial of Zinoviev and Kamenev he was still in the West and found the confessions impossible to believe. He sympathized with friends whose vision of a new world died along with Zinoviev and Kamenev. But when, during the next big trial, he sat in the Moscow courtroom and heard the confessions of Radek and Piatakov with his own ears, his doubts vanished and he accepted the whole fantastic story.

Many Western commentators wondered why the accused, instead of denying the charges, tried to outdo each other in their confessions. Why did they depict themselves as filthy criminals? Why did they not defend themselves, as people on trial usually do? Even if they were exposed, why did they not plead extenuating circumstances instead of making their position worse? If they were revolutionaries and ideologists who believed in Trotsky's theories, why did they not openly support their leader and his theories? Speaking for the last time before the masses, why did they not extol their actions? It is possible, Western observers reasoned, that some of the accused might have resigned themselves, but hardly all of them.

Feuchtwanger tried to answer these questions. He used a primitive, obviously inconsistent version of the argument that the accused co-operated with their accusers because all were part of the Party, all trying to make it function as effectively as possible. He may fairly be charged with dishonesty. Conceding that he could not understand many aspects of the trials, Feuchtwanger reaffirmed his faith by quoting

Socrates on the dark passages in Heraclitus: "What I understand is superb. Hence I conclude that the rest, which I do not understand, is also superb." His explanation of why Stalin staged the political trials, which undermined Soviet prestige in progressive circles abroad, is quite unconvincing. He rejects the suggestion that Stalin was a despot who took pleasure in terror because he was possessed by feelings of inadequacy, lust for power, and a boundless thirst for revenge. Feuchtwanger links the trials to *the democratization of Soviet society*. The government, in his words, did not want the Trotskyites to take advantage of this democratization.[10]

Roosevelt's special ambassador to Moscow, Joseph E. Davies, could not understand the Moscow trials.[11] The distinguished English jurist D. N. Pritt, revealed similar opacity. The Italian Socialist leader Pietro Nenni came closer to understanding, but still fell short. In articles published in *Nuovo Avanti* in 1938, he attributed the Moscow trials to a double degeneration: degeneration of the Party into a bureaucratic and police regime, and degeneration of the opposition into a criminal conspiracy. Thus the repression, in Nenni's opinion, had some legal justification.

But most Western intellectuals saw the Moscow trials in a different light. It was no secret in the West that mass repression began after the first political trials, striking especially at Party cadres and the intelligentsia. No one, it is true, knew the real scale of Stalinist terror. Nonetheless, many reports on the extralegal arrests, shootings, and deportations reached the foreign press through various channels. "When we speak of the great harm done by the cult of personality," writes the former Soviet Ambassador to England, I. M. Maiskii,

> we usually have in mind its effects on the domestic life of the Soviet country. But the cult of personality had no less serious consequences for us abroad. What I said about Wells' reaction to the repression of 1936–38 is only one example of many. Similar, at times even stronger, reactions could be observed among broad circles of the Western intellectuals in general. And those who sympathized with the USSR were shaken most of all.[12]

Romain Rolland, for example, a real friend of the Soviet Union, revealed his torment in a letter to Hermann Hesse on March 5, 1938. Hesse had asked Rolland to intercede for two people arrested in the USSR. Rolland replied that he had tried this several times for his own Soviet friends, that he had written to Stalin but received no answer.

[10] Stalin was quick to use Feuchtwanger's book. A Soviet translation was published, with a huge printing, despite some critical remarks on the cult of Stalin's personality.
[11] See his comments in his *Mission to Moscow*.
[12] *Bernard Shaw i drugie* (Moscow, 1967), p. 82.

While Gorky was alive, I could do a lot through his mediation. Now I can do nothing. The "philosophes" (as they said in the time of Jean-Jacques) no longer matter to those in power. Fortunately, the cause is bigger than they are.[13]

The truth about Stalin's crimes was so frightful that some idealists among progressive Western intellectuals refused to believe it. Bernard Shaw, for example, continued to the end of his life to praise Stalin, identifying his deeds with the ideas of socialism. But then Shaw could not bring himself to believe in German death camps; he could not accept the fact that the Nazis killed almost all the Jews in occupied Europe.[14]

For a long time Bertolt Brecht too did not credit the reports about lawlessness in the Soviet Union. He was cheered by Feuchtwanger's explanation of the trials, and wrote to Feuchtwanger that his book was the best thing on the subject.[15] But when Brecht made a brief visit to the Soviet Union in the spring of 1941, he learned of the arrest of many German antifascists, the closing of the Thälmann Club and the Liebknecht School, and the shooting of his friend and teacher in Marxism, the Soviet writer Tret'iakov. Then Brecht wrote this poem:[16]

IS THE PEOPLE INFALLIBLE?

1

My teacher,
Big, friendly,
Has been shot, condemned by a people's court.
As a spy. His name is damned.
His books are destroyed. Talk about him
Is suspect and hushed.
Suppose he is innocent?

2

Sons of the people have found him guilty.
The *kolkhozy* and factories of the workers,
The most heroic institutions in the world,
Have seen an enemy in him.
No voice has been raised for him.
Suppose he is innocent?

---

[13] *Novyi mir,* 1966, No. 1, pp. 234–35. *Ed.:* See Hesse and Rolland, *Briefe* (Zürich, 1954), pp. 110–11, for the first part of the quotation. I have been unable to discover the source of the final sentence.

[14] Emrys Hughes, *Bernard Shaw* (Moscow, 1966), p. 272. *Ed.:* There is no English edition of this book, which was written for a Soviet publisher.

[15] L. Kopelev, *Brecht* (Moscow, 1966), p. 255.

[16] *Ed.:* B. Brecht, *Gesammelte Werke,* IX (Frankfurt am Main, 1967), pp. 741–43. Medvedev quotes a Russian verse translation by N. Gorskaia. This English prose translation from the German is by D. Joravsky.

. . .

5
To speak of enemies who may be sitting in the people's courts
Is dangerous, for the courts need their authority.
To demand papers on which guilt is proved black on white
Is foolish, for there must be no such papers.
Criminals hold proofs of their innocence in hand.
The innocent often have no proofs.
Suppose he is innocent?

6
What 5000 have built, one can destroy.
Among 50 who are condemned,
One can be innocent.
Suppose he is innocent?

7
Suppose he is innocent
How could he go to his death?

Telegrams and letters sent to Stalin, Vyshinskii, and Kalinin, by leaders of Western science and culture show how disturbed many Western friends of the Soviet Union were. Here is one such letter, written in June, 1938, by three Nobel laureates, Irène and Frédéric Joliot-Curie and Jean Perrin, following the arrest of two outstanding German antifascist physicists:

> The undersigned, friends of the Soviet Union, believe it to be their duty to bring the following facts to your attention:
> The imprisonment of two well-known foreign physicists, Dr. Friedrich Houtermanns, who was arrested on December 1, 1937, in Moscow, and Alexander Weissberg, who was arrested on March 1 of the same year in Kharkov, has shocked scientific circles in Europe and the United States. The names of Houtermanns and Weissberg are so well known in these circles that it is to be feared that their imprisonment may provoke a new political campaign of the sort which has recently done such damage to the prestige of the country of socialism and to the collaboration of the U.S.S.R. with the great Western democracies. The situation has been made more serious by the fact that these scientific men, friends of the U.S.S.R. who have always defended it against the attacks of its enemies, have not been able to obtain any news from Soviet authorities on the cases of Houtermanns and Weissberg in spite of the time which has gone by since their arrest, and thus find themselves unable to explain the step that has been taken.[17]

[17] *Ed.:* This translation, from French to English, is printed in Alexander Weissberg, *The Accused* (New York, 1951), pp. xviii–xix. The complete text declares that Einstein, P. M. S. Blackett, and Niels Bohr also had an active interest in the case.

On May 16, 1938, the greatest physicist of the twentieth century, Albert Einstein, sent a special letter to Stalin, protesting the arrest of many famous scientists. Most such appeals went unanswered.

The Western Socialist parties sharply condemned the terror. In 1937 many believed in the "plot" of Tukhachevskii and his comrades. The Gestapo did its best to have "reliable" reports about this "plot" reach Czechoslovak and French intelligence. From there the reports passed to activists of the Socialist parties. But on the whole European Socialists had no doubts at all about the perversions of socialist democracy in the Soviet Union. Stalin's vengeance on the old Bolshevik guard had nothing in common with justice. The Socialists differed among themselves only in their explanations of the causes of this tragedy. Some thought the Soviet Union, rapidly degenerating into a state of the fascist type, was destroying old revolutionaries who were still true to their ideals. Others argued that a savage struggle for power was going on *within* the Soviet system, with Stalin relying on the new Soviet generation, who were eager for practical action and indifferent to such things as the theoretical quarrels between Trotskyites and Bukharinites. In this view an industrial and agrarian revolution from above is invariably accompanied by reprisals against dissidents. A third group attributed the slaughter of the old Bolsheviks simply to Stalin's megalomania and mania for persecution.

Foreign Communist parties were in an especially difficult position, since their leaders in that period unreservedly endorsed everything that happened in the USSR. Their press usually repeated everything that appeared in *Izvestiia* or *Pravda*. Their main argument was simply that a Soviet court was a proletarian court and therefore had to be just. As for the rumors of torture, the Communist papers rejected them as vicious slander. They did not even raise questions about the arrest and shooting of foreign Communist leaders in Moscow. And most activists really believed, at that time, that dangerous traitors and conspirators were being destroyed in the USSR. The American Communist Hershel Meyer recalls that it was impossible to believe that Stalin was destroying innocent people; such stories were simply dismissed as anti-Soviet propaganda.[18] But this trustfulness of the leaders and activists was by no means always shared by rank-and-file workers, including those who were Communists. Ambassador Maiskii recalls the situation vividly:

> Socialists and reformists of all kinds quickly seized on the news of arrests and repression in the USSR, and popularized it in the factories, saying: "Look what Communism leads to." I well remember

[18] Meyer, *Doklad Khrushcheva i krizis levogo dvizheniia v SShA* (Moscow, 1957), p. 10. For the original, see Hershel D. Meyer, *The Khrushchev Report and the Crisis of the American Left* (New York, 1956).

how English Communists whom I used to see in those years would ask me with bitterness, almost with despair, the same question as Wells: "What is happening in your country? We cannot believe that so many old and honored Party members, tested in battle, have suddenly become traitors." And they told how the events in the USSR were alienating the workers from the Soviet land and undermining Communist influence among the proletariat. The same thing happened in France, Scandinavia, Belgium, Holland, and many other countries.[19]

It is important to analyze the reactions of the varied trends and groups among the Russian émigrés. Many White Guardists rejoiced to see Communists destroying each other. Some saw Stalin's usurpation of power as a step toward a new monarchy, and had hopes in this respect. The supporters of Trotsky, as we have seen, tried to use reports coming from the USSR to split the Communist movement and create a Fourth International.

Some Soviet diplomats and intelligence agents who refused to go back to the Soviet Union addressed appeals to Western public opinion. In December, 1937, European papers (including Paul Miliukov's *Poslednie novosti*) carried the "open letter" of General V. Krivitskii, which he addressed to the French Socialist Party, the Communist Party of France, and the Fourth International. Krivitskii wrote that he had served the Communist cause for a long time, since he joined the Party in 1919. For his services to the Red Army he had received two decorations and constant evidence of trust. But the arrest and shooting of many innocent people had finally obliged him to give up his position and devote himself to the rehabilitation of those who were unjustly accused and destroyed. The letter concluded:

> I know—and I have proof—that a reward has been offered for my head. I know the OGPU will stop at nothing to silence me by murder. Dozens of people, ready for anything, are at Ezhov's disposal and have already been after me. I consider it my duty as a revolutionary fighter to report all this to international working-class opinion.
>
> V. KRIVITSKII (Val'ter)
> December 5, 1937

A few days later many European papers published a similar letter from the former Soviet Ambassador to Greece, A. G. Barmin, which he had sent to the League for the Rights of Man and Citizen. He had been a Communist for nineteen years, he wrote, and now could see preparations for the mass destruction of all those who had made the Revolution and the first working-class state. Thus he was faced with

---

[19] *Bernard Shaw i drugie*, p. 83.

a tragic dilemma: to return to my native land and meet certain death there, or, refusing to see my fatherland, to risk being shot abroad by OGPU agents, who have recently been following my footsteps. To remain in the service of the Soviet government would mean losing all moral right and sharing the responsibility for crimes committed every day against the people in my country. It would mean betraying the cause of socialism to which I have devoted my entire life.

Of special interest is a statement by F. F. Raskol'nikov, hero of the October Revolution and the Civil War, and an outstanding publicist.[20] From 1930 to 1939 he was a Soviet diplomat in Estonia, Denmark, and Bulgaria. After the XVIIth Party Congress in 1934,[21] Raskol'nikov was increasingly alarmed by the cult of personality and the destruction of the best Party cadres. He noticed that he was always followed by NKVD agents. In July, 1939, when he was in France, he learned that he had been declared an enemy of the people and an outlaw. He responded with a public statement, "How They Made Me an Enemy of the People," vigorously defending himself and other innocent victims. Some weeks later he wrote "An Open Letter to Stalin":

> Stalin, you have begun a new stage, which will go down in the history of our revolution as the "epoch of terror." No one feels safe in the Soviet Union. No one, as he goes to bed, knows whether he will escape arrest in the night. . . . You began with bloody vengeance on former Trotskyites, Zinovievites, and Bukharinites, went on to destroy the old Bolsheviks, then slaughtered Party and state cadres who rose in the Civil War and carried through the first Five-Year Plans; you even massacred the Komsomol. You hide under the slogan of a fight against Trotskyite-Bukharinite "spies." But you did not get power only yesterday. No one could be appointed to an important post without your permission. Who placed the so-called "enemies of the people" in the most responsible government, army, Party, and diplomatic positions? . . . Joseph Stalin! Who put the so-called "wreckers" in every pore of the Soviet and Party *apparat*? . . . Joseph Stalin!
>   With the help of dirty forgeries you have staged trials which, in the absurdity of the accusations, surpass the medieval witch trials you know about from seminary textbooks. . . . You have defamed and shot long-time colleagues of Lenin, knowing very well that they were innocent. You have forced them before dying to confess crimes they never committed, to smear themselves in filth from head to toe.
>   . . . You have forced those who go along with you to walk with

[20] Raskol'nikov had been chairman of the Kronstadt Party Committee in 1917, then Deputy Commissar for Naval Affairs, fleet commander on the Volga and the Caspian and then on the Baltic.
[21] According to V. S. Zaitsev, *Voprosy istorii KPSS,* 1963, No. 12.

anguish and disgust through pools of their comrades' and friends' blood. In the lying history of the Party, written under your direction, you have plundered those whom you murdered and defamed, appropriating their feats and accomplishments to yourself.

On the eve of war, you are destroying the Red Army. . . . At a moment of the greatest military danger, you continue to massacre army leaders, middle-rank officers, and junior commanders.

. . . Under pressure from the Soviet people, you are hypocritically reviving the cult of the heroes of Russian history: Alexander Nevskii, Dmitrii Donskoi, Mikhail Kutuzov, hoping they will help you more in the coming war than our executed marshals and generals.

This open letter, as Admiral V. Grishanov rightly said in *Izvestiia* in 1964, is a credit to its author. It appeared in a White-émigré paper, *Novaia Rossiia,* on October 1, 1939, when the Second World War was beginning, and passed almost unnoticed. Raskol'nikov probably had sent it to a French news agency, which served many newspapers, including some émigré ones. He had no other way to reach public opinion. In 1964 his widow, a resident of France, brought the original of the letter to Moscow, where a commission on Raskol'nikov's literary heritage had been set up in the Writers' Union. Raskol'nikov himself died in September, 1939. According to the French newspapers, he committed suicide by jumping—or being thrown?—from a window.

VIII

Illegal Methods of
Investigation and Confinement

1

MASS ARRESTS of innocent Soviet citizens were an unforgivable crime, but they were only the first in the sequence of crimes performed by Stalin's machine of terror. The rest of the sequence must also be examined.

For Stalin, it was not enough merely to isolate or destroy objectionable people. He had to crush their wills, humiliate them, force them to call themselves "enemies of the people" and to confess to various crimes and conspiracies. But it was obvious to Stalin and his accomplices that even partial adherence to legal methods of investigation would make it impossible to achieve this goal. So, in 1937, Stalin prescribed massive application of "physical methods of influence."

The methods of the NKVD are vividly revealed in the deposition of Comrade Rozenblium, a Party member who was arrested in Leningrad in 1937.[1] In the 1955 re-examination of the Komarov case, Rozenblium reported that false testimony was wrung out of him by torture. Then he was taken to the office of L. M. Zakovskii, head of the Leningrad NKVD, who promised him freedom, if he would give false testimony in court in "the case of the Leningrad wrecking, espionage, diversionary, terrorist center," which was then being fabricated. Explaining the matter to Rozenblium, Zakovskii cynically revealed the mechanics of such fabrication:

> To make things clear, Zakovskii sketched a few variants of the proposed center and its branches. . . . After he had acquainted me

[1] Khrushchev retailed this deposition in his speech to the XXth Congress.

with these variants, Zakovskii said that the NKVD was preparing the case, and the trial would be open. The court would be presented with four or five people as the heads of the center: Chudov, Ugarov, Smorodin, Pozern, and Shaposhnikova (Chudov's wife), and with two or three people from each branch. . . . The case had to have a solid basis. Witnesses were of crucial importance. A witness's social position (in the past, of course) and length of Party membership played an important role. You personally, Zakovskii told me, will not have to make up anything; the NKVD will provide you with a detailed report on every branch. Your job will be to learn it by heart, to remember all the questions and answers that may be given in court. Four or five months, maybe half a year, will be spent preparing this case. All this time you will be getting ready, so you will not let down the prosecution—or yourself. Your fate will depend on the course and outcome of the investigation. If you get scared and begin to sing out of tune, you have only yourself to blame. If you hold firm, you will save your neck, and we will feed and clothe you at state expense until your death.

Two years later the investigators themselves fell into their monstrous machine. Party member A. Shan was in the same camp as Zakovskii's deputy, Nikonovich. Nikonovich was supposed to have been shot but escaped death somehow, and got a sentence of twenty years. In constant fear that he would be recognized as a former NKVD leader, he was "stiller than water, lower than grass." He never got into arguments, quarreled with no one, obeyed everyone, even the whims of the most insignificant bosses and guards. Once he told Shan how terribly he and Zakovskii had been tortured by the "new complement" of investigators.

Nowadays some former NKVD officials try to deny that torture was extensively used, despite the reports of thousands of rehabilitated people. One of the memoirs we have is from a person who was a high official in the NKVD: "We declare," he declares, "with full responsibility, that only individual, morally unstable and unprincipled Chekists went so far as to apply physical torture and torment, for which they were shot in 1939, following the November [1938] letter of the Politburo on excesses in investigation." A "responsible" declaration of this sort is a deliberate distortion of the truth. Physical torture was used with the complete approval of the central offices. Of course the policy did not spring up in a single day but developed gradually over several years. Back at the beginning of the first Five-Year Plan, in the campaign to extract gold from alleged nepmen, the OGPU beat arrested people, deprived them of sleep and food, and kept them in prison until they or their relatives handed over gold "for the needs of industrialization."

Beatings, the "conveyor," deprivation of sleep, and the heat, cold, hunger and thirst treatments—all these methods of "investigation" were used extensively against "wreckers" in 1930–31. Arrested Communists, however, were treated more "humanely" at the beginning of the thirties. Until the spring of 1937, torture was used only against certain prisoners, and only by certain specially selected investigators— for example, in the preparation of the trials of the "Trotskyite-Zinovievite" and the "parallel" centers. Other investigators were permitted to use only such methods as the "conveyor." But after the February-March Plenum of 1937, most of them were permitted to apply even the most refined tortures to "stubborn enemies of the people," which meant that almost all prisoners who offered any resistance were tortured. And this was not stopped in 1939, when Ezhov was removed. V. I. Volgin, who was interrogated in one of the prisons of Rostov-on-Don, tells what changes came with the appointment of Beria.

> Previously the investigators would say to us: 'Come on, you gangster, write; we'll make mincemeat of you.' Now they spoke differently: 'Well, Vasili Ivanovich, write, write,' using the polite second person now; 'sign it, buddy; you'll get twenty years anyway.'

The use of torture was one of the worst crimes of Stalin and his terror machine. Torture was, of course, extensively employed during the "inquests" in Russia in the sixteenth and seventeenth centuries. Even then the deficiencies of torture as a method of investigation were recognized. Hence a rule arose: "The informer gets the first knout." That is, the informer should be tortured before the accused, to verify his information. The Western Inquisition, on the other hand, did not punish but encouraged informers, giving them part of the property of the condemned. But then, the Inquisition was least of all interested in finding the truth. Torture provoked such strong protests that Catherine II decreed its end: "No bodily punishments of any kind shall be used on anyone, in any government office, in any cases, for the discovery of the truth." But this ban was by no means always obeyed, especially after the Pugachev rebellion. So Alexander I in 1801 ordered the Senate

> to reaffirm most strictly everywhere and throughout the empire, that nowhere, under no form, neither in higher nor in lower offices or courts, no one shall dare to use or to allow or to undertake, any torture, under pain of unavoidable and severe punishment. . . . The very word "torture," which is a disgrace and reproach to humanity, must be eradicated forever from the nation's memory.[2]

[2] V. G. Korolenko, "Russkaia pytka v starinu," *Sochineniia*, IX (1914), p. 215.

Of course these decrees were not strictly observed by the investigating organs of tsarist Russia. In periods of intense revolutionary conflict tsarist officials and members of the Black Hundreds used the most refined tortures on many revolutionaries, including women. Many embittered counterrevolutionaries revived torture on a mass scale during the Civil War. "The Polish nobles branded our backs with five-pointed stars," wrote Mayakovsky; "Mamontov's bands buried us in the ground alive, up to the head; the Japanese burned us in locomotive furnaces, poured lead and tin in our mouths." But did this inhuman torture of Communists drive the Party to use the same cruel methods of struggle in those grim years?

The following incident is typical of the young Soviet state. In the summer of 1918 the Cheka uncovered a conspiracy against the Soviet regime headed by the British diplomat Bruce Lockhart. The conspirators were arrested and Lockhart was expelled from the Soviet Union. The newspaper reported that "the exposed English diplomatic representative left the Cheka greatly embarrassed."[3] About the same time a small journal, the *Cheka Weekly,* was started in Moscow, An early issue published a letter—"Why the Kid Gloves?"—from the chairmen of the Party committee and the Cheka in Nolinsk, without giving their names or any editorial comments:

> We will say it plainly. . . . The Cheka has not broken with petty-bourgeois ideology, the cursed legacy of the prerevolutionary past. Tell us why you did not subject him, this Lockhart, to the most refined tortures, to get information and addresses, which such a bird must have had a lot of. With those measures you could have easily discovered a whole series of counterrevolutionary organizations, perhaps even have eliminated the possibility of future financing, which is certainly equivalent to wiping them out. Tell us why, instead of subjecting him to such tortures, the mere description of which would make counterrevolutionaries' blood run cold, tell us why you let him "leave" the Cheka greatly embarrassed. Or do you think that subjecting a man to horrible tortures is more inhumane than blowing up bridges and warehouses of food with the purpose of finding an ally, in the torments of starvation, for the overthrow of the Soviet regime? . . . Let every British worker know that an official representative of his country is doing such things that he must be subjected to torture. And it is safe to say that the workers will not approve the system of explosions and bribes carried out by such a rat, directed by rats of higher rank. No more kid gloves. Stop this contemptible game of "diplomacy and representation."[4]

The appeal of the Nolinsk officials was not supported by the Cheka. The same issue of the *Cheka Weekly* carried an article by Dzelon on

[3] *Izvestiia,* Sept. 3, 1918.
[4] *Ezhenedel'nik Chrezvychainykh Kommissii,* 1918, No. 3 (Oct. 6), pp. 7–8.

the interrogation of former members of the tsarist secret police (*okhranniki*):

> In the years of the old regime it seemed to us that all these furious *okhranniki*, gendarmes, and policemen did not have human souls; they did not tremble when they saw all their force sinking into a sea of blood of class-conscious workers and into pools of tears of the dark, tormented Russian muzhik. Often, dying under the gendarmes' tortures, we could not help asking: "Don't you see that you can kill us right away, shoot us or hang us right away, but why torture us?" But now all the *okhranniki* and gendarmes are pitiful, they all tremble, they all faint, when they have to stand before the regime of the proletariat. . . . The proletariat is merciless in its struggle. At the same time it is unshakable and strong. Not a single curse at our most wicked enemies. No tortures and torments! No superfluous words! Vanquished hirelings, former torturers of workers, must be wiped off the face of the earth![5]

According to a writer who was Sverdlov's secretary in 1918, "Why the Kid Gloves?" caused widespread indignation in Party circles.[6] Readers sent the newspapers letters of protest, some of which were published. Sverdlov heard of this polemic. When he read the relevant materials, his indignation was boundless. The question was raised in the highest governmental body, which adopted the following resolution:

> The Presidium of the All-Russian Central Executive Committee, having discussed the article "Why the Kid Gloves?" which appeared in the third issue of the *Cheka Weekly*, has taken note that the thoughts expressed in it on the struggle with the counterrevolution are in gross contradiction with the policy and the tasks of the Soviet regime. Although the Soviet regime resorts of necessity to the most drastic measures of conflict with the counterrevolutionary movement, and remembers that the conflict with the counterrevolution has taken the form of open armed conflict, in which the proletariat and poor peasants cannot renounce the use of terror, the Soviet regime fundamentally rejects the measures advocated in the indicated article, as despicable, dangerous, and contrary to the interests of the struggle for Communism. The Presidium of the Central Executive Committee most severely censures both the authors of the article and the editors of the *Cheka Weekly* who printed this article and provided it with commentary.

It was also decided to close down the *Cheka Weekly* for publishing the article, to dismiss the authors from their jobs, and to forbid their holding office in the Soviet government. At the same time, the Presidium pointed out the need to continue the struggle against counterrevolutionaries.

[5] *Ibid.*, p. 9.
[6] See E. Ia. Drabkina, *Cherneye sukhari* (Moscow, 1961).

Such a resolution was not an accident. Russian revolutionaries of all persuasions had always been intolerant of any form of physical torture. S. L. Zlatopol'skii, for example, a member of the Executive Committee of the People's Will (*Narodnaia volia*),[7] when he was in the Trubetskoi ravelin of Peter-Paul Fortress, in the solitary cells for "especially dangerous state criminals," managed to send the People's Will a long letter, which was then circulated as a sort of proclamation throughout the country. After describing the regime in the Peter-Paul Fortress, particularly in the Trubetskoi ravelin, Zlatopol'skii closed with a dying man's appeal:

> Friends and brothers! From the depths of our dungeon, speaking to you probably for the last time in our life, we send you our bequest: On the day of revolutionary victory, the triumph of progress, may the Revolution not pollute its sacred name by acts of violence and cruelty against the defeated enemy. Oh, if we could serve as a redeeming sacrifice not only for the creation of freedom in Russia but for an increase in humanitarianism in all the rest of the world! Mankind must renounce solitary confinement, force, and torture in any form, as it has renounced the wheel, the rack, the stake, etc. Regards to you, regards to my relatives, regards to everything alive.

Beatings or whippings in prisons of the early twentieth century provoked stormy protests from all the revolutionary parties outside, and many collective hunger strikes, riots, and, in exceptional cases, even mass suicides inside. Even tsarist prison officials were forced to pay attention to these protests. It is not surprising, then, that after the October Revolution the conscience of a true revolutionary could not accept the use of physical torture even against enemies of the revolution. Thus, when Stalin not only permitted but even forced the use of torture, he was committing an outrage to the memory of Russian revolutionaries.

Torture not only conflicts with the principles of a proletarian state, it is the least effective method of investigation. In most cases torture yields not truth but a distortion of the truth, since the accused will agree to say anything to stop the unbearable torment. Thus torture is aimed not so much at finding the guilty person as at making the innocent one guilty, forcing him to calumniate himself or others. Medieval inquisitors were well aware of this when they forced their victims to testify about their contacts with the devil. The intelligence agencies of capitalist countries are also aware of it. The British intelligence agent Oreste Pinto writes:

[7] *Ed.*: The organization that carried out the assassination of Alexander II in 1881.

There is no doubt that physical torture will ultimately break any man, however strong in body or determined in mind. I knew one incredibly brave man who fell into the hands of the Gestapo and who had all his fingernails and toenails forcibly extracted and one leg broken without uttering a word of useful information. But he himself admitted that he was at the end of his resistance. It so happened that his torturers were baffled and gave up at that stage. Had they gone on, even with some minor discomfort compared to the exquisite agony he had so far suffered, he would have broken and confessed all.

. . . Physical torture has one overwhelming disadvantage. Under its spur an innocent man will often confess to some crime he has never committed, merely to gain a respite. . . . He will even invent a crime involving the death penalty, preferring a quick death to a continuation of his agony. Physical torture will ultimately make any man talk but it cannot ensure that he will tell the truth.[8]

Stalin and the NKVD officials understood this very well when they forced devoted Communists to testify about their connections with genuine enemies of our nation.

Even the Inquisition tried to put some limit on the willfulness of the inquisitors. "Heretics" could be whipped, stretched on the rack, or tortured by water, hunger, and thirst. But the rules of the Inquisition forbade the spilling of blood. The "heretic" could be tortured only once in the course of an interrogation, and the torture was supposed to last no more than an hour, so as to let the clerk, the torturer, and the inquisitors rest. The NKVD investigators tortured prisoners for many hours at a stretch, and repeatedly. Brutalized interrogators disfigured prisoners. They not only beat them and kept them from sleep, food, and water; they gouged out eyes and perforated eardrums—that was done to Mamiia Orakhelashvili.

Some survivors' stories make the blood run cold. When sadistic investigators in Butyrskaia Prison did not obtain the testimony they needed from one Communist, they tortured him in front of his wife and then tortured her in front of him. A. V. Snegov tells about torture chambers of the Leningrad NKVD where prisoners would be put on a concrete floor and covered by a box with nails driven in from four sides. On top was a grating through which a doctor looked at the victim once every twenty-four hours. In 1938, both Snegov, a small man, and P. E. Dybenko, who was big, were put into such a box—one cubic meter in size. (This method was borrowed from the Finnish secret police.) One NKVD colonel, on getting a prisoner for interroga-

[8] Pinto, *Spy-catcher* (New York, 1952), pp. 24–25. Medvedev quotes the Soviet translation, *Okhota za shpionami* (Moscow, 1964).

tion, would urinate in a glass and force the prisoner to drink the urine. If he refused, he was liable to be killed without being interrogated.

Suren Gazarian tells what was done to Soso Buachidze, commander of a Georgian division and son of a hero of the Revolution. When he would not give the required testimony, his stomach was ripped open, and he was thrown, dying, into a cell. In the same cell was David Bagration, one of Buachidze's friends, who had just been arrested. Gazarian, who had been an executive in the Transcaucasian NKVD until June, 1937, was also subjected to inhuman torture. This is how he describes it in his still unpublished book:

> Aivazov, the investigator, took some papers off the table and locked them in a drawer. Only my "record" remained on the table.
>
> "Well, I'm going. The brigade knows its job," and, turning to me, he added, "I will leave the record of the interrogation on the table. As soon as you want to sign it, say so."
>
> He left.
>
> . . . The "brigade" came. There were five men. First Iakov Kopetskii came in. He was an old NKVD official; we knew each other well. Tall, strong. He was a very nervous man, they called him "Iasha-psycho." He knew about this name but was not offended. He was followed by Ivan Aivazov, Gurgen's younger brother. He had also worked in the NKVD for several years and knew me well. The third was one of the younger agents of the special section, formerly a student at the inter-*krai* NKVD school. A gawky fellow with big black eyes and long mustaches. He had almost no forehead, thick black hair began practically right above his brows. I have forgotten his name. The last two were students at the inter-*krai* school. One of them held a bucket with the "instruments," as they called them.
>
> Yes, you don't answer back to this choice bunch, all powerful, tough. . . .
>
> "Oho! Look who we'll be working over today," said Kopetskii. "This is a great treat for us."
>
> I remained seated. They surrounded me. Kopetskii took me from behind by my collar, lifted and shoved me with a powerful motion to the middle of the room. Somebody knocked me down with a powerful kick. I fell. . . . A third pulled off my pants. . . . I remembered Bagration being brought into the cell without pants, in his shorts.
>
> The torture began.
>
> The five men beat viciously. They beat with fists, feet, birch rods, ramrods, tightly braided towels; they beat with anything anywhere: on the head, the face, the back, the stomach. . . . Most of all on the legs. Someone noticed that I have sick legs and then they began to beat on my legs.
>
> "We'll fix your legs for you!"
>
> And they beat, they beat. The more they beat, the more brutal they became. What annoyed them most was that I did not scream.

"Will you scream? Will you holler? Will you beg for mercy?" Kopetskii cursed, and beat, beat. . . .

How long they beat me I don't know.

"Well, boys, take a break," Kopetskii commanded.

My fresh shirt had turned to bloody shreds. I lay wet on the floor in a pool of blood. My eyes were swollen. With difficulty I raised my eyelids and as if in a fog saw my torturers. . . .

They were smoking, taking a rest.

They cursed me in gutter talk, insulted me, mocked me, laughed. . . .

Someone came up to me and just then something very painful burned my body. I was convulsed with pain, and to keep from screaming, I clenched my teeth. And they laughed. . . . Then it burned again, again, again. . . . I understood. They were putting out their cigarettes on my body. . . .

The break came to an end and the beating continued with new force.

A strange sensation. The blows became more vicious, but the pain decreased. When I came to, I smelled medicine, saw something white far away.

So. Seems I had passed out and they had brought me to.

"I'm going, everything O.K.," said a nurse.

"Everything O.K.!" That meant they could start all over again. But the "brigade" was smoking. With horror I thought: they're going to put out their cigarettes on my body again. A cigarette burn is very painful. My whole body was aflame from the first burns. Would there be still more? Yes. One finished his cigarette, came up to me, gave the required insult, put out his cigarette, cursed, spat, and went away, to give the next one his turn.

Everything proceeded in a determined sequence. Beating, break, putting out cigarettes, again beating, fainting, coming to, again beating, putting out cigarettes. . . .

It was already growing light but the brigade was still toiling away.

Aivazov appeared.

"Well, boys, go to sleep," he said after greeting them. Why not, he could see the work was done.

"Go to sleep." That meant the "brigade" worked nights and rested days.

The brigade left.

"It'll be the same every day until you sign. Do you understand?" Aivazov called headquarters.

"Send removal men, two."

Just like Bagration the day before, I was dragged back to the cell by two guards.

The same ghastly scene occurs in the memoirs of Ia. I. Drobinskii, the Belorussian Party official. This time we see the methods of "investigation" in the Minsk Central Prison in 1938:

At ten they took him again through that corridor to that room, but what a difference! . . . During the day this was a quiet corridor, with respectable offices in which neat, well-groomed people shuffled papers. In the evening Andrei felt he was running a gauntlet—the screams of the tortured, the filthiest gutter curses of the torturers, coming from every room. Sometimes a glimpse of a body on the floor. Andrei saw a familiar face, turning purple. . . . It was Liubovich, an old Bolshevik, deputy chairman of the republic's council of commissars, chairman of Gosplan. He had been in the first government created by Lenin in 1917. He had entered it as the deputy commissar of communications under Podbel'skii. He had been a member of the Little Council of Commissars, he had worked with Lenin. Now he lay on the floor, they were whipping him with rubber hoses, and he, a sixty-year-old man, was screaming "Mama!" . . . An instant, but it was etched in his memory forever.

. . . A torture room of the sixteenth century. He was taken into an office. As in the daytime, there were two: Dovgalenko and the sportsman. "Well," asked the captain, businesslike, "have you thought it over?" Andrei shook his head. . . .

"Take off your jacket." . . . Andrei didn't move. With a sharp movement the young man tore it off; the jacket split, fell down. "Ah, just once I'll give it to him." Andrei jerked his right fist toward the young man's chin and hit the air. The same instant, he received two karate chops on his arms. A sharp pain pierced them, and his arms hung like vines. And right away the young man hit him hard, once, twice, three times in the chest. . . . Andrei leaned against the wall. Those creatures went to a large closet, took out two thick sticks, and got down to work. From both sides they beat rhythmically, the back of his head, his ribs, his back. Clenching his teeth, Andrei groaned—the main thing was not to scream, not to give those creatures the satisfaction. . . . The pain was unbearable, then it grew dull. Then they poured something on him, iodine or salt water or simply water, and then the pain became horrible, insufferable. His body was being torn by the teeth of some wild beasts, hundreds, thousands of dogs were biting this poor tormented body.

"Well, are you going to write?"

He didn't answer. To answer he had to open his mouth, and then he would begin to scream. He must not scream. They were screaming from other rooms. "Murderers, fascists!" screamed the voice of a young woman, "don't you dare, don't you dare! How can you?" "My God," thought Andrei, "what are they doing to her?" And those creatures were taking a rest. . . .

Most of the victims could not endure the torture and signed fraudulent interrogation records. They should not be judged too harshly. Demoralized and confused, they did not understand what was happening in the country, so their will to fight was unavoidably weakened. Much of their behavior can be explained, if not completely justified. Therefore we cannot agree with General A. V. Gorbatov, whose memoirs reveal anger not so much against the torturers as against the people who succumbed to the torture.[9]

Today we know that prisoners behaved in various ways. Some immediately complied with the desires of the investigators; without any sort of resistance they gave false testimony not only about themselves but about dozens and hundreds of their comrades. M. V. Ostrogorskii tells how the former editor of *Krest'ianskaia gazeta* (*The Peasant Newspaper*), Semen Uritskii, when grabbed by the NKVD, at once began to give false testimony about dozens of his colleagues. Some of these weak-willed people went even further than the investigators demanded; they gained cruel satisfaction out of voluntarily denouncing co-workers and friends, demanding their arrest, though they had no doubt about their innocence. Frequently such people continued to collaborate with the NKVD beyond the investigation; they became stool pigeons (*seksoty, stukachi*), who informed on their mates in the prison cell or the camp barracks.

Many prisoners committed suicide after the first interrogations, by breaking their heads on the washbasin or the prison wall, throwing themselves on the guards during walks, or jumping from a window. Others resisted stubbornly but finally broke down under torture and put their signatures on fraudulent depositions. S. O. Gazarian says that the Georgian Communist David Bagration was tortured for fifteen nights in a row, until he lost control of his actions and signed. I. P. Aleksakhin says that Pavlunovskii, an official in the Commissariat of Heavy Industry, held out for several months. But when they threw him in a solitary cell, full of water and swarming with rats, he caved in, banged on the door, shouting: "Barbarians, write what you want. . . ." And then he signed. M. V. Ostrogorskii tells us that the former Commissar of Justice, N. V. Krylenko, gave in only after cruel tortures. He asked for some paper in his cell, and there, in the presence of his comrades in misfortune, he began to create his counterrevolutionary organization. He would mumble: "Ivanov? No, he's a good official and a man, I won't put him down. But Petrov, he's a louse; let's sign him up. . . ."

When M. R. Maek, an executive of the Leningrad *obkom,* was arrested, he was shown the testimony of B. P. Pozern, who confessed that he had recruited Maek into his counterrevolutionary organization. Maek knew Pozern to be an honest and intelligent man, one of the founders of the Red Guard in 1917. Unable to believe that Pozern could sign such a deposition, Maek demanded a confrontation, which took place the next day. Many years later, after he had been rehabilitated, Maek recalled how an utterly emaciated old man entered the

[9] *Novyi mir,* 1964, Nos. 3–5. *Ed.:* For an English version see Gorbatov, *Years Off My Life* (New York, 1965).

investigator's office, whom he hardly recognized as Pozern. Maek asked him: "How, Boris Pavlovich, how could you write such ridiculous stuff, that you recruited me into an anti-Soviet organization?" But Pozern, looking down, began suddenly to say: "It doesn't matter, it doesn't matter, my friend; I recruited you, I recruited you." Everything was immediately clear to Maek.

Some people would sign any deposition against themselves, but absolutely refused to compromise their comrades. "I don't want to pretend," writes D. Mikhailov in his memoirs,

> that I behaved like a hero during the interrogations and didn't sign any records. I would sign if the matter concerned me alone, or if it was well-known stuff. But when the investigator would tie people to me who were still alive, there I refused. They pinned my first sergeant (*starshina*) to me—I would not give in. They were even more energetic in tying in Boris Gorbatov. I defended him, that is, I disowned him as much as I could. And, it seems, not without success. He died in his bed and not in a camp, although the investigator told me: "Prizewinners aren't worth beans to us, and your military decorations have the same value. Be good a thousand times, but if you fall once, that's all. Understand?"[10]

Many prisoners did not sign anything, despite severe torture. Suren Gazarian, quoted above, signed nothing. N. S. Kuznetsov, North Kazakhstan *obkom* secretary, withstood the most refined tortures. Once he stood before his tormentors without sleep or food for eight days in a row. On the ninth day he lost consciousness and fell, but did not sign the prepared statement.

Nestor Lakoba, poisoned by Beria and posthumously declared an "enemy of the people," left a wife who would not sign any false statements about him. A young and beautiful woman, rumored to be a Georgian princess, she was arrested and put in the Tbilisi prison soon after her husband's death. Nutsa Gogoberidze, the wife of Levan Gogoberidze, who shared a cell with Lakoba's wife, tells how this silent and calm woman was taken away every evening and in the morning was dragged back to the cell, bloody and unconscious. The women cried, asked for a doctor, and revived her. When she came to, she told how they demanded that she sign an essay on the subject "How Lakoba sold Abkhazia to Turkey." Her reply was brief: "I will not defame the memory of my husband." She stood fast even when faced with the ultimate torture: her fourteen-year-old son was shoved crying toward his mother, and she was told he would be killed if she did not sign. (And this threat, as we mentioned earlier, was carried out.) But even then Lakoba's wife would not defame her husband. Finally, after a night of torture, she died in her cell.

[10] Mikhailov is talking here about postwar interrogations.

Kosarev and most of the other leaders of the Komsomol Central Committee were also unyielding. These young and strong people could not be broken by the worst tortures. According to V. F. Pikina, the unyielding behavior of Kosarev and his colleagues kept the NKVD from organizing an open trial of youth. General Gorbatov also did not bear false witness against himself or his comrades.

We cannot help condemning willing false witnesses. Nor can we overlook the fortitude of such people as Gazarian, Kuznetsov, Lakoba's wife, Kosarev, and Gorbatov. But we do not have the right to condemn such people as Bagration or Pavlunovskii, who were demoralized and did not understand what was happening in the country. Gorbatov was wrong when he wrote that these unfortunate people "misled the investigation" when they put their signatures to false statements. What took place in the NKVD torture chambers was not investigation; it was deliberate crime.

Sharing a cell with a friend who had given false testimony against him, N. Kuznetsov did not turn his back; he embraced his comrade. And S. Gazarian did the same. Gorbatov behaved differently with his companions in misfortune. "By your false testimony," he declared, "you have committed a serious crime, for which they are keeping you in prison."[11] This behavior contrasts poorly with the words of Evgeniia Ginzburg, who refuses "to put on the tragic buskins of the hero or the martyr" and does not condemn those who surrendered to unbearable torment. She writes that she was simply lucky—her investigation ended before the massive use of "special methods" began.[12]

The diary of P. I. Shabalkin, who died recently, contains some interesting reflections on the behavior of prisoners. This old Bolshevik was twice subjected to investigation and spent about twenty years in prisons and camps.

Why did so many people who were devoted to the Revolution, ready to die for it, who had endured tsarist prisons and exile and had more than once looked death in the eye, why did so many of these people give in during interrogation and sign false statements, "confessing" to every sort of crime they never committed? The cause of these "confessions" and "self-defamation" consists in the following:

(1) Right after the arrest the prisoner starts to be worked over. First it is done verbally, with the preservation of a certain amount of politeness; then come shouting and cursing, humiliations and insults, spit in his face, light blows, and mockery. "You bastard," "You rat," "You traitor, spy, garbage," and so on and so forth. They humiliate a man without limit, convince him that he is nothing.

[11] *Novyi mir,* 1964, No. 4, p. 119.
[12] *Ed.:* See E. S. Ginzburg, *Journey into the Whirlwind* (New York, 1967).

This goes on day after day, night after night. The so-called conveyor is set up: the interrogators change but the prisoner stands or sits. For days. They kept me, for example, on the conveyor for eight days. They don't let you sleep. They force tea into you. The conveyor is a terrible torture. And all the while they kick you, insult you; if you resist, they beat you. The job of the conveyor is to break a man morally, turn him into a rag.

But if you withstand the conveyor and don't crack, physical torture follows. They get the tortured man to the point where he becomes indifferent to everything, and he is inclined to accept everything they suggest.

"You're a rat." "Yes, a rat."

"You're a traitor." "Yes, a traitor."

"You were a provocateur." "Yes, I was a provocateur."

"You wanted to kill Stalin." "Yes, I wanted to kill Stalin." And so on.

At this time they take stories made up by the investigators and push them on the prisoner, who accepts them without a murmur. The investigators hurry to settle their success. They compile the first record of interrogation, a "hand-written deposition."

(2) Next is the stage of consolidating the "achievements." They begin to feed the prisoner decently. They give him cigarettes, parcels from his family, even let him read books and newspapers. But work on the unfortunate does not stop. They convince him that now he cannot turn back, that he can save himself only by "sincere repentance," that he himself must now think what he can still tell the investigators. They supply him with paper and pen to write "depositions" in his cell, suggest the theme, and check his work.

Frequently the victims of this ordeal started to vacillate. But the NKVD thought up thousands of ways to suppress these vacillations. They would arrange confrontations with other people just as unfortunate. "Interaction" would take place. Additional methods of physical influence would be used. They would take prisoners to see the "procurator," who would be an investigator in disguise. Provocational "court" sessions would be arranged, and so on.

(3) If the prisoner had to be brought before a court—an absolute majority of prisoners were condemned *in absentia* by various troiki, special assemblies (*osobye soveshchaniia*), etc.—then there would be additional work on him, a peculiar rehearsal for the trial. Here every method was used: threats, suggestion, "serious conversations"—"Bear in mind that we will not simply shoot you; we will torture you, tear you to pieces"—and so on. They convinced many people that they would not be shot; that was only for the press, while everybody really remained alive and unharmed. As proof, they would show "shot" people who were still alive. (Afterwards they shot these people anyway, but for the time being they used them to trick the living.) During the trial the torturers were kept right before the prisoner's nose. They were a living reminder of what would happen if he changed his mind. . . .

(4) The investigators developed a complex system of "the individual approach" to the investigated. First they studied him through stool pigeons in his cell, or, if he was in solitary, by brief summons to the investigator. They would work him over in the cell, or in the office. One they would take by fear, another by persuasion, a third by promises, and a fourth by a combination of methods. But the main thing was that they immediately deprived the prisoner of any chance of defending himself.

(5) Yet the main reason why strong-willed people who had more than once looked death in the eye frequently broke down in the investigation, and agreed to monstrous self-accusations, was not the terrible cruelty of the investigation. The crucial thing was that these people were suddenly cut off from the soil on which they grew up. Here a man was like a plant torn from the ground and thrown to the mercy of the winds and weather, deprived of food, moisture, and sun. His ideals were shattered. Facing you were not class enemies. The people, the Soviet people, were against you. You were an "enemy of the people." There was nothing to lean on. A man was flying into a chasm and didn't understand the reason. Why? What for? . . .

Of course there were many who gave in without a fight. The atmosphere of terror in the prison created feelings of hopelessness. Many "fresh" prisoners immediately signed everything that was put in front of them, feeling that resistance was useless and defense impossible. In this way a new phenomenon developed in the investigatory process: the parties would reach a peaceful agreement on the "crime" and the "punishment." Very many military men amazed me by such "softness." They said: "No, I will not let them beat me. If they don't need me, let them shoot me. I'll sign everything they want." And they did this without any struggle or resistance. . . . And this too was a sort of protest against arbitrary rule.

2

As SHABALKIN POINTED OUT, most of the political prisoners were convicted *in absentia* by various special assemblies and troiki. But in many cases—for history, it would seem—a closed trial was held, without spectators, procurators, or defense lawyers. Even in complicated cases this trial did not last more than five or ten minutes. A. Kosarev's trial took fifteen minutes, but that was a rare exception. A. V. Gorbatov, whose trial lasted five minutes, tells how delighted he was when he came to court, convinced that he was going to be acquitted.[13] He not only denied that he had committed any crime. When he was

[13] *Novyi mir,* 1964, No. 4, p. 122. *Ed.:* See the English translation, A. V. Gorbatov, *Years Off My Life* (New York, 1965).

asked why ten condemned people had testified against him, he told the judges how sixteenth-century witchcraft trials had extracted confessions. Immediately the judges pronounced him guilty and sentenced him to fifteen years, which came as such a shock that he fainted on the spot.

Although Evgeniia Ginzburg's trial was supposed to be public, only the Military Collegium of the Supreme Court—three officers and a secretary—faced her and two guards in an empty room. The bored judges were startled by her demand to be told which official she had plotted to kill. They mentioned Kirov's murder. She replied that she had never been in Leningrad, which they dismissed as casuistry. "People with her views" had killed Kirov, and that made her "morally and criminally responsible." About to faint as the sentence was read— she expected death—she was revived by the concluding words: ten years. The whole procedure took seven minutes.

For many prisoners, including most of the high officials, the day of trial was the last day of life. By the law of December 1, 1934, the death sentence was to be executed immediately. Some of those sentenced to be shot were kept in the death chamber for a few days or months, but the majority were killed right after the trial. They were shot in various ways: some in the back of the head on the stairs to the basement; others in the basement of Lefortovskaia Prison, where some prisoners said a tractor engine drowned the shots. E. P. Frolov wrote down the story of one of the soldiers who escorted people condemned to death. He told Frolov that he would take such people to a place of execution in Krasnopresnenskii *raion*. There in a deserted area bordering a cemetery was a lot surrounded by a wall, against which the condemned were shot. This job was done by special people, two of them, who lived in a dugout. When the escort brought condemned people, a hollow-faced man would come out of the dugout, take over the prisoners and their documents, and shoot them on the spot. In the dugout, the soldier said, stood two bottles—one with water, the other with vodka.

Not only men were shot but women, not only young people but old ones, not only healthy but sick. The old Bolshevik A. P. Spunde tells how Gaven died. He had become a Bolshevik before 1905, had done years of heavy labor in tsarist prisons, where he contracted tuberculosis. After the Revolution he was chairman of the Central Executive Committee of the Crimean Autonomous Republic and a leader of Gosplan. In the twenties he had expressed distrust of Stalin. In the thirties he was carried on a stretcher to be shot.

For those who were not killed, there were long years in prison and then in camps. The history of these institutions has not yet been written; only some literary works and memoirs have been published, especially in 1963–64. Some other works of this sort, though not published, have been widely circulated. But all these materials are only a few contributions to a big job that has not yet been done. It is a difficult theme. The history of the Stalinist camps and prisons is probably the most terrible page in Russian history. It is no insignificant episode. It is absurd to regard the truth about the prisons and camps as "a little truth," occupying only a small place in "the larger truth" of our life. Those features of Stalinist arbitrary rule had as much influence on the life and psychology of Soviet society, and on world public opinion, as our industrial development, our victories in the Civil War and the Second World War, and our achievements in science and culture. In the future Stalin will never be forgiven his monstrous crimes. Neither will those historians, political leaders, and writers, who lacked the courage to study the history of Stalin's crimes, be forgiven. Transient political considerations cannot justify this silence.

No contemporary state, including a Socialist one, can do without prisons. As early as the beginning of the twenties some jails for political prisoners were created in the Soviet Union. "Politicals" then referred to S-R's, Mensheviks, and anarchists, that is, members of the "Socialist" parties. The members of other parties—Cadets, Musawatists, and White-Guardists in general—were called counterrevolutionaries and imprisoned together with criminals. The regimen of the political prisoners in the twenties was relatively lenient. They received extra food, were exempt from forced labor, and were not subjected to humiliating inspections. In political jails self-government was allowed; the politicals elected "elders," who dealt with the prison administration. They kept their clothes, books, writing materials, pocket knives; they could subscribe to newspapers and magazines.

Even when the Civil War was hardly finished, on December 30, 1920, the Cheka issued a special order:

> Information received by the Cheka establishes that members of various anti-Soviet parties arrested in political cases are being kept in very bad conditions. . . . The Cheka points out that the above-listed categories of people must not be regarded as undergoing punishment, but as temporarily isolated from society in the interests of the Revolution. The conditions of their detention must not have a punitive character.[14]

When Peter Kropotkin, the anarchist patriarch, died in his home near Moscow—Lenin had taken a personal interest in Kropotkin's living conditions—hundreds of anarchists who had been put in Butyrskaia Prison for anti-Soviet activity demanded permission to attend the funeral of their teacher. Dzerzhinskii ordered that the anarchists be let

---

[14] Cited in Latsis (Sudrabs), *Chrezvychainye kommissii po bor'be s kontrrevoliutsiei* (Moscow, 1921).

out on their honor. After the military funeral, they all returned, to a man. Subsequently they published, from jail, an anthology *On the Death of Kropotkin*.

At the beginning of the twenties the Commissar of Health, N. A. Semashko, pointed with pride to the establishment of a humane prison regime, which could not exist in capitalist countries. To be sure, some deterioration can be noted even in the twenties. At the end of 1923, for example, the exercise period was cut down, which provoked the publicized clash between Social Revolutionaries and guards at Solovketskaia Prison. There were other "excesses," but at the time they were exceptions rather than the rule.

In the early thirties the deterioration continued, but it was the mass repression later in the decade that reduced prisons to the most savage regime imaginable. As we have seen, the cells became brutally over-crowded. Prisoners were forbidden to go to the window, to lie on the bunks in the daytime, sometimes even to talk. On the slightest pretext they were thrown into the *kartser* (punishment hole), deprived of exercise, correspondence, or books. In many cells it was nearly impossible to breathe.

There are many firsthand accounts of the inhuman prison regime during Stalin's time. Here, for example, is an excerpt from the memoirs of M. M. Ishov, onetime military procurator of the West Siberian district, who was put into the Novosibirsk transfer prison in 1938.

I was taken to the second floor and ordered to halt in front of the door to one of the cells. The guard turned the lock with a key, opened the door, and literally squeezed me in. I say squeezed because so many people were there that you could push through only with great difficulty. If you recall the ancient tales about heaven and hell and try to visualize them, then that cell was real hell. Alas, it was no tale but grim reality. About 270 men were kept in a cell 40 square meters in area. They were supposed to find places in the two-tiered system of bunks. People squirmed under the bunks, on the bunks, even on the cover of the big *parasha* [prison slang for chamber pot] standing in the corner. Prisoners piled up at the doors, in the passageway. There was nowhere to sit down and nowhere to move to. Many, standing on their feet, fainted from exhaustion. They wanted just to sit and rest a little. But there was nowhere to sit or lie down. The prisoners, lying on the floor, standing in the passageway, cursed each other. Everyone was extremely irritated and mean.

A more ill-assorted crowd can hardly be imagined. There were big bandits, thieves, crooks, murderers, profiteers, various victims of circumstance, and we, accused of crimes listed in Article 58 of the Criminal Code. In the cell we were called the "counters" [short for counterrevolutionaries]. How depressing it was to hear this! We had many former military men, from various branches of the service. There were officials of big and medium industry, manual workers, office workers, peasants, students. . . . There were juveniles—petty thieves. There were strong people but there were weak and sick people too. At times it became unbearable to be in that cell. A little window, 30 by 40 centimeters [12 by 16 inches], was open all the time, but the flow of air was negligible. The cell was stifling. There was a heavy, noisome stench. It became hard to breathe. Not only the new arrivals but the earlier inmates felt very sick and breathed with great difficulty. It is even hard to imagine how so many people were put into such a small cell.[15]

Some months later Ishov found himself in Lefortovskaia Prison in Moscow, where it was not so crowded: only two people were put into a cell built for one. But the regime was stricter than in the overcrowded provincial prisons. Ishov recalls:

You had to speak with your cellmates and the guards in a whisper. It was strictly forbidden to lie on your cot during the day. At night, when you lay down to sleep, . . . you had to lie with your face toward the door. Covering the head or keeping your hands under the blanket was strictly forbidden. If, while asleep, you accidentally placed your hands over your face or under the blanket, the guard immediately woke the sleeper. Things were no better in the daytime. It was forbidden to sit on the stool with your back to the door. When seated, you had to "keep your direction" constantly toward the slot in the door. In the daytime, not only sleeping but even dozing while sitting was forbidden. If you dozed off accidentally, the guard at once gave the order: "Prisoner, walk around your cell!" And if you dozed off a second time, another order would ring out: "Prisoner, wash!" You went to the tap and washed. Everything was done to wear out the prisoners completely. . . . Light from the street barely penetrated the interior of the cell. An electric bulb mounted in the ceiling burned around the clock. . . . It was cold in the cell. No more than 6–7°C. [44–45°F]. It was impossible to sit in one place for long. We not only walked but literally ran around the cell, trying to warm up a little. . . .

   The food in Lefortovskaia Prison was abominable. In the morning they brought a piece of black bread, a spoon of sugar, and boiling water. For the afternoon meal a dipper of *"balanda."* A blue cabbage leaf floated in it, and the two spoonfuls of groats were watery and bad-tasting. Supper was a few spoonfuls of groats and boiling water. The quantity and caloric value of the food was extremely low. The pots it was served in made for nausea. Sour cabbage soup was poured into a rusty iron basin, and had a disgusting taste and smell. It was almost impossible to take this food.[16]

[15] M. M. Ishov, "Gody potriasenii i tiazhelykh ispytanii" (unpublished manuscript, Leningrad, 1966), pp. 94–95.
[16] *Ibid.,* pp. 141–42, 144.

The regime was just as savage in almost all the prisons. V. I. Volgin, a Rostov agronomist, recalls

> cell Number 47 in the inner prison, around 35 square meters in area. There were always fifty to sixty men in the cell. It was the beginning of June, 1939. It got hot in the courtyard and burning in the cell. We used to press to the cracks in the floor to suck some fresh air and took turns crowding near the door to feel the cross draft through its cracks. The old men could not bear it, and soon were carried away to eternal rest.[17]

Evgeniia Ginzburg tells how the guards in Iaroslav Prison threw an Italian Communist into a cold solitary cell and drenched her with ice water from a hose. In Kuibyshev many prisoners were put into the prison basement, where the central heating pipes passed through. In the summer they counted thirty-three species of insects, including, of course, lice, fleas, and bedbugs. In the winter, heat killed off the insects; the people endured, their bodies covered with painful sores.

After investigation, trial, and imprisonment, inhuman cruelty pursued the prisoners who were being transported. Frequently twenty to thirty prisoners were shoved with rifle butts into each compartment of the "Stolypin" prison cars,[18] intended for only six people. On some trains people stood for days on end, pressed against each other, fed on salted fish and receiving only one cup of water a day, though the train was not crossing a desert. These trains moved east for weeks, and almost every stop was marked by the graves of prisoners. E. G. Veller-Gurevich describes such a journey in her memoirs:

> We came to a freight car standing on a siding; they ordered us to line up and climb into the car by a steep ladder. The car was lighted by one dull lamp in the corner. Inside there were three tiers of bunks in each half of the car. In the middle was a hole in the floor, serving as a "toilet," and an iron stove. A hundred women were put in this car, which was intended for the transport of eight horses. We pressed against each other to warm up a little. My brain could not take in everything that was going on. . . . The journey by stages from Moscow to Tomsk lasted nineteen days. They were infinitely long days: unbelievable crowding, hunger, cold, thirst, parasites, filth, stink, sickness, the impossibility of moving, the struggle between despair and hope.[19]

The Leningrad Communist E. Vladimirova, who made the frightful journey east, described it in her poem "Kolyma," translated here into prose:

[17] *Rasskazy iz kamennogo meshka* (Rostov na Done, 1965), p. 16.
[18] *Ed.*: Named for the minister who put down the Revolution of 1905.
[19] "Iz vospominanii o 37-m." *Ed.*: This seems to be an unpublished manuscript.

The prison train was a new stage in his discoveries. When, calling sheep dogs to help, they got the people ready for the road, dumb with anger and shame, he saw the guards, undressing people until they were naked, twirl their sickly bodies in coarse insulting paws; he saw how they kept people in the trains for two days without drink, feeding them salted fish; saw cripples on crutches and women, locked in cars, with nursing babies in their arms.

Conditions were even worse on the ships taking prisoners from Vladivostok to the Kolyma region. In their crowded holds people often lay on top of each other, and bread was thrown to them through the hatches as if they were beasts. Those who died during the voyage— and they were many—were simply thrown in the sea. A riot or an organized protest was met with icy water, poured into the hold from the Sea of Okhotsk. Thousands of prisoners died after such a bath, or were delivered frostbitten to the hospitals of Magadan.

Many prisons kept politicals and criminals separate, but they met in transports, frequently with tragic results. "The criminals," according to V. I. Volgin,

> robbed the politicals almost openly, because they had the guards' protection. They would let the current victim glimpse a knife in their clothes, and shift his things into their own hands. In most cases resistance was unthinkable, because it could only be bloody and unsuccessful. We would have been slashed, to the guards' joy and with their encouragement. On the road we learned about this frightful experience, and no one wanted to lose his life over a rag. Then we learned too that the transports were the most frightful experience of all for politicals, and that this new torture was maintained by camp administrations as a means of extermination. The rule of separate transit stockades for politicals and criminals had never been repealed; it was even strictly observed in the old days. But in our time it was deliberately not observed, so that politicals might be torn up by criminals.

3

THE FUNDAMENTAL PLACE of detention was not the jails but the thousands of camps that covered the country in Stalin's time. So-called corrective-labor camps were organized in some outlying regions in the early thirties. In Karelia camps were set up to dig the White Sea-Baltic Canal, in Siberia to build the Baikal-Amur Railroad, while the inmates of Siblag, Dmitlag, and others worked at other projects. In 1932, labor camps also began to go up in the Kolyma region. The idea of this form of imprisonment suited the nature of a Socialist society much more than a prison, for the notion was not only to punish but also to correct criminals.

The first codes of Soviet law categorically forbade the use of penal methods that could be considered torture. "For the real implementation of the corrective labor policy," said Article 49 of the RSFSR Criminal Code, "the regime in places of confinement must show no signs of torture, which utterly rules out physical coercion: shackles, handcuffs, the *kartser,* strictly solitary confinement, deprivation of food.[20]

Many cases of extreme cruelty can be found in labor camps of the early thirties, but there was also a sincere attempt to correct criminals. E. P. Berzin, the head of Dal'stroi in 1932–37, tried to solve two problems simultaneously: colonizing an intemperate region and redirecting, while isolating, criminals. These ends were served by examinations, which allowed ten-year sentences to be reduced to two or three years, and by excellent food, clothing, a workday of four to six hours in winter and ten in summer, and by good pay, which enabled prisoners to help their families and to return home with funds.[21] V. Viaktin, a former head of one of the Kolyma camps, also tells about the positive influence this system had on prisoners.[22]

In 1937 all these liberal systems were abolished by Ezhov and Stalin. Such liberalism was declared to be wrecking, with the aim of winning the prisoners' love for "enemy of the people" Berzin and his aides, and to help them separate the Kolyma region from the USSR. The other camps were also changed. The corrective-labor camps were turned into hard-labor camps, calculated not so much to correct as to destroy the prisoners.

Incredibly heavy labor for ten and sometimes twelve to sixteen hours a day, imposed even on people in their seventies, crimes, capricious tyranny, a savage struggle for existence, became the rule rather than the exception. Camps for special punishment and gold mines became virtual death camps.

"In the camp," writes V. Shalamov in one of his tales,

it took twenty to thirty days to turn a healthy man into a wreck. Working in the camp mine sixteen hours a day, without any days off, with systematic starvation, ragged clothes, sleeping in a torn tent at sixty below zero, did the job. Beatings by the foremen, by the ringleaders of the thieves, by the guards, speeded up the process. The period was repeatedly verified. Brigades that began the gold-mining season designated by the names of their brigadiers, at the end of the season did not have a single man left of those who had

---

[20] *Ugolovnyi kodeks RSFSR,* 1930.
[21] Based on the testimony of the writer V. T. Shalamov, a veteran of the Kolyma camps.
    Ed.: See his *Récits de Kolyma* (Paris, 1969), unpublished as yet in the USSR.
[22] *Chelovek rozhdaetsia dvazhdy* (Magadan, 1964).

started, except the brigadier himself, his orderly, and some of his personal friends. The rest of the brigade had been replaced several times during the summer. The gold mine steadily cast its waste products into the hospitals, into the so-called convalescent crews, into invalid settlements, and into fraternal cemeteries [common graves].

The exhaustion of prisoners was so great that in the first postwar years there were frequent cases of two thousand to three thousand enrolled men turning out about one hundred to work in the mines.

The regime of most Kolyma and northern camps was deliberately calculated to destroy people. "In the first place," writes V. I. Volgin in his memoirs,

> they handed out a ration that clearly meant starvation on a ten-hour day. The ration was intentionally harmful to health. . . . Prisoners were taken out to work during the worst frosts. The barracks were not given enough heat, clothing would not dry out. In the fall they kept people, soaked to the skin, out in the rain and the cold to fulfill norms that such hopeless wrecks could never fulfill. . . . Prisoners were not dressed for the climate in the Kolyma region, for example. They were given third-hand clothing, mere rags, and often had only cloth wrapping on their feet. Their torn jackets did not protect them from the bitter frost, and people froze in droves.
>
> In such conditions there was a mass of sick people. Their treatment was often directed, as the staff put it, towards *"padëzh"* [murrain, the death of a herd of cattle]. The sick looked for salvation only where the doctors were themselves prisoners. . . . In the Kolyma region there were so-called *slabosilki* [infirmaries], where they kept convalescents after discharge from the hospital. Here they were confined for three weeks. The ration was indeed better: 700 grams of bread [about 1½ pounds]. But three weeks for a wreck were the same as a bone for a hungry dog. I regarded those infirmaries as a way of covering up the *padëzh* of the arrested cattle. As if to say, "We took suitable measures, but they did not want to work and live."[23]

And over the gates of all the camps in the Kolyma region was the inscription required by the camp statute: "Labor is a matter of honor, valor, and heroism." (Can we fail to recall here that the gates of Auschwitz carried the inscription *"Arbeit macht frei"*?)

The destruction of political prisoners was not achieved only through exhausting work. By putting both types of prisoners in the same camp, the administration was in fact sicking the criminals on the politicals. "On every suitable occasion," writes a former criminal, Minaev,

[23] V. I. Volgin, "Vospominaniia," pp. 42–43. *Ed.:* This seems to be an unpublished manuscript.

> they tried to let us know that we thieves were still not lost to the homeland; prodigal, so to speak, but nevertheless sons. But for "fascists" and "counters" [i.e., politicals] there was no place on this mortal earth and never would be in all ages to come. . . . And if we were thieves, then our place was beside the stove, while "phrasemongers" and all that sort had their place by the doors and in the corners.

Criminals traditionally have some sort of organization dating back for decades, in some countries for centuries. Prisons and camps do not destroy this organization but often strengthen it. The idea of the Stalinist punitive agencies to thrust criminals and politicals into the same camps was no better or worse than the idea of creating gas ovens in Auschwitz, Treblinka, and the other Nazi death camps.

Many of the camp bosses taunted the political prisoners and delighted in dreaming up humiliations. A boss in a large northern camp, on receiving a group of prisoners exhausted by a long journey, lined them up in front of the gates and ordered: "Those with higher education, one step forward." Some took the step, hoping apparently that their knowledge would be used somehow in the camp. "Everyone into the barracks, rest," the boss then ordered. "But you scholars," he said to those who had stepped out, "forward, march! Clean the outhouses!"

Undisguised terror on a massive scale struck down thousands of innocent people without trial or investigation, following charges of sabotage or attempted rebellion. According to A. I. Todorskii, in 1938 commissions were sent to the northern camps, where they finished off political prisoners who had received five- and ten-year sentences. One such commission, consisting of a special NKVD official, Kashketin, the head of the special section of Camp Administration, Grigorishin, and the head of the operations section of the NKVD, Chuchelov, sentenced many prisoners in the Ukhtin camp in the Komi Autonomous Republic to be shot. This same Kashketin commission also terrorized Vorkuta. Covering themselves with declarations about some kind of counterrevolutionary organization preparing a prison rebellion, they shot several thousand political prisoners. Many were machine-gunned at the Vorkuta brick factory as they were going from one part of the camp to another, not suspecting what was in store for them.[24]

Local camp authorities did not lag behind these central commissions. In 1938, on charges of sabotage, at least 40,000 prisoners were shot in the Kolyma region by the head of Dal'stroi, Pavlov, his assistant Garanin, and their apprentices. Colonel Garanin went especially wild. Arriving at a camp, he would order all "shirkers" to be lined up. This usually meant sick people and physical wrecks. Some could not

---

[24] From a statement by A. P—, a former Vorkuta inmate, who by some miracle survived.

stand on their feet. Garanin would walk down the line in a fury, shooting many at close range. Two soldiers followed him, taking turns at reloading his revolver. The guards often stacked the corpses at the gates like a dam of timbers, and the work brigades passing by would be told, "The same thing will happen to you for shirking."[25]

4

SOMETHING MUST BE SAID about the people who worked the system of terror that Stalin organized, who ran the machine of suppression, only parts of which have been sketched here. There were, of course, different types in the NKVD even during the height of the Stalinist terror. Some honestly believed that they were fighting enemies of the Soviet regime, wreckers, and spies. Many soldiers and junior officers in the NKVD troops did not know that they were being forced to guard not only criminals but millions of worthy people. Others knew the truth, but did not fully understand the causes of this frightful tragedy. Such officials often tried somehow to help prisoners. There is considerable evidence of this in the writings of B. D'iakov, E. S. Ginzburg, V. T. Shalamov, S. O. Gazarian, and other published and unpublished materials.

E. Ia. Drabkina has given the author a curious example. There was an industrial enterprise in the north, where the workers were mostly politicals, while all but the highest offices were held by thieves. For a long time it had not fulfilled its production plan. At the beginning of the war a new director, V. A. Kundush, was sent out from Leningrad, as a punishment for his "liberalism." He asked the factory controller, a former Party member, for a list of former Communists in the work brigades. Then he picked from this list replacements for all the thieves in important jobs. The enterprise immediately became a pacemaker, and throughout the war held the Red Banner for Management. After the war Kundush obtained the early release of many prisoners "for good work" but soon found himself a prisoner.

The majority of Ezhov's and Beria's subordinates were men of a different type. They understood very well that their bosses were criminals, their victims innocent, but the realization only intensified their sadistic ardor in fabricating cases and extracting confessions. The writer Boris D'iakov tells how investigator Mel'nikov sneered at him: "Prove to us that you are 100 per cent crystal pure and you'll get ten years, otherwise a piece of lead."[26]

[25] Both Garanin and Kashketin were themselves shot in 1939 for "espionage and wrecking." A superfluous lesson for all torturers.
[26] *Oktiabr'*, 1964, No. 7, p. 82.

Gazarian tells of an old teacher in Barnaul, Siberia, A. A. Afanas'ev, who was originally accused of creating a terrorist group in the city back in the Civil War, to kill Lenin *if he should come to Barnaul.* But the chief would not endorse the case because the accusation was so fanciful. So the investigator made a new accusation: Afanas'ev was a Japanese spy. "Well, so what," said the sick old man, "I can become a Japanese spy." But once again the case was not endorsed by the central office, because there was no indication of how Afanas'ev sent his reports to Japan. So new searches began in Barnaul, for the spy's accomplices. This time they found the "resident" of Japanese intelligence in the city—a railroad worker. And all these people were shot. Fritz Platten, the Swiss Communist, was accused of being a German spy since 1917, when he arranged Lenin's return to Russia. In spite of savage torture, he refused to sign the deposition, because it would have cast a shadow on Lenin. Finally he and the investigator compromised: he would confess to spying for some other country than Germany—America or Argentina, our source does not recall exactly which.[27]

In Rostov-on-Don, a captain of the river fleet was asked to sign a statement that when he was commander of the tanker *Smelyi* he had sunk the torpedo boat *Burnyi* with an explosive shell. The captain laughed and asked the investigator if he knew what a tanker was. "Tanker, tank," the interrogator muttered, "it's an armed boat." "No, not at all," explained the captain. "It's a boat that carries oil and cannot destroy a torpedo boat." "Well, the hell with you," said the investigator calmly. "Write it the other way round, the way it has to be, and you can go to a camp with fresh air. But here you'll rot."[28] Twenty-seven people in the same cell were forced to sign a statement that they had burned down the Rostov mill for diversionary purposes, while thirteen men "confessed" to having blown up a railway drawbridge over the Don. But both the mill and the bridge are still standing in Rostov, unhurt except for the damage done during the war.

According to Ia. I. Drobinskii, one of the commanders of the Belorussian military district, Povarov, admitted that he had formed a counterrevolutionary military organization and named more than forty people whom he had allegedly recruited—made-up names of nonexistent commanders. On the basis of this "evidence," Povarov was tried and condemned. The investigators did not know that the people named were nonexistent, but they knew very well that anyone named in an investigation would not run away. So these names could be put "in reserve," for future arrest.

---

[27] M. F. Pozigun, Party member since 1920, heard this from Platten in a prison hospital.
[28] Reported by V. I. Volgin.

The *oblasti* received their arrest plans from Moscow. Telegrams in code reported that "in your *oblast,* according to the information of the central investigating agencies, there are so many terrorists or ASA's (anti-Soviet agitators). Find them and try them." The NKVD agencies had to fulfill these quotas and wait for a new quota the next month or quarter.

One day in 1937 the chief editor of a Ukrainian newspaper, A. I. Ba——, was summoned to the NKVD. He was told to edit the introductory part of an indictment of "a kulak terrorist center." Working at night in the NKVD director's office, Ba—— heard the director calling the regional offices of the NKVD, demanding increases in the "index figures" of the fight against "enemies of the people." "How many did you take today?" he would shout. "Twelve! Not enough, far from enough. And you?" he would say to another *raion.* "Sixty? Good, great work. Only watch you don't drop off at the end of the month." To a third: "What! You arrested only five people? Have you already built complete Communism in your *raion,* or what?" And then, turning to Ba——, he said, "I have to put the pressure on. Soon they'll phone from Moscow, and then what could I tell them, what sort of report could I make?"

It is astonishing—and instructive—to see how careless most NKVD searches were. In making the arrests, the agents usually seized papers and letters but did not bother to open floors, sofas, mattresses, and the like. They knew from experience that they would not find "compromising" documents and did not want to waste time. It was much easier and faster to think up some story and get its confirmation by torture. Neither did they waste much time analyzing papers seized during arrests; after a brief examination, such material would as a rule be destroyed. A vast number of precious manuscripts and papers were taken from Academician Vavilov and other scientists, from hundreds of writers and poets, from prominent government and Party leaders. All vanished without a trace. Almost none of the investigators regarded confiscated papers as evidence they could use to expose the criminal. One arrested scholar, to take an especially instructive example, had three original letters of Immanuel Kant. One would think that these letters, written in German, would attract the investigators' special attention. Not at all. The letters were burned without even being translated. In the record they are listed as three letters "by an unknown author" in a foreign language.

In a number of cases arrests, even of important officials, were made with no searches at all. The Moscow apartment of Livshits, Deputy Commissar of Communications and one of the main defendants in the trial of the "parallel" center, was not searched. Livshits was arrested in Khabarovsk, brought to Moscow, and after several months of investigation and trial was shot. During all this time, according to his widow, their Moscow apartment was never searched. No one showed any interest in the contents of his desks, his papers, letters, or notes. After he had been tried and shot, she phoned the appropriate agency to come and take her husband's gun.

Most of the judges and procurators must have known what they were doing when they sanctioned the arrest of innocent people and then sentenced them to be shot or imprisoned. These officers of the law knew that they were creating lawlessness, but they chose to be its creators rather than its victims. "Without a shudder constricting my heart," writes M. M. Ishov, a military procurator who refused to serve the terror machine,

> it is impossible for me to recall the name of Sonia Ul'ianova. She worked in the second section of the Chief Military Procuracy. All the cases fabricated in the NKVD against good Soviet citizens passed through the bloodstained hands of this woman, who was ready to climb over mountains of corpses of loyal Communists to save her own worthless life.

Likewise, many camp directors and officers understood what kind of prisoners they were dealing with but went ahead with their savage job anyhow.

What turned many NKVD officials into sadists? What forced them to break all the laws of humanity? Many of them were once good Communists or Komsomol members, who joined the NKVD on orders, not at all by inclination. Many influences were at work on them. In the first place, there was the fear of becoming prisoners themselves, which overrode all other feelings. Secondly, a terrible selection went on within the NKVD, sifting out some officials, leaving the worst. Many—and this must not be overlooked—were corrupted by the unlimited power over the prisoners that Stalin gave to the NKVD. As Dostoevsky wrote in his *Notes from the House of the Dead*:

> Whoever has experienced the power, the complete ability, to humiliate another being . . . with the most extreme humiliation, willy-nilly loses power over his own sensations. Tyranny is a habit, it has a capacity for development, it develops finally into a disease. I insist that the habit can dull and coarsen the very best man to the level of a beast. Blood and power are intoxicating. . . . The man and the citizen die within the tyrant forever; return to human dignity, to repentance, to regeneration, becomes almost impossible.[29]

NKVD personnel were specially trained to be capable of carrying out any order, even the most criminal. The special brigades of tor-

---

[29] Dostoevsky, *Sobranie sochinenii*, III (1956), p. 595.

turers, for example, usually included students from the NKVD schools, young people eighteen to twenty years old. They were taken to torture chambers as medical students are to dissection laboratories, and thus were turned into sadists. Many of Ezhov's and Beria's torturers were destroyed during the Stalinist period, and others were punished in 1953–55 and in the period following the XXth Congress. But quite a few got off with only a mild scare: they were dismissed from their jobs and retired or given other work. Most of them attributed—and continue to attribute—their crimes and inhuman cruelty to orders from above, to the decrees of Stalin, Ezhov, Beria and other "bosses." But the International Military Tribunal at Nürnberg decided—and the Soviet Union endorsed the decision—that orders which contradict basic rules of morality, which flout the ethical imperatives on which human society is founded, which destroy the very foundations of human community, cannot serve as a moral or legal justification for those who carry out such orders.

Part Two

———◆———

THE PRECONDITIONS
OF STALINISM

IX

The Problem of
Stalin's Responsibility

1

To MANY PEOPLE in the Soviet Union, the mass repression of 1937–38 was an incomprehensible calamity that suddenly broke upon the country and seemed to have no end. Explanations abounded, some of them representing a search for the truth, but more attempting to escape the cruel truth, to find some formula that would preserve faith in the Party and Stalin. Some of these legends and stories are worth examining, especially since many people still believe them.

One widespread story was that Stalin did not know about the terror, that all those crimes were committed behind his back. Of course it was ridiculous to suppose that Stalin, master of everyone and everything, did not know about the arrest and shooting of members of the Politburo and the Central Committee, about the killing of most commissars, about the devastation of almost all *oblast* Party committees, about the arrest of the military high command and the Comintern leaders, about the death of leading writers and scholars, of his own relatives and friends. It was naïve and ridiculous to picture Stalin as a man completely cut off from reality, ignorant of what was happening on this earth, and still to worship him. But that is a peculiarity of the mind blinded by faith in a higher being, following a logic that has nothing in common with normal human logic, living in a world of illusions and fantasies. It is this peculiarity of the religious mentality that explains the stories about Stalin's ignorance of what was going on.

"We thought," wrote Ilya Ehrenburg, "(probably because we wanted to think so) that Stalin did not know about the senseless ravaging of Communists, of the Soviet intelligentsia."[1] Many people thought

---

[1] *Novyi mir*, 1962, No. 5, p. 152.

that wreckers, headed by Ezhov, had wormed their way into the NKVD, and were destroying the Party's best cadres without Stalin's knowledge. A typical conversation occurred between the commissar of the 29th Rifle Division, F. A. Stebenev, and the commander of the Viazemskii Military District, A. Ia. Vedenin, the future commandant of the Kremlin.[2]

> "What's going on, Andrei Iakovlevich?" Stebenev asked me. "What's going on?" He walked nervously about the room. "I don't believe there are so many enemies in the Party. I don't believe it. Can it be that in some high Party office, in the security organs, there are alien people? It's as if they are deliberately destroying the Party's cadres. I would bet my head that Joseph Vissarionovich doesn't know about this. Warnings, complaints, protests are being intercepted and don't reach him. Stalin must be informed. Otherwise, disaster. Tomorrow they'll take you, and after you me. We can't keep quiet."

That was the opinion of hundreds and thousands of officials, rank-and-file Party members, even many prisoners and their relatives. D. A. Lazurkina, an official in the Leningrad *obkom,* survived to tell the XXIInd Congress:

> When they arrested me . . . I felt such a horror, not for myself but for the Party. I couldn't understand why they were arresting old Bolsheviks. For what? . . . I told myself something horrible was happening in the Party, probably wrecking. And this gave me no rest. Not for one minute, though I spent two and a half years in prison, then was sent to camp, then into exile, . . . did I ever accuse Stalin. I always stood up for Stalin when other prisoners cursed him. I would say: "No, it cannot be that Stalin has permitted all that has happened in the Party. It cannot be."

This naïve conviction of Stalin's ignorance was reflected in the word *ezhovshchina,* "the Ezhov thing," the popular name for the tragedy of the thirties. The sudden disappearance of Ezhov seemed to confirm this story, which was only a new version of the common people's faith in a good tsar surrounded by lying and wicked ministers.

But it must also be acknowledged that this story had some basis in Stalin's behavior. Secretive and self-contained, Stalin avoided the public eye. Although his name was on everyone's lips, he acted through unseen channels. He tried to direct events from behind the scenes, making basic decisions by himself or with a few aides. He rarely addressed meetings in 1936–38, and never advertised his part in the mass repression, preferring to put the spotlight on other perpetrators of these crimes, thereby retaining his own freedom of movement. More-

[2] Reported in A. Ia. Vedenin, *Gody i liudi* (Moscow, 1964), p. 55.

over, many of his speeches gave the impression that he was not well informed about the repression. For example, at the February-March Plenum of the Central Committee in 1937 he demanded that there be no arrests of Trotskyites and Zinovievites who had broken all ties with Trotsky and ended oppositional activity. At that very time, thousands of such people were being arrested. Stalin also rebuked those who considered it a trifle to expel tens of thousands from the Party. At that very time not tens but hundreds of thousands were being expelled and arrested.

Shortly before the arrest of the Civil War hero D. F. Serdich, Stalin toasted him at a reception, suggesting that they drink to *"Brüderschaft."*[3] Just a few days before Bliukher's destruction, Stalin spoke of him warmly at a meeting. When an Armenian delegation came to him, Stalin asked about the poet Charents and said he should not be touched,[4] but a few months later Charents was arrested and killed. The wife of Ordzhonikidze's Deputy Commissar, A. Serebrovskii, tells about an unexpected phone call from Stalin one evening in 1937. "I hear you are going about on foot," Stalin said. "That's no good. People might think what they shouldn't. I'll send you a car if yours is being repaired." And the next morning a car from the Kremlin garage arrived for Mrs. Serebrovskii's use. But two days later her husband was arrested, taken right from the hospital.

The famous historian and publicist Iu. Steklov, disturbed by all the arrests, phoned Stalin and asked for an appointment. "Of course, come on over," Stalin said, and reassured him when they met: "What's the matter with you? The Party knows and trusts you; you have nothing to worry about." Steklov returned home to his friends and family, and that very evening the NKVD came for him. Naturally the first thought of his friends and family was to appeal to Stalin, who seemed unaware of what was going on.[5] It was much easier to believe in Stalin's ignorance than in subtle perfidy. In 1938 I. A. Akulov, onetime Procurator of the USSR and later Secretary of the Central Executive Committee, fell while skating and suffered an almost fatal concussion. On Stalin's suggestion, outstanding surgeons were brought from abroad to save his life. After a long and difficult recovery, Akulov returned to work, whereupon he was arrested and shot.[6]

It was Stalin who called a special Plenum of the Central Committee in January, 1938, at the height of the repression, to pass the resolution "On the mistakes of Party organizations in expelling Communists, on the bureaucratic handling of the appeals of those ex-

[3] See I. D. Ochak, *D. Serdich* (Moscow, 1964).
[4] The artist M. Sar'ian told Ehrenburg of this incident.
[5] This episode is reported by I. P. Aleksakhin.
[6] M. V. Ostrogorskii reports this incident.

pelled, and on measures to eliminate these shortcomings." Presenting scattered figures on expulsions that had been rescinded by the Control Commission, and on "enemy" accusations that had been proved groundless by the NKVD, the resolution attacked the expellers and the accusers:

> All these facts show that many of our Party organizations . . . have not exposed the cleverly masked enemy who hides . . . behind shouts for vigilance, . . . and tries to slaughter our Bolshevik cadres and sow distrust and excessive suspiciousness in our ranks.[7]

Whereupon the Central Committee ordered all Party organizations to cease "mass, wholesale expulsions," to decide each case on an individual basis, to get rid of Party officials who did not take the individual approach, and to review the appeals of expelled members within a three-month period.

Much of this resolution, edited and in parts actually written by Stalin himself, was ambiguous, but it roused great hopes of an end to mass repression and a review of arrests already made. Those hopes were strengthened by press reports that some expelled Communists had been reinstated in the Party and some false accusers had been punished. But the January Plenum was nothing more than a political diversion. When the victims of Stalinist terror are counted, historians will probably establish that more Communists—CC members included —were expelled from the Party, arrested, and shot in 1938 than in 1937.

Stalin's personal role in the activities of the punitive organs was discussed in many *oblast* and republic Party meetings in 1937–38. When Kaganovich, Andreev, Malenkov, Mikoian, Shkiriatov, *et al.* came out to the provinces to direct the repression, they made it clear that they were acting on Stalin's orders. These speeches, however, rarely appeared in the press.

Only on the eve of the XVIIIth Party Congress, after Ezhov's dismissal, did the press begin to emphasize Stalin's leading role in the assault on "enemies of the people." The theme was continued by many speakers at the Congress in March, 1939. Shkiriatov, for example, declared:

> Comrade Stalin has directed the work of purging enemies who have wormed their way into the Party. Comrade Stalin taught us how to fight new wreckers in a new way; he taught us how to get rid of these hostile elements quickly and decisively.[8]

[7] *KPSS v rezoliutsiiakh,* III (1953), p. 855.
[8] *Sten. otchet XVIII s'ezda VKP (b)* (Moscow, 1939), p. 175.

Some delegates gave enthusiastic details. Mishakova, for example, told how Stalin helped her purge the Komsomol. She began on her own in Chuvashia, but the Komsomol CC tried to curb her.

> Kosarev's gang . . . were entrenched in the CC. . . . I sent a letter to Comrade Stalin telling him of the irregularities in the Komsomol Central Committee. Although he was very busy, Comrade Stalin found time to read my letter. The result was an investigation . . . and the Stalinist resolution adopted at the VIIth Komsomol Plenum.[9]

Many years later, further details were made public. At first Shkiriatov was given the job of checking Mishakova's accusations. He supported her, but only to the extent of suggesting that Kosarev be reprimanded for "persecuting" Mishakova. Shkiriatov sent this proposal to Stalin, with a covering note: "Dear Joseph Vissarionovich: As always, I am sending this memo to you. If something is not right, you will correct me." And Stalin did "correct" Shkiriatov. In his speech to the VIIth Plenum of the Komsomol CC, Shkiriatov shouted: "You, Kosarev, wanted to kill everything Stalinist and Bolshevik in Mishakova, but you didn't succeed, because Stalin interfered in this affair."[10]

Even then, however, Stalin continued to cover up the traces of his crimes. He told a group of delegates to the XVIIIth Congress that Ezhov had arrested many more people than he was "allowed." After the Congress, too, when the acute shortage of qualified people became apparent, Stalin tried to throw the blame on Ezhov. The engineer A. S. Iakovlev recalls

> a conversation in the summer of 1940, when Stalin said these precise words to me:
> "Ezhov is a rat; in 1938 he killed many innocent people. We shot him for that."
> I wrote these words down immediately after returning from the Kremlin.[11]

Iakovlev seems to believe even today that Stalin did not know what Ezhov was doing behind his back.

Many new documents have confirmed beyond any doubt that Stalin not only knew about all the main acts of repression; they were done on his direct instructions. Here is one such document, read to the XXIInd Congress by Z. T. Serdiuk:

[9] *Ibid.*, p. 561.
[10] From the speech of V. F. Pikina to the meeting in the Museum of the Revolution, dedicated to the sixtieth birthday of A. Kosarev, Nov. 21, 1963. For Kosarev's fate, see above, pp. 208–09.
[11] A. S. Iakovlev, *Tsel' zhizni; zapiski konstruktora* (Moscow, 1966), p. 179.

Comrade Stalin:
I am sending for confirmation four lists of people whose cases are
before the Military Collegium:
    (1) List No. 1 (general)
    (2) List No. 2 (former military personnel)
    (3) List No. 3 (former NKVD personnel)
    (4) List No. 4 (wives of enemies of the people).
    I request approval for first-degree condemnation of all these
people.

EZHOV

Condemnation of the first degree (*pervaia kategoriia*) meant shooting.
These lists were signed by Stalin and Molotov. On each one is the
sanction: "Approved. J. Stalin, V. Molotov." Stalin signed around
four hundred such lists in 1937–39. They bear the names of 44,000
people, mostly Party and government officials, military personnel, and
cultural leaders.

While personally directing repression at the center, Stalin drove
his aides in the provinces. Armenia provides a typical example. After
Ter-Gabrielian was fired—he had been chairman of the Armenian
Council of Commissars—and after Khandzhian was murdered—he
had been First Secretary of the Armenian Central Committee—state
and Party cadres were subjected to mass terror. The new Party chiefs
(G. Amatuni, S. Akopov, G. Tsaturov, and K. Mugdusi), striving to
win the favor of Stalin and Beria, killed many leading officials, including Ter-Gabrielian. But Stalin was still dissatisfied with their
work. On September 8, 1937, he sent a letter to the Buro of the
Armenian Central Committee, criticizing the republic's economic and
cultural development, its disorderly agriculture and industrial stagnation, its toleration of Trotskyite and anti-Party elements. In this
context Stalin rebuked the Armenian Party leaders for "protecting"
enemies of the people, asserting that "enemy of the people" Ter-
Gabrielian had been killed prematurely to prevent the exposure of
other enemies. "It is intolerable," the letter said, "that enemies of the
Armenian people should be playing around freely in Armenia." Consequently Amatuni and Akopov were removed from their positions,
expelled from the Party, and arrested. G. A. Arutiunian was made
First Secretary, and repression became especially massive and bloody.[12]

A similar letter was sent by Stalin and Molotov to Uzbekistan and
read before a Central Committee Plenum. Ikramov, the local First
Secretary, was accused of political blindness towards bourgeois na-
tionalists, allegedly headed by F. Khodzhaev in league with Bukharin,
Antipov, and other ex-oppositionists who had already been arrested.
After the letter was read, a special committee was set up in the

[12] *Ocherki po istorii KP Armenii* (Erevan, 1964), p. 355.

Plenum, which hastily "established" the justice of the charges against Ikramov. The Plenum then expelled Ikramov from the Party and handed the matter over to the investigating organs.[13]

In the Ukraine Stalin gave his personal public endorsement to the vicious Nikolaenko, who had been expelled from the Party for slandering local Party leaders.[14] Stalin proclaimed Nikolaenko a "heroine-unmasker," and called on all Party members to follow her example. "Who is Nikolaenko?" Stalin asked the February-March Plenum in 1937.

> Nikolaenko is a rank-and-file Party member. She is an ordinary "little person." For a whole year she kept warning that something was wrong in the Kiev Party organization. . . . She was brushed off, like a pesky fly. Finally, to get rid of her, they took and expelled her from the Party. Neither the Kiev organization nor the Ukrainian Central Committee helped her achieve justice. Only the intervention of the All-Union Central Committee unraveled this tangled knot. . . . It was found that Nikolaenko was right and the Kiev organization was wrong. . . . And she was not a member of the Central Committee, not a commissar, not the *obkom* secretary of Kiev, not even the secretary of some Party cell. She was a simple, rank-and-file Party member.
>
> As you can see, sometimes ordinary people come closer to the truth than some high institutions.[15]

Stalin not only ordered arrests; he also closely followed many investigations. Sometimes he interrogated prisoners himself, in his office. G. I. Petrovskii told his friends about one such interrogation:

> They brought Stanislav Kosior to Stalin for interrogation. In Stalin's office were Molotov, Kaganovich, and Voroshilov. They sat Kosior in a chair. He sat there depressed; it was obvious he had been through a lot. "Well, talk!" "What can I say?" Kosior replied. "You know I'm a Polish spy." Petrovskii asked Kosior, "Stasik, why do you tell lies about yourself and me?" "I made depositions," said Kosior, "and I won't take them back." Then Stalin remarked triumphantly: "There, you see, Petrovskii, and you didn't believe Kosior became a spy. Now do you believe he's an enemy of the people?" To this Petrovskii answered: "Yes, I believe; he's the same kind of spy as myself." Stalin ordered that Petrovskii's file be brought in. The file contained only one piece of paper. Stalin, irritated, asked: "Is that all?" "Yes, that's all," he was told. "We shoot people like you," Stalin shouted at Petrovskii, "but I will have mercy on you."

Following this confrontation Petrovskii went to the Ukraine,

---

[13] *Ocherki istorii KP Uzbekistana* (Tashkent, 1964), p. 295–6.
[14] See *Ocherki po istorii KPU* (Kiev, 1964), p. 466.
[15] *Pravda*, Apr. 1, 1937.

where he was fired from his job and deprived of his apartment and *dacha*.[16]

On occasion Stalin even gave orders about what kind of torture was to be used on one or another Party official. And if the investigator still could not obtain the desired testimony, Stalin reprimanded the NKVD agents for "defects in their work." When the depositions of tortured prisoners included the names of their "accomplices," Stalin, without seeking any further proof, wrote on the record "Arrest," or "Arrest everyone."[17] When Ezhov, in one of his reports, told about the arrest of a group of officials—with the list attached—and declared that information on other persons was being checked, Stalin underlined Ezhov's final words and wrote: "No need to check, arrest them."[18]

The old Communist P. I. Shabalkin met, in a camp, a Chekist who had been in Stalin's personal bodyguard in 1937–38. He told Shabalkin that Ezhov came to Stalin almost daily with a thick file of papers. Stalin would give orders about arrests and tortures, and when an investigation was finished, he would sanction the punishment recommended by the NKVD, *before the trial*. Thus the court needed only a few minutes to rubber-stamp the sentence approved by Stalin.

In 1935–38 Stalin almost never made public pronouncements on scholarly questions. But his interference determined the tragic outcome of many scholarly discussions. The most outstanding Soviet writers who perished in the years of terror were arrested on Stalin's orders.

Many officials repeatedly appealed to Stalin to put an end to the lawlessness. He responded in various ways. Sometimes he promised to look into the matter but did nothing; other times he sent the petitioner to Molotov and Ezhov. Usually he cut these appeals short, telling people not to meddle in the affairs of the NKVD, which knew what it was doing. A typical conversation occurred in September, 1937, between Stalin and the secretary of the Far East *kraikom*, Vareikis.

> "What did he tell you?" Vareikis' wife asked him. "It's terrible even to say," Vareikis replied. "At first I thought it wasn't Stalin but someone else on the phone. But it was him. . . . Yes, him. Stalin shouted: 'It's none of your business! Don't mix in where you don't belong. The NKVD knows what it's doing.' Then he said that only an enemy of the Soviet regime could defend Tukhachevskii and the others, and he slammed down the receiver."[19]

[16] From the archive of the Petrovskii family.
[17] N. R. Mironov, *Programma KPSS i voprosy dal'neishego ukrepleniia zakonnosti i pravoporiadka* (Moscow, 1962), pp. 7–8.
[18] *Ibid.*
[19] *Pravda,* Sept. 18, 1964.

A few days later Vareikis was urgently summoned to Moscow and arrested. Four days later his wife was also arrested in Khabarovsk.

As for torture, Stalin not only knew about it; he initiated that method of "investigation." After the removal of Ezhov, many local Party leaders began to criticize NKVD agents for using torture, whereupon Stalin sent a coded telegram to *obkom* and *kraikom* secretaries, and to officials of the NKVD, saying:

> The Central Committee explains that from 1937 on the NKVD was given permission by the Central Committee to use physical influence. All bourgeois intelligence agencies use physical influence against representatives of the socialist proletariat. . . . Why should the socialist intelligence agency be more humane in relation to dedicated agents of the bourgeoisie, sworn enemies of the working class and the collective farmers? The Central Committee believes that the method of physical influence must necessarily be used in the future too, as an exception, against obvious and stubborn enemies of the people, as a completely correct and expedient method.[20]

Stalin was also the initiator of the inhuman conditions in the prisons and camps. Early in 1938 a group of officials in the Kolyma region sent Stalin a telegram complaining about the lawless regime of Pavlov, the new chief of Dal'stroi, and his aide, Garanin. Stalin replied:

> To Nagaevo. The newspaper *Sovetskaia Kolyma*. To Os'makov, Romashev, Iagnenkov. Copy to Pavlov of Dal'stroi. . . . Received long telegram of Os'makov, Romashev, and Iagnenkov with complaint about the regime in Dal'stroi and the shortcomings in the work of Pavlov. The telegram does not take into consideration the difficulties in the work at Dal'stroi and the specific conditions of Pavlov's work. I consider your telegram demagogical and unfounded. The newspaper should help Pavlov, not throw a wrench in the works.
>
> STALIN[21]

This telegram provoked an even greater orgy of terror in the Kolyma region, against Chekists as well as prisoners.

Of course Stalin did not and could not know about all the lawlessness. Much of it was the result of "local initiative." But the fundamental arrests and directives originated from Stalin. He created and encouraged the system of arbitrary rule and terror that caused the death of millions. In other words, we have no reason to place the main responsibility on Ezhov or any other official supposedly acting without Stalin's knowledge. The main responsibility lies unconditionally with

[20] *Ed.*: Khrushchev quoted this telegram to the XXth Party Congress.
[21] *Sovietskaia Kolyma*, Jan. 17, 1938.

Stalin—which does not relieve his aides of responsibility. Ezhov did not deceive Stalin; Stalin deceived Ezhov, using him to carry out his plot and then, as was his wont, destroying him.

What drove Stalin to such unprecedented crimes, to the mass destruction, not of "class hostile" elements but of the basic cadres of the Soviet state and the Communist Party?

2

THE CONTRAST between the people's image of Stalin and the terrible truth revealed after the XXth Party Congress was so great that it was only natural for people to try to soften that contrast, to ease the pain a man feels on suddenly learning that his father, his best friend, or his favorite teacher is a criminal. This natural human desire gave rise to a new story, which many people still believe: the tragedy of the "deceived" Stalin. Conceding that Stalin killed tens of thousands of innocent people, that he was personally responsible for the mass repression of the thirties, these people argue that he intended no evil, that he was led astray by careerists, adventurers, and foreign intelligence agents, who wormed their way into the NKVD, in order to wipe out the best cadres and demoralize the people. Stalin, in this legend, believed to the end of his days that he was fighting real enemies of the revolution.

Anna Louise Strong, for example, finds

> the key [to the terror], most probably, in actual, extensive penetration of the GPU by a Nazi fifth column, in many actual plots and in the impact of these on a highly suspicious man who saw his own assassination plotted and believed he was saving the Revolution by drastic purge. . . . Stalin engineered [the country's modernization] ruthlessly, for he was born in a ruthless land and endured ruthlessness from childhood. He engineered suspiciously, for he had been five times exiled and must have been often betrayed. [As if other Bolsheviks had not gone through the same hard experiences. —R.M.] He condoned, and even authorized, outrageous acts of the political police against innocent people, but so far no evidence is produced that he consciously framed them.[22]

Even after the XXIInd Party Congress this legend was repeated. I. Verkhovtsev, for example, pictured "Stalin's nasty and sick suspicious nature playing into the hands of foreign intelligence agencies, and also careerists, adventurers, and hostile elements, who wormed their way into the security organs and fabricated cases against leading Party and state officials."[23] M. I. Petrosian adds "historically unavoidable limitations" of democracy as conditions that enabled such

[22] A. L. Strong, *The Stalin Era* (New York, 1956), pp. 68, 125.
[23] I. Verkhovtsev, *Leninskie normy partiinoi zhizni* (Moscow, 1962), p. 29.

wicked people to do their dirty work.[24] And V. Tarianov follows the same line to conclude that Ezhov, Merkulov, Beria, and Abakumov were responsible, not Stalin.[25] Stalin's daughter, Svetlana, puts up the same defense of her father. Listing the many relatives and friends who were arrested and shot with his knowledge and consent, she exclaims:

> How could father have done that? I know only one thing: he could not have thought it up by himself. . . . I believe that Beria was craftier, sneakier, more treacherous, more brazen, clearer in his goal, firmer and consequently stronger than my father. My father had his weak points—he could feel doubts, he was more gullible, coarser, and rougher; he was simpler and could be taken in by a trickster like Beria.[26]

Some Western Communists have indulged in even wilder fancies, picturing Ezhov and Beria as the leaders of deep conspiratorial organizations, which systematically deceived Stalin on the direct orders of bourgeois intelligence agencies. The primitive quality of such explanations is obvious. In the final analysis they are attempts to preserve somehow former illusions.

Of course Stalin was not clairvoyant. He was a very limited and suspicious man. Thus it is not surprising that at Stalin's "court," as at the court of every despot and tyrant, all kinds of intrigues and a fierce struggle for power and influence were constantly in progress among his retinue. Cut off from the people by a wall of armor, Stalin was ill informed about the state of affairs in the country and the Party. This made it easy to lead him astray and to deceive him. Thus it is probable that some of his aides used slander and provocation to rouse his suspicions of individuals whom he had trusted, so as to obtain his sanction for their arrest and execution. Beria was a master of such provocations. The 1955 trial of Beria's creatures in Georgia established, for example, that an attempt on Beria's and Stalin's lives during a boat ride on the Black Sea was organized by Beria himself, and that Stalin's life was not actually threatened. Some hoodlums hired by Beria shot in the air from the mountains, deliberately missing the target—and when they came to collect their reward, they were killed. This gave Beria the pretext he wanted to take vengeance on Lakoba, Chairman of the Central Executive Committee of Abkhazia, and on other devoted Communists.

Some foreign intelligence agencies tried similar provocations. Raskol'nikov, for example, tells how Bulgarian counterintelligence palmed off forged documents on Ezhov's agents, and succeeded in

---

[24] M. I. Petrosian, *Gumanizm* (Moscow, 1964), p. 228.

[25] V. Tarianov, *Nevidimye boi* (Moscow, 1964), pp. 74–75.

[26] *Ed.:* S. Allilueva, *Dvadtsat' pisem k drugu* (New York and Evanston: Harper and Row, 1968), pp. 74, 130.

provoking the arrest of almost all the members of the Soviet embassy in Bulgaria, from the chauffeur, M. I. Kazakov, to the military attaché, V. T. Sukhorukov.

But it would be a mistake to see such intrigues and provocations as the main cause of the mass repression. The tragic fate of Tukhachevskii is illuminating in this respect. As early as the twenties the Western press tried to compromise him, attributing overweening ambition to the "red Napoleon."[27] German generals, many of whom knew Tukhachevskii and other Soviet military leaders from the time they studied in Western military academies and from meetings during maneuvers, appreciated the formidable talents of their prospective adversaries. Appreciating also what was happening in the Soviet Union in the thirties, German leaders attempted to compromise Tukhachevskii and his colleagues.

In 1937 the Gestapo forged a letter allegedly sent by Tukhachevskii to his "friends" in Germany, telling of the intentions of himself and his "sympathizers" to overcome civilian control by a coup d'état. Not only the handwriting but even the characteristic style of Tukhachevskii was imitated. On the forged letter were genuine *Abwehr* stamps: "top secret" and "confidential." Hitler himself wrote a note on it—an order to shadow the German generals who supposedly were in contact with Tukhachevskii. Today even the name of the engraver who forged Tukhachevskii's signature is known. To reach Stalin with this letter and other materials, there was a fake theft of Tukhachevskii's "dossier" by Czechoslovak intelligence agents during a fire in the *Abwehr* building. Eduard Beneš tells in his memoirs how he received unofficial information in January, 1937, that Hitler was negotiating with Tukhachevskii, Rykov, and others to overthrow Stalin and set up a pro-German government. Beneš immediately passed all this information on to the Soviet Ambassador in Prague, Aleksandrovskii.[28]

Thus one might think that, with respect to Tukhachevskii, Stalin really was tricked by German intelligence. But the true story of Tukhachevskii's destruction is more complicated, and much remains unclear. Reinhard Heydrich, second in command of the Gestapo, did not think up the idea of the Tukhachevskii "plot" himself; it was suggested to him by a Russian émigré general, Nikolai Skoblin, who had connections with the NKVD as well as the Gestapo.[29] Stalin had

[27] See A. I. Todorskii, *Marshal Tukhachevskii* (Moscow, 1963), p. 5.
[28] E. Beneš, *Memoirs* (London, 1954), pp. 19–20, 47.
[29] See A. M. Nekrich, *1941. 22 iunia* (Moscow, 1965), pp. 86–87. See also Wilhelm Hoettl (pseudonym: Walter Hagen), *The Secret Front* (London, 1954), pp. 77–85, and Victor Alexandrov, *L'Affaire Toukhatchevski* (Paris, 1962). *Ed.:* There is an English translation of Alexandrov, *The Tukhachevsky Affair* (Englewood Cliffs, N.J., 1964). There is also an English translation of Nekrich, which appeared under the name of V. Petrov, *June 22, 1941* (New York, 1968).

"reliable information" about Tukhachevskii's "treason" at the very beginning of 1937, but he let him continue as Deputy Commissar of Defense. Moreover, the forged letters did not figure either in his trial or in the pretrial Military Soviet that met June 1–4, 1937, to examine the case. At this meeting Stalin made unsubstantiated charges against Tukhachevskii, Iakir, and others, simply expressing his desire to get rid of them. The members of the Military Soviet were given fraudulent "depositions" by officers who had already been arrested, accusing Tukhachevskii and the others of planning a coup d'état. The forgeries made by the Gestapo were tacked onto the Tukhachevskii case only *after* Tukhachevskii and his comrades had been shot.

Stalin never told anyone of his true intentions and plans. In this sense —and only in this sense—he had no accomplices or trusted friends. This opens the door to all sorts of speculation about his motives. To the end of his days he insisted both in conversation and in his writings that all the people he destroyed were enemies of the people. Actually, Stalin was totally preoccupied with the preservation of his unlimited power, and contemptuous of almost everyone around him and of human life in general. The elimination of hundreds of thousands of people posed no moral problem to him. He undoubtedly knew that thousands of Party leaders arrested on his orders were neither spies nor traitors. All his behavior shows that his accusations against these people were deliberate slander.

After Stalin's death huge amounts of slanderous materials were discovered in the NKVD offices. If one goes by these materials, far-flung networks of "right-Trotskyite, spy-terrorist, diversionist-wrecking organizations and centers" existed in almost every *krai, oblast,* and republic, for some reason always headed by the local First Secretaries of the Party organizations.[30] It was not hard to see that the great bulk of these false accusations did not come to the NKVD from without; they were fabricated by its own investigators. A real factory of lies was in operation, turning out hundreds of thousands of false stories about all kinds of "plots," "terrorist acts," "espionage," and "diversions."

It would be a mistake to think that these false accusations were the main cause of the destruction of the best cadres. They were only a pretext. The real causes of the mass repression go much deeper. Any serious investigation would have exposed the Nazi forgery against Tukhachevskii, but Stalin did not order an expert investigation. It would have been even easier to establish the falseness of many other

[30] For example, the Sverdlovsk *oblast* NKVD "uncovered" the "insurrectionary staff of the Urals—the organ of a bloc of rightists, Trotskyites, S-R's, and church people," headed by Kabakov, the First Secretary of the Sverdlosk *obkom* and a member of the All-Union Central Committee.

materials produced by the NKVD, but neither Stalin nor his closest aides checked or wanted to check the authenticity of these materials. Stalin, when sanctioning the arrest and execution of his former colleagues and friends, rarely expressed a desire to meet and interrogate these people himself. When such rare meetings did take place, Stalin, as we saw in the cases of Petrovskii and Kosior, did not want to listen to the accused man but simply demanded an unconditional confession. He closely followed the reports of many investigations, so he knew that some prisoners did not admit their guilt despite the cruelest tortures. Nonetheless, he sanctioned their executions. He was also given last letters and declarations by many of his former colleagues, in which they reaffirmed their innocence, their devotion to the Party and to Stalin, and asked Stalin to see them and listen to them. But he invariably ignored these declarations and requests.

Eikhe's appeal, which was read to the XXth Party Congress, was especially moving. Writing on October 29, 1939, he confessed to one genuinely criminal act: signing a false confession. He described the torture that had extracted this confession from him: he had an imperfectly mended spine, which was used by the NKVD investigator to cause him unbearable pain. He pointed out the absurd disregard for facts that the investigator had displayed, and pleaded with Stalin to save the Party from its real enemies, the people who were destroying innocent cadres. Stalin paid no more attention to this than to any other appeal. It was simply passed on to Beria, and Eikhe was shot on February 4, 1940.

Another candidate member of the Politburo, Rudzutak, completely repudiated his confession at his trial before the Military Collegium of the Supreme Court. His hard-hitting accusation of his accusers and affirmation of his utter loyalty also went unanswered.[31] Stalin refused to talk with him, and Rudzutak was shot.[32]

If we assume that Stalin was deeply convinced of the guilt of people repressed on his orders, then it is impossible to explain why he took such pains to keep the investigations secret, making sure that no outside person, not even the procurator, could gain admittance into the torture chambers of the NKVD. Why did he take pains to revoke all due process with respect to political prisoners? Why did he take away their right to defense, to prove their innocence? Why did the usual political trial take place in prison and last only a few minutes? Why was such a trial an empty formality, with the sentence typed in advance? Why were many political prisoners given long prison terms *in absentia,* without any trial at all, by the decision of so-called

[31] *Ed.:* Rudzutak's statement was also read by Khrushchev to the XXth Party Congress.
[32] Lion Feuchtwanger reports, in *Moscow 1937,* that Stalin told him about a long letter from Radek, protesting his innocence. But Stalin didn't want to meet Radek, and the very next day Radek "confessed" to his crimes.

troiki? Why were individuals labeled enemies of the people and expelled from the Party as soon as they were arrested, long before investigations were finished? Why did Stalin establish the illegal system whereby the NKVD all by itself did the arrests, the investigations, the trials, the sentencing, and the executions? Such questions can never be satisfactorily answered if we start with the story of a "deceived" Stalin.

In some *oblasti* the NKVD, unable to handle its huge quota of repression, drastically simplified the investigation. M. M. Ishov, the former military procurator, tells how NKVD agents in Novosibirsk not only made up stories themselves; they even signed for the prisoners. Then the sentence was pronounced *in absentia,* often a death sentence. And people were shot, without being tortured, without even being interrogated. Very frequently arrests were made without the sanction of the procurator's office.

In Moscow, however, as in many large cities, and also in most big cases the NKVD tried to preserve some legality. Forcing prisoners to tell lies against themselves and to invent all sorts of conspiracies, NKVD investigators demanded that they sign depositions in their own hand. In case of resistance, the signature would be secured by days, even months, of torture, a procedure that seems strange to some commentators. The idea was not only to break the prisoner's will, to degrade him, but also to cover up the crime, to give murder some semblance of legality. That is why torture was introduced in the NKVD on Stalin's insistence.

Only the same motives can explain the terrible conditions that were created on Stalin's orders in the camps. When the Nazis sent millions of people to Auschwitz and the other death camps, they would write on the accompanying documents: "Return undesirable." Stalin and his aides behaved more hypocritically. On many files is the inscription "Use only for hard physical labor." But the meaning was the same, since "hard physical work" under existing conditions meant death 99 per cent of the time. All this shows that Stalin deliberately tried to erase all traces of his crimes.

In 1955–58 some open trials of former NKVD executives were held in various cities. The trials revealed that the NKVD leadership became, in the years of the cult, a rallying point for all sorts of adventurers and careerists, some with dark political and criminal pasts. The low moral character of many was matched by their low intellectual level. Khrushchev described one such person—Rodos, who had interrogated Kosior, Chubar', and Kosarev—as

> an insignificant man with the mental horizon of a chicken, and the morality, literally, of a degenerate. . . . Could such a man on his own possibly have carried out an investigation to prove the guilt

of men such as Kosior? No, he could not have done much without appropriate instructions. He said to the Presidium [i.e., the Politburo]: "They told me Kosior and Chubar' were enemies of the people; therefore I, as the investigator, had to extract from them the confession that they were enemies.[33]

One of Beria's closest assistants, Paramonov, long chief of the investigation section of the NKVD, had only a fourth-grade education. Someone once played a joke on him by sending in a denunciation of Georgii Saakadze, a famous Georgian of the seventeenth century. According to S. O. Gazarian, Paramonov ordered a search for Saakadze. There were, of course, some NKVD officials with well-developed intellects, such as Vyshinskii and L. Sheinin, an investigator for special affairs who even did some creative writing. But morally they were hardly different from Rodos.

How did the NKVD, which was under Stalin's personal control, fall into the hands of adventurers, careerists, and semiliterates? It was not by accident. Stalin needed precisely such people in the punitive organs. They had one priceless virtue: they were completely dependent on the man who gave them almost unlimited power, and they were ready to do anything he ordered without thinking, without pangs of conscience. There was nothing new in this situation. Louis XI, for example, the founder of absolutism in France, chose his chief of police, Tristan the Hermit, for the same reasons. There was Ivan the Terrible and his *oprichniki,* especially his favorite *oprichnik,* Maliuta Skuratov, who took part in almost all the tsar's crimes. It is not surprising that Ivan was Stalin's favorite among the tsars. Stalin kept firm control of the punitive organs, removing some officials and promoting others. And all these facts lead once again to a single conclusion: Stalin's orders and actions were deliberate crimes.

It is not hard to imagine a man with weak nerves, mistrustful and fearful, finding himself at the head of the only socialist state in the world. Such a man would begin to see enemies and conspiracies everywhere. He would thrash about, not knowing what to do, wind up killing his best and most devoted friends, surrendering the country to a small group of incompetent but ambitious adventurers who knew how to win his confidence. But Stalin bore no resemblance to such a leader. He was unquestionably a man of strong nerves, inflexible will, and iron self-control. He had a forceful personality, which was, to a great extent, the secret of his influence over those around him. His fundamental actions and orders were not the product of fear or deception; they were the well-calculated moves of a man determined to stop at nothing to reach his goals. "It's not so easy to fool Comrade Stalin," he once said about himself.[34]

[33] Khrushchev's speech to the XXth Congress.
[34] *Sochineniia,* XII, p. 113.

3

HISTORIANS HAVE OFTEN been obliged to turn to psychiatry, for history offers many cases of rulers with abnormal minds. Obviously pathological traits, developing as a result of hereditary predisposition and unlimited power, can be detected in the behavior of such despots as Sennacherib, Nero, Caligula, Philip II, Ivan the Terrible, and Paul.[35] Pathological traits are apparent in the behavior of Hitler and some of his colleagues. It is therefore not surprising that Stalin's behavior is also attributed to acute mental illness. For example, at a meeting of old Bolsheviks with delegates to the XXIInd Party Congress in 1961, N. A. Alekseev, a Party member since 1897 and a physician by profession, argued that Stalin was mentally sick and incompetent (*nevmeniaemyi*). Another old Party member, I. P. Aleksakhin, who returned to Moscow aften seventeen years in confinement, propounded the same story to the Party *aktiv* of Krasnopresnenskii *raion* in 1961. Many foreign Communists argued the same way after the XXth Party Congress obliged them to face the facts of Stalin's terror. For example, the American Communist Hershel Meyer, denying that the development of socialism necessitated terror, tried to show that an accident was to blame: Stalin's paranoid psyche. In this interpretation Stalin was convinced that he was destroying real enemies and saving the Revolution from those who sought to restore capitalism.[36]

According to medical textbooks, paranoia is a psychological disorder characterized by wildly distorted, frenzied ideas, which, however, affect only a limited area of perceptions and develop with little or no hallucinations and without a marked change in personality.[37] Paranoia develops primarily among men in their early forties, of strong but uneven temper. The sickness is accompanied, as a rule, both by megalomania and by a persecution mania. Other typical symptoms are egocentrism, grudge-bearing, unsociability, obstinacy, and a striving for dominance. Paranoiacs get special satisfaction from unmasking their "enemies." They hate people who once helped them and to whom they are somehow obligated. "A paranoiac," writes psychiatrist P. I. Kovalevskii, "has no friends. . . . Suspiciousness, mistrust, secretiveness, and cruelty show through all his actions. . . . Often the

---

[35] *Ed.:* Paul was a Russian emperor, 1796–1801, who was overthrown and killed by a palace revolution.

[36] See Meyer, *Doklad Khrushcheva i krizis levogo dvizheniia v SShA* (Moscow, 1957), pp. 15–20. The original is Hershel D. Meyer, *The Khrushchev Report and the Crisis in the American Left* (New York, 1956).

[37] *Bol'shaia meditsinskaia entsiklopediia*, XXIII (1961), p. 224. The story that Stalin had schizophrenia must be rejected out of hand, for the symptoms—splitting of the psyche, atrophy in the emotional and volitional sphere, disintegration of the logical thought processes, aural and other hallucinations—were clearly absent.

cruelty is joined with a thirst for blood . . . and with great cunning."[38] At the same time, the paranoiac retains his memory and intellect, and frequently manages to carry on his professional functions.

From this description it is clear that the story about Stalin's mental sickness is not entirely unfounded. It is not difficult to detect pathological elements in his behavior. Morbid suspiciousness, noticeable throughout his life and especially intense in his last years, intolerance of criticism, grudge-bearing, an overestimation of himself bordering on megalomania, cruelty approaching sadism—all these traits, it would seem, demonstrate that Stalin was a typical paranoiac. Nevertheless this view is inadequate.

Medicine makes a serious distinction between a real mental illness, in which a man is acknowledged incompetent and must be placed in a psychiatric hospital, and various abnormal states of personality, in which a person knows what he is doing and bears a complete responsibility for his behavior. This distinction between the person with psychopathic traits and the person who is genuinely sick must be applied to Stalin. Despite all the pathological changes in his personality during the last twenty years of his life, which took on the characteristic features of paranoid psychopathology, despite the fact that his behavior clearly shows not only acute moral degeneration but also serious psychic derangement—I am profoundly convinced that *Stalin was beyond doubt a responsible* (vmeniaemyi) *man, and in most cases was fully aware of what he was doing.* And no court, including the court of history, can excuse and explain Stalin's actions by reference to incompetence.

For all his suspiciousness and mistrust, Stalin acted with great self-control. After he chose a victim, he almost never struck without preparations. His were not the actions of an abnormal man, driven only by a persecution mania. Before taking vengeance, he organized vilification of his victim, entangling him in a web of slander.

There were basically two different methods of assault on the cadres. One could be called "from the top down." First, in a chosen *oblast,* republic, or institution, the entire complement of leaders would be thrown out by an unexpected swift move, using depositions fabricated in Moscow. The leaders, labeled Trotskyites, enemies of the people, and spies, would be arrested. Then came the turn of lesser officials— members of editorial boards, directors of institutions and enterprises, heads of *raion* Party committees and *raion* executive committees, and, in the central institutions in Moscow, department and section heads and many rank-and-file staff members. It was considered self-evident

---

[38] P. I. Kovalevskii, *Psikhiatricheskie eskizy iz istorii,* III [Kharkov? 1893?], pp. 65–75. Many historians and psychiatrists call Ivan the Terrible a typical paranoiac. See, for example, Kovalevskii's article "Ioann Groznyi i ego dushevnye sostoianiia," *ibid.,* and also A. Lichko, "Glazami psikhiatra," *Nauka i religiia,* 1965, Nos. 10, 11.

that "enemies of the people" who had headed an *oblast* or an institution for years had planted their agents everywhere.

The second method could be called "from the bottom up." The NKVD, without consulting the leaders of the chosen *oblast,* republic, or commissariat, would arrest several rank-and-file officials and label them wreckers, enemies of the people, spies. The central newspapers, and frequently the local ones too, would raise a great hullabaloo: What had the local leaders been doing? Why had they overlooked enemy activity? Then arrests spread, reaching individual officials in the *oblast* or republic *apparat,* or section heads in the commissariat. At the same time some close associates of the leaders would be taken: a personal chauffeur, a researcher, an editor, a secretary, a relative. The natural desire of the leaders to save people they knew to be honest and loyal would be interpreted as protection of enemies of the people. The newspapers' tone would become more wild and menacing, openly charging that some leaders were helping enemies of the people, alluding to Trotskyite or other compromising connections of these leaders. All this stimulated the flow of denunciations. In some cases the central press even appealed over the heads of the *oblast* or commissariat leaders, inviting rank-and-file Communists to come out against their chiefs. A typical article in *Pravda* was headlined "Time for the Bolsheviks of Omsk to Speak Up," and continued: "If the leaders of the Omsk *obkom* do nothing, and protect Trotskyite-Bukharinite spies, then it is time the Omsk Bolsheviks began to make their voices heard."[39] The leaders would thus be isolated from the rank and file, demoralized, paralyzed. All sorts of careerists and time-servers would be mobilized and united. The business would end with the destruction of the victim selected by Stalin and the NKVD.

These actions bear little resemblance to those of a paranoiac.

It is also instructive to observe how Stalin frequently limited himself, at the outset, to shifting a major figure without arresting him, although the NKVD already had fabricated testimony against him. The man would be transferred to a less important or sometimes a more important post; he would be sent from Moscow to a province, or he would be called from a province to Moscow. One way or another, Stalin would remove his "opponent" from his familiar milieu, from the collective that knew and trusted him. There were cases in 1937–38 when a leading Communist would be transferred three or four times. Dybenko, for example, was relieved of his command in the Privolga military district in 1937 and appointed commander of the Leningrad military district. But a few months later he was removed from this post for "insufficient vigilance," appointed Deputy Commissar of Forest Industry, and sent to the Urals. There, in April, 1938.

[39] *Pravda,* Sept. 28, 1937.

he was finally arrested.[40] Postyshev was sent, before his arrest, to be
the *obkom* secretary in Kuibyshev, Chubar' to be *gorkom* secretary
in Solikamsk. Tukhachevskii, a few weeks before he was shot, was
sent from Moscow to Kuibyshev, as commander of the Privolga military district. Kosior, dismissed as First Secretary of the Ukrainian
Central Committee, was moved from Kiev to Moscow to be Deputy
Chairman of the All-Union Council of Commissars. Iagoda, after he
ceased to be Commissar of Internal Affairs, became Commissar of
Communications. On September 27, 1936, his picture appeared in
all the newspapers beside that of Ezhov. A. Kosarev was not arrested
right after the VIIth Plenum of the Komsomol Central Committee,
which practically declared him an enemy of the people. His wife says
that he was watched from behind every tree at his dacha but for some
time was not touched. Even Ezhov, dismissed from the NKVD in
December, 1938, was arrested only many weeks later, during which
time he was Commissar of Water Transport and even appeared together with Stalin.

These maneuvers also have little resemblance to those of an incompetent man.

It is also significant that many people who had been close to Lenin
were not arrested, though they were out of Stalin's favor and had been
close friends with those already condemned as enemies. These individuals were merely demoted. Stalin did not arrest Podvoiskii, Kon,
Petrovskii, Stasova, Mikha Tskhakaia, F. Makharadze, or many other
once prominent leaders whose names often were mentioned in slanderous denunciations and confessions.

Why did Stalin order the destruction of some old Bolsheviks but
spare others? Why did he sometimes cross out names on the lists of
people to be arrested? Why, looking over interrogation records that
named dozens of "accomplices" and "accessories," did Stalin refrain
from noting that this, that, or the other individual should be arrested?
Did Stalin, like many tyrants, enjoy his unlimited power not only to
break and kill people but also to leave some alive, to show that he
was free to "execute and to pardon"? This does not seem to be the
chief factor. Stalin's main considerations were political. He had identified himself as Lenin's closest friend and colleague. It was therefore
necessary and desirable that genuine friends and colleagues of Lenin
remain alive, to demonstrate the continuity between the time of Lenin
and the epoch of Stalin. These people were continually forced to praise
Stalin; on his birthday they signed collective congratulations to Stalin,
"the true Leninist." All this shows that Stalin was not guided by the
frenzy of an abnormal person but by clear-cut political calculations.

An illuminating case in point is the fate of M. M. Litvinov, Com-

---

[40] See *Voenno-istoricheskii zhurnal*, 1965, No. 10.

missar of Foreign Affairs and a close comrade of Lenin. Litvinov was not arrested, unlike nearly everyone else in his Commissariat. The story goes that in 1907 during the Vth Party Congress in London, Stalin got in a fight with some dock workers and Litvinov helped him out. In 1937–38 Litvinov expected to be arrested any night and even had a suitcase with underwear ready. But arrest did not come. Later on Litvinov asked Stalin the reason for this "indulgence." "I haven't forgotten that time in London," answered Stalin. Even if this story is authentic, Stalin was not sincere. Gratitude was never one of his characteristics, but he realized that he needed Litvinov (as well as I. Maiskii) as a diplomat. Litvinov could not be replaced as easily as other commissars or *obkom* secretaries.

The same was true of many cultural leaders. In the fabricated depositions of arrested artists, writers, and film workers there were allegations against hundreds who were not arrested. For example, Boris Pasternak and Iurii Olesha were named as accomplices of Babel and Meyerhold in the so-called diversionary organization of literary people. But Stalin did not order the arrest of Pasternak and Olesha. Nor did he permit the arrest of many leading film directors, although the NKVD prepared more than one case against them. Stalin liked to watch films when he was relaxing; he saw some favorites fifty or a hundred times—and forced his retinue to watch them too.[41] His weakness for the cinema obviously saved many Soviet directors.

The careful calculation in Stalin's crimes is also apparent in those cases where he arrested the wife or some other close relative of a leader, but kept the leader in his important job and continued to meet him both officially and socially. We have already mentioned the arrest of Kalinin's wife in 1937, and of Molotov's after the war. Similarly arrested were two of Mikoian's sons, Ordzhonikidze's brother, the wife and the son of Otto Kuusinen,[42] the wife of A. V. Khrulev, and others. Sometimes Stalin made a show of mercy by releasing one of his aides' relatives. Kalinin's wife, for example, was released a few days before he died—and later was exiled once again. Iu. K—— says that one day Stalin, while talking with Kuusinen, asked him why he didn't try to get his son freed. "Evidently there were serious reasons for his arrest," he answered. Stalin grinned, and ordered the release of Kuusinen's son. The case of Poskrebyshev, Stalin's personal secre-

---

[41] Stalin's favorites, according to M. I. Romm, were *The Great Waltz, Lights of the Big City, Lenin in October,* and *Volga, Volga.*

[42] Aina Kuusinen, like Otto, was a Comintern official. M. A. Solntseva tells how she shared bunks with Aina and moved through the same transit prisons with her in 1938–41. She used to receive parcels from Otto, addressed by a domestic servant. "Once," Solntseva writes, "on New Year's Eve they put a screechy radio receiver in our barracks. Aina Kuusinen, dressed in rags, listened to a New Year's speech by Otto Kuusinen in the Kremlin."

tary, is instructive. His wife was the sister of Sedov's wife, and Sedov was Trotsky's son. But that did not prevent Poskrebyshev from being one of the closest people to Stalin. Stalin did finally order the arrest of Poskrebyshev's wife but kept him as his secretary. Poskrebyshev was fired only a few months before Stalin's death and still was not arrested.

Neither did Lazar Kaganovich's relatives escape Stalin's attention. Mikhail Moiseevich, Lazar's brother, was Minister of the Aviation Industry before the war. He was a Stalinist, responsible for the repression of many people. But after the war he fell out of Stalin's favor. As a result, some arrested officials, who had allegedly set up an underground "fascist center," named Mikhail Kaganovich as an accomplice. They made the obviously inspired (and utterly preposterous) assertion that he (a Jew) was to be vice-president of the fascist government if the Hitlerites took Moscow. When Stalin learned of these depositions, which he obviously expected, he phoned Lazar Kaganovich and said that his brother would have to be arrested because he had connections with fascists. "Well, so what?" said Lazar. "If it's necessary, arrest him!" At a Politburo discussion of this subject, Stalin praised Lazar Kaganovich for his "principles": he had agreed to his brother's arrest. But Stalin then added that the arrest should not be made hastily. Mikhail Moiseevich had been in the Party many years, Stalin said, and all the depositions should be checked once more. So Mikoian was instructed to arrange a confrontation between M.M. and the person who had testified against him. The confrontation was held in Mikoian's office. A man was brought in who repeated his testimony in Kaganovich's presence, adding that some airplane factories were deliberately built near the border before the war so that the Germans might capture them more easily. When Mikhail Kaganovich had heard the testimony, he asked permission to go to a little toilet adjoining Mikoian's office. A few seconds later a shot was heard there.[43]

These accounts reveal Stalin's great contempt for his aides, not any fear of them. And they simply cannot be reconciled with the notion of Stalin's incompetence.

Equally incompatible with that view are the cases of people arrested on Stalin's orders, but a few months or years later, after torture and severe sentences, released—again on Stalin's orders, often without explanations—and appointed to high offices. Consider, for example, Stalin's strange behavior towards his old comrade Sergei Ivanovich Kavtaradze, who had once helped him hide from detectives in St. Petersburg. In the twenties Kavtaradze joined the Trotskyite

[43] Mikoian recounted these events to A. V. Snegov, who does not remember the name of the false witness.

opposition, and left it only when the Trotskyite center called on its supporters to stop oppositional activity. After Kirov's murder, Kavtaradze, exiled to Kazan as an ex-Trotskyite, wrote a letter to Stalin saying that he was not working against the Party. Stalin immediately brought Kavtaradze back from exile. Soon many central newspapers carried an article by Kavtaradze recounting an incident of his underground work with Stalin. Stalin liked the article, but Kavtaradze did not write any more on this subject. He did not even rejoin the Party, and lived by doing very modest editorial work. At the end of 1936 he and his wife were suddenly arrested and, after torture, were sentenced to be shot. He was accused of planning, with Budu Mdivani, to murder Stalin. Soon after sentencing, Mdivani was shot. Kavtaradze, however, was kept in the death cell for a long time. Then he was suddenly taken to Beria's office, where he met his wife, who had aged beyond recognition. Both were released. First he lived in a hotel; then he got two rooms in a communal apartment and started to work. Stalin began to show him various signs of favor, inviting him to dinner and once even paying him a surprise visit along with Beria. (This visit caused great excitement in the communal apartment. One of Kavtaradze's neighbors fainted when, in her words, "the portrait of Comrade Stalin" appeared on the threshold.) When he had Kavtaradze to dinner, Stalin himself would pour the soup, tell jokes, and reminisce. But during one of these dinners, Stalin suddenly went up to his guest and said, "And still you wanted to kill me."[44]

Some historians may see this comment as proof of Stalin's paranoia. But Stalin knew very well that Kavtaradze never tried to kill him. However, he could not admit this openly, for then he would have had to reconsider the execution of Budu Mdivani and many other Communists involved in the case. It was much simpler to "forgive "Kavtaradze alone. Similarly, he sent word to Alesha Svanidze that he would be "forgiven" if he asked Stalin's pardon. Svanidze, considering himself innocent, refused to ask for pardon and was shot. All these actions reveal a misanthropic tyrant, not a mentally ill person who did not know what he was doing.

Stalin usually turned down appeals to free people. We have already seen that he not only rejected an appeal by Einstein and the Joliot-Curies on behalf of two foreign physicists, Houtermanns and Weissberg, who had been arrested in the USSR; in 1939 he turned them over to the Gestapo. Still, in a number of cases, Stalin had to give in. The physicist L. D. Landau tells how he

> was arrested because of a ridiculous denunciation. I was accused of being a German spy. . . . I spent a year in prison and it was clear I wouldn't last another six months. I was simply dying. Kapitsa went

[44] Recounted by S. I. Kavtaradze.

to the Kremlin and declared that he was demanding my release. If
it was not granted, he would be forced to leave the Institute. I
was freed.[45]

It stands to reason that Kapitsa's fame as a scientist did not influence
Stalin as much as the need for Kapitsa as head of the Institute.[46]

After the Soviet-Finnish War and in the first months of World
War II, Stalin allowed the release of several thousand Red Army
officers. Many of them were promoted to high posts during the war.
Stalin used to meet and talk with them. On the other hand, in October
of 1941 and the summer of 1942, Stalin ordered a large group of
leading Red Army officers to be shot in the camps; he considered them
a threat to himself in the event of unfavorable developments on the
Soviet-German Front.[47]

A man suffering from a persecution mania would not, after
destroying thousands of devoted Party leaders, have replaced them
with men with such murky political records as Beria and Abakumov.
Stalin knew the true nature of these people. At the June, 1937,
Plenum, G. N. Kaminskii, then Commissar of Health, who had been
Secretary of the Central Committee of Azerbaijan and Chairman of
the Baku Soviet in 1922, told about the suspected ties between Beria
and Mussawat intelligence.[48] Stalin knew that under Kerensky the
Menshevik Vyshinskii had been head of the militia in Arbat *raion*,
and in the summer of 1917 signed orders for the arrest of Bolsheviks.
Why did Stalin entrust the procuracy of the USSR to this man? Why
did he prefer Vyshinskii and Beria to members of the old Leninist
guard? His motive was clearly political. Deliberately seeking to usurp
all power, he knew that he could get rid of the Leninist core of the
Party only by using such people as Ezhov, Beria, and Vyshinskii.

Stalin received much compromising material on many of his aides,
whom he nevertheless kept in high places. Voroshilov's name was included in the fabricated depositions of some military officers.[49] An old
Party member, F. Z——, says that in Sverdlovsk *oblast* alone several
poods of depositions against Kaganovich and Molotov were "prepared." Many against Molotov and Gorkin were stored in Kuibyshev
oblast. Investigators tortured President Kalinin's wife until she signed
statements compromising her husband. Stalin was aware of all this;
he suggested some of these depositions himself. But for the time being
he ignored them.

[45] *Komsomol'skaia pravda,* July 8, 1964.
[46] *Ed.:* The Institute of Physical Problems, specially created for P. I. Kapitsa on his
      return from a long stay in England (1923–35), was mainly devoted to the study of
      low-temperature physics and superconductivity. In 1946 Kapitsa ceased to be
      director, reportedly because he refused to work on the development of nuclear
      arms. After Stalin's death he was made director once again.
[47] Recounted by Konstantin Simonov.
[48] See *Voprosy istorii KPSS,* 1965, No. 11.
[49] V. Shalamov has informed me of this.

Stalin was a morbidly suspicious man who could not understand the sincere, honorable, and simple personalities of many old Leninists. "If one's heart is so constructed," Krylov wrote long ago, "that it feels neither friendship nor love, . . . one sees everyone as an enemy." Many criminals, afraid of exposure, begin to fear those around them, and the result may be more and more crimes. Something of this sort must have happened to Stalin. Having wiped out most of the Leninist old guard, and almost all his erstwhile friends and comrades, having cast aside all laws, of the Party and state, of friendship, of simple humanity, Stalin had good reason to be afraid of people. And this fear steadily increased throughout his life. "Evil rulers," says an Eastern proverb, "are always haunted by fear of their subjects." Stalin's fear of exposure and retribution drove him to commit more and more crimes. But we should not attribute the tidal wave of repression in the thirties to maniacal suspiciousness. Every despot is suspicious, but suspicion does not explain despotism.

4

IN THE LATE 1950's the author first heard, from a high-placed official, a strange explanation of the blood purges of the thirties. Yes, he said, Stalin knew very well that his victims were not spies and wreckers. All those charges were deliberately fabricated. Judged by the usual moral and state rules, Stalin's actions were of course lawless. Still they were necessary for the further development of the Revolution. The people Stalin got rid of were powerful and popular. They could not have been simply fired from their jobs or expelled from the Party. They had to be accused of monstrous crimes, of plotting against the Soviet regime and attempting to restore capitalism, of espionage and conspiring with the imperialists. Then, with the masses deceived, those people could be destroyed.

"But why," I asked, "was it necessary for the Revolution to get rid of its active participants?"

That is the logic of all revolutions, he answered. Many of the people Stalin destroyed had stopped being revolutionaries by the mid-thirties. They had degenerated into officeholders and bureaucrats. They were pushing the Party and state machine not toward socialism but toward state capitalism. Stalin had to get rid of those who were interfering with the further development of the socialist Revolution; he had to push up[50] young officials who were capable of leading the revolution forward.

This story is essentially the same as the appeal of the Maoist Red

[50] *Ed.:* The verb *vydvinut'*, to push up or advance, and the noun *vydvizhenets,* the person pushed up or advanced, were endlessly used in the thirties to describe the official policy of placing lower-class people in top jobs.

Guards to open fire on "headquarters" and to overthrow those "who hold power but are taking the road to capitalism." I have discovered that it has wide currency among Party and state officials, both active and retired. Of course it is not expounded publicly but retailed "confidentially," especially in conversation with young officials. It may even have its source in some comments of Stalin himself.

What can be said of this legend?

The degeneration[51] of many officials did occur in the postrevolutionary period, as will be seen in Chapter XI. To some extent it was inevitable in a huge and relatively backward country where, in 1917 alone, the Party increased more than a hundredfold as it was transformed from an underground political organization into the ruling party. And, from 1918, it did not share its power with any other party; it ruled by dictatorial methods, uncontrolled for all practical purposes.

Who were affected by bureaucratic degeneration? First of all, petty-bourgeois revolutionaries who had joined the proletarian cause but were unable to overcome the temptations of the transitional period. Also some proletarian revolutionaries, who were firm in the struggle against tsarism and the bourgeoisie but could not cope with the exercise of governmental power. There were tens of thousands of old officeholders whom the Soviet regime was forced to bring into the state *apparat*. They did not need to degenerate; they knew no other methods of governing than bureaucratic.

It was not inevitable that degeneration would affect the entire regime and the Party as a whole. In its first decades the Soviet regime waged a struggle against bureaucratism, careerism, and petty-bourgeois degeneration, raising a whole stratum of young and talented officials in this spirit. Was Stalin so dissatisfied with this struggle that he wanted a swift, massive purge of bureaucratic officials, even if he had to use barbaric methods, in order to accelerate the socialist Revolution? Such a suggestion does not withstand the slightest criticism.

In the first place, not only were bureaucratized leaders repressed in 1936–39; an enormous number of devoted officials, as well as army officers, business managers, scientists, and artists, were arrested. And not only high-placed leaders but masses of middle-rank officials perished; not only members of alien classes but also the most educated section of the Party intelligentsia, who had been carefully trained by the Soviet regime. In the second place, most of these people were replaced by less experienced, less reliable, less educated cadres. We will not even mention the triumph of people like Molotov, Beria, Ezhov, Mekhlis, Bagirov, Malenkov, and Voroshilov. They—and Stalin

[51] *Ed.:* The word is *pererozhdenie;* see the definition in the Glossary.

—were the most complete degenerates, the real renegades from Marxism-Leninism.

The enormous scale of repression resulted in a grave shortage of cadres. Hundreds of thousands of officials had to be pushed up from below. Tens of thousands of Stakhanovite workers became factory directors. Ordinary soldiers became platoon and company commanders, company commanders were placed in charge of battalions and regiments, battalion and regimental commanders rose to command divisions and entire armies. Many rank-and-file scientists took over laboratories and big institutes. Most of these *vydvizhentsy*—"pushed-up people"—were subjectively honest; they wanted to work for the good of the Soviet regime. But the situation created by the repression was hardly conducive to honesty. Many *vydvizhentsy* were soon corrupted by power, as will be shown in detail later.

5

THE TSARIST SECRET POLICE fought the revolutionary movement, especially the Bolshevik Party, with agents and provocateurs, including Party members who made deals with the police out of fear or some base motive. Many local and even central Party organizations were penetrated by such agents. In 1918 a Moscow publishing house brought out a collection of documents on the history of Bolshevism, taken from the archives of the secret police.[52] Twelve agents who had operated in the Social Democratic Party were named:

M. I. Brandinskii, Ia. A. Zhitomirskii, I. G. Krivov, A. I. Lobov, R. V. Malinovskii, A. K. Marakushev, A. A. Poliakov, A. S. Romanov, I. P. Sesitskii, M. E. Chernomazov, V. E. Shurkhanov, and a "Vasilii" whose identity was not disclosed.

According to these police files, agents had even participated in the Prague Party Conference of 1912, sending in reports of its resolutions and practical decisions.[53]

Most of the police spies were exposed right after the February Revolution of 1917. But some were exposed only much later. For example, Serebriakova, who had betrayed many Bolsheviks to the tsarist secret police, was the center of a celebrated case in the twenties. In the mass repression of the thirties Stalin and the NKVD made use of the popular hatred for police spies. False accusations of this kind were directed against such respected Party members as Zelenskii,

[52] *Bol'sheviki (Dokumenty po istorii bol'shevizma s 1903 po 1916 gg byvshego Moskovskogo Okhrannogo Otdeleniia)* (Moscow: Zadruga, 1918).
[53] *Ed.:* At the Prague Conference Stalin was nominated for membership in the Central Committee. For the possible significance of "Vasilii," see pp. 318–20.

Piatnitskii, Razumov, and many other officials who have now been completely rehabilitated. Even Meyerhold was accused in 1938 of having worked for the tsarist secret police under the name Semenych. Few realize that similar accusations have repeatedly been made against Stalin himself.

As early as the twenties, émigré papers carried reports that Stalin had been an agent of the tsarist secret police. One of the first to make this charge was the leading Georgian Menshevik Noah Zhordania, who recounted what Stepan Shaumian had told him about his, Shaumian's, arrest in Tiflis. He was apprehended on the first day of an illegal visit to that city, when only one person knew the date of his arrival and the address where he was supposed to stay. That person, if we can believe Zhordania's report of what Shaumian said, was Stalin.[54] In the late thirties such reports were retailed by Trotskyite publications. In 1952 a collection of such stories appeared in Paris.[55] Still more publications of this sort came out in the West after the XXth Party Congress of 1956. Some authors even tried to attribute Khrushchev's unexpected speech, "On the Cult of Personality and Its Consequences," to the pressure of army officers who showed him supposedly irrefutable proof of Stalin's former treachery. That was the story told, for example, in "Stalin's Sensational Secret," published by the American magazine *Life* for April 23, 1956.

The author, Alexander Orlov, had been a leading NKVD official in the first half of the thirties, spending much of his time abroad as a resident of Soviet intelligence. At the height of the repression, Orlov decided not to return to the USSR. Until 1953 he made no exposés, but after Stalin's death he published a series of articles, later incorporated in a book, *The Secret History of Stalin's Crimes* (New York, 1953). In these publications Stalin was accused of killing Kirov and organizing mass repression, but there was no mention of his working for the tsarist police. Then, in the 1956 article, Orlov tried to explain the mass repression by Stalin's fear of being exposed as a former police spy.

In February, 1937, when Orlov was in a French clinic with a bad back, he was visited by his cousin Zinovii Borisovich Katsnel'son, an NKVD plenipotentiary in the Ukraine and a member of the Central Committee. Katsnel'son was a great friend of Kosior and often met with Stalin. He said to Orlov that Stalin told Iagoda, when they were preparing the first Moscow trial, that it would be useful to connect some of the intended victims with the tsarist secret police. Iagoda

---

[54] Similar materials were published in the early thirties by the Dashnak journal *Airinik*, in Boston, Mass. *Ed.:* Dashnak refers to an Armenian nationalist party that held power for a time during the Civil War.

[55] *Byl li Stalin provokatorom tsarskoi okhrany? Ed.:* I have been unable to locate or authenticate this reference.

decided to try and find a former officer of the secret police, which at that time was not an easy matter. The largest collection of police archives was kept in the Lubianka office of Iagoda's predecessor, Menzhinskii. An NKVD official named Shtein was told to search these archives. He discovered a file in which a police official named Vissarionov had kept his papers. "There," wrote Orlov in his 1956 article,

> were reports and letters in longhand, addressed to Vissarionov, in the handwriting of the dictator that was so familiar to Shtein. The file, as Shtein discovered, concerned Stalin all right—not Stalin the revolutionary but Stalin the *agent provocateur* who had worked assiduously for the tsarist secret police.

Shtein then went to the Ukraine, to his former chief and friend, V. A. Balitskii, head of the Ukrainian NKVD. Balitskii submitted the papers to expert analysis and established their authenticity. Then Balitskii informed Katsnel'son, Iakir, Kosior, and other high-placed officials. Many photocopies of the documents were made, and Iakir flew to Moscow and told Tukhachevskii, Gamarnik, Kork, and others. The military commanders drew up a plan to destroy Stalin. They proposed to pick two Red Army units loyal to them to accomplish an overturn in the Kremlin, without any disturbances in the country. All this Katsnel'son is supposed to have told Orlov in February, 1937, four months before the arrest of Tukhachevskii and his friends. Orlov wrote that he went to Spain soon after receiving this report, and there he heard the news of Tukhachevskii's arrest over the French radio. Subsequently everyone who could possibly have been involved in the affair was arrested and shot. In short, a large part of the repression was due to Shtein's accidental discovery.

In fact, Orlov's allegations do not withstand even superficial criticism. Katsnel'son, to begin with, was neither a member nor a candidate member of the Central Committee in 1937. The "conspirators" Orlov names were not arrested all at once but over a long period of time, and none of them tried to hide on learning that their "plot" had failed. Kosior was arrested and shot almost a year after Tukhachevskii's arrest. As for the many photocopies that were allegedly made of the "Vissarionov file," not one is extant, although many of the "conspirators" could easily have sent them to friends abroad. We know the details of the arrest of the military leaders and these facts are utterly incompatible with the existence of a widespread conspiracy to kill Stalin. It is also improbable that no one had searched the archives of the tsarist secret police before 1937. Also, many of the Ukrainian officials who were close to Kosior and Iakir—G. Petrovskii, for example—were not arrested. Orlov is even wrong in his account of Khrushchev's speech to the XXth Party Congress. Khrushchev said nothing in that speech about the case of Marshal Tukhachevskii and the other generals, who were rehabilitated only in 1957. There are many more such distortions and errors in Orlov's article. His explanation of why he was silent for so long, and why, even in his 1953 book on Stalin's crimes, he did not mention Katsnel'son's story, sounds unconvincing. It is obvious, in short, that Orlov's 1956 article is a clumsy fabrication.

That same year, 1956, Isaac Don Levine, who had written the first foreign biography of Stalin, published another book, containing a letter dated July 12, 1913, from a certain Eremin to the chief of the Enisei department of the secret police, A. F. Zhelezniakov:

> Iosif Vissarionovich Stalin, who has been administratively exiled to the Turukhansk region, gave the head of the Tiflis Agency of S[tate] G[endarmes] valuable undercover information when he was arrested in 1906.
>
> In 1908, the Head of the Baku Secret Police got a number of reports from Stalin, and later, when Stalin arrived in St. Petersburg, Stalin became an agent of the Petersburg Division of the Secret Police.
>
> Stalin's work was distinguished by precision, but it was sporadic.
>
> After Stalin's election to the Party's Central Committee in Prague, Stalin, upon his return to Petersburg, became completely opposed to the government and entirely broke off his connection with the Secret Police.[56]

This letter contradicts Orlov's claim that Stalin worked for the police *after* the Prague Conference of 1912. Levine's attempt to explain the discrepancy, without disavowing Orlov's material, is unconvincing. His account of the document's history fails to explain how it could have passed through several owners over a thirty-year period without being published. The reference to Stalin's arrest in 1906 is entirely unsubstantiated. Levine argues that Stalin could have been arrested when the Avlabar secret printing press was destroyed in April, 1906. But Stalin was not involved in that affair, many Caucasian Bolsheviks tell us. Anyhow, in April, 1906, he was participating in the IVth Unity Congress of the RSDLP in Stockholm. Levine tried to authenticate Eremin's signature, but the evidence he offers, largely based on his amateur expertise, is not convincing.[57] A similar lack of credibility marks all the materials published abroad purporting to establish Stalin's connections with the secret police.

Following the XXth Party Congress, stories on this subject began to circulate in the USSR. As the reader has already seen, a 1918 collection of police documents indicated that an unidentified Vasilii was

---

[56] *Ed.:* See frontispiece of Levine, *Stalin's Great Secret* (New York, 1956), for a photograph of this document.

[57] *Ed.:* For further evidence that the document is a fabrication, see Edward Ellis Smith, *The Young Stalin* (New York, 1967), pp. 306–309.

an agent within the Party; old Bolsheviks now recall that Stalin had the pseudonym Vasilii in 1912.[58] And here are a few more stories of this sort, which the author has heard.

(1) In the early thirties, the historian Professor Sepp, author of *The October Revolution in Documents,* happened upon the file of a police agent, Iosif Dzhugashvili. The file contained Dzhugashvili's request to be released from arrest. A note was written on this request: "Free him, if he agrees to give the Gendarme Department information about the activity of the Social Democratic Party." Sepp at that time was working in the Agitprop section of the Central Committee of Georgia. He went to Beria and showed him the file. Beria took it and flew to Moscow to see Stalin. Stalin looked through the file, destroyed the documents, and told Beria that it was all nonsense but Sepp had to be taken care of. Following Beria's return to Tiflis, Sepp was arrested and shot.[59]

(2) In the mid-thirties Beria had Transcaucasian NKVD officials gathering materials from police archives on the activity of the Social Democratic Party. (Beria needed this material for his book on the history of Marxist organizations in Transcaucasia.) In the Kutais archives, a denunciation of a group of Social Democrats was found, signed by Iosif Dzughashvili. The denunciation was brought to Kabulov, Beria's closest aide, who gave it to Beria himself.[60]

(3) The old Bolshevik V—— has told how he once dropped in on Stalin in a conspiratorial apartment in Tiflis and found a high-ranking gendarme with him. After the gendarme left, V—— asked Stalin: "What do you have in common with the gendarmes? Why was that gendarme here?"

"Ah . . . , he's helping us, in the gendarmerie," Stalin answered.[61]

(4) At the end of 1916, because of the deteriorating situation at the front, the army decided to draft a group of Social Democrats exiled in Siberia, including Stalin. After the exiles had arrived at Krasnoiarsk under guard, Stalin asked for a day's leave in the city. He did not return and did not go to the front. Although he lived in Krasnoiarsk practically without hiding, the police showed no evidence of interest in his activity.[62]

(5) Following the Prague Conference of 1912, Ordzhonikidze was assigned a number of important jobs by the Central Committee and set out on a trip to many Russian cities. As soon as he crossed the border, detectives "latched onto" him, and shadowed him during his whole long journey. At one station Stalin came in the train and sat down

[58] See Iu. Trifonov, *Otblesk kostra* (Moscow, 1966), p. 52.
[59] From the personal papers of E. P. Frolov, Party member since 1918.
[60] The story was told to S. O. Gazarian by a member of Kabulov's family.
[61] From the papers of E. P. Frolov.
[62] From the memoirs of the old Bolshevik B. I. Ivanov.

with Ordzhonikidze, who told him about the decisions of the conference. They went to sleep in the railway car. But in the morning
Stalin was gone. Five years later, after the February Revolution,
Ordzhonikidze asked Stalin where he had gone to. "I noticed someone
following me and didn't want to get involved," answered Stalin. Later,
in the police files, the report of the agents who had followed Ordzhonikidze was found. It described his entire journey, without one word
about his meeting with Stalin.[63]

(6) During the Revolution of 1905 Stalin organized a number of
"expropriations," that is, armed robberies. (The Bolsheviks considered
expropriations permissible in the context of a revolutionary situation.)
In some cases guards were killed. The legal penalty was very severe,
up to and including death. Stalin's participation was no secret to the
police. But when he was arrested early in 1908, he received an unusually light sentence: two years' exile in Solvychegodsk. Some historians feel that such lenience was not accidental.

For most procurators in the Stalinist period these stories would have
justified an order for the arrest of Joseph Dzhugashvili if he had not
been the head of the NKVD, the Party, and the state. But it is not
hard to see that all these "proofs" of Stalin's connections with the
tsarist secret police are based on questionable second- or even third-
hand reports. They have as little credibility as the accounts in the
foreign press. Why, for example, did Stalin order Sepp to be shot, but
not Beria and Kabulov? Who can vouch for the truthfulness of the
story of the old Bolshevik V———, who supposedly saw a high-ranking
gendarme in Stalin's apartment? Stalin made such monstrous false
charges against so many of his former comrades that the desire to pay
him back in kind could easily arise.

The coincidence between Stalin's pseudonym in 1912 and that
of some unidentified police spy also tells us nothing. Stalin had a
great variety of cover names. On the other hand, many other Bolsheviks could have had the cover name Vasilii. According to police reports, Stalin customarily used the pseudonyms Koba and Kavkazets.

T. Firsova's story about Stalin and Ordzhonikidze's trip is also
unconvincing. In fact, the police did have reports about their meeting,
which noted that Stalin met Sergo in Moscow and went with him to
St. Petersburg on April 9, 1912. A Colonel Zavarzin sent a telegram
to this effect to the head of the Petersburg secret police. Three experienced detectives were sent along to tail Stalin and Sergo. Sergo was
arrested in St. Petersburg on April 14, Stalin on April 22. It is possible
that this happened precisely because he slipped away from the train.

[63] Recounted by G. L. Mekhanik, who heard it from T. Firsova, who heard it from
Zinaida Gavrilovna Ordzhonikidze.

There was undoubtedly a special file on each Bolshevik leader in the central offices of the gendarmerie. But during the February Revolution a crowd of workers and soldiers broke into the Petrograd police archives, threw a lot of papers from cabinets and safes into the courtyard, and burned them. Many documents were thereby irretrievably lost. There is, it is true, a report to the effect that a principal archive dealing with the leaders of the RSDLP was stolen by the former Russian Ambassador to France, Maklakov, and taken abroad, and that he gave it to the Hoover Institution Library in the United States. The future will tell how much truth there is in this report.[64] In any case, we have at our disposal almost no essential police records relating to Stalin: protocols of his interrogations, denunciations of him, and so on.

The few such documents that have been unearthed in the archives have not confirmed the story of Stalin's connections with the tsarist secret police. Here, for example, are two letters that passed between the chiefs of the Moscow and the Vologda branches of the secret police in 1911:

Absolutely Secret
Personal

M.V.D. Chief of the Division
for the Preservation of Social
Safety and Order in Moscow
August 17, 1911
To: The Chief of the Vologda *Guberniia* Gendarme Administration

According to repeated and trustworthy information given to my Department by secret agents, at the present time an active and very serious member of the Russian Social Democratic Labor Party, bearing the pseudonym "Koba," is living in Vologda, where he is serving, or has already served, a term of administrative exile.

The above-named "Koba" has been in direct touch with the Party center abroad and has now been told to go abroad for the necessary instructions to fulfill the obligations of a traveling agent for the Central Committee.

The following address is used for communication with the above-named "Koba": Peter Alekseevich Chizhikov, Ishmematov's Store, Vologda; money for Koba's traveling expenses will be sent to this address.

Absolutely Secret
Chief of the Vologda *Guberniia* Gendarme Administration
To: The Chief of the Moscow Branch of the Secret Police
August 21, 1911

[64] *Ed.:* See Edward Ellis Smith, *The Young Stalin* (New York, 1967), p. vii, for confirmation by a man who searched this archive. In the main text Smith makes it seem that the archive conclusively proves Stalin's connection with the tsarist police. Smith's notes reveal something quite different: he found few documents relating to Stalin, and none of them asserts or even suggests that Stalin was an informer.

The nickname "Koba" indicated in your communication of August 17, No. 260990, belongs to the former political exile Joseph Vissarionov Dzhugashvili, who is temporarily living in Vologda. A copy of the report on him addressed to the Director of the Department of Police on March 14 of this year, No. 53, was at the same time forwarded to you by the Chief of the Tiflis *Guberniia* Gendarme Administration.

From the files of the Administration entrusted to me it appears that on February 27, 1909, Dzhugashvili arrived under guard in the place of exile designated for him, Sol'vychegodsk, whence, on July 24 of the same year, he disappeared. Arrested in Baku on March 24, 1910, he was taken back to Sol'vychegodsk, whence, on July 27, 1911, upon finishing his term of exile, he was released, and with a transit document arrived in Vologda, where in accordance with his petition, he was permitted to stay temporarily, for two months until September 19 of this year.

According to our agents' information, *Dzhugashvili* together with other exiles (Ivan Petrov *Petrov,* Ivan Mikhailov *Golubev,* Nikolai Matveev *Il'in,* Aleksandr Iankelev *Shur,* Irodion Isaakov *Khasimov,* Fedor Ignat'ev *Siaponovskii,* Mikhail Alekseev *Kalandatze,* Georgii Alekseev *Korostylev,* and Grigorii Ivanov *Zhavoronkov*), tried to organize a Social Democratic faction in Sol'vychegodsk, and held meetings at which papers were read and political questions were discussed. The goal of these meetings was to produce experienced propagandists. This information of our agents was forwarded by my predecessor to the *Raion* on May 17 of this year, No. 216. On his arrival in Vologda on July 19, Dzhugashvili moved into the house of Bobrova on Malo-Kozlenskaia Street, and from July 24 came under observation under the nickname "Kavkazets."

. . . Since Dzhugashvili will probably soon be going to St. Petersburg or Moscow to see representatives of organizations there, he will be accompanied by an observer on his departure from Vologda.

Taking into consideration the fact that Dzhugashvili is very careful and could therefore be lost by an observer, it would be better to make a search and arrest him now in Vologda. To this end, please inform me whether you have at your disposal information necessary to make a case against Dzhugashvili, and whether there are any objections on your part to a search of this person now.

We might add to the foregoing that it is impossible to count on favorable results from a search of him in Vologda, in view of the extremely conspiratorial nature of his actions.

Simultaneously with the search of Dzhugashvili all the people with whom he is in contact here will also be searched.

Certified signature:

COLONEL KONISSKII[65]

---

[65] Ts.G.I.A. [i.e., Central State Historical Archives] f. 102, ed. kh. $\frac{267}{1911 \text{ g.}}$ D.O. 1911.

It is hard to suppose that such letters would be exchanged concerning a provocateur. Thus we cannot accept the insistent story that Stalin had connections with the Tsarist secret police, that fear of exposure drove him to mass repression of Bolsheviks. Stalin did not serve the tsarist secret police; he served only himself and his insatiable ambition.

Nevertheless, even if we leave to future historians the final settlement of this question, we must note that Stalin was a typical provocateur, though in another sense of the word. In his struggle for power, provocation was his favorite weapon, and he used it with great skill. As early as the intraparty struggle of the twenties he inflated disagreements, set leaders against each other, encouraged enmity among them. Whatever is believed about Kirov's murder, it cannot be denied that Stalin used the murder for provocative ends, cleverly directing popular anger against the former opposition. And the "open" political trials of the thirties were beyond all doubt one of the most monstrous provocations in history.

In 1937 Stalin announced to a meeting of the Military Soviet of the USSR that he had received a denunciation of Bliukher signed by one of his deputies. Stalin added that he did not believe the denunciation. In fact he had not received it; he merely wanted Bliukher to quarrel with one of his colleagues, who was soon arrested with Bliukher's tacit consent.[66] Stalin often gave his agents and subordinates criminal orders—verbally, of course—and then punished them for carrying them out. And it was impossible to refer to Stalin during an investigation; if one did, one would have had to answer for slander as well as for everything else.

Under Stalin's influence, NKVD investigators used provocation as well as torture. Playing on the blind fanaticism and patriotism of citizens who were not too bright, they would ask for help in exposing dangerous "enemies of the people," and thus would obtain false depositions.[67] NKVD officials who became useless to Stalin were frequent victims of provocation. For example, an NKVD general was told to go at once to a certain border point in order to capture a dangerous spy who was supposed to be crossing there. When the general arrived, he was arrested and accused of trying to flee abroad. The postwar "Leningrad case" and the "doctors' case" were typical provocative actions organized by Stalin and some NKVD executives.[68]

Actions of this kind have caused Stalin to be compared not only to Ivan the Terrible and other tyrants but also to famous provocateurs. G. S. Pomerants, for example, compares Stalin to E. F. Azev, the

[66] Recounted by P. Iakir.
[67] E. S. Ginzburg tells of one such provocation in her *Journey into the Whirlwind* (New York, 1967). See the chapter "Pugachev Tower," pp. 180–88.
[68] *Ed.:* For these cases, see below, pp. 480–95.

leader of the fighting organization of the Social Revolutionary Party, who was at the same time an agent of the secret police.[69] M. P. Iakubovich makes the same comparison in his interesting notes on Stalin. "Why," Iakubovich asks,

> did Azev play with human lives, destroying people on both sides—his revolutionary comrades and his superiors in the police? I believe that such activity was above all his way to satisfy his love, his lust for power, in the manner available to him in those times. The power of life and death is the greatest power, of all its possible variations; to kill people is the sharpest and fullest satisfaction of this lust for power. Of course, if a power-hungry man is characterized by blood-thirsty cruelty as well, by a capacity for ruthlessness, by contempt for people and lack of faith in any ideas, then he has the capacity to play with ideas and juggle them at will, just as pragmatism requires.
>
> All these qualities were possessed in full by E. F. Azev and like-wise by J. V. Stalin. In the same cold blood, without any regret or pangs of conscience, Stalin sent his Party comrades to be shot, just as Azev sent them to the tsarist gallows. And the motives of both were the same—an unchecked, boundless thirst for power, which was satisfied most fully by the murders they committed. The only difference between them was that they lived in dissimilar historical contexts: Stalin realized his power through the *apparat* of the organs of state security subordinated to him, while Azev did so through the *apparat* of the tsarist courts and the tsarist police, or by the hands of the "fighting organization." . . . The psychological similarity between them is remarkably great. They are soul brothers.[70]

6

THUS WE HAVE COME to the conclusion that neither the intrigues of Stalin's aides nor his own morbid suspiciousness played the decisive role in the events of 1936–39, although it would be wrong to deny the significance of these factors altogether. What, then, were the basic motives of Stalin's crimes?

The first and most important was undoubtedly Stalin's *measureless ambition*. This incessant though carefully hidden lust for unlimited power appeared in Stalin much earlier than 1937. Even though he

[69] G. Pomerants, "Nravstvennyi oblik istoricheskoi lichnosti," an unpublished manuscript.
[70] M. P. Iakubovich, "Zapiski o Staline," unpublished manuscript. *Ed.:* Medvedev's four-page quotation from this manuscript has been greatly abridged here, for much of it tells the familiar story of Azev.

had great power, it was not enough—he wanted absolute power and unlimited submission to his will. The norms for Party life established by Lenin got in his way. He was constantly irritated by the need to consider the opinions and criticism of other leaders, among whom he was only the first among equals after Lenin's death. Although Stalin corrupted many old Party leaders before 1937, he was quite aware that these people would not become simple cogs in the state machine he wanted to create. These leaders felt that they too had taken part in the creation of the state and the Party and demanded their share of the leadership. But Stalin did not want to share power with any of his comrades.

Stalin did not usurp all power because he stopped trusting his aides, or because he developed a persecution mania and began to see traitors all around him. For a long time he consciously strove for unlimited personal power. As early as 1926, when Kirov was elected First Secretary of the Leningrad Party Committee, Stalin revealed himself at a dinner celebrating the event. The conversation turned to a favorite question of that period: how to govern the Party without Lenin? Everyone, of course, agreed that the Party should be governed by a collective. Stalin at first did not take part in the discussion, but then he got up and, walking around the table, said: "Don't forget we are living in Russia, the land of the tsars. The Russian people like to have one man standing at the head of the state. Of course, this man should carry out the will of the collective." It was characteristic of the time that no one present thought Stalin had himself in mind as this great chief of Russia.[71]

Stalin may have been serious in his argument that class struggle would intensify as the country moved toward socialism. Inclined to schematic thinking, to a simplified, mechanistic understanding of reality, Stalin was often deeply convinced that the schemes he created were uniquely correct. But he was certainly not sincere when he extended this argument beyond members of former exploiting classes to veterans of the Revolution and the basic cadres of the Party and state. Stalin spoke respectfully of some of his victims even after he had destroyed them. At a Politburo meeting, discussing the case of A. I. Egorov just before his arrest—he had been Chief of Staff and Deputy Commissar of Defense—Stalin spoke well of Egorov's predecessor, Tukhachevskii. Stalin noted Tukhachevskii's unquestioned military talent, his great sense of responsibility when given a job, and his striving to master the theory, technology, and practice of military affairs.[72] And after Uborevich had been shot, Stalin said to K. A.

[71] Recounted by Peter Chagin, who was present at the dinner. He was a leader of the Leningrad organization and a close friend of Kirov.
[72] Recounted by A. I. Todorskii.

Meretskov: "Train our troops the same way you trained them under Uborevich."[73]

Generally, though, Stalin referred to his victims with bitterness and hatred. He feared many of his colleagues and he feared conspiracies. Politburo members who met each other for tea or visited each other's homes could fall under suspicion. They too were under constant surveillance by the NKVD. But Stalin's behavior also reveals that he was worried about his power as usurper and tyrant, not about the first proletarian state in the world.

Stalin's destruction of the Party's old guard was a deliberate policy. He and the NKVD leadership planned to destroy Party, state, and military cadres, and this plan, to use A. Todorskii's expression, was not inferior to the mobilization plan of a great army. It was carefully thought out, richly supplied, and masterfully executed. It was a crime whose equal is hard to find in world history.

A leader's excessive ambition does not automatically lead to mass repression of his opponents and rivals. When considering the personal aspect of the repression in the thirties we must take into account not only the ambition but also the cruelty and viciousness of Stalin. We must also note the contradiction between Stalin's limitless ambition and his limited abilities. It was this very contradiction that drove Stalin into conflict not only with those he saw as his present or future opponents but also with many old Bolsheviks who were personally devoted to him, never said anything against him, and carried out all his orders. From his early years Stalin had an inferiority complex. Combined with ambition and vanity, it engendered spiteful envy. Without any serious or systematic education, knowing no foreign languages, he became in 1917 a member of a government that was called, even by its enemies, the best educated in Europe. Surrounded by many brilliant people, Stalin must have felt his inferiority as a political leader, a theorist, and an orator. Hence his envy toward every truly educated Party intellectual. He wanted not only unlimited power but also unlimited glory; no one must upstage him in the historical drama. Thus many people became his enemies not because they were opposed to the regime but because they performed great services for it.

Nero, fancying himself a great actor and poet, sometimes killed not only those who gave him too little applause, but also people who excelled him in versifying or declaiming. When he took part in competitions of singers or actors, he was always the victor, but that was not enough; he ordered that the statues of past winners be dragged into privies. Many of Stalin's actions amounted to the same thing. People who had done as much or more than he for the Revolution

[73] See *Komandarm Uborevich* (Moscow, 1964).

merited destruction by that very fact. And everywhere he put up monuments to himself—thousands upon thousands of factories and firms named for Stalin, and many cities: Stalinsk, Stalino, Stalinir, Stalingrad, Stalinbad, Stalinkan, Stalin, Stalinovarosh—more than can be counted. This again recalls Nero, who wanted to name Rome Neropolis.

Stalin was first elected to the Central Committee only in 1912, and at that time he did not belong to the nucleus of leaders grouped around Lenin. Stalin's role among the Transcaucasian Bolsheviks was also much more modest than later legends asserted. Lenin was only slightly acquainted with Stalin before the Revolution, despite the story which dates their "friendship" from their first meeting at the Tammerfors Conference in 1905. It was in 1913 that Lenin, having met Stalin once again and read his article on the national question, wrote to Gorky: "A wonderful Georgian has joined us and is writing a big article." Lenin's natural enthusiasm for people often led him into mistakes. In the same period he spoke very warmly of Malinovskii, who turned out to be a veteran agent of the tsarist police. In any case Lenin's acquaintance with Stalin in 1913 was short-lived. By November, 1915, Lenin was writing to Karpinskii from Bern: "Do me a big favor: find out (from Stepko or Mikha or someone) the last name of 'Koba.' (Joseph Dzh . . . ? We have forgotten.) "[74]

But when Stalin was encouraging the cult of his personality, he wanted praise for his entire biography. He and his cohorts shamelessly falsified Party history, twisting and suppressing many facts and producing a flood of books, articles, and pamphlets filled with distortions. People who knew Party history at first hand got in Stalin's way. So Stalin arranged deliberate provocations to remove these people, from life and—so he thought—from history as well. In 1935, for example, fulsome praise was manufactured for Beria's history of Bolshevik organizations in Transcaucasia. The real author was not Beria, who was incapable of anything creative, but a commissar of education, Bediia, and some other individuals. After the book appeared, Bediia was falsely accused and destroyed. In any case the book ascribed to Beria grossly distorted history. It asserted that Stalin had directed the second center of the Party's origin. The newspaper *Brdzola*, a sheet slightly larger than a leaflet that had appeared only four times, was put on the same level as Lenin's *Iskra*.[75] Beria credited Stalin with founding the famous underground press in Baku, although Stalin had

---

[74] *Sochineniia*, 4th edn., XLIII, p. 426. *Ed.:* Stepko was N. D. Kiknadze, Mikha was M. G. Tskhakaia—both Georgians. Cf. *ibid.*, p. 401, for a letter from Lenin to Zinoviev in July, 1915, asking: "Do you remember Koba's last name?" Evidently Zinoviev could not.

[75] *Ed.: Iskra* was the Russian newspaper, published abroad in 1900–1903, as the chief means of organizing the Russian Social Democratic Party. *Brdzola* ("The Struggle") was an underground Georgian newspaper whose four issues appeared in 1901–1902.

never been in Baku at the time. Such lies upset Party leaders, especially in Transcaucasia. Stalin and Beria destroyed them.

By destroying almost all the members of the Central Committee, Stalin created the preconditions for claiming that there were two chiefs of the October Revolution. The same motives explain—in part, of course—the repression of many Red Army leaders. All the victories of the Civil War were attributed to Stalin's military genius. This is not to deny Stalin's achievements in the Civil War. But his contributions to victory were no greater, and sometimes smaller, than those of Kuibyshev, Frunze, Ordzhonikidze, Sklianskii, Tukhachevskii, Gusev, Egorov, Iakir, Bliukher, and many others. And thousands of officers who fought in the Civil War knew this. Stalin decided to "correct" history by getting rid of these people.

From his first years of political activity, Stalin nourished a dream of the godlike chief. His first meeting with Lenin was therefore disappointing, as he confessed in 1924:

> Lenin had been drawn in my imagination as a giant, stately and imposing. How disenchanted I was to see a most ordinary man, below average height, in no way, literally in no way, different from ordinary mortals. . . .
>
> Usually a "great man" is expected to arrive late at a meeting, so that the members of the meeting should wait for his appearance with bated breath, should warn each other . . . "Shhh . . . quiet . . . he's coming." Such ceremony seemed to me not superfluous, because it was impressive and inspired respect. How disenchanted I was when I learned that Lenin had arrived at the meeting before the delegates and, hiding in some corner, was simply having a conversation, a very ordinary conversation with very ordinary delegates. I won't conceal the fact that this seemed to me at that time a kind of violation of a kind of necessary rule.[76]

In 1924 Stalin went on to praise Lenin's simplicity and accessibility. But when he became a "great man," he established other rules for himself and took cruel vengeance on those who disapproved.

Such were the basic motives, though of course not the only ones, that impelled Stalin to his crimes. Today most memoir writers stress not only his ambition, vanity, and cruelty, but also his coarseness, his lack of culture, of intellectuality. K. K. Ordzhonikidze tells the following incident:

> It is common knowledge that Stalin and Sergo were good friends. Since I was often at my brother Sergo's place, I got to know not only Stalin but also many eminent leaders of the Communist Party and our country, in the first place Dzerzhinskii, Voroshilov, and Mikoian. I especially remember Stalin's arrival in Tiflis in June,

[76] Stalin, *Sochineniia*, VI, p. 54.

1926. He came on the first of June and stayed in Tiflis more than a week. A. I. Mikoian arrived with him in Tiflis. Sergo then lived on Ganovskaia Street (now it is called Tabidze Street). Stalin and Mikoian stayed in Sergo's apartment. Then I got to know them well.

In connection with Stalin's arrival, leading Georgian and Caucasian officials gathered at Sergo's apartment. The table was set. We drank a lot of wine and sang drinking songs. Stalin poured me a tumbler of Georgian wine, which I tossed off at one draft. Then he poured me another tumblerful, which I also drank, and continued to sing along with everybody.

There was a moment of silence, and Stalin, taking advantage of it, began to sing in the Georgian language. It was an indecent song. He went on singing even though women were sitting at the table. Maria Platonovna Orakhelashvili did not need a translation, but Zinaida Gavrilovna [Sergo's wife], who did not know Georgian, asked Sergo to translate the words of the song into Russian. At first Sergo refused, but she kept insisting, seeing the embarrassment of many and the unusual reaction of those present. When Sergo whispered a few words of this obscene song to Zinaida Gavrilovna, she blushed from shame and embarrassment.

That Stalin was foul-mouthed is well known, but that incident graphically convinced me that he was so used to foul words that he even sang songs abounding in them, and what was most astonishing was that he was not at all inhibited by the presence of such highly moral women as Maria Platonovna Orakhelashvili and Zinaida Gavrilovna Ordzhonikidze.

On the day of Stalin's departure from Tiflis, there were guests at Sergo's again. There was abundant refreshment. Then the guests went from Sergo's to Mamiia Orakhelashvili's place. Mamiia Dmitrievich lived at that time not far from Sergo, on Paskevich Street (now it is called Philip Makharadze Street). Stalin did not want to go to Orakhelashvili's but Sergo talked him into it. Stalin was visibly convinced by words of Sergo that I still remember: "How can you do that! He's the head of our government—it will be awkward if you avoid him." At that time Mamiia Orakhelashvili was Chairman of the Council of Commissars of the Transcaucasian Republic.

Subsequent years would show that Stalin hated Orakhelashvili. Evidently he had come to dislike him long before and thus showed such reluctance to go to his house.

At the same time Stalin's great willpower was frequently noted. In 1939 F. F. Raskol'nikov wrote in his diary:

The fundamental psychological trait of Stalin, which gave him a decisive advantage, as the lion's strength makes him king of the jungle, is his unusual, superhuman strength of will. He always knows what he wants and, with unwavering, implacable methodicalness, gradually reaches his goal. "Inasmuch as power is in my

hands," he once said to me, "I am a gradualist." In the silence of
his office, in deep solitude, he carefully figures out a plan of action
and with fine calculation strikes sudden and true. Stalin's strength
of will suffocates, destroys the individuality of people who come
under his influence. He easily succeeded in "crushing" not only the
soft and weak-willed M. I. Kalinin but even such willful people as
L. M. Kaganovich. Stalin does not need advisers, he needs only
executors. Therefore he demands from his closest aides complete
submission, obedience, subjection—unprotesting, slavish discipline.
He does not like people who have their own opinion, and with his
usual nastiness drives them away.

He is poorly educated. . . . He lacks the realism that Lenin possessed and, to a lesser degree, Rykov. He is not farsighted. When he
undertakes some step, he is unable to weigh its consequences. He is
after-the-fact. He does not foresee events and does not guide the
spontaneous flow, as Lenin did, but drags at the tail of events,
swims with the current. Like all semi-intellectuals who have picked
up scraps of knowledge, Stalin hates the genuine cultured intelligentsia, Party and nonparty in equal measure. Stalin lacks the flex-
ibility of a man of state. He has the psychology of Zelim Khan, the
Caucasian robber, who greedily seized one-man rule.[77] Scorning
people, he considers himself complete master over their life and
death. A narrow sectarian, he proceeds from a preconceived
scheme. He is the same kind of schematist as N. I. Bukharin, with
this difference, that Bukharin was a theoretically educated man.
Stalin tries to force life into a ready-made framework. The more
life resists being forced into the narrow Procrustean bed, the more
forcefully he mangles and breaks it, chopping limbs off it. He
knows the laws of formal logic, and his conclusions logically follow
from his premises. But against the background of more outstanding
contemporaries, he has never shone intellectually. Instead he is
unusually tricky . . . [sic]. No one can compete with Stalin in the
art of tricking. At the same he is sneaky, treacherous, and vengeful.
"Friendship" is an empty word for him. He flung aside and sent to
execution such a close friend as Enukidze. In his home life Stalin
is a man with the requirements of an exile. He lives very simply and
modestly, because with the fanaticism of an ascetic he scorns the
good things of life: life's comforts, such as good food, simply do not
interest him. He does not even need friends.

Raskol'nikov knew Stalin well, and he drew a basically accurate
portrait of the man's psyche. But the portrait is not exhaustive. Of
course, Stalin was a strong-willed man, unwavering in attaining his
goals. His quiet firmness and taciturnity impressed many Bolsheviks,

[77] Here Raskol'nikov is mistaken. Zelim Khan was not a Caucasian robber. He was one
    of the active, though peculiar, participants in the national liberation struggle of
    the Caucasian peoples against tsarism.

won him the reputation of an unflinching fighter, even gave him a certain attraction in the eyes of many Party members. But his strong will is not a sufficient explanation of his ascendancy. An assassin who shoots from ambush hardly needs a stronger will than his victim. An honorable man abstains from crimes not because he lacks a strong character; his character is simply directed towards other goals. Too often we call a man strong who violates all the accepted norms of human relations and all the rules of honorable struggle; the more he flouts these rules, the stronger and more resolute he seems to some people. In fact, most crimes evince not strength of will, only weakness of moral principles.

Stalin was in his way a strong man. But he did not have the super-human strength of will that some of his contemporaries attributed to him. He simply lacked firm moral principles and Communist convictions; he never loved or respected people, never tried to serve them, never was a true Communist. And he never recognized any rules of honorable political struggle. Taking advantage of his superior position in the Party, striking from ambush, he could break and destroy a great many people. But we do not know how he would have behaved if *he* had been tortured in the cellars of the NKVD. What would have happened to his superhuman will and firmness? His victims perished not because their will power was weaker than Stalin's. The weakness was in the guarantees and barriers that should have been set up in our Party and state against the rise of leaders like Stalin.

Raskol'nikov is also inadequate on Stalin's cunning. Stalin was not simply crafty; he was a man of unusual hypocrisy. He achieved a great deal by his ability to put on any mask. He was also extraordinarily cruel, even to those closest to him. One of the first victims was his wife, Nadezhda Allilueva, a charming and honorable woman, who committed suicide in 1932. Zinaida Ordzhonikidze used to tell her friends that she always found it unpleasant to visit Stalin, who liked to make fun of his "friends." His personal secretary Poskrebyshev was a frequent butt. One New Year's Eve Stalin rolled pieces of paper into little tubes and put them on Poskrebyshev's fingers. Then he lit them in place of New Year's candles. Poskrebyshev writhed in pain but did not dare take them off.

Yet Stalin could also be the most charming host, even tender, offering his guests compliments, serving them a Caucasian dish with his own hands or bringing them roses from the garden. (We may note, only as a chance coincidence, that Hitler also liked to make gifts of flowers and to smell roses.) Stalin played this role especially with foreign guests, which misled many of them. We have already cited Lion Feuchtwanger's enraptured comments on Stalin. H. G. Wells also failed to understand Stalin, who received him in 1934.

I confess that I approached Stalin with a certain amount of suspicion and prejudice. A picture had been built up in my mind of a very reserved and self-centred fanatic, a despot without vices, a jealous monopolizer of power. I had been inclined to take the part of Trotsky against him. . . . All such shadowy undertow, all suspicion of hidden emotional tensions, ceased for ever, after I had talked to him for a few minutes. . . . I have never met a man more candid, fair and honest, and to these qualities it is, and to nothing occult and sinister, that he owes his tremendous undisputed ascendancy in Russia. I had thought before I saw him that he might be where he was because men were afraid of him, but I realize that he owes his position to the fact that no one is afraid of him and everybody trusts him. The Russians are a people at once childish and subtle, and they have a justifiable fear of subtlety in themselves and others. Stalin is an exceptionally unsubtle Georgian. His unaffected orthodoxy is an assurance to his associates that whatever he does would be done without fundamental complications and in the best possible spirit. They had been fascinated by Lenin, and they feared new departures from his talismanic directions.[78]

This is obviously a portrait of Wells rather than Stalin.

Many Soviet politicians and cultural figures also succumbed to Stalin's favors, especially the younger ones who rose during and after the war. A marshal, for example, resting at his dacha in 1947, was invited by phone to dinner with "the boss." The dinner was quite relaxed, with Stalin often rising and walking about the room. At one point he went up to the marshal and asked: "I heard recently that you were in confinement?" "Yes, Comrade Stalin," was the reply. "I was in confinement. But, as you see, they figured out my case and let me go. But how many good and remarkable people perished there," the marshal unexpectedly concluded.

"Yes," said Stalin slowly. "We have a lot of good, remarkable people." He turned quickly and went out into the garden. Everyone at the table fell into a frightened silence. "What did you say to Stalin?" Malenkov whispered indignantly. "Why?" A few minutes later Stalin came back, carrying roses. He gave one bouquet to the marshal, another to his wife. The marshal, who had been preparing himself for the worst, was overcome, and never again reminded Stalin of his fallen comrades.[79]

For people he wanted to impress, Stalin sometimes put on elaborate acts. After the war, for example, when he was receiving an admiral in his office, he suddenly called Poskrebyshev, who put on his desk a pile of books on linguistics, and running down a list, which included prerevolutionary works, said that he had been unable to get to some

[78] H. G. Wells, *Experiment in Autobiography* (New York, 1934), pp. 684–89.
[79] *Ed.:* Medvedev does not cite the source of this reminiscence.

of them as yet. "What doesn't Stalin study!" thought the admiral.

In 1935, at a banquet for the graduates of the military academies, Stalin proposed a toast to Bukharin. "Let us drink, comrades, to Nikolai Ivanovich Bukharin. We all know and love him, and whoever remembers the past—get out of my sight!" Another typical example of this hypocrisy was recalled by Kosarev's widow, at the meeting dedicated to his memory.

> When Papanin's group[80] returned to Moscow in the summer of 1938, there was a reception and a big banquet in the Kremlin. Molotov proposed a toast to those present, including Kosarev. Everyone who was toasted went up to Stalin to clink glasses. Sasha also went up. Stalin not only clinked his glass but embraced and kissed him. Returning to his seat, Sasha, pale and agitated, said to me: "Let's go home." When we had left, I asked him why he was so upset. He replied: "When Stalin kissed me, he said in my ear, 'If you're a traitor, I'll kill you.'" Some months later Sasha was in fact killed, although he had not acted against Stalin.[81]

While it is a mistake to consider Stalin a superman of invincible will, it is also wrong to regard him simply as an ambitious, sadistic hypocrite who gained control of the Party by intrigues and crimes. Both as a person and as a leader, Stalin was a much more complex and contradictory figure. We must face the question whether he was guided by Marxist principles, as the Chinese leaders and some Soviet historians and officials still insist.

In fact Stalin was not a Marxist, though he wrote such things as *Marxism and the Nationality Question* and *The Foundations of Leninism*. The schematism evident in all his published works is alien to Marxism-Leninism. If Lenin could write that it was highly doubtful whether Bukharin's theoretical views were entirely Marxist, Stalin's works deserve such an appraisal even more. Of course, Stalin often wrote and spoke like a Marxist. He could not ignore the Party's ideology or avoid the use of Marxist terminology. But he was never a Marxist in essence, especially during his last twenty-five years. For Marxism represents not only a certain system of concepts; it is also a system of convictions and moral principles, and devotion to the achievement of happiness for all working people is one of the fundamental principles. Those moral qualities are precisely what Stalin lacked. At the outset his political views were formed under the influence of Marx and Lenin, but they did not grow into convictions, into a system of Communist moral principles. Thus, when he came to

---

[80] *Ed.:* I. D. Papanin directed an Arctic expedition, which determined ocean currents by drifting on a floe for an extended period.

[81] See the stenographic report of the meeting in the Museum of the Revolution on the sixtieth anniversary of A. V. Kosarev, Nov. 21, 1963, p. 49.

power, he easily degenerated and quickly lost even the superficial traits of a Marxist and a proletarian revolutionary. We say "superficial" because Stalin can hardly be considered a revolutionary in essence. He was only a fellow traveler [*poputchik*] of revolution.

There are many historical examples of unstable and dishonorable people who join a revolutionary movement and later degenerate into tyrants. Joseph Fouché, for example, the all-powerful Minister of Police in Napoleon's government and in the Bourbon restoration, one of the richest men in France, began as one of the most radical Jacobins. When he was proconsul of a province he threatened moderates, confiscated the property of the rich, and attacked the Church. In Lyons he had hundreds of people shot, on accusations of being enemies of the people. In 1794 he was elected president of the Jacobin Club. But ten years later the same Fouché hunted down Jacobins, and ten years after that he pursued Bonapartists. Stalin referred to Fouché with respect: "There was a man for you. He outwitted everyone, made them all look like fools." Mussolini is another case in point. He began as a member of the most radical wing of the Italian Socialist Party and wound up as a fascist dictator.

In his novel *Devils* (also known as *The Possessed*), Dostoevsky gives a distorted picture of the Russian revolutionary movement in the second half of the nineteenth century, but some of the types he portrays deserve scrutiny. The Russian revolutionary movement included not only the heroic types pictured in Chernyshevsky's novel *What Is To Be Done?* but also people like Dostoevsky's Liputin, a petty provincial official, envious, a coarse despot, a miser and a usurer; and like his Verkhovenskii, a cheat, scoundrel, and murderer, who wanted to unite his few followers not by common ideals but by joint responsibility for the crimes they committed. That such "socialists" did exist is proved by the activity of Nechaev in the late 1860's. He sincerely believed that he was a socialist, which he understood as follows:

> To become a good socialist, one must reject all tender, soft feelings of kinship, friendship, love, gratitude, and even honor itself. . . . He is not a revolutionary who pities anything in this world. . . . A revolutionary knows only one science—the science of destruction and extermination. He lives in the world with this sole aim. To leave not one stone on another, as many ruins as possible, the extinction of most of the revolutionaries—that is the perspective. Poison, the knife, the noose—the Revolution consecrates everything.

Blind obedience to the chief, a system of mutual spying and involuted deception of all members of the organization—such were Nechaev's methods for the triumph of socialism. He murdered Ivanov, a student in the Agricultural Academy, accusing him of betrayal, although Ivanov had only opposed Nechaev's arbitrary ways. In an interesting article on Dostoevsky,[82] Iu. Kariakin has drawn an analogy between Stalin and Nechaev that has some validity. Kariakin has also informed the author of a suggestive fact: Nechaev's archive, thought to be lost, was returned to its place after 1953, "from Stalin's office."

In 1917–18 Maxim Gorky often wrote in the semi-Menshevik paper *Novaia zhizn'*, which was opposed to the October Revolution. But some of his remarks were quite penetrating. He distinguished, for example, two types of revolutionary: the revolutionary for all time and the revolutionary for this day. The first type is eternally Promethean, dissatisfied in any social system, because he believes humanity can go on creating the better out of the good forever. The second type has a keen feeling for the wrongs of contemporary society and accepts current revolutionary ideas, but

> in the whole structure of his feelings he remains a conservative. He presents the sorry, often tragicomic spectacle of a being who seems to have been put on earth only to take the cultural, humanitarian, all-human content of revolutionary ideas and to distort and degrade them, to make them ridiculous, repulsive, and stupid.
>
> He feels offended above all for himself, for the fact that he is not talented, not strong, that he has been insulted, even for the fact that he has been in jail. . . . He thinks he is completely emancipated, but inside he is chained by the heavy conservatism of zoological instincts, fathered by a thick mesh of petty grudges, which he has no power to rise above. The habits of his thought drive him to seek in life and in man above all the negative phenomena; in the depths of his soul he is full of contempt for man, on whose behalf he suffered once or a hundred times, but who has himself suffered too much to notice or appreciate the torment of another. . . . He has toward people the attitude that an untalented scientist has toward the dogs and frogs picked for cruel scientific experiments, with the difference that the untalented scientist, though uselessly tormenting the animals, does it in the interests of man, while the revolutionary for this day is not constantly sincere in his experiments on people.
>
> People for him are material: more suitable the less exalted it is. . . . He is a cold fanatic, an ascetic; he emasculates the creative force of the revolutionary idea.[83]

Gorky's definition of a revolutionary for this day, astonishing in its pointed precision, is completely applicable to Stalin.[84] It is strange

---

[82] See *Problemy mira i sotsializma,* 1963, No. 5. An English translation is in *World Marxist Review,* 1963, No. 5.

[83] *Ed.:* See Gorky, *Untimely Thoughts* (New York, 1968), pp. 229–33, for the complete essay. The translation given here is by Taylor and Joravsky.

[84] The degeneration of a revolutionary socialist into a tyrant has been treated in science fiction, notably in H. G. Wells, *The Holy Terror* (London, 1939), which was obviously influenced by contemporaneous events in the Soviet Union. See Iu. Kagarlitskii, *Gerbert Uells; ocherk zhizni i tvorchestvo* (Moscow, 1963), pp. 263–65.

that Gorky himself did not notice this; in the thirties he was very close to Stalin.

Stalin's degeneration both as a man and a statesman, which began of course long before 1934, explains many of his actions in the late 1930's. He never sought to restore capitalism. Nevertheless, his criminal actions did great harm to the cause of socialism. He almost completely liquidated the socialist democracy that was one of the main achievements of the October Revolution. By relying primarily on the punitive organs, to which he gave unlimited authority, he markedly undermined the leading role of the Party. He also caused serious damage to the alliance of workers and peasants.

Although Stalin was extremely destructive, he was often obliged to adapt himself to socialist society. He was not only required to take correct Marxist positions in words; on occasion he had to act like a Marxist. Though he devastated the Soviet intelligentsia, he could not do without them. Therefore he could not help advancing, to some degree, the cultural revolution, the formation of a new proletarian intelligentsia. Though his repression in the Red Army and the Comintern was a great service to fascism, he opposed fascism after Germany's attack on the Soviet Union, and thereby helped the worldwide fight against it. Exaggerating his services to the people and the Party, Stalin thought to establish the cult of his personality to last for ages. He did not foresee that within ten years after his death nearly all his monuments would be destroyed along with many—though by no means all—remnants of his cult.

People are drawn to socialism for various reasons. Lenin was prompted by a conviction that Marx and Engels were right and by his ardent love for the toilers and the oppressed of the world. "When I stood at Vladimir Il'ich's grave," said Krupskaia at the memorial meeting of the Congress of Soviets,

> I thought over his entire life and this is what I want to tell you. His heart beat with ardent love for all toilers, for all the oppressed. He never said this himself, nor would I, probably, at another less solemn moment. . . . This was his heritage from the heroic revolutionary movement of Russia. . . . He never approached Marx as a bookworm. He approached Marx as a man seeking answers to questions which tormented him.[85]

Lunacharskii also stressed Lenin's combination of moral and intellectual greatness.[86] And Clara Zetkin noted the complete absence in Lenin of any effort to lord it over his comrades: "Lenin behaved as

[85] N. K. Krupskaia, *O Lenine* (Moscow, 1960), p. 13.
[86] See A. V. Lunacharskii, *Lenin* (Leningrad, 1924).

an equal among equals, with whom he was joined by every fiber of his being."[87]

Stalin treated the Party cadres quite differently. It was not love for suffering humanity, for the working class, that brought Stalin to the Revolution, but his thirst for power, his vanity, his desire to rise above people and subject them to his will. The son of a shoemaker and a peasant woman—even today in Georgia there are rumors that attempt to give Stalin higher status, as the illegitimate son of some aristocrat or high-placed clergyman—he clearly saw the impossibility of "making a career" in the Russian Empire. That, at bottom, is what drove Stalin into the ranks of the revolutionaries. When he joined the most radical wing of the revolutionary movement, he already believed in his special mission. The son of a famous Bolshevik tells this revealing episode. In 1912, when he was only nine, a Caucasian came to his parents' apartment in Moscow. After a little talk his father went out, leaving the Caucasian, who was pleased by the boy's conversation. Four hours later the doorbell rang. The boy jumped up but the man stopped him. "Wait, wait," he said, taking him by the shoulder and hitting him on the check as hard as he could. "Don't cry," the Caucasian said, "don't cry, little boy. Remember, today Stalin talked to you." When the boy told his parents about their guest's strange behavior, they were outraged and baffled, until, later on, they heard of a custom in many mountain villages of Georgia: If a prince came to a peasant's hut, the peasant would call in his son and hit him hard on the cheek, saying, "Remember that today Prince So-and-so visited our house."[88]

For Stalin, the Party was always just an instrument, a means of reaching his own goals. To be sure, the propagandists of his cult pictured him as a man who constantly thought of the people's needs, as a simple, accessible, sensitive man. In reality, Stalin was inaccessible to rank-and-file workers; he met no ordinary people and felt no need to do so. He did not visit the factories and farms where socialism was being built. He was indifferent to the fate of individual people; for him they were merely cogs in the enormous, soulless state mechanism. Thus the ideas of socialism lost the meaning given them by Marx, Engels, and Lenin; they were only arid dogma for Stalin. His socialism took on many features of Nechaev's. "What a splendid model of barrack communism!" Marx exclaimed about Nechaev's *Bases of the Future Social Structure,* where people must "produce as much as possible and use as little as possible," and where all personal relations are strictly regimented.[89]

---

[87] Klara Tsetkin, *Vospominaniia o Lenine* (Moscow, 1955), pp. 9–10. Cf. the comments of *Novyi mir,* 1963, No. 7, p. 5.

[88] Recounted by M. I. Romm, a friend of the one who got slapped.

[89] Marx and Engels, *Sochineniia,* 2nd edn., XVIII, pp. 414–15.

Believing in his uniqueness and infallibility, Stalin lost his sense of reality. He evidently assumed that his crimes would seem insignificant in comparison with the magnificence of his historical deeds, the unavoidable price of progress. In fact no enemies could have done more harm to the struggle for socialism and communism.

X

Other Causes of Mass Repression

1

BESIDES DESTROYING the old Leninist guard, most of whom were well known to Stalin, the repression of 1936–38 struck millions of people who were unknown to him and were no serious threat to his power. Only the intertwining of many causes and processes can explain this mass repression. I shall try to unravel some of them.

The most widely used formula during Stalin's lifetime, to help justify the unjustifiable, was the old Russian saying "When you chop wood, chips fly." In other words, there really was a far-reaching counterrevolutionary organization, based on the former oppositions, with many "degenerated" officials in it. And the further implication is that some excesses and distortions were unavoidable in the decisive assault on this counterrevolutionary organization.

Ezhov, for example, in a speech to NKVD executives, declared that the Soviet Union was going through a dangerous period, that a war with fascism was imminent, and therefore the NKVD had to destroy all the nests of fascists in the country. "Of course," Ezhov said,

> there will be some innocent victims in this fight against fascist agents. We are launching a major attack on the enemy; let there be no resentment if we bump someone with an elbow. Better that ten innocent people should suffer than one spy get away. When you chop wood, chips fly.[1]

There is a certain weird sense in this argument. As we have seen, the destruction of every Party leader was accompanied by the arrest of hundreds, even thousands, of people directly or indirectly connected

[1] Recounted by the old Bolshevik E. P. Frolov.

with him. Stalin spread the story of a vast fascist underground, a fifth column permeating every pore of Soviet society. By means of terrible tortures, arrested people were obliged not only to confess their own guilt but also to reveal their "accomplices" and "confederates." In some NKVD agencies there were even norms: if the second secretary of an *oblast* committee had to name at least twenty "confederates," then the first secretary had to implicate at least forty.

Some of those arrested conceived a peculiar theory, which they tried to pass on to other prisoners. If, they argued, we confess to any and every imaginary crime, and name hundreds of innocent people as our "confederates," more and more innocent people will be arrested, until the Party wakes up to the monstrous stupidity of the whole process and restrains the NKVD. Evgeniia Ginzburg tells how one of Bukharin's students, the biologist Slepkov, named 150 people as his "confederates" in Kazan alone. "You must disarm yourselves before the Party!" he would shout at the confrontation with the people who had been arrested because of him, although none of them had ever armed themselves in the first place.[2] General Gorbatov tells of a fellow prisoner who denounced more than three hundred innocent people.[3] And S. O. Gazarian writes of a prisoner who on his own initiative denounced all the Party officials and even all the ordinary Communists he knew in his *raion*. He too believed that the more people arrested, the sooner the absurdity of his depositions would come to light. But his expectations were disappointed. A court accepted his depositions and sentenced him to be shot. The people he denounced were also severely punished.

"In the Minsk central prison at the end of 1937, . . . there were two conflicting points of view," writes Ia. I. Drobinskii in his memoirs.

> The first was: "Write more, fulfill and overfulfill the investigator's demands. The repressions are a provocation, a festering boil; the faster it grows, the sooner it will burst. To make it grow, drag in more people. Every action has an equal and opposite reaction." . . .
> The other point of view was to fight, to make no compromises. Do not bear false witness against yourself or against others. Endure all tortures, torment, hunger; if you have not endured, if you have slipped, rise again, tear into them, even if they rip your skin off; to your last ounce of strength, fight, fight, fight.

The same arguments went on in other prisons. N. K. Iliukhov tells how he met Sokol'nikov, who urged him not only to sign the interrogation records but to think up denunciations against all those who were helping Stalin—against Postyshev, against the Party *apparatchiki,* against NKVD officials. "Drag down with you as many bad people

[2] E. S. Ginzburg, *Journey into the Whirlwind* (New York, 1967), pp. 135–36.
[3] A. V. Gorbatov, *Years Off My Life* (New York, 1965), p. 127.

as you can, protect good ones." Obviously such a position was not correct or moral; it suited Stalin's plans completely. It enabled him to destroy the basic Party cadres as well as former oppositionists. The huge scale of the repression did not frighten Stalin. Moreover, voluntary cooperation with the NKVD demoralized the prisoners, deprived them of unity in the face of lawlessness. However, even without such voluntary "testimony," the NKVD often arrested many colleagues, friends, even chance acquaintances of the "enemies of the people," for "prophylactic" purposes. Thus, almost every arrest started a series of new arrests, and the chain reaction was hard to stop.

Another reason the repression of 1936–38 became so massive was the practice of arresting relatives of "enemies," especially wives, grown children, and often brothers, sisters, and parents. The family of Tukhachevskii, for example, was cruelly ravaged: his wife and brother died in prison, his daughter and four sisters were arrested. Even many women rumored to be close to Tukhachevskii were arrested. Eight members of Enukidze's family perished, and the same fate struck hundreds of thousands of completely innocent people.

"In May of 1938, seven months after Sasha, they took me," recalls Kaledina-Shver.

> They took Sasha. . . . He died in the NKVD's child reception [*detpriemnik*]. . . . In our prison cell there were forty or fifty *"ChSIR"*—"members of families of traitors to the native land." Gritting our teeth, we endured mockery and humiliation. We believed in a happy ending, we were waiting for it. But three months went by, and we were taken away. Where, why—no one knew. . . . For two weeks we were transported in cattle cars. . . . A long, long train, filled only with women. . . . Once the train stopped in a field. An officer climbed into the car, opened a briefcase, and started to take out one folder after another, reading off names and terms. . . . "For what?"—this question burned in my head, in my soul. . . . "Eight years! . . . Five! . . . Eight! . . . Eight! Five!" I heard my name: "Kaledina-Shver—eight years!"
>
> Someone asked: "Why do some get eight, others five? We all have the same fault: we're the wives of our husbands—Communists! And many of us are Communists ourselves."
>
> The officer was slow in answering, then smiled and said: "Loved wives got eight years, and unloved five!" He made some other jokes too, that defender of despotic caprice! They took us to Akmolinsk. Thirty kilometers away, in Point 26, behind barbed wire, barracks for three to four hundred people. Up to eight thousand women were jammed into the camp. We called it *ALZHIR* [i.e., Algiers, and also an acronym for] Akmolinsk Camp for Wives of Traitors to the Native Land.[4]

[4] Boris D'iakov, *Povest' o perezhitom* (Moscow, 1966), pp. 180–81.

According to another former inmate, M. E. Lebedeva, the same camp
held the wives of Krestinskii, Dybenko, Khitarov, Pilnyak, Kudriav-
tsev, and Sulimov. And there were many such camps in all the remote
regions of our country—in Kolyma, for example, where tens of thousands of women did construction and agricultural labor.

This shocking lawlessness is not excused by the law, adopted a
few years before the mass repression, providing that all members of
traitors' families be exiled to remote regions. Both in letter and in
spirit that law applied to the families of people who were beyond the
reach of the courts because they had fled abroad. Even in such cases
it was unjust to punish not the traitor himself but his relatives, most
of whom were quite innocent. But in 1936–37, and frequently in later
years too, this savage law was unjustly extended to "enemies of the
people" who had made no attempt to flee. According to A. I. Todorskii,
in 1937, the year of the bloodiest terror, it was a law, after the head
of a family had been sentenced, to arrest his wife and grown-up children, and give the wife eight years in the camps, the children five.
Some minor children of "enemies" were arrested and even shot. In
Georgia, S. O. Gazarian informs us, the son of Nestor Lakoba, age
fourteen, and three of his schoolmates were killed on Beria's orders.
The sons of Ikram, of Tomskii, of Iakir, and the daughter of Antonov-
Ovseenko were arrested at age fourteen or fifteen. Many children
of "enemies" were arrested and exiled in the 1940's. In 1944, for
example, the children of Bubnov and Lominadze were arrested, and in
1949 there was a big campaign for such arrests in Leningrad and
Moscow. The victims included young students from the families of the
writer Artem Veselyi, of Army Commander Bazilevich, of Shliapnikov,
the former leader of the "workers' opposition," of Peter Smorodin,
and many others.

                                    2

HISTORY SHOWS that the establishment of a personal dictatorship is
usually accompanied by mass repression; not only the immediate
entourage of the new dictator but also people quite remote from him
are struck down. Usually this happens because the new regime defines
many new things as political crimes. A host of new prohibitions and
taboos arise, and people are trained to them not only by ideological
pummeling but also by the executioner.[5]

According to Soviet law, thoughts, beliefs, or intentions that do
not result in concrete action cannot be regarded as crimes. Marx con-

[5] *Ed.:* At this point Medvedev quotes Camille Desmoulins at great length, describing
  many forms of behavior that provoke the suspicion of newly established tyrants.
  See Gérard Walter, *La révolution française* (Paris, 1948), pp. 331–34.

sidered this a basic rule of any democratic state. Stalin and the NKVD cast it aside. Not actions, not even intentions, but opinions became the basis for prosecution. At first this antidemocratic doctrine was an ex post facto justification of punishments already carried out, but then it became the legal basis for mass repression. Throughout Stalin's rule, the label "state and political criminal" was applied not only to a person who opposed the Soviet regime and socialism, who undertook some action against the dictatorship of the proletariat, but also to many persons who simply had different opinions, who did not share the prevailing ideology but at the same time were completely loyal to the Soviet regime.

The existence of people with different political convictions did not represent any threat to the dictatorship of the proletariat. On the contrary, the history of mankind shows that the persecution of people for their beliefs does not attain its goal; usually it is self-defeating. But that is not the only issue. As centralization and bureaucracy increased, not only nonsocialist beliefs but disapproval of particular measures of the Soviet state or disagreement with some aspects of the Party line marked people for prosecution as "enemies." And because of the large number of incorrect decisions during the years of the cult, the number of people who became "enemies" this way was considerable. Moreover, after 1934–35 the label "state and political criminal" was applied to any person, however devoted to the idea of socialism, who talked against Stalin personally, expressed disapproval of his actions, or spoke or acted in a way that could be interpreted even indirectly as belittling Stalin. In subsequent years this protection of the chief's prestige assumed monstrous forms. It was enough to tell an anecdote about Stalin, to damage a picture of him accidentally,[6] or to express doubt about one of his pronouncements on theory for a person to become an "enemy of the people." In Germany the Academy of Law declared love for the Führer to be a legal concept and therefore dislike of the Führer to be a crime. In the USSR, love of Stalin became obligatory for all Soviet people, and dislike of him or even the slightest criticism of his activities was a crime. In the course of time such "crimes" were considered even more serious than opposition to socialism and the Soviet regime.

In the first years of the Soviet regime, some leaders expounded the false thesis that the "subjective" and "objective" aspects of a person's behavior were identical. But the real triumph of this thesis occurred in the years of the cult. It was declared unimportant whether a person was subjectively devoted to the Soviet regime. If, in the opinion of the leadership, that person hurt the proletarian dictatorship and helped

---

[6] In 1922, when Lenin heard that a woman had been arrested in Novgorod for treating his picture disrespectfully, he sent a telegram demanding her immediate release.

the country's enemies by some theoretical or practical mistake, then he had to be considered an enemy of the Soviet people, regardless of his subjective motives. "Conciliators," people who themselves committed no mistakes but called for leniency toward those who were being criticized and repressed, were also cruelly persecuted.

3

BY CREATING a mass psychosis about enemies, Stalin was able to destroy inconvenient people. Many of his aides took the same advantage of the same situation, advancing their careers by removing people they disliked. As Stalin drew these careerists into his crimes, he had to give them carte blanche to deal with people they found inconvenient. And they took full advantage. In Georgia, for example, thousands of people Beria and his gang found objectionable were destroyed. In Azerbaijan more than ten thousand people were shot on the charge of attempting to murder Bagirov. (Both in Georgia and in Azerbaijan the mass repression of 1937–38 was probably worse than in the other republics, which makes it all the more strange that today the most stubborn attempts to restore the cult of Stalin are being made in those republics.)

It is axiomatic that the system of personal dictatorship could not be limited to the higher organs of power. Thousands of people exercised extraordinary power during the years of the cult. New commissars, directors of major enterprises, *obkom* and *raikom* secretaries, state security officials, heads of "special departments," and so on, got the right to decide the fate of Soviet citizens. Each of them was almost absolute master of his domain, and many used their power to get rid of people they did not like. Cliques of unprincipled careerists took shape, dedicated to the preservation of their power. Imitating Stalin, they set up little cults of their own personalities, turning any criticism into a state crime. Thus a basis was created for ceaseless mass repression.

In this connection, the roles of Molotov, Malenkov, Kaganovich, Voroshilov, and some other close aides of Stalin must be stressed. The whole truth was not told at the XXth Party Congress, where the impression was given that only Stalin, Ezhov, and Beria were responsible for the repression of the thirties. Moreover, right after the Congress the word went out that the other Politburo members took no part in the mass lawlessness but tried as much as possible to restrain Stalin. This story was reflected in the Central Committee Resolution of June 30, 1956, "Overcoming the Cult of Personality and its Consequences." Written jointly by Molotov, Malenkov, Kaganovich, and

Voroshilov, who were still members of the Politburo (or Presidium), this resolution declared that the basic Leninist nucleus of the Central Committee was preserved even under Stalin, and tried to restrain him although it was not able to remove him.

It would be ridiculous to repeat this story today. The speeches at the XXIInd Congress contained a multitude of facts irrefutably proving that Molotov, Kaganovich, Malenkov, and Voroshilov not only did not restrain Stalin but actively helped his lawlessness. A. N. Shelepin, for example, told the Congress of documents showing that Molotov and Kaganovich together with Stalin sanctioned the arrest and shooting of many outstanding leaders. When Iakir wrote to Stalin protesting his innocence, Stalin inscribed the letter: "A scoundrel and a prostitute," to which Voroshilov added: "A completely precise description." Molotov signed his name underneath, and Kaganovich added: "For this traitor, bastard [*svoloch'*], and ———— [an obscene word] [insertion by R. M.] there is only one punishment—execution."

These three, and also Malenkov, Shkiriatov, Mekhlis, Poskrebyshev, and several other close aides of Stalin, often took the initiative in the destruction of Party cadres. Molotov's role was especially prominent and venomous. Early in his career he was noted for his inclination to intrigue, demagogy, and bureaucratic methods. In July, 1920, the Nizhnii Novgorod *guberniia* Party conference adopted a resolution censuring Molotov, then chairman of the *guberniia* executive committee, because he had indulged in rumormongering and character assassination in an effort to block the election of people he disliked to the committee.[7] In 1922, when Molotov was the CC secretary responsible for assignment and registration in the Central Committee *apparat,* Lenin wrote him a letter demanding immediate action to improve his work. "Otherwise," Lenin wrote,

> we ourselves ("in struggle with bureaucracy") are producing the most stupid and shameful bureaucracy right under our own noses.
>
> The Central Committee's power is enormous. The possibilities are gigantic. We assign 200,000–400,000 Party officials, and through them thousands and thousands of nonparty people.
>
> And this gigantic Communist process is completely ruined by obtuse bureaucracy.[8]

When Molotov became Chairman of the Council of People's Commissars at the beginning of the thirties, he quickly revealed himself in this high post as the same heartless and obtuse bureaucrat. He was a worthy adjutant to Stalin in his crimes. The fate of old Bolshevik G. I. Lomov, which was discussed above, is typical. Stalin, receiving a denunciation of Lomov, wrote on it: "Comrade Molotov. What will

[7] See the document quoted in *Stenograficheskii otchet XXII s'ezda,* pp. 351–52.
[8] *Sochineniia,* 4th edn., XLV, p. 397.

it be?" Molotov noted: "For immediate arrest of that bastard Lomov. V. Molotov." Within a few days Lomov was arrested, charged with belonging to a rightist organization, and shot.[9] Molotov instigated the arrest of the First Secretary of the Ural *obkom,* I. D. Kabakov, the Chairman of the Far Eastern *krai* Executive Committee, Krutov, and the Commissar of Light Industry, K. V. Ukhanov.[10] M. A. Suslov notes that Molotov often tried to be a "better Catholic than the Pope." For example, on a document sanctioning the imprisonment of a large group of wives of repressed officials, Molotov wrote next to one name: "VMN," i.e., the supreme penalty. Sh. Ol'gin tells how Motolov began to persecute Ordzhonikidze long before his suicide. Molotov refused to fulfill many requests of the Commissariat of Heavy Industry, which Ordzhonikidze headed. Fearing that this personal enmity would hurt the Soviet economy, Ordzhonikidze offered his resignation to Stalin.

It was Molotov who, in 1937, put forward the theory that an "enemy of the people" could actively participate in the building of socialism, support all Party decisions, never in any way show his enemy essence—so that he might rise to a higher place and strike a harder blow against the Soviet regime. "The special danger of present-day diversionary wrecking organizations," Molotov told the February-March Plenum in 1937, "is that these wreckers, diversionists, and spies make themselves out to be Communists, ardent supporters of the Soviet regime." Molotov also played a special role in falsifying history. In his own hand he wrote, for the conclusions of the *Short Course,*[11] that Stalin was the only man who moved Marxist theory forward after Lenin's death. He also inserted remarks blaming the excesses of collectivization entirely on local Party leaders, though—or because—he had been the secretary of the Central Committee who dealt with agricultural problems during the years of collectivization. He also put into the *Short Course* the assertion that local nationalism was in league with counterrevolutionary interventionists.[12]

Kaganovich played an especially large role in the extermination of the best Party cadres. In the early twenties, when he was promoted to important work in the Central Committee, he was already distinguished by his vicious, underhanded way with people. By the early thirties he was a finished Stalinist, ready to commit any crime for the sake of his career. His methods of grain procurement in the Northern Caucasus in 1932 have already been described. Returning to Moscow *oblast* as Party secretary, he applied his experience there. He went, for

[9] See Shelepin's speech to the XXIInd Party Congress.
[10] *Ibid.*
[11] *Ed.:* See above, p. 30, n. 1. For the remark in question, see *History of the CPSU* (B) (New York, 1939), p. 358.
[12] See V. S. Zaitsev's comments in *Vsesoiuznoe soveshchanie istorikov* (Moscow, 1964), p. 289.

example, to Efremov *raion* (then in Moscow *oblast*) in the fall of 1933, and began collecting grain by taking possession of the Party card of Utkin, chairman of the *raion* executive committee and secretary of the Party *raikom*. If, Kaganovich warned, the grain-procurement plan was not fulfilled in three days, Utkin would be expelled from the Party, fired from his job, and put in jail. To Utkin's proof that the plan was unrealistic because the harvest predicted in May was twice as great as the amount of grain and potatoes actually harvested, Kaganovich replied with a stream of obscene abuse, accusing Utkin of right opportunism. The plenipotentiaries of the Moscow Party Committee worked in the countryside until late fall, taking from the peasants and collective farms even the grain and potatoes they needed for food and seed, but the procurement plan was fulfilled only by 68 per cent. Utkin was expelled from the Party. So was Gaidukov, Proletarskii *raikom* secretary and chief of the grain-procurement plenipotentiaries. Nearly half of the local population boarded up their huts and left Efremov *raion,* which had to import seed grain and potatoes for three years.[13] Such methods of leadership were typical of Kaganovich, who became Stalin's right-hand man during the mass repression.

The decimation of the cadres in Cheliabinsk, Ivanovo, Iaroslavl, and a number of other Party organizations are on Kaganovich's conscience. The cruelty of his approach is exemplified by his descent on Ivanovo. As soon as he arrived, a telegram went off to Stalin in Moscow: "First study of records shows that *obkom* secretary Epanchikov must be arrested at once. Director of *obkom* propaganda department Mikhailov must also be arrested." Very soon a second telegram went to Moscow:

> Study of situation shows that right-Trotskyite wrecking has assumed broad dimensions here—in industry, agriculture, supply, health care, trade, education, and political work. *Apparaty* of *oblast* organizations and Party *obkom* exceptionally infested.[14]

Receiving Stalin's sanction, Kaganovich decimated the Ivanovo *obkom.* In August, 1937, at the plenum of the ravaged committee, Kaganovich accused the entire *oblast* Party organization of conniving with "enemies of the people."

> The secretary of the Ivanovo Party *gorkom,* A. A. Vasil'ev, began to express doubt about the "enemy activity" of the arrested *obkom* officials, but Kaganovich rudely interrupted him. Right there at the plenum A. A. Vasil'ev was expelled from the Party, and then arrested as an "enemy of the people." The same fate befell I. N.

[13] This episode is recounted by the old Communist I. P. Aleksakhin.
[14] See *XXII s'ezd KPSS, Stenograficheskii otchet,* II.

Semagin, a Party member since 1905, chairman of the *oblast* trade-union council.[15]

When Kaganovich became Commissar of Means of Communication, railway officials began to suffer mass arrests.[16] He personally made unfounded charges against innocent people, and preached to Party activists the omnipresence of disguised enemies, the necessity of intensifying work to unmask them. At a meeting of railway activists on March 10, 1937, he said: "I cannot name a single line, a single road, where there is no Trotskyite-Japanese wrecking. . . . What is more, there's not a single branch of railway transport where such wreckers have not turned up. . . ." Under Kaganovich, railway officials were arrested according to lists, including all the deputy commissars, almost all the directors of roads, and the heads of the political sections. Today they have been rehabilitated, many of them posthumously. By 1961 the Party Control Commission had found thirty-two letters from Kaganovich to the NKVD demanding the arrest of eighty-three leading transportation officials. A letter of August 10, 1937, is an example of Kaganovich's readiness to make groundless accusations. He demanded the arrest of ten executives in his commissariat simply because their behavior seemed suspicious. "There are documents," Shelepin told the XXIInd Congress,

> which prove that Kaganovich, before the conclusion of various court cases, personally edited drafts of the verdicts, and arbitrarily introduced any changes he felt like—for example, that terrorist acts had been planned against his person.

Malenkov also took an active part in the repression. In 1937 he and Ezhov decimated the Belorussian Party organization. More than half of its members were expelled and arrested. Then he did the same in Armenia, working with his friend Beria.[17] Malenkov personally interrogated prisoners and used torture. The former head of Lefortovskaia Prison has told how Beria and Malenkov took turns coming to the prison to torture imprisoned Communists, without even going through the formalities of summoning the prisoners to be interrogated.[18] As for Voroshilov, he gave more than formal sanction to the arrest of leading army officers. He called some of them to Moscow to report to the Commissar of Defense, and they were arrested in Voroshilov's waiting room.[19] Among Stalin's aides Zhdanov claimed the role of a theorist.

---

[15] *Ocherki istorii Ivanovskoi partiinoi organizatsii* (Ivanovo, 1967), p. 296.
[16] See Shvernik's speech to the XXIInd Party Congress.
[17] See Shvernik's speech to the XXIInd Party Congress.
[18] Reported in a letter that I. Piatnitskii sent to the Presidium of the XXIInd Party Congress.
[19] According to M. Ishov, that is how A. P. Prokof'ev, Soviet military attaché to Mongolia, was arrested.

In view of the extremely low level of theoretical work in the time of the cult, some of his articles are distinguished by originality and clarity. But in his methods of work Zhdanov was unquestionably a typical Stalinist, whose role in the repression was far from modest.

The behavior of M. I. Kalinin is confusing and unclear. As Chairman of the Central Executive Committee, then chairman of the Presidium of the Supreme Soviet, Kalinin obviously knew about the flood of repression. Hundreds of people passed through his waiting room every day in 1936–41, and thousands of letters were sent to him, bringing complaints and protests against lawlessness.[20] In a number of cases Kalinin tried to defend people. His personal intervention, for example, won the release of Johann Makhmastel', a diplomatic courier, and Theodor Nette, who defended the Soviet diplomatic pouch against an attack of White Guards.[21] Kalinin also tried to help such personal friends as Akulov, Shotman, and Enukidze. But Stalin ordered Kalinin not to interfere in NKVD affairs. Kalinin's weaknesses, such as indecision and acquiescence, kept him in Stalin's grip. Stalin even had his wife arrested. She remained in prison seven years and was released only a few days before Kalinin's death.[22] The epoch of the cult is epitomized in that situation: the country had a President whose wife was kept in a concentration camp. (Stalin used the same technique with Molotov.) On the pretext of protecting Kalinin, Stalin kept him under virtual house arrest for a long time, with NKVD agents constantly in his apartment. Kalinin completely surrendered to Stalin, covering up the dictator's crimes with his great prestige.

The old Party leader Emilian Iaroslavskii also helped Stalin a great deal.[23] In the twenties Iaroslavskii's authoritative *History of the Party* did not stress the role of Stalin; indeed, the fourth volume mentioned Stalin's incorrect position in March, 1917. It is therefore not surprising that Stalin's 1931 pronunciamento, "On the History of Bolshevism," attacked Iaroslavskii's "mistakes."[24] The mistakes were not specified, but the press picked up the attack, accusing Iaroslavskii of Trotskyism, Menshevism, and all the mortal sins. He wrote several letters to Stalin, arguing in one that conditions on the historical front were intolerable, that honorable Bolsheviks were being labeled falsifiers and counterrevolutionaries, that this was hurting Party work on the theoretical level, that no one was planning a new Party program.

[20] *Ed.:* Petitions for the redress of grievances are customarily addressed to the chairman of the Presidium of the Supreme Soviet.

[21] See *Neva,* 1963, No. 4, p. 187.

[22] See the 1963 biographical sketch of Kalinin in the series "Lives of Remarkable People," published by Molodaia Gvardiia. After Kalinin died his widow was exiled from Moscow.

[23] Some light was shed on their relations by E. N. Gorodetskii at the All-Union Meeting of Historians in 1962.

[24] See Stalin, *Sochineniia,* XIII, pp. 84–102.

No reply came from Stalin and the campaign of abuse was continued, whereupon Iaroslavskii caved in. He published a letter confessing all the errors ascribed to him, and wrote a biography of Stalin in which Stalin's role was "fully reflected."[25] He surrendered to Stalin not only as a historian but also as a leader of the Party Control Commission. The many appeals against lawlessness that Communists sent to this Commission went unanswered. Thus, instead of protecting legality and the rights of Party members, the Commission gave "rear-guard" protection to Ezhov's and Beria's gangs.

The question of N. S. Khrushchev's role is often raised. As First Secretary of the Moscow *oblast* Committee in 1938–39, Khrushchev's services in "destroying enemies of the people" were great enough to be praised at the XVIIIth Party Congress in 1939. Thus it came as a surprise to Molotov, Malenkov, Kaganovich, and Voroshilov when Khrushchev took the initiative in exposing Stalin's crimes at the XXth Congress in 1956.

As a comparatively young politician, easily impressed (and not very bright), Khrushchev in the thirties was strongly influenced by Stalin, had faith in him and feared him. Of course we also know that later on, when Khrushchev was First Secretary of the Party and chairman of the Council of Ministers, he committed many serious errors; he was arbitrary and voluntaristic, especially in the economic field; he violated the principles of collective leadership and began to revive the cult of personality—his own. Still and all, in exposing Stalin's crimes, in freeing hundreds of thousands of innocent citizens, and in rehabilitating the millions who perished under Stalin's arbitrary rule, Khrushchev performed an indisputable service that will never be forgotten. It is that which obliges us to take a completely different view of his role in the repression—and also of Mikoian's—than we do of Molotov, Malenkov, Kaganovich, and Stalin's other aides.

4

ONE OF THE MOST TERRIBLE FEATURES of the repression in the thirties was that the masses, trusting the Party and Stalin, were drawn into it. Hundreds of thousands of simple and essentially honorable folk, guided by the best motives, were drawn into the campaign against "enemies of the people." Millions were poisoned by suspicion. They believed Stalin's story about a ubiquitous underground and were caught up in the spy mania. The campaign against "enemies" and "wreckers" acquired a mass character, like the Stakhanovite movement. The central newspapers were especially zealous in inflaming

[25] See *Vsesoiuznoe soveshchanie istorikov*, pp. 362–63.

this mass psychosis. Almost every issue of *Pravda* and *Izvestiia* called upon the workers to seek out and expose enemies of the people. "Enemies and Their Protectors," "Wrecking in the Selection of Cadres," "Wreckers in Radio Stations," "Who's in Charge of Priazhinskii *Raion*?," "Uproot Enemy Nests in the Commissariat of Trade," "Enemy Outburst in Sverdlovsk"—hundreds of such articles roused the masses to struggle.

"Enemies of the people" were to be sought everywhere. "Not one disorder," *Pravda* declared,

> not one accident, should go unnoticed. We know that assembly lines do not stop by themselves, machines do not break by themselves, boilers do not burst by themselves. Someone's hand is behind every such act. Is it the hand of the enemy? That is the first question we should ask in such cases.[26]

Pravda denounced officials who believed in the inevitability of accidents and hesitated to expose enemies.[27] R. I. Eikhe, First Secretary of the West Siberian *oblast* Committee, told a Novosibirsk Party meeting: "We are now so well equipped and have so many devoted people that there can be no breakdowns. When accidents and failures begin to take place in a factory, the first thing to do is to look for an enemy."[28] And in May, 1937, the Moscow Party Conference adopted this resolution: "For every drop of blood they spill, the enemies of the USSR will pay with gallons of the blood of spies and diversionaries." All the *oblast* papers published this resolution, calling for mass executions, as an example to be imitated.

Such appeals had mass results. The smallest error of a manager, miscalculation of an engineer, misprint overlooked by an editor or proofreader, publication of a bad book, was taken to be deliberate wrecking and cause for arrest. People looked everywhere for secret signs or fascist symbols, and found them in drawings in books, in notebooks, in scout badges. Even such difficulties as the low pay of teachers, shortages of funds, high dropout rates from high school, the wearing out of equipment, were demagogically attributed to sabotage.

There were even such absurdities as a report that bayonets were bending as a result of wrecking. A special commission sent from Moscow established that a certain ordnance technician had started the fuss. One day he decided to fasten the end of a bayonet in a big vise, and, putting the weight of his whole body against the rifle stock, to try and bend the bayonet. He succeeded. After a careful investigation the commission declared that the bayonets were eminently suitable for battle.[29]

[26] *Pravda,* Feb. 2, 1937.
[27] See, for example, *Pravda,* Apr. 21, 1937.
[28] See the newspaper *Sovetskaia Sibir',* January, 1937.
[29] Marshal N. N. Voronov, *Na sluzhbe voennoi* (Moscow, 1963), pp. 118–19.

An anonymous denunciation of A. Ia. Vedenin, military commander of the Kirghiz Republic, said that he deliberately chose spotted horses for the army in order to spoil the camouflage of the cavalry before its future enemy.[30] One Communist, the head of a fire department, was asked during a political lesson who had commanded the Red Guard in Moscow in 1917. Upon answering, quite correctly, that Muralov had, he was immediately arrested as a counter-revolutionary. People were put in prisons or camps for "disseminating the verses of Pasternak or Esenin," and "for connections with Ilya Ehrenburg," although none of these writers was arrested. "Plotting to resurrect Austria-Hungary" was another charge, and even "suspicion of intending to betray the Native Land." In one of the Ufa prisons, R. G. Zakharova met a teacher who was accused of a connection with Finland: after the overthrow of the Soviet regime, she was to be proclaimed Queen of the Mari, a Finnic-speaking nationality in the Volga-Ural region. In a Minsk clothing factory, according to Ia. Drobinskii, an old cutter and Communist, Solnyshkov, was accused of fomenting discontent among the people by designing too narrow pockets in the pants of work clothes. M. Ishov tells how the military procurator of Leningrad, Kuznetsov, was charged with joining the Party in 1904 just to "disrupt it from within." In Novosibirsk a group of construction workers born in 1913–14 were accused of supporting Kolchak's armies in the Civil War of 1918–21. One of the directors of a lying-in hospital in Gomel was accused of instructing the chief doctor to infect all the babies with syphilis. The artist V. I. Shukhaev and his wife were accused of belonging to the *Borot'bist* Party. The naïve artist, poorly prepared for the new way of life, kept asking his cellmates who these *Borot'bisty* were.[31] In Moscow a large group of stamp collectors were arrested for exchanging stamps with foreign collectors. According to L. M. Portnov they were accused of sending secret information abroad. V. T. Shalamov tells how an Esperanto society in Moscow was arrested; the name of this artificial language apparently frightened the security organs. Dozens of athletes, especially those who had participated in international competitions, were arrested on absurd charges. A denunciation to the NKVD was an easy way to get rid of athletic rivals. The world champion swimmer, Semen Boichenko, was removed from competition that way, as were the Starostin brothers, soccer players on the Spartak team.

It was enough for a Vladivostok cinema to show a newsreel that included a shot of a Moscow official arrested two months earlier, and

[30] See Vedenin, *Gody i liudi* (Moscow, 1964), p. 58.

[31] *Ed.:* They were a Ukrainian peasant party, which was fused with the Bolshevik Party in 1920 on the recommendation of Lenin and Stalin. See, e.g., Stalin, *Sochineniia*, IV, p. 304.

Pravda carried an article, "Enemy Outburst," calling for an investigation to see if there were enemies of the people among the officials in this cinema, in the film organization of Vladivostok, and in the Main Repertory Commission in Moscow. Even such an innocuous book as *An Index of Literature for Viola and Viola d'Amore* was declared by *Pravda* to be subversive and fascistic, because the works of some contemporary German composers were included in it.

Pravda and *Izvestiia* also kept a careful eye on other newspapers, whipping up laggards. "If you study the Kiev paper *Proletarskaia Pravda*," wrote *Pravda*, "you are struck by a strange fact. Not one enemy of the people has been unmasked by the paper. As a rule, the paper exposes enemies who have already been exposed."

Even Komsomol members and schoolchildren were dragged into the feverish search for "enemies of the people." On July 10, 1937, *Pravda* reported elections in 1,525 primary Komsomol organizations, complaining that "you can count on the fingers of one hand the electoral meetings at which . . . the offspring of fascist agents who had wormed their way into the Komsomol were unmasked." Whereupon arrests of Komsomol members and leaders increased significantly.

Thousands of plenipotentiaries traveled around the country during those years, feverishly checking on reports from the provinces. Some of these officials were prompted by the best motives, others by stupidity or careerist considerations; still others were simply mad with fear. But almost all of them ordered or sanctioned the arrest of innocent people. The work of one of these officials, Zemtsov, is typical. With nothing but unverified newspaper articles about "enemy" activity in a rural *raion,* Zemtsov called a *raion* Party meeting without making any kind of check and declared that the *raion* leaders were enemies. Then he ordered the arrest of the *raikom* secretary, and it was done. Zemtsov put together a list of Communists to be expelled and told the *raikom* (*raion* Party committee) to do it. By evening of that day seventeen Communists were expelled from the Party. Then Zemtsov took away the keys and seal from the members of the *raikom,* handed them over to the *raion* division of the NKVD, and, sealing up the *raikom* building, left. In one single day he had liquidated the *raikom.*[32] Today this story sounds like a bad joke, but that was precisely the mode of operation of higher-ranking officials, such as Kaganovich in the Kuban and in Ivanovo *oblast,* and Malenkov in Belorussia and Armenia. In Kiev special commissions were attached to the *raikomy* to gather compromising materials on Party members and candidate members. Thousands of libelous statements were collected. In Kiev's Petrovskii *raion,* 111 people in a single Party organi-

[32] *XVIII s'ezd VKP/b. Stenograficheskii otchet* (Moscow, 1939), p. 569.

zation in the Academy of Sciences were denounced, although there were only 130 Communists in the entire Academy.[33]

The Holy Inquisition, set up in the Middle Ages to defend the Christian faith, encouraged denunciations in every way possible and persecuted everyone who refused to report "heretics."[34] The Stalinist punitive organs did much the same thing in 1936–39—and to a considerable degree right up to the death of Stalin. Instead of punishment for slander—the few show trials of slanderers early in 1938 were only a feint, not an announcement of basic policy—in most cases it was encouraged, as an expression of vigilance. In such conditions all sorts of careerists and scoundrels tried to use slander to destroy their enemies, to get a good job, an apartment or a neighbor's room, or simply to get revenge for an insult. Some pathological types crawled out of their holes to write hundreds of denunciations. In short, the abolition of law and justice aroused the basest instincts.

Lenin warned the Cheka about false accusations and urged the severest punishment for them. But under Stalin most slanderers went unpunished, and a flood poured into the NKVD offices, where big receptacles "for statements" were placed in reception rooms. The usual NKVD response to a denunciation was to arrest the victim and only later to bother about "checking" the charges made against him.

In fairness it should be noted that in 1937–38 there were protests against this flood of slander and encouragement of slanderers. Mikhail Kol'tsov, for example, wrote several hard-hitting articles. He distinguished three types of informers: the javelin thrower, intent on striking down as many victims as possible; the careerist, seeking domination of his institution by terrorizing it; and the coward, determined to protect himself by destroying others.[35] But articles like Kol'tsov's could not stop the flood of denunciation and repression inundating the land. Individual protests, expressed not in concrete action but in written reports and conversations, merely increased the number of victims, for the leaders to whom such protests were addressed were the chief organizers of the terror.

---

[33] *Ibid.*
[34] For some interesting reflections on this subject, see B. Danem, *Geroi i eretiki* (Moscow, 1967), pp. 275–78.
[35] See *Pravda,* Jan. 17, 1938.

XI

The Conditions Facilitating Stalin's Usurpation of Power

1

SOME CONFUSION about the nature of Stalin's power must be cleared away. By the end of the twenties and the early thirties he was already called a dictator, a one-man ruler, and not without reason. But the unlimited dictatorship that he established after 1936–38 was without historical precedent. For the last fifteen years of his bloody career Stalin wielded such power as no Russian tsar ever possessed—indeed, no dictator of the past thousand years. In the years of the cult, Stalin held not only all political power; he was master of the economy, the military, foreign policy; even in literature, the arts, and science he was the supreme arbiter, his subjective judgments the decisive criteria.

It is therefore astonishing to find historical works that picture 1936–38 as a time when socialist democracy flourished. According to these historians, Stalin slowed but could not stop the democratization of Soviet society:

> The cult of personality . . . could not alter the nature of the socialist system, could not shake the Leninist foundations of the Party. The Party and its local organs lived their own active, autonomous life. In continuous conflict with the unhealthy tendencies engendered by the cult of personality, *the genuinely Leninist principles on which the Party was founded invariably won out.*[1]

In other words, the shooting of hundreds of thousands, the arrest of millions, the mushroom growth of concentration camps, were merely

---

[1] *Gody ratnykh trudov i podvigov* (Moscow, 1966), p. 9. Italics added. One of the series "Molodezh' ob istorii KPSS."

"unhealthy tendencies"; Stalin's crimes, committed in outer space, did not affect the Party, which continued to "live its own active, autonomous life."

An especially crude distortion is contained in a textbook for schools teaching the foundations of Marxism-Leninism.[2] "The Victory and Consolidation of Socialism" is the title of the section dealing with the late thirties. It tells about the democratization of the electoral system, the development of democracy within the Party, broadening of Party members' rights, etc., but says nothing about mass repression. In this section not a single victim of Stalinist tyranny is named. There is only a cryptic reference to Stalin's mistaken thesis about the intensification of class struggle, and to abuses of power. Although this textbook was not officially endorsed by the Central Committee, it has gone through two editions with printings of more than two million copies.

Of course the change from indirect and limited to direct and universal voting for the Supreme Soviet and all the local Soviets, and the introduction of the secret ballot, should not be belittled. These are important characteristics of Soviet democracy, though they are merely formal. Many dictators, after a forceful seizure of power, maintained a formal show of democratic institutions. Cornelius Sulla, for example, retained the consulship, though the consul elected was either Sulla himself or the man he picked. The Senate was preserved, though three hundred of Sulla's supporters were added to it. The tribunes of the people remained, though they lost most of their power. The popular assembly continued to meet, if only to hear Sulla's will.

Stalin followed this ancient tradition. He did not repeal the laws of the Soviet regime; he simply did not enforce them. He did not abolish the Central Committee or the Supreme Soviet; he simply changed their personnel by force. He utterly ignored all laws, traditions, and norms.

Consider, for example, the rule that a member of the Party's Central Committee could be removed only by a two-thirds vote of the Central Committee Plenum. (Point 58 of the Party statute in effect between the XVIIth and XVIIIth Party Congresses.) In 1937–38 the fate of Central Committee members was decided by Stalin after consulting a few close aides. Only a few members were expelled after discussion of their cases at a Plenum, or even in the Politburo. Most were expelled and arrested without the least observance of legal formalities. Commander Iakir, suddenly called to Moscow, was arrested en route. NKVD agents came into his sleeping car in the middle of the night, at Briansk, removed the pistol from under Iakir's pillow, woke him up, and declared him under arrest. "Where is the Central Com-

[2] *Ocherki po istorii KPSS* (2 edns.: Moscow, 1966, 1967). Ed. by S. P. Trapeznikov; written by G. N. Golikov, *et al.*

mittee decision?" Iakir asked. "Come to Moscow," said the agents, "and they'll show you all the decisions and sanctions."[3] Rudzutak was arrested at his dacha, in his study, in the midst of a lively conversation with the painters V. N. Meshkov, A. M. Gerasimov and P. M. Shukhmin.[4] Ia. A. Iakovlev, head of the Agricultural Section of the Central Committee, was taken in his office at CC headquarters. "Are we having a counterrevolutionary coup?" he asked the NKVD men who came for him. "I am a member of the Central Committee and a member of the government. What right do you have to arrest me without the sanction of the Central Committee?"[5] In October, 1937, the Kremlin guards refused to allow A. S. Bubnov and V. P. Zatonskii to attend a Central Committee Plenum. Extremely upset, Bubnov went to the Commissariat of Education—he was in charge of it—and stayed there until late in the evening, when he learned, from the radio news report, that he was no longer Commissar of Education. A few days later he was arrested and soon died in prison.[6]

Stalin also ignored the rule concerning periodic sessions of Party Congresses and Central Committee Plenums. Under Lenin, in the first six years after the October Revolution, there were six Party congresses, five conferences, and seventy-nine Central Committee Plenums. In the first decade after Lenin's death, there were four congresses, five conferences, and forty-three Plenums. During the next two decades, 1934–53, there were only three congresses—and thirteen years elapsed between the XVIIIth and XIXth Party Congresses—one conference, and twenty-three Plenums, most of them before the war. In 1941, 1942, 1943, 1945, 1946, 1948, 1950, and 1951, there was not a single plenary session of the Central Committee.[7] In short, Stalin gradually transformed the Central Committee from the organ of democracy that it was supposed to be, into a big and unwieldy chancellery.

As mentioned earlier, some émigrés saw Stalin's usurpation of power as a sort of monarchist coup, a step toward the founding of a new dynasty. Miliukov, for example, wrote to a friend on September 18, 1936:

> In your opinion, these shootings [occur] because the line has been lost. [But] the line does continue, and so, whatever is being lost, let them continue to believe in the correctness of the line right to the place of execution. Though I regard the means (the external form) as barbarism, I believe the end for which these means are used to be

[3] See the collection of reminiscences *Komandarm Iakir* (Moscow, 1963).
[4] G. A. Trukan, *Ian Rudzutak* (Moscow, 1963).
[5] Recounted by D. Iu. Zorina, former "instructor" of the Central Committee.
[6] See *Andrei Bubnov* (Moscow, 1964).
[7] See *Sovetskaia istoricheskaia entsiklopediia*, VIII (1965), p. 275.

completely correct. . . . All the more reason why I wish Stalin good health, so there will be no zigzags backwards.[8]

"I am happy," said an old monarchist officer, who had been in prison since 1920, to his young Communist cellmate in the late thirties: "At last the dreams of our beloved Nicholas [II], which he was too soft to carry out, are being fulfilled. The prisons are full of Jews and Bolsheviks. Can't you see that a new dynasty is being created in Russia?"[9]

These people were, of course, mistaken. Stalin was not planning to restore the monarchy or to bring back the exiled landowners and capitalists. He was trying to combine the new social system with an anti-democratic regime of absolute personal power. In this respect his usurpation of power can be compared to Napoleon's in postrevolutionary France. But there was a big difference. Napoleon, acting in the interests of the bourgeoisie and supported by it, behaved openly and proclaimed himself Emperor. Stalin's usurpation of power, on the other hand, in no way corresponded to the interests of the proletariat, and he was forced to resort to camouflage and deception. Until the end of the 1930's he held no governmental posts, aside from his membership in the Presidium of the Central Executive Committee and later the Presidium of the Supreme Soviet. Just before the war he became Chairman of the Council of Ministers. Later he assumed the title of Marshal, then Generalissimo. But without royal titles Stalin had, in the last fifteen years of his life, such absolute power as Napoleon never had or could have had. E. H. Carr notes a further paradox here:

> The Bolsheviks knew that the French revolution had ended in a Napoleon, and feared that their own revolution might end in the same way. They therefore mistrusted Trotsky, who among their leaders looked most like a Napoleon, and trusted Stalin, who looked least like a Napoleon.[10]

We have analyzed Stalin's motives, but there is a more important problem than his motives: How did he manage to carry out his criminal plans? Why did the Party allow so much bloodshed? Why was it powerless to resist such enormous tyranny? What was inevitable in this frightful tragedy, and what was accidental?

Marx and Engels often referred to the possibility, or even the inevitability, that a revolution would degenerate if it occurred in objective historical conditions that did not correspond to its ideals.

[8] The letter was found in the Kuskova Archive in Prague, in 1945. Reported by S. Petrikovskii, member of the CPSU.
[9] Reported by M. B. Kuznets, who was the young Communist to whom the officer made these remarks in Butyrskaia Prison.
[10] Carr, *What Is History?* (New York, 1962), p. 90.

Plekhanov also wrote about this several times in his arguments with the populists. If the people, Plekhanov declared, approach power when social conditions are not ripe, then "the revolution may result in a political monstrosity, such as the ancient Chinese or Peruvian empires, i.e., in a tsarist despotism renovated with a Communist lining."[11] Some of the people we have talked to see prophetic truth in these words. They try to prove that it was inevitable, in the Soviet Union of the twenties, for the likes of Stalin to come to power. "If Lenin had lived another ten or twenty years," the writer V. K——— told me, "he would certainly have been pushed out of the leadership by the 'new' people, whose embodiment was Stalin." "The system created after the October Revolution," said the economist I. P———,

> was based on outright dictatorship, on force, to an excessive degree. Disregard of some elementary rules of democracy and lawful order inevitably had to degenerate into Stalinist dictatorship. It was Stalin who fitted this system ideally, and he only developed its latent possibilities to the maximum degree. The whole trouble was that a socialist revolution in a country like Russia was premature. In a country that has not gone through a period of bourgeois democracy, where the people in its majority is illiterate and uncultivated, in such a country genuine socialism cannot be built without the support of other more developed socialist countries. By prematurely destroying all the old forms of social life, the Bolsheviks raised up and turned loose such forces as must inevitably have led to some form of Stalinism. Approximately the same thing is happening today in China and in Albania.

This point of view, as applied to the Soviet Union, is one-sided and incorrect. If the political and social system created after the October Revolution inevitably engendered Stalinism, if history offered no other possibilities of development, if everything was strictly determined, then the October Revolution must also have been determined by the monstrous system of Russian autocracy. Thus we must conclude that the October and the February revolutions were not at all premature or accidental events. In other words, to explain Stalinism we have to return to earlier and earlier epochs of Russian history, very likely to the Tartar yoke. But that would be wrong; it would be a historical justification of Stalinism, not a condemnation.

I proceed from the assumption that different possibilities of development exist in almost every political system and situation. The triumph of one of these possibilities depends not only on objective factors and conditions, but also on many subjective ones, and some of these factors are clearly accidental.

Even Russian tsarism in the early twentieth century had various

[11] Plekhanov, *Izbrannye filosofskie proizvedeniia,* I (1956), p. 323.

possibilities of development. With a more capable leadership, with a sensible system of concessions, the February Revolution might not have taken place. The tsarist regime took some steps in that direction. The State Duma comes to mind, where even Bolsheviks were represented; one recalls the fact that *Pravda* was established legally, for the most part, in 1912–14, and so on. But there was also the Rasputin affair, there were incompetent generals who suffered one defeat after another in the war. Thus the tsarist regime was unable to utilize the possibilities of peaceful evolution, and revolution became inevitable. There was likewise more than one possibility for the development of bourgeois democracy after the February Revolution. If the war had been ended, or the government had decided on a truce, if the Social Revolutionary Party had made greater concessions to the peasants— Kerensky's promise of land to the peasants came one or two days before October 25, when it was meaningless—if Lenin had not managed to arrive in Russia in time, then the bourgeois democratic system could have become stronger and lasted longer. But these things did not happen, and the October Revolution became inevitable.

To speak of various historical possibilities is to raise the question of probability: which line of development was more likely, which less? The question requires concrete investigation of all the objective and subjective circumstances in a given situation. Even a small possibility of a given line of development does not constitute an impossibility.

From this point of view Stalinism was by no means inevitable, despite the defects in the political conception that the Bolsheviks brought to the October Revolution and despite the defects of the new Soviet regime. It also had many merits. The contest between various alternatives began under Lenin and was bound to grow more intense. But if he had not died in 1924, the victory of genuinely democratic and socialist tendencies would have been more probable than the victory of Stalinism.

Many foreign thinkers, including Communists, have studied this problem. After the XXth Congress, in March, 1956, Palmiro Togliatti published his famous objection to a simple inversion of the cult of personality: blaming all evil on the superman who had formerly been praised for all good. Togliatti suggested that the system called Stalinist was to be explained by reference to the development of bureaucracy, deriving from prerevolutionary conditions and from the desperate need for centralized power during the Civil War. This context favored the rise of Stalin, a typical *apparatchik*.[12]

---

[12] See P. Togliatti, *Problemi del movimento operaio internazionale (1956–61)* (Rome, 1962), pp. 99–106. *Ed.:* A convenient English translation may be found in *The Anti-Stalin Campaign and International Communism; A Selection of Documents* (New York, 1956), pp. 97–139.

Some Yugoslav thinkers have given much stronger expression to the view that the Stalinist system was foreordained. Veljko Korać, for example, follows a vivid characterization of the system—"a specific etatism and bureaucratic despotism, . . . the heartless destroying of men in the name of an ineffable mystic of the future, making politics and ideology absolute and the negation of human freedom"—with a declaration of its inevitability. He finds its causes in the occurrence of a socialist revolution without an adequate material base. The working class was too small, the culture of the masses too low. The poor peasants were an effective force for overthrowing the old order but not for self-disciplined participation in building the new. Political organization, power, compensated for the weakness of the material base.

> Technical advance only enforced the ascendancy of this techno-bureaucracy. . . . In the name of Marxism, Stalin distorted Marx's ideas into a closed system of dogmas making of himself the sole and absolute interpreter of those dogmas. . . . [The Stalinist system did] not come into being as a historical caprice or as the pressure of tradition of tsarist despotism. Instead it appears as a *necessary accompaniment to the development of an undeveloped country which has undergone socialist revolution before industrial revolution.*[13]

Korać gives an accurate description of the historical and economic background, but he is wrong in his main argument. It is hard to agree that in an economically backward country, the socialist transformation of society and the industrial revolution must be accompanied by mass violence. Too many historical facts simply will not fit in this simplistic scheme. Were not the hundreds of thousands of officials destroyed in 1937–38 the best promoters of industrialization? Why did the machine of state power, which they had created together with Stalin, have to fall on them?

The mass repression of the thirties cannot be attributed to any significant resistance to Stalin's arbitrary rule. The sad fact is that Stalin's drive for unlimited personal dictatorship encountered no significant resistance, even from the officials who were being struck down. The only forces opposed to Stalin were those which had been enemies of the proletarian dictatorship all along—world imperialism and the White Russian émigrés. Feeble resistance came from the remnants of the Socialist Revolutionary and Menshevik parties, which considered themselves the defenders of democratic socialism. The comparative ease of Stalin's usurpation of power cannot be explained by theories such as Korać's.

[13] V. Korać, "Socialism in Underdeveloped Countries," *Praxis* (Zagreb), 1964, No. 1, pp. 300–301.

It was an historical accident that Stalin, the embodiment of all the worst elements in the Russian revolutionary movement, came to power after Lenin, the embodiment of all that was best. Nevertheless, the possibility of such an accident, and the factors that transformed the possibility into reality, demand close analysis. For the Party must not only condemn Stalin's crimes; it must also eliminate the conditions that facilitated them.

We are also confronted with another question: How did Stalin manage to preserve not only power but also the respect and trust of the majority of Soviet people? It is an unavoidable fact that Stalin never relied on force alone. Throughout the period of his one-man rule he was popular. The longer this tyrant ruled the USSR, cold-bloodedly destroying millions of people, the greater seems to have been the dedication to him, even the love, of the majority of people. These sentiments reached their peak in the last years of his life. When he died in March, 1953, the grief of hundreds of millions, both in the Soviet Union and around the world, was quite sincere.

How can this unprecedented historical paradox be explained? We must look more closely at the conditions that facilitated Stalin's usurpation of power.

2

ONE CONDITION that made it easy for Stalin to bend the Party to his will was the hugely inflated cult of his personality. "For 1938," Ilya Ehrenburg writes in his memoirs,

> it is more correct simply to use the word "cult" in its original religious meaning. In the minds of millions Stalin was transformed into a mythical demigod; everyone trembled as they said his name, believed that he alone could save the Soviet Union from invasion and collapse.[14]

The deification of Stalin justified in advance everything he did, everything connected with his name, including new crimes and abuses of power. All the achievements and virtues of socialism were embodied in him. The activism of other leaders was paralyzed. Not conscious discipline but blind faith in Stalin was required. Like every cult, this one tended to transform the Communist Party into an ecclesiastical organization, with a sharp distinction between ordinary people and leader-priests headed by their infallible pope. The gulf between the people and Stalin was not only deepened but idealized. The business of state in the Kremlin became as remote and incomprehensible for the unconsecrated as the affairs of the gods on Olympus.

[14] *Novyi mir,* 1962, No. 5, p. 152.

The social consciousness of the people took on elements of religious psychology: illusions, autosuggestion, the inability to think critically, intolerance towards dissidents, and fanaticism.[15] Perceptions of reality were distorted. It was difficult, for example, to believe the terrible crimes charged against the old Bolsheviks, but it was even more difficult to think that Stalin was engaged in a monstrous provocation to destroy his former friends and comrades.

The religious cult of Stalin's personality was accompanied by the belittling of everyone else, especially ordinary working people. Conformism, uniformity of behavior and thought, was implanted in the Soviet people. Serving socialism was transformed into serving Stalin; it was not he who served the people but they who served him. His praise, his encouragement, his smile were considered the highest reward. Soldiers in battle were trained to shout "For the homeland, for Stalin!"—laying down their lives not so much for socialism as for Stalin. For the sake of future beatitude, the religious believer is expected to endure without complaint any misfortune in his present earthly life.[16] Just as believers attribute everything good to God and everything bad to the devil, so everything good was attributed to Stalin and everything bad to evil forces that Stalin himself was fighting. "Long live Stalin!" some officials shouted as they were taken to be shot.

This religious outlook crippled the will even of those people who had stopped believing in Stalin and had begun to see where Stalin was taking the Party. Why did Ordzhonikidze shoot himself rather than Stalin? Why was there not one real attempt to remove Stalin during his fifteen years of bloody crimes? Those who were capable of such an act were stopped not so much by fear for their lives as by fear of the social consequences, which could not be predicted in the conditions of the cult. The hero of a novel of the mid-1960's puts the case clearly:

> It's terrible that we ourselves helped to strengthen blind faith in *him*, and now are powerless before that faith. Sacred truth looks like a terrible lie if it does not correspond to people's actual beliefs. You can imagine what would happen if today someone got on the radio, say, and told the entire country what was going on, told the truth about Stalin. From that instant even a person who had his doubts would believe that we are surrounded by enemies; he would believe everything. And any cruelty would be justified.[17]

In the time of Ivan the Terrible people created an earthly god and then could not raise a finger against the idol they had created. A

[15] See Iu. Kariakin, "Epizod iz sovremmennoi bor'by idei," *Problemy mir i sotsializma,* 1964, No. 9.

[16] See Iu. Levada, *Sotsial'naia priroda religii* (Moscow, 1965).

[17] G. Baklanov, "Iiul' 41 goda," *Znamia,* 1965, No. 2, p. 16.

radical historian tells with horror how "Prince Repnin, impaled on a stake and dying slowly, . . . praised the Tsar, his lord and executioner." The radical historian ascribes such behavior to "the inculcation of distorted views, with the result that force of spirit served merely to stifle indignation and the natural impulse to rebel."[18] A conservative historian is awed rather than horrified by the passivity of Ivan's subjects, who blamed themselves for the divine wrath that their tyrannical sovereign wreaked upon them.[19]

A recent student of religious psychology notes the frequency with which rulers are turned into fetishes.[20] And indeed the historian finds many such cases in the most diverse ages and societies, from ancient Egypt to the fascist regimes of the twentieth century. Elements of this attitude are even found in modern revolutionary movements, for example in the Russian populist theory of the hero leading the crowd. But why did the cult of personality arise and exist for so long in the Soviet Union, a strange secular variety of religious consciousness in a socialist society? Why was this cult supported by the Bolshevik Party, which grew up in battle against populist illusions about heroes and the crowd?

It has been seen that the boundless praise of Stalin did not arise spontaneously; it was organized by Stalin and his creatures. And this well-organized campaign did its job. From their earliest years schoolchildren were taught that everything good came from Stalin. But it would be naïve to attribute the success of Stalin's cult only to clever propaganda. That is what simpleminded opponents of Christianity do when they attribute its spread to deception and stupidity, instead of studying the historical conditions that explain its success.[21]

Some historians think that the success of Stalin's cult was considerably facilitated by the petty-bourgeois character of tsarist Russia, which carried over into the postrevolutionary era. They also point to the low educational and cultural level of the masses, and the absence of strong democratic traditions in a country so recently emancipated from despotism. For centuries the cult of the tsar, the ideology of absolutism, had been ingrained in Russia. While taking this notion into consideration, it would be a mistake to regard the ignorance of the masses or the religious illusions of peasants and petty artisans as the only preconditions of Stalin's cult. There were others, inherent in

[18] See S. M. Stepniak-Kravchinskii, *Rossiia pod vlast'iu tsarei* (Moscow, 1965), pp. 59–60. *Ed.:* This is a reprint of a famous work by a nineteenth-century populist (*narodnik*).

[19] See N. M. Karamzin, *Istoriia gosudarstva Rossiiskogo,* IX (St. Petersburg, 1892), p. 106.

[20] Iu. A. Levada, *Sotsial'naia priroda religii* (Moscow, 1965), p. 232.

[21] Cf. Marx and Engels, *Sochineniia,* 2nd edn., XIX, p. 307.

the Revolution itself. It brought such sweeping change in such a short time that the leaders seemed to be miracle makers. Indeed, the tendency of the masses to glorify their leaders appears spontaneously in every mass revolution. It is an expression of the masses' great enthusiasm, pride in their revolution, their gratitude to the leaders who did so much for their liberation. Of course this idealization of the leaders need not inevitably lead to a cult of the leaders, or become idol worship. Much depends on concrete historical circumstances and on the character and world view of the leaders themselves.

Paradoxical as it may seem, another important factor explaining the triumph of Stalin's cult was the crimes he committed. He did not commit them by himself. Taking advantage of the people's revolutionary enthusiasm and trustfulness, the enormous power of Party and state discipline, and the low educational level of the proletariat and the peasantry, Stalin involved millions of people in his crimes. Not only the punitive organs but the entire Party and government *apparat* participated actively in the campaigns of the 1930's. Thousands of officials were members of the *troiki* that condemned innocent people. Tens of thousands of officials sanctioned the arrest of their subordinates, as required by a Politburo resolution in 1937. Commissars had to sanction the arrest of their deputies, *obkom* secretaries the arrest of Party officials in their *oblasti,* while the Chairman of the Union of Writers sanctioned the arrest of many writers. Hundreds of thousands of Communists voted for the expulsion of "enemies of the people." Millions of ordinary people took part in meetings and demonstrations demanding severe reprisals against "enemies." Frequently people demanded such penalties against their former friends.

The majority of Soviet people believed in Stalin and the NKVD in those years, and were sincere in their indignation against "enemies of the people." But many citizens, even in the NKVD, had their doubts, if not about the general trend, then at least about particular acts of repression. These people reacted to the voice of conscience in different ways. Some took a stand against the particular acts they questioned. Others resigned themselves and kept quiet. Either way, people who felt some doubts could not admit to themselves that they were in some measure accomplices in crimes. So they forced themselves to believe in Stalin, who knew everything and could not make mistakes. They found mitigation for themselves in the cult of his personality.

"Of course," says the writer A. Pis'mennyi in one of his last works,

> I could not believe that Ivan Kataev, Zarudin, Guber, Pantraiger or Mikhail Loskutov, or Sergei Urnis, or many other friends of mine were spies, bomb-throwing anarchists planning to kill Stalin, loathsome poisoners of reservoirs, or enemy agents trying to restore the

power of Riabushinskii and von Mekk.[22] However I might try today to ridicule my tossing and turning and—why hide it, when everything is being said?—my search for spiritual peace, the fact is that then above all I wanted to understand. Yes, yes, I repeat once again, I wanted not only to believe but to understand what was happening. . . . But in those years it was impossible to understand what was happening. You could become an informer, go mad, commit suicide, but if you wanted to live, the most convenient way for an unhappy, distraught, but honorable person clinging with his last ounce of strength to his place in society—I repeat and will go on repeating a thousand times—was to *believe*. To believe without reasoning, without second thoughts, without proofs, as people believe in omens, in god, in the devil, in life beyond the grave. The thought that all social actions could be prompted by the criminal designs of a single man who had appropriated the full plenitude of power, and that this man was Stalin, was blasphemous, was unbelievable.

And in fact this complex mixture of contradictory feelings was one of the main sources of strength for Stalin's cult, especially among officials, many of whom feel this way even now.

Thus there was a two-way cause-and-effect relationship between the terror and the cult of Stalin's personality. Stalin's cult facilitated his usurpation of power and the destruction of inconvenient people, while his crimes, supported by the *apparat* and also by the deluded masses, extended and reinforced the cult of personality.

The cult of personality does not automatically lead to mass repression—much depends on the personality. Not every deified emperor or pharaoh was a cruel and bloodthirsty despot. But the most dangerous feature of the cult of a personality is that the leader's conduct depends not on laws or other rules but on his own arbitrary will. The Party and state cannot endure such a situation, when the only guarantee of a citizen's rights, indeed of his very life, is the personal qualities of the leader.

3

IT WAS FAIRLY EASY for Stalin to convince the Soviet people that he was fighting real enemies, destroying traitors. The dimensions of the fraud helped it to succeed. The charges were piled so high and repeated so often that deliberate deception seemed absolutely impossible. Goebbels said that the bigger the lie and the more often it is repeated,

[22] *Ed.*: For Riabushinskii, see above, pp. 119–20. N. K. von Mekk was a railroad tycoon who stayed in Russia after the Revolution and worked for the Commissariat of Transportation. In 1929 he was accused of counterrevolutionary activity and shot.

the easier it is for people to believe it. Stalin was a master of this cynical technique.

Secrecy was important. The investigations of political crimes were strictly *in camera,* and any attempt to penetrate this secrecy was itself regarded as a political crime. The newspapers in 1936 and the first half of 1937 published many reports on the "unmasking" of Trotsky-ites and Bukharinites; but later in 1937 such reports became progressively fewer in number, although the flood of repression continued to rise. A wall of silence surrounded the fate of Postyshev, Kosior, Chubar', Eikhe, and Rudzutak. The arrest of hundreds of other leaders was not reported in any newspaper, and could only be deduced from certain hints or from brief oral reports given in *raion* and city Party committees. The charges against most of Stalin's victims were never made public. Even well-informed people knew only of arrests in their own *oblast,* in their own line of work, in their own circle of acquaintances. The scale of the terror escaped them. This ignorance was heightened by the orgy of transferring officials from one *oblast* to another, from one post to another, that characterized that time of troubles. At times people did not know whether an official had been arrested or transferred. In many cases even the relatives did not know. The NKVD as a rule did not inform relatives of execution or death by other causes. Playing on hopes and illusions, the NKVD invented a formula about the exile of "enemies of the people" (even those who had been shot) to distant camps "without the right of correspondence."

Stalin and the NKVD often preferred methods of disguised terror to straightforward arrest. Many were arrested without a warrant or the sanction of the procurator. Prisoners tortured to death were reported dead of a heart attack or some other disease. Sometimes the NKVD staged "robberies," during which the intended victim would be killed. That is how the actress Zinaida Raikh, Meyerhold's wife, died, while she was struggling for her husband's release. The robbers who raided her apartment stabbed her seventeen times, took all her papers, and left many valuables untouched.[23] Agents were sent abroad to kill certain émigrés, Soviet diplomats, and intelligence agents. Some officials were murdered in their homes, in hotels, on hunting parties, in their offices, thrown out of windows, poisoned—and then were reported dead of heart attacks, accidents, or suicides. The body of Nestor Lakoba, who was supposed to have died of a heart attack, was sent from Tbilisi to Sukhumi with great ceremony.

The First Secretary of the Armenian Central Committee, A. Khandzhian, was murdered on July 9, 1936, in Beria's office in Tbilisi by Beria himself.[24] A. Ivanova, who was then an official in the Party

[23] Recounted by Ilya Ehrenburg.
[24] Reported by Shelepin at the XXIInd Party Congress.

Control Commission, happened to be in the office next to Beria's on the day of the murder, where she heard the shot. Khandzhian's body was taken to the hotel where Armenian officials usually stayed. Beria's accomplices put the body on a bed and fired a shot in the air. In the corpse's pockets they placed two forged letters:[25] a farewell to his wife, Rosa, and a confession to Beria, saying he had made a mess of his affairs and had decided to put an end to himself. Beria and his clique then insulted the memory of the dead man, accusing him of shameful cowardice. Meetings were held throughout Transcaucasia in July of 1936 to condemn Khandzhian's "cowardly act." The lead article in the Armenian Party paper declared suicide

> an especially shameful act of treacherous cowardice when committed by a Party leader. . . . For the past three or four years . . . the steadfast leader of the Transcaucasian Bolsheviks, Lavrentii Beria, has extended enormous help to the Communist Party of Armenia . . . and its former leader Khandzhian . . ., [who] shot himself at a time when he had been raised to lofty heights as leader of the entire Party organization. That shot we cannot help calling a traitor's shot.[26]

There were hints that Khandzhian had connections with suspicious people, and a few months later he was retroactively named an enemy of the people. On this basis almost the entire leadership of the Armenian Party was cut down.

Sergo Ordzhonikidze's death was attributed to a heart attack, and the doctors who signed the false autopsy report were arrested and destroyed. This procedure was not new. In 1932 the suicide of Stalin's wife, Nadezhda Allilueva, was reported as death from appendicitis, and subsequently, at the very beginning of the mass repression, the doctors who signed the report were executed.

Stalinist officials committed ordinary as well as political crimes. They built themselves luxurious private houses and villas, illegally spending millions of rubles of state funds. Some, like G. F. Aleksandrov, a leading ideologist and administrator, created dens of debauchery near Moscow. Beria used to drive around Moscow in his car, looking for young women who were then delivered to his dacha. And all this was made possible by the lack of a free press. To get proper leaders, Lenin said, there must be full public disclosure of all the activities and qualities of the candidates. The masses should have the right to check up on every step of their leaders' activities.[27]

Freedom of speech and of the press have been demanded by every truly democratic revolution. As the French "Declaration of the Rights

[25] Reported by S. O. Gazarian.
[26] The Armenian newspaper *Kommunist*, July 15, 1936.
[27] Lenin, *Polnoe sobranie*, VIII, p. 96.

of Man and Citizen" pointed out, the necessity of making the demand is itself evidence of despotism.[28] For Marx, freedom of the press was never even a debatable question. From the very beginning of his revolutionary activity he expressed his complete hostility to censorship, which

> does not abolish conflict but makes it one-sided, transforms . . . the conflict of principles into conflict between a powerless principle and an unprincipled power. . . . A censored press has a demoralizing effect. The greatest vice, hypocrisy, is inseparable from it, and hence . . . the vice of passivity. The government hears only its own voice, . . . yet keeps up the self-deception that it hears the voice of the people, and demands that the people support this self-deception. On their side the people either fall into political superstition and political skepticism or turn completely away from state affairs, become transformed into a crowd of individuals living their private lives.[29]

Lenin, in September, 1917, wrote a special article on freedom of the press, outlining the method by which the Soviet government would guarantee the freedom to all groups of citizens.[30] A few days after the October Revolution he signed the "Decree on the Press," which allowed restrictions on the press only in moments of crisis and promised full freedom "within the limits of responsibility, as judged by a court, in accordance with the broadest and most progressive law."[31] The Civil War prevented this decree from being put into effect. The proletarian revolution had to liquidate bourgeois newspapers and journals that called for the overthrow of the Soviet regime. But a few months after the Civil War ended, Lenin projected a number of measures to extend freedom of speech and press.

A survey of the journals and newspapers published in 1921–22 shows how freely problems were discussed in that period. Of course censorship, military for the most part, was preserved. In a keynote article, "Freedom of the Press and the State," which set out government policy at the beginning of 1921, Lunacharskii wrote that censorship was necessary to prevent the dissemination of counterrevolutionary ideas.

> But the person who says "Down with all these prejudices about free speech; state control of literature suits our Communist system; censorship is not a horrible feature of the transitional period but something inherent in a well-ordered socialized life"—the person who

---

[28] See F. Buonarrotti, *Zagovor vo imia ravenstva* (Moscow, 1948), p. 89. *Ed.*: A translation of Filippo Buonarrotti, *Conspiration pour l'égalité dite de Babeuf* (Brussels, 1828).

[29] Marx and Engels, *Sochineniia*, 2nd edn., I, p. 69.

[30] Lenin, *Sochineniia*, 3rd edn., XXI, p. 152.

[31] *Dekrety Sovetskoi vlasti*, I (1957), p. 24.

infers from this that criticism should be transformed into some sort of denunciation, or into cutting down a work of art to fit primitive revolutionary patterns, such a person shows only that under the Communist, if you scratch him a little, you will find a Derzhimorda.[32] Whatever power he gets, he sees nothing in it but the pleasure of throwing his weight around, the pleasure of bullying, and especially of grab-'em-and-don't-let-'em-go. . . . We do show such symptoms; we cannot help it, we are a people with too low a level of culture. The danger of a strong proletarian regime, vested in junior agents and accidental spokesmen, being transformed into a police regime, an Arakcheev regime,[33] is real and present, and must be avoided by every means.[34]

Stalin was one of the "junior agents" Lunacharskii warned against. Under his direct influence, from the mid-twenties, there was a steady restriction in the publicity attending Party and state affairs. When Stalin achieved one-man rule he extended his personal control of all sources of information to an unheard-of degree. Party members and citizens in general were given no other information than Stalin and his aides thought necessary. The idea of a proletarian monopoly on the press was perverted; freedom of speech was simply liquidated. The press was closed not only to enemy criticism and mudslinging, which was quite proper, but also to criticism from Party positions, to criticism of the political, economic, and cultural perversions that abounded in the years of the cult.

The absence of publicity enabled Stalin to cover up his crimes and also to be the complete master, especially when even the most important officials were denied information that he knew about. It seemed to everyone that Stalin knew much more than they, which deprived them of confidence in their own powers and initiative. In her open letter to *Izvestiia* on the fifteenth anniversary of Stalin's death, Lydia Chukovskaia described the situation:

> What got us into this unprecedented trouble? Into this utter defenselessness of people in front of a machine rolling over them? Into this historically unexampled merger, fusion, union, of the state security organs (which were breaking the law every minute of the day and night) with the procuratorial organs that exist to uphold the law (yet became obsequiously blind for years on end), and finally with the newspapers, which are supposed to defend justice but instead excreted planned, mechanized slander on the persecuted—millions of millions of lying words—on "hardened," "vicious" enemies of

[32] *Ed.:* A character in Gogol's *Inspector General,* whose name—its literal meaning is "Hold the snout"—has become an eponym for officials who rule by browbeating and force.

[33] *Ed.:* Arakcheev was a prominent martinet under Alexander I. His name became an eponym for militaristic despotism.

[34] *Pechat' i revoliutsiia,* 1921, No. 1, p. 7.

the people, who had "sold themselves to foreign intelligence services," and are now rehabilitated? When and how was this accomplished, this combination, undoubtedly the most dangerous of all the chemical combinations known to scientists? How was it possible? . . . *The murder of the truthful word*—it too derives from the cursed time of Stalin. And it was one of the blackest crimes in all history. The loss of the right to independent thought closed the door in Stalin's time to doubt, questioning, cries of alarm, and opened it to the self-confident, shameless, multi-copied and multi-persistent lie. The hourly repeated lie kept people from finding out what was being done in their native country to their fellow citizens; some did not know because of their simplicity, their naïveté, others because they did not want to know. Whoever knew or guessed was condemned to shut up, keep quiet, for fear of perishing the next day; not fear of trouble at work, unemployment or poverty, but plain physical destruction. What a great honor was shown to words in that time: for them people were killed.

Of course state secrets are necessary. But Stalin put a curtain of secrecy around matters that require maximum publicity. He turned the Party's monopoly of the press against the Party and the people.

4

NEVER HAVE THE HEROIC and the tragic been intertwined as they were in the Soviet Union during the thirties. As a recent author points out, "the meaning of those years is too complex and contradictory to permit, only two or three decades later, a completely dispassionate and conclusive judgment."[35] Still we can say with assurance that it was an epoch not only of political reaction but also of revolutionary progress, which influenced Stalin as well as everyone else.

Stalin knew that he could keep his power only if he declared himself a supporter of democracy, socialism, Marxism-Leninism. A dual personality can be detected in Stalin's behavior. He did more than issue orders for arrests and shootings. As the leader of the first socialist state in the world, he had to decide many questions of economic and cultural development, of foreign policy and the international workers' movement. He made many mistakes which cost the Soviet people dear. But he had to consider the ideology and the collective will of the Party, Lenin's heritage, the socialist aspirations of the workers. Thus the cult of Stalin's personality could restrain but could not entirely stop the rapid development of Soviet society in some areas. That is one reason why it was difficult to expose the crimes of Stalin, for the offi-

[35] S. S. Smirnov, "Smert' Komsomolki," *Komsomol'skaia pravda*, Nov. 16, 1966.

cial propaganda attributed all the achievements of the Soviet people to him.

It was known that Party and state leaders were being arrested as "enemies of the people," but at the same time new schools, factories, and palaces of culture were rising everywhere. Military leaders were being arrested as spies, but the Party was building a strong, modern army. Scientists were being arrested as wreckers, but Soviet science had developed rapidly with the Party's support. Writers were being arrested as Trotskyites and counterrevolutionaries, but some literary works appeared that were real masterpieces. Leaders in the union republics were being arrested as nationalists, but the formerly oppressed nationalities were improving their lot, and friendship among the peoples of the USSR was growing. And this obvious progress filled Soviet hearts with pride, engendering confidence in the Party that was organizing it and in the man who stood at the head of the Party. Stalin even profited from the accidental fact that 1937, the most frightful year of repression, happened to be blessed with the most bountiful harvest of the prewar period. Claude Roy has compared Stalin to the savage warriors who move into battle driving the wives and children of their opponents before them. Stalin sheltered himself behind a people advancing out of ignorance and backwardness. His opponents could not strike at him without striking their loved ones.[36] Though the metaphor does not give a completely accurate picture of the period, there is a great deal of truth in it.

Some writers and memoirists try to explain the behavior of people in the thirties primarily by fear. Nikolai Aseev, for example, describes people's feelings on the death of Stalin, in his poem "Faithful to Lenin":

> Why the crowd at the grave?
> People run from all sides
> To check, to see for sure,
> What he will leave after death.
>   . . .
> And then, by the mortal remains,
> We didn't know how to behave.
> Remain petrified with fear
> Or begin to talk loudly?

Such an interpretation of the recent past is misleading and insincere. Of course many people were afraid of Stalin, especially those close to him; Stalin knew how to inspire dread. Many people feared the NKVD, feared repression. Evtushenko writes of these fears very graphically:

[36] *Liberation,* June 25, 1963.

> I remember their power and force
> In the court of the conquering lie.
> Fears slid everywhere like shadows,
> Penetrated every storey.
> Quietly they trained people,
> And left their mark on everything,
> Taught shouting where silence should be
> And silence where one ought to shout.

In reminiscences of the mid-thirties, a former section chief of the Red Army General Staff, V. A. Novobranets, describes

that very complex feeling of fear which possessed us all in the years of the cult of personality. We were afraid to bring on ourselves the charge of lack of "vigilance." We were afraid to break Party discipline; senior comrades overwhelmed us with their authority. We were afraid we would be accused of a "right deviation," a "left exaggeration," a "right-leftish bloc." We were scared of the word "Trotskyite" as little children are scared of "the big bad wolf." Finally, we were simply afraid for our own composure, were afraid to overload our strained days of study by examination of some doubts and questions that were unclear to us.

A. Pis'mennyi writes about the same thing in his memoirs:

There was something animal-like—this must be admitted—probably some affinity with the zoological instinct of self-preservation, in the complex, I would even say diseased, process of learning to believe, of submitting to the implacable and at the same time dubious logic of social life in the thirties. Perhaps this was the most unbearable part. Behind all the lofty reasoning, the vast calculations, the ideological and political conjectures, hiding and dancing in my noble mind was a little demon of ordinary fear. It was not preaching lofty principles and was not given to the speechifying cant that had become so customary. The little demon of the instinct of self-preservation, with its ugly lewd face, was naïve and shrewd. It did not get involved with political analysis. In its common sense there was more wisdom of everyday life than in dozens of learned books. Its skeptical ideas about the surrounding world had to be kept hidden from other people because, though these ideas were perhaps closest of all to the truth of everyday life, they might have been considered philistine and even reactionary.

For many people, however, fear of repression was not simply blind animal fear for their lives, as Pis'mennyi himself explains further on. Many Bolsheviks who feared repression in the thirties had boldly faced up to prison, forced labor, and execution in the tsarist period. They knew that the revolutionary movement was dangerous, but they were not afraid. In the years of the cult people were possessed by fear of being disgraced. For the majority trusted Stalin, believed that he was sincerely serving the people, saw the growth of socialism around them, and feared being outside this mainstream. "It would take a really talented writer . . . to reproduce the thoughts and feelings that possessed thousands and thousands of people in that period," writes another memoirist.

> There was agonizing bewilderment and a passionate desire to understand something; there was unspeakable fear and faith in common sense; there was hope flooding the heart and despair laying waste the soul. How can one describe the condition of people who sensed with all their being the approach of a terrible disaster and did not know how to escape it, how to save themselves, and remained bound and helpless as in a nightmare? . . . How can one describe the mood of people who had no possibility of explaining anything because questions were lacking, who had no possibility of vindicating themselves because there were no charges against them, who understood the full horror of their position, the ominous danger hanging over them and those close to them, and at the same time had to act as if there was no cause for concern, as if everything was all right, had to preserve their cheerfulness and capacity to work?[37]

To understand why it was easy for Stalin to convince people about the existence of an extensive fascist underground, we must also recall the grim atmosphere of the thirties. As early as 1907, A. Bogdanov, who was still a Bolshevik at the time, foresaw the possibility that the first socialist states might be islands in a sea of capitalist states, which would try to destroy them by repeated attacks.

> It is difficult to predict the outcome of those clashes. But even where socialism would hold out and emerge the victor, its character would be profoundly and lastingly distorted by the many years of its besieged condition, of unavoidable terror and a military regime. . . . That would be very different from our socialism.[38]

Much of this prediction came painfully close to reality. The Soviet Union was a besieged fortress, and its citizens realized that a death struggle with fascism was inevitable. The result was an atmosphere of alarm as well as exaltation.

The memory of the intense and cruel class struggle of the preceding decade was fresh in everyone's memory. Some of those who had been defeated formed counterrevolutionary organizations, though as a rule

---

[37] B. E. Efimov, *Mikhail Kol'tsov, kakim on byl* (Moscow, 1965), p. 69. Efimov is an artist.
[38] A. Bogdanov, *Krasnaia zvezda* (St. Petersburg, 1907), p. 119. "Our" refers to the ideal socialism of the Martian who gives this speech in a science-fiction novel.

they were small and uncoordinated. They agitated against the Soviet regime, and in some cases actually committed acts of sabotage in factories, burned down *kolkhoz* buildings, or planned terrorist attacks. Party propaganda ceaselessly played upon these actions to heighten the spirit of vigilance.

The espionage and subversive activities of imperialist intelligence agencies, especially those of the fascist states, were stepped up in those years. They sent in spies, drawing them from the numerous émigré organizations, and also tried to recruit spies among unstable or hostile citizens within the country. Even in the 1920's hundreds of foreign agents and dozens of armed bands were arrested at the borders every year.

But even the alarming international situation of the thirties did not justify the spy mania, the artificial incitement of passions, the vast exaggeration in reports of enemy organizations. Ordinary people and even most leading officials lacked sufficient information to appraise these reports. Thus Stalin's charges of espionage against his former political opponents and his myth of a widespread counterrevolutionary underground seemed believable to many people. Konstantin Simonov testifies to the overwhelming influence of the conviction that war was near at hand:

> In the spring of 1937, when I heard about the trial of Tukhachev- skii, Iakir, and the other military commanders—as a boy in the twenties I had seen Tukhachevskii several times—I trembled, but I believed that what I read was true, that a military conspiracy really did exist, and the participants were connected with Germany and wanted to carry out a fascist coup in our country. At the time I had no other explanation for what was happening.[39]

In short, the widespread belief in the existence of an extensive under- ground facilitated Stalin's realization of his criminal plans. His cruelty and mistrust even seemed desirable qualities to many people.

Today some Communists call Stalin a counterrevolutionary, and consider the events of 1936–38 a counterrevolutionary coup. This is an oversimplification. It is true that Stalin did more than slow down the development of socialist society. (The widespread cliché about this "slowing down" [*tormozhenie*] is also an oversimplification.) In many respects he and his accomplices turned the Revolution back- ward, forcing the Soviet Union to diverge far from the principles of socialism proclaimed by the October Revolution. In these respects he can properly be called a counterrevolutionary. But he also continued to rely on the masses, which was the chief peculiarity of Stalin's actions and the ultimate determinant of his success.

[39] K. Simonov, *"Kommentarii k voennym dnevnikam 1941 goda,"* p. 64. *Ed.:* This seems to be an unpublished manuscript.

Napoleon discarded revolutionary phraseology as he secured one-man rule. Stalin behaved differently, masking his usurpation of power in ultrarevolutionary phrases. Thus he secured the support of the people, without which even such a despot as Stalin could not have maintained himself. And he was obliged to refrain from complete subversion of socialist principles.

Of course Stalin's usurpation of power may be considered a coup d'état. But it was a very unusual coup. It was accomplished "from above," gradually, over the course of many years, with revolutionary slogans. It destroyed some of the gains of the Revolution, but not all.

The "before-the-storm" atmosphere also helps to explain why officials who understood that innocent people were perishing refrained from opposing Stalin and the NKVD. "Stalin had already managed to get a death grip on power," writes G. S. Pomerants,

> and to strike at Stalin meant to strike at the Soviet system. But the Soviet system was one of the strongest obstacles to fascism. Not by reason of Stalin's dislike for Hitler—he may have liked him—but by the logic of the system itself, which was stronger than Stalin's will. And it was impossible to perform surgical operations, to strike at the Soviet system even to cure it, with Hitler standing there.[40]

Pomerants runs together the war and the prewar years, so his reasoning is only partly correct. The dilemma—Stalin or Hitler?—arose in the war, not before. When it did, even White émigrés were faced with the choice. Some took Hitler's side, some took neutral positions, but many, including Miliukov, supported the Red Army.[41] If even émigrés supported Stalin during the war, Soviet people were all the more obliged to do so. This choice was not so categorical in the years before the war. Stalin's crimes were so great that, had they been known, it would have been impossible to support him even by reference to the threat of fascism. But that, once again, was the problem: almost none of the Communists at the time knew the scale of these crimes or realized how dangerous they were. Thus, misgivings did not lead as a rule to concrete actions. "Of course there was a lot we did not know, and did not even suspect about Stalin's monstrous plans," one old Bolshevik has said to the author. (He helped build Magnitogorsk and then spent many years in jails and camps.)

[40] G. Pomerants, op. cit., on p. 324.
[41] In 1941, in an émigré paper published in Vichy France, Miliukov endorsed the formula "If you're not for Stalin, that means you're for Hitler." The fact that Milukov chose the Soviet side is to his credit. But the reasons he gave for his choice are curious. He saw in Stalin's "new form of one-man dictatorship . . . a new step forward in the evolution of the Russian state organization."

However, we did see all around us many faults, mistakes, even crimes. Why did we not immediately rise up against them? In the thirties we felt as if we were at war, at war with the entire old world, and we believed that in war you should act like there's a war on. In other words, we should swear at the blunders of the high command not during the conflict but after the battle. While the conflict was on, a conflict to the death, it was necessary to maintain iron discipline no matter what. We considered it natural to ignore the successes of the enemy, and to exaggerate our own still very modest successes in every way possible. That's always how it is in a war.

E. Vladimirova speaks about these reflections somewhat differently in one of her prison poems:

> Afraid to break the structure of customary thoughts,
> Fearing to see the truth naked,
> We seek grounds to preserve our calm
> And avoid spiritual schism.
>
> Hiding our cowardly heads under our wings,
> Submissively accepting any evil,
> We say, "Let it be hard on us,
> We will forgive our homeland anything."
> Forgive . . . whom? and what?
> If only the country needed our pain, then we would accept
> Pain and any sentence without a word about forgiveness.
>
> In the dread hour that has come upon our land,
> Under storm clouds of war that threaten every hour,
> We should not forgive, but answer,
> Where is the truth and where the lie, where the
>   path and where the danger?
>
> We must give an answer: Who needed
> The monstrous destruction of the generation
> That the country, severe and tender,
> Raised for twenty years in work and battle?

Such misgivings, such insights into Stalinism, can be found to a much greater extent among prisoners than among those who remained free. Only when people landed in prison did they come to see the frightful inside truth of the Stalinist dictatorship and the extraordinary dimensions of the terror. As the Polish writer Jerzy Lec puts it: "Certain thoughts come into your head only when you're under guard."

5

LONG BEFORE the October Revolution, the Bolshevik Party was based on strict centralization. Indeed, this was one of its distinguishing

features; many arguments between Bolsheviks and Mensheviks focused
on the relationship between democracy and centralism. The Mensheviks protested against strict organization, the increasing authority of
Party centers, and the transformation of Party members into "cogs in
the Party machine." Plekhanov's article "Centralism or Bonapartism"[42]
is characteristic. Opposing the concentration of too much authority in
the Central Committee, he declared that centralism was a noose chok-
ing the Party, that it was Bonapartism if not absolute monarchy. Lenin
decisively rejected such charges: "The answer to the gossip about
Bonapartism is: Nonsense! It's beneath our dignity to reply."[43] Lenin
perceived the danger of extreme centralism, but he also saw that it was
the centralized discipline of the Bolsheviks, no less than their correct
policies, that gave them the lead in the revolutionary struggle.

In the first years after the October Revolution, centralism was
intensified. Beating back the imperialist intervention, mobilizing an
exhausted and devastated country for struggle with the enemy, the
Bolsheviks had to centralize power and limit democracy. "The idea of
revolution," Lunacharskii wrote in 1921,

> is firmly connected in most people's minds with the idea of freedom.
> . . . In fact no revolution creates a regime of freedom or can create
> it. Revolution is civil war, invariably accompanied by external war.
> . . . That is why even a socialist revolution, which announces an
> end to all wars and the abolition of all state power as its ultimate
> ideals, is forced in its first stage to intensify the spirit of its own
> kind of militarism, to intensify the dictatorial quality of state power
> and even, so to speak, its quality as a police state.[44]

The Comintern too was committed to the strictest centralization. Each
of its member parties was regarded only as a section of the central
organization, and a tight, almost military discipline was maintained
within these sections.[45]

How appropriate for all Communist parties were the various elements of centralization adopted by the Bolshevik Party during the
Civil War? That question is subject to debate, but one cannot deny
that many of the restrictions on democracy in the USSR were considered temporary, connected only with a certain period of development. As the Civil War was coming to an end, the Party adopted a
number of measures to decrease centralization and develop democracy.
The IXth Party Conference of September 22–25, 1920, resolved that

> It is necessary in the internal life of the Party to achieve broader
> criticism, both of local and of central Party institutions. The Central

[42] Plekhanov, *Sobranie sochinenii,* XIII, pp. 81–93.
[43] Lenin, *Polnoe sobranie,* VIII, p. 423.
[44] *Pechat' i revoliutsiia,* 1921, No. 1, pp. 3–4.
[45] See Lenin, *Sochineniia,* 4th edn., XXXI, p. 185.

Committee is instructed to indicate ways to broaden intraparty criticism at general meetings. Publications should be created that would be capable of achieving a more systematic and broader criticism of the Party's mistakes (discussion leaflets, etc.) . . . Any repression of comrades for being dissidents on certain issues that the Party has already decided is intolerable.[46]

Six months later the Xth Party Congress, which worked under Lenin's direction, warned once again that there were many negative aspects of excessive centralization: bureaucracy, isolation from the masses, rule by force, decline in Party morale. The resolutions of the Congress called for a revival of intraparty democracy to correct these abuses.[47] Of course, elimination of centralization was out of the question. Even after the Civil War a powerful state was necessary for defense and for the mobilization of resources to achieve industrialization. The huge and ever-growing economic machine of a modern society creates a basis for centralization by requiring coordinated, effective, firm leadership. But one cannot agree that "socialist democracy was absolutely excluded," or that "Stalin was right in quickly abolishing NEP," because "the creation of socialism in a ruined backward country required a period of 'primitive accumulation,' " with the state "directly exploiting workers and peasants."[48] The Soviet Union needed not blind, thoughtless, unlimited centralism but a wise combination of centralization with local initiative and individual creativity, of state discipline with personal freedom. Stalin did not find—he did not even seek—such a combination. Covering himself with the thesis that the class struggle was intensifying, he constantly pressed for greater one-sided centralization. The repression of the thirties completed the process. Centralization was transformed into absolutism. But this repression became possible only when Stalin's power had already exceeded all reasonable bounds. Such excessive power could corrupt even the best people; in the hands of a limited, ambitious, and spiteful careerist, it inevitably led to the criminal abuse of power.

In short, centralization was necessary, but it should have been accompanied by effective guarantees against the abuse of power. Without such counterweights, centralized power was bound to degenerate from democratic centralism into bureaucratic centralism, and then into despotism. What is more; bureaucratic centralism not only leads to despotism; at a certain stage of development it makes that despotism almost insuperable.

It was difficult to draw a line between reasonable and unreasonable centralization in the before-the-storm atmosphere of the thirties—all

[46] *KPSS v rezoliutsiiakh,* I (1953), p. 509.
[47] *Ibid.,* pp. 517–19.
[48] *Ed.:* Medvedev does not indicate the source or author of this quotation, which has been greatly abridged.

the more reason to establish definite guarantees today. A proletarian state based on the trust of the masses, welded together by Marxist-Leninist ideology, and led by one party, has immeasurable force. We must make sure that this force does not fall into the hands of political adventurers and irresponsible promoters (*prozhektery*),[49] that it is always used in the interests of the people, not against the people.

Another important factor in explaining Stalinism is the lack of a system for regularly changing the Party and state leadership. Lenin was chief of the Party continuously for a quarter of a century. But he was also the founder of the Bolshevik Party and the Soviet State; he was a genius of a type that appears in the political arena perhaps once in a century. A different system and other terms of power were necessary for Lenin's successors. Yet after his death as before, the Party had no system of limits on the length of time an individual might remain at the head of the Party and the state.

Today social psychologists are investigating the psychology of the masses, of various social and professional groups. They should also examine the psychology of power, of leadership, its normal and pathological forms. Gorky called attention to this problem back in 1934, in a conversation with some writers. He tried to distinguish the concepts of "the chief" (*vozhd'*) and "chiefism" (*vozhdizm*).

> Chiefs are needed as leaders (*rukovoditeli*) who know the shorter routes to the goal set by the people. By the people, in the name of the people, and not by the chief, in the name of his personal goal. . . . The chief of working people is always a model of the lofty morality of self-sacrifice. I would even claim that the most important trait of a popular chief is his modesty, his revulsion against phrasemaking and striking poses. A pseudo chief is very pleased by honors and glorification. His high position intoxicates him, he loses the last remnants of reason, like the Pythia. . . . It is a complex phenomenon, but undoubtedly chiefism is a disease of the psyche, in which the ego grows like a sarcoma, corrupting the mind. In this disease the personal principle hypertrophies, the collective principle atrophies. Without a doubt chiefism is a chronic disease. It can become acute. . . . Stricken with chiefism, a person is infected by megalomania, and following after it like a dark shadow is a persecution mania. . . . He was a man, and is not a man any longer.[50]

Research into the psychology of leadership (*liderstvo*) should include methods of curing its pathological forms; not the least effective method is regular replacement of people in power.

[49] *Ed.:* This term was used by the Central Committee to explain the dismissal of Khrushchev at the end of 1964, when it was commonly translated as "harebrained schemer." A *prozhekter,* says a Soviet dictionary, is "a fancier of unrealizable projects."

[50] Quoted by I. Shkap, *Sem' let s Gor'kim* (Moscow, 1964), pp. 249–50.

Something must also be said about the Party's monopoly of political activity. Just after the October Revolution Lenin strongly opposed the creation of a united "socialist" government, which would have included Right Social Revolutionaries and Mensheviks. But Lenin did not at that time come out for a one-party government. The Bolsheviks invited the Left S-R's to enter the Council of People's Commissars, giving them seven of the eighteen seats, including the Commissariats of Agriculture, Justice, and City and Local Self-Government. Nor was the political activity of many other parties banned right after the October Revolution. Only on June 14, 1918, in view of Right S-R and Menshevik participation in the fight against the Soviet regime, the All-Russian Central Executive Committee decreed the expulsion of Right S-R's and Mensheviks from all Soviets. In July, 1918, after the rising of the Left S-R's, the same decree was issued for them. But even after their expulsion from the Soviets, the S-R and Menshevik parties continued to exist as legal, active political organizations. Moreover, when the Menshevik Central Committee at the end of 1918 opposed foreign intervention and collaboration with the bourgeoisie and rejected the proposal for a Constituent Assembly, the Central Executive Committee rescinded the decree of June 14 with respect to the Mensheviks. In February, 1919, the same was done with respect to Right S-R's who opposed intervention.[51] Maximalist S-R's and Bundists opposed Kolchak in 1919, and the Party did not decline temporary agreements with these groups. During 1919 the S-R's and Mensheviks held legal congresses and other meetings in the Soviet Republic.

An analysis of Lenin's speeches and articles during 1917–21 shows that he did not assume the existence of only the Bolshevik Party and a complete ban on others. On the contrary, he said that after basic revolutionary changes had been carried out, free elections should be held. He did not doubt that the Bolsheviks would win, but it was taken for granted that other parties would have a chance to present their programs in these elections. The Civil War, devastation, and famine all delayed, but by no means ruled out, the holding of such elections.

When the Civil War ended, the issue took a new turn, which has not been adequately studied. In 1920, the Left S-R's, the Maximalists, and the Populist Communists decided to end their existence as parties. In March, 1920, the Borot'bists and left S-R's of the Ukraine were taken into the Ukrainian Communist Party. In 1921 the left wing of the Bund also decided to join the Communist Party. The Right S-R's, the Mensheviks, and the Anarchists went through a serious crisis at the beginning of the decade, and could not work out any definite program

[51] See E. G. Gimpel'son, "Iz istorii obrazovaniia odnopartiinoi sistemy v SSSR," *Voprosy istorii,* 1965, No. 11, p. 21.

or enduring organization. Many of the leftists in these parties joined the Bolsheviks, some for careerist reasons. Some took part in the counterrevolutionary outbursts of 1920–21 (the Kronstadt rising, the kulak riots in Tambov, etc.). The Anarchist Party supported Makhno's action against the Soviet regime.[52]

Nevertheless it is also apparent that the Soviet government's policy towards some of these parties was not irreproachable. The open trial of the leaders of the Right S-R's is a case in point. From the end of May through the summer of 1922, Lenin was seriously ill. The trial, which lasted from June 8 to August 7, was evidently organized by the General Secretary, Stalin. (The chairman of the Supreme Tribunal of the Central Executive Committee was Piatakov, and the chief prosecutor was N. V. Krylenko.) A number of people, including Gorky, issued strong protests against the trial. Of course the Right S-R's had a long record of crimes against the Soviet government. Suffice it to recall Fanny Kaplan's attempt to kill Lenin in 1918, the assassination of Uritskii and Volodarskii, and the crimes of S-R authorities in the Volga region during the summer of 1918, and in Arkhangelsk. Nonetheless, in 1919 the Soviet government declared an amnesty and legalized the Right S-R Party, which began to publish its newspaper, *Delo naroda,* in Moscow. But in 1920, kulak uprisings broke out in many *oblasti,* headed for the most part by Right S-R's. The Party's conference in 1920 heard appeals for terror, and that same year an alliance against the Bolsheviks was formed between Right S-R's and left-wing Cadets. Evidently there was sufficient basis for a criminal investigation of the Right S-R's.

Of course the Soviet court should have proceeded carefully and objectively. Deliberate crimes had to be distinguished from political mistakes, and the personal responsibility of each leader had to be established, for the S-R Party was never a tightly centralized organization. In painful fact, the trial took a very different course. It is probable that the organizers of the trial even had recourse to provocation, to achieve greater political impact. In addition to the real leaders of the Right S-R's, who strove to defend themselves and justify their Party's activities, there were defendants who had not been leaders and, in a number of cases, had not even been members. These people zealously agreed with the indictment and repented for crimes they had taken no part in.

One such defendant was Rufina Stavitskaia (or Faina Stavskaia). She was well known to many eminent Bolsheviks as an activist of the Anarcho-Communists. In 1922 she had applied for admission to the

[52] *Ed.:* For a concise analysis of Nestor Makhno's complex relations with the Soviet regime during the Civil War, see E. H. Carr, *The Bolshevik Revolution,* I, pp. 302–304.

Bolshevik Party. A peculiar test was set for her: to expose the Right S-R's at the trial.[53] She agreed, and today her husband tries to justify her action, which is a disgrace for a true revolutionary.

> 1922 was an extremely hard year for Rufina Stavitskaia. In her youth she had taken the revolutionary path and ceaselessly sought to give her life to the cause of world social revolution. Now she was faced with the prospect of giving not her life but something that is dearer for every revolutionary. In the interests of the dictatorship of the proletariat and its socialist revolution, she was asked to give her revolutionary honor, as the old revolutionaries and political prisoners understood that honor. She was obliged by the will of the leading force of the proletarian revolution to take part in a big trial that exposed and destroyed the enemies of the proletarian regime who were at that time ideologically and politically the most wicked, the most dangerous. . . . Soon afterward she was admitted to the Communist Party, which she had served as well as she could until then.[54]

The Supreme Tribunal sentenced her to two years of solitary confinement. But the same decision also stated:

> With respect to Semenov, Konopleva, Efimov, Usov, Zubkov, Fedorov-Kozlov, Pelevin, Stavskaia, Dashevskii, the Supreme Tribunal finds: these defendants were honestly mistaken when they committed their serious crimes, for they believed that they were fighting in the interests of the Revolution. . . . The above-named defendants have completely recognized the full gravity of the crime they committed, and the Tribunal, in complete confidence that they will courageously and selflessly fight for the Soviet regime in the ranks of the working class . . . petitions the Presidium of the Central Executive Committee to release them from all punishment.

And in fact Stavitskaia was freed, sent to work in the Crimea, and accepted as a member of the Communist Party. Later she became director of a historical library, but in 1937 she was arrested and shot.

After this trial, both the Right S-R and the Menshevik parties were banned. Legal political activity was now possible only for the Communist Party. Since the S-R's and Mensheviks had lost their connections with the masses, their repeated attempts to resume illegal activity were unsuccessful. Lacking a uniform program or tactics, they broke into many small groups. Both of these fragmented parties included revolutionaries who were striving for socialism, though they had a different vision of it than the Bolsheviks. Their leaflets and other publications, including newspapers—the *Sotsialisticheskii vestnik* of

[53] V. Baranchenko, "Vozvrashchenie chesti. Zhizn' i gibel' Fainy Stavskoi" (manuscript). Baranchenko, an old Bolshevik, was her husband.
[54] *Ibid.*

the Mensheviks and *Revoliutsionnaia Rossiia* of the S-R's—which were printed abroad and illegally distributed in the USSR, contained some just criticism of the Bolsheviks. For example, the S-R's, while fully supporting socialist agrarian cooperatives—that was one of the main points in their own program—criticized Stalin's methods of establishing cooperatives. S-R and Menshevik publications attacked the bureaucratization of the state *apparat*, the repression of technical specialists, the trial of the "Industrial Party" and the "Union Bureau." At the same time a significant fraction of the S-R's opposed terror, declaring themselves in favor of "ethical socialism." The movement toward the goal, they reasoned, should be advanced not by any means whatever but by means that would educate militants for communism. They also spoke out against all arbitrary rule and even against the state itself, for they continued to draw their ideas from Lavrov and Chernyshevskii.

However, despite hard times and widespread dissatisfaction in the USSR during the late twenties and early thirties, the S-R's and Mensheviks had no success with their propaganda. Their publications were printed in insignificant numbers, their agitators were easily caught by the OGPU, their illegal organizations were invariably liquidated a few months after formation. For neither the S-R's nor the Mensheviks had persuasive answers to the questions that disturbed the people. They were too closely connected in people's minds with the discredited Provisional Government, the attempt to assassinate Lenin, the Civil War terror in the north and in the Volga region, and conciliation with the capitalists. In their criticism of the Bolsheviks, they belittled the social gains of the October Revolution and the Soviet regime. For all these reasons they failed to reach the masses, and by the beginning of the thirties almost all their illegal organizations had dwindled from insignificance to nonexistence.

Although the Bolsheviks' treatment of the other democratic parties was not beyond reproach, it should be pointed out that the Communist Party's monopoly of political activity was a product of history; in a certain period it was an important condition for the realization of the dictatorship of the proletariat. But while the one-party system has some positive aspects, negative tendencies result from its prolonged existence. Serious mistakes of the leadership are not discussed in the open, the leaders' responsibility for their actions is reduced, bureaucratic degeneration and even a transition to a despotic system are facilitated. That was the evolutionary pattern of the Stalinist regime. It is not surprising that today almost all the Communist Parties of Western Europe have declared their opposition to a one-party system.

Of course, in the Soviet Union today a change to any sort of multiparty system is not possible or feasible. But this very fact greatly reinforces the need to create specific safeguards against arbitrary rule and bureaucratic distortions, safeguards built into the structure and working methods of the ruling Party itself.

6

PARTY DISCIPLINE cannot be discussed in the abstract, outside the context of the members' beliefs or the policies of the Party centers. According to Lenin, the necessary conditions for discipline in a revolutionary party are: (1) the consciousness of the proletarian vanguard, its devotion to the revolution and its readiness for self-sacrifice; (2) the ability of the vanguard to merge with the broad masses; and (3) correct policies, on condition that the broad masses become convinced of this correctness by their own experience.[55] Thus Party unity must not be construed to mean absolute suppression of any and all groups and tendencies in the Party, independently of concrete historical conditions and of the actual policies of the Party leaders at a given time. Unity obviously gives any party great strength. But sometimes unity is a manifestation of weakness, especially when an entire party is moving as one man in the wrong direction.

Under Lenin, there were always various tendencies and groups within the Party, which was considered natural and normal. Lenin never demanded the excommunication of comrades who agreed with the Party program as a whole but disagreed with the leaders on certain issues of policy. Only when the country was emerging from the Civil War, when difficulties were growing to the point that a split between the workers and the peasants was threatening, only then did Lenin denounce arguments among Bolsheviks and present a special resolution on Party unity that contained a categorical demand: dissolve all groups and factions based on political platforms that had been rejected by the Xth Party Congress.[56] This resolution, including a secret seventh point permitting expulsion from the Party of Central Committee members elected at the Xth Congress, was frequently cited by Stalin in his struggle for power. But Stalin seriously distorted the meaning of the resolution. It condemned factions, but it did not take away the members' right to criticize Party policy. Indeed, the resolution said that criticism was obligatory, and that Party members had the right to control Party decisions. To ensure the exercise of these prerogatives,

[55] See Lenin, *Left-wing Communism: An Infantile Disorder.* Cf. also his *Polnoe sobranie,* XX, pp. 300–304, where he declares that denunciation of factionalism distracts attention from what is really important: the policy of the various factions. Cf. also *Voprosy istorii KPSS,* 1965, No. 2, p. 34.

[56] *X-yi S'ezd RKP. Stenograficheskii otchet* (Moscow, 1963), p. 521 and *passim.*

the Congress ordered regular publication of a "Discussion Leaflet" and of "special collections" of articles.[57]

Lenin opposed factions but he did not demand that their members immediately change their views and convictions; he only proposed a halt in mass propaganda of these views. Indeed he stressed the necessity of publishing divergent views.[58] Secondly, in proposing the resolution for Party unity, Lenin emphasized that it applied to the current period and to the disagreements under discussion at the Xth Congress. He strongly opposed a broad interpretation of the resolution. When D. B. Riazanov proposed an amendment forbidding not only factional activity but also election campaigns to future congresses on the basis of platforms, Lenin disapproved:

> I think that Comrade Riazanov's wish is, however unfortunate that may be, unrealizable. *We cannot deprive the Party and the members of the Central Committee of the right to appeal to the Party, if a basic question provokes disagreement.* I can't imagine how we could do this. The present Congress cannot in some way control elections to a future congress. Suppose some question like the Treaty of Brest-Litovsk comes up.[59] . . . If circumstances give rise to fundamental disagreements, can we prohibit their presentation to the judgment of the entire Party? We cannot![60]

Collective leadership, another major difference between Lenin's concept of Party organization and Stalin's, is inconceivable without a constant exchange of opinions. A unanimous resolution of the Central Committee in 1923 stressed the need for

> collective discussion of important issues. . . . The leading Party organs must listen to the voice of the Party masses, must not regard any criticism as a manifestation of factionalism, for that would push conscientious and disciplined Party members onto the road of internal isolation or factionalism.[61]

These rules were especially important for a Party in power, facing a multitude of problems that Marxist parties had never before dealt with. Discussion should not have been feared; it should have been encouraged. It should have proceeded in a comradely atmosphere instead of turning into an organized campaign against dissidents.

The suppression of discussion took place gradually, beginning with attempts to interpret the resolution of the Xth Party Congress in a dogmatic and tendentious manner. Zinoviev and Kamenev were among

[57] *Ibid.*, pp. 572–73.
[58] *Ibid.*, p. 523.
[59] *Ed.:* Lenin was originally outvoted on this issue within the Central Committee. He threatened to resign and take his case to the Party at large.
[60] *Ibid.*, p. 540.
[61] *XIII s'ezd VKP. Stenograficheskii otchet* (Moscow, 1963), pp. 152–53.

the first to use this tactic, against the Trotskyites in 1923–24. For example, on December 1, 1923, Zinoviev told a Party conference in Leningrad:

> We prefer sometimes to cut off a very considerable section of the Party . . . in order to achieve a single monolithic Communist Party rather than a "parliament of opinions." . . . Freedom for factions within a party that is governing a state means freedom to form parallel embryonic governments. . . . The slightest division of power means ruin for the dictatorship of the proletariat.

A few days later, at a meeting of Moscow activists, Zinoviev challenged the Trotskyites:

> If you think the time has come to legalize factions and groups, then say so openly. We believe the time has not come and will not come during the period of the dictatorship of the proletariat. [Stormy applause] It cannot come because this issue is connected with the issue of freedom of the press, and in general with the issue of political rights for the nonproletarian strata of the population.[62]

Later on, Zinoviev's distortion of the rule on factions was turned against his own opposition group.

In the mid-twenties most Party activists understood the rule differently: when there are serious differences on important questions, Party members have the right to criticize the upper echelons. In short, they had the right of opposition. The right was implicitly recognized in a typical resolution of the Central Committee, such as that adopted July 23, 1926:

> The Party hoped that the opposition would in the process of day-to-day work realize and correct its mistakes. Thus the opposition was given full opportunity to defend its views in the normal Party way when disagreements arose on various questions. Although the opposition persisted in its mistakes, which were pointed out by the XIVth Party Congress, and introduced elements of flagrant factional irreconcilability into the work of the Politburo and the Central Committee, the opposition's defense of its views within the Central Committee in the normal Party way did not arouse serious concern about the preservation of unity either in the Central Committee or in the Central Control Commission.[63]

The resolution went on to accuse the opposition of overstepping the limits of permissible discussion, a charge that will not be assessed here. The point is that the resolution acknowledged the opposition's right to uphold its views.

As Stalin became master of the Party, he began to denounce not

[62] Zinoviev, *Sud'by nashei partii* (Moscow, 1924), pp. 95–96.
[63] *KPSS v rezoliutsiiakh*, II (1953), p. 161.

only the views of particular opposition groups but opposition in general. The very word "opposition" was given an increasingly sinister meaning until all opposition was represented as the work of petty-bourgeois circles, and finally of bourgeois-imperialist circles. Party unity increasingly came to mean unconditional and universal submission to the will of the General Secretary.

Stalin used the slogan of Communist unity to split the Party, to excommunicate and exterminate anyone he found unsuitable. Thus he did in fact achieve "unprecedented unity." But he also destroyed the main condition for genuine unity, as described in the first point of Lenin's resolution: mutual trust among the Party's members and leaders. To Stalin, unity meant a total ban on any criticism of the leaders, even on the most minor issues.

7

THE SYSTEM OF PERSONAL DICTATORSHIP that Stalin created was complex and strong. The deceived masses were its ultimate foundation. Another very important support was the *apparat* of Party and state, both central and local. But the special role of the punitive organs must not be overlooked. The Cheka, or Extraordinary Commission to Combat Counterrevolution and Sabotage, was organized in December, 1917. During the Civil War, 1918–20, it reached a peak of activity near the fronts. In that period its units were thought of not as juridical or investigative agencies. They were military-administrative *punitive* agencies. Just as a soldier at the front kills his opponent simply because he sees him with a weapon in his hand, so the Cheka's mission was to seek out and destroy counterrevolutionaries and saboteurs, the internal enemy. A civil war is a special kind of conflict; the front passes through every city, every village, every house. In 1921 M. I. Latsis (or Sudrabs), head of a secret section of the Cheka, proudly described the nonjuridical, purely administrative use of force by his organization.[64] Active counterrevolutionaries, he said, were summarily shot; others were

> confined in concentration camps. This measure must be used rather extensively against all anti-Soviet parties. Common sense tells us to protect ourselves from a knife in the back. But this cannot be accomplished if we search for material evidence in every case. It is enough if a given person belongs to a counterrevolutionary class and formerly held posts in the government and revealed himself as an active man in strengthening the foundations of the old order, for him to be isolated from society. Excessive caution never hurts. It is such

[64] Latsis, *Chrezvychainye Komissii po bor'be s Kontrrevoliutsiei* (Moscow, 1921).

considerations that prompt us to isolate from society almost all the Right and Left S-R's and some of the active Mensheviks and Anarchists. Even if these parties did not actively fight the Soviet regime, we still must clear them off the road, since every obstacle in our path and every restraint and weakening of our forces in this last and decisive struggle may turn victory over to the counterrevolutionaries.[65]

It must be noted that Lenin took strong exception to Latsis' scornful attitude toward "material evidence" and his readiness to put members of anti-Soviet parties into concentration camps.[66] Latsis' brochure—and frequently the actions of the Cheka—also deserved criticism for too broad an interpretation of the concept "counterrevolutionary element," and also of the slogan "Whoever is not with us is against us." When "teachers, students, and all youth in school" were declared to be "in their overwhelming majority a petty-bourgeois element, . . . the fighting force of our opponent, from which White Guard regiments are created," abuses of power were bound to occur. An additional cause of such abuses was the fact, noted by Latsis himself, that the Cheka attracted to its ranks psychotics and also "swindlers and simply the criminal element, who use the title 'agent of the Cheka' for blackmail, extortion, and lining their pockets." It was during the Civil War that careerists like Beria and Bagirov joined the Cheka.

A special circular letter, signed by Dzerzhinskii and Latsis on December 17, 1918, reveals the nature of some abuses by demanding an end to them. The two leaders deplored the tendency to arrest specialists simply because most of them were of bourgeois or even noble origin:

> We must hire bourgeois brains and make them work for the Soviet regime. Therefore a specialist should be arrested only if it is established that he is working for the overthrow of the Soviet regime. Do not arrest him only because he is an ex-nobleman or a former exploiter, if he is working properly. . . . The Cheka very often has recourse to arrests when it is not expedient to do so. There is no need to arrest someone on the basis of mere rumor or suspicion or because of some petty crime.[67]

It should be noted that the dimensions of the Cheka's abuses and mistakes have always been exaggerated by ideological opponents of the Soviet Union. John Reed had reason to say, in evaluating the Cheka, that "the proletariat was self-restrained and gentle." During the first six months of the Cheka's activity only twenty-two people

[65] *Ibid.*, pp. 15–16.
[66] Lenin, *Sochineniia*, 4th edn., XXVIII, pp. 365–66.
[67] Latsis, *op. cit.*, p. 55.

were shot. In the second half of 1918 a wave of conspiracies and terrorist acts swept over the young Soviet Republic and the Party was obliged to respond with the red terror. "And so," Latsis writes,

> in the second half of 1918 more than 6,000 people were shot, and during the entire three years (1918–20) 12,733 people. In all of Russia. Compare this figure with the martyrology of our comrades killed by the White Guards, and you will agree that if the Cheka can be accused of anything, it is not excessive zeal in shooting, but insufficient application of the supreme penalty.[68]

Far more people were put in concentration camps, but this confinement was usually regarded as only for the duration of the Civil War. I have already quoted order No. 186, signed on December 30, 1920, by Dzerzhinskii and Iagoda, insisting that political prisoners were to be regarded as temporary detainees, and were not to be treated as harshly as criminals.[69]

Even during the Civil War the Party adopted a number of measures to improve the Cheka.[70] As soon as the war had ended, the Cheka leadership began a campaign to empty the prisons and camps and to change its working methods. A Cheka decree of January 8, 1921, acknowledged that

> prisons are filled to overflowing, not with bourgeois but for the most part with workers and peasants [involved in theft or speculation]. This legacy [of the Civil War] must be done away with; the prisons must be emptied and we must carefully see to it that only those who are really dangerous to the Soviet regime should be put there.

The decree went on to stress the self-defeating nature of mass repression, which increases the number of discontented people. A great program of patient re-education was now the proper way to deal with ordinary people; to catch genuine enemies, very careful investigation must replace "the crude distinction between ours and not-ours simply according to class character."[71]

Change in the Cheka's methods was not enough. With the end of the Civil War the necessity for a swift-striking punitive agency gradually disappeared. A special investigative *apparat* was still needed to catch spies, subversives, and counterrevolutionaries. But this *apparat* had to be deprived of the right to punish without a trial, that is, as an act of administration. The functions of judgment and punishment had to be transferred to juridical agencies. That is why in 1921, under

[68] *Ibid.*, p. 9.
[69] See above, p. 274.
[70] See, e.g., the instructions quoted by E. Drabkina, *Chernye sukhari* (Moscow, 1963), pp. 460–61.
[71] Quoted in Latsis, *op. cit.*, pp. 19–21.

peacetime conditions, when the main problem was to guarantee greater legality and the rights of the individual, Lenin raised the question of limiting the functions of the Cheka. On his initiative, the IXth Congress of Soviets adopted a resolution that led to a major reorganization of the Cheka.[72] On February 7, 1922, it was transformed into the GPU (*Glavnoe politicheskoe upravlenie*—Main Political Administration). The GPU was given the job of combating only especially dangerous state crimes: political and economic counterrevolution, espionage, and banditry. Moreover the GPU did not have the right to apply repressive measures against criminals. In all cases, including those which were investigated by the GPU, the power of judgment belonged exclusively to the courts.

The reconstruction of the Cheka-GPU went on for some years in the first half of the twenties. But it slowed down after the deaths of Lenin and Dzerzhinskii; indeed things started moving in an entirely different direction. The GPU gradually began to resume the functions that were appropriate only for a period of civil war. Under pressure from Stalin, a punitive organization reappeared, with the right to put people in jail and camps, to exile them to remote places, and later even to shoot them without any juridical procedure, simply as an administrative act.

V. R. Menzhinskii, the head of the GPU after Dzerzhinskii's death, was an old Party official, but he lacked the influence and authority of his predecessor. He decried the tendency to make the GPU a private power base of a few individuals,[73] but he was sick for long periods and rarely interfered in the day-to-day activity of the GPU. The real boss by the late twenties was his deputy, Iagoda, who was strongly influenced by Stalin. Those two introduced a new style of work, for example, in the seizure of valuables from nepmen by massive use of violence and arbitrary force. The GPU was also assigned the job of transporting hundreds of thousands of kulak families to the eastern districts of the country. The families of "subkulaks" were also deported, which meant that hundreds of thousands of middle and even poor peasants were arbitrarily exiled. Collective farms were ravaged by the GPU during the grain-procurement campaigns of 1932 and 1933. It also administered the lawless repression of the intelligentsia in the late twenties and early thirties. At that time some GPU employees, with tacit support from above, were already creating false evidence, forcing prisoners to sign false interrogation records, inventing all kinds of plots and organizations, and beating and torturing prisoners. When one victim, M. P. Iakubovich, told his interrogator at the end of 1930 that such methods would have been impossible

[72] See *Izvestiia*, Dec. 30, 1921.
[73] See *Izvestiia*, Aug. 31, 1964.

under Dzerzhinskii, the interrogator laughed: "You've found someone to remember! Dzerzhinskii—that's a bygone stage in our revolution."

This lawlessness was cloaked with various ideological arguments about the class struggle. But even if it was justified against members of hostile classes—and it was not—it still corrupted many employees of the punitive organs, developing the worst sides of their characters, training them to blind obedience and callousness toward the citizenry. At the same time the GPU's influence and members grew; as early as 1926 Stalin signed a directive to increase its staff. For a while men of principle held on, but especially after 1934, when Menzhinskii died and Iagoda took his place, Stalin's unlimited control of the agency was assured.

After the murder of Kirov and especially after the first "open" political trial in 1936, a purge left adventurers and careerists in most of the leading positions within the NKVD.[74] It is important to note that in 1937 the pay of NKVD employees was approximately quadrupled. Previously a relatively low pay scale had hindered recruitment; after 1937 the NKVD scale was higher than that of any other government agency. NKVD employees were also given the best apartments, rest homes, and hospitals. They were awarded medals and orders for success in their activities. And, in the latter half of the thirties, their numbers were so swollen as to become a whole army, with divisions and regiments, with hundreds of thousands of security workers and tens of thousands of officers. NKVD agencies were set up not only in every *oblast* center but in each city, even in each *raion* center. Special sections were organized in every large enterprise, in many middle-size ones, in railroad stations, in major organizations and educational institutions. Parks, theaters, libraries—almost all gathering places (even smoking rooms) came under constant observation by special NKVD operatives. An enormous network of informers and stool pigeons was created in almost every institution, including prisons and camps.

Dossiers were kept on tens of millions of people. In addition to the sections that kept tabs on Cadets and monarchists, S-R's and Mensheviks, and other counterrevolutionary parties, in the Fourth Administration (*upravlenie*) of the NKVD a section was created for the Communist Party. It maintained surveillance over all Party organizations, including the Central Committee. All *raikom, gorkom,* and *obkom* secretaries were confirmed in their posts only after the approval of the appropriate NKVD agencies. Special sections were also created to watch the Chekists themselves, and a special section to watch the special sections. The Chekists were trained to believe that Chekist

[74] *Ed.:* The OGPU was dissolved in 1934, and its functions were transferred to the NKVD (People's Commissariat of Internal Affairs).

discipline was higher than Party discipline. "First of all," they were told, "you are a Chekist, and only then a Communist." Their training included learning the history of the trade, beginning with a very serious study of the Inquisition.

Stalin paid special attention to surveillance of his closest aides, the members of the Politburo. "The secret service of the sovereign," says an ancient Indian book, "must keep its eyes on all the high officials, directors of affairs, friends and relatives of the ruler, and likewise his rivals."[75] Stalin watched every step of his closest aides, using the notorious law "On the protection of chiefs," enacted after Kirov's murder. While Stalin personally selected his own bodyguard and completely controlled it, the protection of other leaders was entrusted to the NKVD. They could not go anywhere without the knowledge of their guard, could not receive any visitor without a check by the guard, and so on.

Although the powers of the NKVD were unusually great in the early thirties, in the summer of 1936 the Central Committee passed a resolution, on Stalin's proposal, to grant the NKVD extraordinary powers for one year—to destroy completely the "enemies of the people." At the June Plenum of the Central Committee in 1937 these powers were extended for an indefinite period. The result was a significant extension of the NKVD's juridical functions.

Before the repression began, a Special Assembly (*Osoboe Soveshchanie*) was set up in the NKVD. Then throughout the country an extensive system of *troiki,* or three-man boards, was created, subordinated to this Special Assembly. These illegal bodies, whose very existence violated the Constitution of the USSR, independently examined political cases and passed sentences, completely ignoring the norms of jurisprudence. In this way the punitive organs were exempt from any control by the Party and the Soviets, the courts, and the procurator. Even when the NKVD investigators passed cases to the procurator's office or the courts, the latter obediently handed down verdicts prepared beforehand by the agency. In many *oblasti* procurators issued back-dated sanctions several months after an arrest, or even signed blank forms on which the NKVD subsequently entered any names they wanted. In reality, only one man had the right to control the activity of the punitive organs—Stalin himself.

Why did Stalin need this huge punitive *apparat,* the like of which history has never seen? No external danger justified its existence. It was directed primarily against "internal enemies," and it had to find these "enemies," if only to justify its own existence. Thus the ever-

[75] *Tirukaral. Kniga o dobrodeteli, o politike i o liubvi* (Moscow, 1963), p. 79. *Ed.:* This is a translation of the Tamil classic Tirukkural. See C. and H. Jesudasan, *A History of Tamil Literature* (Calcutta, 1961), pp. 41–51.

expanding punitive agencies, besides being a firm foundation of the Stalinist regime, became a source of never-ending repression.

Mention must also be made of the demand for labor by the great network of labor camps. According to an old Communist, Iu. Fr———, at the very beginning of the thirties Stalin received a report from a former political prisoner, who later made a career for himself in the NKVD. This report said little about the reformation of criminals by labor; it argued that keeping people in labor camps was far more "economical" than detaining them in prisons. It also argued that labor camps would facilitate industrial construction in regions where it was hard to attract free labor, especially in the North European part of the country, the Urals, Siberia, and the Far East.

These ideas were endorsed by Stalin and approved in the Politburo. The Main Camp Administration (GULAG) and some of the first camp *raiony* were created. As industrial construction spread through the country, so did the number of labor camps. State plans assigned an increasingly important role to GULAG. By the end of the thirties GULAG was responsible for much of the country's lumbering and extraction of copper, gold, and coal. GULAG built important canals, strategic roads, and many industrial enterprises in remote regions. This widespread use of forced labor had dangerous consequences. In the first place, the harsh regime established in 1937 used up labor quickly, with a consequent need for rapid replacement. Secondly, because Stalin did not find a rational solution for the problem of building in remote regions, he constantly increased the number of projects assigned to GULAG. The planning agencies frequently put pressure on the NKVD to speed up certain projects. Planning was done not only for projects assigned to GULAG but also for the growth of its labor force. Planning even encompassed the mortality rate in the camps—and in this respect achievement far exceeded plan goals. Before some large construction projects were begun, many *oblast* NKVD agncies would receive an order to provide the necessary labor force. Thus another vicious circle: the system of forced labor became a cause as well as an effect of mass repression.

8

THE SOCIALIST REVOLUTION sets itself great and humane goals: the elimination of all exploitation, the end of wars and violence, and the harmonious, all-round development of the human personality. But to reach these goals the proletariat must go through a long struggle, both with its enemies and with the vestiges of its own past. Thus revolutionaries become involved in the problem of choosing ways of fighting, in the relationship between ends and means.

There have been many responses to this problem. The great Indian leader Gandhi was so impressed by the interaction between means and ends that he virtually denied the significance of ends. "We do not know the goal," he wrote. "For me it is enough to know the means. Means and ends are interchangeable terms in my philosophy of life."[76] Such disregard for the concept of a goal is foreign to Marxism-Leninism. Nor does Marxism-Leninism renounce violent means in the revolutionary struggle, as Gandhi did. But true Marxism must not and cannot take the position that the revolutionary goal justifies in advance any means used to reach it. The proposition "the end justifies the means" was not devised by revolutionaries. Its most extreme expression is found in the medieval Church. "The Church," wrote Bishop Dietrich von Nieheim in 1411,

> is freed from the rules of morality if its existence is threatened. Unity as a necessary goal justifies all means: simony, treachery, treason, prison, fetters, and death. The social system exists for the goals of society and the individual must be sacrificed for the common good.[77]

The Jesuits' name was applied to this point of view, and another version of it was endorsed by the fascists in modern times. "When we win," asked Goebbels, "who will question us about our methods?"[78]

This point of view has frequently passed from the enemies of revolution to its advocates. Since Robespierre and Saint-Just, in Marx's words, were unable to understand society's ills, they saw the cause only in counterrevolutionary thoughts, the cure in chopping off heads.[79] And in fact the Convention, on the urging of the Jacobin leaders, authorized arrests and executions on the basis of suspicion. Many revolutionaries objected. Jacques Roux, for example, a leader of the *enragés,* denounced

> this frightful law, the enforcement of which is entrusted to intriguers, who abuse it to satiate their fury, their rage, their vengefulness against those who have the courage to expose their swindling and their treachery. . . . Our revolution will never conquer the world by transforming all of France into a huge Bastille. . . .[80]

Subsequently, by a decree of June 10, 1794—which is fully comparable to the Central Executive Committee's decree of December 1, 1934

[76] M. K. Gandhi, *Moia zhizn'* (Moscow, 1959), p. 23. Cf. also J. Nehru, *Otkrytie Indii* (Moscow, 1955), p. 390, and Nehru, *Avtobiografiia* (Moscow, 1955), p. 531.

[77] *Ed.:* I have been unable to find the source of this quotation.

[78] Quoted from Goebbels' diary, in E. Rzhevskaia, *Berlin, mai, 1945* (Moscow, 1965), p. 73.

[79] Marx and Engels, *Sochineniia,* 2nd edn., I, p. 439.

[80] Quoted by E. Plimak, "Radishchev i Robesp'er," *Novyi mir,* 1966, No. 6, pp. 161–62.

—the few legal restraints on the execution of suspects were removed.[81] By the end of their dictatorship seven weeks later, the Jacobins were using terror against discontented poor people, foreshadowing Stalin's Draconian punishments for minor violations of labor discipline.

In the nineteenth century there were many revolutionaries who recognized no restrictions in their choice of means. Nechaev has already been discussed. Bakunin also saw revolution as universal destruction, as revenge, whose weapons could be "poison, the knife, the noose." Only a little while before his death did Bakunin realize that Jesuitism and revolution were incompatible, that "you will build nothing vital or strong by Jesuitical trickery, that, for the sake of success itself, revolutionary activity must seek support not in low, base passions; without the highest human ideal, no revolution triumphs."[82]

In the Soviet revolution, some people preached—and sometimes practiced—the proposition that the revolutionary goal justifies any methods. In the first months after the October insurrection, lynching (*samosud*) of "suspects" was fairly frequent. Former ministers of the Provisional Government, A. I. Shingarev and F. Kokoshkin, came to an end that way, and John Reed barely escaped. The Civil War was accompanied not only by historically justified forms of revolutionary violence but also by superfluous cruelty. B. M. Dumenko, who organized the first cavalry units of the Red Army, was shot, and so was the commander of the Second Horse Army, F. Mironov. (They were not rehabilitated until 1964–65.) Sholokhov has given a vivid description of the mass shooting of Cossacks on the Upper Don, which was a major cause of the Veshenskaia Cossack rising against the Soviet regime.[83]

Trotsky, Commissar of War and head of the Revolutionary-Military Soviet, frequently misused violence. To deal with a regiment that quit its battle position and refused to obey orders, Trotsky ordered that the commander, the commissar, and every tenth man in the regiment be shot. (The tenth-man technique derives from the military customs of the ancient Romans.) S. I. Gusev, a member of the Revolutionary Military Soviet, approved, and the order was carried out. Many Communists were indignant—S. I. Berdichevskaia recalls how she sheltered a fugitive officer—while many others agreed that the critical situation at the front required the harshest measures. But in 1921, when some Red Army regiments, tired of continual war, refused to attack the Kronstadt insurgents, V. Putna without any shootings persuaded them to fight.

[81] See A. Levandovskii, *Robesp'er* (Moscow, 1965), pp. 256–57.
[82] Quoted in *Voprosy istorii*, 1964, No. 10, p. 85.
[83] See Iu. Trifonov, *Otblesk kostra* (Moscow, 1966), pp. 163–64, and Sholokhov, *The Don Flows Home to the Sea*.

Many of the executions carried out by the Cheka were unnecessary, especially some shooting of hostages. In 1920 the Soviet government proclaimed an amnesty for all former White Guardists hiding in the Crimean mountains, but the local authorities shot some of those who gave themselves up, including some who had been forcibly drafted into the White Army.

The conclusion of the Civil War required an end even to the violent methods that had been justified. But many leaders considered the introduction of legality as equivalent to "disarming the Revolution."[84] As Kalinin noted:

> The Civil War has created huge cadres of people for whom the only law is expedience, ordering, power. To govern, as far as they are concerned, means to issue orders in complete independence, without submitting to the regulating articles of the law.[85]

The transition to new methods was difficult even for Lenin. In the spring of 1922, when the Commissariat of Justice was preparing the first Criminal Code of the RSFSR, Lenin sent a letter to the Commissar concerning the definition of counterrevolutionary activity. He urged that the definition should be

> a politically truthful (and not only a juridically narrow) proposition, giving the grounds for and justification of terror, its necessity, its limits.
>
> The courts should not eliminate terror—to promise that would be self-deception or deception—but should give it a legitimate basis, principled, clear, without hypocrisy or adornment. The formulation must be as broad as possible, for only revolutionary morality (*pravosoznanie*) and revolutionary conscience will provide the conditions for a wider or narrower application in each case.[86]

Lenin then sketched three possible drafts, two of which were indeed "as broad as possible," for they held a person guilty of counterrevolutionary crime and subject to execution if he engaged in propaganda or agitation that "objectively aided" or might be "capable of aiding" the international bourgeois enemy.[87] These formulations, which would have encouraged a multitude of abuses, did not appear in Article 57 of the Criminal Code of the RSFSR, published June 15, 1922. That article defined a counterrevolutionary action as one "*directed* toward the overthrow" of the Soviet regime or toward aid to its foreign enemies.[88] Nevertheless, Lenin's letter, which was pub-

---

[84] See, e.g., V. M. Kuritsyn, "NEP i revoliutsionnaia zakonnost'," *Voprosy istorii*, 1967. No. 9.

[85] M. I. Kalinin, *O sotsialisticheskoi zakonnosti* (Moscow, 1959), p. 166.

[86] Lenin, *Sochineniia*, 4th edn., XXVII, p. 296.

[87] *Ibid.*, pp. 296–97.

[88] *Ed.:* Italics added. In other words, the burden of proving treasonable *intent* was placed upon the prosecution, whereas Lenin's formulation removed that burden.

lished in 1924, hardly contributed to the development of the fledgling judiciary.

If various abuses of revolutionary legality were possible during Lenin's lifetime, it is easy to imagine how quickly they increased once Stalin became leader of the Party. Long before the mid-thirties he pressed upon official cadres the belief that there could be no restrictions on the methods used to fight those he proclaimed to be enemies of the Revolution. Mass terror against peasants who were prosperous or simply lacked class consciousness, lawless repression of the bourgeois intelligentsia, arbitrary treatment of the oppositions and all dissidents—all these were practical applications of "the end justifies the means." And torture made its appearance during collectivization: kulaks and "subkulaks" were beaten, and drenched in cold water during winter. In Sholokhov's *Virgin Soil Upturned*, Nagul'nov summed up the Stalinist attitude: "Place in front of him dozens of old men, children and old women," and if he is told that it is necessary for the Revolution, he will "finish them all off with a machine gun."[89]

Stalin was not the only proponent of such methods; many other leaders and also rank-and-file participants in the Revolution agreed. This attitude was undoubtedly ascribable to the cultural backwardness of the masses, the elemental nature of the movement, the inability of many people in it to think for themselves. Stalin cleverly exploited the most backward attitudes still rampant among many officials. All he had to do was to say "enemies of the people" and those unfortunates were outside the law; any cruelty, torture, or violence against them was immediately justified.

By no means all officials willingly took part in the expulsion of hundreds of thousands of peasant families to Siberia in 1930–32. Many activists sent to the countryside during collectivization returned home sick over what they had experienced. In 1936–38 numerous officials found it hard to sanction mass arrests of Party comrades. Many NKVD employees obeyed the instructions to use torture with grave misgivings. But the customary logic—it is necessary for the Revolution—eased their consciences and clouded their brains, preventing a realistic appraisal of events, transforming honorable revolutionaries into blind instruments of Stalin's arbitrary rule—and often into his victims, too.

N. V. Krylenko is a typical case. A decade after the Civil War, when its terroristic methods were revived against technical specialists, many of whom were arrested and severely punished simply by fiat without any trial, the first to protest should have been the Commissar of Justice, Krylenko. Instead he was an especially zealous defender of extralegal repression:

[89] *Ed.:* See Sholokhov, *Podniataia tselina* (Moscow, 1931). Translated as *Seeds of Tomorrow* (New York, 1935).

To bourgeois Europe and to broad circles of the liberalish intelligentsia, it may seem monstrous that the Soviet regime does not always deal with wreckers by putting them on trial. But every class-conscious worker and peasant will agree that the Soviet regime is behaving correctly.[90]

Nor did Krylenko protest the unconstitutional edict of December 1, 1934, or the lawless acts of the NKVD in 1935–37. He probably realized his mistake in 1938, when he was condemned and shot without any legal procedure.

Another typical case is that of B. P. Sheboldaev, first secretary of the North Caucasus *kraikom*. In the early thirties he joined with Kaganovich in deporting from the Kuban not only groups of people belonging to hostile classes but whole villages. On November 12, 1932, in Rostov, Shelboldaev said:

We openly proclaimed that we would send off to northern regions malicious saboteurs and kulak agents who do not want to sow. Didn't we in previous years deport kulak counterrevolutionary elements from this same Kuban? We did, in sufficient numbers. And today when these remnants of the kulak class try to organize sabotage, oppose the demands of the Soviet regime, it is more correct to give away the fertile Kuban land to collective farmers who live in other *krais* on poor land, and not enough even of that poor land. . . . And those who do not want to work, who defile our land, we'll send them to other places. That's fair. We may be told: "What? Earlier you deported kulaks, and now you're talking about a whole village, where there are both collective farms and conscientious individual peasants? How can that be?" Yes, we must raise the question of a whole village, because the collective farms, because the really conscientious individual peasants, in the present situation, *must answer for the condition of their neighbors.* What kind of support for the Soviet regime is a collective farm, if right next to it another collective farm or a whole group of individual farms oppose the measures of the Soviet regime?[91]

Five years later Sheboldaev himself fell victim to a savage purge of "the people's enemies."

In 1936 the old Bolshevik M. I. Stakun, secretary of the Gomel *obkom*, in a speech to his activists criticized even the NKVD for "liberalism" and demanded the arrest of an old woman who had cursed the Soviet regime for the bread shortage. A year later the NKVD was sufficiently illiberal to arrest Stakun himself. In 1936–37 V. F. Sharangovich, as first secretary of the Belorussian Central Committee, decimated Belorussian cadres, under Ezhov's and Malenkov's direc-

[90] Krylenko, *Klassovaia bor'ba putem vreditel'stva* (Moscow, 1930).
[91] See A. Radin and L. Shaumian, *Za chto zhiteli stanitsy Poltavskoi vyseliaiutsia s Kubani v severnye kraia* (Rostov-on-Don, 1933), p. 14.

tion. When A. G. Cherviakov committed suicide after Sharangovich publicly demanded his removal, Sharangovich declared at a Party congress in Minsk: "A dog's death for a dog." A year later he himself was shot.

Some old Bolsheviks in their memoirs assert that everything bad began in 1937. For example, in "The Return of Honor" V. Baranchenko writes of the twenties and thirties in the most enthusiastic tones; everything was fine until that cursed 1937 arrived. Ia. I. Drobinskii takes a different view. The hero of his memoirs, Andrei Fomin, brought before the Military Collegium, delivers a silent soliloquy:

> People! Communists! How did you come to this? . . . You have suddenly changed! . . . But that's the rub, Andrei, it wasn't sudden. It was prepared for imperceptibly—no, not even imperceptibly, but before our eyes. Gradually, slowly, but in systematic small doses, this poison of infamy was administered, and cadres were prepared for this operation. The poison accumulated in the organism, and when the defensive forces had weakened, it took over the entire organism. It was being prepared back then when muzhiks' families were broken up, when the muzhik's ancient nests were broken up, when he was driven to the end of the earth, into camps, when he was labeled a subkulak for daring to say that it was wrong to dekulakize his friend, a middle peasant, a laboring man! This poison was accumulating back then when they forced a peasant to turn in flax though they knew very well that it had not grown, when directives were issued to crack down on sabotage, to bring saboteurs to trial, though they knew once again that there was no sabotage and no saboteurs, because there was no flax, it had not grown. When they brought such "saboteurs" to trial, and seized the last little cow, the procurator knew that there was no sabotage at all, but still he sanctioned the arrest. The judges also knew that the muzhik was honest, but they tried him. And now the same procurator has sanctioned your arrest and the same judges are trying you. The principle hasn't changed. It is simply being given wider application. Back then you didn't understand this. But that was when the cadres were being prepared for these cases, cadres of people for whom it's not important whether you are guilty of anything; but it is important that there is a directive to consider you guilty. Remember how you said to Gikalo back then: "Nikolai Fedorovich, that flax did not grow." "I know that myself," answered Gikalo, "but the country needs flax and Moscow believes neither tears nor objective reasons."

The vile methods of the Bolsheviks are a favorite theme of Western anti-Soviet literature. In Koestler's novel *Darkness at Noon,* for example, the investigator Ivanov tries to convince himself and others that the repression of 1937 is justified. Dostoevsky's Raskolnikov, he argues, would have been in the right if he had killed the old woman on Party orders, to get money, say, for a strike fund. There are only two possibilities in ethics: the Christian, humanist rule that the individual is sacred and rational calculation is therefore excluded from morality, or the socialist rule that the individual must be sacrificed to the rationally calculated good of the collective. Ivanov sarcastically contrasts the indifference of Christians and humanists to millions of premature deaths under the old order with the outrage of Christians and humanists over the shooting of thousands in the Soviet Union. "Nature," he concludes, "is generous in her senseless experiments on mankind. Why should mankind not have the right to experiment on itself?"[92] ". . . You talk of the atrocities of the Revolution," says a Chekist in another anti-Soviet book. "That's an empty word. Atrocities remain atrocities only when there are not enough of them. When they achieve their purpose, they become a holy sacrifice. . . ." Such arguments are a slanderous caricature of Marxism-Leninism. But it must be recognized that they are very similar to the arguments of a great many Stalinists.

"The goal is not a road sign," Ilya Ehrenburg has justly remarked,

> but something entirely real, an actuality, not a picture of tomorrow but the actions of the present day. The goal predetermines not only political strategy but also morality. You cannot establish justice by knowingly performing unjust acts; you cannot fight for equality by turning the people into "cogs and screws" and yourself into a mythical divinity. The means always have an effect on the goal, elevating or deforming it.[93]

Of course, a revolution has a vast arsenal of means to choose from, and much depends on the concrete circumstances. In the Soviet revolution there have been situations when extremely cruel methods had to be used, such as the shooting of the Tsar's family in Ekaterinburg, the sinking of the Black Sea Fleet, and the Red Terror of 1918. Still, not all such methods are permissible. The true revolutionary must carefully study each concrete situation and decide what means will reach the goal by the shortest route at the least cost. Which methods should not be used in a given situation, and which should not be used in any situation, should also be determined. Two Soviet philosophers, arguing that the great moral goal of communism requires the use of moral methods to reach it, discern a certain autonomy in morality. Some objective criteria of morality are above the practice of a given moment and set limits to the choice of methods. Rigorous observance of these limits will help Communists achieve their long-run goal by helping them to win and hold the confidence of the masses.[94]

[92] *Ed.:* A. Koestler, *Darkness at Noon* (New York, 1961), p. 141.
[93] *Novyi mir,* 1965, No. 4, p. 63. Cf. the remarks of Iu. Kariakin in *Problemy mira i sotsializma,* 1963, No. 5, p. 36.
[94] See M. G. Makarov, *Filosofiia marksizma-leninizma o kategorii "tsel'"* (Leningrad, 1960), p. 12, and the comments of M. Livshits in *Voprosy filosofii,* 1967, No. 1, p. 122.

The revolutionary who does not recognize this truth can have only temporary successes. A revolutionary party that uses vile methods inevitably loses the trust and support of the people, and this in turn limits its possibilities of choosing methods that depend on mass action and popular initiative. Thus, vile methods are evidence not of a leader's strength but of his weakness, and in the final analysis they aggravate his weakness.

9

THE FACT THAT MOST of the Soviet people trusted Stalin, the Party leadership, and the punitive agencies placed the victims of repression in a tragic position. They were not guilty, but most people did not believe them, and turned their backs. An incident in the interrogation of Antonov-Ovseenko reveals the terrible situation. The radio happened to be on when the investigator called the old revolutionary an enemy of the people, and was answered back, "You're the enemy of the people, you're a real fascist." At that moment some sort of meeting was being broadcast on the radio. "Do you hear," said the investigator, "how the people hail us? They trust us completely, and you will be destroyed. I've already received a medal for you."[95]

Incomprehension was even more serious than a sense of isolation in depriving many people of the strength to resist. Even such a well-informed and intelligent man as M. E. Kol'tsov could not comprehend what was going on.

> "What is happening?" Kol'tsov used to repeat, walking up and down in his office. . . . "I feel I'm going crazy. I am a member of the editorial board of *Pravda,* a well-known journalist, a deputy [to the Supreme Soviet]; it would seem that I should be able to explain to others the meaning of what is happening, the reasons for so many exposés and arrests. But in fact I, like any terrified philistine, know nothing, understand nothing. I am bewildered, in the dark."[96]

Many of those arrested thought that there had been some accidental mistake, that soon everything would be cleared up and things would return to normal. "I'll be home tomorrow," Ian Gamarnik's deputy G. Osepian told his wife when the NKVD came to his apartment one night. A similar "constitutional illusion" was revealed by V. I. Mezhlauk, the former chairman of Gosplan. In prison he continued to think about the problems that occupied him when he was free. Just before he was shot, he wrote "On Planning and Ways to Improve It."[97] Similarly, when A. Bubnov was expelled from the Central Committee

[95] See *Novyi mir,* 1964, No. 11, p. 212. Reported by Iu. Tomskii, who heard it from Antonov-Ovseenko in prison.
[96] *Mikhail Kol'tsov, kakim on byl* (Moscow, 1965), p. 71.
[97] *Izvestiia,* Feb. 19, 1963.

and fired as Commissar of Education, he simply turned things over to the new Commissar and went to the construction site of the State Public Library, which he had been supervising.[98] He was convinced that the injustice being done to him would be corrected, but he did not imagine that this would happen only many years after his execution. Calm, self-control, and nonresistance were also the parting advice to his friends from I. A. Piatnitskii, a close colleague of Lenin's. On the day before his arrest Piatnitskii met Tsivtsivadze, who had been expelled from the Party, though his loyalty could not be doubted. "For the Party," said Piatnitskii, "we must endure everything, if only it is alive."[99] Even after torture, many arrested people continued to believe that legality would prevail, if not during the investigation then at the trial. Another reaction reveals the same underlying lack of comprehension: When the entire membership of the Party committee in a Siberian city were grabbed one night and put into a single cell, they decided that a counterrevolutionary coup had taken place in their city, and, expecting to be shot at once, they began to sing the "Intei national."

Isolation and incomprehension engendered confusion, passivity, and even resignation. "The impunity and relative ease with which Stalin took vengeance on millions of people," V. Shalamov wrote in one of his stories, "were due precisely to the fact that these people were not guilty of anything." Most people, even when they were expecting arrest, did not try to hide and escape destruction. Many even turned themselves in. For example, after Iakir was shot, the head of the political administration of the Kiev Military District, M. P. Amepin, was called to Moscow. He knew quite well what was in store for him. "I don't know whether I'll come back," he told his friends and family, "but believe me, I have never been an enemy of my country or my country's government."[100]

I. P. Belov, commander of the Belorussian Military District, also had forebodings when he was suddenly summoned to Moscow. Through the entire journey he kept walking up and down the empty corridor of the official railway car, or stood at the dark window for long periods. Several times he turned to his traveling companion with questions, from which it was easy to see that he was thinking of his predecessor, I. P. Uborevich, who had also been suddenly called to Moscow and had not returned. Belov's anxiety was not groundless. As soon as he arrived in Moscow he was arrested and quickly perished.[101]

---

[98] *Andrei Bubnov* (Moscow, 1964).
[99] Recounted in the diary of Piatnitskii's wife, which is in the possession of S. Petrikovskii.
[100] *Voenno-istoricheskii zhurnal*, 1964, No. 7, p. 119.
[101] *Ibid.*, 1963, No. 6, p. 76. The traveling companion was L. M. Sandalov, who survived to tell the story.

P. I. Shabalkin was unusual in his refusal to submit to arrest when NKVD agents came to his office. A member of the Buro of the Far Eastern *kraikom,* he demanded that his case be discussed in the *obkom* buro. But the *obkom* secretary, who also did not understand what was going on, told Shabalkin to submit. And Shabalkin did so, surrendering his gun to the NKVD agents.[102] Even diplomats who were recalled from abroad, and usually knew what would happen to them, almost always obeyed the order to return.[103]

Sometimes, after long and painful expectation of arrest, people felt a certain relief to be finally in jail. "Well, comrades," the old Bolshevik Dvoretskii told his cellmates when he was brought into Minsk Prison, "Tonight I will probably get a good night's sleep. The first in three months. . . . For three months I've been in torment, waiting for them to come for me. Every day they took people but didn't come for me. They took all the Commissars, but me they just would not take. I was simply worn out. Why don't they call me? Why don't they take me? And then, glory be! . . . Today a phone call from the NKVD. And I've been in bed for almost a year, my legs don't function. Some director calls up. 'Can't you come over for an hour? We need to consult with you,' he says. 'Of course I can,' I say. 'Send over a car.' "[104]

The same passivity, so strange at first sight, was manifested by most primary Party organizations. The newspapers of the thirties and forties reveal that many Party organizations did defend their members against the slanderous accusations that were hurled at virtually every Party member, but only until the NKVD stepped in. Once he was arrested, a man's Party organization took a sharply different attitude toward him. Hardly any of the primary Party organizations defended its repressed members before the NKVD or vouched for their honesty and loyalty. Nearly all the expulsions of "enemies of the people" were adopted by Party organizations unanimously, without any discussion of the charges.

But what could rank-and-file Communists—and many leaders— have done? If a primary Party organization did not take a "correct" position, then the *raikom* or *gorkom* would "correct" it, savagely purging all the defenders of "enemies of the people." "And what could Communists say at meetings?" an old Communist has written to the author.

---

[102] Recounted to the author by Shabalkin.
[103] At this point Medvedev appends a defense of the few who refused to return, most notably F. F. Raskol'nikov. Medvedev concedes that the nonreturnees broke the law, but defends their right to do so on the ground that Stalin had already destroyed the rule of law.
[104] Told to the author by Ia. I. Drobinskii.

Give new material to informers? The whole problem was that no one dared to tell anybody anything bad about Stalin; everyone was obliged—even if he knew something, even if he knew or guessed the truth—to shout hallelujah. Try not to shout hallelujah, if you're, say, a district agitator. Try not to "give a rebuff to the enemy outburst"! The result was that everyone had to work out his world view in solitude, disregarding everything he heard from people around him. And anyone who worked out his own view, but could not play the hypocrite for ten years and somehow gave himself away, ended up in a camp.

It is impossible to agree with such logic, although it was fairly widespread during the years of the cult. There is a frightful paradox here. Thousands upon thousands of people, arrested in 1937–38 on charges of plotting against Stalin and his aides, could be reproached today for insufficient resistance to evil and for excessive faith in their leaders.

This complex mixture of contradictory feelings—incomprehension and panic, faith in Stalin and fear of the terror—fragmented the Party and made it fairly easy for Stalin to usurp total power. Of course he did more than take advantage of a confused situation; he encouraged dissension in every way, pitting people against each other, one part of the Central Committee against another, thus enabling him to destroy people in groups. The ban on factions did not end quarrels among separate groups of leaders on various issues, both principled and unprincipled. Denied an open forum, these quarrels became distorted and vicious. Stalin, a master of treacherous intrigue, encouraged such quarrels for his own ends. It was probably Stalin who kept alive the antagonism among Molotov, Kaganovich, Malenkov, Beria, and Voroshilov. Covering himself with the slogan of unity, Stalin fostered an atmosphere of mutual distrust among Party leaders, always trying to have his dirty work done by other people, to divide and conquer.

The lack of solidarity was felt at every level. Military leaders like Belov, Bliukher, Dybenko, and Alksnis, who were arrested and shot in 1938, had been members the year before of the Military Collegium that imposed death sentences on Tukhachevskii, Iakir, Uborevich, Primakov, and the other generals. It had not been easy for them to sign the sentences. "I remember a terrible day at Meyerhold's," Ilya Ehrenburg writes in his memoirs.

> We were sitting and peacefully examining a monograph on Renoir when one of Meyerhold's friends, Army Commander I. P. Belov, came in. He was very excited. Ignoring the fact that, besides Meyerhold, Liuba and I were in the room, he began to tell how they had tried Tukhachevskii and other military men. Belov was a member of the Supreme Court's Military Collegium. "They sat just like this,

opposite us. Uborevich looked me in the eye. . . ." I still remember
Belov's remark: "And tomorrow I'll be put in their place."[105]

Examples of this kind can be adduced endlessly. V. Smirnov,
appointed Commissar of the Navy in 1938, made a special tour of the
fleets to purge "enemies of the people." He was highly successful, but
at the end of the year he himself was arrested and shot. And Eikhe,
as First Secretary of the West Siberian *kraikom,* sanctioned many arrests of so-called Trotskyites and Bukharinites, who were forced to
bear false witness against Eikhe, with the result that he was shot as
the leader of the Trotskyite-Bukharinite underground in West Siberia.
And K. A. Bauman and Ia. A. Iakovlev, as heads of the Central Committee Divisions of Science and of Agriculture, supported the persecution of many outstanding scientists in 1936–37—until their own turn
came.

P. P. Postyshev is an especially egregious case in point. As Secretary of the Ukrainian CC, he worked hard to decimate the national
cadres of that republic. In 1932–33, together with Stalin, he organized
the persecution of Skrypnik, driving him to suicide. In 1937 Postyshev
sent V. A. Balitskii, the NKVD plenipotentiary in the Ukraine, dozens
of lists containing the names of hundreds of innocent people. To be
sure, Postyshev became alarmed when some people close to him were
repressed on orders from Moscow. Speaking at the February-March
Plenum of the Central Committee in 1937, he expressed doubts about
the justice of some arrests. He could not understand how close associates, such as Karpov, who had gone through the savage struggle that
attended industrialization and collectivization, could have joined the
Trotskyites.[106] But these misgivings did not stop Postyshev from continuing to sanction thousands of arrests in the Ukraine. He did not
stop even when, in 1937, his wife was arrested. He was nevertheless
demoted "for insufficient vigilance," to the post of First Secretary of
the Kuibyshev *kraikom.* Even then he did not change his mind. In
1938 the Kuibyshev *krai,* which then included Mordvinia, was purged
of "enemies" with a savagery unexampled even in other *oblasti.* Postyshev sanctioned the decimation of almost all organizations on the *krai*
level and also 110 *raion* committees. He organized the open trial of
the *krai* agricultural administration, as a result of which many agricultural officials were shot. He changed many of the sentences sent to
him for his signature, requiring death where the procurator and
investigator thought eight or ten years in confinement were sufficient.
And then, when the *krai* had been purged, Postyshev was removed
from his job on the charge of "exterminating cadres"—Stalin must

[105] *Novyi mir,* 1962, No. 3, pp. 152–53.
[106] *Ed.:* Medvedev quotes at length the words of Postyshev that were cited by Khrushchev
in his speech to the XXth Party Congress.

have grinned when he mouthed this formula—and arrested and shot.

Examples of such reciprocating viciousness and blindness could be multiplied. Even a Central Committee decree in January, 1938, noted that many Party organizations were expelling members as enemies of the people when the NKVD found no basis for their arrest. A similar process occurred in organizations of artists, writers, and scholars. The slogan of "unity" usually meant that a particular school or trend was trying to establish its monopoly. Some of the candidates for such dominance were driven into a frenzy by any resistance; they attacked their opponents so savagely that they seemed to desire the destruction of everyone who disagreed with them. In fact, as the normal protection of individual rights disappeared, some literary and scientific groups did everything they could to incite the NKVD against "enemies of the people" in their particular fields.

Of course incomprehension and confusion were not universal. There were people who had a good idea of what was going on. A seventy-five-year-old Bolshevik explained the situation to two former officials who could not understand why they were in Sol'-Iletskaia Prison:

> Your logic is childish. You have understood nothing. Don't you see that Lenin predicted present events twenty years ago? To be sure, these words of Lenin have been kept under lock and key. The broad Party masses cannot know what Lenin said could happen if a *nonobjective* man concentrated *unlimited* power in his hands. Lenin's words of genius have come true. All those who could at some time have stopped this man from realizing his unlimited power, from carrying out his policy without consulting anyone, all those people are physically destroyed.[107]

Even some young people mistrusted the adulation of Stalin, though it had been drilled into their heads since infancy. Mikhail Molochko, a Komsomol member and student from Minsk, wrote in his diary on February 3, 1935:

> It is interesting to read the newspapers, especially *Komsomolets*. Interesting materials of the VIIth Congress [of Soviets]. I read the inspired, colorful speech of the writer A——, devoted to Comrade Stalin. To tell the truth, I don't like the constant adulation of this "great strategist," "wise chief," and so on. This is systematic, unceasing ruination of the man. Well, speak, write, give some reward; but they are giving only epithets as rewards. All the speeches at the Congress are permeated with a single spirit, the spirit of tacking

---

[107] S. Gazarian, "Eto ne dolzhno povtorit'sia" (unpublished manuscript). The old Bolshevik was I. I. Radchenko, former head of Glavtorf [the Central Peat Agency]. His audience was M. Belotskii, former Secretary of the Kirghiz Central Committee, and Gazarian, former NKVD official. *Ed.:* Part of the quotation, predicting the triumph of the Party over Stalin, is omitted.

Stalin's name on every place and district. I don't see and I can't see why everyone praises and loves Stalin so much. I personally do not feel this love or even great respect.[108]

The question inevitably arises about people who understood: what should they have done? After the XXIInd Party Congress in 1962 a famous poet wrote:

> We are all his regimental mates,
> Who were silent when
> From our silence grew
> A national disaster.
>
> Hiding from each other,
> Spending sleepless nights,
> While out of our circle
> He was making executioners.
>
> Let our grandsons score us
> With their contempt
> All alike, equally,
> We do not hide our shame.[109]

The author of these lines won a Stalin Prize in the years of the cult. He was not silent at all; he heaped praise on Stalin. Now ashamed, he is trying to hide behind all of Stalin's contemporaries, all equally disgraced, or so he would have us believe. It will not work. People behaved in various ways and have varying degrees of responsibility. Much depended on their distance from the epicenter of the catastrophe, on the choices they faced. The responsibility of a commissar or even a writer cannot be equated with that of a rank-and-file Party member, worker, or collective farmer. The responsibility of the head of a concentration camp or prison cannot be equated with that of a simple guard. Much also depended on the degree of comprehension. And finally, a great deal depended on qualities of personality, on courage and sense of honor.

Many people actively helped Stalin in his crimes and made for lawlessness themselves, slandering citizens on their own initiative. Such aides to the executioner should be covered with shame and punished by a court. There were many free people, called in by the NKVD to act as witnesses, who out of fear would sign any deposition put before them. Many groveled and shouted Stalin's praise of their own free will, with genuine zeal.

But there were also individuals who in one way or other resisted. Some officials, sensing imminent arrest, fled their home towns, some-

---

[108] *Neman,* 1962, No. 4, p. 141. Molochko joined the Red Army as a volunteer during the war with Finland and died in 1940.
[109] *Ed.:* The poet is not identified by Medvedev.

times even became illegal and changed their names. (Iu. Borev based the scenario for "Resurrected from the Living" on one such case.) There were also many petitioners and protesters. The Central Committee, the Procurator's office, and Stalin personally received letters not only from relatives and friends of prisoners but also from leading cultural, scientific, government, and Party figures. Kapitsa's demand for Landau's release, which was granted, has been mentioned. Academician D. N. Prianishnikov was not so fortunate in his stubborn efforts on behalf of N. I. Vavilov. After having been rejected by Molotov and Beria, he decided on a desperate step; he recommended the imprisoned Vavilov for a Stalin Prize. Marietta Shaginian, in her brief note "A Page of the Past," tells how the arrested poet David Vygodskii was defended by fellow writers. At considerable risk to themselves Iurii Tynianov, Boris Lavrenev, Konstantin Fedin, M. Slonimskii, M. Zoshchenko, and Viktor Shklovskii wrote declarations and guarantees, pleading for the release of their comrade. Vygodskii, like Vavilov, was not released; both died in prison. When the old Bolshevik N. N. Kuliabko, who had recommended Tukhachevskii for Party membership, learned of his friend's arrest, he sent a letter of protest to Stalin—and was immediately arrested.[110] The ineffectiveness of millions of analogous protests forced many people to shrink into themselves and be silent.

There were also people in the Party *apparat,* with access to investigatory materials, who tried to oppose lawlessness. N. S. Kuznetsov, an *obkom* secretary in Kazakhstan, sanctioned the arrest of many Communists in the first months of the mass repression. Then he began to have doubts. He went to the *oblast* prison to interrogate some friends, became convinced of their innocence, sent *obkom* Party officials into the NKVD *apparat,* and took control of NKVD operations in his *oblast.* He obtained the release of many Communists and forbade the use of torture. Gathering an enormous amount of material on the lawlessness of the NKVD and its penetration by all sorts of suspicious people, including former White Guard officers, Kuznetsov went to Moscow and obtained a meeting with Stalin. Stalin listened only a few minutes and broke off the conference, advising Kuznetsov to report the whole thing to Malenkov. Malenkov also brushed him off, telling him to go back to Kazakhstan and send in a written report by governmental courier. Returning, Kuznetsov learned that he had been transferred to another *obkom.* A few months later he was called to a meeting in Alma Ata and arrested in his hotel. The two *oblast* committees he had headed were decimated and the Communists who had been released on Kuznetsov's demand were rearrested.[111]

[110] See *Marshal Tukhachevskii: sbornik vospominanii* (Moscow, 1965), p. 30.
[111] From the reminiscences of N. S. Kuznetsov, kept in the archives of the Marx-Engels-Lenin Institute.

The Party Central Committee in Kirgizia tried in 1937 to interfere in the actions of the security organs. The Buro of the Central Committee, hearing of the torture of prisoners, set up a special commission to investigate—with tragic results: the entire commission was repressed by the NKVD.[112] In Leningrad a self-sacrificing hero appeared within the NKVD itself. At a 1936 meeting of the Party *aktiv* of the Leningrad NKVD, Shapiro, one of the local leaders, gave the obligatory speech calling for intensified exposure of enemies. Then Drovianikov, another leading official of the *oblast* NKVD, mounted the rostrum. "Comrades," he said,

> we are not discovering conspiracies, we are manufacturing them. We should tell our Party the truth—that we are persecuting and destroying people on the basis of slanderous and untrue accusations. I know what's in store for me, but I cannot remain silent about what's going on in the NKVD.

The chairman of the Leningrad Soviet, I. F. Kodatskii, who was attending the meeting, then delivered a violent speech, calling for merciless vengeance on all enemies of the people. "And Drovianikov's speech," he declared, "shows that enemies of the people have infiltrated the NKVD. They must be mercilessly rooted out." Drovianikov was arrested right there in the meeting hall and was shot the same night. A year later Kodatskii was also arrested and perished.[113]

The Belorussian NKVD also had a heroic though futile defender of justice: Bikson, a Bolshevik since 1905 and a comrade of Dzerzhinskii's. In 1937, as chairman of the Special Collegium of the Supreme Court of Belorussia, he refused to consider many baseless cases. Hearing of the use of torture, he went to the Belorussian Central Committee, only to be asked by its secretary, Volkov: "What intelligence agency are you serving? The Polish or the English?" Bikson replied: "I have been a Bolshevik since 1905." "We know these old Bolsheviks," Volkov shouted, and phoned the head of the Belorussian NKVD, Berman. "There is an old counterrevolutionary here, an agent of Polish intelligence, your employee Bikson. He's going to a lot of trouble for enemies of the people." Bikson was arrested in the Central Committee office and soon died in prison. A few months later Volkov was removed from his post and given a less important position in Tambov, where he committed suicide in a hotel.[114]

M. M. Ishov, a military procurator in the West Siberian Military District, also tried to oppose the terror. On an inspection tour in Tomsk, he discovered that the local NKVD investigators humiliated the prisoners, deprived them of food and water, and beat them during interrogations. Many prisoners were not questioned at all; the investi-

---

[112] See *Ocherki istorii kommunisticheskoi partii Kirgizii* (Frunze, 1966), p. 289.
[113] Recounted by the former Chekist V. A. Kundush.
[114] Recounted by Ia. I. Drobinskii.

gators made up interrogation records and signed them themselves. Cases were sent to a *troika*, which handed out death sentences *in absentia*. Ishov arrested some of these investigators, including Puchkin, Vavrish, and Sveshnikov, and sent them under guard to Novosibirsk. He then gathered material on the activities of four NKVD agencies in the West Siberian Military District, and began sending reports on their lawlessness to the Chief Military Procurator of the USSR, Rozovskii, to the General Procurator of the USSR, Vyshinskii, and to Stalin, Molotov, and Kaganovich. He achieved a discussion of the problem by the *obkom* Party Buro, and he managed to save a few Red Army officers and civilian officials from being shot. But otherwise he was unsuccessful. His appeals to Moscow usually went unanswered. The *obkom* Buro, after listening to his speech, instructed the head of the Novosibirsk NKVD agency to "correct the situation." The result was the arrest of Ishov's sister and brother, and an NKVD report to Moscow:

> Military Procurator Ishov is opposing the NKVD, impeding the investigation of the cases of enemies of the people, refusing to sanction their arrest. He has taken the law in his own hands, arresting NKVD agents. By his actions he is undermining the authority of the agencies. We ask that he be removed from his post and that his arrest be sanctioned.

In March, 1938, Ishov went to Moscow, and submitted additional material on NKVD terror to the Chief Military Procurator's Office. In July he went to Moscow again, and was seen by Vyshinskii. "When we entered his office," Ishov recounts in his memoirs,

> Vyshinskii pointed to a chair alongside his desk, asked me to sit down, and asked for what reason and precisely with what business I had come to him. Taking documents out of my briefcase and putting them on the desk, I asked him to hear me out. . . . .I asked him to pay special attention to the techniques and methods used to extract false testimony: beating, humiliation, the medieval methods of the Inquisition. When he had heard me out, Vyshinskii responded with words that stuck deep in my memory, for my whole life. He said: "Comrade Ishov, since when have the Bolsheviks decided to treat enemies of the people in a liberal fashion? You, Comrade Ishov, have lost your sense of Party and class. We don't intend to pat enemies of the people on the head. There's nothing wrong with beating enemies of the people on their snouts. And don't forget what the great proletarian writer Maxim Gorky said, that if the enemy doesn't surrender, he must be destroyed. We will have no mercy on enemies of the people."

Ishov tried to show Vyshinskii that it was not enemies but innocent people whom the NKVD had forced to lie. But Vyshinskii reacted coldly, and only for appearance' sake told Rozovskii, who attended the conversation, to check on Ishov's materials. No check, of course, was ever made. Returning to Novosibirsk a few days later, Ishov was arrested through Vyshinskii's personal sanction.

All these attempts at resistance failed. For one thing, they were uncoordinated and isolated. Also, it was too late to do much. Stalin could have been stopped at the end of the twenties, and some chances of removing him by regular Party procedure still existed at the beginning of the thirties. But after 1934 Stalin could have been removed only by force, and no one was prepared to take that step for fear of the possible consequences. Besides, that was a practical impossibility. In addition no one understood that Stalin was engaged in a premeditated usurpation of power; so people turned to the usual forms of protest. They wrote to the proper office and hoped for help "from above." They did not understand that entirely different forms of struggle were required than complaints and petitions to the very people who were ruling illegally. The usual ways of fighting the enemy were unsuitable, and so were the usual methods of correcting the mistakes of individual Party members. No one could think of ways to combat lawlessness that came from the Party's own leaders. It is difficult to blame the Soviet people. In their overwhelming majority they were honorable workers and fighters, who overcame countless difficulties to build socialist industry and agriculture, destroyed fascism, and helped to liberate many European and Asian nations. Their descendants will always be grateful to the people of the thirties and forties for their self-sacrificing heroism. The Party was prepared to stand up to any danger from without, but hardly from within. It was helpless for a time, attacked by its own chiefs.

10

ANTI-COMMUNIST LITERATURE includes many attempts to connect Stalin's cult and his totalitarian regime not only with peculiarities of Russian historical development—such explanations contain some truth —but also with peculiarities of the "Russian soul," and with the Russian school of eschatological thought that is supposed to be akin to Communist ideology. Such pseudoscholarly inventions must be firmly rejected. Nevertheless, it is mistaken to attribute the ideology and the practice of Stalinism only to the international position of the USSR or to Stalin's personal faults. It is necessary to analyze the social processes that began after the Revolution; the struggle between the proletariat and the bourgeoisie, and also the struggle between proletarian and petty-bourgeois, bureaucratic elements in the Party.

Marxist sociology includes in the petty bourgeoisie not only peasants, artisans, small merchants, and the lower sections of office workers and professionals, but also déclassé elements at the bottom of society, a large group in Russia and many other backward capitalist countries. They are people who have lost or have never had even petty property; they have not grown accustomed to labor in capitalist industry, and live by occasional earnings. Despite great diversity, all these petty-bourgeois strata have certain features in common, including political instability and vacillation, a degree of anarchism, and small-proprietor individualism. Because of their political instability they may provide the reserves for revolution or for reaction, depending on circumstances. Unsettled and disoriented after the First World War, they supported fascist dictatorship in some European countries. The disintegration of the tsarist regime made such people revolutionary in Russia, and the Bolshevik Party drew many to its side. Several million proletarians were victorious only because they were supported by tens of millions of semiproletarian and petty-bourgeois elements.

It would be naïve to think that these petty-bourgeois elements would be completely transformed by several years of revolutionary struggle. It would also be a mistake to idealize the proletariat, picturing it as purely virtuous. Not only in Russia but also in many industrially developed countries, a good part of the proletariat were infected with petty-bourgeois faults and moods. Thus petty-bourgeois elements penetrated workers' parties everywhere long before the October Revolution. That provided the social basis for the bureaucratic degeneration of Party functionaries, especially at the peak of the hierarchy, in the parties of the Second International before the First World War. The Bolshevik Party was not, of course, immune to this process.

Most professional revolutionaries, who formed the backbone of the Party, derived from the intelligentsia, the lesser gentry, or the civil service. These origins did not prevent most of these people from merging heart and soul with the proletariat, directing it, and thus becoming proletarian revolutionaries in the full sense of the word. But by no means all the leaders of the Party experienced a complete transformation. Besides, the Revolution and the Civil War produced many new leaders who had not gone through the rigorous school of political and ideological struggle. The fact that many individuals who were not true proletarian revolutionaries became leaders of the Party after Lenin's death was therefore not an accident or the result of insufficient wisdom. It was the natural result of a proletarian revolution in a petty-bourgeois country like Russia.

Lenin was well aware that one of the most difficult problems of the proletarian revolution was to safeguard the Party cadres from bureaucratic degeneration. The transformation of the Bolshevik Party from an underground organization to a ruling party would greatly increase petty-bourgeois and careerist tendencies among old Party members and also bring into the Party a host of petty-bourgeois and careerist elements that had previously been outside. "A situation is gradually taking shape," said a resolution adopted in 1921 on Lenin's initiative, "in which one can 'rise in the world,' make a career for himself, get a bit of power, only by entering the service of the Soviet regime."[115] In his last writings Lenin concentrated on this very problem: the interrelationships between petty-bourgeis and proletarian elements in the state, and the bureacratization of the *apparat*. "We call ours," he wrote in 1922,

> an *apparat* that is in fact still thoroughly alien to us and constitutes a bourgeois and tsarist mishmash. . . . There is no doubt that the insignificant percent of Soviet and Sovietized workers will drown in this sea of chauvinistic Great Russian riffraff like a fly in milk.[116]

It is only fair to note that degeneration of a part of the revolutionary cadres is the rule in every revolution, which attracts many people who are motivated by a desire for power or wealth. The French Revolution brought to the fore not only leaders like Marat but also careerists like Fouché, Talleyrand, Barras, and Tallien. The October Revolution did not escape the same fate. "Every revolution has its scum," Lenin said once. "Why should we be any exception?" Stalin combined the character traits and ideology of a proletarian revolutionary with those of a petty-bourgeois revolutionary inclined toward degeneration via careerism. But the problem did not lie in Stalin alone.

In the late twenties and early thirties, degeneration affected a significant part of the Leninist old guard. Great progress in socialist construction and great power turned their heads. The increasing centralization of power among the leaders was not matched by an increase of control from below. Communist conceit (*komchvanstvo*), susceptibility to adulation and flattery, began to develop among once modest revolutionaries. In their way of life many of them moved too far away from the people. Mikhail Razumov provides a typical example. A party member since 1912, secretary of the Tartar and then of the Irkutsk *obkom,* he turned into a magnate before the startled eyes of Evgeniia Ginzburg, who records the process in her memoirs. As late as 1930 he occupied one room in a communal apartment. A year later he was building a "Tartar Livadia," including a separate cottage for himself. In 1933, when Tartary was awarded the Order of Lenin for success in the *kolkhoz* movement, portraits of the "First Brigadier of Tartary" were carried through the city with singing. At an agricultural exhibition his portraits were done in mosaics of various crops, ranging from oats to lentils. Similar stories are told about Betal Kalmykov,

[115] *Pravda,* July 27, 1921.
[116] Lenin, *Sochineniia,* 4th edn., XXXVI, p. 554.

the leader of the Kabardin-Balkar Bolsheviks; about E. P. Berzin, the head of Dal'stroi; about Ia. S. Ganetskii and many old-guard Leninists.

There were various causes of such developments. It is easy to understand why Vyshinskii, a Menshevik turncoat, persecuted first his former Menshevik comrades and later his new comrades, the Bolsheviks. He was an unprincipled, cowardly politician, hungry for power. It is harder to understand why staunch Bolsheviks like Iaroslavskii or Kalinin broke and began to help Stalin. Personalities aside, the general rule is apparent. It was not the struggle with the autocracy, not jail or exile, that were the real tests for revolutionaries. Much harder was the test of power, at a time when the Party acquired almost unlimited power.

In most cases bureaucratic degeneration did not reach the criminal extremes that it did in such individuals as Postyshev and Krylenko. Usually "playing the magnate" was not accompanied by deeper moral and political degeneration. Razumov, Kalmykov, Berzin, and thousands of other such leaders retained their basic loyalty to the Party. But they gradually acquired the habit of commanding, of administration by fiat, ignoring the opinion of the masses. Cut off from the people, they lost the ability to criticize Stalin's behavior and the cult of his personality; on the contrary, they became increasingly dependent on him. Their change in life style aroused dissatisfaction among workers and rank-and-file Party members. One result was the relative ease with which Stalin subsequently destroyed such people, for he could picture their fall as a result of the people's struggle against corrupt bureaucrats. In the same way Mao Tse-tung calls for struggle against "people who are in power but are moving along the capitalist road." Stalin's demagogy is widely used in contemporary China.

The purge did not make the Party more proletarian or bring its leaders closer to the people. To be sure, many young and subjectively honorable leaders appeared in the higher circles of the Party at the end of the thirties. But in the conditions of the cult many of them became magnates even faster than their predecessors. The large number of unprincipled careerists who got into leading Party posts did not need to degenerate, for they had never had such qualities as devotion to the people, a desire to serve the workers, and commitment to Marxist ideas. The old Leninist guard were an obstruction to these petty-bourgeois careerists, who therefore supported Stalin's crimes and later constituted the strongest bastion of support for his personal dictatorship. To be sure, the concrete circumstances of the Soviet system obliged these petty-bourgeois careerist elements to endorse Communism, if only in words. They learned to hide their true goals, their actual code of ethics, behind ostentatious revolutionism. Thus a whole stratum of "Soviet" philistines and "Party" bourgeois took shape. They had some purely external features of socialist ideology and morality, and therefore differed from traditional bourgeois philistines only by their greater sanctimoniousness and hypocrisy. The influence of such petty-bourgeois elements was especially strong in the union republics where the proletarian nucleus was not as great and the Revolution not as profound as in the basic regions of Russia.

It must also be recognized that the people who rose during the mass repression, who made careers out of persecutions and arrests, were hardly interested in democracy. Uncontrolled dictatorship suited these Stalinists, since they could retain their power only under such conditions. Timeserving and complete submission to those above was their defense against those beneath, the people. Thus the cult of personality was not only a religious and ideological phenomenon; it also had a well-defined class content. It was based on the petty-bourgeois, bureacratic degeneration of some cadres and the extensive penetration of petty-bourgeois and careerist elements into the *apparat*. Stalin was not simply a dictator, he stood at the peak of a whole system of smaller dictators; he was the head bureaucrat over hundreds of thousands of smaller bureaucrats.

This is not to say that there was a complete transformation of the Party between Lenin's lifetime, when the bureaucratic elements were held in check, and Stalin's time, when they won total ascendancy. Some observers hold to this view, though it is oversimplified to the point of extreme distortion.

The extremely complex social processes of the period after Lenin's death are still waiting for genuine scientific analysis. But certain trends are apparent. On the one hand, the working class, growing with exceptional speed, absorbed the déclassé urban bourgeoisie and petty bourgeoisie, and the millions of peasant migrants to the cities. In 1929–35 new workers of these types were several times more numerous than the working class of the past. This rapid change in the composition of the working class was bound to affect its psychology and behavior, and also the composition of the Party, facilitating the degeneration of some parts of the *apparat*. At the same time, an opposite process was taking place: the transformation of the semiproletarian masses by the propagation of Marxist-Leninist ideology and socialist morality. It was in those years that profound social processes prepared the way for an ultimate strengthening of socialist elements. Though many people acquired only the externals of socialist ideology and morality, many more internalized them. In 1922 Lenin could write that the Party was still not sufficiently proletarian, the state *apparat* still a bourgeois mishmash. Ten years later the picture had substantially changed. The *apparat* was working much better, coping with more complex problems.

The socialist transformation proceeded in various ways at various levels. The spread of proletarian ideology and Communist morality was most intensive at the end of the twenties and the beginning of the thirties, and on the lower levels of society. During the mass repression that followed, all levels of the *apparat* suffered losses, but the lower suffered less than the upper. Thus, even during the years of the cult, genuinely proletarian Marxist-Leninist cadres and a basically Soviet atmosphere prevailed in most of the primary Party organizations. Of course, they too were affected by the distortions connected with the cult. Many wrong and even criminal directives were carried out by primary Party organizations. But there was far more sincere error and honest self-deception on these lower levels than there was higher up. Most of the directives sent down to them breathed the spirit of revolution, speaking about struggle with the enemies of socialism, concern for individuals, the need to advance the cause of Marxism-Leninism. The lower organizations, failing to see the gap between the words and deeds of Stalin and his associates, tried to adhere to political and moral norms that many people at the top did not consider binding on themselves.

On the middle levels of the Party and the state, the situation was more complex. Many devoted Leninists rose to take the places vacated by repression, but too many replacements were unprincipled careerists and bureaucrats. At the top levels there was a reverse process: Leninist elements were replaced by people whom we today call Stalinists. Even at the top, however, there was some variety. One group, the Stalinist guard, were cruel, unprincipled men, ready to destroy anything that blocked their way to power. Some used physical methods directly, a type that Stalin preferred for the top leadership of the punitive agencies. Others were criminals of a new type, who did their bloody deeds at a desk, jailing, torturing, and shooting by pen and telephone. But these people were incapable of managing a big, complex governmental organism. Therefore Stalin had to bring into the leadership people of another type. They were comparatively young leaders who supported Stalin in almost everything but were not informed of many of his crimes. Though they shared certain characteristic faults of Stalin's entourage, they also wanted to serve the people. They lacked sufficient political experience to analyze and rectify the tragic events of the Stalinist period, and some of them perished toward the end of it. But others survived, and after Stalin's death gave varying degrees of support to the struggle against the cult.

11

PETTY-BOURGEOIS ELEMENTS and degenerated cadres were not the only source of Stalin's strength. In the proletarian core of the Party

there were conservative tendencies that facilitated the rise and extended hegemony of Stalinism. The proletariat is the most advanced
class of bourgeois society, but it would be a mistake to idealize it. In
it, as in every class, there are people who are incapable of thinking.[117]
Such individuals are not attracted by the creative approach that is
the essence of Marxism-Leninism. On the contrary, they prefer dogmatism, which frees them from the need to think. Instead of studying
ever-changing reality, they use a few fixed rules. Although a revolution
represents the victory of the new ideas over old dogmas, in time a
revolution becomes overgrown with its own dogmas. In tsarist Russia
such a tendency was more likely than usual, for a great many revolutionaries lacked education. In such a situation Stalin's ability to make
extreme simplifications of complex ideas was not the least factor in
his rise. Many Party cadres knew Leninism only in its schematic
Stalinist exposition, unaware that Stalin was vulgarizing Marxism-
Leninism, transforming it from a developing, creative doctrine into a
peculiar religion. Thus it would be wrong to attribute every mistake
of former revolutionaries to petty-bourgeois degeneration. Many of
their errors were due not to a change in their earlier views but to an
incapacity for change, in other words, to dogmatism.

Many dedicated revolutionaries, indifferent to personal advantage,
were nevertheless incapable of carrying the Revolution forward when
a new stage required new methods. More and more their thought revealed the doctrinaire rigidity, the sectarian ossification, that Thomas
Mann had in mind when he spoke of "revolutionary conservatism."
Many leaders who excelled in the period of Civil War were not effective at building a new society. Accustomed to resolving most conflicts
by force of arms, they were incapable of complex educational work,
which had to be the chief method in the new period. Instead of learning, some Communists even began to boast of their lack of education.
"We never finished *gimnazii* [secondary schools], but we are governing *gubernii* [provinces]," a well-known Bolshevik declared at the end
of the twenties, and his audience applauded. When such people ran
into difficulties, they often turned into simple executors of orders from
above, valuing blind discipline most of all. The closed mind, the refusal to think independently, was the epistemological basis of the cult of
personality. It was not only degenerates and careerists who supported
the cult; there were also sincere believers, genuinely convinced that
everything they did was necessary for the revolution. They believed
in the political trials of 1936–38, they believed that the class struggle
was intensifying, they believed in the necessity of repression. They
became participants—and many of them subsequently became victims.

[117] *Ed.:* Medvedev quotes Lenin, *Sochineniia,* 4th edn., XXXI, without giving a page
reference. I cannot find the quotation.

How narrow and dogmatic such people could be is revealed in a song composed by wives of "enemies of the people" at a transit prison.

> In accord with severe Soviet laws
> Answering for our husbands,
> We have lost our honor and freedom,
> We have lost our beloved children.
> We don't cry, though we feel bad.
> With our faith firm we will go anywhere,
> And to any part of our measureless country
> We will take our ardent labor.
> This labor will give us the right to freedom.
> Our country, like a mother, will accept us again.
> And under the banner of Lenin and Stalin,
> We will give our labor to the country.[118]

Rigidity of this type was manifested by many leaders in the period under review, and is well portrayed by a novelist in a character named Onisimov. He is an old Bolshevik who has become an important manager, a commissar, devoted to socialism, scrupulously honest, simple in his way of life, never using his high post for personal advantage, but also a conservative, a worshipper of blind discipline. He is a zealous servant, who thinks only of how to carry out his orders "from above," from "the boss." Nothing else interests him. Though he hates Beria personally, like Beria he is a pillar of the Stalinist regime.

> When he was reporting to Stalin on the problem of East Siberian metallurgy, he had no idea of the paradoxes, of the contradictions of the era. Questions that might have disturbed his reason and conscience as a Communist were set aside, avoided in the simplest way: It's not my business; it doesn't concern me; it's not for me to judge. His favorite brother died in prison; in his soul he mourned for Vania, but even then remained firm in his "don't argue!" For him the expression "soldier of the Party" was no empty phrase. Later, when "soldier of Stalin" came into use, he considered himself such a soldier, with pride and undoubtedly with reason.[119]

Besides being incapable of finding solutions for new problems, a dogmatist often cannot understand that many problems have several possible solutions. The many forms of socialism depend on circumstances of place and time, national peculiarities and historical traditions. The dogmatist does not see this; he regards any deviation from his schemes as something anti-Communist, to be condemned and punished. Not only leaders but to a large extent the masses had their

---

[118] Quoted in E. G. Veller-Gurevich, "Iz vospominanii o 37-om." *Ed.:* This seems to be an unpublished manuscript.

[119] A. Bek, *Novoe naznachenie. Ed.:* I have been unable to locate this novel; Medvedev simply calls it a *roman* and doesn't give the place or date of publication.

rigidity drilled into them during the years of the cult. "I used to open the journal *Searchlight* with the greatest interest," a poet reminisces.

> Lying down on the floor I would draw a kulak with a sawed-off gun. I recall how, before a holiday, I would spare neither India ink nor whiting; I would divide the whole world unconditionally into Whites and Reds. Eager, skinny, short, I marched gaily, and suspected a bourgeois in every fat man.

And in fact, during the twenties and thirties the slogan "Whoever is not with us is against us" was inculcated both in the Party and in the people. When Lenin uttered it during the Civil War, the fate of the Soviet regime hung by a hair. To keep on shouting it after the Civil War was a sign of sectarian and dogmatic thinking.

12

LET US EXAMINE the problem of bureaucratic degeneration more closely. It played a part in nineteenth-century socialist arguments concerning the postrevolutionary state. Should the victorious proletariat use the old state *apparat* or destroy it? If destruction was the answer, a question still remained: should a new proletarian state be created on the ruins of the old, or could the proletariat do without a state altogether? Might not a proletarian state turn into a clique of privileged functionaries standing above the people?

Revolutionaries expressed many different views on these questions. The anarchists, for example, drew a sharp line between society and the state. In any society the state was the main conservative force, the most serious obstacle to the development of equality and freedom. Therefore the revolution meant the immediate destruction of any state. For the anarchists there was no problem of a transitional period to put down the upper classes and re-educate the lower in the spirit of socialism. They believed that any proletarian state would inevitably degenerate into the rule of the minority over the majority, and would represent a new form of the oppression of the masses. "What does it mean to say that the proletariat will be elevated to be the ruling class?" asked Bakunin.

> Can the entire proletariat stand at the head of the government? . . . Then there would be no government, there would be no state. . . . This dilemma is easily resolved in the theory of the Marxists. By popular government they mean government of the people by a small number of representatives elected by the people. . . . And so, whatever way you look at this problem, you reach the same sorry conclusion: the government of the enormous majority of the popular masses by a privileged minority. But this minority, say the Marxists,

will consist of workers. Yes, of former workers, who, as soon as they become rulers or representatives of the people, will cease to be workers and will begin to look upon the whole world of common laborers from the heights of the state system. They will represent not the people but themselves and their claims to govern the people.[120]

Marx and Engels objected strongly to this gloomy picture. Socialist society cannot arise in a single day; it can be created only by many years of struggle to reconstruct the social organism on new principles and to suppress the opposition of the overthrown exploiting classes. In other words, a more or less prolonged transitional period would be needed between capitalist and communist societies. After destroying the old state machine the proletariat would have to create its own, the dictatorship of the proletariat, giving this state a "revolutionary and transitional form."[121] In a famous critique of antiauthoritarian revolutionaries, Engels wondered whether they had ever seen a revolution.

Revolution is without doubt the most authoritarian thing possible. Revolution is an act in which part of the population forces its will on another part by means of guns, bayonets, cannon, that is, by extremely authoritarian instruments. And the victorious party is necessarily obliged to maintain its rule by means of the same fear that its weapons inspire in the reactionaries.[122]

Marx and Engels also faced the problem of how to keep the proletarian state from degeneration, from becoming transformed from society's servant to its master. But this problem was never satisfactorily solved in nineteenth-century Marxist writings. There were good reasons. In the first place, it was hard to work out rules for a proletarian state without any concrete experience of building such a state. Marx and Engels made some recommendations on this matter only after the Paris Commune: every official should be subject to recall at any moment, and the salary of any official should be no higher than a workman's pay. But the experiment of the Paris Commune lasted only seventy-two days, which was too short to test the efficacy of these measures or to discover what else might be necessary to prevent degeneration.

In the second place, Marx and Engels assumed that the socialist revolution would triumph in all the major capitalist countries at the same time. Therefore the revolutionary state would be necessary only for a short period. They regarded the state as a necessary evil, to be endured only "until the generation that grows up in the new free social

[120] M. A. Bakunin, *Polnoe sobranie sochinenii*, II (S.P., 1907), p. 217.
[121] Marx and Engels, *Sochineniia*, 2nd edn., XVIII, p. 297.
[122] *Ibid.*, p. 305.

situation will be in a condition to cast aside this whole rubbish of state systems."[123]

In the most famous comment of all, Engels summed it up:

> The first act in which the state really comes forward as the representative of society as a whole—the taking possession of the means of production in the name of society—is at the same time its last independent act as a state. The interference of the state power in social relations becomes superfluous in one sphere after another, and then ceases of itself. The government of persons is replaced by the administration of things and the direction of the processes of production. The state is not "abolished," it *withers away*.[124]

Lenin took the same point of view in *State and Revolution* (1917), though of course he was primarily concerned with the establishment of proletarian hegemony over the bourgeoisie. Lenin did not believe in the simultaneous victory of the socialist revolution in the major capitalist countries. He considered it more likely that socialism would triumph first in one country, which would lead to an inevitably savage struggle between the proletariat and the overthrown exploiting classes, lending new urgency to the maintenance of a strong proletarian state.[125] "We are not utopians," Lenin wrote.

> We do not "dream" of suddenly doing without all government, all subordination. Those are anarchist dreams, essentially foreign to Marxism, based on a failure to understand the tasks of the dictatorship of the proletariat. In fact, they only serve to put off the socialist revolution until people are different.[126]

In 1917, since the possible degeneration of the proletarian state did not seem to be an urgent problem, Lenin merely repeated some of Marx's and Engels' ideas without elaboration. The new state *apparat*, he said in *State and Revolution*, would be staffed with industrial and white-collar workers who would be prevented from turning into bureaucrats by election and recall, by limiting their salaries to the level of workingmen's pay, and by universal involvement in the functions of supervision and control, ". . . so that all will become 'bureaucrats' for a time, and therefore no one can become a 'bureaucrat.' "[127]

After the October Revolution the situation changed. On the one hand, a powerful state *apparat* developed very quickly, to consolidate the gains of the Revolution and to defeat the enemies of the proletariat in savage warfare. On the other hand, certain alarming processes began to manifest themselves in this *apparat*. Because of the shortage of

[123] *Ibid.*, XXII, p. 201.
[124] *Ibid.*, XX, pp. 291–92. *Ed.:* The English translation is by Emile Burns. See Engels, *Herr Eugen Dühring's Revolution in Science (Anti-Dühring)* (New York, 1939), pp. 306–307.
[125] See, e.g., Lenin, *Sochineniia*, 3rd edn., XXIII, p. 354, and XXV, p. 173.
[126] Lenin, *Polnoe sobranie*, XXXIII, p. 49.
[127] Lenin, *Sochineniia*, 4th edn., XXV, p. 452.

literate, trained workers, many alien class elements began to appear in the government. And some Communists, finding themselves in power, began to abuse their position and to display very un-Communist traits: conceit, scorn for the workers' interests, the bureaucratic syndrome. They turned into officeholders, standing above the people and pursuing first and foremost their own goals.

The Communist Party did much to keep these processes in check. The Party's best people were placed in key government posts, and all state organizations were obliged to account for themselves before Party organizations and to carry out directives issued by Party organizations. But these measures could not entirely stop the process of bureaucratic degeneration. As has been pointed out, the Party was itself subject to the danger of degeneration. Further, the Party ceased to be only a union of like-minded people; the Party *apparat* directed the state, and thus the Party organizations—above all the Central Committee and the Party congresses—became the legislative organs of the Soviet regime. This was a positive development in that the Party, forged in the fire of two revolutions, was the bearer of socialist ideas; it tied together all the parts of the new social organism. But there were also some negative results. Since officials in the Party *apparat* had much more power than officials in the state *apparat,* some of the former were inclined to misuse their power. For example, some of the necessary privileges of the top leaders, i.e., privileges that facilitated their work, became fetishes for certain Party members. Finally, the heightening of the Party's significance depressed that of the soviets. They no longer discussed legislation but gave formal endorsement to Party directives.

Lenin, who watched these processes closely, planned to write a second part of *State and Revolution* which would generalize the experience of the young Soviet state. But he never managed to carry out this plan. We can infer his views from his actions. He waged an unrelenting struggle against the various kinds of bureaucratic degeneration, trying to erect barriers against it. In line with Marx's proposal, which was endorsed in *State and Revolution,* the famous Party maximum was established: a limit was placed on the salary of any Party member. (Lenin himself received a modest salary, and made sure that it was not arbitrarily raised.) Any Party official could be quickly removed from any government post. The Party was regularly purged, with the participation of manual and white-collar workers who were not Party members. As a result of these purges, the membership dropped from 730,000 in March, 1921, to 472,000 at the beginning of 1924.[128] And other efforts were made to bring the Party under popular control.

[128] *Ed.:* The reader should bear in mind that purges before the thirties were not "blood purges." They were an examination of members' records in order to expel unworthy members.

In practice these measures were insufficient. They were especially unavailing with respect to the higher echelons. Some Party leaders, wielding enormous power, could easily get around the existing restrictions. Nor were there sufficient guarantees against a struggle for power among particular leaders. Lenin was very much aware of this; almost all his last articles and memoranda are permeated with anxiety over the future development of the Soviet state.

After Lenin's death, barriers against bureaucratic degeneration were not erected. On the contrary, Stalin skillfully used the incompleteness, both in theory and practice, of the proletarian state. The absence of effective mechanisms to check the abuse of power by the highest leaders enabled Stalin to strengthen his own position and gradually to usurp all power. Indeed, he steadily weakened the anti-bureaucratic measures that had begun to be developed under Lenin. The Party maximum was gradually abolished. As soon as Lenin was dead, admission to the Party was greatly broadened. In the three years from 1924 to 1927 the membership increased by two and a half times, reaching 1,148,000 at the beginning of 1927. Even the masses' intense feeling at Lenin's death was used by Stalin: the "Lenin enrollment" brought into the Party all at once hundreds of thousands of inadequately educated workers, which greatly increased the power of the *apparat*. The principle that all officials are subject to recall was used by Stalin to eliminate people he did not like, while he himself and his chosen aides were made irreplaceable. The system of Party, state, and popular control that had begun to take shape under Lenin was gradually destroyed.

These complex processes stand in need of profound analysis. Below we shall try to outline only one: the decline of popular control over government institutions.

13

CAPITALIST SOCIETY cannot do without bureaucracy, government by privileged people elevated above the masses. But the capitalist class maintains control of these officials, by many informal as well as formal methods. Indeed, the upper strata of the bureaucracy belong to the exploiting class and cannot become an independent social force.

The proletariat destroyed the old state machine and created its own, but the possibility existed that its officials, given power in the name of the people, would begin to use it against the people. This can happen, as in the years of Stalin's cult, in the case of officials endowed with the plenitude of state power. The result is a difficult position for the popular masses. Protected against their former rulers and external enemies, they are practically helpless against the arbitrary rule of their own leaders. Thus one of the most important tasks of the proletarian revolution should be the establishment of effective control by the working class over its representatives in the state and Party *apparat*.

This sort of problem was recognized long before the Russian Revolution. Robespierre, for example, noting that the people's sovereign power is unlimited, asked who would control the individuals to whom such power is delegated.[129] He had an incorrect answer to that sensible question: the benefactor of the people would exercise control. The Babouvists saw the danger more clearly[130] and proposed a more sensible solution: bodies of popular supervisors checking up on officials. Marx and Engels' sensitivity to the problem has already been noted. Perhaps the most forceful formulation came from Engels:

> When the working class comes to power, . . . it must, in order not to lose its newly won supremacy, on the one hand, get rid of the old machine of oppression which had been used against it, and on the other hand, *protect itself against its own deputies and functionaries.*[131]

This problem was one of the most important facing the Bolsheviks after the October Revolution. It was not possible to rely merely on the personal qualities of the leaders. A system of control had to be developed, to keep officials constantly reminded that they were servants of the people. This was especially necessary in view of the new government's unavoidable reliance on bourgeois specialists and functionaries taken over from the old state *apparat*.

Within days after the Revolution, by the end of October, a special collegium was selected by the Central Executive Committee to begin state control. In May, 1918, this Central Control Collegium was transformed into the People's Commissariat of State Control. At the same time many workers' and peasants' inspection organizations came into being. In 1920 they were fused with the Commissariat of State Control to form the Commissariat of Workers' and Peasants' Inspection, *Rabkrin*. Control organs were also set up in the Party. In September, 1920, on Lenin's motion, the IXth Party Conference created the Central Control Commission (TsKK) and local control commissions, whose tasks were to

> fight encroaching bureaucratism, careerism, the abuse of their Party and Soviet positions by Party members, the violation of comradely

---

[129] M. Robespierre, *Revoliutsionnaia zakonnost' i pravosudie* (Moscow, 1959), p. 209.

[130] See F. Buonarroti, *Zagovor vo imia ravenstva* (Moscow, 1948), I, pp. 316–17. *Ed.:* A translation of Filippo Buonarroti, *Conspiration pour l'égalité dite de Babeuf* (Brussels, 1828).

[131] Marx and Engels, *Sochineniia,* 2nd edn., XXII, p. 199. Italics added.

relations within the Party, the spread of unfounded and unverified rumors and insinuations, which discredit the Party or its individual members, and other such reports that damage the Party's unity and authority.[132]

These agencies accomplished a considerable amount, but they were not efficient. Lenin was especially critical of *Rabkrin,* which was headed in 1919–21 by Stalin. "Let us speak plainly," Lenin wrote:

> At present *Rabkrin* does not have an ounce of authority. Everyone knows that there are no institutions more poorly organized than the institutions of *Rabkrin,* and that in its present state nothing can be expected of this Commissariat.[133]

In the last years of his life Lenin gave a great deal of attention to this issue. He wrote that the struggle with bureaucratism was "just as complex as the struggle with petty-bourgeois elements,"[134] that "bureaucratism can be completely defeated only when the entire population will take part in government,"[135] that this struggle "can be successful only if we are enormously persistent over a long period."[136]

In 1922 Lenin worked out a new system of popular control. He proposed the creation of joint Party and state control agencies that would rely above all on masses of workers and peasants. The particulars were: (1) expansion of the Central Control Commission by adding seventy-five to a hundred workers and peasants, who were to be carefully screened from the Party point of view, since they would enjoy all the rights of Central Committee members. (2) The assignment of some members of the Central Control Commission to *Rabkrin,* where they would be members of its directing *apparat* and thus maintain a vital link between the two agencies of control. At the same time the *apparat* of *Rabkrin* was to be reduced to three or four hundred people. One of the most important tasks of the new control organs was to prevent a split in the Central Committee, and also to limit the "boundless power" of the Party's General Secretary. "Our Central Committee," Lenin wrote,

> has become a strictly centralized and highly authoritative group, but the work of this group is not set up in conditions appropriate to its authority. The reform I am proposing should improve things: the members of the Central Control Commission, a certain number of whom would be obligatory attendants at every meeting of the

[132] *KPSS v rezoliutsiiakh,* I (1953), p. 533. The quotation is taken from the corresponding resolution of the Xth Congress.
[133] *Sochineniia,* 4th edn., XXXIII, p. 448.
[134] *Ibid.,* XXXII, p. 167.
[135] *Ibid.,* XXIX, p. 161.
[136] *Ibid.,* XXXII, p. 367.

Politburo, should form a solid group, which should see to it, "without respect to persons," that no authority—neither that of the General Secretary nor that of any other Central Committee member —stops them from making an inquiry, from checking documents, and in general from achieving unconditional information and the strictest accuracy.[137]

Stalin did not continue Lenin's effort to create genuine agencies of popular control. Quite to the contrary, he limited the existing agencies to checking up on lower organizations and controlling opposition groups, while the higher administrative bodies became increasingly immune to effective control. As Stalin's power grew, the importance of the control agencies declined. In December, 1930, he proposed that an Executive Commission be attached to the All-Union Council of Peoples' Commissars, to take over important functions of the Central Control Commission and *Rabkrin* in checking on the execution of government decrees. In February, 1931, the same reorganization was carried out in the autonomous republics. Just before the XVIIth Party Congress of 1934, the press carried a proposal by Kaganovich to replace the Central Control Commission and *Rabkrin* by two new agencies: a Commission of Party Control (KPK) and a Commission of Soviet Control (KSK). Stalin told the Congress that there was no need for the two existing agencies. Now, he said, an organization was required that "would not have the universal goal of inspecting everyone and everything, but could concentrate all its attention on the work of control, on the work of verifying the execution of the decisions of the Soviet regime's central institutions."[138] Thus the functions of control were restricted. Such problems as fighting bureaucratic abuses or perfecting the state *apparat* were not even mentioned. The section of the resolution that the Congress adopted in response to Stalin's dicta drew a sharp distinction between Party and state control agencies: one commission was to check up on governmental decisions, the other on Party decisions.[139]

The functions of the Commission of Soviet Control, which later became the Commissariat of State Control, were essentially limited to inspection, auditing, and reporting on violations discovered this way. As for the Commission of Party Control, it had almost no control functions at all; its main job was the review of personnel problems

[137] *Polnoe Sobranie*, XLV, p. 387. From a memorandum, "How We Should Reorganize *Rabkrin*," published in *Pravda* of Jan. 25, 1923, while Lenin was still alive. However, in this and in all subsequent publications until Stalin's death, the words "neither that of the General Secretary nor that of any other Central Committee member" were deleted.

[138] Stalin, *Sochineniia*, XIII, pp. 373–74.

[139] See *Leninskaia sistema partiino-gosudarstvennogo kontrolia i ego rol' v stroitel'stve sotsializma, 1917–1932gg.* (Moscow, 1965), pp. 196–98.

and appeals of Communists. Rank-and-file Party members and the popular masses were entirely excluded from the control function. The whole system of *Rabkrin*—groups and cells, sections, complaint bureaus, the "light cavalry," and so on—was dismantled.

14

IN THE FINAL ANALYSIS, the attitude of the masses is decisive. Sooner or later they overthrow all sorts of tyrants and despots, but at other times the same masses are the strongest support of despotism. "Every people," said Marx, "has the rulers it deserves." An Arab thinker and social activist of the nineteenth century expressed the idea at greater length:

> The common people are the despot's sustenance and his power; he rules over them and with their help oppresses others. He holds them captive and they extol his might; he robs them and they bless him for sparing their lives. He degrades them and they praise his grandeur; he turns them against each other, and they take pride in his craftiness. And if the despot squanders their wealth, they say he is generous; if he kills without torturing, they consider him merciful; if he drives them into mortal danger, they submit, fearing punishment; and if some of them are reproachful, rejecting despotism, the people will fight the rejectors as if they were tyrants. In short, the common people cut their own throats through fear, which derives from ignorance. If ignorance is destroyed, fear will disappear, the situation will change.[140]

This interpretation can be applied to the Soviet Union only in part. We have already argued that Stalin was supported by the majority of the Soviet people, not only because he was clever enough to deceive them but also because they were backward enough to be deceived. The severe oppression that made the population of the tsarist empire revolutionary also kept them on a low cultural level. As the novelist V. G. Korolenko wrote in a letter to Lunacharskii: "The ease with which you got our popular masses to follow you indicates not our readiness for a socialist system but, on the contrary, the immaturity of our people."[141] And that partly just remark was often made by Lenin in a different form: in Russia it was comparatively easy to begin a socialist revolution, but it would also be much harder to carry it through to the end, in the minds of people as well as in the economy.

[140] 'Abd al Raḥmān al-Kawākibī, *Priroda despotizma i gibel'nost' poraboshcheniia* (Moscow, 1964), pp. 25–26. *Ed.*: Translated from an Arabic edition (Aleppo, 1957).
[141] *Ed.*: The quotation derives from Korolenko, *Pis'ma k Lunacharskomu* (Paris, 1922), p. 33.

The Stalinist dictatorship was undoubtedly parasitic on the short-comings of the masses in revolutionary Russia. Stalin cleverly used the revolutionary passion of the masses, their hatred for enemies of the revolution, and their low level of culture. The oversimplified slogans he issued in the thirties—the intensification of the class struggle under socialism, the destruction of "enemies of the people"—captivated the mass mood, becoming thus a powerful material force that supported Stalin's dictatorship. But saying this, we are still far from exhausting the problem of the relationship between Stalin's cult and the masses. The problem cannot be reduced simply to the masses' lack of education.

Efforts have been made to connect the cult of Stalin with the peculiarities of the Russian peasantry, its tsarist illusions and religiosity. Some comrades draw a comparison with the French peasants, who supported Napoleon as a guarantee against the return of the feudal landowners. This "peasant origin" of Stalinism was expounded at an ideological conference in the Central Committee in November, 1965. And G. Pomerants defends it in a pamphlet:

> Centuries of Tartar rule and serfdom left a considerable tradition of servility and shamelessness (*khamstvo*). The Revolution shook it, but, on the other hand, the Revolution wrenched masses of peasants away from their old nesting places, transformed whole strata of a patriarchal people into masses, who lost their old main-stays and assimilated not much of the new ideology. These masses wanted nothing like an extension and strengthening of freedom; they hardly understood what freedom of the individual is. They wanted a boss and order. That was Stalin's mandate No. 2. Mandate No. 3 was a decapitated religion. The muzhik believed in God; in pictures of the Savior and the Kazan Mother of God he found something to love, to worship unselfishly. . . . They explained to the muzhik that there is no god, but that did not destroy his religious feeling. And Stalin gave the toilers a god, an earthly god, of whom it was impossible to say that he did not exist. He did exist, he existed in the Kremlin, and now and then he would appear on a platform and wave his hand. He was endlessly concerned that not a hair should fall from a toiler's head.[142]

Such explanations are oversimplified. The new cult of the live god did not replace the muzhik's old god. The old religion, though weakened, retained great rural strength in the thirties and especially in the forties. Religion was not decapitated, and therefore faith in Stalin could hardly be considered the result of the peasants' unsatisfied religious feelings. Secondly, Stalin's cult proceeded not from the vil-lage to the city but from the city to the village. It originated in the early thirties, when conditions were very bad in the newly collectivized

---

[142] G. Pomerants, "Nravstvennyi oblik istoricheskoi lichnosti," unpublished manuscript.

villages. Millions of peasant families had been deported to the north and to Siberia. In many *oblasti* there was famine. The peasant masses were dissatisfied with the policy of forced state procurements at arbitrary prices. In some areas grain strikes broke out. Thus conditions in the countryside were obviously unfavorable to the rise and consolidation of Stalin's cult, which probably had its fewest devotees in the rural areas.

The cult also had little appeal to the petty-bourgeois urban masses. They too were dissatisfied in the early thirties, but they were also tired and politically apathetic as a result of the long years of war, first imperialist and then civil. Such apolitical petty bourgeois were unlikely to grow ecstatic over Stalin, but they also apathetically turned their backs on the agitation of the S-R's and Mensheviks.

In the thirties, Stalin's cult was strongest among workers, especially in the Party stratum of the working class, and also among the new young intelligentsia, particularly those of worker and peasant origin. It was also strong in the Party and state *apparat,* especially in the *apparat* that took shape after the repression of 1936–38. In short, appraisal of the cult's influence requires a differential approach; the people cannot be regarded as a single mass. Furthermore, all these problems require concrete sociological analysis.

The same rule applies to the low educational and cultural level of the masses. Obviously ignorance, lack of education, defects in moral values, and an abundance of potentially authoritarian personality types played a very important role in the establishment of the Stalinist dictatorship. "Ignorance," wrote the young Marx, "is a demonic force, and we fear that it will serve as the cause of still more tragedies."[143]

The theory that genuine socialism is impossible without a certain cultural and moral level in society is not new. In the nineteenth century Herbert Spencer argued this case at great length, against liberal reformers as well as socialists. He noted that voluntary associations of these people invariably acquired an authoritarian structure, and asked what could be expected if they achieved state power. Drawing analogies with such disparate states as those of medieval Europe, Japan, and contemporary Germany, where Bismarck showed "leanings towards State socialism," Spencer envisioned a centralized bureaucratic despotism if socialists came to power. If the socialist state became involved in foreign war or internal dissension, he predicted "a grinding tyranny like that of ancient Peru," with a revival of forced labor and universal surveillance. Analogies and prophecies aside, the heart of Spencer's analysis was his insistence that

> the machinery of communism, like existing social machinery, has to
> be framed out of existing human nature; and the defects of existing

[143] *Sochineniia,* 2nd edn., I, p. 112.

human nature will generate in the one the same evils as in the other. . . . The belief, not only of the socialists but also of those so-called liberals who are diligently preparing the way for them, is that by due skill an ill-working humanity may be framed into well-working institutions. It is a delusion. . . . There is no political alchemy by which you can get golden conduct out of leaden instincts.[144]

No Marxist could agree with Spencer's argument, which derives the forms of social organization directly from biological and social instincts inherent in humanity at a given moment. If it is true that the morality of the majority influences the social organization, it is also true that the social organization influences morality. Nevertheless the problem that Spencer raised was not satisfactorily dealt with in Marxist writings of the nineteenth century. Both Marx and Engels expected that the socialist revolution would simultaneously triumph in the most culturally advanced countries of Europe. In the early twentieth century, as the center of the revolutionary movement shifted to Russia, the interrelation of socialism and culture was debated among the Russian Social Democrats. Not only the Mensheviks but even some Bolsheviks felt that a socialist revolution could not triumph in Russia, because of its backwardness. In 1917 Gorky took a similar position, since he feared that the revolution would cause too many losses to the Russian intelligentsia, which was still small in numbers, and would thus retard the development of society. Lenin rejected these misgivings.

> If a certain cultural level is required for the creation of socialism (though no one can say just what this "cultural level" is, for it is different in each West European country), then why can we not begin from the beginning by winning the preconditions for this certain level through revolution, and then, on the basis of the workers' and peasants' power and the Soviet system, move to catch up with other nations? . . . For the creation of socialism, you will say, people must be civilized. Very good. But why could we not begin by creating such preconditions for the civilization of people as getting rid of noble landlords and . . . capitalists?[145]

And in fact the Bolsheviks undertook a cultural as well as a social revolution. But while the level of culture was rapidly rising among the masses, thereby confirming Lenin's prognosis, an opposite process was taking place within the leading circles. The first Soviet government was, as I noted previously, the most "educated" government in Europe. Nevertheless, a large part of the highest cadres and a huge part of the middle and lower cadres were extremely lacking in culture

---

[144] Spencer, *The Man versus the State* (London, 1881), pp. 40–43. Medvedev cites the Russian translation, *Lichnost' i gosudarstvo* (St. Petersburg, 1908), pp. 31–33.
[145] Lenin, *Sochineniia*, 4th edn., XXXIII, pp. 438–39.

and education. Lenin perceived this clearly: "The economic forces under the control of the proletarian state of Russia are quite sufficient to ensure the transition to communism. What then is lacking? What is lacking is culture in the stratum of Communists that is governing."[146]

With Stalin's rise to power, the general cultural level of the leadership dropped even more. At a time when the number of specialists and educated people was increasing at the lower and middle levels of the state and economic administration, many of those in Stalin's retinue were distinguished by shocking ignorance and stupidity—for example Molotov, Voroshilov, Ezhov, and Beria. And Malenkov, Khrushchev, Shkiriatov, and Budennyi were not distinguished by excessive culture. Stalin himself remained to the end of his life an uneducated man, although he pretended to be a "scholar of genius" and "a coryphaeus of science." The NKVD *apparat* was recruited from ignorant people who despised the intelligentsia. A glaring lack of culture was also the hallmark of many in the new intelligentsia who took prominent places in literature, art, and science in the thirties and forties.

The lack of general culture was accompanied by a special kind of ignorance: that of a socialist society's patterns of operation, incomprehension of the contradictions in the new social system and of the ways to overcome them. These people could not adapt Marxism-Leninism to new conditions. As a result, the political and cultural development of the masses became one-sided. The working class and the core of the Party kept their revolutionary spirit, their desire to build socialism and communism and to fight fascism and imperialism, but this spirit was not supplemented by the necessary political education.

[146] *Ibid.*, p. 258.

Part Three

THE CONSEQUENCES
OF STALINISM

Prologue

STALIN'S ONE-MAN RULE took shape gradually, beginning in the mid-twenties, reaching the level of a cult in the early thirties,[1] and achieving its finished form as a result of the repression in 1936–38. Now we shall examine the aftereffects, as they revealed themselves in the last fifteen years of the Stalinist dictatorship, 1939–53.

Of course those years were a time of great achievements. The Soviet Union played a decisive role in defeating fascism, helped in the creation of the world socialist camp, and quickly restored its war-shattered economy. But it would be a mistake to remember only those great feats. The cult of Stalin and its consequences were not an essential part of socialist society—they were indeed a complete contradiction of its principles—but the reality as well as the principles of socialism did manage to survive. The Party was bled white, but it was not killed; it lived and led the people onward. There were forces that limited the effects of the cult and prevented the destruction of much that had been created by Lenin and the Revolution. Therefore we must not exaggerate the consequences of the cult, but we cannot—

[1] Some historians have argued that the two decades from 1933 to 1953 should not be called "the period of the cult of personality." See, for example, the letter by E. Zhukov, V. Trukhanovskii, and V. Shunkov, *Pravda*, Jan. 30, 1966. They say that "exaggeration of the role of one person willy-nilly led to belittlement of the heroic efforts of the Party and the people in the struggle for socialism. . . ." This exercise in sophistry ignores the fact that "the period of the cult of personality" is the description used not only by "certain historical works" but also by the resolutions of the XXIInd Party Congress. It also ignores the logic of the philosopher A. V. Gulyga and the historians N. A. Erofeev, I. M. Lemin, D. E. Melamed, A. M. Nekrich, and G. B. Fedorov, who said, in a joint letter to the Central Committee:

> Every historical epoch is a complex conglomerate of various phenomena, which can be characterized only by many-sided definitions. The end of the thirties was a period in Party history marked by the building of socialism in the field of the economy, of social relations, etc. It was also the period of the cult of Stalin's personality, distinguished by senseless mass repression. If we refuse to define this period as the period of the cult of Stalin's personality and speak only of the period of extended socialist construction, then it will seem that the mass repression of Soviet people was hardly a characteristic feature of the period of extended socialist construction. It stands to reason that this is not so. In reality the mass repression only hindered socialist construction.

we have no right to—minimize them, to forget that Stalinism did immeasurable harm to the cause of socialism both at home and abroad.

We cannot agree with those historians who would reduce the whole problem to the personal tragedy of the victims of repression. The Party and the people, they argue, lived their lives largely independently of Stalin and his retinue and built socialism knowing nothing of the crimes that were being committed in the country. Stalin did destroy many outstanding leaders, these historians concede, and we deeply regret it, but the victims were replaced by other leaders who successfully continued their work. Such arguments are wrong. In the first place, many of the new leaders could not replace leaders of the Leninist type. But more than that, it was not only leaders who changed during the cult; the conditions under which leaders work were fundamentally changed. In the new situation even the most capable and dedicated of the new leaders could not perform the work done by their predecessors.

Today it is often said that Stalin's cult did not change the nature of socialist society, but that is only a half truth. Stalin's long rule led to the most serious distortions in the theory and practice of socialist construction. Many of the basic principles of a socialist society were perverted, and enormous harm was done to the cause of socialism. Thus it would be quite wrong to compare Stalinism with some mild illness of a healthy man. It was an extremely serious disease, which threatened the total destruction of the greatest achievements of the October Revolution.

XII

Diplomacy and War

1

THE PROBLEMS THAT CONFRONT the leaders of a great power in the modern world are extremely diverse and complex. Not only miscalculations in the diplomatic arena or in military strategy but even errors in evaluating discoveries in natural science can have disastrous effects. No one leader, not even one of genius, can master the flow of information needed to solve state problems. Collective decision making and some decentralization of power are imperative.

In the early thirties Stalin seemed to understand these simple truths. At least he stated them well to the German writer Emil Ludwig:

> On the basis of the experience of three revolutions, we know that out of a hundred one-man decisions, which are not tested, not corrected collectively, about ninety of the decisions are one-sided. In our directing agency, the Central Committee of our Party, which directs all our Soviet and Party organizations, there are about seventy members. . . . In this areopagus is concentrated the wisdom of our Party. Each member has the chance to correct any personal opinion or proposal. Each member has the chance to bring in his own experience. If this were not so, if decisions were made by one person, we would have very serious mistakes in our work.[1]

Those were fine words, but they were only words. Convinced of his own infallibility, Stalin set up a system of government from which collective decision making on important matters was virtually excluded. Of course he often consulted his aides and various officials. Sometimes he even listened to objections, presented, of course, very carefully—anyone who seriously disputed Stalin's opinions was likely to end up as an "enemy of the people." But these limited consulta-

[1] Stalin, *Sochineniia*, XIII, p. 107.

tions, which usually occurred not in the conference room but at private receptions or dinners, were no substitute for genuinely collective decision making. In such a situation the wisest ruler would soon lose his bearings. For he receives from his subjects above all the information he wants to hear, and thus loses more and more the basis for distinguishing between illusion and reality.

In a number of cases Stalin did make the right decisions. It was not his intention to weaken the Soviet Union economically or militarily; he had other goals. But once he had usurped all power, his chance of making correct judgments was so greatly reduced that he committed many errors. And that was not the worst part; the system he set up made mistakes not only inevitable, numerous, and grave, but extremely difficult to correct. That was one of the most dangerous consequences of the cult.

2

IN THE THIRTIES Communist parties struggled vigorously against fascism. But Stalin, as the recognized leader of the Comintern, held them rigidly to a point of view that derived from the Russian Revolution. Years of conflict with the Mensheviks, culminating in the choice between the Provisional Government and the Soviet regime, had inculcated into Bolsheviks a special animus against Menshevism. An analogous situation took shape in parts of Western Europe between 1918 and 1923, when the Social Democratic parties helped to sustain bourgeois regimes and to suppress the revolutionary movement. Thus it was natural for the young Communist parties to oppose Social Democrats, but it was wrong to call them "social fascists," the "moderate wing of fascism," "the main social support for fascism." Stalin was not alone in this mistake. Bukharin, Kamenev, and Zinoviev made the same charges, and they were included in the 1928 Program of the Comintern, of which Bukharin was a chief author.

Whatever may be said for Comintern policy toward the Social Democratic parties in the early and middle twenties, it is impossible to approve the policy of 1929–34. In this period fascist movements developed rapidly in many European countries. The Social Democrats, excluded from power almost everywhere, went into opposition. Many of them took a clear if not always consistent antifascist stand. But Stalin, instead of changing Comintern policy, continued to insist on fighting Social Democracy. For example, in 1931 the XIth Plenum of the Comintern Executive Committee passed the following resolution:

A successful struggle against fascism requires the mobilization of the masses by Communist parties on the basis of a united front from below. . . .[2] It requires immediate and decisive correction of mistakes that are reducible to the liberal juxtaposition of fascism and bourgeois democracy, of the parliamentary forms of the bourgeois dictatorship and its openly fascist forms. This is a reflection of Social Democratic influences in the Communist ranks.[3]

This hostility to all forms of bourgeois democracy had its own logic for Stalin. Constantly violating the elementary norms of any democracy instead of developing a proletarian socialist democracy, Stalin could not acknowledge any positive value in bourgeois democracy.

At the beginning of the thirties Stalin came down hardest on the left Social Democrats, who enjoyed considerable influence among the working class in several European countries. He called them the most dangerous part of Social Democracy because they concealed their opportunism with phony revolutionism, and thus drew the people away from the Communists. This sectarian policy was especially harmful in Germany, where the fascist threat was greatest. The German Communist Party stuck to the policy of a united front only "from below," which meant that it preached Stalin's thesis of "social fascism" even in its appeals to Social Democratic workers.[4] Likewise in their trade-union policy: instead of struggling against reformists within the existing unions, the Communists decided to withdraw and organize independent unions. This isolated the German Communist Party from a large section of the workers. The same stupidity, with the same result, was manifested in the Communist propaganda that ignored the great value to the working class of bourgeois democratic freedoms. The Neumann-Remmele group were especially zealous Stalinists. In 1931 Remmele even declared in the Reichstag: "Fascist rule, a fascist government, does not frighten us. It will collapse sooner than any other."[5] In the summer of 1932 this group was defeated within the German Party, but sectarian influence remained strong.

The Soviet publicist Ernst Henri has described the situation vividly in a letter to Ilya Ehrenburg:

Stalin's words were just as much an order for the Comintern as his instructions were for the Red Army or the NKVD. They divided

[2] *Ed.*: A united front "from below" signified a refusal to form a political alliance with existing Social Democratic organizations. A united front was to be sought by winning rank-and-file Social Democrats away from their existing organizations.

[3] *Kompartii i krizis kapitalizma; XI Plenum IKKI, Sten. otchet* (Moscow, 1932), p. 626.

[4] See the materials cited by L. I. Gintsberg in the collection of essays *Evropa v novoe i noveishee vremia* (Moscow, 1966), pp. 675–76. Note especially the declaration by the German Communist Party, as late as July, 1932, that "the working class will be incapable of a united struggle against fascism and the bourgeoisie as long as the Social Democratic leaders have any influence on the masses."

[5] Quoted in *ibid.*, p. 676. *Ed.*: Both Heinz Neumann and Hermann Remmele were subsequently arrested by the NKVD. See above, p. 222.

workers from each other as if with a barricade.... Old Social Democratic workers everywhere were not only insulted to the depth of
their souls; they were infuriated. They could not forgive the Communists for this. And the Communists, gritting their teeth, carried
out the order for a "battle to the death." An order is an order, Party
discipline is discipline. Everywhere, as if they had gone out of their
minds, Communists and Social Democrats raved at each other
before the eyes of the fascists. I remember it well. I lived in Germany during those years and will never forget how old comrades
clenched their fists seeing how everything was going to ruin, how
the Social Democratic leaders rejoiced, how the theory of social
fascism month by month, week by week, was paving the way for
Hitler. They clenched their fists as they submitted to the "mind"
and "will" [of Stalin], and went to meet the death awaiting them
in S.S. prisons.

In August, 1935, the VIIth Comintern Congress corrected many
of these mistakes, largely on the initiative of Georgii Dimitrov. But
even then the Stalinist sectarian attitude interfered with the practical
implementation of the united front in many countries. It is revealing
that Stalin never spoke at the VIIth Comintern Congress. Nor did he
publicly express his attitude toward the new Comintern line. Even in
his report to the XVIIIth Party Congress in 1939, he said nothing
about the decisions of the Comintern.

In August, 1939, antifascists around the world were stunned by
the news of Stalin's nonaggression pact with Germany. The complex
origins of this treaty, which have not been adequately clarified in
Soviet historiography, are presented here in a preliminary outline.

The prologue to the sharp change was the dismissal of Maxim
Litvinov. On April 16, 1939, Litvinov received the British ambassador
and gave him a formal proposal for a mutual-assistance pact among
Great Britain, France, and the Soviet Union. At the May Day parade
that year, Litvinov still stood beside Stalin, which was duly noted by
diplomats in Moscow. But on May 3 the newspapers contained a short
notice: "M. Litvinov at his own request is being relieved of his duties
as People's Commissar of Foreign Affairs." To Hitler this was "a gun
shot, a sign of change in Moscow's relations to the Western powers."[6]
In the month that followed, many Soviet ambassadors were recalled
and a good number of them, along with many officials of the Commissariat of Foreign Affairs, were arrested. Molotov was put in charge.
At the same time the Soviet Union moved toward a change in relations
with Germany. On May 5, the Soviet chargé d'affaires, G. Astakhov,
called on Julius Schnurre in the German Ministry of Foreign Affairs

---

[6] From a speech in August, 1939. Quoted in W. L. Shirer, *The Rise and Fall of the Third
    Reich* (New York, 1960), p. 531.

to explain how Litvinov's retirement could have a positive effect on German-Soviet relations. The conversation was repeated on May 17. In Moscow the same topic was discussed by Molotov and the German ambassador, Count Werner von der Schulenburg, on May 20 and June 28. The purpose of these moves was to put pressure on the French and British, and to have some insurance in case the negotiations with their countries failed to achieve a mutual-assistance pact.

In July and early August, Germany showed great eagerness for a nonaggression pact with the Soviet Union. Hitler pressed his diplomats to hurry. He had not stopped thinking about aggression against the USSR, but he wanted to postpone it until he had defeated his Western enemies and Poland. For the Soviet Union and the peaceful forces of the world, a German-Soviet nonaggression pact was far from ideal; it would have been preferable to conclude a collective-security agreement among all the antifascist powers. But the United States at that time was isolated from European affairs, while Great Britain and France were playing a dangerous political game: they were still hoping for an agreement with Hitler and were trying to direct German aggression eastward. In the summer of 1939, they were conducting their negotiations with the Soviet Union in such a way as to ruin them.[7] The Soviet Union had to choose the lesser of two evils by accepting Germany's proposal for a nonaggression pact. Stalin made the decision on August 19. That same day Molotov finally agreed to receive Joachim von Ribbentrop, the German Minister of Foreign Affairs, in Moscow. On August 23 the German delegation arrived and the pact was signed.

Many biased Western writers make it seem that the Soviet Union unleashed Hitler by signing this pact. I do not intend to justify Stalin's entire policy. I have already shown how he obstructed a united front in Germany, decimated the Comintern, dissolved the Polish Communist Party, killed the best Red Army commanders. All this greatly facilitated Hitler's drive to war. But the nonaggression pact should not be added to this list of Stalin's errors and crimes. The Soviet government was compelled to sign the pact because Britain and France had been encouraging German fascism, and were frustrating the negotiations for a mutual-assistance pact with the Soviet Union. It was the British and French ruling circles, and also some in the United States, that had helped Germany re-create a strong military machine, in the hope that it would be used against Bolshevism. It was Britain and France that allowed Germany to seize Austria, betrayed Czechoslovakia by the infamous Munich agreement, and by their policy of nonintervention helped Hitler and Mussolini crush the Spanish Republic. These cir-

---

[7] For details of the negotiations, see P. A. Zhilin, *Kak fashistskaia Germaniia gotovila napadenie na Sovetskii Soiuz* (Moscow, 1966).

cumstances compelled the Soviet Union to protect itself by taking advantage of the conflicts among the imperialist states. In 1939 the nonaggression pact with Germany could serve such a purpose.

Stalin's blunder was not the pact itself but the attendant psychological and political atmosphere that he created. He put too much trust in his pact with Hitler. As Konstantin Simonov has written:

> It still seems to me that the pact of 1939 was founded on *raison d'état,* in the almost hopeless situation we were in back then, the summer of 1939, when the danger of the Western states pushing fascist Germany against us became immediate and real. And yet, when you look back, you feel that for all the logic of *raison d'état* in this pact, much that accompanied its conclusion took away from us, simply as people, for almost two years, some part of that exceptionally important sense of ourselves, which was and is our precious peculiarity, connected with such a concept as "the first socialist state in the world." . . . That is, something happened which was in a moral sense very bad.[8]

Another mistake was the signing, on September 29, 1939, of the German-Soviet Boundary and Friendship Pact. The public articles were quite unnecessary.[9] The secret protocols were quite unprincipled. In the second, for example, each party pledged to suppress any agitation against the other, and to keep each other informed of efforts in this direction.[10] The result was a complete halt to all antifascist propaganda in the USSR. Worse yet, Soviet leaders began almost to justify Germany, as if she were being attacked by England and France. Molotov, for example, declared in the fall of 1939:

> During the last few months such concepts as "aggression" and "aggressor" have acquired a new concrete content, have taken on another meaning. . . . Now . . . it is Germany that is striving for a quick end to the war, for peace, while England and France, who only yesterday were campaigning against aggression, are for continuation of the war and against concluding a peace. Roles, as you see, change. . . . The ideology of Hitlerism, like any other ideological system, can be accepted or rejected—that is a matter of one's political views. But everyone can see that an ideology cannot be

---

[8] *Ed.:* Medvedev seems to be quoting from an unpublished manuscript, probably the same as that cited on p. 375 or on p. 454.

[9] A month earlier, when Ribbentrop had proposed that a preamble on the friendly nature of German-Soviet relations be added to the nonaggression pact, Stalin himself categorically refused. "The Soviet government," he declared, "could not honestly assure the Soviet people that friendly relations exist with Germany, when for six years the Nazi government has been pouring buckets of slop on the Soviet government." Quoted in P. A. Zhilin, *Kak fashistskaia Germaniia gotovila napadenie na Sovetskii Soiuz* (Moscow, 1966), p. 61.

[10] Shirer, p. 631.

destroyed by force. . . . Thus it is not only senseless, it is *criminal* to wage such a war as a war for "the destruction of Hitlerism," under the false flag of a struggle for democracy.[11]

After this speech, Beria gave a secret order to the GULAG administration forbidding camp guards to call political prisoners "fascists." The order was rescinded only in June, 1941.

Stalin did not merely stop antifascist propaganda in the Soviet Union. In plain violation of the resolutions of the VIIth Comintern Congress, he sent a directive to all Communist parties demanding curtailment of the struggle against German fascism, naming Anglo-French imperialism as the basic aggressive force, which was to become the main target of Communist propaganda. This sudden about-face caught the Western Communist parties by surprise. One result was the paralysis of the Rumanian Communist Party, which had been making great progress, as shown by the massive May Day demonstrations of 1939 in Bucharest. The Communists in other European countries were also thrown into complete disarray. At that time they were considered sections of the Comintern, obliged to submit to discipline. Thus the Comintern's declaration that France and Great Britain were the aggressors, while Germany wanted peace, put the French and British Communists in an especially difficult position. The logic of the directive required Communists in those countries to take a defeatist stand,[12] or at least to refuse support to the military efforts of their bourgeois governments.

This policy did not have much significance in Britain, where the Communist Party was relatively small. But in France, where the Party was strong, this antiwar position markedly weakened national resistance to German aggression, and facilitated a government ban on the Communist Party. The resulting political tension worked to Hitler's advantage in those months. At the turn of the year some illegal French Communist publications were demanding that the French government end the imperialist war with Germany. To be sure, the French Party changed its line in the spring of 1940, when German armies invaded France. The underground Central Committee informed the government that it would consider the surrender of Paris treason, and called on it to arm the people and turn Paris into an impregnable fortress. After the fall of France in June, the Communists called for resistance to the occupiers. But even then some French activists believed that the German-Soviet nonaggression pact meant a nonaggression pact between Nazism and Communism. Late in 1940 some of them had serious hopes

[11] *Stenograficheskii otchet vneocherednoi piatoi sessii Verkhovnogo Soveta SSSR* (Moscow, 1939) pp. 8–10.

[12] *Ed.:* "Defeatism" refers to the Leninist program in World War I: Stand for the defeat of one's own country.

of legal activity in occupied territory, and even prepared to publish *L'Humanité* legally in Paris. Only at the beginning of 1941, when Communists were arrested and shot en masse, did such illusions dissolve, and the Central Committee begin to take a more clear-cut antifascist stand. However, armed struggle against the Nazis began in earnest only after the German attack on the USSR.

The left Socialists, who after the VIIth Comintern Congress had worked with the Communists in the antifascist struggle in France, Spain, Italy and elsewhere, were indignant over the "friendship" between the USSR and Germany in 1939–40. Their press declared outright that the USSR had deserted the front, that Moscow had destroyed solidarity with the proletariat fighting Nazism.[13]

Soviet-German "friendship" did delay the USSR's entry into the war by two years. But that delay was used more effectively by Germany than by the USSR. Seizing one country after another, Germany increased its military potential in those years much faster than the Soviet Union. If Great Britain had also been defeated in 1940, the fate of the world, including the USSR, might have been very different. When Stalin planned his foreign policy in 1939, he did not expect France to be defeated so quickly. In general he underestimated the strength of fascist Germany and overestimated the resources of the Soviet Union.

In the spring of 1940 Hitler first seized Denmark and Norway, then Holland, Belgium, and France. These acts of aggression proved once again that fascist Germany would tear up any international agreement when it seemed advantageous to do so. What should Stalin have done? Immediately declare war on Germany, thus creating an antifascist coalition in the summer of 1940? Some historians say so, but I cannot agree. However, the Soviet Union should *at least* have denounced the nonaggression pact. On the contrary, after the defeat of France the press emphasized the creation, by the German-Soviet agreements, of a peaceful Eastern Front for Germany. *Pravda* quoted complacent statements from Nazi newspapers to this effect.[14]

Moreover, Stalin did not stop at "friendship" with Hitler. In 1940 he entered negotiations concerning spheres of influence after the presumed defeat of Great Britain. These negotiations were begun on Hitler's initiative, since he wanted to divert Stalin's attention from German preparations for war against the USSR. And Stalin, to a certain extent, took the bait. He even agreed to negotiations concerning the adherence of the USSR to the Tripartite (Anti-Comintern) Pact. These negotiations were interrupted, though not by Stalin; Hitler simply stopped answering Stalin's letters on the subject.

[13] See, for example, the articles in *Nuovo Avanti* in August, 1939.
[14] See *Pravda,* Aug. 26, 1940, for such quotations.

Another major blunder in this period was the war with Finland. The Soviet government's desire to secure Leningrad and its northwest border was natural. But there were various ways of going about this. As could have been expected, Finland turned down a Soviet proposal to exchange the Karelian Isthmus bordering on Leningrad, well populated by Finns, for a much larger but sparsely populated territory north of Lakes Ladoga and Onega. This rejection was by no means a sufficient cause for war. In 1939 Finland was largely under the influence of France and Great Britain though it took a neutral stand when they declared war on Germany. This small country with three million inhabitants could not by itself be a threat to the Soviet Union. As for Britain and France, they were beginning a war with Germany and could not seriously consider war against the Soviet Union with Finland as a *place d'armes*. The danger of a British and French attack on the USSR in 1939 existed only in the imagination of propagandists. Stalin did not take into consideration the real danger that the Nazis might use Finland for such a purpose, and did not use it as the pretext for preventive war against Finland.

Stalin thought the war would last only a few days. Not long before it began, the Chief Military Soviet met in Moscow to outline the campaign. The plan prepared by Marshal B. M. Shaposhnikov, Chief of the General Staff, was harshly criticized by Stalin, who accused him of underestimating the strength of the Red Army and overestimating that of the Finns. The plan was rejected, and the command of the Leningrad Military District was told to draw up a new scheme, based on the discussion in the Chief Military Soviet. The result was a plan for fighting with "little loss of blood," counting on a rapid victory, using limited forces, without a concentration of reserves. It was this plan that doomed Soviet troops to long weeks of failures and heavy losses.[15]

Stalin and Voroshilov were so sure of a quick victory that Shaposhnikov was not even given advance notice; he was on leave when he heard that war had begun. It did not produce a quick victory. The Red Army did not have enough experience or experienced officers (after the recent "purges") to break through the Mannerheim Line in a sudden rush. It was also an obvious error for Stalin to set up a new "people's government of Finland" in the first days of the war, headed by Otto Kuusinen in Terioki. (It greatly hindered military operations, and by the time peace talks began was completely forgotten.) The Soviet Union was obliged, in the course of a bloody war, to concentrate on the Finnish Front almost as many troops as the entire male population of Finland. Although they were not given winter clothing

[15] From the documentary novel of A. Chakovskii, "Blokada," *Znamia*, 1968, No. 10.

and skis in time, they had to conduct a winter campaign. Only after great losses was the Mannerheim Line finally broken in the spring of 1940.

The Soviet victory, achieved at great expense, not only of lives but also of a socialist state's basic principles in foreign policy, slipped out of Stalin's hands. From a political standpoint, the war only created difficulties for the USSR, and even from a narrow military standpoint, the results in no way justified the huge Soviet losses. Stalin displayed most unusual moderation in the peace talks. He stuck to his original demands, and did not create guarantees against the predictable triumph of *revanchiste* tendencies. Incomprehensibly, Stalin calmly watched the rise of such tendencies, the restoration of the Finnish Army, the turn away from a British and French orientation to acceptance of German protection, and the accumulation of German troops on Finnish soil. (By June, 1941, the Germans had five divisions in Finland.)

Clearly it was the defeat of 1939–40 that pushed Finland into Hitler's arms. In other words, it was Stalin's irrational foreign policy that moved Finland into the German camp, when it might have joined the antifascist coalition or in any case have remained neutral. This is not to justify the Finnish militarists for their participation in the German attack on the USSR. But it was Stalin who helped them dominate public opinion in Finland for some time.

3

THE MOST SERIOUS of Stalin's mistakes in foreign policy was his misreading of the military situation in the spring and summer of 1941.[16] Of course he, and the Soviet government as a whole, did foresee in general terms the possibility of war with Germany and Japan, and they did make preparations by creating a modern defense industry, military aviation, an up-to-date navy, civil-defense training for the whole population, and so on. In 1939–41, the army increased by 2.5 times, many troops and supplies were transferred to the western districts, war production increased, and the number of military schools grew. Especially after the war with Finland, military training was intensified. The development of new weapons was speeded up. The fortification of the new western borders was begun. Taken all together this was truly impressive preparation, but it was scheduled for completion no earlier than 1942. And overwhelming evidence in the spring of 1941 showed

[16] Cf. Stalin's own comment in 1933: "No people can respect its government if it sees the danger of attack and does not prepare for self-defense." *Sochineniia*, XIII, p. 279.

that war could not be postponed that long. The time bought by the nonaggression pact was clearly coming to an end; Stalin's calculation that war could be postponed until 1942 or later was obviously unreal.

The intensive transfer of German troops to the Soviet border began in 1940.[17] Early in 1941 it was sharply increased, becoming an uninterrupted flood in March and April. After May 25 as many as a hundred echelons were moved up each day.[18] On the eve of June 22, 1941, the deployment of the Germany army of invasion was complete. One hundred and ninety fully equipped divisions, both German and satellite, 3,500 tanks, around 4,000 planes, and 50,000 guns and mortars were massed on the Soviet borders.

Efforts were made to keep these movements secret and to mislead Soviet intelligence, but so huge an operation could not be concealed. Numerous reports steadily poured in through various channels: Soviet intelligence, the diplomatic corps, foreign friends of the Soviet Union, officials of the British and US governments, deserters, and so on. For example, the Soviet military attachés in Paris and Berlin, Generals Susloparov and Tupikov, and the naval attaché in Berlin, Admiral Vorontsov, reported by the end of May, 1941, that the frontier zones were almost saturated with men and equipment. The Soviet embassy in Berlin reported constant rumors of the impending attack. The rumored dates were quite varied, evidently to sow confusion: April 6, April 20, May 18, finally June 22—all Sundays. The embassy sent these rumors to Moscow regularly, and toward the end of May submitted a thorough report, which concluded that Germany's preparations for war against the USSR were virtually complete, that the concentration of forces was too great to be intended for political pressure. But Stalin did not react to this report in any way.[19]

Very important information came from President Roosevelt. From his agents in Germany he had received precise information about the date and direction of the main German strikes and almost all the basic elements of the Barbarossa plan. He gave this information to Soviet Ambassador Konstantin Umanskii.[20] Details also came from the NKGB.[21] On June 6 the NKGB presented Stalin with intelligence

---

[17] The former chief of the Information Division of the General Staff, V. A. Novobranets, writes in his memoirs that this transfer went on all through 1940; by December of that year around a hundred divisions, including eleven tank divisions, were concentrated on Soviet borders. Novobranets says that F. I. Golikov, the chief of *Razvedupr* (Intelligence Administration), systematically lowered these figures to please Stalin. This report needs additional verification.

[18] *Voenno-istoricheskii zhurnal*, 1965, No. 10, pp. 33–39.

[19] V. Berezhkov, *S diplomaticheskoi missiei v Berlin* (Moscow, 1966). Berezhkov worked in the Berlin embassy at the time.

[20] A. M. Nekrich, *1941, 22 Iiunia* (Moscow, 1965), p. 121.

[21] By this time the NKVD was divided into two commissariats: Internal Affairs (NKVD) and State Security (NKGB).

reports that four million German troops were concentrated on the border; on June 10 that the German army group stationed in East Prussia had received an order to occupy, three days later, their take-off positions for the attack on the USSR; on June 11 that the German embassy in Moscow had been ordered by Berlin to prepare for evacuation in seven days, and that diplomats were burning documents in the basement of the embassy.[22]

In the months preceding the war, Soviet military intelligence even acquired the stenographic record of Field Marshal Walther von Brauchitsch's analysis of the German Army's military exercises in the spring of 1941, which worked out various details of the assault on the USSR.[23] From agent Richard Sorge in Japan came information of enormous importance. In May of 1941 and again in June, he reported not only the precise timing of the German attack but also the size of the army, the operational plans, and the directions of the main strikes. These reports were immediately given to Stalin, who wrote on them "For the archives," and "To be filed," and put them out of his mind. Some people say that Stalin and Golikov intended to recall Sorge and punish him as a "panicmonger" and a "misinformer." And others say that even the German ambassador to the USSR, Schulenburg, a secret enemy of Hitler's, decided to warn the Soviet government a few weeks before the attack. The Soviet ambassador to Germany, V. G. Dekanozov, a friend of Beria and confidant of Stalin's, happened to be in Moscow. Schulenburg invited him to dinner, and asked him to tell Stalin that Hitler might strike at the USSR in the near future.[24] But Stalin did not believe Schulenburg any more than Sorge, Roosevelt, and the others. He decided that the report of the German ambassador was only a blackmailing trick of Hitler's, to get new concessions from the USSR.

Stalin blindly believed that Hitler would not break his pact with the USSR. Any facts that did not fit the abstract scheme in Stalin's head were rejected. Indeed, he made a public show of his confidence in peace. When Yosuke Matsuoka, the Japanese Minister of Foreign Affairs, left Moscow in April, 1941, Stalin and Molotov surprised everybody by seeing him off. The German ambassador, who was at the railroad station, tells how Stalin came over, hugged him, and remarked for all the crowd to hear: "We must remain friends, and you must now do everything to that end."[25]

The disgraceful behavior of the Soviet government during the

---

[22] See *Voprosy istorii*, 1965, No. 5, pp. 27–28. One of the intelligence groups on German territory, which sent important information on the impending German attack, has been described in the documentary tale "Ee zvali Al'ta," *Pravda*, July, 1967.

[23] Reported by V. A. Novobranets.

[24] Also present were Gustav Hilger, of the German embassy, and Stalin's translator, Pavlov.

[25] See Shirer, p. 839.

German attack on Yugoslavia is also revealing. At the end of 1940 and the beginning of 1941, German troops entered Hungary, Bulgaria, and Rumania with the consent of their reactionary governments. The pressure on Yugoslavia increased, until in March, 1941, Yugoslav Premier Dragiša Cvetković signed an agreement to join the Tripartite Pact. The result was a national uprising; a group of patriotic officers overthrew the pro-German government. The Soviet Union not only recognized the new government but, on April 5, 1941, signed a treaty of friendship and nonaggression with it. Less than twenty-four hours later, German troops invaded Yugoslavia and subjected Belgrade to savage bombardment. Stalin did not condemn this aggression against a fraternal Slavic country. The report of German war against Yugoslavia appeared on the last page of *Pravda,* on April 7. Nothing was said about the bombardment of Belgrade. Moreover, the Soviet government closed the embassies of Yugoslavia, Greece, and Belgium, which signified recognition and encouragement of German aggression.

The massing of the German Army on Russian borders worried the Soviet command so much—they even knew the numbers of the German divisions—that they sought permission to move troops to defensive positions and put them on military alert. Stalin refused. Indeed, all military organizations and industry were unprepared for the attack both psychologically and materially. Most divisions were short of their full wartime staffs. Many tank units did not have their full complement of men and equipment. There was a general shortage of spare parts and repairs were slow. Airplane, tank, and artillery factories were producing obsolete models. A large part of the military equipment was stored not in the rear but in the threatened districts. The network of roads in border areas was inadequate. Airfields had to be enlarged for new types of planes, so construction companies of the NKVD went to work on most military airfields all at once, putting them out of use until the late fall. As a result most military planes were transferred to civilian airports, which were located near the border and poorly defended against bombing attacks. A major reorganization of tank divisions was also undertaken in the first months of 1941. At the end of June many tank troops did not have their tanks, and many tanks were without crews.[26]

[26] Such examples could be greatly multiplied. See such books as *Istoriia Velikoi Otechestvennoi voiny,* I–VI (Moscow, 1962–64); *Istoriia Velikoi Otechestvennoi voiny, Kratkii ocherk* (Moscow, 1965); *Vsemirnaia istoriia,* X (Moscow, 1965); *Istoriia mezhdunarodnykh otnoshenii i vneshnei politiki SSSR,* II (Moscow, 1962); A. M. Nekrich, *22 Iiunia 1941 g.* (Moscow, 1965); *et al.* Nekrich's book has been subjected to harsh and tendentious criticism, which is surprising since most of the facts in it are no different from those adduced by other Soviet historians or by diplomats, military leaders, and intelligence agents. The book has its faults, but they cannot justify the savage attacks published by *Voprosy istorii KPSS,* 1967, No. 9.

Incredible as it may seem, military leaders testify that the army did not have definite plans of operation in the event of a German attack. The former Commissar of the Navy, N. G. Kuznetzov, describes the situation:

> Stalin kept military matters under his personal control. No system existed that would unfailingly go into operation in the event of war, no matter which individual might be put out of action at the critical moment. In this respect the war caught us unprepared. . . . Stalin had ideas on how to wage war, but, with his usual pathological mistrust, he kept them secret from the future executors of his ideas. Mistaken about the probable date of the conflict, he thought there was still enough time. And when the course of history speeded up, the ideas, the thoughts about a future war, could not be transformed into clear strategic conceptions and concrete plans.[27]

Undoubtedly informed of the Soviet Union's unpreparedness, the fascist command became brazenly open in May, 1941. Artillery units brought up to the border were not even camouflaged. In May and June combat patrols reconnoitered more and more openly, encroaching on Soviet territory and opening fire on Soviet border guards. According to Marshal I. Kh. Bagramian, at the end of May German planes flew over Soviet territory unopposed, photographing installations along the border. At one point, shortly before the attack, an entire flight of German reconnaissance planes landed at a Soviet airfield. The pilots said they were lost, and were released to go "home." When the commander of a military district, Colonel-General M. P. Kirponos, asked Moscow for permission to direct at least warning fire at the fascist planes, he was rebuked: "What do you want to do, provoke a war?" Moscow also forbade troops in the Kiev Military District to occupy lightly fortified fields in front of uncompleted heavy fortifications.

On June 14, when Hitler was holding the final military council before the attack, Soviet newspapers published a government declaration:

> According to the information of the USSR, Germany is observing the terms of the Soviet-German nonaggression pact as strictly as the USSR. Therefore, in the opinion of Soviet circles, rumors about Germany's plan to break the pact and to undertake an attack on the USSR are quite unfounded. The recent transfer of German troops, released from operations in the Balkans, to the eastern and northeastern areas of Germany is connected, is must be supposed, with other motives, which have no bearing on Soviet-German relations.

[27] *Oktiabr'*, 1965, No. 11, pp. 162, 147–48.

The effect of this declaration is described by L. M. Sandalov:

> The anxious mood, which had become especially acute by the middle of the month, was somewhat relieved. Such a statement coming from an authoritative state agency dulled the vigilance of the troops. Among the command staff it generated confidence that there were some unknown circumstances which enabled our government to remain calm and confident about the security of the Soviet borders. Officers stopped sleeping in the barracks. Soldiers began to undress at night.[28]

The blindness of Stalin and his advisers in those fateful weeks was simply unbelievable. While the German embassy in Moscow was systematically reducing the number of German citizens in the USSR, almost every day new Soviet officials were arriving in Germany with their families. Deliveries of Soviet goods to Germany continued without pause, though Germany had sharply reduced the flow of its goods as specified in the trade commitments of 1939. Shortly before the attack, all German ships left Soviet ports without even finishing unloading. In Riga, for example, more than two dozen German ships, some of which had only begun to unload, weighed anchor on June 21. The Riga harbor master, sensing something wrong, at his own risk detained the German ships and quickly got in touch with the Commissariat of Foreign Trade in Moscow. Stalin was told at once, but he ordered that the German ships be allowed to leave. At the same time Soviet ships, given no instructions, continued to unload in German harbors. On June 22 they were seized as spoils of war.[29]

The Commissariat of Defense warned Stalin once again about the possibility of a German attack a few days before it happened. "You are creating panic over nothing," he replied. According to Marshal Bagramian, on the afternoon of June 19 the command of the Kiev Military District was warned by the Commissariat of Defense that Hitler might attack within a few days without a declaration of war. But even then Stalin did not put the troops in border areas on military alert, not even the air force. Marshal Rodion Ia. Malinovskii writes that troops in the border areas

> continued their peacetime training: the artillery belonging to infantry divisions was in artillery camps and on firing ranges, antiaircraft guns were on antiaircraft firing ranges, engineer units were in engineer camps and "stripped" infantry divisions were in their separate camps. Given the threat of imminent war, this very crude blunder bordered on the criminal. Could it have been avoided? It could and should have been.[30]

[28] Sandalov, *Perezhitoe* (Moscow, 1961), p. 78.
[29] See V. Berezhkov, *op. cit.,* pp. 91 and 116.
[30] "Dvadtsatiletie nachala Velikoi Otechestvennoi voiny," *Voenno-istoricheskii zhurnal,* 1961, No. 6.

On the evening of June 21 Molotov summoned Ambassador
Schulenburg to ascertain the causes of Germany's "dissatisfaction."
But Schulenburg, uninformed about Hitler's immediate plans, could
not answer Molotov's worried questions. Returning to the embassy, he
found instructions from Ribbentrop waiting for him: he was to visit
Molotov and read a document containing Hitler's usual obscene denunciation of a nation about to be invaded. It was virtually a declaration
of war. In Schulenburg's words, Molotov heard him out in silence and
then said bitterly: "This is war. Do you believe that we deserved
that?"[31] Molotov had good reason to ask such a question. Not until
that night, Marshal Malinovskii tells us, was a coded telegram sent to
the military districts, warning of a German attack on the twenty-
second or twenty-third. Troops were ordered to move quietly into
firing positions in the fortified areas, to disperse aircraft, to put all
units on alert, and to take no other actions without special orders. To
the question whether the troops could open fire if the enemy invaded
Soviet territory, the reply was that they should not give in to provocation and should not open fire. But this directive did not even reach
the troops, for at dawn on June 22 the German Army attacked.[32]

The systematic inaction during the weeks and days preceding the
war cannot be blamed on Stalin alone. Voroshilov (whose boastful
speeches of the prewar years were often recalled by army commanders
in the terrible first period of the war), Commissar of Defense S. K.
Timoshenko, F. I. Golikov, chief of *Razvedupr* (the Intelligence
Administration), and G. K. Zhukov, who was chief of the General
Staff in the first half of 1941, must all share the blame. But the main
responsibility was Stalin's. As Konstantin Simonov justly remarks, in
his notes on the first days of the war:[33]

> . . . If one considers the surprise [of the attack] and the resulting
> scale of the initial defeats, then precisely here everything from the
> bottom up, beginning with the reports of intelligence agents and
> border guards, through the summaries and communications of the
> military districts, through the reports of the Commissariat of De-
> fense and the General Staff—everything in the last analysis came to
> Stalin personally and rested on him, on his firm confidence that it
> was precisely he who should succeed, by precisely those measures
> that he considered necessary, in preventing the impending disaster.
> Conversely, it was precisely from him, through the Commissariat
> of Defense, through the General Staff, through the staffs of the

---

[31] A. Werth, *Rossiia v voine 1941–1945* (Moscow, 1967), p. 75. *Ed.:* See Werth, *Russia at War, 1941–1945* (New York, 1964), p. 127.

[32] *Voenno-istoricheskii zhurnal*, 1961, No. 6.

[33] *Ed.:* This seems to be an unpublished manuscript. Medvedev calls it "zapiski o pervykh dniakh voiny," without any underlining or quote marks to indicate a formal title.

military districts, right down to the bottom, that all the pressure went, all the administrative and moral pressure that ultimately made the war far more of a surprise than it would have been in other circumstances.

The incongruity between reality and Stalin's actions is so striking that many people are now asking why. N. G. Kuznetsov suggests the following explanation:

> Under the pressure of inexorable facts, Stalin began to realize, early in 1941, that an attack by Hitler was really possible. But once he was convinced that his expectation of a later war had been proved wrong, that our armed forces and the country as a whole were inadequately prepared for war in the next few months, he tried to take advantage of everything that he thought might postpone the conflict, to carry on in such a way as to give Hitler no pretext for attack, to provoke no war.

But such an explanation is not entirely convincing; Kuznetsov himself a few lines earlier notes that Stalin,

> as a man of great experience, a major politician, was obviously aware that the aggressor could be sobered up only by our readiness to give him the proper response—a blow for a blow! If the aggressor raises his fist, that means he must be shown a fist in return.[34]

It is possible to argue that Stalin was deceived by Nazi counter-intelligence. In 1941 the Nazis sedulously circulated rumors that the massing of German troops on the Soviet borders was "the greatest camouflage operation in military history, designed to divert attention from final preparations for the invasion of Britain."[35] But it was not difficult to see through these tricks, especially since they were far outweighed by other information. To be sure, some leaders of the NKGB and *Razvedupr,* fearing Stalin's wrath, gave him the enemy's rumors as reliable information, while truly reliable information was included in summaries of unreliable rumors. Still, there were many who, at great risk to themselves, tried to make Stalin aware of the truth. But Stalin did not want to listen to the voice of reason. As Simonov writes:

> Stalin is responsible not only for the fact that he refused, with incomprehensible stubbornness, to consider very important intelligence reports; his worst sin is that he created a disastrous atmosphere in which dozens of competent people who had irrefutable documented information did not have a chance to show the chief

---

[34] *Oktiabr'*, 1965, No. 11, p. 163.

[35] Quoted in *Voprosy istorii,* 1966, No. 8, p. 79. Cf. E. Rzhevskaia, *Berlin, mai 1945* (Moscow, 1965), for several episodes in this campaign, directed by Goebbels himself. *Ed.:* The quotation is from a secret memorandum of the German High Command. See Paul Carell, *Hitler Moves East, 1941–1943* (Boston, 1964), p. 12.

of state the extent of the danger, and did not have the right to take sufficient measures to avert it.[36]

Inability to understand may well have been reinforced by fear. Afraid of a great war with Germany, Stalin shunned any display of vigilance that could be used by the Nazis as an excuse for war. He did not understand that a Germany determined on war would always find an excuse, or would do without one altogether.

But the main cause of Stalin's mistakes in 1941 was the system of one-man rule combined with the one man's limitations. Unlimited power was in the hands of a limited tactician and a limited strategist. He did not perceive all the weaknesses of the Red Army, which he had caused to lose its finest officers. He did not perceive many of the difficulties still troubling the cities and villages. He overestimated Soviet strength and therefore hoped that Hitler would not dare to attack the USSR. Of course attacking the USSR *was* a risky adventure for Germany, especially since Hitler gambled on victory within a few weeks, in any case before winter. The German war plan did not provide for adequate reserves of manpower or industrial production. The Nazi Army could beat the Red Army in some battles, but Germany could not enslave the whole Soviet people in addition to all the nations of Europe. Considering that the German Army suffered defeat in spite of its unbelievably favorable situation in 1941, it is useful to imagine what would have happened to it if the Soviet government had been properly prepared. Hitler was also a dictator; he too based his actions on imaginary rather than real factors. Intoxicated by the German victories in the West, he overestimated the strength of the German Army, and underestimated the strength of the Soviet people and the cohesion of Soviet society. He thought that after early defeats the USSR would collapse like a house of cards. Hitler was an adventurist and a reckless maniac, but Stalin perceived him as a rational statesman. Stalin's tendency to mistake illusions for reality prevented him from seeing the same fault in Hitler.[37] That is one of the main reasons why both Hitler and Stalin miscalculated in 1941.

4

IT IS ACKNOWLEDGED by historians of all persuasions that Stalin was responsible for the Germans' great advantage of surprise and for the

---

[36] Konstantin Simonov, "Uroki istorii i dolg pisatelia." *Ed.:* This seems to be an unpublished manuscript.

[37] The lesson of 1941 must not be forgotten today in our relations with China. Mao Tse-tung also has a tendency to confuse reality and his frenzied perceptions of it. Thus we should consider the possibility of irrational adventures being attempted by the Maoist leadership.

Soviet troops' unpreparedness. It is also generally acknowledged that the Soviet Union entered the worst war in history with its best military and civilian leaders recently destroyed. Yet some authors try to salvage Stalin's reputation by arguing that whatever his faults before the war, *during* it he proved to be an excellent commander in chief. This partial rehabilitation became especially insistent in memoirs published in 1967–68.[38]

In 1969 the authoritative journal *Kommunist* carried a review article that endorsed this argument: "For all the complexity and contradictions of his character, Stalin emerges from the generals' memoirs as an outstanding military leader."[39] The historian who wrote this review-article is obviously polemicizing with Khrushchev, in particular with the section of his speech to the XXth Party Congress that harshly yet fairly demolished the myth of Stalin's military genius. The facts cited by Khrushchev in 1956 have not been disproved; in the decade following his speech they were supplemented by hundreds of authoritative accounts, most of them published in the Soviet press. The case against Stalin's military record has become so overwhelming that prevarication and sophistry are the only recourse of his apologists.

They also exploit a widespread feeling derived from the cult of personality. Stalin's name became a sort of symbol existing in the popular mentality independently of its actual bearer. During the war years, as the Soviet people were battered by unbelievable miseries, the name of Stalin and faith in him to some degree pulled the Soviet people together, giving them hope of victory. The logic of any cult was at work, attributing all defeats to other commanders or to treason, all victories to Stalin. To this day, many of the soldiers and officers who went into battle with Stalin's name on their lips find it hard to reconsider their attitude toward him and the wartime events connected with his image. The historian may sympathize with this primitive psychology, but inexorable facts oblige him to oppose it.

Stalin was in fact a mediocre commander. He did make correct decisions, gave his subordinates correct orders, and accepted from them —often after arguments and resistance—much good advice. But his personal qualities—his nastiness and narrow-mindedness, his contempt for people and boundless love of power, his suspiciousness and his bureaucratic style of leadership—were bound to affect his behavior as a commander. The result was something much worse than the mistakes that cannot be avoided in any war. Most of Stalin's wrong decisions were so extravagantly and senselessly costly that they cannot be condoned.

[38] See those of Marshals A. Grechko, I. Konev, K. Meretskov, K. Rokossovskii, General S. M. Shtemenko, and the second installment of N. Kuznetsov's reminiscences.

[39] E. Boltin, writing in *Kommunist,* 1969, No. 2, p. 127.

The historian cannot overlook, for example, the great damage done by Stalin's two basic dogmas: "We will not surrender an inch of our land to the enemy," and "We will carry the war to the enemy's territory." Because of these dogmas he rejected proposals for a defense in depth. His strategic plan excluded the possibility that the enemy might break through the first line of defense. Thus neither factories nor people in the western areas were prepared for possible evacuation. Worse yet, the first line of defense was simply drawn along the national border, with all its convolutions. That made encirclement difficult to avoid and natural defense lines—such as the Neman River and the Augustow Canal—difficult to take advantage of. Major General P. G. Grigorenko tells, for example, how half the troops in the Western Military District were concentrated in the so-called Belostok salient, that is, in a state of semiencirclement. They were completely encircled in the first days of the war, which opened the way to Minsk and enabled the Germans to surround another big army group by the eighth day. Twelve armies were distributed along the borders in such a pattern as to be easily outnumbered and outflanked by the German attack.[40]

Some years before, the Revolutionary Military Soviet of the USSR, foreseeing the possibility of a temporary retreat at the beginning of a war, began to organize partisan units in frontier districts. The chiefs of this plan were Iakir, Uborevich, Bliukher, and Ia. K. Berzin, and it died with them in 1937–38. Their organization of secret partisan bases was alleged to reveal "lack of confidence in the power of the Soviet state," and even "preparation for hostile actions in the rear of the Soviet armies." Many commanders of the projected guerrilla units, who were in civilian work in peacetime, were arrested as "enemies of the people" and "diversionists."[41]

The same kind of blunder followed the acquisition of new territory in 1939–40. The old frontier had been heavily fortified at considerable expense. Considering the highly mobile nature of warfare, that old line of defense should have been maintained, with only covering armies deployed in the newly acquired districts. Indeed, a third line of defense, for strategic reserves, should have been created, along the Dnepr, for example. Stalin took different measures. He ordered the transfer of basic artillery and other equipment into the new terri-

---

[40] See *Voenno-istoricheskii zhurnal*, 1965, No. 10, pp. 33–39. Cf. Goebbels' entry in his diary in June, 1941: "The Russians were concentrated right on the border. We couldn't hope for anything better. If they had been distributed in depth, they would have been a great danger." Quoted in E. Rzhevskaia, *Berlin, mai 1945* (Moscow, 1965), p. 71. Cf. also the German historian K. Tippelskirch, *Istoriia vtoroi mirovoi voiny* (Moscow, 1956), p. 177, a translation of his *Geschichte des zweiten Weltkrieges* (Bonn, 1951).

[41] See I. G. Starinov, *Miny zhdut svoego chasa* (Moscow, 1964).

tories, and the old fortified areas were dismantled. Some bunkers were blown up, others were handed over to collective farms for storing vegetables. Construction of the new fortifications proceeded slowly, and the Nazis attacked when the artillery, dismantled in the old areas, had not yet been reassembled in the new ones.

In spite of the confidence implied by this strategy, Stalin's behavior in the first hours and days of the war was flustered. A. S. Iakovlev, who was Deputy Minister of the Aviation Industry in 1941, recalls how the order to fight came from Commissar of Defense Timoshenko only at 7:15 A.M., when the German attack was well under way, and even then the order to fight revealed a strange residuum of continuing caution. Soviet troops were ordered "to attack and destroy enemy forces in the regions where they have violated the Soviet border. Until receipt of special instructions, ground troops will not cross the border." Soviet bombers and fighter planes were not to fly more than 100 to 150 kilometers [60 to 90 miles] into Germany. Iakovlev is still amazed by these limitations. "War was already under way. Did not the high command know what it was? An accidental incursion? A mistake of the Germans? Provocation?"[42]

The absurdity of Timoshenko's order can be traced back to Stalin. Called from his bed at the dawn of June 22, he came to the Kremlin and heard the reports of Commissar Timoshenko and Chief of Staff Zhukov. War was under way along the entire border, but Stalin did not want to believe it. He still thought some sort of massive provocation was going on. He ordered Molotov to get in touch with the Germany embassy, with Berlin. Only after Molotov had met Schulenburg and returned to say that Germany had declared war did Stalin realize it really was war. Still he told Timoshenko to order the troops to repulse the enemy attack but not to cross the border.

Khrushchev told the XXth Party Congress how Stalin, on hearing of the Red Army's defeats, believed that the end had come, that everything created by Lenin had been irretrievably lost. Thereupon Stalin withdrew from direction of the war effort, until some Politburo members came to him and said that immediate measures had to be taken to correct the situation at the front. All the marshals of the USSR were at the XXth Congress; so were Molotov, Malenkov, Kaganovich, Voroshilov, and Bulganin, and none of them found it necessary to correct Khrushchev. Was his sensational report disproved later? The central archives of the Soviet Army contain many directives issued during the opening days of the war but not a single document signed by Stalin in the period from June 24 to July 2, 1941. Nor does any order from the Commissar of Defense or any other military leader refer to any directive from Stalin. What did he do, where was he in those

---

[42] A. S. Iakovlev, *Tsel' zhizni* (Moscow, 1966), pp. 240–41.

crucial days? An answer has recently been given in a documented tale that was passed by special military censorship.[43]

> ... Late in the evening Stalin, accompanied by some members of the Politburo, unexpectedly appeared at the Commissariat of Defense on Frunze Street. As he entered the Commissar's office, Stalin was calm and self-assured. However, it was there at the directing center of the country's military effort that he first sensed concretely the magnitude of the growing danger. Enemy tank groups were forming a pincers on Minsk and it seemed that nothing could stop them. Contact with our retreating armies had been lost. . . . Stalin, usually so outwardly calm and deliberate in his speech and motions, this time could not restrain himself. He burst out with angry, insulting scolding. Then, without looking at anyone, head down and stooped over, he left the building, got into his car, and went home. . . .
>
> No one knew what was going on in Stalin's mind during the next few days. No one saw him. He did not appear in the Kremlin. No one heard his voice on the telephone. He summoned no one. And none of those who hour by hour waited for his summons dared go to him unsummoned. . . . The members of the Politburo, the Peoples' Commissars, the leaders of the Commissariat of Defense, of the General Staff and the Army's Political Administration, were overwhelmed with thousands of matters, great and small, connected with the implementation of military measures throughout the country and at the fronts. But as they worked on these problems from morning to late at night, they asked themselves time and again: Where is Stalin? Why is he silent? What was he doing, what was he thinking about, this apparently omnipotent and omniscient man, in those long terrible hours?

The author goes on to guess the answers, rather unconvincingly. In an unofficial conversation Khrushchev once said that Stalin simply drank, and that sounds more like the truth. And when the Politburo members came to see him, he was frightened, thinking they had come to arrest him. It must be borne in mind that the management of the war could not proceed normally without Stalin. Because of the strict centralization he had established, neither Zhukov nor Timoshenko nor Molotov nor Beria had the authority to give certain necessary orders. Stalin's absence from his post as head of the state and the Party from June 23 to the beginning of July was an important reason why the Nazis penetrated so swiftly and deeply into the USSR.

The terrible losses suffered by Soviet forces in the opening hours and days of the war are attested by both Soviet and German historians. There is accordingly a painful irony in an order, issued on the evening of June 22, calling for counterattacks in depth, with the aim

[43] See A. Chakovskii, "Blokada," *Znamia*, 1968, No. 11, p. 49.

of "transferring action onto enemy territory."[44] Troops could not even form a firm line of defense on Soviet territory. Marshal Grechko describes how "the enemy managed in three weeks to put 28 of our divisions out of action, while more than 70 divisions lost 50 per cent or more of their men and equipment."[45] "No organized defense," writes I. V. Tiulenev,

> could be created or maintained in the first days of the war. Battles had an uncoordinated character. Instead of a solid front of defense, which could not be created because of the disorganized movement into battle of cover units, there were isolated centers of fighting.[46]

Although overall direction improved somewhat with Stalin's return to his post, the situation remained critical. And still, in July and August of 1941, Stalin could not overcome his confusion. N. N. Voronov, who was Deputy Commissar of Defense and representative of the General Staff on many fronts, recalls:

> I rarely saw Stalin in the first days of the war. He was depressed, nervous, and off balance. When he gave assignments, he demanded that they be completed in unbelievably short times, without considering real possibilities. In the first weeks of the war, in my opinion, he misconceived the scale of the war, and the forces and equipment that could actually stop the advancing enemy on a front stretching from sea to sea. . . . He was constantly expressing the assumption that the enemy would be defeated in a very short time.[47]

Even with Nazi armies moving quickly and deeply into the country, Stalin would not give up his dogma about carrying the war to enemy territory. As a result he forbade retreat even when it was absolutely necessary. At the beginning of September, 1941, for example, remnants of the armies of the Southwest Front fell into a pincers from the west and east. The commander of the front, General M. P. Kirponos, decided to organize a defense on the Sula River and along the southern branch of the Dnepr. He and his chief of staff, General Tupikov, sent Stalin a detailed report of their desperate situation, concluding with a request for permission to withdraw. An hour and a half later they got a reply: "Kiev was, is, and will be Soviet. I do not permit you to retreat to the Sula River. I order you to hold Kiev and the Dnepr. Stalin."[48] The commander in chief of the southwest armies, Marshal Budennyi, tried to change Stalin's mind. In a report to head-

[44] *Voenno-istoricheskii zhurnal*, 1961, No. 1, p. 9.
[45] *Ibid.*, 1966, No. 6, pp. 7–8.
[46] *Cherez tri voiny* (Moscow, 1962) pp. 147–48.
[47] N. N. Voronov, *Na sluzhbe voennoi* (Moscow, 1963), p. 179.
[48] Reported by S. M. Iakimenko, who was an intelligence officer on the staff of the Southwest Front.

quarters he stressed that "Delay in the withdrawal of the Southwest Front may lead to the loss of troops and an enormous amount of matériel. . . ." But Stalin ignored him.

Marshal Bagramian also recalls this catastrophe. When the encirclement was already clearly formed, General Tupikov wrote another report plainly stating that headquarters must allow a retreat or be responsible for the destruction of hundreds of thousands of people. The commander of the front would not sign the report, so Tupikov sent it on his own. In reply he was accused of panicmongering—and the very next day the enemy cut through the last lines connecting the front with the rest of the country.[49] Kirponos' troops were crushed on the left bank of the Dnepr. A huge breach was opened in the south, through which the German armies poured into new areas in the east and the south.

Only in the fall of 1941, when the Germans had occupied almost the entire Ukraine, all of Belorussia and the Baltic republics, and had reached Leningrad and the outskirts of Moscow, did Stalin finally give up the thought of quickly destroying the enemy "in the districts where he has violated the Soviet border." He finally issued a directive that is aptly summed up in the witty remark of one officer: "It is necessary to stop the offensive and start the defense."

Another cause of chaos in these first months was the lack of a well-organized chain of command. "Only when the war had begun was organized leadership hurriedly formed," writes former Commissar of the Navy Kuznetsov.[50] On June 23 the headquarters of the Chief Command of the Armed Forces was set up under Commissar of Defense Timoshenko. Stalin was listed only as a member of this headquarters. On July 10 the headquarters of the Supreme Command was created. On July 19, almost a month after the beginning of the war, Stalin was named Commissar of Defense, and only on August 8 was the headquarters of the Supreme Command of the Armed Forces reorganized into the headquarters of the Supreme Commander in Chief—Stalin.

From June to September, despite stubborn resistance on individual sectors of the fronts, the Soviet armies were forced to retreat hundreds of kilometers. More than three million soldiers were killed or taken prisoner. (German losses up to September 30, 1941, numbered 550,000 men.[51]) Since it was the basic cadres of the regular army that suffered the losses, they were especially serious. Losses of equipment were also enormous. As the Nazis began their drive on Moscow, they enjoyed a great advantage in men and equipment. Marshal Vasilevskii

[49] *Literaturnaia gazeta*, Apr. 17, 1965.
[50] *Voenno-istoricheskii zhurnal*, 1965, No. 9, p. 66.
[51] *Kommunist*, 1966, No. 17, p. 49.

attributes the critical situation not only to the lack of strategic reserves in the Moscow district but also to the bungling of headquarters and the General Staff.[52] Stalin was flustered. Many examples can be given of his confusing, inconsistent, and sometimes impossible orders in the most crucial days of October, 1941. Colonel General P. A. Belov, who had last seen Stalin in 1933, on meeting him again during the defense of Moscow was startled to see

> a short man with a tired, drawn face. In eight years he had aged by twenty. His eyes lacked their former firmness, and confidence was no longer sensed in his voice. But I was even more surprised by Zhukov's behavior. [At that time Zhukov was commander of the Western Front.] He spoke sharply in an imperious tone, giving the impression that he was the senior commander here. And Stalin accepted this as necessary. Sometimes his face even showed signs of being flustered.[53]

Marshals Konev and Zhukov also tell about Stalin's serious mistakes in directing military operations near Moscow in October-November, 1941.[54] Konev, for example, could not get permission for a strategic withdrawal early in October that would have saved four armies from encirclement. And Zhukov, a month later, was compelled to launch attacks before his troops were prepared to do so effectively.[55] It must also be noted that Stalin hurried away from Moscow during the panic that broke out on October 16, 1941,[56] undoubtedly intensifying the panic by his flight. He did, to be sure, gain control of himself and return. And he must be given credit for accumulating some reserves at the height of the fighting near Moscow, in order to launch an attack later. In November and December, while the major government departments remained in Kuibyshev and Gorky, Stalin was in Moscow, inspiring the troops with confidence of victory. But these pluses hardly outweigh his unforgivable minuses.

The winter offensive of 1941–42 had great significance for the people's morale, since it dispelled the myth of German invincibility. Unfortunately Stalin refused to recognize that the Soviet Army still had fewer men and less equipment than the German army, and issued a premature order for a general attack on all fronts. Zhukov recalls the evening of January 2, 1942, when he was called to Moscow to discuss strategy. After Stalin had laid out the plan for a general offensive, Zhukov argued the case for restricting the attack to the Moscow front. N. A. Voznesenskii supported him, pointing out the lack of necessary

---

[52] *Ibid.*, pp. 52–53.
[53] P. A. Belov, *Za nami Moskva* (Moscow, 1963), p. 43.
[54] See *Bitva za Moskvu* (Moscow, 1966), pp. 33, 40.
[55] *Ibid.*, pp. 68–69.
[56] *Ed.:* See Werth, *Russia at War*, pp. 232–42, for one of several accounts.

forces and equipment. Stalin, supported by Malenkov and Beria, brushed aside these objections. As they were leaving, Shaposhnikov told Zhukov that it had been pointless to argue; directives had already been sent to the fronts; the attack would begin the following day.[57]

The result was a predictable failure. Not one of the main German army groups was fully broken up. A recent history[58] points out that this effort to achieve the impossible spoiled the attack on the Central Front, where a German army group could have been surrounded if Soviet reserves had been concentrated on that task. Worse yet, when the winter offensive had spent itself and there was an urgent need to go on the defensive, Stalin insisted that the attack be continued. Zhukov recalls his repeated rejection of appeals for rest and consolidation right through March and into April.[59] Soviet troops were therefore exhausted when the German spring and summer campaign of 1942 began. That was undoubtedly one of the reasons for the Soviet defeats that summer. Another was the concentration of forces in the center, on the mistaken assumption that the Germans would focus their efforts once again on the drive toward Moscow. Intelligence reports in mid-March indicating a German concentration in the south were simply ignored.[60] Moreover, Stalin would not completely give up the thought of ending the war in 1942. Though he accepted the General Staff plan for a defensive strategy that summer, he ordered some offensives, around Kharkov, for example, and in the Crimea. These were places where the Germans were also preparing for an offensive, and they had the superiority to justify it. Within a single month about 200,000 men concentrated on the Crimean Front were lost, along with all their heavy artillery, which was subsequently used against the defenders of Sevastopol.

Konstantin Simonov considers the fighting on Kerch Peninsula in the spring of 1942 a typical example of

> the contrast between the right way to run a war and the false, slogan-ridden ideas of how a war should be run, which were based not only on military illiteracy but also on the mistrust of people engendered by 1937. . . . Seven years ago one of our front-line correspondents wrote me: "I was on the Kerch Peninsula in 1942. The reason for the shameful defeat is quite clear to me: the complete mistrust of the army and front commanders that emanated from Mekhlis, the stupid tyranny and wildly arbitrary ways of this military illiterate. . . . He forbade the digging of trenches so that the offensive spirit of the soldiers would not be undermined. He moved up heavy artillery and army staffs to the very front lines, and

[57] *Voenno-istoricheski zhurnal,* 1966, No. 10, pp. 79–80.
[58] *Kratkaia istoriia Velikoi Otechestvennoi voiny* (Moscow, 1965), p. 138.
[59] *Voenno-istoricheskii zhurnal,* 1966, No. 10, p. 84.
[60] *Kratkaia istoriia Velikoi Otechestvennoi voiny* (Moscow, 1965), pp. 153–54.

so on. Three armies were placed on a 16-kilometer front, a division occupied 600–700 meters of the front—never, nowhere, have I seen such a saturation of troops. And they all were mashed into a bloody porridge, they were thrown into the sea, they perished only because the front was commanded by a madman instead of a commander."

I was at the same place as the author of this letter, and although I don't quite agree with his choice of words, I subscribe to the substance of what he says. I have brought this up not in order to run down Mekhlis one more time; incidentally, he was a man of irreproachable personal courage and did nothing for his own glory. He was deeply convinced that he was doing right; and precisely for that reason, from a historical viewpoint, his actions on the Kerch Peninsula are of major interest.

Here was a man of that period; regardless of circumstances, he considered everyone a coward who preferred a suitable position one hundred meters from the enemy to an unsuitable position thirty meters away.

He considered everyone a panicmonger who wanted to take elementary security measures against possible failures, considered everyone unsure of our own forces who made a realistic appraisal of the enemy's. For all his personal readiness to give his life for the homeland, Mekhlis was an obvious product of the atmosphere of 1937–38.

The commander of the front, Kozlov, to whom Mekhlis came as Stalin's representative, an educated and experienced military man, was also a product of the atmosphere of '37–'38, only in a different sense: he was afraid to take on full responsibility, afraid to pit a reasonable argument against a stupid onslaught—"everyone and everything forward"—afraid of the risk to himself in taking his argument with Mekhlis to headquarters.[61]

The attack near Kharkov also ended in disaster. Soviet troops managed to advance several dozen kilometers, but they were unable to consolidate their gains. On May 17, 1942, the Nazis took the offensive and threatened to encircle the Soviet armies. The Chief of the General Staff, A. M. Vasilevskii, proposed an immediate halt in the Soviet offensive. But Stalin, after talks with Timoshenko, rejected this proposal and ordered a continuation of the offensive. On the evening of May 18 Khrushchev asked Stalin to call off the offensive, but Stalin refused once again. Only when it was too late did he issue the order to stop. The situation was then hopeless; at least two armies were surrounded. Most of the men were killed or taken prisoner. The South and Southwest Fronts, which had insufficient troops to begin with, were extremely weakened by the Kharkov and Crimean disasters. The

[61] Simonov, "Uroki istorii i dolg pistaelia." *Ed.:* This seems to be an unpublished manuscript.

Germans were soon moving forward along the entire Southern Front.[62]

The heroism of the Red Army finally stopped the enemy very deep in Russia, at Stalingrad and in the Caucasus. Having exhausted the enemy in savage battles, the Army resumed the offensive in November, 1942, and surrounded and destroyed hundreds of thousands of enemy soldiers at Stalingrad. Once again Stalin revealed his inability to assess the relative strength of the Soviet armies and the enemy's. In this second winter offensive as in the first, he did not know when to stop the attack and go on the defensive. It took one more major defeat of Soviet troops, in the spring of 1943, to make Stalin see the real balance of forces. The enemy withdrew into the Don Basin, to regroup and prepare a counterattack. Stalin imagined that the Nazis were moving further west, beyond the Dnepr. So, although Soviet troops had outrun their supply bases and air support, Stalin demanded not a halt but an intensification of the offensive, to prevent the enemy from getting behind the Dnepr. The result was a powerful German attack that caught Soviet forces completely by surprise. After heavy fighting they were forced to retreat behind the North Donets and to abandon Kharkov and Belgorod once again. Reserves had to be sent to the southern sector of the front, and the move westward was accordingly slowed down.

I will not attempt to examine the whole war and all of Stalin's actions as Supreme Commander in Chief. War is a complex process, whose result depends on a host of contributory elements. But such consequences of the war as the immense wave of patriotism among the people and the renewed importance of the Communist Party cannot be overlooked. Millions of new members joined, and the influence of Party organizations recovered from the decline suffered during the repression. It was not the NKVD but the Party which organized the people for the fight against fascism. Many officials acquired considerable autonomy in deciding important problems, and thousands of new leaders came to the fore, genuinely talented and devoted to the people. The course of events forced Stalin to rely on such individuals.

The patriotism of the Soviet people and the increasing experience of its army were chief factors that ensured a Soviet victory, despite Stalin's poor leadership.[63] Of course he too learned something in the course of the war. He did a lot—though his myth did a lot more. By 1943–45 his orders to the troops were more judicious than in the first two years. Still, his progress was much less noticeable than most of

[62] See *Kratkaia istoriia Velikoi Otechestvennoi Voiny* (Moscow, 1965), p. 162, for criticism of the Kharkov offensive.
[63] To point out Stalin's blunders is not to belittle the victory. On the contrary, that feat was belittled during Stalin's time, when it was wrongly attributed to him rather than the people.

his subordinates'. He did not command in the sense of directing troops in battle. Zhukov testifies that Stalin had very little understanding of tactical problems; the action of military units smaller than armies was obscure to him. As for his "organizational talent," it rested largely on fear of repression, which did not stop during the war, as we shall see later.

Whether the armies were retreating or advancing, Stalin stayed in his office. He had a poor picture of front-line conditions; he did not visit the army, to say nothing of the army in action.

Marshal Biriuzov is quite explicit on this point:

> He stood at a distance from the army. He was the Supreme Commander in Chief, but the troops never saw him at the front, and not once did his eyes behold a soldier in combat. Moreover, during the very difficult initial period of the war the army in action did not even receive operational orders signed by Stalin himself. Almost all such documents were signed by B. M. Shaposhnikov, "on the instructions of the Supreme Commander in Chief." Only when Soviet troops began to win one victory after another did orders appear over Stalin's signature.[64]

This isolation became a serious liability when Stalin tried to force his ideas on front-line commanders in contravention of the views of the front-line staff. Some commanders made independent decisions that were later attributed to Stalin's military genius.[65] He was also given credit for decisions that were worked out by many minds at meetings of the General Staff.

In short, Stalin was in several respects a poor commander, with a weakness for abstract schematizing, for underestimating the enemy and overestimating his own forces. He was shortsighted and cruel, careless of losses, unwilling or unable to fight with little loss of blood, little interested in the fate of soldiers or the common people. He had much more to do with the reverses of the beginning of the war than with the victories at the end. Those military historians are wrong who accept this simple syllogism: since the war ended in victory, and Stalin was the Supreme Commander in Chief, he was a very good commander. A careful examination of the record supports a very different view. With other leadership the army could have defeated the Nazi aggressor not at Stalingrad and Kursk, but much farther west and much sooner. Hundreds of towns and tens of thousands of villages would not have been destroyed. Victory would not have cost twenty million lives.

---

[64] S. S. Biriuzov, *Sovetskii soldat na Balkanakh* (Moscow, 1963), p. 242.

[65] See, for example, the beginning of the Kursk battle, as recounted in the memoirs of General Malinin, *Na ognennoi duge,* pp. 109–11. *Ed.:* I have been unable to locate this source. It may be part of V. I. Malinin, comp., *Vyrosli my v plameni* (Moscow, 1964), which I have been unable to consult.

Finally, something must be said about repression during the war and immediately after it. In the first days of the war, for example:

> General D. G. Pavlov, commander of the Western Front, was arrested and shot. General V. E. Klimovskii, a leading participant in the Spanish Civil War and chief of staff at the front, was arrested and shot. General N. A. Klich was arrested and shot. Major General S. I. Oborin, commander of the 14th Mechanized Corps, arrested on the charge that it was not ready for action. Korobkov, commander of the 4th Army, was arrested.

All these officers, scapegoats for Stalin's blunders, have today been rehabilitated.[66] Many of the generals who died in battle in the first months of the war—e.g., V. Ia. Kachalov, Kirillov, and Ponedelin— were also made scapegoats. They were proclaimed traitors, and their families were exiled from Moscow.[67]

At the beginning of the war Stalin sometimes issued confused orders for arrests, then abruptly ordered the release of the victims. I have already mentioned the brief imprisonment of Vannikov, Minister of the Defense Industry.[68] A Deputy Minister of the Aviation Industry, V. P. Balandin, had a similar experience. He was in prison while his colleagues were anxiously consulting with Stalin about the air defense of Moscow.

> Stalin repeated several times: "There are no people you can count on.... There aren't enough people." When Stalin began to talk about people, Dement'ev whispered to me: "Let's ask about Balandin." I nodded, and we took advantage of a pause in the conversation: "Comrade Stalin, it's been over a month since they arrested our Deputy Commissar in Charge of Engines, Balandin. We don't know why he's doing time, but we can't imagine that he is an enemy. The Commissariat needs him, the supervision of engine building has become very poor. We beg you to review this case, we have no doubts about him."
>
> "Yes," Stalin replied, "he's been doing time for forty days, and hasn't signed any depositions. Maybe there's nothing on him.... It's very possible.... That does happen...." The following day Vasilii Petrovich Balandin, with sunken cheeks and shaved head, was back in his office in the Commissariat, continuing his work.[69]

Soldiers who broke out of encirclements were often rewarded with arrest. The agents of SMERSH[70] were actively engaged in repression both at the front and in the immediate rear. Of course, German intelli-

---

[66] See *Kratkaia istoriia Velikoi Otechestvennoi voiny* (Moscow, 1965), p. 68, and I. G. Starinov, *Miny zhdut svoego chasa* (Moscow, 1964).

[67] *Ogonek*, 1964, No. 47.

[68] See above, p. 248.

[69] A. S. Iakovlev, *Tsel' zhizni* (Moscow, 1966), p. 265.

[70] *Ed.:* An acronym formed from *smert' shpionam*—death to spies.

gence and the Gestapo did send many spies into rear lines, and tried to recruit traitors. But the reports of SMERSH, which tell of uncovering huge numbers of foreign agents, anti-Soviet elements, and plots and betrayals, leave the impression that many such discoveries were deliberately contrived.

The home front was also subjected to repression. For example, a group of philosophers—F. Gorokhov, I. M. Kulagin, and others—were arrested on the charge of defeatist tendencies. Before the end of the war the NKGB also subjected some commissariats to savage "purges," especially the Commissariat of Means of Communication, which was ravaged on March 16, 1944, with the knowledge of Stalin and Kaganovich.[71]

Stalin's attitude toward prisoners of war is one of the grimmest pages in his record. In the first two years of the war at least two million Soviet soldiers, perhaps three million, were taken prisoner. Many surrendered only when they found themselves in a hopeless position: surrounded, without arms or supplies, without food, wounded. And Stalin himself was largely to blame for the disastrous experience of large Red Army units. It is quite possible that he sensed his responsibility—if only subconsciously—and this may have inspired his savage attitude toward prisoners of war. He refused to sign the Hague Convention, with the result that Soviet prisoners received no help through the International Red Cross. Many of the Soviet prisoners who joined General A. A. Vlasov's "Russian Liberation Army" were only trying to save themselves from starvation, hoping at a suitable moment to cross over to the Soviet Army or the partisans.

When the war ended, special officers visited the prisoner-of-war camps in the Anglo-American zone, and read to the inmates an official letter, which declared that prisoners of war would not be prosecuted in their native land. This promise was not kept. Returning prisoners of war were treated like traitors. Into the concentration camps went not only real traitors but also many war heroes, defenders of Sevastopol, Odessa, and Brest, partisans, people who had been tortured in Nazi camps. The fate of Major N. S. Tkachuk is typical. A tank officer, seriously wounded near Dorogobuzh during a desperate attack on an enemy breakthrough, he was hidden and nursed by collective farmers. When he was barely recovered, Tkachuk tried to pick his way eastward but was captured by the Nazis and put in a prisoner-of-war camp. In February, 1942, he escaped but was recaptured. After a third flight, Tkachuk made contact with French partisans, and for two

[71] It is noteworthy that the victims in this commissariat were rehabilitated only in 1959, i.e., after the defeat of the antiparty group, Kaganovich included. *Ed.*: "The antiparty group" refers to Khrushchev's opponents in the Politburo who were removed from office in 1957 by action of the Central Committee.

years actively fought the Nazis. In January, 1945, he was again taken prisoner but was freed by British forces. He joined a British unit—asking to have a Soviet uniform made for him—and fought the Nazis once again. But when Tkachuk returned to his native land, he was put in a "filtration" camp for a year, and then was arrested and condemned on the basis of ridiculous charges.[72]

Even such a hero as V. I. Us was arrested. A former school principal, he was badly wounded and taken prisoner in 1941. On recovering, he escaped, got through to his native village, and created there an underground youth organization, *Nabat* (Tocsin). In November, 1943, *Nabat* rose, seized the village, and created a bridgehead on the west bank of the Dnepr, where a whole corps of the Second Ukrainian Front soon landed. *Nabat* was highly commended by the political division of the Fourth Guards Army. But soon after the liberation of the Ukraine, Us was arrested and sentenced to twenty years, for "voluntarily surrendering and creating a nationalist organization." To be sure, he was freed four years later, but he and his organization received full political rehabilitation[73] only after Stalin's death, thanks in the main to the journalist V. Dubovik.

Others who were arrested on their return from captivity were Major Gavrilov, one of the leaders in the defense of Brest fortress, and participants in the concentration-camp underground in Norway: General Samokhin, the prisoners' poet I. E. Kovalevskii, Lieutenant Colonel V. A. Novobranets. Many thousands of such cases could be cited. Even the Tartar priest Musa Dzhalil, who was killed in Nazi captivity, was proclaimed an enemy of the people just after the war.

Thus punishment fell, not on those who were really responsible for the defeat of many Soviet armies in 1941–42, but on the victims, on those who had already paid for the myopia and the blunders of the "greatest military leader of our time."[74] Moreover, officers who had never been taken prisoner were also arrested after the war, among them:

S. A. Khudakov-Khanferiants, Marshal of Aviation and war hero.[75] Admiral L. M. Galler, Deputy Commissar of the Navy and head of the Naval Engineering Academy. V. A. Alafuzov, Naval Chief of Staff. G. A. Stepanov, his deputy.

[72] The story is told by S. S. Smirnov in *Pravda*, Apr. 5, 1964. Cf. the fate of A. Karapetian, P. Chkuaseli, and V. Moskalets, imprisoned pilots who seized three German airplanes in the summer of 1944 and escaped to a partisan base in the Naluboks forest in Belorussia. After the liberation of Belorussia they were arrested and sentenced to ten years in prison. See *Izvestiia*, July 9, 1964.

[73] *Ed.:* There are basically two types of rehabilitation: civil, which simply voids the criminal conviction, and political, which also restores Party membership.

[74] Stalin's own son, Jacob Stalin, was taken prisoner at the beginning of the war. After Stalingrad the Germans proposed to exchange him for Field Marshal Friedrich Paulus. Stalin refused, and Jacob was shot by the Nazis.

[75] See *Bakinskii rabochii*, Oct. 2, 1964.

The last two were released and rehabilitated in 1953, but Galler died in prison. These three veteran admirals were accused of giving away the secret of the parachute torpedo—when sketches of it were sold at bookstalls.[76]

At the request of Stalin's son Vasilii,[77] Marshal of Aviation A. A. Novikov was arrested. Marshal Zhukov fell out of Stalin's favor, was demoted, and sent away from Moscow. The names of many other famous wartime commanders also vanished from the press: F. I. Tolbukhin, K. K. Rokossovskii, K. A. Meretskov, N. N. Voronov, N. F. Vatutin, I. D. Cherniakhovskii, I. Kh. Bagramian, I. S. Konev, R. Ia. Malinovskii. Stalin, revealing once again his limitless vanity, was determined that no one would share his military glory.

5

DURING STALIN'S LAST DECADE world politics moved through two periods. Until 1947 or 1948 the anti-Nazi coalition continued to exist, though rapidly disintegrating, giving rise to two opposed blocs involved in a steadily intensifying cold war. These two different periods raised different problems for Soviet foreign policy. In the first period the Soviet Union had to define its relationship as the center of the world revolutionary movement to revolutionary movements on the rise in many countries. At the same time the Soviet Union had to define its relationship to its allies in the anti-Nazi coalition, especially to the ruling circles of the United States and Great Britain. Needless to say, these relationships were often at odds: the interests of the world revolutionary process were completely opposed to the interests of the American and British imperialists.

Even before the Second World War, Soviet political writers frequently declared that just as the First World War had led to the victory of the socialist revolution in Russia, so the Second World War would inevitably lead to the victory of the socialist revolution in most European and in many Asian countries. That was not empty talk. Very real chances for the victory of the socialist revolution arose throughout continental Europe during the Second World War. Much depended on the fortunes of the German-Soviet conflict. If it had been less successful for Hitler in 1941, he would not have declared war on the United States in December. The Red Army would have moved into Western Europe while Britain had not yet recovered from her defeats.

---

[76] N. K. Kuznetsov, *Nakanune* (Moscow, 1966), p. 212.

[77] Vasilii Stalin was a coarse, semiliterate alcoholic, who began the war as a captain and rose to lieutenant general after the war. He was even put in charge of the Air Forces of Moscow Military District.

Not only Eastern but also Western Europe would have been liberated
by the Red Army. The face of Europe today would be quite different.
In actuality Soviet troops came to free neighboring countries from
Nazi tyranny only in 1944. By then Britain had rebuilt a large and
strong army, and the United States was in the war with a huge, well-
equipped military machine. In 1943 Anglo-American forces entered
Italy and in June, 1944, landed in France. In the same year British
troops also landed in Greece. Thus a situation arose that was much
more complicated for the Soviet Union and for the national liberation
movements than would have been the case if the Soviet-German War
had followed a different course.

In the countries liberated by the Soviet Union, people's democracies were set up, which was a great victory of the world socialist
revolution. For the progressive and socialist movements in countries
liberated by Anglo-American forces, the situation was difficult. The
revolutionary movement was strong in some of these countries. In
Italy it was stronger than in Hungary, in France stronger than in
Poland, in Greece stronger than in Rumania. In France, for example,
all antifascist parties were joined in a powerful resistance movement.
Communists played a major role, especially in the organization of the
August insurrection that liberated Paris before the arrival of the
Anglo-American troops and de Gaulle's forces. As the Germans beat
a hasty retreat from France, real power in the localities passed to the
units of the Resistance. In the last ten days of August the situation was
favorable for the assumption of all power by the National Front of
Resistance. But the Front did not even try to form its own government
during those days. It supported de Gaulle as he moved into power,
helping him form a coalition government that included Communists.

What if the forces of the Resistance had tried to take power in
August of 1944? This question was discussed at the first postwar conference of Communist and Workers' parties in 1947.[78] Some speakers,
particularly Wladyslaw Gomulka of Poland, reproached the French
Communist Party for its indecision. Analogous charges were made in
1952 by one of the French leaders, André Marty. Together with
Charles Tillon, he had headed detachments of the maquis during the
war, but in 1952 both were declared to be enemies of the French
Communist Party and expelled, in part, no doubt, because of Marty's
charges against the other French leaders, and indirectly against Stalin.
(Marty died shortly after; Tillon was reinstated in the Party after
1956.) The same charges are made today by some historians, who
accuse Stalin of withholding the signal for insurrection in 1944,

[78] Ed.: Medvedev is referring to the conference of nine European parties that met in
  Warsaw in September, 1947, and founded the Cominform. The major speeches
  were published in various languages, e.g. Informatsionnoe soveshchanie nekotorykh
  . . . partii . . . (Moscow, 1948). See also For a Lasting Peace, For a People's
  Democracy, the newspaper of the Cominform.

indeed of forbidding the French Party to push toward a socialist revolution lest it create problems in his relations with the allies, on the Polish question among others.

At present there is not enough information to support this charge. It is quite likely that an opportunity was lost in August, 1944, to transfer power to the National Resistance Front, and that Stalin was involved. De Gaulle's memoirs reveal that he perceived such a possibility. The Soviet journalist Ernst Henri argues that neither the Americans nor the British in August, 1944, could have prevented the creation of a National Front government in Paris.[79] Nor would de Gaulle have started a civil war in the rear of armies in action. A large and still strong German army stood on the French borders, and neither the British nor the Americans wanted any complications in their rear. However, even if some revolutionary opportunities were missed in France in August, 1944, this was not the single irretrievable opportunity that, if seized, would have changed the postwar history of Western Europe. The major chance for a socialist France and a socialist Italy was lost not in August, 1944, but on the Soviet-German Front in the summer campaigns of 1941 and 1942.

Moreover, the assumption of power by the National Front in August, 1944, would not have been a socialist revolution. A democratic united front was then the only possibility in France, not a dictatorship of the proletariat. The National Front was a bloc of several parties, including not only Communists but Socialists, Radicals, and Catholics, while Gaullists also collaborated with it. The chairman was the Catholic Georges Bidault. Although Communists held crucial positions in many local units and in many armed detachments, the Communist Party did not have a majority in the central organs of the Front. Thus a government of the Front would have had to be a coalition, necessarily including members of the Gaullist émigré government, which was already establishing itself in France and was officially recognized by all the allies. The chairman of such a government could not have been a Communist. He would probably have been de Gaulle, though with much less authority than in the government that he actually created.

Of course the Communists would have had much more influence than they briefly enjoyed in de Gaulle's government. (They were part of it until 1947.) But the whole situation—including the presence of the Anglo-American forces and the rapid revival of bourgeois parties and newspapers and of private industry—made it impossible for the Communists to destroy the coalition and rule by themselves. No government could have come to power in postwar France by insurrection. only by universal elections. The most that the Communists could

[79] *Ed.:* Medvedev cites Henri's—or Genri's—memorandum (*zapiska*), "O vneshnei politike Stalina v poslevoennyi period." It seems to be an unpublished manuscript.

expect to get in such elections was 30 or 35 percent of the votes, and perhaps four or five ministerial portfolios in a National Front government. They might have been forced to leave the government not in 1947 but in 1948 or 1949, which would have given them a better position for further struggle. But that still would not have meant a decisive victory for them. In short, even if we grant that Stalin and Maurice Thorez made a mistake in their August, 1944, directives to Communists in the French Resistance, there is no ground for calling this the blunder that decided the fate of postwar Europe.

The socialist revolution had even less chance of success in Italy in 1944–45. After allied forces entered Sicily in 1943, Marshal Pietro Badoglio formed a government that declared war on Germany and collaborated with the Anglo-American troops. The Communist Party was not yet strong enough to demand more than participation in a coalition antifascist government. That is what the Italian Communists did. Together with the Socialists they achieved a democratic republic on the ruins of the fascist and monarchist state. The risk of losing these gains was too great to allow an effort to achieve more.

The situation in Greece was more complicated. The resistance movement was very strong, with Communists controlling the National Liberation Front (EAM) and the Liberation Army (ELAS). The émigré monarchist government, taking little or no part in the resistance, counted on returning to Greece with the help of Anglo-American armies. When the Soviet offensive in the Balkans forced the Germans to leave Greece quickly, most of the country fell under the authority of the ELAS-EAM. British forces controlled only sections of a few cities. Members of the EAM were represented in the provisional government of George Papandreou. But the compromise that was possible in France was impossible in Greece—and in Yugoslavia too. Both the British forces and the Greek reactionaries were bent on disarming the resistance movement and creating a "national" army that would support a monarchist regime. A bitter conflict was unavoidable. On December 1, 1944, the leaders of the EAM left the Papandreou government, and a general strike was called in Athens. The British commander, General Scobie, ordered the ELAS detachments to evacuate Athens and the Piraeus, and when they refused, Churchill gave the order to open fire. He telegraphed Scobie on December 5, 1944:

> It would be well of course if your commands were reinforced by the authority of some Greek Government, and Papandreou is being told by Leeper to stop and help. *Do not, however, hesitate to act as if you were in a conquered city where a local rebellion is in progress.*[80]

[80] Winston S. Churchill, *Triumph and Tragedy* (Boston, 1953), p. 289. Medvedev cites the Russian translation (Moscow, 1955).

In the conflict that followed, the Greek Communists received no real help from the Soviet Union. Stalin recalled the Soviet military mission from Greece. With excessive punctiliousness he lived up to the secret oral agreement that he had recently made with Churchill, which put Greece in the British sphere of influence. While there was widespread outrage over the British action in Greece, the Soviet Union withheld even moral support to the Greek antifascists. Churchill noted the startling discrepancy in his memoirs:

> The vast majority of the American Press violently condemned our action, which they declared falsified the cause for which they had gone to war. . . . The State Department, in the charge of Mr. Stettinius, issued a markedly critical pronouncement. . . . In England there was perturbation. The *Times* and the *Manchester Guardian* pronounced their censures upon what they considered our reactionary policy. Stalin however adhered strictly and faithfully to our agreement of October, and during all the long weeks of fighting the Communists in the streets of Athens not one word of reproach came from *Pravda* or *Izvestia*.[81]

At the height of the punitive operations, Churchill wrote to Anthony Eden: "I am now even more impressed by the loyalty with which Stalin got out of Greece according to our deal, despite the great temptation, and the possibly great pressure put on him." The forces of the EAM-ELAS, without support or hope, were forced to end their armed struggle. An armistice was concluded. A government was formed without the participation of the EAM. The policies of this government led a few years later to a new uprising and civil war. And once again, the Greek Communists did not receive the moral and material support they needed from Stalin and the Soviet Union.

The relations between the Soviet Union and the national liberation movements in Asia in 1944–47 have not yet been adequately studied. The destruction of fascism, in which the Soviet Union played the decisive role, created the conditions for the downfall of the entire colonial system of imperialism. As for direct aid, the Soviet Army helped not only to free North Korea from the Japanese but also to win a victory for the socialist movement in that part of the country. In Manchuria, the Soviet army handed over to the Chinese People's Liberation Army most of the weapons taken from the Kwantung Army of the Japanese. The power of the people triumphed virtually all over Manchuria. Thus the northeastern provinces of China became a strong base from which the struggle against Chiang Kai-shek could unfold. That was the crucial turning point in the national democratic and agrarian revolution in China.

Stalin grossly underestimated the chances of this revolution. Brit-

[81] *Ibid.*, pp. 292, 293.

ish, Yugoslav, and Chinese publications have made the facts fairly clear. Shortly after the war Stalin invited representatives of the Chinese Communist Party to Moscow and advised them to find some acceptable compromise with Chiang Kai-shek. Stalin thought that a major offensive against Chiang would bring open intervention by the United States instead of victory for the Communists, thus complicating the international situation. The leaders of the Chinese Communist Party disagreed with Stalin and went their own way. He recognized his error in 1948, when the offensive of the People's Liberation Army was moving toward success.

In 1947–48 a new period in international relations began. By that time the world was rather clearly divided in three camps: the socialist, the neutralist, and the imperialist. Soviet foreign policy was accordingly faced with three different sets of problems.

Eastern Europe provides the best examples for studying Soviet relations with socialist countries. With Soviet aid war-ruined economies were restored, land was turned over to peasants and factories to the working class—an irreversible, revolutionary transformation headed by the Communist parties. Stalin could not avoid going along. But to a great extent he also hindered the development of a truly democratic and socialist revolution in these countries.

He introduced many perversions in the relationships of the Soviet Union with the people's democracies, and the effects can be felt to this day. In Ernst Henri's telling phrase, Stalin followed a policy of "socialist Caesarism." He regarded the leaders of the new socialist countries as his vassals, obliged to obey him without demur in foreign and internal policy. He saw the extension of the socialist camp as the extension of his personal domain, his alodium (*votchina*). And if the interests of some country, even the national interests of the Soviet Union, came into conflict with his vainglorious pretensions, he unhesitatingly gave priority to his pretensions. Ignoring the political and economic individuality of each East European country, their specific interests and needs, he tried to convert them into protectorates rather than independent, friendly allies of the Soviet Union. Discontent was the unavoidable result, not only among the petty-bourgeois masses, who were very sensitive to national restrictions, but also among the working class and the Communist parties. Many Communist leaders in Eastern Europe were unwilling, in all important matters, to follow blindly the orders from Moscow.

The inevitable conflict was most acute in relations with Yugoslavia. That country developed the greatest antifascist struggle during the war, with the clearest Communist leadership. It was the country that, right after liberation, carried out the most radical socialist transformation, including agrarian reform, the nationalization of industry, and the liquidation of counterrevolutionary and proimperialist groups. In short, right after liberation the dictatorship of the proletariat was established, in the form of a people's democracy. It was this vanguard role of Yugoslavia, both in fighting the fascist occupation and in effecting a socialist transformation, that enhanced the popularity of the Yugoslav leaders at home and in the other people's democracies. Not all of Tito's foreign and internal policies were correct, but it is beyond the scope of this book to appraise Yugoslav history. The essential point here is the source of Stalin's fury. It was not the mistakes of Tito, whether real or imaginary, it was Tito's growing popularity, and his reluctance to accept all of Stalin's recommendations on the economic and political development of Yugoslavia, that enraged Stalin. The striving for autonomy, in foreign as well as internal policy, finally led to a complete break between the USSR and Yugoslavia, and Stalin was chiefly responsible. The Yugoslav Communist leaders were branded a band of Trotskyite-Bukharinite murderers and agents of imperialism. The world Communist press joined in a campaign of unrestrained slander, calling this socialist country a terrorist fascist dictatorship, a center for British and American intelligence and anti-Communist propaganda. Economic relations were broken off. Soviet troops were moved up to the Yugoslav borders. The Soviet press virtually demanded civil war in Yugoslavia.

After the break, collectivization and industrialization were accelerated in almost all the people's democracies. The concrete conditions and pecularities of the various countries were widely ignored. Many countries were subjected to a stereotyped, instead of a creative, application of Soviet experience. As a result the standard of living fell and discontent grew, among Communists as well as the populace at large. But Stalin and his obedient servants, such as Mátyás Rákosi in Hungary, Boleslaw Bierut in Poland, Vlko Chervenkov in Bulgaria, and Enver Hoxha in Albania, responded to criticism with mass repression. They resurrected Stalin's argument that class struggle in socialist countries grows more intense as socialism develops. On this basis they created tales of counterrevolutionary, Titoist underground organizations, directed from Belgrade, Washington, and London.

With the Soviet punitive agencies providing direction, from 1948 to 1952 "enemies of the people" were discovered among the leaders of Hungary, Bulgaria, Rumania, Poland, Czechoslovakia, and Albania. Many of them were brought to the Soviet Union for investigation and punishment. Vladimir Prison, according to V. V. Zurabov, who was there in the early fifties, was filled with Communists from the people's democracies.

In almost all the socialist countries, "open" political trials were staged, clearly imitating the Soviet originals of 1936–38. Most of the accused were brought by torture to make obedient confessions of monstrous crimes. Lászlo Rajk, for example, the former Minister of Foreign Affairs and of Internal Affairs in the Hungarian People's Republic, and long before that a leader of the Hungarian workers' movement and of the resistance to Admiral Horthy's fascist regime, confessed that he had been an agent provocateur of that regime. From 1931 on he had allegedly betrayed more than two hundred Communists to the police. He declared that he was in the service of Yugoslav and British intelligence services, that he was not a Hungarian Jew but a German, and so on.

The same kind of ridiculous fabrications were recited in Bulgaria. Tribute should be paid to the behavior of the chief defendant, Traicho Kostov, who flatly denied the charges against him. When the procurator saw that it was impossible to force a confession out of Kostov in open court, he stopped direct questioning and began to read the depositions that Kostov had allegedly signed during the pretrial investigation. After hearing these fabrications, which took three hours to read, the court turned to the examination of other defendants, though Kostov categorically denied the authenticity of the depositions attributed to him. In his final speech he tried to expose the whole shameful production. In Poland the big show concerned an "espionage diversionary organization" allegedly operating in the Polish Army. The defendants were military leaders, headed by Marian Spychalski, Minister of Defense. Perhaps the biggest surprise was his replacement by the Soviet Marshal Konstantin Rokossovskii.

In Czechoslovakia many leaders were jailed—such as Vladimir Clementis, Gustav Husak, Josef Smrkovsky, Eduard Goldstücker, Maria Svermova, Josef Goldman, and Eugen Loebl. General Ludvik Svoboda, one of the main organizers of the Czechoslovak Army, was sent to a village to be the chairman of an agricultural cooperative. Much of this repression was done under pressure from Stalin and with the knowledge of Klement Gottwald. Antonin Novotný took an active part, and so did Rudolf Slanský, General Secretary of the Party. But then Slanský himself was arrested and brought to trial.

The Slanský trial is worth considering in detail. We have a thorough knowledge of its mechanics, which, we may assume, were essentially similar in the other trials. The principal source is Eugen Loebl, Party member since 1931 and Deputy Minister of Foreign Trade at the time of his arrest in November, 1949. Loebl survived to win complete rehabilitation in 1963, and in 1968 published an account of his experiences.[82] He describes the treatment that got him to the

---

[82] *Ed.:* See Eugen Loebl and Dusan Pokorny, *Die Revolution rehabilitiert ihre Kinder. Hinter den Kulissen des Slansky-Prozesses* (Vienna, 1968). Translated into English as *Stalinism in Prague* (New York, 1969).

point where he would sign anything. He was forbidden to sit down during interrogation and even in his cell. He was wakened thirty or forty times a night, kept on hunger rations, and given an injection of some narcotic that weakened his will to resist. (Other prisoners were worked over by such methods as the torture of a wife in her husband's presence.) The depositions Loebl was forced to sign changed with the passage of time. First he was an agent of Tito, then of international Zionism and Israel, and finally of Slanský's underground committee. He had to memorize each of these depositions in turn, and go through rehearsals. When he cooperated, he received good food and even medical care. The whole business was directed by agents of the Soviet security organs. Loebl knew nothing about Slanský's affairs, but fear prompted him to testify that Slanský was trying to restore capitalism.

When this "investigation" began, Slanský was still the Party's general secretary. As late as July, 1951, though he had lost that post, there was an elaborate celebration of his fiftieth birthday. And then, in November, his arrest was announced. At that point, Loebl recalls, rehearsals for the trial were intensified, sometimes with individual participants, sometimes all together. If someone forgot his lines, he was shouted at. Better food was given for good performances. Inconsistencies were eliminated. Immediate translations were provided for the Soviet security officers who attended the rehearsals. They made comments and suggested corrections that were included in the record and memorized by the prisoners. In the last days before the trial, Novotný's name was put in the record—as a key figure in the exposure of Slanský's group. Opening on November 20, 1952, the trial ran smoothly. Most of the accused were shot; Loebl got life imprisonment.

As in the Soviet Union, the open trials generated a mass psychosis and a multitude of arrests. In Hungary, for example, more than 150,000 political prisoners were in prisons and camps when Stalin died. Among the leaders of the people's democracies who served time in those years were Gomulka, First Secretary of the Polish Party, and Z. Kliszko, another Polish leader; János Kádár, Secretary of the Hungarian Party; Lucretiu Patrascanu, General Secretary of the Rumanian Party during the underground and organizer of the revolt; V. Luca, Deputy Chairman of the Rumanian Council of Ministers; Ana Pauker, Rumanian Minister of Foreign Affairs. In Albania Kotchi Dzodze (Koci Xoxe), Secretary of the Central Committee, was shot. The ultimate consequences of such lawlessness became apparent in Hungary in October, 1956.

Stalin's policy of "socialist Caesarism" extended beyond the people's democracies. He tried once again to subject all the Communist parties of the world to his control. Palmiro Togliatti has noted the postwar revival, in a masked form, of the centralized international organization that had been dissolved in order to affirm the necessity of autonomy in each party's struggle for democracy and socialism.[83] The result, he says, was a period of stagnation, during which all Communist publications revived the habit of calling the leaders of Western Social Democracy nothing more than bourgeois agents, who were allegedly turning their parties into instruments of American imperialism. In 1956 the XXth Congress struck the decisive blow at such dogmatism.[84]

Toward the new national states of Asia and Africa Stalin revealed remarkable ineptitude in 1945–52. Back in the twenties he had correctly perceived the importance of the national bourgeoisie in such areas. "Revolution in the imperialist countries," he said in 1927,

> is one thing. There the bourgeoisie is the oppressor of other nations; there it is counterrevolutionary at every stage of the revolution; there the national element, as an element of the struggle for liberation, is absent. Revolution in colonial and dependent countries is a different thing. There the yoke of foreign imperialism is one of the factors of revolution; there this yoke cannot but press also on the national bourgeoisie; there the national bourgeoisie, at a certain stage and for a certain time, may support the revolutionary movement of their own country against imperialism; there the national element, as an element of the struggle for liberation, is a factor of revolution.[85]

In the postwar period Stalin lost sight of this distinction. He declared that the bourgeoisie in colonial areas had abandoned the banner of national independence, that only Communists could carry it forward.

The many real gains won in Asia and Africa under the leadership of the national bourgeoisie were declared to be a fraud, the result of a deal between the local bourgeoisie and the imperialists. Independent states such as India, Indonesia, and Egypt were called pseudosovereign puppet states in our press. Stalin regarded nonalignment, neutrality, as a fiction. Almost all the leaders of the Asian and African nationalist bourgeoisie—Sukarno and Nehru, for example—were called imperialist agents. The *Great Soviet Encyclopedia* said that Gandhi "demagogically made himself out to be a partisan of Indian independence and an opponent of the English," when he was in fact their agent.[86] Such an attitude made for serious mistakes in the tactics of many Asian Communist parties. Together with Mao Tse-tung, who began to play an active role in working out strategy for the Asian parties, Stalin diverted them from a broad national struggle toward an adventurous

[83] See the quotation in B. M. Leibzon and K. K. Shirin', *Povorot v politike Kominterna* (Moscow, 1965), pp. 339–40. *Ed.:* Togliatti is alluding to the dissolution of the Comintern in 1943 and the establishment of the Cominform in 1947.

[84] *Ibid.*

[85] Stalin, *Sochineniia*, X, p. 11.

[86] *Bol'shaia Sovetskaia Entsiklopediia*, 2nd edn., X, p. 203.

policy of armed insurrections and peasant wars of the Chinese type. In Burma, for example, which had just won its independence, an insurrection was started, a liberated region created—and a defeat was suffered. In Indonesia the Communist leader, Musso, demanded in 1948 an end to cooperation with the national bourgeoisie and Sukarno. An insurrection began in Java and ended in the execution of two hundred Party leaders, including Musso and Amir Sjarifuddin. Defeat was the end result of partisan operations in Malaya and the Philippines. Even in Japan a revolutionary situation was proclaimed in 1950, and preparations for armed insurrection began. The result was a sharp decline in the electoral strength of the Japanese Communist Party. Only in Vietnam did armed struggle develop successfully. That was due not only to the proximity of China but also to the fact that Vietnam continued beyond 1945 to be a virtual colony of France. The state there really was a pseudosovereign puppet.

Toward the major capitalist states Stalin took a very hard line, beginning in 1947–48. The struggle for peaceful coexistence was not the chief task of Soviet foreign policy in that period. The clearest example of this hard line was Stalin's policy with respect to Germany, especially the so-called Berlin crisis, which greatly exacerbated the situation in Europe. Also in the Far East the situation was greatly exacerbated by the long and bloody war in Korea. In both cases the Soviet Union and its allies were finally obliged to retreat to their original positions. The struggle ended formally in a draw, but under the circumstances the result favored our opponents far more than ourselves. As Ernst Henri writes:

> It is completely wrong to consider the outcome of the Korean War a draw. The fact is that at the time it helped Truman to turn against us people all over the world who were vacillating, and it considerably weakened the moral authority won by the Soviet Union during the Second World War.

Of course some failures are inevitable in foreign policy, where it is difficult to foresee all the actions of one's opponent. Both the Berlin crisis and the Korean War were a kind of reconnaissance in force on Stalin's part. These events showed both camps the boundaries that they could not cross without provoking a threat of general war, which is equally intolerable to both the Soviet Union and the United States. In some cases such a reconnaissance is necessary and useful. Only when historians have more documents and information will it be possible to say precisely how sensible it was to pursue a policy of reconnaissance in force in 1948–52, whether less dangerous and less costly forms of reconnaissance could not have been tried.

XIII

Domestic Policy

1

THE VICTORY in the Fatherland War, though won at the price of enormous sacrifices, engendered great exaltation. People tried to heal the wounds of war as quickly as possible; they lived on the hope of a better and happier future. The land was so bloodsoaked that any thought of new deaths seemed unbearable. Indeed, right after the war the Presidium of the Supreme Soviet decreed an end to the death penalty, even for the most serious crimes. The spymania and universal suspicion that prevailed before the war tended to disappear, especially in view of the drastic change in the international situation. The Soviet Union was no longer isolated. But repression continued in the postwar period, though on a somewhat smaller scale than in the prewar years.

In 1949–51 some *oblast* Party organizations were decimated. The "Leningrad Affair" was the most serious of such cases. On Stalin's order, and with the active participation of Beria and Malenkov, the Leningrad *obkom* first secretary, P. S. Popkov, was arrested, and with him a number of other leading officials, including the former Commissar of Education and director of the "Ice Line,"[1] Tiurkin. Indeed, nearly the entire staff of the Leningrad *obkom* was arrested, and mass repression fell on officials of the local *Komsomol,* the Soviet executive committee, on *raikom* leaders, factory managers, scientific personnel, and people in higher education. Thousands of innocent people were arrested, and many of them died in confinement. Among the victims of the Leningrad Affair were:

> N. A. Voznesenskii, member of the Politburo, Deputy Chairman of the Council of Ministers and chairman of Gosplan. A. A. Kuznetsov, Secre-

[1] *Ed.:* The road across the ice of Lake Ladoga, which brought supplies to besieged Leningrad.

tary of the Central Committee and a leader of the defense of Leningrad.
M. I. Rodionov, Chairman of the Council of Ministers of the RSFSR.
A. A. Voznesenskii, Minister of Education of the RSFSR.

Many of the officials who were cut down in 1949–52 belonged to
the new generation of leaders who rose to prominence after 1936–37.
They were significantly different from the preceding generation. As a
rule they completely accepted the cult of Stalin's personality. As their
careers progressed, some of them acquired the characteristic features
of Stalinists: rudeness and unjustified abruptness in their treatment of
subordinates, dictatorial manners, vanity. But many of these younger
officials had not yet perceived the grave consequences of Stalin's cult
and knew little about the lawlessness he had created. They were basically honorable people who tried to do their jobs as well as possible.
An anecdote by N. A. Voznesenskii's secretary is revealing:[2]

> Late one night I received a package from Beria addressed to Voz-
> nesenskii. As usual, I opened the package and took out a thick
> bundle of papers fastened together. On the first sheet was printed:
> "List of people subject to . . ." In my hands was a long list of peo-
> ple condemned to be shot. . . . At the end of the list, diagonally,
> Beria, Shkiriatov, and Malenkov had signed their names.
> The list had been sent to Voznesenskii for his approval. This
> was a first in my long years of working in the Kremlin. Till that
> day nothing of the sort had ever come to Voznesenskii. I went at
> once to Nikolai Alekseevich's office and gave him the list that was
> burning my fingers. Voznesenskii began to read it attentively. He
> would read a page or two, stop, think for a while, return to the
> page he had read, and read further. When he had finished reading
> the list, looking at the signatures underneath, Nikolai Alekseevich
> said indignantly: "Return this list by courier where you got it
> from, and inform the proper person by telephone that I will never
> sign such lists. I am not a judge, and don't know whether the peo-
> ple on the list need to be shot. And tell them never to send such
> lists to me again."
> Beria could not but remember Voznesenskii's categorical refusal
> to sign the sentences of "enemies of the people."

In the first years following the war the influence of these younger
officials, who had distinguished themselves during the war, increased
markedly. Voznesenskii, for example, was made first deputy chairman
of the USSR Council of Ministers, which meant that men like Voroshilov, Molotov, and Kaganovich became his subordinates. Kuznetsov,
rising to a secretaryship in the *apparat* of the Central Committee, was
given the job of checking the activity of the security organs. This
caused acute dissatisfaction among Stalin's former favorites. The young

[2] From V. V. Kolotov, "Ustremlennyi v budushchee" (unpublished manuscript).

leaders were threatened from another direction as well. The rigid framework of Stalin's cult was too confining for the most capable of them. Sooner or later some of them would have to become a nuisance to Stalin, as people who might diminish his own authority. That is how death came to N. A. Voznesenskii, after he had been in charge of Gosplan for eleven years, since December, 1937.

A major factor was Voznesenskii's book on the war economy of the USSR, which was issued in 1947.[3] Its detailed analysis was based on much new factual material, and despite certain mistakes, it soon became popular among economists. Some of its theses began to be cited on the same level as theses from Stalin. Although Stalin had read the manuscript in 1947 and had even signed the authorization for publication, the book was suddenly declared to be anti-Marxist and was withdrawn. At the beginning of 1949 Stalin removed Voznesenskii from all his posts, including membership in the Central Committee. Stalin also refused to see his former aide and hear him out.

Voznesenskii remained at liberty for several months following his "disgrace." Apparently there was not even a pretext for his arrest. Beria tried to create one—an excuse for decimating the Gosplan leadership—by concocting a case about the loss of some secret papers in Gosplan. Not only the Chairman of Gosplan but the First Deputy, A. D. Panov, the Deputy Chairman, A. V. Kuptsov, and several other officials were brought to trial. Voznesenskii spoiled the show by flatly denying the charges and exposing the provocative nature of the trial in his first statement. Fearing further exposure, Beria ordered that Voznesenskii appear in court no more and that the other defendants be condemned.[4]

But this was only a postponement for Voznesenskii. And even then, out of office, with Beria after him, he did not lose his faith in Stalin. His wife tells how he repeatedly phoned A. N. Poskrebyshev, Stalin's secretary, asking him to send over a courier, with whom he sent back memoranda pleading for work and assuring Stalin of his devotion and honesty. But he did not get an answer. He believed that there was some sort of misunderstanding. "While Stalin is getting to the bottom of this," he told his family, "I must not lose time." And he continued to work on a new book, "The Political Economy of Communism," which he had begun in 1948. But it remained unfinished. In 1950 he was shot.[5]

The Soviet intelligentsia was raked over once more. Of course there were mistakes, there were apolitical and unideological tendencies,

[3] Ed.: See Voznesenskii, Voennaia ekonomika SSSR v period otechestvennoi voiny (Moscow, 1947). There is an English translation (New York, 1948).
[4] Recounted by V. Kolotov in Literaturnaia gazeta, Nov. 30, 1963.
[5] See ibid., and Voprosy istorii KPSS, 1963, No. 6, p. 98.

which had to be criticized by the Party. But there are various kinds of criticism. Instead of serious, dispassionate analysis, Stalin and Zhdanov launched pogroms, one after another, which severely damaged Soviet culture at home and prestige abroad. The persecution of writers, composers, and drama critics began in 1946–47 with a series of speeches by Zhdanov, resulting in the expulsion of Mikhail Zoshchenko and Anna Akhmatova from the Union of Writers. Other artists were subjected to mudslinging: Boris Pasternak, Dmitri Shostakovich, V. I. Muradeli, Sergei Prokofiev, Aram Khachaturian, Sergei Eisenstein, Vsevolod I. Pudovkin, V. Ia. Shebalin, N. Ia. Miaskovskii, Nokolai Pogodin, I. Sel'vinskii, V. Kirsanov, V. S. Grossman, Olga Bergol'ts, and A. Gladkov.

Soon the arrests began. Among the many writers, poets, and critics arrested in 1948–50 were:

Perets Markish, Gladkov, D. Bergelson, B. D. Chetverikov, S. Galkin, D. Gofshtein, I. Fefer, L. Kvitko, B. D'iakov, Ia. Smeliakov, A. Efremin, A. Isbakh, I. M. Nusinov, and G. A. Gukovskii.

The Jewish theater was in fact destroyed by the NKVD.[6] Emmanuel d'Astier de la Vigerie[7] tells how Stalin, on Kaganovich's advice, invited S. M. Mikhoels to play the role of King Lear for him in 1946. This remarkable actor was repeatedly invited to give private performances of Shakespearean roles for Stalin. Each time Stalin thanked Mikhoels and praised his acting. But in 1948, with Stalin's knowledge, Mikhoels was killed in Minsk. A few years later he was posthumously labeled a spy for Anglo-American intelligence.

The leaders and the creative intelligentsia of the Ukraine were also threatened by repression in the first years after the war. Kaganovich was first secretary of the Ukrainian Party for only nine months in 1947, but to this day many Ukrainian officials call those months the "black days" of the Ukraine. Identifying himself as the chief of the Ukrainian people, Kaganovich insulted, denounced, and terrorized their leading cadres. Without justification he accused writers and Party officials of nationalism.[8]

Those were the years of an ugly campaign against "cosmopolitanism" and "worship of things foreign," bringing dozens of arrests and thousands of dismissals. It was dangerous even to quote foreign sources, to say nothing of corresponding with foreign scholars. Driven from their work and hounded to early deaths by nervous strain were I. I. Iuzovskii, a major theatrical and literary critic, I. S. Zvavich, a

---

[6] For the arrest of the actor Zuskin and many others see "Evreiskaia literatura," in *Kratkaia literaturnaia entsiklopediia; Voprosy literatury,* 1966, No. 8, p. 75; Ehrenburg's memoirs in *Novyi mir,* 1965, No. 2; and B. D'iakov's memoirs in *Oktiabr',* 1964, No. 7.

[7] *Sur Staline* (Paris, 1964).

[8] See *Ocherki po istorii kommunisticheskoi partii Ukrainy* (Kiev, 1964), pp. 574–75.

publicist, I. L. Al'tman, A. S. Gurvich, B. Dairedzhiev, and S. M. Mokul'skii. After the 1948 meeting of the Academy of Agricultural Sciences and the 1950 meeting of the Academy of Medical Sciences, the medical and biological sciences were subjected to unprecedented devastation. Dozens of leading scientists were repressed and thousands were fired or demoted. Among the victims were L. A. Orbeli, V. V. Parin, N. P. Dubinin, M. M. Zavadovskii, I. I. Shmal'gauzen, P. N. Konstantinov, P. K. Anokhin, and I. S. Beritashavili. Many years of persecution finally drove D. A. Sabinin, the leading Russian plant physiologist, to suicide.

The intense, adulatory publicity given to Zhdanov's speeches on ideological questions increased his authority to the point where Stalin grew envious. Using as an excuse Zhdanov's supposedly incorrect position on the activity of T. D. Lysenko, whom Zhdanov proposed to remove from the presidency of the Agricultural Academy, Stalin sent Zhdanov into retirement. Shortly afterwards Zhdanov passed away in his dacha, from an infarction of the myocardium, the reports said. Later Stalin accused a group of doctors at the Kremlin hospital of murdering Zhdanov.

Repression touched other sciences as well as biology. Among those arrested were Doctor of Technical Sciences and General of Artillery P. A. Gel'vikh; Professor S. Iudin, an outstanding physician, and originator of many operative techniques; and the historian E. L. Shteinberg.

At the end of the forties the NKVD cooked up a story about the existence of a "pro-American Jewish conspiracy" in the USSR, which was followed by the arrests of leading officials of Jewish origin. S. A. Lozovskii (Dridzo), who had just turned seventy-four, an old Bolshevik member of the Central Committee and Deputy Minister of Foreign Affairs, was arrested and shot. Almost all the members of the Jewish Antifascist Committee were arrested, and most were shot. (Academician Lena Shtern was exiled.)

Early in 1949 Mikhail Borodin was arrested. In the twenties he had been the chief political adviser to Sun Yat-sen and the National Revolutionary government of China. Sun Yat-sen, just before his death in 1925, had given him a letter to the Central Executive Committee of the USSR. It was the political testament of that great Chinese revolutionary, which the present leaders in Peking want to forget.[9] After the Second World War Borodin worked as editor in chief of the English-language newspaper *Moscow Daily News;* later he transferred to the Communist Information Bureau. Almost the entire editorial staff of the paper was arrested along with him, including the American journalist Anna Louise Strong, who was accused of espionage and

[9] *Ed.:* The letter is quoted in Lyon Sharman, *Sun Yat-sen. His Life and Its Meaning* (New York, 1934), pp. 308–9.

expelled from the USSR. The accusations against these individuals were not voided until 1955.[10]

In 1949 Transcaucasia was hit by another wave of mass repression. Beria and his henchmen, with Stalin's approval, made up a story about the existence of a Dashnak counterrevolutionary underground, and exiled thousands of Armenian families to the Altai region.[11]

The repression of former political prisoners in 1948 and 1949 deserves special attention. While the war was on they remained in confinement, even those whose terms ended in 1942–43. The great victory, one would think, should have relieved the tension and permitted a general amnesty. It was expected, and an amnesty was in fact declared—but not for "enemies of the people." On the contrary, in the first years after the war a wave of terror swept through the camps. A vast number of prisoners received "additions" (*doveski*)—illegal extensions of their sentences by five, eight, or ten years. Many politicals were transferred from general to special camps with an "intensified regime." On completion of their sentences, some were released from the camps but condemned to "eternal settlement" in the northern *raiony*, in the Kolyma region, Siberia, and Kazakhstan. A very few received permission to return to European Russia, but not, as a rule, to the big cities. And these few were arrested again in 1948–49. They were sent back to prisons and camps, often without any concrete charges, simply for preventive confinement, as it was called. Those few who by some oversight were not rearrested found themselves in a terrible position. No one would hire them or register their right to live anywhere; they often wandered through the country for months and years without roofs over their heads. Some were so desperate they committed suicide, others became beggars; there were even some who returned to "their" camp, hoping to find work as wage laborers.

2

THE DECLINE in agricultural production during the first Five-Year Plan[12] was arrested in the mid-thirties. Despite many administrative abuses and arbitrarily low state procurement prices, the advantages of large-scale collectivized and mechanized farms began to show results. From 1934 agriculture started to improve, though slowly and unevenly. After many years of inflated reports it is now known that agricultural output in 1937 was 25 per cent greater than in 1932. The rationing

[10] See Anna Louise Strong, *The Stalin Era* (New York, 1956), and the newspaper *Moskovskaia pravda*, June 30, 1964. *Ed.*: Borodin died in confinement in 1951.
[11] See *Istoriia kommunisticheskoi partii Armenii* (Erevan, 1964), p. 432. Mass arrests were also inflicted upon the leading cadres of the Moscow automobile plant.
[12] See Chapter III, Section 4.

system was abolished, but agricultural abundance was still a distant dream. The third Five-Year Plan projected further progress, which was not realized. In 1938 and 1939 agricultural output fell below the 1937 level; in 1940 that level was surpassed by 5 to 6 per cent. Instead of the planned yearly grain harvest of 8 billion poods, the average for 1938–40 was 4.756 billion poods [1 pood = 36.113 lbs.].

An enormous gap had developed by the end of the thirties between the rapid development of industry and the slow development of agriculture. A good relationship between the city and the countryside, between the working class and the peasantry, became increasingly difficult to achieve. The heart of the problem was the forced transfer, the "pumping" (perekachka) of funds from agriculture to industry. In the late twenties and the early thirties it was an unavoidable necessity. In 1929 Stalin spoke about it quite frankly, conceding that a "supertax," "something like tribute," was being extracted from the peasantry. He promised that this emergency measure would soon be stopped.[13] The promise was not kept. Because of the serious mistakes in its agricultural policy, the Soviet state could not liquidate the notorious "scissors" effect, that is, the disparity between agricultural and industrial prices. The prices paid to collective and state farms at the end of the thirties remained very low, while they continued to be overcharged for manufactured goods and for the services of the Machine Tractor Stations. Thus the forced transfer of funds from the countryside to the city, far from ending, was increasing.

The war threw Soviet agriculture even further back. Agriculture suffered greater losses than any other branch of the national economy. In 1945 agricultural output was only 86 per cent of the 1913 level. The number of farm machines had decreased severalfold, and labor was in short supply. Many collective farms were staffed only by women, old men, and boys. In other words, the effort to improve agriculture had to start all over again. In 1946 the fourth Five-Year Plan began, with ambitious goals for agriculture. Not one of them was reached. In 1950 gross agricultural production was 99 per cent of the 1940 level, instead of the planned 127 per cent. Only 85 million tons of grain were harvested in 1950, instead of the projected 127 million tons. Livestock passed the 1940 count but remained far below the planned estimates. Though the number of horned cattle exceeded the 1940 level, it was still lower than in 1916 and 1928. In 1951 the fifth Five-Year Plan began. Once again all indicators pointed to non-fulfillment of the agricultural targets. In 1953 gross production was only 4 per cent higher than in 1940. The average yearly grain harvest in 1949–53 was around 81 million tons. Per capita grain production in 1953 was 19 per cent lower than in 1913. It is hardly surprising

[12] Stalin, Sochineniia, XII, pp. 49 ff.

that virtually no grain was available for fodder or export. The average yield of most crops was lower in 1949–53 than in 1913.

The main reason for the postwar stagnation in agriculture was Stalin's violation of the principle that farmers need personal material incentives. Although industry quickly reached and surpassed its pre-war level, the forced transfer, the "pumping" of funds from the countryside to the cities, continued to increase in the last years of Stalin's life. The prices paid for agricultural products were barely raised at all in a period when the real value of money was sharply declining. Farms had to sell the bulk of their produce at prices much lower than the cost of production. In 1953 one ruble was paid for a centner [100 kg] of sugar beets—little more than half the average cost of production. A centner of grain brought 90 kopecks—four to five times less than the average cost of production. The price of potatoes did not even cover the cost of transporting them to the state procurement centers. Most of the marketable meat was surrendered by the collective farms as payment in kind for the work of Machine Tractor Stations, or at procurement prices equal to only a few percentage points of the retail price on meat. (At that time even in the United States the farmers' share in the retail price of their products was 40 to 60 per cent.)

Moreover, in the last years under Stalin a perverse system of planning state procurements was established, which assigned to collective farms a total sum of deliveries exceeding both the overall state plans and the capabilities of many collective farms. The result was a huge accumulation of arrears, while grain procurements took on the character of forced confiscations.[14] In many areas, especially outside the black-earth (chernozem) zone, virtually all the farms' surplus was being pumped out of the countryside and even a part of their subsistence requirements. If farming in these regions was not entirely ruined by this perverse policy but sometimes even made a little progress, the reason was that millions upon millions of collective farmers were working without pay, were working not for money or for produce but for marks (*palochki*) in their labor books. As for means of subsistence, they had to be obtained not by collective-farm work but by work on the household plots, which were less encumbered by taxes and obligatory deliveries. Without their private plots the collective farmers simply could not have survived; in return for their collective-farm labor days they did not receive even the minimum necessities of life. Frequently it was the desire to keep the household plots that forced the peasants to work on the collective-farm fields, since only members of collective farms had the right to those plots.

[14] *Ed.: Prodrazverstka*, Medvedev's word here, was the term used to describe grain requisitions during the Civil War.

In other words, unpaid labor on the collective-farm fields was turned into a strange payment the peasant made for the right to use his own little plot of land. Instead of developing truly collective and socialist relations in the countryside, this system preserved and intensified the commitment to private property.

Moreover, even the private farming of the collective farmers suffered from Stalin's shortsighted policies in the postwar years. Despite the increase in obligatory procurements, shortages of grain and animal products became even more acute. Stalin could find no better solution to the problem than to start imposing more and more taxes and requisitions on the private plots. Every head of livestock, every fruit tree, was subjected to tax and to obligatory deliveries. After nearly destroying the incentive to collective-farm work, Stalin was weakening the incentive to work on the private plot. Many peasant families quit raising livestock and even chopped down the fruit trees in their gardens. Many found themselves in a truly hopeless situation; they did not get enough to live on either from the collective farm or from their own plot. Want became their constant companion. Many were also prevented from quitting agriculture and moving to the city. The passport system set up under Stalin withheld passports from many collective farmers, who therefore could not leave their villages without permission. At the same time traditional peasant crafts began to be restricted and banned, which made the situation even worse, especially in the non-black-earth area.[15]

The agricultural system that developed under Stalin completely contradicted the basic principles of socialist society, especially the central one: "From each according to his abilities; to each according to his labor." Stalin tried to base agriculture not on personal material incentives and not even on enthusiasm, but above all on orders, on compulsion. That was the chief cause of the stagnation that characterized agriculture during the period of the cult.

The final irony was the influence of this system on industry. After producing some initial gains in the accumulation of funds for industrial development, agriculture based on compulsion ceased to make up the enormous losses that the whole economy suffered because of agricultural shortages. The poverty of the peasants in the final analysis caused a drop in the real wages of industrial and white-collar workers, for they could not get the food products they needed. Moreover the agricultural population decreased very slowly under Stalin's system, and this also held back the growth of industry. The affluence of a society depends, as Marx noted, on the degree to which it can shift labor from agriculture to industrial production and services.[16]

[15] *Ed.:* Cottage industry provided an important supplement to agricultural income for peasants in non-chernozem areas.
[16] See *Arkhiv Marksa i Engel'sa,* IV (1935), p. 119.

3

DURING THE FIRST Five-Year Plan, Stalin's industrial goals were unrealistic adventures, heedless of cost. Nonfulfillment of all the major targets as expressed in physical units, along with many difficulties that unexpectedly emerged, had a certain sobering effect on Stalin. But then he went to the other extreme. When the second Five-Year Plan was drawn up, he demanded a decrease in the rates of industrial development, from an estimated 22 per cent average annual growth rate in the first plan to a projected rate of 13 or 14 per cent for the second.[17]

Industrial managers, workers, technicians, and engineers did not, however, accept these lowered growth rates. Because the new factories and equipment built during the first Five-Year Plan had begun to play a major role in production, and because of the experience and knowledge acquired, the rate of industrial development accelerated during the second plan. Although—or because—Stalin drove industrial managers much less and did not assign them any insuperable targets, the rate of industrial development rose from 19 per cent in 1934 to 23 per cent in 1935, and rose again to 29 per cent in 1936. And it must be borne in mind that every percentage point of growth in the second plan meant a much larger increase in actual volume of production than a percentage point in the first plan.

When large-scale attacks on "wreckers" began, growth rates suffered a sharp slowdown. In 1937 the rate for industry as a whole was 11 per cent, in 1938 12 per cent, in 1939 16 per cent, in 1940 12 per cent. These rates did not correspond to the country's potentialities in that period. Indeed, there were branches of industry where mass repression led to an actual halt in growth. Consider metallurgy, for example, which was extremely important for defense. Kaganovich, who was directly involved in the repression of metallurgists, declared that "an energetic and decisive liquidation of the consequences of the wrecking done by Japanese-German Trotskyite-Bukharinite diversionaries and spies is the basis for a new upsurge in the work of factories and of all ferrous metallurgy as a whole."[18] The actual situation belied his prognosis. Repression of specialists caused ferrous metallurgy to deteriorate. In 1939 less pig iron and steel were poured and less steel was rolled than in 1938. The chemical industry also suffered a virtual standstill in 1938–40, and the output of mineral fertilizers and soda remained at the 1937 level. The rate of growth in the production of motor-vehicle tires and rubber footwear fell off sharply. The total power capacity of turbines manufactured in 1940 merely equaled that of 1937. Automobile production reached almost 200,000 in 1937 and

[17] Stalin, *Sochineniia,* XIII, pp. 185–86.
[18] Quoted in *Voprosy istorii KPSS,* 1964, No. 11, p. 72.

declined in 1940 to 145,390. Tractor production dropped from 51,000 in 1937 to 31,600 in 1940. The production of engine bearings remained all but stationary, as did tree cuttings; the output of paper and cardboard declined. In three years (1938–40) the manufacture of cement increased by only 200,000 tons, while the production of lime and gypsum declined. There was a drop in the production of roofing materials and in window glass by almost 50 per cent. Textiles slowed down sharply; the targets for 1938–40 were not fulfilled. Sugar and many other products of the food industry declined. At the same time important branches of the defense industry developed slowly.[19]

After the war, industrial growth rates rose sharply. As early as 1947 most indices were back to prewar levels or above them. The country's great moral and political exaltation had a marked effect on the development of the national economy. Stalin, intoxicated by his glory and power, no longer went into the "petty details" of the economy, which helped industrial development, as did the rise of new, experienced managers during the war. In the last years of his life Stalin began to display a characteristic of many monarchs: neglect of affairs. A revealing episode was recounted to the June Plenum of the Central Committee in 1963. Not long before Stalin's death there was a meeting of the Council of Ministers to ratify the yearly plan. Usually Stalin did not preside in the Council of Ministers, but this time he took the chair, picked up the bundle of plan projects, and said: "Here is the plan. Who's against it?" The ministers sat staring and silent. "Then we accept it," Stalin declared. With that the meeting ended. When they had left, Stalin said: "Let's go and see a movie." And when he got to the film auditorium he said: "We fooled them good."

Stalin's Olympian isolation, his ignorance of conditions in the country, reached the point where he almost always caused a great deal of trouble when he intervened. The "great Stalin plan for the transformation of nature,"[20] the erection of tall buildings in Moscow, the beginning of the Turkmen Canal, the dozens of ostentatious and expensive pavilions at the Agricultural Exhibition in Moscow—these are a few examples of Stalin's blunders. They were intended to be grandiose monuments of his epoch, though they were utterly at variance with the real needs of the time. In 1949, to take another spectacular example, Stalin ordered the Salekhard-Igarka railway line, which was supposed to duplicate on land the Great Northern sea route. Over hundreds of kilometers through northern wasteland, rails were laid and settlements for railway workers were built, along with stations

[19] See the yearbooks, *Narodnoe khoziaistvo SSSR,* published by Tsentral'noe statisti-cheskoe upravlenie.

[20] *Ed.:* A plan to change the climate by planting millions of hectares of trees and reversing the flow of rivers.

and bridges. And then, when billions of rubles had been spent, the whole construction was stopped "because the railway was unnecessary." Meanwhile, because Stalin underestimated the importance of oil and gas, those vital industries developed very slowly. He intensified extraction of coal and peat and cutting of firewood, in a country with inexhaustible oil and gas resources. A by-product of this blunder was a slowdown in development of the chemical industry and the diversified technical progress dependent on it.

The standard of living of industrial workers improved only slowly in those years. The construction of new housing was almost at a standstill, while the urban population was markedly increasing. In general Stalin followed a labor policy based on compulsion. Workers were forbidden to change jobs and were punished severely for the smallest infraction, such as lateness. Workers' participation in management was not developed, and the role of the trade unions was weakened. All this was bound to have a negative effect on the productivity of labor and the industrial growth rate.

A recent article declares that Stalin "was a great revolutionary and government leader. Judging by many oral and printed reminiscences, we find that he knew how to take care of state funds and how to listen to specialists."[21] The reader may judge such declarations for himself.

4

STALIN CONSIDERED HIMSELF an expert on the nationality question, but he had a highly biased view of the different nationalities inhabiting the USSR. To some small nationalities he applied the criminal policy of mass deportation. The Kalmyks, Chechentsy, Ingushi, Karachaevtsy, Kurds, Balkartsy, Crimean Tartars, and Volga Germans were deported en masse from their national territories. In the Transcaucasian republics and the Crimea all Germans and many Greeks, Bulgars, and Turks were likewise torn away from their homes. All references to the disgraced nationalities disappeared from history books and encyclopedias, as if they had never existed. Hundreds of thousands of people, including women, children and old men, were removed in this way, their property confiscated; they were permitted to take only a few things with them. The author happened once to see a special train of nomadic Kurds being deported to the east. The dirty freight cars were packed with women and children, most of them weeping and wailing.

More than five million people were deported. Set down in wartime conditions in sparsely populated, undeveloped districts of Kazakhstan,

[21] V. Chivilikhin, "Zemlia v bede," *Moskva*, 1968, No. 2, p. 175.

Siberia, and Central Asia, hundreds of thousands died of hunger, cold, and disease. The Crimean Tartars, for example, lost around half their people, mostly old folks and children. Aside from the loss of life and the damage to morale, whose results are felt to this day, these deportations did serious economic damage to the districts from which the disgraced peoples were torn away.

The pretext was treason. Some portion of some of these nationalities collaborated with the fascist enemy. The same was true of the Russians, Ukrainians, and other Soviet nationalities. As has been noted, a "Russian Liberation Army" was created in Germany under Vlasov. Divisions of White Cossacks fought against the Red Army. In the Ukraine the followers of Bandera and Mel'nikov battled Soviet partisans. The Nazi forces included an SS division called Galichina and many other national legions, such as the Georgian and Latvian. So there was no reason to single out for repression certain nationalities in the Caucasus, the Crimea, and the Volga valley.

Nor was there any reason to deport the Soviet Germans, who had nothing in common with Nazi Germany. This has been recognized by a decree of the Presidium of the Supreme Soviet of August 24, 1964, which voided all unjust charges against the Soviet Germans. Mikoian, chairman of the Presidium, in a meeting with a delegation of Volga Germans on June 7, 1965, acknowledged their good behavior both during the war and afterwards.

In the immediate aftermath of the war the population of the Western Ukraine, West Belorussia, Bessarabia, and the Baltic republics were subjected to mass repression. To be sure, there were numerous underground counterrevolutionary groups and bands in these areas that had to be destroyed. But it was also necessary to distinguish between bandit leaders and disoriented people who were accidentally drawn into underground groups. The NKVD struck indiscriminately at all members of nationalist groups, and at their families as well. Thousands of peasants, from whom the terrorists took food by armed threats, were also repressed. Armenians living in Georgia were subjected to restrictions, deprived of their rights as Soviet citizens, and in many cases deported. The national rights of the Abkhazians were also restricted.

In general, exaggerated attention was paid to a person's nationality in the years of the cult. The line for nationality on passports and applications, though actually unnecessary, became very important. Signs of great-power chauvinism grew constantly stronger. The Russian element in the USSR was stressed to the point that a cult of the Russian nation was created. Orienting himself toward surviving Great Russian prejudices, Stalin increasingly replaced internationalism by a nationalist outlook. A symbol of the time was the absence in Moscow of a monument to Marx, to Engels, or even to Lenin, while a statue of Yurii Dolgorukii, a stupid and cruel twelfth-century prince, went up on Soviet Square, replacing the Obelisk of Freedom that had been erected at Lenin's suggestion.

At the same time the rights of the union republics were increasingly curtailed. As a reaction to this policy, and also as a result of the petty-bourgeois degeneration of some local cadres, there was a revival of nationalist feelings, which had almost vanished in the thirties. Manifestations of national dissension reappeared, especially in the Caucasus.

Great damage was done to the country's international reputation by the resurgence of anti-Semitism. In 1931 Stalin had declared that anti-Semitism, as an extreme form of racial chauvinism, was a dangerous survival of cannibalism.

> Anti-Semitism is dangerous for the workers as a false path, leading them off the correct road and taking them into the jungle. Therefore Communists, as consistent internationalists, cannot but be consistent and sworn enemies of anti-Semitism.[22]

Stalin forgot his own words. During the war he studiously ignored anti-Semitism. Every month, for example, the Chief Political Administration of the Soviet Army sent out to the Army's political *apparat* themes for political studies and lectures. Not once in the four years of the war was one lesson or one lecture devoted to anti-Semitism, its role in Nazi policy, or the Nazis' murder of almost the entire Jewish population of Europe.

After the war Stalin began to exclude all Jews from the Party and government *apparat,* covering his actions with talk about the counterrevolutionary activities of international Zionist organizations, ignoring the existence in foreign parts of many White Guard Russian, Ukrainian, Georgian, and other nationalist organizations. In 1948 almost the entire staff of the Jewish Antifascist Committee was arrested, though it had been set up during the war on the initiative of the Central Committee. Of course the members of this committee had had various contacts with Jewish nationalist organizations abroad. But there was nothing illegal about that; the Committee had been set up to establish such contacts.

After the arrest of the Committee members, anti-Jewish measures increased. For "prophylaxis" a limit was placed on the admission of children of Jews to many university faculties and to many other institutions of higher education. Jews were barred from the diplomatic service and were gradually squeezed out of the courts and the procu-

---

[22] *Sochineniia,* XIII, p. 28. The statement was made in response to a question from the Jewish Telegraph Agency in the United States.

ratorial agencies, except as defense lawyers. In most higher educational institutions, in scientific institutes, even in many factories, a secret quota was introduced for Jews, like the one that the tsarist government established at Pobedonostsev's request.[23] Even in the defense of academic dissertations Jews were admitted only as a certain percentage of Russians and other nationalities. Though Jews had played a great role in the Revolution and the Civil War—Sverdlov and many other members of Lenin's Central Committee were Jews—under Stalin in the forties and early fifties there was hardly a single Jew even among *raikom* secretaries. Anti-Semitism was plain to see in the campaign against "cosmopolitanism," which was used to close down Jewish schools, theaters, newspapers, and magazines.

Most anti-Jewish measures were not given publicity; they were usually carried out on oral instructions. But the anti-Semitic feelings of Stalin and his retinue, including Kaganovich, a Jew, were no secret. And then, in the last years of his life, Stalin cast aside almost all ideological screens and made anti-Semitism an open, obvious part of state policy. Everything indicated that he was beginning preparations for a mass deportation of Jews to remote districts. They were to be another one of the scapegoats that Stalinist despotism constantly sought to shed responsibility for its blunders.

At the end of 1952 the "doctors' case" was organized. Lidia Timashuk, a radiologist in the Kremlin Hospital and a secret agent of the MGB, wrote Stalin an obviously inspired letter, saying that she had observed many eminent doctors applying wrong methods of treatment.[24] Her letter alarmed some MGB officials, who feared that they might be accused of insufficient vigilance. The Minister of State Security (MGB), V. S. Abakumov, ordered the head of the Investigation Department, M. D. Riumin, not to investigate the letter and even arrested him. But Stalin ordered Riumin's release, dismissed Abakumov, and appointed S. D. Ignat'ev Minister of State Security. Moreover, Stalin took personal charge of the investigation of the Kremlin doctors' case, summoning and instructing the agents. "If you don't get the doctors' confessions," he told Ignat'ev, "you'll lose your head."

After that warning, the MGB went to work in earnest on the doctors. On January 13, 1953, the central newspapers reported the "unmasking" of an organization of wrecking doctors, including such major physicians as V. N. Vinogradov,[25] M. S. Vovsi, M. Kogan, B.

---

[23] *Ed.*: Konstantin Pobedonostsev, chief bureaucrat of the Russian Church and adviser to the last two tsars, is generally regarded as the *ne plus ultra* of reactionaries.

[24] She was given the Order of Lenin for her "heroic feat." After Stalin's death, and even after the XXth Party Congress, she continued to work as a radiologist in the Kremlin Hospital. When some old Bolsheviks learned of this, they refused to be X-rayed.

[25] According to Stalin's daughter, he had treated Stalin for more than twenty years.

Klin, B. G. Egorov, A. Feld'man, A. Grinshtein, Ia. Etinger, and G. Maiorov. They had allegedly murdered Zhdanov, shortened the life of Shcherbakov, and tried to do the same to many admirals and marshals. The report claimed that the doctors were hired agents of foreign intelligence, and that most of them were also connected with the international Jewish nationalist organization Joint.[26] The intermediaries between the doctors and foreign intelligence agencies were supposed to be the head physician of Botkin Hospital, Shimeliovich, and the actor S. M. Mikhoels, who had been murdered in Minsk in 1948.

This slanderous report marked the beginning of an anti-Semitic campaign that should have been unimaginable in the Soviet system. In medical schools, hospitals and many other institutions, thousands of Jewish specialists were expelled as a "prophylactic measure." Many university departments, hospitals, and laboratories lost as much as half their staffs. Many books by Jews were removed from the forthcoming lists of publishing houses. Even some medicines developed by the arrested doctors were banned, although they had won general recognition. In some places hooligan elements beat up Jews. This anti-Semitic campaign, which recalled the pogroms, aroused sharp protests abroad and disturbed the friends of the Soviet Union. Two leaders of the World Peace Council, Frédéric Joliot-Curie and Paul Robeson, were reported to have flown to Moscow to meet with Stalin, but he refused to see them.

Some historians still deny Stalin's anti-Semitism. Khrushchev tried to deny it. But hundreds of facts prove the contrary. The archives of the old Bolshevik E. P. Frolov contain a document entitled "The Anti-Semitism of J. V. Stalin," a compilation of the most obvious manifestations. Here is that list:

> Repeated statements that there were many Jews in the opposition groups. An attempt to represent the "united opposition" of Trotsky, Kamenev, and Zinoviev as a conspiracy of "three dissatisfied Jewish intellectuals" against the Party.
>
> His daughter Svetlana's divorce from her husband, Grigorii Moroz, a Jew, and of his son Vasilii from his Jewish wife.
>
> His rejection, at the beginning of the war, of a list of editors for front-line and Army newspapers, on the ground that many of the nominees were Jews.
>
> The termination of the only Jewish-language magazine published in Moscow.
>
> The closing of the Soviet-Polish border to Jews fleeing from the Nazis, and their death in the Warsaw ghetto.

[26] *Ed.:* The Joint Distribution Agency, a charitable organization.

The termination of the Jewish newspaper *Emes* [*Truth, Pravda*] at the end of 1948.

The termination of a Jewish paper in Birobidzhan.

The closing of the Jewish theater.

The liquidation of the Antifascist Jewish Committee at the end of 1948, and the arrest of its leaders.

The arrest of Jewish poets and prose writers who used Yiddish—Perets Markish, Kvitko, Fefer, Bergel'son, *et al.*

The murder of Mikhoels, and the ban on an investigation.

The creation of the [S. A.] Lozovskii case, and Lozovskii's arrest.

The campaign against cosmopolitanism.

The doctors' case.

The preparation for resettlement of Jews in a ghetto: the building of barracks, the preparation of an Appeal to the Jewish People by I. L. Mints, the collection of signatures on the Appeal by Ia. S. Khavinson, a meeting at the Stalingrad Tractor Factory and the adoption of a resolution to resettle the Jews.

The arrest of the leading Jewish officials in the Dynamo Factory on the charge of belonging to a Jewish counterrevolutionary organization.

The arrest of a group of leading Jewish officials in the Likhachev Factory and in the Metro Administration.

The purge of Jews from the Central Committee, the Moscow Committee, the Moscow City Committee, the *raion* committees, the newspaper *Pravda,* the MVD, the Procurator's office, the courts, military organizations, the Ministry of the Soviet Information Bureau, the Radio Committee, ministries, and other organizations.

The discharge of most Jewish political officials in the Army in the second half of the war.

The arrest of Jews who declared a desire to go to Israel.

The fabrication of the Slanský case on the charge of contacts with a Zionist organization.

Pogrom-type articles in *Kul'tura i Zhizn', Meditsinskii rabotnik, Pravda, Izvestiia,* and other central newspapers.

An anti-Semitic cover on *Krokodil* (Romm reading André Gide).[27]

The exposé of "rootless cosmopolitans" hiding under pseudonyms.[28]

K. Simonov's article against the campaign, and Sholokhov's article in defense of the campaign.

The fabrication of the "case" of the anti-Party group of theater critics (A. Gurvich, Iuzovskii, *et al.*) in January, 1949.

[27] *Ed.:* In the Cyrillic alphabet the name Gide is identical with *zhid,* a pejorative for Jew. M. I. Romm is a leading Soviet film director.

[28] *Ed.:* Frolov is referring to attacks on Jewish writers who used non-Jewish pen names.

The fabrication of the "case" of Jewish poets and film directors.

Percentage quotas for Jews entering institutions of higher education.

Restricted registration of Jews in big cities.

Denial of jobs to Jews.

The organization of pogroms in the Ukraine.

The list is far from complete. But it is enough to show that Stalin himself took the path that, in his own words, could lead only back to the jungle.

XIV

The Impact of Stalinism
on Art and Science

1

STALINISM DESTROYED thousands of creative people and established grotesque monopolies over all fields of culture. But the most serious cultural aftereffect was the perversion resulting within the arts and sciences, in their content.

The social sciences were especially vulnerable. As 'Abd al-Raḥmān al-Kawākibī wrote in the nineteenth century:

> A despot's knees do shake, from fear of learning connected with real life, such as theoretical thought, rationalist philosophy, the study of the rights of nations, civics, the detailed study of history, rhetoric, and other sciences. . . . A despot invariably feels wretched in the presence of a man who knows more than he, the despot. Therefore he does not tolerate the presence of a talented scholar and, if he must have [the services of a scholar] . . ., he chooses a cringing flatterer.[1]

And, though Stalin said that "no science can develop and prosper without conflict of opinions, without freedom of criticism," though he said that an "Arakcheev regime" in science is intolerable, in fact an Arakcheev regime was established in every social science without exception.[2] Because of his intervention, free discussion of scientific problems was virtually prohibited. The "discussions" of those years

---

[1] *Priroda despotizma i gibel'nost' poraboshcheniia* (Moscow, 1964), pp. 24–25.
[2] *Ed.:* The quotation is from Stalin's articles on linguistics, published in *Pravda*, June 20, July 4, and Aug. 2, 1950, and widely republished in many languages, English included. Arakcheev was an aide to Alexander I whose name became a byword for a martinet.

were almost always organized campaigns ending in the "rout" of dissidents (*inakomysliashchikh*).

In most of the social sciences Stalin alone had the right to make discoveries and draw major conclusions; everyone else was assigned the role of a popularizer or a commentator. Dogmatism, rote learning (*nachetnichestvo*), stagnation, and inertia were the results. Between 1946 and 1952 no less than six hundred books and pamphlets, in a total printing of twenty million copies, were devoted to Stalin's speeches and articles.

The deification of Stalin, the creation of stories about his infallibility and omniscience, generated a quasi-religious perception of reality in the scholarly community. The truth was not what corresponded to facts, to empirical research, but what Comrade Stalin had declared to be true. Quotations from "the classics of Marxism-Leninism," and above all from the newly canonized classics of Stalin, became the main proof that a given proposition was true. Inconvenient facts were juggled, distorted, or simply ignored.

The study of history was already near a standstill in the early thirties. What happened thereafter is well described in a recent work on Soviet historiography.[3]

Toward the mid-thirties the possibility of scholarly investigation of contemporary history was reduced to a minimum. The increasingly limited amount of publishable information no longer permitted a scholarly analysis of industrial and agricultural development. Critical verification of this information became impossible. The investigator was deprived of information about the standard of living in the city and the countryside, the social structure, and many other aspects of sociopolitical life. The accessible area of archival sources was sharply limited.[4] At the same time the fight against "vulgar sociologism," "the antihistorical school" of M. N. Pokrovskii, conditioned the historian against independent theoretical work. Theoretical analysis and generalization became the monopoly of one man—J. V. Stalin. . . .

The biggest event in the development of the historiography of Soviet society was the publication in 1938 of *The History of the CPSU; Short Course.* The extremely one-sided and schematic conception of this book was subordinated in the final analysis to the task of exalting and glorifying Stalin, validating and justifying all his actions. . . . The truly outstanding triumphs and achievements of the Soviet people, of the Communist Party, were recounted in a panegyrical spirit, were represented as one undiluted triumph, with difficulties, mistakes, and shortcomings virtually excluded. The

[3] *Ed.:* Medvedev does not give a precise citation. He may have in mind the item cited below, p. 518, n. 58.

[4] Note by Medvedev: In 1938 all major archives came under NKVD administration. The publication of documents on the history of Soviet society virtually ended.

narrative itself . . . was accomplished by stringing together quotations from Stalin's works or paraphrases of them. . . . The final
chapters of the *Short Course,* which reflect most fully the characteristic features of the ideology of Stalin's cult, are a monstrous
blend of whitewashing and mudslinging, of panegyrics and slander.
Since this book was not meant to give a scholarly elucidation and
explanation of the historical process, it was written in the form of
expounding axioms, which required no proof and did not have to
be understood but memorized, learned by heart. The moment the
Short Course appeared it was proclaimed "an encyclopedia of basic
knowledge in the field of Marxism-Leninism," "a means of heightening political vigilance," . . . the sole and official "guide to Party
history," "permitting no willful interpretations." . . . Historical
science was denied the opportunity to examine the phenomena of
social life, to analyze facts creatively. The loss of many historians
in the mass repression of the thirties and the postwar period also
left its mark. . . . The result of all this was a sharp drop in the
number of works on the history of Soviet society, and a shift from
scholarly research to mass agitation, at best to works of popularization.

Almost all the previous achievements of Soviet historians were
canceled out. The value of source material was put in doubt; original
sources ceased to be studied. Stalin and his obedient historians were
brazenly voluntaristic in writing the history of the USSR and the
CPSU, willfully twisting facts and crossing out inconvenient names.
For example, the *Short Course* declared that the slogan "Make all
kolkhozniki prosperous," which Stalin formulated in 1933, was realized by 1937. All the officials who had fallen victim to repression
were pictured as agents of foreign powers who had been plotting
against the Soviet state "for twenty years." No proofs or arguments
were given, only invective and labels: "Trotskyite-Bukharinite out-
laws," "a band of murderers and spies" "White Guard insects," "useless trash," "fascist lackeys," "the dregs of the human race," and so
on.[5]

The short biography of Stalin published after the war was an
equally glaring example of fraudulence. Indeed, it is impossible to
list all the distortions contained in this little book. Here is only one
example:

In the second half of 1911 the Petersburg period of Comrade
Stalin's revolutionary activity began. On September 6, 1911, Comrade Stalin illegally left Vologda for Petersburg. In Petersburg

---

[5] Thirty million copies of this book were published in the first ten years of its life,
despite four years of war and such economic problems as the paper shortage. See
G. Malenkov, *Doklad na soveshchanii predstavitelei nekotorykh kompartii v
Pol'she v 1947* (Moscow, 1947), p. 27.

Comrade Stalin made contact with the Petersburg Party organization; he directed its attention to the fight against the Menshevik liquidationists and the Trotskyites, to uniting and strengthening the Bolshevik organizations of Petersburg. On September 9, 1911, Comrade Stalin was arrested in Petersburg and exiled to Vologda province.[6]

If Stalin left Vologda on September 6, he could have arrived in Petersburg no earlier than the seventh, and on the ninth he was already arrested. In those two days, his biographers would have us believe, he managed not only to make contact with some Petersburg comrades, but to direct, unite, and strengthen them.

Such crude falsification became a matter of course. Zhdanov, for for example, told a conference[7] that the exiled Chechentsy and Ingushi had been the chief obstacles to friendship among the North Caucasian peoples as far back as the Civil War period. Some photographs allegedly portraying Stalin's life were pure montage. Genuinely historical photos were subjected to careful retouching, so that inconvenient people would disappear. Some figures were even removed from the negatives. Stalin's relationship with Lenin was transformed into a tale that "surpasses all the most touching fables of the ancients concerning human friendship."[8]

And all the time that Stalin's obedient historians were creating these brazen fabrications, Stalin was making public attacks on vulgarizing, oversimplifying, and varnishing history. Those were the years when it was standard form to denounce the thesis ascribed to Pokrovskii and his school: "History is politics projected into the past."

Economics was also in deep trouble. The central problems of this discipline, especially those involved in the political economy of socialism, were hardly worked on. The publication of books on concrete issues was sharply curtailed, many research institutes were closed, scholarly discussions were stopped. For twenty years the country had no textbook on political economy. Agricultural economics was particularly degraded. Almost no work was done on such fundamental topics as agricultural costs and prices, accounting (*khozraschet*) and profitability (*rentabel'nost*), increasing the marketed proportion

[6] Institut Marksa-Engel'sa-Lenina, *Iosif Vissarionovich Stalin. Kratkaia biografiia* (Moscow, 1947), pp. 48–49. The authors of this book were G. F. Aleksandrov, M. B. Mitin, P. N. Pospelov, *et al. Ed.:* There is an English translation: Marx-Engels-Lenin Institute, *Joseph Stalin: A Political Biography* (New York, 1949).

[7] It was a conference of musical critics and composers, called by the Central Committee to criticize V. I. Muradeli's opera "The Great Friendship." *Ed.:* An abridged translation of Zhdanov's speech can be found in his *Essays on Literature, Philosophy, and Music* (New York, 1950).

[8] S. Petrov wrote this in *Pravda*, Apr. 24, 1950.

(*tovarnost'*) of agricultural output, payment of labor, differential land rent, and so on. Such a vital branch of economics as the science of management was neglected, while the administration of the economy became increasingly petrified, overcentralized, bureaucratic paper shuffling. Systems to encourage workers by material incentives were poorly developed. Economics was cut off from the natural sciences, from concrete planning work, from statistics. A large part of statistical materials was classified as top secret. Thus the science of economics had little contact with economic reality; theory was not developed but simply decreed.

Jurisprudence also deteriorated, with Vyshinskii as the dictatorial plenipotentiary. He it was who established the principles that a court cannot aspire to absolute truth and must accordingly be satisfied with some degree of probability; that evaluation of evidence is based only on inner conviction; that the law is an algebraic formula, which is corrected in the process of application by the judge. Vyshinskii even suggested that the law should not be applied at all, if it has "lagged behind life." "We must remember Stalin's teaching," he told a meeting of the Party *aktiv* in the USSR Procuracy in March, 1937, "that there are periods, there are moments in the life of a society, particularly our society, when laws turn out to be obsolete and must be set aside."[9] It was Vyshinskii who established that an accomplice must bear responsibility for all the activity of the group he belongs to, even though he had nothing to do with the commission of a crime and did not give his consent to it. In cases involving crimes against the state Vyshinskii held that the confession of the accused was sufficient proof. He cynically declared that a prisoner who denied his guilt had to prove himself innocent. Completely ignoring the educative and organizing function of the law, he reduced it to mere compulsion. In the same way he gave "scientific" justification to the new regime in the camps and prisons.

Thus the science that should have defended legality was converted into a pseudoscientific defense of Stalinist willfulness. It must also be borne in mind that Stalin not only ignored the basic laws of the state, including the Constitution. The system of legislation was itself perverted. At Stalin's first suggestion the legislators would pass any law, even if it contradicted the fundamental norms of socialist society.

In philosophy, Stalin's little pamphlet *On Dialectical and Historical Materialism* was proclaimed the ultimate classic of Marxism-Leninism. In fact it held back the development of real philosophical inquiry for many years. Problems in the theory of knowledge, logic, and the methodology of science were hardly studied by Soviet philoso-

[9] Quoted in *Voprosy istorii KPSS*, 1964, No. 2, p. 19.

phers. Not progress but regress was the rule in many areas of the history of philosophy, particularly in the study of German idealism. The richness of Lenin's *Philosophical Notebooks* was ignored; indeed they were excluded from his collected works.[10]

In the field of historical materialism, concrete sociological investigations were halted in favor of expounding general theoretical schemes. Philosophers did not analyze the data of science; they usually limited themselves to the rehearsal of examples and illustrations chosen to fit predetermined stereotypes. Thus philosophy was transformed into scholasticism. In much the same way many philosophers violated Lenin's program for a union of dialectical materialism with natural science. Theories that they found inconvenient or simply incomprehensible were declared idealistic or metaphysical. This pasting of derogatory labels on concrete scientific trends did great harm not only to philosophy but also to natural science. Many scientists were automatically classified as proponents of reactionary ideology. Major scientists were driven out of science and even physically destroyed. Some leading philosophers pasted the label of idealistic philosophy on the theory of relativity, the study of genes, the chemical theory of resonance, cybernetics, and mathematical logic. All this created a gulf between the philosophy of dialectical materialism and natural science, with effects that can be felt to this day.

Pedagogy also suffered during the cult. On the pretext of combating "distortions," some top officials began to repudiate all the achievements of the twenties and early thirties. I. G. Lobov, for example, head of the School Sector of the Central Committee, declared in 1936 that every aspect of Soviet education had been corrupted by the theory that the schools should wither away.[11] The only evidence he could give consisted of quotations from old publications by a couple of educational theorists, V. N. Shul'gin and M. V. Krupenina, who had not been in any influential positions since 1931. P. V. Rudnev, Krupskaia's secretary and a former official in the Commissariat of Education, has described the real state of affairs in 1936:

> In essence an entire period in the history of Soviet pedagogy was being canceled out—the period of its formation, when the basic principles of Communist education were worked out, a Soviet system of preschool education and polytechnical schools joining labor and learning. . . . That was a period when the Communist chil-

[10] In 1952 V. Kruzhkov reported to Stalin the plan for completing the fourth edition of Lenin's *Collected Works.* When Stalin saw the *Philosophical Notebooks,* and a number of other things, in the plan, he remarked with irritation: "Don't stretch it too far, don't stretch the Leninist heritage too far." Kruzhkov took the hint, and excluded a number of Lenin's works. Recounted by T. Bachelis.

[11] *Ed.:* Medvedev quotes at length from "Lobov's pamphlet (Sept., 1936)," without giving its title.

dren's movement was created, when enormous political and educational work was done among the teachers, when old specialists were drawn into the building of a new system, when a rapprochement was effected between them and the Soviet regime, and the great mass of bourgeois and petty-bourgeois pedagogical theories was re-evaluated in the light of Marxist theory. It was a period of bold creativity . . ., of passionate arguments . . ., of training new young pedagogical cadres, of boldly promoting the best representatives of the teachers to leading posts in administration and teacher training. It was the period . . . of Lunacharskii, Krupskaia, Bubnov, Skrypnik . . ., of the founding of pedagogical journals not only in Moscow, Leningrad, and Kharkov but also in the provinces (Novosibirsk, Sverdlovsk, Gorky, Rostov, Ivanovo, and so on), when there was a large methodological literature, not only of a didactic nature but also describing the actual experience of Soviet schoolwork in the period 1918–36.

The assessment of this period's pedagogy in the Central Committee resolution of 1936 promoted distortions concerning educational theory and practice that are of more than historical importance to us.[12]

The hue and cry about "excesses" signified the curtailment of polytechnical education, a tacit abandonment of the Leninist principle of combining study with productive work. The very modest program of this sort, which had been decreed by the Central Committee in 1931–32 but never really put into practice, was now abandoned. The 1933–34 curricula in physics, chemistry, biology, mathematics, and geography virtually ignored practical applications in industry and agriculture. At the same time labor training was increasingly confined to work in the school's shop and garden. Contacts with factories and farms were weakened, and attempts to give pupils direct experience of production were abandoned.

In 1937 Krupskaia sent a vigorous protest to the Orgburo. She recalled how Marx and Lenin had insisted on the union of mental and physical labor in the educational process, in order to train many-sided individuals.

On this issue we fought with teachers of the old gymnasia, who scorn labor. . . . In recent years the teaching of labor in the schools has been reduced to nothing. Some sort of handicraft "labor processes" are taught; labor is isolated from study more than ever. . . . In a few days the question of abolishing the teaching of labor in the schools, of closing down school shops, will be voted on in the

[12] Rudnev, "K voprosu o vosstanovlenii istoricheskoi pravdy v pedagogicheskoi nauke." *Ed.:* This memorandum, as Medvedev calls it, seems to be an unpublished manuscript. The Central Committee resolution of 1936 refers to a decree of July 4 condemning "pedology." See *Direktivy i postanovleniia sovetskogo pravitel'stva o narodnom obrazovanii* (Moscow, 1947), I, pp. 190–93.

Central Committee. *Not the reorganization of labor, but its liquidation.* This question was not discussed with engineers, agronomists, workers, collective farmers, young people. Only old teachers, instructors of various subjects, have been consulted.[13]

Stalin and Zhdanov ignored Krupskaia's letter. Under their leadership the schools were gradually transformed into "Soviet gymnasia." Not only was labor completely abolished; many long-forgotten features of the old gymnasium were revived, such as the teaching of Latin and separate schools for boys and girls. Thus basic principles of Communist education were perverted, a scornful attitude was fostered toward physical labor and toward laboring people.

2

THE SOCIAL SCIENCES were also damaged by surreptitious efforts to make Stalin seem greater than Lenin. Stalin hypocritically declared: "I am only a pupil of Lenin, and the goal of my life is to be a worthy pupil of him."[14] In reality Stalin was envious of Lenin's place in history and tried to appropriate it for himself.

As early as 1920, while speaking at the celebration of Lenin's fiftieth birthday, Stalin unexpectedly remarked—"no one," he said, "has yet spoken" about this—that "Comrade Lenin acknowledged his shortcomings in matters of enormous importance." He portrayed Lenin as a theorist with a poor idea of what was going on in the country, who gave the Party incorrect instructions at the most critical moment before the October Revolution. Twisting the facts, Stalin claimed that he, Stalin, had seen more clearly than Lenin the "pitfalls and abysses on our way." He made it seem that Lenin, who was hiding in the fall of 1917, had left the armed insurrection to the "practical leaders," presumably Stalin above all. He pictured Lenin as saying "Yes, you were right," when he emerged from hiding to greet the victorious Congress of Soviets.

In 1946, when Stalin's collected works were being published, the part of this speech that dealt with Lenin's mistakes was made significantly stronger. B. V. Iakovlev has counted more than a hundred changes that Stalin made in the text. He inserted, for example, this extremely misleading remark: "Despite all Lenin's demands, we did not listen to him; we kept to the path of strengthening the Soviets and arrived at the Congress of Soviets of October 25, at a successful insurrection."[15]

[13] Quoted in *Uchitel'skaia gazeta*, Feb. 20, 1962.
[14] Stalin, *Sochineniia*, XIII, p. 105.
[15] *Ibid.*, IV, p. 317. The original text was published in the *sbornik, 50-letie V. I. Lenina* (Moscow, 1920).

The picture of two chiefs in the October Revolution finally reached the point of making Stalin seem to have been Number 1. On the twentieth anniversary of the Revolution, *Pravda* asserted that the armed insurrection in Petrograd was prepared by the Central Committee, "headed by Stalin." A contemporaneous historical journal spelled out this fable in detail, and assigned Stalin a role in the Civil War far more important than Lenin's.[16] After 1945, the fable of the two chiefs was extended to all the periods of Party history, beginning with the Revolution of 1905.[17] A number of authors even claimed that Stalin, together with Lenin, had created the Party, had always shared the leadership with him, and that Lenin, in the last years of his life, was greatly influenced by Stalin. Kalinin, to take a notable example, wrote: ". . . Comrade Stalin together with Lenin created, built, and strengthened our Party. With Lenin he led the Party, the revolutionary movement, and the October armed insurrection."[18]

Stalin arbitrarily decided what could be published not only *about* Lenin but even *by* him. The recent *Complete Works* of Lenin—the fifth edition—contain many "new" documents, letters and articles that had been lying in the safes of the Institute of Marxism-Leninism, and sometimes in Stalin's personal files. Some items that had been included in the second or third editions, published in the twenties and thirties, were excluded from the fourth edition, published in the forties and fifties. Reminiscences of Lenin were blocked from publication, and a scholarly biography of him was made impossible to write or publish.[19] Libraries were obliged to get rid of reminiscences not only by Bolsheviks who had been proclaimed "enemies of the people"—such as V. I. Nevskii, V. A. Antonov-Ovseenko, and G. I. Lomov—but also by Krupskaia, V. D. Bonch-Bruevich, and Lunacharskii.

Kaganovich was especially zealous in this process of elevating Stalin over Lenin. "We all say Leninism, Leninism," he remarked one day at Stalin's dacha; "but Lenin has been gone for a long time. Stalin

[16] See *Istoricheskii zhurnal*, 1937, No. 10, especially pp. 24–26, 66, for articles by A. Fokht and M. Lur'e. See also Stalin's *Kratkaia biografiia*, pp. 82–83, for Stalin's role in the Civil War.

[17] See, e.g., I. Riabtsev, *Razrabotka V. I. Leninym i I. V. Stalinym ideologicheskikh osnov marksistskoi partii, 1902–1905 gody* (Moscow, 1951).

[18] Kalinin, *K shestidesiatiletiu so dnia rozhdeniia tovarishcha Stalina* (Moscow, 1939), p. 89.

[19] On August 5, 1938, Marietta Shaginian's novel *Bilet po istorii, chast' I: Sem'ia Ul'ianovykh* (Moscow, 1938), was the subject of a CC resolution, and on Aug. 26, 1947, *Shest' let s Leninym; vospominaniia lichnogo shofera*, by S. K. Gil', received similar treatment in the CC Secretariat. These books were published only after the XXth Party Congress revoked the resolutions. (See *Spravochnik partiinogo rabotnika* [Moscow, 1957], p. 364.) In the period while the resolutions were in force, they virtually blocked publication of works about Lenin.

has done more than Lenin and we should talk about 'Stalinism.' We've had enough about Leninism."[20]

At the beginning of the thirties Stalin objected to a proposal by Gorky and Iaroslavskii for a biography of himself. "The time has not yet come to write such a biography," was his oracular remark. In 1937, when the Children's Publishing House (*Detgiz*) produced a book of "Stories about Stalin's Childhood" and sent it to Stalin for approval, he sent *Detgiz* the following letter:

> February 16, 1938
>
> I am strongly opposed to the publication of "Stories about Stalin's Childhood." The book is filled with a mass of factual distortions, untruths, exaggerations, and undeserved encomia. The author has been misled by lovers of fairy tales—by liars (perhaps "honest liars") and timeservers. A pity for the author, but facts remain facts. But that isn't the main thing. The main thing is that the book has the tendency to inculcate in Soviet people (and people in general) the cult of the personality of chiefs and infallible heroes. That is dangerous, harmful. The theory of "heroes and the mob" is not Bolshevik but Socialist Revolutionary. The Socialist Revolutionaries say that "Heroes make a people, turn it from a mob into a people." "The people makes heroes," reply the Bolsheviks. This book is grist for the Socialist Revolutionaries' mill, it will harm our general Bolshevik cause. My advice is to burn the book.
>
> J. STALIN[21]

In the postwar period Stalin abandoned such hypocritical disclaimers. In the late forties he not only endorsed the proposal for a biography of himself but closely followed the writing of it, inserting many handwritten remarks in the manuscript, especially where he found insufficient praise for himself. Some of these tributes to himself were read to the XXth Party Congress by Khrushchev. The most astonishing was the solemn declaration that "Stalin did not permit himself a trace of self-importance, conceit, or vanity."

Stalin's seventieth birthday was celebrated with unbelievable pomp. One major writer declared that people of the future would call Stalin's time "the epoch of justice," and might choose his birthday as the beginning of a new calendar, calling it "the Day of Thanksgiving" of the Year One.[22] Two months later another writer put these reverent words in the same newspaper:

[20] The ridiculous lengths to which Stalin's flatterers were willing to go can be seen in a poem, published by *Komsomol'skaia pravda* in the early fifties, in which Stalin is given credit for GOELRO, the plan for the electrification of Russia. It is also noteworthy that the number of books by Stalin printed during the period of the cult was ten times greater than the books of Marx and Engels, and two and a half times greater than Lenin's.

[21] *Voprosy istorii*, 1953, No. 11, p. 21.

[22] *Pravda*, Dec. 18, 1949.

. . . If you meet with difficulties in your work, or suddenly doubt your abilities, think of him, of Stalin, and you will find the confidence you need. If you feel tired in an hour when you should not— think of him, of Stalin, and your work will go well. If you are seeking a correct decision, think of him, of Stalin, and you will find that decision. . . . "Stalin said"—that means the people think so. "The people said"—that means Stalin thought so.[23]

Stalin himself, the XXth Party Congress was told, chose the text of the Soviet national anthem, which said not a word about the Communist Party but contained a paean to Stalin: "Stalin has trained us to faith in the people, to labor, to great deeds, inspired has he us." For a long time the Museum of the Revolution in Moscow was turned into a museum of gifts to Stalin.

While he was still alive new monuments were constantly being raised to him all over the country. On July 2, 1951, Stalin signed a decree of the Council of Ministers providing for the erection of a monumental statue of himself on the Volga-Don Canal, and on September 4 of the same year he ordered thirty-three tons of bronze for it. His megalomania grew along with his power and glory. In the thirties he demonstratively wore a simple soldier's coat; now he never parted with a marshal's uniform. He even took the title of Generalissimo, previously borne by only three men in Russian history: Peter the Great's favorite, A. D. Men'shikov; Prince Anton Ulrich, the consort of Empress Anna; and A. V. Suvorov. In foreign countries, during Stalin's lifetime, the title was pinned to Chiang Kai-shek and Francisco Franco.

3

TODAY IT IS QUITE OBVIOUS that Stalin left a poor theoretical legacy. The list of theoretical problems that he helped to solve is small. On the other hand, there is a long list of important problems that should have been solved in "Stalin's era" but were not.

Stalin's theoretical works can be divided into three main groups. The first consists of his popularizations, such as *The Foundations of Leninism*. These works contain little that was original. They are largely commentary on quotations from the writings of Marx, Engels, and Lenin. It can be argued that they are superb popularizations,[24] but

[23] *Pravda*, Feb. 17, 1950.
[24] An eminent Soviet historian, for example, told a June, 1965, conference in Kiev that he still considers Stalin's *On Dialectical and Historical Materialism* to be a classic popularization of Marxism.

careful study reveals their weakness. Stalin did not try to raise the masses to an understanding of genuine theory; he usually reduced the theory to simplified schemes. Indeed, he was a master of that art. He constantly promoted simple slogans and formulas that would appeal to the masses, without caring whether these slogans corresponded to reality. In this respect Stalin's actions reveal an experienced demagogue; here we see one of the main reasons for his success. Many other demagogues have used similar methods. Hitler once said: "Political problems are complicated and confused. . . . I . . . simplified them and reduced them to the simplest terms. The masses understood that and followed me."[25]

It is also noteworthy that Stalin borrowed much of his commentary—without acknowledgment. His prerevolutionary article on the national question is a good example. Endlessly acclaimed during the years of the cult as *the* fundamental work on the national question, it was in fact merely part of a body of Marxist writings on the problem. Lenin called it "a very good article,"[26] but he spoke just as highly of a number of other articles and pamphlets on the national question in that period, for example those of O. N. Lola (Stepaniuk) and P. I. Stuchka (Vetern). In retrospect the historical significance of Stalin's contribution shrinks to small proportions. Iu. I. Semenov,[27] for example, has shown the difference between Stalin's analysis, which rests on an abstract definition of *"a nation,"* and the genuinely Leninist approach, which rests on concrete appraisal of a real national *movement*. What is more, the characteristics by which Stalin defined "a nation" were obviously borrowed, without acknowledgement, from Karl Kautsky and Otto Bauer. Stalin merely changed the wording a bit, turning national character, for example, into "the psychological constitution (*sklad*), manifesting itself in a community of culture."[28]

The origins of Stalin's *Foundations of Leninism* are even more revealing. Delivered as lectures at Sverdlovsk University in early April, 1924, they appeared in *Pravda* during April and May of the same year. At that very time Stalin had the manuscript of F. A. Ksenofontov's treatise *Lenin's Doctrine of Revolution*. Ksenofontov, who had been helping Stalin in theoretical matters, was sent to work in Tashkent soon after Stalin read his manuscript. Rumors circulated that Ksenofontov was protesting Stalin's appropriation of many formu-

[25] Quoted in Iu. A. Levada, *Sotsial'naia priroda religii* (Moscow, 1965), p. 235.
[26] Lenin, *Polnoe Sobranie*, XLVIII, p. 169.
[27] See his article "Iz istorii teoreticheskoi razrabotki V. I. Leninym national'nogo voprosa," *Narody Azii i Afriki*, 1966, No. 4, p. 121 and *passim*.
[28] Stalin, *Sochineniia*, II, p. 296. In this volume of his collected works, which was prepared for publication in 1946, Stalin changed his definition somewhat, but as Semenov points out, the new one is no better than the old, for a simple list of characteristics cannot be a successful definition of "a nation."

lations. These rumors were soon substantiated by the appearance of Ksenofontov's book. The author took pains in the preface to specify the exact date and place of writing:

> Sverdlovsk University, October-November, 1923. The comparatively late publication [1925] is due to the fact that the manuscript was first reviewed by M. N. Liadov, and then was in the possession of Comrade Stalin for final review (April–June).[29]

The preface was dated January, 1925, and, to drive home the fact of priority, the date of completion of the main text was put at the end of the book: March 13, 1924.

A simple collation of Stalin's and Ksenofontov's book shows their great similarity in organization, in exposition of central ideas, in basic definitions. Ksenofontov rejected the notion that Leninism is simply "Marxism in practice," or "the Marxism of Russian reality." He insisted that Leninism is much more: "the science of the revolutionary politics of the working class in conditions of imperialism, i.e., the theory and practice of the proletarian revolution."[30] Stalin rejected the same notions and came to the same conclusion:

> Leninism is Marxism of the era of imperialism and of the proletarian revolution. More precisely, Leninism is the theory and tactics of the proletarian revolution in general, the theory and tactics of the dictatorship of the proletariat in particular.[31]

Stalin also echoed Ksenofontov on the connection between the national question in colonial countries and the proletarian revolution in advanced countries.[32] Their analyses of the dictatorship of the proletariat are also strikingly similar. In a private letter to Ksenofontov in July, 1924, Stalin gave him some credit for helping prepare *The Foundations of Leninism*. But in 1926, when Ksenofontov asked for Stalin's permission to cite the letter, Stalin refused.[33] This disagreement over priority ended in the typical Stalinist manner. Ksenofontov was arrested in 1937 and killed during interrogation.

The second group of Stalin's works deals with concrete problems of socialist construction and with theoretical issues that had not previously confronted Marxism. Here again, originality is notable by its absence. Propositions that were hailed as great discoveries by propagandists of the cult were actually trivial platitudes. But it must be granted that Stalin was a master at making these platitudes seem important. And once again many of these supposedly new insights

---

[29] F. Ksenofontov, *Uchenie Lenina o revoliutsii* (Moscow, 1925).
[30] *Ibid.*, p. 16.
[31] Stalin, *Sochineniia*, VI, pp. 70–71.
[32] Compare pp. 82–83 of Ksenofontov with Stalin, *Sochineniia*, VI, pp. 141–43.
[33] Stalin, *ibid.*, IX, p. 152.

were unacknowledged borrowings. For example, he was long credited with the comprehensive criticism of mechanistic and idealistic distortions of Marxist philosophy. In fact he merely appended a highly oversimplified summary to a prolonged discussion. Likewise his famous six conditions of economic construction were merely a summation of the debates at a June, 1931, conference of business managers. All six conditions had been presented both separately and together by many managers, both at the conference and in a number of preliminary documents—for example in the report of one of the Central Committee's commissions, which had investigated the factories of the Moscow region.[34]

The same was true of Stalin's "discovery" of socialist realism. Iu. B. Borev has shown that the search for the term was a large-scale collective enterprise in the late twenties and early thirties. Some writers suggested "proletarian realism" as the best description of Soviet literature. Mayakovsky preferred "tendentious realism." In May, 1932, an editorial in *Literaturnaia gazeta* chose "revolutionary socialist realism." In June, I. Kulik, the leader of the Ukrainian writers' organization, gave a clear explanation to a meeting in Kharkhov:

> If a writer gives a truthful reflection of reality, then he is essentially a realist, and his method is realistic. If he is a writer who supports the platform of the Soviet regime, then that means he is a revolutionary writer, and his method is revolutionary. If this writer tries to participate in the building of socialism, to create a socialist literature, then his method will be socialist. Thus, comrades, the method which should guide us all ought to be called "revolutionary-socialist realism."[35]

About forty-five people met at Gorky's house on October 26, 1932, and talked about socialist realism. Stalin, who spoke at the end of the meeting, was simply repeating what many had already said when he called the method of Soviet literature "socialist realism." An obvious lack of originality also marked Stalin's overdue criticism of N. Ia. Marr's school of linguistics. Long before 1950, when Stalin published his articles on linguistics, the ideas he endorsed had been repeatedly argued by Marr's opponents, including Academician V. V. Vinogradov, who gave Stalin much help in preparing the articles.[36]

The *History of the CPSU: Short Course* was written by a special brigade, but it was endlessly referred to as a book by Stalin. In 1938 the director of the Museum of the Revolution, M. Samoilov, a former Bolshevik deputy to the national Duma, wrote to Stalin requesting

[34] For Stalin's formulation, see *ibid.,* XIII, pp. 51–80.
[35] Quoted in Borev, *Vvedenie v estetiku* (Moscow, 1965), pp. 231–32.
[36] See above, p. 498.

some pages of the manuscript for display in the museum. Stalin returned the letter with the following reply scrawled across it:

> Comrade Samoilov, I didn't think that in your old age you would occupy yourself with such trifles. If the book is already published in millions of copies, why do you want the manuscript? To put your mind at rest, I burned all the manuscripts.
>
> J. STALIN.

In other words, he had burned manuscripts that never existed.

Neither was Stalin the author of the Constitution, though it was called the "Stalin Constitution." A large collective worked it up, including Bukharin and Iakovlev, who were subsequently killed. A commission also worked on the Model Charter for collective farms, which was also called the "Stalin Charter." The theory of constant and variable factors of warfare, which was advertised as Stalin's greatest discovery in military science, was strikingly similar to the views of General Samokhin. Working in headquarters at the beginning of the war, he was told by Stalin to make a comparative analysis of the military potential of Germany and the USSR. The resulting paper was called "Constant Factors of War."[37]

The third group of Stalin's works do contain some original thoughts. He has far less to his credit than other eminent colleagues of Lenin, and most of that was written before 1930. Of course, it would be wrong to reject these works just because they belong to Stalin. (By the same token, the many valuable theoretical works of Bukharin and other former leaders of the opposition should not be rejected.) But it must be said that Stalin's few original works contain more incorrect than correct views. The list of his theoretical achievements is short, the list of his theoretical errors is long.

A common source of Stalin's theoretical errors was his basic limitations: poor theoretical background, inadequate knowledge, and his innate penchant for the schematization of reality. He frequently took some view of Lenin's, which was valid in a bygone historical setting, and turned it into an absolute law for all times. His approach to theory was wrong in essence. He did not derive theoretical positions from concrete reality; he forced theory to fit his wishes, subordinated it to transient situations—in a word, he politicized theory. On top of that he inculcated in Party cadres and scholarly circles a servile attitude toward theory. No one except Stalin could challenge or correct a theoretical proposition in the Marxist-Leninist classics. This law applied especially to his own propositions. They could only be slavishly repeated, without the slightest alteration.

Only a few examples can be given here, and even those without

[37] Reported by V. Novobranets.

the detailed analysis they deserve. As early as 1936, long before the USSR had begun to overtake the capitalist countries economically, Stalin declared that it had already built the economic basis of a socialist society. Only "a much easier task" remained: to crown this base with the corresponding superstructures. In fact the creation of socialist superstructures, especially socialist morality, is an exceptionally long and difficult job, even more difficult than taking factories from capitalists. Yet Stalin, only three years later, told the XVIIIth Party Congress that socialism had already been completely built. In 1938–39 it was dangerously premature to make such a claim. Similarly with the cultural revolution.[38] Stalin told the XVIIIth Congress that it had been accomplished since the XVIIth Congress in 1934. As L. M. Zak has shown in his dissertation, this compression of the cultural revolution into a few years tended to arrogate to Stalin alone command of the basic cultural transformations.

On the problem of class struggle in the USSR Stalin was inconsistent. In 1934 he set the goal of liquidating classes by fulfilling the second Five-Year Plan. And, in the 1936 interview with the American newspaper publisher Roy Howard, he said that classes had been liquidated. On the other hand, he insisted that the class struggle would intensify as the country moved toward the complete triumph of socialism. In fact, the class struggle should have died down, if only because the victory of socialism meant the complete liquidation of exploiting classes in the USSR.

The stages and functions of the Soviet state were all mixed up by Stalin. According to his oversimplified scheme, the organization of the economy and the transformation of culture were not seriously developed functions of the state in its first stage.[39] The function of safeguarding socialist property also appeared only in the second stage. He limited the external functions of the Soviet state to military defense against foreign attack. He did not point out such important functions as the struggle for peace and equal rights among the nations, or the development of economic and cultural relations among nations.

The periodization of the October Revolution that Stalin gave in his speech "Trotskyism or Leninism," subsequently adopted by Soviet historians, was also wrong and tendentious.[40] Nor can one agree with

[38] *Ed.:* The cultural revolution signified the effort to create "red culture" in place of "bourgeois culture"; that is, to transform the intelligentsia from its characteristic hostility or neutrality vis-à-vis the Soviet regime to an attitude of reverent eagerness to be of service.

[39] *Ed.:* The point here, as in the matter of the cultural revolution, is that Stalin's policy made a sharp turn from considerable laissez-faire in the twenties to an extreme of state intervention in the thirties. He ascribed this turn to a change in the stage of development of the state.

[40] See the criticism of this periodization in the collection *Lenin i Oktiabr'skoe vooruzhennoe vosstanie v Petrograde* (Moscow, 1964), pp. 37–38.

Stalin's assertion that the collectivization of agriculture was a revolution as important in its consequences as the October Revolution.

Lenin described the dictatorship of the proletariat as political rule based on force, not on law. If his comments are taken out of context, they become misleading half-truths. He certainly did not hold the view that any means to a given end are acceptable. Even in the most difficult situations Lenin and the other genuine Bolsheviks never considered themselves exempt from all rules. Moreover, when Lenin spoke of power based on force, not law, he usually emphasized that he was speaking of the laws of the bourgeois state, which had to be broken in order to bring about the proletarian revolution.[41] He always stressed the necessity of unwavering adherence to the new Soviet laws, which should support the dictatorship of the proletariat in its struggle with its enemies.[42] The extreme conditions of the Civil War necessitated extreme measures, but Lenin stressed the exceptional nature of these infractions of the rule of law.[43] Stalin, on the other hand, willfully extended the thesis that the proletarian dictatorship is force unlimited by law, applying it to the entire transitional period from capitalism to socialism. In other words, not revolutionary legality but lawlessness was to be considered a hallmark of the proletarian dictatorship.

Stalin also blighted the theory of the socialist revolution. He took Lenin's thesis about the possibility of socialism in one country and proclaimed it a new and complete theory of revolution. In this way a rigid limit was imposed on the further development of the theory of socialist revolution and an essential element of Leninism was separated from Marxism. In other ways too the history of Marxism was blighted. Doubting the existence of Communist ideals before Marx, scorning the utopian socialists, in part because he was ignorant of them, Stalin distorted the origins of scientific socialism. He also gave rise to a distorted evaluation of the Russian populists (*narodniki*). The *History of the CPSU: Short Course* labeled them all "opponents of Marxism," even though the first populists were active before Marxism appeared in Russia. Only their faults were brought out, which was completely at variance with the assessments made by Marx, Engels, and Lenin. The populists' views on terror and on the relationship between the individual and the mass were presented in an extremely vulgarized and distorted form. The *Short Course* declared that the "People's Will"[44] brought nothing but harm to the revolu-

[41] See, e.g., Lenin, *Polnoe sobranie*, XX, p. 16.
[42] See, e.g., *ibid.*, XXXVII, p. 129; XXXIX, pp. 55–56.
[43] See *ibid.*, XXXVII, p. 129, for his insistence on formal reports of extraordinary situations requiring the suspension of the rule of law.
[44] *Ed.:* The revolutionary organization that assassinated Alexander II in 1881.

tionary movement in our country. For all practical purposes the populist movement was portrayed as an antirevolutionary force. As for
Plekhanov, who effected the transition from populism to Marxism, his
theoretical heritage was subjected to one-sided and prejudiced
appraisal.

K. L. Seleznev has pointed out serious errors in the Stalinist treatment of Marx's and Engels' theoretical heritage. Such important topics
as the class struggle of the proletariat under capitalism, including the
problems of war and peace, were largely ignored. Similar disregard
was shown to Marx's views on the essence of communism, and the
phases of transition to its highest form. His and Engels' writings on
the problems of a proletarian party and the hegemony of the working
class were brushed aside by Stalin as nothing more than "rough
drafts."[45] Engels' contributions to socialist thought were not only
neglected but unfairly criticized. For example, in a letter to the Politburo in 1934 Stalin misinterpreted Engels' views on the tactics that
the proletariat should adopt when faced with an expansionist war.[46]
Stalin violated the principle of historicism by applying criteria suitable only for the epoch of imperialism.[47] Engels was also unfairly
attacked for his comment in 1891 that a democratic republic was a
possible form of the dictatorship of the proletariat.[48] The *Short Course*
cited this remark as evidence that Marx's idea concerning the Commune as the form of proletarian dictatorship was "consigned to
oblivion."[49] In fact, during that same year, 1891, Engels called
attention to the Commune as a form of the proletarian dictatorship.[50]

The Bolshevik struggle with opportunism in the Second International was also distorted in Stalinist theory. This was the issue that
touched off Stalin's letter to the historical journal *Proletarskaia revo-
luitsiia*, in 1931.[51] The article that aroused Stalin's wrath—A. G.
Slutskii on Bolshevism and German Social Democracy in the prewar
period—did contain a number of incorrect assertions, but they had
been criticized before Stalin's letter appeared.[52] Slutskii had put in-

---

[45] Stalin, *Sochineniia*, X, p. 96.
[46] The letter was published in *Bol'shevik*, 1941, No. 9, pp. 1–5. See also the article
"Raboty poslednikh let zhizni Engel'sa," *Pravda*, Mar. 23, 1937. The main item of
concern was Engels' article on the foreign policy of tsarism. *Ed.*: A convenient
reprint of Stalin's letter may be found in his *Sochineniia*, I (XIV) (Stanford, 1967),
pp. 2–10.
[47] See the editor's comment in Marx and Engels, *Sochineniia*, 2nd edn., XXII, p. xxxiii.
[48] See Engels' critique of the Erfurt Program, *ibid.*, pp. 237–40.
[49] See *History of the CPSU (Bolsheviks)*; *Short Course* (New York, 1939), p. 356.
[50] See Marx and Engels, *Sochineniia*, 2nd edn., XXII, p. 201. This was the final point of
his introduction to Marx's *Civil War in France*.
[51] See above, p. 143.
[52] See V. A. Dunaevskii, "Bol'sheviki i germanskie levye na mezhdunarodnoi arene," in
the collection *Evropa v novoe i noveishee vremia* (Moscow, 1966).

sufficient stress on the Leninist struggle against centrism.[53] Stalin, accurate but unoriginal on this point, went on to make errors of his own, which impelled Soviet historians to distort the relationship between Bolshevism and the international socialist movement. Lenin was pictured as trying to split the movement from the very beginning of the Bolsheviks' activity. Actually, as late as 1915 Lenin rejected the idea that the Bolsheviks should leave the Second International. Slutskii was right when he said that a split in those years would only have narrowed the base of Bolshevism and transformed it into a purely national phenomenon.[54]

The left wing of German Social Democracy was misinterpreted by Stalin, who was so wide of the mark as to attribute the theory of permanent revolution to Rosa Luxemburg, though it was actually the creation of A. L. Parvus and Trotsky.[55] In general Stalinist historiography gave a misleading picture of the Second International. Dunaevskii has summed up accurately:

> By stressing the mistakes of the left Social Democrats—both real and imaginary—and presenting as axiomatic the thesis that opportunism completely dominated the Second International, Stalin put all its activity in a false light and belittled the role of the Social Democratic parties in it (especially their left-wing groups). Such an approach contradicted the position of Lenin, who believed that the Second International did "extraordinarily important and useful work in spreading socialism and in preliminary, basic organization of its forces."[56] . . . At the same time Stalin's form of expression— his harsh words about the authors he mentioned, his political description of them as "rotten liberals," "Trotskyite smugglers," etc.—made creative discussion on matters of principle impossible, and subsequently led to repression of the people who were criticized.[57]

Stalin's approach to Party history deserves special attention. Aside from the deliberate falsifications in the *Short Course*—which reflects Stalin's views though it was written by other people—its striking quality is its unabashed dogmatism and schematism. The Soviet historian M. Ia. Gefter has described this very well:

> Any historical scheme involves a simplification, a straightening out of reality, achieved by excluding atypical features and elements.

[53] *Ed.:* Centrism here means the effort to reconcile the left and right wings of the socialist movement.

[54] See Dunaevskii, *ibid.,* p. 506.

[55] See V. V. Chistiakov, "V. I. Lenin o nemetskikh levykh sotsial-demokratakh," *Ukrainskii istoricheskii zhurnal,* 1965, No. 9, for evidence that Rosa Luxemburg's writings of the period not only lack explicit reference to "permanent revolution" but are implicitly opposed to that theory.

[56] Lenin, *Polnoe sobranie,* XXVI, p. 103.

[57] V. A. Dunaevskii, *op. cit.,* pp. 507–08.

Every scheme is a reconstruction of the past, making it seem above all a preparation for the present condition of society, so that the beginning stages of a process are defined in one way or another by its result. Stalin turned this particular feature of historical cognition into an absolute. For him the result was the *one and only* important thing; the current result was transformed from a criterion of historical truth into an instrument for constructing it. Hence such a characteristic feature of the *Short Course* as its self-evident style. Living reality served as an illustration of the obvious truth of some ideas and propositions and the obvious falsehood of others. Building the conclusion into the point of departure imparted the quality of predestination to historical development: *it could have happened only this way and no other.*

How Marxist determinism, the unusually rich dialectical idea of the patterned (*zakonomernoe, gesetzmässig*) movement of history, was turned into the "iron" and bureaucratized conception of Stalin is a subject in itself. One thing is certain: this is no longer Marxism. Only now can we appreciate the harm done by this metamorphosis both to the theory itself and to the new generations in our country and abroad who came to accept it. They lost the feeling for, the understanding of, that genuine innovative creativity which was characteristic of the ideas of Bolshevism at their birth, in contrast not only with conscious opportunistic distortion of Marxism but also with the Marxist orthodoxy of the preceding time (which besides its weak points had definite accomplishments). Harm was done to the study of the patterned (*zakonomernaia*) struggle of ideas, of policies. Scientific analysis of the rise and development of differences within the workers' and socialist movement, analysis of the transformation of the struggle of ideas into a conflict of social forces, was replaced by a scheme reduced to the most primitive level: behind every disagreement, behind every nuance of thought, from the very beginning there is supposed to be a direct class interest. History was drained of blood, and the possibilities of training Communist cadres on the experience of our Revolution were thereby cut down. Indeed, if the outcome of the struggle is essentially predestined, if the positions of every single one of the opposing sides are apparent in advance, if all parties, groups, and individuals have not changed but only manifested or exposed themselves in the course of the struggle, then it is impossible to explain the gigantic difficulties the Bolsheviks had to overcome in working out their political line and even more in winning the proletarian vanguard and the multimillioned masses to their side.

But that is still not all, by no means all. The concrete form and function of the a priori method of the *Short Course* were no less crucial if not more so. To what end was Party history straightened out? Naturally for the victory of socialism in our country. But that end—and here is the "secret" of the conception—was doubled, was united with another: the defeat and destruction of "internal enemies," of "Bukharinite-Trotskyite spies, wreckers, traitors to the homeland." (See the title of Chapter XII, Section 4, of the *Short Course.*) The *entire* preceding journey was examined from that decisive point of view. Therefore the intraparty struggle occupied the central place in the *Short Course,* and even more in the postrevolutionary than in the pre-October section. And accordingly entire strata of reality, of the Party's positive activity and policies, were cut out. Events were included merely as the external setting for this struggle, and the real historical patterns (*zakonomernosti, Gesetzmässigkeiten*), the internal contradictions, which *drove* the Revolution and the building of socialism were replaced by a scheme essentially void of development, reduced to an ever-recurrent clash of politicians, some of whom were always loyal to Lenin, while others were hostile to Leninism from the beginning and therefore logically, step by step, approached treason to the state and the nation.[58]

Another characteristic of the Stalinist conception of history was, as Ia. S. Drabkin remarked at the same meeting, nationalism, in some cases verging on chauvinism. The *Short Course* almost completely ignores the world Communist movement, does not show that our Party is a part of it. Marx and Engels are discussed only in connection with the activity of the Group for the Emancipation of Labor.[59] International Social Democracy is discussed only to support an exposé of revisionism. The theorists of the Second International are described only as "burying" the ideas of Marx and Engels. The chapter on the First World War speaks very scornfully of the internationalists in other socialist parties. Rosa Luxemburg and Karl Liebknecht are called "inconsistent internationalists," whom Lenin criticized. There are a few words on the founding of the Comintern but next to nothing on the revolutionary movement thereafter. Even the VIIth Comintern Congress gets no mention, although it was held only a few years before the book appeared. Not a word is said about the united front or the popular front.

"But more important than what is not said in the *Short Course,*" notes Drabkin,

> is what *is* said there. The whole book, from the first to the last page, is permeated with the idea that all Social Democracy (literally all, and not just the right-wing Socialist leaders) is the worst enemy of any progress, that no agreements, alliances, even temporary and loose ones, are possible with it. How can there be any talk of a united front, when the Conclusion, generalizing the whole historical

[58] From M. Ia. Gefter's speech to the joint meeting of the historiographical group and the methodological sector of the Institute of History, on Apr. 29, 1966, devoted to the report of N. N. Maslov, "Sostoianie i razvitie istoriko-partiinoi nauki v 1935–1955 gg." *Ed.*: This seems to be an unpublished manuscript.

[59] *Ed.*: The first Russian organization of Marxists.

experience, says: "The history of the Party teaches that without the destruction of the petty-bourgeois parties that operate within the ranks of the working class, pushing the backward sections of the working class into the embrace of the bourgeoisie, thus splitting the unity of the working class, the victory of the proletarian revolution is impossible. . . . Unless such parties are overcome and driven out of the ranks of the working class, it will be impossible to achieve the unity of the working class."

In the field of Russian history, Stalin not only completely justified Ivan the Terrible and his *oprichnina*; he even considered Maliuta Skuratov a great, progressive statesman.[60] Ivan's only mistake, according to Stalin, was that he let his conscience bother him too much; he spent too much time praying for forgiveness after destroying each big feudal family. Thus he was unable to wipe out all the boyar families completely. (History repeats itself. Today in China Genghis Khan, a tyrant as monstrously cruel as Ivan, is being rehabilitated.) Under Stalin's influence, works of history and art glorified many other tsars and princes, portrayed in an extremely distorted fashion. Thus the legend of Alexander Nevskii was revived. The tsars and the Orthodox Church had accounted him a divine protector of the imperial throne, hushing up the fact that he called the Tartars into Novgorod to suppress a popular rebellion. Many of the tsarist wars of conquest were justified in Stalinist historiography, including Nicholas I's wars in the Caucasus. At the same time Shamil, the hero of the national liberation struggle of the Caucasian peoples, was depicted as an agent of British imperialism and of the Ottoman Empire.

Finally, one must note Stalinist misinterpretation of the feudal and the slaveholding social formations. The diversity in forms of land use and landownership under feudalism was ignored, in favor of simplistic generalities about the feudal lords' monopoly of landownership and their proprietary relationship to peasants. Stalin simply identified the feudal formation with one of its variants—serfdom. It was also wrong to insist that slaves in revolt struck the fatal blow at the slaveholding social formation.

In philosophy Stalin was at best a dilettante. He lacked both systematic training and genuine self-education. He never made a real study of Hegel, Kant, Ludwig Feuerbach, the French materialists, or, judging by his pronouncements, the philosophical works of Marx, Engels, and Lenin. All his philosophical writings are marked by primitivism, oversimplification, superficiality, and a penchant for dogmatic schematization. In his first philosophical pamphlet, *Anarchism and Socialism,* he contrasted the two outlooks as follows: The

[60] *Ed.:* The *oprichnina* was Ivan's agency of terror. Skuratov was a particularly violent official of it.

chief principle of anarchism is "everything for the individual"; "the emancipation of the individual is the chief condition for the emancipation of the mass, the collective." The main principle of Marxism is "everything for the mass"; "the emancipation of the mass, the collective, is the chief condition for the emancipation of the individual." Such opposition between the collective and the individual is of course alien to Marxism. It was Marx and Engels, not the anarchists, who wrote in *The Communist Manifesto* that the full development of each individual is the condition for the full development of all. In the same pamphlet of Stalin's—essentially a student exercise—there are such other clumsy errors as an artificial distinction between the theory and the method of dialectical materialism. The comments on irritability and sensation, and on Neo-Darwinism and Neo-Lamarckism are superficial or simply wrong.

The subsequent philosophical writings of Stalin multiplied such oversimplified distortions. The achievements of modern science went unexamined; materialism and dialectics continued to be mechanically separated as theory and method, respectively; the unity and struggle of opposites was misconstrued to emphasize the struggle and ignore the unity. The interaction between forces and relations of production and the problem of contradictions in a socialist society, were bungled. His assertion that the entire old superstructure was liquidated along with the old base was completely unfounded, implying that the entire cultural legacy of the past had been destroyed, since it could be considered the superstructure of the old base. We owe to Stalin the nihilist attitude toward German classical philosophy, which dismissed Hegelian philosophy as an aristocratic reaction to the French Revolution.

Economic theory also felt the impact of Stalin's ignorant willfulness. He misinterpreted the operation of the law of value in a socialist society. He denied the commodity character of production in the USSR, maintaining that under socialism the law of value did not apply to the means of production. Thus the principle of equivalence in funding the expenses of production was violated, which further obstructed the operation of material incentives. According to Stalin, in a socialist society the law of value operates merely in the sphere of circulation and only "influences" production. He also completely ignored differential rent in agricultural production. He noted with satisfaction that consumer purchasing power was growing faster than production, thereby transforming shortages and queues into a law of life. He even denied the existence of a surplus product[61] under socialism, and underestimated the very important principle of material incentives.

He asserted that the collective property of the *kolkhozy* held back

[61] *Ed.:* Marx's term for the difference between the worker's wage and the amount of value he produces.

the development of agricultural production. He urged the transformation of such property to public ownership, by means of an accelerated replacement of commodity circulation by a system of direct exchange of products. He excluded the basic means of production from *kolkhoz* property, and opposed the sale of agricultural machinery to the *kolkhozy*. He declared that collective and state farms could make do with a minimum of profit, even none at all. In fact state farms that made no profit covered their losses at the expense of the state budget, which had the effect, among others, of obstructing the improvement of the farms. As for the collective farms, which could not tap the state budget, they shifted their financial difficulties onto their members. And of course, Stalin's principle of "higher profitability" (*rentabel'-nost*), according to which all *kolkhozy* were profitable in some higher sense of the word, although they suffered losses individually, was not much help to those farms and their members. In general, the Stalinist view of agriculture concentrated on the fulfillment of obligatory deliveries, not on the increase of productivity and profitability.

On the development of capitalist economies, Stalin was confused and superficial. He failed to perceive the increasing role of the state—see, for example, his interview with H. G. Wells—and believed that capitalism would keep sliding downhill through successive crises. He insisted on the absolute impoverishment of the workers under capitalism, although the facts did not fit this theory. The underemployment of industrial capacity that was so characteristic of the capitalist economy in the thirties and forties he attributed to the loss of foreign markets, particularly the big Russian market, though the main cause was the shrinking of domestic markets.

Jurisprudence was seriously hurt by Stalinism. Revolutionary legality was reduced to the protection of socialist property, to be achieved by intensification of repressive measures. Such legal tasks as ensuring state and social discipline, the development of culture, the education of Soviet people, and most important of all, the protection of the rights and legal interests of Soviet citizens—all were beyond the limits of the Stalinist formula. Stalin gave Soviet legality a one-sided repressive character.

Stalin made numerous mistakes in military science, though he was hailed as a classic writer in this field, while the works of Clausewitz were denied any value—on the authority of Stalin.[62] A number of issues in military strategy were deliberately distorted in order to justify Stalin's blunders during the war:

> Poor preparedness for war on the part of nonaggressive nations was raised to the level of a principle, and so was the theory of active defense, which was a postdated justification of our army's retreat

[62] See his letter to Colonel E. Razin, in *Bol'shevik*, 1947, No. 3, pp. 6–8.

deep into the country and its cession of much territory to the enemy. And so was counterattack, as an allegedly unavoidable form of strategic operations in wartime.[63]

In the postwar years, Stalin's subjective approach to the potentialities of nuclear weapons held back the development of their application in combat and also of defenses against them.

On the nationality question, the many ways of building and federating national states were reduced to various kinds of autonomy. Stalin declared that the national question was no longer a live issue in capitalist Europe, that it was still significant only in the colonial and semicolonial world. To the XIXth Party Congress in 1952 he announced that the bourgeoisie had discarded the banner of national independence and only the Communists could raise it. This is not only an obvious untruth in Asia and Africa; the last decade has shown that bourgeois circles in Europe (e.g., in France) and America (e.g., Canada, Mexico, Chile) are still capable of using the slogan of national independence.

The Stalinist distortion of pedagogy has already been discussed. It remains to add that his *Economic Problems of Socialism* mentioned the necessity of polytechnical education only in connection with the question of the free choice of a profession. This important principle of Marxist-Leninist pedagogy was for all practical purposes discarded. Even primitive school shops were shut down in 1937.

Stalin made many mistakes in appraising the prospects of the Chinese Revolution. In 1929–35 the Chinese Communist Party, as its leaders now admit, clashed internally over Stalin's line. Stalin's name was never mentioned, but Chinese Communists who held the same views as Stalin were the explicit targets of criticism.

These are only some of Stalin's theoretical mistakes, which have already been criticized in the press. If it is possible to speak of a Stalinist stage in the theoretical field, then it is one of temporary decline and stagnation; to overcome it is the main task of historians, philosophers, economists, and other social scientists. The first step must be the complete debunking of the legend that Stalin was "the greatest theorist and classic of Marxism-Leninism," which even today is being revived.

4

ALL THE NATURAL SCIENCES were hampered by the cult, in some cases directly through Stalin's personal intervention, in most cases indirectly, by the bureaucratic system. Stalin frequently made himself

[63] See *Voennaia strategiia* (Moscow, 1962), p. 5.

an uninvited arbiter, giving scientists instructions that as a rule were quite incompetent. He told geologists where and how to look for oil, advised doctors on their specialties,[64] instructed biologists on problems of heredity. Frequently his stupid example was followed by Zhdanov, Malenkov, Molotov, and others in his entourage. The bureaucratic system in many scientific institutions fostered little specialized cults on the model of Stalin's big one. A particular scientist would be proclaimed the only source of basic truth, immune to criticism. Great damage was done by the savage character of scientific discussions, the constant attempts to politicize science, to divide it into Soviet and bourgeois camps. Not only philosophers but many scientists picked up the habit of pasting defamatory labels on their rivals. These conditions guaranteed the rise of adventurers and careerists, who used the support of powerful but ignorant administrators to push true scientists into subjection.

Biology was the most severely damaged.[65] The tragic history of the thirty-year war in biology and agronomy has been presented in detail in Zhores A. Medvedev's book, to which I refer the reader.[66] I shall note here only that Stalin's support enabled Lysenko to set up the August, 1948, session of the Agricultural Academy, which started a pogrom in biology. The existence of two biologies was proclaimed—proletarian and bourgeois—and the most promising developments were assigned to the bourgeois camp. The majority of foreign and Soviet biologists were labeled idealists and lackeys of imperialism, just as in Nazi Germany physics had been divided into "Aryan" and "non-Aryan" schools. Not only was truth banned; illiterate fantasy was officially enthroned. Heredity became a mysterious property unattached to any material structure but "permeating" all the "granules" of a living being. Vitality was a no less mysterious property, invoked to explain the growth and development of organisms, and their equally mysterious capacity to remove themselves for the good of the species. The Darwinian thesis of intraspecific competition was denied, and sudden transformations of species were proclaimed—wheat turning into rye, pine into spruce, oats into wild oats—along with the Lamarckian pattern of species transformation. Lysenko's fantasies became absolute truths, immune to criticism, as soon as he announced

---

[64] See *Novyi Mir,* 1966, No. 8, p. 282.

[65] Stalin considered himself practically a specialist in this field. In an article on Stalin's seventieth birthday, his secretary, Poskrebyshev, declared him not only the organizer of citrus cultivation in the Black Sea district but the researcher who investigated the possibility of such cultivation—and that of eucalyptus trees in the Moscow region, the breeding of branched wheat, etc.

[66] *Ed.:* It has been published in the West—*The Rise and Fall of T. D. Lysenko* (New York, 1969)—but not yet in the Soviet Union. Cf. D. Joravsky, *The Lysenko Affair* (Cambridge, Mass., 1970), pp. 184–85, for the publication history.

them. Great harm was done to agriculture as well as biology. With Stalin's support, V. R. Williams' school of soil science was given dominion in agronomy. After the August, 1948, session of the Agricultural Academy, and after a special government decree issued on Stalin's initiative, Williams' grassland system of crop rotation was forcibly introduced into all agricultural zones of the country.[67]

For years O. B. Lepeshinskaia's rejection of cytology enjoyed official Lysenkoite approval, again with Stalin's support. Medical science also suffered from methods of work modeled on Lysenko's. In 1950 the Academy of Sciences and the Academy of Medical Sciences, in a joint meeting, dogmatically enthroned one part of the rich heritage of I. P. Pavlov, his theory of higher nervous activity. As S. Mordashev has pointed out, certain scientists assumed the role of infallible interpreters of Pavlov's work, his only direct heirs. All trends in physiology other than theirs—various ways of studying the nervous system, evolutionary physiology, cellular physiology, endocrinology—were banned. Almost all departments of physiology and psychiatric clinics were committed to this dogmatic scheme. Even Pavlov's work on the physiology of the digestive system, which had won him the Nobel Prize, was neglected. Instead of developing Pavlov's fruitful legacy, these dogmatic physiologists ruined it.[68]

Bookburning was another characteristic of Stalin's cult. When people were suppressed, their books were too, though the books usually had no relation to the false charges against their authors. Thus millions of books were removed from public libraries, and only a few individuals dared to keep them in their homes. Even magazines and newspapers were destroyed or put away in "special collections" (*spetskhranenie*), that is, restricted to a few people. Some extremely important scientific works were taken out of scholarly circulation, and the continuous development of scientific ideas was often broken. A ban fell on the works of such leading social and natural scientists as V. I. Nevskii, A. S. Bubnov, M. N. Pokrovskii, Iu. M. Steklov, N. I. Vavilov, G. K. Meister, N. K. Kol'tsov, E. B. Pashukanis, and Gaster. The same was done to the military writings of Tukhachevskii, Iakir, Egorov, and the other condemned generals. Books which merely referred to "enemies of the people" in a favorable way were banned. Even *Ten Days That Shook the World* was banned, because it did not show "the leading role of Stalin during the October Revolution."

Un-Marxist distortions marred the history of science during the years of the cult. As B. M. Kedrov told the conference of historians in

---

[67] *Ed.*: For an explanation see Zh. A. Medvedev, *op. cit.*, pp. 86–99, and Joravsky, *op. cit.*, pp. 293–305.
[68] See *Pravda*, June 11, 1965.

1962, the question of priority was examined not from the internationalist viewpoint, which searches for the participation of all nations in the enrichment of world civilization, but from the point of view of national rivalry. The claims of certain nations were unjustifiably denied, while Russian scientists were credited with every imaginable discovery. The authors of these ridiculous claims were protected against criticism, since it was known that their trend of thought corresponded to Stalin's. Most Soviet scientists were denied communication with foreign colleagues, whether by attendance at international meetings or by correspondence. Even exchanges of printed material were reduced, and international meetings all but ceased to be held on Soviet soil. The greatest harm was done to Soviet, not to foreign, science. Soviet science did make progress during the years of the cult, but the progress would have been much greater without the stupid dictatorship that was established in the thirties and forties. That was one of the most serious consequences of Stalin's cult.

5

DESPITE THEIR IMPERFECTIONS, Soviet literature and art made great strides in the twenties and early thirties. Many "infantile disorders" were overcome, and Soviet artists of all kinds grew both in numbers and in skills. At the First Congress of Soviet Writers in 1934, energetic optimism was the dominant mood. It seemed as if literature and art were getting a new impetus to further development. But mass repression decimated the arts, destroying not only people but their works. Most of those who remained at large were morally damaged. All the conditions for cultural creativity suffered disastrous change.

Many important works were still created, which had a beneficial effect on Soviet citizens, particularly the youth. Suffice it to recall such films as *Chapaev, We Are from Kronstadt, Baltic Deputy,* and *Lenin in October* and novels by N. A. Ostrovskii, Tvardovskii, Makarenko, A. A. Fadeev, and M. A. Sholokhov. But it would be wrong to list the notable works of those years and ignore the fact that cultural development slowed down markedly. The number of notable works was far less than Soviet artists were capable of producing, and one-sidedness became the characteristic feature of the Soviet arts.

The pernicious influence of Stalinism was felt in many ways. A notable example was the triumph of a narrow concept of socialist realism. Senseless restrictions were imposed not only on the content but also on the form of art. Analogous narrowness and distortion were pressed upon Lenin's principle of "partyness" (*partiinost'*). His article "Party Organization and Party Literature"[69] was misinterpreted. It

[69] Lenin, *Sochineniia,* 4th edn., X, pp. 26–31.

was written late in 1905, when many censorship restrictions had been lifted, and legal Bolshevik publications could oppose the enormous flood of bourgeois literature. Lenin used "literature" in the broad sense of the word, meaning journalistic writing as well as belles-lettres. What he wrote is still meaningful, but it cannot be mechanically transferred from the conditions of 1905, when the Party was only struggling for power, to the conditions of a one-party state. Neither should one overlook Lenin's clear warnings:

> It is self-evident that literary work is least of all amenable to mechanical uniformity, to leveling, to the rule of the majority over the minority. It is self-evident that in this work it is absolutely necessary to guarantee great scope to individual initiative, to individual propensities, scope for thought and fantasy, form and content.[70]

Properly understood, the principle of "partyness" requires a writer and artist to defend the interests of the masses, to struggle for socialist and communist ideals and against the faults that hinder realization of those ideals. In short, the principle requires a truthful picture of reality. But during the cult, "partyness" was taken to mean subordination of writers and artists to the decisions of various Party officials. Artists were supposed to be only "soldiers of the Party," in the most primitive sense of the word. They were deprived of the chance to discover reality independently; they were told not only what but how to create. In 1905 Lenin was concerned with the development of legal Party literature; in the years of the cult *only* Party literature—understood in an extremely narrow way—was permitted. There was much talk about ideological struggle, though in practice it was avoided. A great many creative things that could not be considered "Party" works simply went unpublished.[71]

"Partyness" and objectivity were supposed to coincide, because the proletariat and its Party do not need to conceal their shortcomings or to distort the truth. That is basically true, but it is also true that certain groups and strata in the Party, and certain individuals who usurped the right to speak for the Party, had an interest in concealing the truth. These officials did not want objectivity; they maintained their power and privileges by lies and demagogy. That was the origin of the distortions that were covered with talk about the interests of the people. The little bosses of the arts only talked of "partyness"; in fact they were dominated by the most cynical pragmatism: what was to their advantage was true.

Incompetent but powerful officials interfered at will with literature and art. Forgotten was the June, 1925, resolution of the Central Committee, which noted that literary matters must be handled with

[70] *Ibid.,* p. 28.
[71] Examples are the recently published works of Mikhail Bulgakov and Andrei Platonov.

great tact, caution, and patience, banishing the tone of literary command, all pretentious, semi-literate and complacent Communist conceit. . . . The Party must utterly extirpate attempts at crude, incompetent administrative interference in literary matters.[72]

In the Party bosses' actual dealings with literary people there was no tact, caution, or patience. A complex bureaucratic hierarchy was set up to choose and approve works of art. Many censors and administrators, most of them incompetent, handled a book before it might reach Stalin, who was quite ready to intervene in the crudest possible ways.

Emilian Iaroslavskii, in his book *On Comrade Stalin,* told how the great man not only liked to read belles-lettres; in his youth he had written "very good poems," which were printed in the paper *Iveriia* over the pseudonym "Soselo." Admittedly, Stalin was not, like Mao Tse-tung, proclaimed the greatest poet of modern times. But he did have a considerable impact on Soviet literature. In many cases his comments determined the fate of a creative work—sometimes of the creator as well. For example, he forbade the performance of A. N. Afinogenov's play *The Lie,* which was in rehearsal at three hundred theaters. Stalin did not like the way the heroine condemned the falsehood that had crept into Soviet lives.[73] Then there was the case of Bulgakov's play *Flight.* Gorky wrote of it: "This is a superb comedy, with deeply hidden satirical content. I am firmly convinced that *Flight* will be a triumph when the Moscow Art Theater puts it on, a tremendous success." But Stalin expressed a negative opinion, and, in a letter to V. Bill'-Belotserkovskii, opined that Bulgakov did not deserve the success of his play *Days of the Turbins.* As a result, *Flight* and most of Bulgakov's other plays were banned from the stage.[74] Stalin's personal interference cut off Shostakovich's opera *Katerina Izmailova* (*Lady Macbeth of Mtsensk*), which had been playing successfully in a number of theaters for two years. For some reason Stalin did not like the music. Stalin also banned many classics. Just before the Moscow Art Theater went on tour to Paris, it was forbidden to perform Pushkin's *Boris Godunov.* The director of the theater, M. Arkad'ev, wrote Stalin a "letter of repentance" in July, 1937, after he had been fired. He listed the "dubious" elements in Pushkin's tragedy, which had been pointed out to him "from above." Noble Poland is contrasted with poor Russia. "Dmitrii is not presented by Pushkin for what he really was—an agent of foreign intervention."[75]

[72] Reprinted in *O partiinoi i sovetskoi pechati. Sbornik dokumentov* (Moscow, 1954), pp. 346–47.
[73] See *Znamia,* 1963, No. 1, p. 211.
[74] M. Bulgakov, *Izbrannaia proza* (Moscow, 1966), pp. 29–30.
[75] From materials belonging to the cultural historian L. M. Zak.

It was in the years of the cult that the political censor acquired enormous power, the ultimate say-so, in any publishing house. Back in the twenties Lunacharskii had called for a different arrangement:

> We need a flourishing, diversified literature. Obviously the censor should not allow clearly counterrevolutionary stuff to pass. But apart from that, everything that shows talent should have free access to the book market. Only when we have such a broad literature will we have a genuine loudspeaker into which all strata and groups of our enormous country will speak; only then will we have sufficient material, both in the subjective statements of these writers as representatives of these groups, and in objective observations of our reality seen from various points of view.[76]

No one in the censorship organs of Stalin's times followed Lunacharskii's sensible advice. Indeed, many leading publishers, editors, and members of arts councils owed their positions to excessive caution, their refusal to allow a multitude of films and plays and books.

In the 1936–37 season ten out of nineteen new plays in major theaters were taken off the stage, including the ballet *The Bright Stream,* with music by Shostakovich; M. Svetlov's play *Deep in the Provinces*; the comic opera *Knights,* with words by Demian Bedny; the comedy *The Death of Tarelkin* by Sukhovo-Kobylin; and Afinogenov's play *Salute to Spain.* In that same year more than ten theaters were closed down in Moscow alone, and ten others in Leningrad. Zak calculates, for 1937 alone, fifty-six plays removed from the repertoire and banned, including all the works of V. Kirshon, B. Jasienski, I. Mikitenko, and other arrested playwrights.

The same arbitrary rule governed the film industry. In 1935 thirty-four films were stopped in production, in 1936 fifty-five, and in 1937, when the number of movies permitted to start production had sharply dropped, thirteen were still stopped in midcourse. During the same years more than twenty films were taken out of circulation after they had already been shown. It is therefore understandable why no more than ten feature films were released in any one of the postwar years, despite an abundance of studios.

That was the time, incidentally, when Stalin encouraged biographical films, not about revolutionaries but about Russian tsars, princes, and military leaders. He ordered color films about Ivan the Terrible, Peter the Great, Alexander Nevskii, Suvorov, Kutuzov, and Admiral Ushakov. He reviewed the scenarios and even chose the directors. The famous director M. I. Romm has aptly described the resulting stereotype, using his own film, *Admiral Ushakov,* as an example. The people were depicted as a faceless mass, clay in the omnipotent hands of the

---

[76] *Literaturnoe nasledstvo,* No. 74 (Moscow, 1965), p. 31.

flawless hero—and he too ultimately lacked individuality, since he had no inner contradictions and therefore no development of character.[77]

The great director and writer Dovzhenko was subjected to ridicule and threats in the postwar period when he wrote the film story *The Ukraine on Fire*. Stalin would not allow it to be published or screened. He and Beria baited Dovzhenko, calling him a nationalist, objecting to the retreat of Soviet soldiers that he put in his story, and threatening him with punishment.[78] But Dovzhenko did not waver. He knew he was in the right, as he explained in his diary:

> Comrade Stalin, even if you were God, I would not take your word that I am a nationalist who should be branded and dragged in the mud. When there is no hate as a matter of principle, and no scorn and no ill will for a single people in the world, not for any people's fate, or for its happiness, or for its achievements or prosperity, is love for my own people nationalism?
>
> Or is it nationalism to be short-tempered with the stupidity of bureaucrats, with cold self-seekers, or to be incapable as an artist of restraining tears when the people are suffering?
>
> Why have you turned my life into torment? Why did you take joy away from me? Why did you trample on my name?
>
> Still I forgive you, for I am a part of the people. I am nevertheless greater than you.
>
> Since I am very small, I forgive you your smallness and malice, for you are imperfect, even though people pray to you. God exists. But his name is chance.[79]

I. Zuzanek has discerned a further paradox in the mass culture fostered during the period of the cult.

> Frequently it dulled the active creative elements of mass consciousness, paralyzed the healthy critical moods without which socialism cannot develop. Paradoxical as it may seem, in terms of function this was an "elitist" culture, intended to strengthen the belief that people are as the bureaucratized mind of the official or the critic conceives them, the mind that is remote from the problems of real life but has ready-made stereotyped formulas and recipes for all occasions.[80]

Artistic and literary criticism were on a very low level during the cult. The principles of socialist realism were turned into a code of prescriptions and dead dogmas. "Socialist realism requires . . ." became a common introduction to an assertion of some normative aesthetics. The theory of conflict only between the good and the better, the theory

---

[77] See *Pravda*, Apr. 17, 1962.
[78] See S. Plachynda, *Oleksandr Dovzhenko* (Kiev, 1964), p. 238.
[79] Quoted in Iu. Barabash, *Chisto zoloto pravdy* (Moscow, 1966) pp. 124–25.
[80] I. Zuzanek, "Kul'tura i massy," *Problemy mira i sotsializma*, 1965, No. 7, p. 44.

of the ideal hero, based not on real life but on speculative norms, were expressions of the same phenomenon: the tendency to make an absolute of anything connected with Stalin, to raise such things to the level of "eternal truths."[81]

The oversimplified sociological approach to art, which arose in the first decade of Soviet literature, gained ground in the period of the cult. The works of many talented writers, such as Sergei Esenin, were indiscriminately denigrated. The same treatment was given to the literary groups of the twenties, such as RAPP, the Smithy, LEF, the Serapion Brothers, and *Pereval*.[82] One noisy assault followed another. Vicious campaigns were waged against "Meyerholdism," against "formalism" in Shostakovich's music, against the film director Sergei Eisenstein, against the artist A. V. Fonvizin, against "Artistic Daubers," as the illustrators of a children's book were called in an article. Those were malicious attacks, not criticism. Even the few fair remarks in such articles were expressed in an insulting form. The talented painters V. Lebedev and Kovishevich were called "daubers," "smearers," "dabblers."

Verbal beatings of this sort became especially common in the postwar period. We have already mentioned Zhdanov's speech concerning the journals *Zvezda* and *Leningrad*, which set off attacks on various writers.[83] Indiscriminate assaults were also made on the works of leading composers. A 1948 campaign against a small group of theater critics turned into a major pogrom against "cosmopolitans," with very serious consequences. Konstantin Simonov, who took part in that campaign, gave a revealing account of it in 1956. Playwrights, under pressure to accentuate the positive, were turning out rosy pictures of a world free of conflict, where life's problems either did not exist at all or were solved with ridiculous ease. Some critics tried, very timidly, to suggest the need for greater realism. Simonov is ashamed to recall a plenary meeting of the board of directors of the Writers' Union at the end of 1948, where such critics were denounced for attacking the Soviet theater "from an alien point of view." Demagogic extrapolation was the chief method of proof. If a critic had made fun of a pasteboard Party organizer in a play, he was implicitly mocking the Party. If he had written that the patriotic speeches in a play were bombastic, he was undermining patriotism. Soon afterward *Pravda* carried an article, "An Antipatriotic Group of Theater Critics," that virtually carried such demagogy to the point of criminal indictment.

[81] See A. Metchenko in *Novyi Mir*, 1956, No. 12, p. 233. He should be reminded today of his just remark back then that the serious consequences of the cult have still to be overcome in literature and literary criticism.

[82] *Ed.:* For identification of these groups see *Kratkaia literaturnaia entsiklopediia*, or, in English, E. J. Brown, *Russian Literature Since the Revolution* (New York, 1963).

[83] See above, p. 483.

With word going around that Stalin had a direct hand in the article, the effect on the literary world can easily be imagined.[84]

Above all, one is struck by the monotony of the literature resulting from such pressures. The best works published in the thirties were devoted for the most part to Civil War themes, and in general to the first decade of the Soviet regime. In the forties the major works dealt with the Fatherland War. Other themes was simply ignored or whitewashed. Lawlessness and repression, bureaucracy and the degeneration of a part of the *apparat*, were forbidden topics. The embellishment of reality became the hallmark of many writers; the desirable was often indistinguishable from the real. Writing about collective farms was especially prone to this vice. "Fiction," A. Tvardovskii has justly remarked,

> was devoted to a simple-minded, to put it mildly, embellishment of the life of the *kolkhoz* village, to the construction of uncomplicated and tested thematic frames, into which reality was forced, freed of its complexity, contradictions, its genuine uncontrived problems.[85]

A typical product was S. P. Babaevskii's novel *Cavalier of the Gold Star,* which received the Stalin Prize, first class. For a typical cinematic embellishment of rural life, there was *Cossacks of the Kuban.* Another favored genre of late Stalinist art was the panegyric exalting Stalin himself. Toward his sixtieth and seventieth birthdays (1939 and 1949) the press was full of sham folk epistles in verse, on the Father of the Peoples and the like. Painting and sculpture became pompous, overdecorated, cold portraiture. Ostentatious façades and utterly useless decoration dominated architecture.

Many writers and painters sought escape in historical subjects, or in international themes, often without knowledge of the subject matter. But Simonov recalls that half-truths about contemporary Soviet life were the really dangerous enemy of art.

> It was too easy for many of us to reconcile ourselves to a facile portrayal of postwar life . . ., to fall into the trap of a "beneficent" elevation of literature above life, an elevation that supposedly corresponded to the interests of building socialism. Lacking principles, we reconciled ourselves to gliding over the surfaces of life, not writing lies but avoiding grim truths. In most cases this did not reflect the writers' insincerity, because many of them in the final analysis sincerely believed, say, that it was not the time, in a grim situation, to write the hard truth; they could return to it later, they said, when it would be in the past.[86]

---

[84] See *Novyi mir,* 1956, No. 12, pp. 249–51.
[85] *Ibid.,* 1965, No. 1, p. 6.
[86] Simonov, *op. cit.,* pp. 241–42.

These protestations are true only in part. Soviet literature and art, like its historiography, presented not only half-truths but often plain distortions and falsifications. Suffice it to recall O. Mal'tsev's book *The Yugoslav Tragedy*, which depicted the leaders of the Yugoslav Communist Party as spies and traitors. As for the historical novel, recall V. Kostylev's trilogy, *Ivan the Terrible,* which portrays its hero not only as a just and wise ruler but even as an affable and affectionate man in his relations with common people. The author justified Ivan's executions and even sympathized with him: ". . . it was rather hard for the sovereign-father!" And Maliuta Skuratov, that bloody executioner, emerges "staid, businesslike, an impartial public servant, an avid partisan of the middle and petty gentry." Skuratov had "a humane, Russian heart"; "in his life and death he was a model of love for the homeland." The same brazen falsification of history can be seen in V. Iazvitskii's five-volume novel *Ivan III, Lord of All Rus,* and in many other books, plays, and films on historical subjects.

Deliberate distortions were especially numerous in works on revolutionary subjects, such as Alexis Tolstoy's novel *Bread,* and such films as *The Vow, Unforgettable 1919, The Great Citizen, Lenin in October,* and *Lenin in 1918.* Director Romm and actor Shchukin achieved a remarkable portrait of Lenin, but his constant adviser and friend is Stalin. As for Bukharin, Zinoviev, and Lenin's other colleagues, they are depicted even in 1918 as agents of bourgeois intelligence services, dreaming with the Left S-R's of murdering Lenin.

In his book *Far from Moscow,* V. Azhaev deliberately conceals the fact that almost all the workers building the oil pipeline on Sakhalin were prisoners, while the directors of the project were commanders of the Far Eastern concentration camps. (The character of Batmanov is based on V. A. Barabanov, formerly chief of Vorkuta.) Similarly in books on the building of Komsomol'sk on the Amur, nothing is said of the thousands of prisoners who often performed the most laborious work.

Artistic quality was bound to be very low. A vast quantity of gray, uninteresting works appeared in all fields of literature and art. As early as 1940 a group of leading filmmakers sent a special letter to Stalin concerning the difficulty of their situation, the appearance of stereotyped dullness in films. This letter, signed by L. Trauberg, M. L. Romm, A. Kapler, S. Vasil'ev, F. Ermler, and G. Aleksandrov, went unanswered. The same diseases afflicted the arts in the people's democracies. One recalls, for example, the nasty attacks on Bertolt Brecht in the German Democratic Republic, and the eloquent article by Peter Karvash demonstrating what is bound to happen when artists are pressured to depict the politician's dream as reality: the public simply loses interest and turns aside.[87] But he speaks only of illusions and mistakes, and the spread of conscious fraud must be pointed out. Moral degeneration infected a portion of the artistic intelligentsia.

Increasing cultural isolation was another feature of the postwar period. The Soviet people knew less and less about cultural developments outside the socialist countries. Under the guise of struggling against cosmopolitanism and "foreign fads," Soviet writers were fenced off from the progressive intelligentsia of the West. For example, in 1949 Soviet newspapers called Hemingway "a snob who has lost his conscience"; the antifascist writer Lion Feuchtwanger was identified as a "literary huckster"; while Sinclair Lewis was said to have "a dirty little soul."

Finally the suppression of democracy in cultural organizations must be noted. Congresses of writers were no longer held on the union level. The board of directors of the Writers' Union was not re-elected. More and more openly, the move was toward monopoly rule, the formation of cliques assuming the power to lay down the law in literature, painting, architecture, the cinema, and the theater.

[87] See *Problemy mira i sotsializma*, 1965, No. 1, prilozhenie.

XV

Socialism and Pseudosocialism

1

THE TRADE UNIONS were originally supposed to be a bulwark of democracy. They were to defend workers against bureaucratic elements in the *apparat*. Opposing the view that the unions should be made part of the state, Lenin wrote: "Our state right now is such that the whole organized proletariat must defend itself against it." The trade unions, he said, cannot lose

> such a basic function as nonclass "economic struggle," in the sense of struggle against bureaucratic perversions in the Soviet *apparat*, in the sense of protecting the material and spiritual interests of the toiling masses by ways and means unavailable to that *apparat*. . . .[1]

What is more, Lenin suggested that in fifteen or twenty years the trade unions would take on a major share of management. But nothing of the sort happened. Stalin did not try even as an experiment to introduce elements of workers' participation in management. The trade unions were for all practical purposes made part of the state. They were transformed into a simple appendage of Party and economic agencies. They did not study the standard of living of the various strata of workers, or the real cost of living, or the minimum level of subsistence, much less fight to improve the material position of the workers. They took almost no part in the discussion of major economic problems. Their basic job became the handling of petty problems of daily life.[2]

The Soviets were designed to be organs of democracy, the direct instruments of the people's rule. Stalin retained them in form, but in

---

[1] *Sochineniia*, 4th edn., XXXII, p. 79.
[2] *Ed.*: Medvedev is evidently referring to the processing of individual grievances.

reality they "were plunged into a lethargic sleep."[3] Stalin talked frequently about reviving them, but he never got beyond talk. Both at the center and in the provinces they became mere appendages of Party committees, mute executors of directives coming from Party agencies.

The Constitution of 1936 did not arrest this process. To be sure, elections to the Soviets became more democratic from a formal point of view. Deputies to local Soviets had been elected by open voting in factories and other institutions; now they were elected in polling places scattered through territorial districts. The entire adult population cast secret ballots. Once the voters elected deputies directly only to the local Soviets; the local Soviets elected deputies to the next higher Soviets, and so on. Now all elections became direct. The voters of each district elected deputies to the local Soviet, the city Soviet, the *oblast* Soviet, the republic Soviet, and the Supreme Soviet of the USSR. But in reality this system, which copied procedures in bourgeois democracies with their multiparty system, was hardly a step forward for the Soviet state. The change from open voting to a secret ballot was the only genuine progress. Otherwise the new system was even regressive. Factories and other institutions lost the chance to influence the Soviets. Interaction between deputies and voters was considerably weakened. It became much harder for the voters to follow the activities of a deputy or to recall him. When elections were held directly at factories and other institutions, voters could discuss the relative merits of various candidates and choose the best man. Now voters had no choice but the one name presented for each office.

All this decreased the deputies' responsibility to their constituents, and the voters too lost a sense of responsibility—many of them quickly forgot whom they had voted for in the last elections. The interdependence of Soviets on different levels also declined. Formerly, when local Soviets elected higher ones, the lower had some claim to control the higher; now control passed only from the top down. In other words, the local Soviets differed little from the municipalities in centralized bourgeois states.[4] Many workers and peasants continued to be elected as deputies, but this meant little, for the work of government was done more and more in the Soviets' executive committees, which carried out directives from the center and paid little attention to local initiative. The Soviets were not convened regularly. The supreme Soviets of the republics generally met only to ratify the budgets and the decrees issued by their presidiums. Even the ratification of the budget was secured, as a rule, only several months after the budget had gone into effect. Legislation originated only in the executive arm or most often

---

[3] *Problemy mira i sotsializma,* 1963, No. 5, p. 60.
[4] Paul Miliukov noted this with satisfaction in his article "Pravda o bol'shevizme": "The Constitution of 1936 . . . restored normal forms of government."

in the Party's Central Committee, not among the deputies. The
Supreme Soviet almost never engaged in real discussion of the bills
presented to it for discussion. Deputies never criticized bills—until the
executive organs proposed the revocation of bills that had been passed
without a murmur.

The Party also suffered from violations of democracy during these
years. Stalin's disregard for the Central Committee as an organ of
collective leadership has been discussed. Regular meetings of plenary
organizations were not convened. All questions were decided in the
buro or by the First Secretary and other officials of the *apparat*.
Candidates for elections to Party offices were never discussed, except
in the primary Party organizations. The secretaries and buro members
of the *obkom* and the *raikom* were appointed "from above," with no
one asking the opinions of ordinary Party members. Naturally, Party
leaders appointed in such a way considered themselves responsible not
to those below them but only to those above them. Gradually many
of them turned into simple executors of instructions, into *chinovniki,*
as functionaries were called in the old regime.

Thus, while a democratic system was preserved in form, in fact a
hierarchy of cults arose, each covering a certain territory or field of
action. Certainly there was an enormous difference between the big
cult of Stalin and the little cults of an *obkom* secretary or some scientific boss: Stalin alone was god. But there were also similarities.
Wladyslaw Gomulka has given a good characterization of the hierarchy:[5]

> The chief figure in a cult of personality understood everything,
> knew everything, decided everything, and directed everything in the
> field of his activity. He was the most intelligent person, regardless
> of his actual knowledge, abilities, and personal qualities. It was not
> so bad when a reasonable and modest man was arrayed in the
> garment of a cult. Such a man usually felt bad in such attire. It can
> be said that he was ashamed and did not want to wear it, though he
> could not entirely take it off. . . . Matters were worse or even quite
> bad when a limited man, a stupid agent for someone else, or a rotten
> careerist, got power, i.e., the right to a cult. Such people buried
> socialism, unthinkingly but surely. Given the system of the cult,
> the Party as a whole could act independently only within the frame-
> work of subordination to the chief cult. If anyone tried to get out-
> side this framework, he was threatened with anathema by his
> comrades. If an entire party was involved, then the other parties
> anathematized it. . . .
> The system of the cult of the personality shaped the minds,
> shaped the mode of thinking of Party leaders and members. Some

[5] *Rech' na VIII plenume TSK PORP, 20 oktiabria* (Warsaw, 1956), pp. 39–40.

believed and were convinced that the only infallible interpreter of Marxist science, the only person who was developing and enriching it correctly, showing the only correct road to socialism, was Stalin. It followed that everything that did not correspond to his ideas and orders was harmful, was bound to entail abandonment of Marxism-Leninism, was a heresy. Others, who had their doubts, were also convinced that any attempt to express their thoughts in public not only would change nothing but would end with unpleasant consequences for themselves. Still others were indifferent to everything except the path that would take them to a soft chair and guarantee that chair.

"The state," Lenin said, "gets its strength from the consciousness of the masses. It is strong when the masses know everything, can pass judgment on everything and do everything consciously." Of course such consciousness does not come by itself; it can only be the result of prolonged education of the people. The Communist Party and its chiefs are supposed to educate the masses to independence and a sense of responsibility, to conscious discipline, to democracy and love of freedom, to hatred of injustice and arbitrary rule. And the Party accomplished much in that direction even in the thirties and forties. It would be wrong to think that our propaganda did nothing but extol Stalin and cover up his crimes. Using other examples and object lessons, both domestic and foreign, the Party continued to educate the Soviet people and Soviet youth in the spirit of socialism. Thus it is indisputable that during the years of the cult the consciousness and activism of the masses grew, *within certain limits*. The people became more educated and cultured, Leninist ideas penetrated everywhere. Proletarian influences reached the petty-bourgeois masses; the authority of the Communist Party increased markedly. But at the same time the masses were educated in another, unproletarian spirit, in the spirit of blind subjection to the authority of the chiefs, above all Stalin.

Stalin mistrusted and despised the people. He belonged to a workers' party but did not respect workers. He said of a man from a working-class milieu: "This one's come from under his machine. What's he doing mixing in?" Neither the people nor the Party were really involved in the solution of fundamental problems; even most officials in the *apparat* were not involved. Political passivity was encouraged among Party members as well as in the masses at large. Criticism of the leaders' actions, especially of Stalin himself, was ruled out at any level. Everything that issued from the Kremlin was always accepted as right or in any case as inevitable.

Stalin often discussed the need of criticism from below, saying that criticism and authority were compatible. But he never put that objective into effect with respect to most Party leaders, certainly not with respect to himself. In 1928 he described the danger inherent in such a situation:

> The fact that the chiefs rising to the top become separated from the masses, while the masses begin to look up at them from below, not daring to criticize them—this fact cannot but create a certain danger of isolation and estrangement between the chiefs and the masses. This danger may reach the point where the chiefs get conceited and consider themselves infallible. And what good can come of the leaders on top growing conceited and beginning to look down on the masses from above? Clearly, nothing but disaster for the Party can come from this.[6]

In this matter as in so many others, Stalin talked one way and behaved another.

Marx and Engels, who foresaw the possibility of the bureaucratic degeneration of a proletarian state, thought two measures would provide effective protection: universal election and recall of all officials, and a level of salaries not exceeding workers' wages.[7] But during the cult, as we have seen, the right to recall officials, like the right of free democratic elections, became a fiction; it ceased to exist, for in the Soviet social mechanism there were no means, no organizations, no political institutions, to guarantee the exercise of the people's democratic rights.

The restrictions on official salaries also turned out to be a weak protection against degeneration. The Soviet regime did not blindly imitate the Paris Commune; the Council of People's Commissars, following the socialist principle of payment according to work performed, set the minimum monthly wages of workers' helpers at 120 rubles, while the chairman of the Council received 600 rubles. Thus, the ratio between the lowest worker's wages and the highest official's salary was 1 to 5. In the ensuing Civil War and economic collapse, real wages dropped far below the subsistence minimum. For a long time, manual and white-collar workers were obliged to deny themselves necessities, to live half-starved. Most of them were willing to make these necessary sacrifices. On the other hand, specialists, most of whom were of the bourgeois intelligentsia, could not be drawn into the service of the young Soviet state without salaries that were fairly high for the time.

With respect to Communists, even those who held the highest posts, Lenin demanded moderation. He showed concern for their health and food and living accommodations, but insisted that their salaries,

---

[6] Stalin, *Sochineniia*, XI, p. 31.
[7] See, e.g., Marx and Engels, *Sochineniia*, 2nd edn., XXII, p. 200. This is Engels' introduction to the 1891 edition of Marx's *Civil War in France*.

his own included, be kept within certain limits. No luxuries were allowed. Lenin took this issue very seriously. He repeatedly stressed the need for "gradual equalization of all wages and salaries in all professions and job categories."[8] He insisted that high salaries for bourgeois specialists were "a compromise, a retreat from the principles of a Communist Party and of any proletarian regime, which require that all salaries be reduced to the level of an average worker's pay, that careerism be fought with action, not with words."[9] He acknowledged that "the corrupting influence of high salaries is indisputable, both on the Soviet regime . . . and on the working class masses."[10]

In general, Lenin opposed both the equalization of all wages and excessively high salaries, especially for Party members. This policy resulted in the so-called Party maximum—a wage ceiling for all Communists. In August, 1922, a Party conference decreed a table of ranks for Party members, and required any member whose salary exceeded the highest rank by more than 50 per cent to contribute a large portion of the excess to a mutual-assistance fund.[11] In October, 1923, the Central Committee and the Central Control Commission sent all Party organizations and Party members a special circular concerning misappropriation of state funds and goods. In particular the circular ordered a halt to the furnishing of apartments and private dachas at state expense. Grants of goods to Party members were to be tapered off; the standard of living appropriate to responsible officials was to be achieved by raising salaries, which would be subject to strict accounting, as grants of goods were not.[12]

For the most part the Party maximum was an operative rule until the end of the twenties and early thirties. Then it began to be undermined, primarily by the decline in the real wages of most workers. The limited increase in money wages did not cover the rapid rise in prices; a considerable number of workers found their income sinking below the subsistence minimum. At the same time the small circle of high officials was protected by the creation of a system of special stores, distributing centers, and dining rooms, where goods could be obtained at fixed prices. Gradually they acquired other privileges too: their own hospitals, free rest homes, dachas, and so on. In the same period a peculiar habit began to appear: the Party *aktiv* were given expensive gifts for holidays, congresses, and conferences. On February

[8] *Sochineniia*, 4th edn., XXVII, p. 132.
[9] *Ibid.*, p. 220.
[10] *Ibid.*, p. 222. Cf. 221, for his flat declaration: "To conceal from the masses the fact that attracting bourgeois specialists by excessively high salaries is a retreat from the principles of the Commune would be to sink to the level of bourgeois politicians, to deceive the masses."
[11] *Spravochnik partrabotnika, vypusk* III (Moscow, 1923), pp. 95–96.
[12] No. 58, Oct. 19, 1923. *Ed.:* This is the entire reference in Medvedev's manuscript.

8, 1932, the Party maximum was formally abolished, bringing a new increase in the real income of leading officials.

When the economic situation improved, permitting the abolition of rationing in 1935 and a steady increase in real wages, the privileges of high officials were not terminated. On the contrary, they were increased. A system of representatives' subsidies (*predstavitel'skie dotatsii*) was established for all officials at the level of the chairman of a city Soviet and higher. Moreover, the direct salaries of higher officials rose much faster than wages of ordinary workers. Many officials increased their salaries even more through a system of pluralism (*sovmestitel'stvo*); that is, one man held several offices, receiving full pay for each. Thus the 1-to-5 ratio between an average worker's salary and that of the highest official, which Lenin evidently considered optimal, was violated even before the war.

Subsequently the ratio grew still greater. During the war and the first postwar years, when the real wages of ordinary workers were falling once again, the salaries of the highest officials continued to rise. That was the period when the disgraceful system of "packets" (*pakety*) was introduced in the higher state and Party institutions. Each month almost every high official would receive an envelope or packet containing a large sum, often much higher than the salary formally designated for his post. These payments passed through special financial channels, were not subject to taxes, and were kept secret from the rank-and-file officials of the institution. Some Communists found the courage to refuse these packets. E. P. Frolov tells how M. D. Kammari, an editor of the journal *Kommunist,* never went to get his packets from the bookkeeper's office, which put the head bookkeeper in a difficult position. "I don't need so much money," Kammari used to say. "My salary is enough for me." But he had few imitators among his colleagues. On the contrary many of them began to look at him suspiciously, regarding his behavior as a challenge and a protest.

In the postwar years the ratio between the real wages of an average worker and the salary of the highest official became scandalously large. (We will not even bring into the comparison the very lowest wages, twenty-seven to thirty rubles in present prices, which was three to four times less than the subsistence minimum.) If we estimate not only formal direct money salary but the whole system of payments, then the ratio was 1 to 40, 1 to 50, and for some officials even 1 to 100.

As for members of the Politburo and Stalin himself, the cost of keeping them does not submit to calculation. The numerous dachas and apartments, the huge domestic staffs, the expenses for their staffs and guards, rose to millions of rubles yearly. Stalin alone cost the state tens of millions of rubles a year. It is said that he once asked the head of his guard, General Vlasik, to calculate this sum. With the help of specialists Vlasik made extremely careful calculations, and came up with a figure so astronomical that even Stalin was not only astonished but upset. "It cannot be," he told Vlasik. "That's a lie." Beria immediately assured Stalin that Vlasik's calculations were nonsense, and Vlasik was fired. We do not know whether this story is true, but we can be sure that Vlasik was closer to the truth than Beria. Maintaining Stalin cost the state much more than the American people pay for their President, and it may not have been much more expensive to support Nicholas II.

The political passivity of the masses, the lack of criticism, the serious violations of democracy both in the Party and in the Soviets, high salaries and "packets"—all generated an amazingly rapid growth of bureaucracy. A bureaucrat is not simply a government functionary who sits in his office and directs certain affairs. A bureaucrat is a privileged functionary, cut off from real life, from the people, from the needs and interests of common folk. He is interested in his job as a position to be preserved and improved, not as a task to be done. He will knowingly do something unnecessary or even harmful for the people if it will preserve his position. Careerism and subservience, red tape and protocol, are his constant companions. Basic ignorance, especially of cultural achievements, emotional dullness, and a limited intellect are, as E. Gnedin rightly remarks, typical characteristics of the bureaucrat.[13]

Bureaucracy, as has been said above, provided fertile soil for the cult of personality. Marx put it very well:

> Bureaucracy considers itself the ultimate purpose of the state. . . . The higher circles rely on the lower in everything involving a knowledge of particulars; the lower circles trust the upper in everything involving an understanding of the universal, and thus they lead each other into delusions. . . . The universal spirit of bureaucracy is mystery, sacrament. Observance of this sacrament is ensured from within by hierarchical organization, and with relation to the outside world by its closed corporative character. Authority is therefore the criterion of knowledge, and the deification of authority is its manner of thought.[14]

The lack of effective controls, the passivity of the masses, and bureaucracy inevitably generated corruption. The venality of many officials during the cult of personality reached such proportions that the countermeasures taken since Stalin's death have not been sufficiently effective. Extreme measures had to be used; in 1962 the death penalty was authorized for certain cases of bribetaking. Lenin in his

[13] See "Biurokratiia xx-go veka," *Novyi mir*, 1966, No. 2, p. 199.
[14] Marx-Engels, *Sochineniia*, 2nd edn., I, pp. 271–72.

time also demanded "at least ten years of prison, and on top of that ten years of hard labor" for bribetaking.[15] "We must struggle against bribery," he said in another letter, "and punish it by shooting after trial."[16]

Bureaucracy and corruption during the cult of personality destroyed the masses' belief that they, the simple people, were the real masters of their country. Among workers and peasants there was a blunting of the feeling of responsibility for everything going on around them, an important moral stimulus for the development of our society. Moreover, there was a decline in the sense of responsibility among the leaders themselves. A bureaucrat rises not by the will and demands of those beneath him. He is solely dependent on those above him. An *oblast* might not like or respect its first secretary, but it had to put up with his leadership as long as he was on good terms with his superiors. Under these conditions many officials stopped taking the feelings and opinions of ordinary people into account altogether, and became accustomed to commanding those beneath them and fawning upon their superiors.[17]

Not all the leaders during the cult were corrupt bureaucrats. As has been pointed out, the mid-thirties witnessed the rise of a whole new generation of able and dedicated young officials. But the conditions of the cult militated against their rise to the top. Cruel and unprincipled careerists could best adapt to the situation. Under Stalin's dictatorship the disciplined, imperious leader was the most likely to succeed, intolerant of criticism from below, saying one thing and doing another, incapable even of talking with the common people, relying on force and intimidation in dealings with them.[18]

A Stalinist was usually a careerist, who combined arrogance and conceit with political instability and hypocrisy. Many of these "Communists" wanted not only power but ostentatious luxury, a clear demonstration of their elevation above the people. The majority of Stalinists did not hesitate to put their hands in the public till, to use state property as their own. Some Western theorists have argued that a new class arose in our country, a class of bourgeoisified officials. Such a theory is incorrect. Part of the leading cadres degenerated, but the process did not go so far as to create a new class. On the other hand, the possibility of such a result cannot be ruled out. For a Stalinist is not simply a certain type of leader who appeared during the cult of personality. During the long years of the Stalinist dictator-

[15] *Sochineniia*, 4th edn., XXXV, p. 27.
[16] *Leninskii sbornik*, XXXVI, p. 441.
[17] See the penetrating remarks of I. Vinogradov, concerning the agrarian sketches of E. Dorosh and V. Ovechkin, in *Novyi mir*, 1965, No. 7, p. 244.
[18] For an effective contrast between the Leninist and Stalinist types of leader, see E. Drabkina, *ibid.*, 1963, No. 7, and A. Metchenko, *Kommunist*, 1964, No. 12.

ship, clearly defined elements of a bureaucratic oligarchy and a caste system arose in the higher and middle levels of leadership; a clearly defined part of these leaders began to consider their position and privileges a right that must be defended by any means.

After Stalin's death, authors such as Vladimir Dudintsev exposed the ugly truth about such leaders. His novel *Not by Bread Alone* was a social event, as Konstantin Paustovskii said.

> The new caste of Drozdovs[19] is still with us, . . . there are still thousands and thousands of them. . . . Recently I took a trip around Europe on the steamer *Pobeda.* In the second and third classes there were workers, engineers, artists, musicians, writers; in the first class were the Drozdovs. I need not tell you that they had and could have absolutely no contact with the second and third classes. They revealed hostility to everything except their position, they astounded us by their ignorance. They and we had completely different ideas about what constituted the prestige and honor of our country. One of the Drozdovs, standing before "The Last Judgment," asked: "Is that the judgment of Mussolini?" Another, looking at the Acropolis, said: "How could the proletariat allow the Acropolis to be built?" A third, overhearing a comment on the amazing color of the Mediterranean, asked severely: "And is our water back home worse?" These predators, proprietors, cynics, and obscurantists, openly, without fear or embarrassment, carried on anti-Semitic conversations worthy of true Nazis. They were jobbers, quite, quite indifferent to anything else. . . . Where did they come from, these bootlickers and traitors, who think they have the right to speak in the name of the people? Where did they originate? They are the consequence of the cult; the situation trained them to regard the people as dung to fertilize their career. Intrigues, slander, moral assassination, and just plain assassination—these are their weapons, as a result of which Meyerhold, Babel, Artem Vesely are not in this hall with us today. The Drozdovs destroyed them. The cause that moved them was their own prosperity. Dudintsev has given one example of their terrible work. . . . We must fight the corruption that can ruin the country. The behavior of these Drozdovs is encased in slogans, they give blasphemous speeches, saying that they are acting for the good of the people. Who gave them the right to represent the people? Dudintsev has only begun the battle; the task of our literature is to fight it to the end.

The fresh stream of the last decade has swept most of these Stalinists, these Drozdovs and Borzovs,[20] into the sump pit of our political life. But not all of them are cutting roses at their dachas. Many have adapted to the new situation.

[19] *Ed.:* Drozdov is the chief villain of Dudintsev's novel, a masterful caricature of the Stalinist official.

[20] *Ed.:* A character in V. V. Ovechkin's story "Raion Routine." See his *Upriamyi Khutor; rasskazy i ocherki* (Moscow, 1960), pp. 221 *ff.*

Stalin's cult gave rise to similar systems in many Communist parties, not only in socialist but also in capitalist countries. The deification of Mao Tse-tung in China, the cults of Rákosi in Hungary, of Vlko Chervenkov in Bulgaria, of Enver Hoxha in Albania, are comparable to the cult of Stalin; accompanied by lawlessness, the rise of mistrust in relations among Communists, and a dangerous gulf between the Communist parties and the masses, all of which has greatly helped our enemies in their anti-Communist propaganda.

Bureaucracy among the governors and political passivity among the governed were the most dangerous consequences of the cult of personality. When Beria prepared a *coup d'état* in 1953, he counted most of all, not on the MVD divisions that he moved toward Moscow but on the political passivity of the majority of people and also on the discipline of the bureaucracy, who were trained not to interfere in Kremlin affairs.

2

WHILE DOGMATISM and rote learning reigned in ideology, political life was afflicted with sectarianism. Sectarianism has always been one of the most widespread and dangerous diseases of the revolutionary and socialist movement. Marx, Engels, and Lenin provided us with models of the way to resist this disease, by making the movement as broad as possible. Lenin's nonsectarian policy toward bourgeois specialists, and his refusal to excommunicate comrades who erred have been noted. Indeed, he could pay eloquent tribute to people with whom he had had many sharp disagreements, such as Plekhanov, Rosa Luxemburg, and Kautsky. In each case Lenin insisted that their works be published in full and studied by all Communists.[21] The obituary he wrote on a Left S-R, P. P. Prosh'ian, is remarkably revealing. "Comrade Prosh'ian," as Lenin did not hesitate to call him, "did more before July, 1918, to strengthen the Soviet regime than he did in July, 1918, to damage it." Lenin knew very well that Prosh'ian had been sentenced to three years in prison for taking part in the Left S-R insurrection against the Soviet regime, that he had not served his sen-

---

[21] For some of his tributes to Plekhanov, see Lenin, *Polnoe sobranie*, XXV, p. 222, and XLII, p. 290. For Kautsky, see *ibid.*, XXXII, p. 104. For Luxemburg, see *Sochineniia*, 4th edn., XXXIII, pp. 183–84. Some of Stalin's admirers claim that we should treat him as Lenin treated Plekhanov. This is a poor analogy. Despite his mistakes, Plekhanov was an outstanding Marxist theorist, who never committed any crimes. While we condemn Stalin unreservedly, we can have a different attitude toward those of his former colleagues who today are deeply repentant of their pasts, who sincerely condemn the crimes of the Stalinist period and help to expose and correct them. Stalin never repented; on the contrary, he moved steadily from one crime to ever more monstrous ones.

tence but had gone into hiding with a false passport, and had died in a dilapidated hospital.[22]

Lenin's attitude toward N. N. Nakoriakov (Nazar Ural'skii) provides another illuminating example. An old Bolshevik, Nakoriakov had done much revolutionary work in various Russian cities and abroad. In 1916, however, he took a defensist position [i.e., supported the Russian war effort], and after the February Revolution supported the Provisional Government. In 1919–20 he served in Denikin's army, but became disillusioned with the White Guard movement, left it, and entered the service of the Soviet government. Lenin followed his political evolution closely, considering him a valuable official of the Soviet regime. In November, 1921, Lenin arranged a meeting with Nakoriakov, and on January 4, 1922, wrote to Preobrazhenskii: "Please drop me a few lines about Nazar Nakoriakov. Has he got a job? What are his political feelings—have they changed lately or are they the same as before?"[23] Preobrazhenskii replied that the conversation with Lenin had made a great impression on Nakoriakov, but his political evolution was very slow and he was working in an unimportant job in the Trade Union Council. In 1922, with Lenin's influence, Nakoriakov was appointed director of the State Publishing House of Artistic Literature. In 1925 he joined the Bolshevik Party once again.

Stalin's way was utterly different. Sectarianism and indiscriminate mistrust were characteristic of him from the start. We have already described his refusal to trust any of the military specialists during the Civil War, in spite of the Party's clearly expressed policy. In the late twenties and early thirties he showed the same unjustified mistrust toward almost all the bourgeois specialists. As for Party comrades who made mistakes, Stalin never forgot or forgave. They were forced to make repeated declarations of repentance, and if they were destroyed, the historical record was changed to make all their past activity seem an unbroken chain of crimes and blunders.

Worse yet, from the end of the thirties huge groups of Soviet people were placed under suspicion regardless of their actual behavior, on the basis of completely arbitrary and subjective criteria. It was then, when Stalin's despotism was utterly unlimited, that sectarianism became one of the most important elements of Party and state policy. Talking about "prophylactic" measures against the intensification of the class struggle, Stalin divided all citizens into two categories: the politically reliable and the politically unreliable. He said that a son is not answerable for his father, and vigilance should

[22] See *Katorga i ssylka,* 1924, No. 2, pp. 222–23. The obituary is reprinted in Lenin, *Sochineniia,* 4th edn., XXXVI, pp. 456–57.
[23] *Polnoe sobranie,* LIV, p. 107.

not be confused with suspiciousness, but his actions belied his words. Many of the "unreliable" were barred from any responsible positions and confined to routine jobs regardless of their abilities. As an *obkom* secretary once said: "The Party does not need talent; it needs loyal people."

Who were classified as "unreliable"? (Former capitalists and counterrevolutionaries are not considered; only a few of them remained in the country.) First, there were children and close relatives of "enemies of the people"—numbering in the millions. Then there were children, even grandchildren, of former kulaks and other members of the exploiting classes—again millions of people. There were millions more who had relatives abroad. After the war almost all former prisoners of war and repatriated people, their children and close relatives, were put into this category. The tens of millions who spent the war in territory occupied by the Germans were also suspect, their rights and opportunities restricted.

A final peculiarity of this sectarianism must be noted. As far as Stalin and his entourage were concerned, it was not the result of anxiety about the purity of the Party or the leading agencies of the state. They made many exceptions for themselves and for people who suited their purposes. Relatives of "enemies of the people," former oppositionists, former Mensheviks, and so on, could be found at the highest levels. No agency was stricter in selection of personnel than the NKVD, yet that agency had the most alien elements, people who had once been expelled from the Party, people with criminal records and dubious political histories. Thus, for Stalinists sectarianism was only one more means of preserving their own rights and privileges.

3

TURGENEV WROTE of an old liar who gave this clever advice: "When you do a rotten thing, shout louder than anyone about the foulness of such things. When you rob the treasury, shout louder than anyone about the infamy of embezzlement!" Machiavelli gave analogous advice to rulers. They should express

> piety, fidelity, humaneness, sincerity, religion. . . . Everyone sees what you seem to be, a few will sense what you are, and these few will not dare to speak against the opinion of the crowd, on whom the grandeur of the state rests.

Stalin may not have read Turgenev or Machiavelli, but he was a master of this cynical rule.

This book has cited numerous examples of Stalin's brazen hypocrisy. Thousands of times he said one thing and did the opposite. He spoke of collective leadership and made decisions on his own. He said the alliance between the workers and peasants should be strengthened, at the very time he was destroying that alliance. He advocated voluntary collectivization and sanctioned force. While systematically falsifying history and contemporary news, he sanctimoniously exclaimed: "God forbid that we should be infected with the disease of fearing the truth. The Bolsheviks differ from all other parties in that they do not fear the truth, are not afraid to look truth in the eye, however bitter it may be."[24] Accusing tens of thousands of innocent citizens of plotting against the Soviet regime, Stalin himself carried out a plot against the Leninist leadership of the Party and state. Mass repression coincided with the promulgation of a new and more democratic constitution. Persecuting the intelligentsia, Stalin denounced *Makhaevshchina*[25] and called the intelligentsia the salt of the Soviet earth. In January, 1938, at the height of the repression, he had the Central Committee adopt a resolution calling for due process in expulsions from the Party. Several thousand expelled and arrested Communists were in fact released and reinstated, with considerable press coverage. But at the same time a new political trial was begun, bringing in its train the arrest of hundreds of thousands of innocent people.

Stalin even denounced the cult of personality. In 1932, when the Society of Old Bolsheviks asked for permission to open an exhibition of documents concerning his life and activity, he refused: "I am against it because such enterprises lead to the establishment of a 'cult of personality,' which is harmful and incompatible with the spirit of the Party."[26] Only a few years later dozens of such exhibitions celebrated "the greatest genius of modern times." In 1930 he wrote a letter to Shatunovskii, urging him not to speak of devotion to Stalin or to any individual. "That is not a Bolshevik principle. Have devotion to the working class, to its Party, to its state, but don't mix that up with devotion to individuals, which is an inane and unnecessary toy of the intelligentsia."[27] This letter was first published in 1951, at a time when every newspaper and every speech expressed personal devotion to Stalin much more frequently than devotion to the Party and the people.

A profound connoisseur of human failings, a brilliant master of bureaucratic psychology, Stalin systematically inculcated respect for rank in every field of life. All sorts of tables of ranks were worked out, and promotion was accompanied by privileges, rigorously defined

---

[24] Stalin, *Sochineniia,* XII, p. 9.
[25] A left-wing form of anti-intellectualism. The Polish radical Jan Machajski urged the exclusion of intellectuals from the proletarian movement.
[26] Central Party Archive, Institute of Marxism-Leninism (F. 558, *op.* 1, *d.* 4572, *l.* 1).
[27] Stalin, *Sochineniia,* XIII, p. 19.

for each rank, as well as by increased responsibility and pay. Special uniforms and insignia were worn not only in the army but by railway workers, juridical officials, and diplomats. For himself Stalin devised the special rank of Generalissimo. Yet he declared, "For the most part I am not an admirer of those who worship rank."[28]

And how many times did Stalin call for criticism and self-criticism! For example:

> Sometimes people say that self-criticism is a good thing for a party that has not yet come to power and has "nothing to lose," but self-criticism is dangerous and harmful for a party that has come to power, that is surrounded by hostile forces, against which enemies can use exposure of its weaknesses.
>
> . . . That is completely untrue! On the contrary, it is precisely because the Bolsheviks have come to power, precisely because the Bolsheviks may get conceited about their achievements, precisely because the Bolsheviks may not notice their weaknesses, and thus may make the enemy's work easier, precisely for these reasons self-criticism is especially necessary now, after the taking of power.
>
> The purpose of self-criticism is to reveal and liquidate our weaknesses. Is it not clear that self-criticism in a dictatorship of the proletariat can only facilitate the Bolsheviks' struggle against the enemies of the working class? . . .
>
> To put off self-criticism is to make things easier for our enemies, to aggravate our weaknesses and mistakes. But to do all this is impossible without . . . involving the working class and the peasantry in the liquidation of our weaknesses, our mistakes.[29]

Fine preaching, often quoted in the years of the cult, but not practiced, for the author did not practice it. And how sharply Stalin denounced arbitrary rule in the Party! "I am absolutely against a policy of expelling all dissident (*inakomysliashchie*) comrades," he wrote to a German Communist.

> I am against such a policy not because I feel sorry for dissidents but because such a policy generates in the Party a regime of intimidation, a regime of fright, a regime that kills the spirit of self-criticism and initiative. It is not good if the Party chiefs are feared but not respected.[30]

Comment would be superfluous.

"Stalin's school was a very rough school," A. V. Snegov told the All-Union Conference of Historians in 1962. "Besides destroying honorable people, he corrupted live ones. He forced people to carry out dirty missions, and on the ideological front taught them to lie."[31]

[28] *Ibid.*, XII, p. 114.
[29] *Ibid.*, XI, pp. 128–30.
[30] *Ibid.*, VII, pp. 44–45.
[31] *Vsesoiuznoe soveshchanie istorikov*, p. 270.

All media of communication varnished reality, ignored most difficulties, injustice, and arbitrary rule. Many good decisions were made and never carried out. But the incongruity between words and deeds consisted not just in saying one thing and doing another but in saying nothing about much that was done.

4

SOCIALISM MEANS not only that social ownership replaces private ownership in the means of production, not only a change in the relationship of man to machine, but also a change in the relations of men to each other. Socialism was supposed to be a profoundly humane social system created for man, for the happiness of the toilers. Back in 1845 Engels found the essence of socialism in "the creation for all people of such conditions that everyone will get the chance to develop his human nature freely, to live in human relationships with his neighbors, without fear of violent destruction of his well-being."[32] The most famous statement of this theme occurs in *The Communist Manifesto:* "The free development of each is the condition for the free development of all."[33] In 1894, a year before Engels' death, he recalled these words as the briefest possible expression of the basic idea of socialism.[34] Thus not only the absence of exploitation but also love for people, concern for their everyday needs both spiritual and material, and genuine democracy, order, and legality—all these are essential features of a socialist society.

The Communist Party started to build such a society in the Soviet Union. Millions of people guided by the ideas of Marxism-Leninism moved toward that goal. The October Revolution brought power to the toilers, factories to the workers, land to the peasants. Thus a solid foundation was laid for a truly socialist democracy. The workers won extensive social rights and freedoms, women received equal rights with men, the road to culture and education was opened to the masses, and also the way to abolition of national and class antagonisms. It would be wrong to deny these achievements by referring to the deformities of the Stalinist period. An ever-expanding sector of the Soviet population has relationships not of enmity, rivalry, and exploitation but of friendship and cooperation. Such relationships existed and developed during the first Five-Year Plans, the Second World War, and the postwar period. Various forms of these truly socialist relationships have also developed in the people's democracies.

[32] Marx and Engels, *Sochineniia,* 2nd edn., II, p. 554.
[33] *Ibid.,* IV, p. 447.
[34] *Ibid.,* XXXIX, pp. 166–67.

But it must be acknowledged with equal clarity that Soviet philosophy, sociology, and history have so far examined these relationships in a one-sided fashion. They show only the contrast between socialism and capitalism, or between socialism and vestiges of precapitalist social formations. That is an important aspect of the problem, but not the only one.

Capitalism and feudalism have often been veiled in outwardly attractive forms. A good example of such social mimicry is the "Christian republic" created by the Jesuits in Paraguay in 1610 and lasting for more than 150 years. Jesuit missionaries drove tens of thousands of Indians into special settlements, where they were condemned to backbreaking work and semistarvation under conditions of regimentation and complete lack of personal freedom. They were shut up in their settlements like rabbits in a pen. Their law was the will of the priest. They worked four to five days a week "for God" and only two for themselves. But the Jesuits declared that this was a "Christian communist republic," which realized the ideals of equality and happiness.

There have been many projects for pseudosocialism. Iu. A. Kariakin has made an original analysis of Marx's and Engels' comments on such "crude," "primitive," "instinctual," "leveling," "unreasoned," "ascetic," "barrack" types of socialism. (All the adjectives are Marx's or Engels'.) They all involve the transformation of a very limited perception into a world view. Repudiation of the individual is the beginning and the end of this ideology. Repudiation of the individual generates envy, a striving to level, the rule of universal grayness, mediocrity, militant ignorance, blind hatred of "educated people," the transformation of the great democratic demand for equality into the reduction of all "ordinary people" to the lowest or the mean level, willful instead of scientific politics, a peculiar secular religion in which "truth" is presented to the faithful as a revelation from above, as a miraculous gift, more often as a command requiring unquestioning obedience. Talk about democracy is turned into organized enthusiasm for these commandments. The relations between shepherds and sheep is actually a case of the blind leading the blind. Jesuitry, at first spontaneous and unconscious, develops, improves, and may attain a degree of self-consciousness.[35] The proclaimed goals may gradually fade into the background and become only a means to

[35] See Marx and Engels, *Iz rannykh proizvedenii,* p. 586; *Sochineniia,* 2nd edn., I, pp. 444–45; XXXIV, p. 235; XXXV, p. 186; XXI, pp. 217–22; XXVII, pp. 202, 306; etc. *Ed.:* Medvedev's manuscript does not make it clear how much of this passage, which has been abridged in translation, is quotation from Marx and Engels, quotation from Kariakin, or Medvedev's own words. Kariakin's article is entitled "Marksistskaia traditsiia bor'by protiv 'Kazarmennogo Kommunizma.'" Place of publication, if any, is not specified.

realize the one genuine goal: to seize and hold personal power. "We already know," warned Marx, "what a role stupidity plays in revolutions, and how scoundrels are able to exploit it."[36]

Despite the spread of Marxism and the triumph of the October Revolution, pseudosocialism has not disappeared but has actually gained ground. That is not surprising. Pseudosocialism is a weed that is very hard to extirpate, for it spreads together with genuine socialism, always changing its appearance. By no means all ideologists and politicians who are essentially bourgeois express *open* hostility to socialism and communism. Many try to take advantage of the ideas and slogans of socialism, which are popular among the masses. Leaders of petty-bourgeois movements are especially given to this tactic. German fascism, for example, masked its archreactionary content with the term "National Socialism." Of course there was not a grain of socialism in either the "Christian republic" in Paraguay or the "National Socialist" state in Germany. But many social systems and states have arisen in recent decades that combine features of real and sham socialism. And that was the case in the USSR in the period of Stalin's cult.

The open forms of capitalism and feudalism were destroyed in our country as a result of fierce class struggle, but the complete hegemony of socialist relationships and structures did not follow. It was not just that certain "vestiges of capitalism" remained. Marx showed that socialism is distinguished from communism by its retention of certain "birthmarks" of capitalism.[37] Some people imagine that these "marks" will stand out in a socialist society like stains on a white tablecloth. But that has not been the case. The complexity of a modern socialist society is ascribable to the very fact that these "birthmarks" of capitalism and feudalism almost never stand out; they are the same "color" as the surrounding social reality. Only profound economic, political, and sociological analysis reveals the true nature of these "spots." Of course, we frequently encounter some defects of the former social formations in their traditional form. Stealing and bribe-taking are obvious examples. But more often the inherited defects are camouflaged as "socialist virtues."

Eighteenth-century philosophers argued about the interaction of social environment and human nature. "Man must be re-educated," some would say, "and then the social environment will change." "The social environment must be reshaped," said others, "and then people

---

[36] Marx-Engels, *Sochineniia,* 2nd edn., XXX, p. 226.
[37] *Ed.:* Medvedev is referring to Marx's *Critique of the Gotha Program,* which distinguishes a lower stage of socialism from a higher—the higher is called communism by the Leninists. On the lower stage such things as wage labor and the state are retained.

will change." The revolutionary experience of the twentieth century has given a fairly clear-cut answer to the question of the interaction between education and social environment. The October Revolution drastically changed almost all the old economic and political institutions. The old distinctions of class and property were erased. In the process, people also changed, especially those who took part in the Revolution. But changes in the nature and character of people proceeded much more slowly than economic and political transformations. It is therefore hardly surprising that many defects of the old society appeared in the new setting, often in a new form. Sometimes these defects distorted social relationships so pervasively that only the external form of a new relationship was preserved, while its essence became alien to socialism.

The analysis of these processes is crucial to an understanding of Soviet society. We cannot overlook the fact that along with the genuine thing sham socialism, or barrack socialism, became part of Soviet reality. The distinguishing feature of Stalinist pseudosocialism was the gross violation of humane principles, under cover of lying talk about love for the people and socialist ideals. There was of course nothing socialist in mass arrests and murders of innocent people, in the huge machine of terror, the system of prisons and camps with their semislave labor. Other features of pseudosocialism can be perceived outside the institutions of terror: in the countryside, where many collective farmers received next to nothing for their labor on the communal land and could live only off the produce of their household plots. Pseudosocialism is evident in official indifference and nastiness to ordinary people, in disregard for their needs, in bureaucracy and sectarianism. Laws that made criminals of people who were late to work or quit their jobs, even teenagers and women who had just miscarried, that sent *kolkhoz* women to Siberian exile for taking a bit of grain ("*za koloski*")—all these are examples of Stalinist pseudosocialism. It was not socialism to restrict the freedom to choose one's place of work or the right to change it.

A precise description of Stalinist pseudosocialism has been provided by the Soviet economist L. El'konin:[38]

> In broad historical perspective the Stalinist system can be regarded as a zigzag away from socialism on the USSR's path toward socialism. . . . But it was not simply a zigzag, not simply an unsuccessful variant of the movement toward socialism. In many essential features it was an *abandonment* of socialism. The great economic and cultural achievements won by the talent, labor, and heroism of our people for the sake of socialism were not placed in the service of socialism by the Stalinist system, with its ignorant, bureaucratic, and

[38] *Ed.:* This seems to be an unpublished manuscript.

antihuman methods borrowed from the terrorist forms of capitalism, and even from feudalism. . . .

But as the Stalinist system took our country, which was growing economically and culturally, with growing opportunities and growing demands, further and further away from socialism, the people were led to believe that they were not only building but had already built a socialist society. Thus, little by little, inevitably, the notion was fixed in people's minds that everything which constituted the political, ideological, and moral basis of Soviet society under Stalin was socialism: the cult of the state and worship of rank, the irresponsibility of those who hold power and the population's lack of rights, the hierarchy of privileges and the canonization of hypocrisy, the barrack system of social and intellectual life, the suppression of the individual and the destruction of independent thought, the environment of terror and suspicion, the atomization of people and the notorious "vigilance," the uncontrolled violence and the legalized cruelty. All of this was taken to be socialism.

But that is precisely how socialist society has been lampooned by ideologists of capitalism ever since the socialist movement appeared. The Stalinist system converted this hostile slander into reality. It could do this only by parasitizing the great works of our people, which was roused by October to the construction of socialism, by parasitizing its great faith in the final triumph of Leninist socialism and its great readiness to endure everything for the sake of that triumph. . . . The greatest tragedy of proletarian socialism, perhaps the greatest in its entire history, was the debasement and discrediting of socialism under the banner and in the name of socialism, in the epoch when mankind had begun the socialist revolution, in the very country that first began it and was called to serve as an example for other countries, and in the name of Lenin, a name connected by all people everywhere with the ideals of the socialist revolution. Without doubt this is Stalin's greatest crime, this besmirching, this betrayal of the cause of revolutionary socialism, the socialism of Marx and Lenin. This was a service to world capitalism unequalled by any of the enemies of socialism.

The task of Soviet historians, sociologists, philosophers, and economists is to disentangle the diverse elements of the Stalinist system, which included not only socialist relationships but also state-capitalist, semifeudal, and even—in the camps—state slaveholding relationships. There should be neither exaggeration nor minimizing of these elements of pseudosocialism. Many people, both counter-revolutionary enemies and also Social Democrats, have pointed out the pseudosocialist features of Soviet society, sometimes with considerable accuracy. But they usually reduce the whole political and economic system to forms of pseudosocialism, and therefore they have been unable to see the true nature of our social system, its sources of strength and perspectives of development.

A counterrevolutionary who escaped from a camp and reached Finland before the war is a good example. In the White émigré press he described the inhuman conditions in the camps, and the many defects of the Stalinist agrarian policy, from which he concluded:

> The country is waiting for a war to rebel. One cannot conceive of any defense of the "socialist fatherland" by the popular masses. On the contrary, no matter with whom the war may be and whatever the consequences of a military defeat, all bayonets and all pitchforks that can possibly be plunged in the back of the Red Army will surely be plunged. . . . Every muzhik knows that at the first shots of the war he will first of all knife the nearest chairman of a rural soviet, the chairman of his collective farm, etc., and those people know perfectly well that they will be knifed in the first days of a war. . . .

The Nazi leaders must have fed on just such prophecies when they shouted that Russia was a colossus with feet of clay, that Russia would collapse like a house of cards with the first Red Army defeat. Those prophets of doom were savagely mocked by the actual course of events.

But the Soviet people and its friends abroad frequently fell into an opposite error. Observing the achievements of the Soviet Union and the elements of truly socialist relationships, they did not see and did not want to see many manifestations of pseudosocialism. As a result they could not understand the nature of the complex social and political processes in the Soviet Union, and therefore the exposure of the cult of Stalin's personality took them by surprise. It is impossible to comprehend Soviet society if one recognizes only the features of barrack pseudosocialism that were established by Stalin and the Stalinists. But it is also impossible if one sees only the truly socialist relationships. The distinguishing characteristic of the Stalinist epoch and of the succeeding period has been not only the struggle between socialism and capitalism in their open manifestations but also the struggle between socialism and barrack pseudosocialism. Some form of that struggle was unavoidable. But the particularly savage forms, and the temporary triumph of pseudosocialism, were avoidable. With different leadership there would have been very different results.

5

ONLY THE MOST DANGEROUS consequences of Stalin's arbitrary rule have been discussed. They affected social and national relationships and moral norms; they altered many forms of political organization, methods of government and of economic management. Social psychology, ideology, literature, science, art, even everyday patterns of life suffered perverse change. Yet the consequences of Stalin's cult are not irreversible. Reform began immediately after his death. The effects of the cult were perversions and diseased growths, but they did not destroy the main features of the epoch of transition from capitalism to socialism and the downfall of imperialism.

However great the influence of certain individuals on the course of history, it cannot cancel out the basic patterns (*zakonomernosti, Gesetzmässigkeiten*) of the historical process. Stalin was not the only leader in the country. Many other forces were at work. Both the people and the Party worked for socialism and put it into effect despite many internal and external obstacles. Stalin tried to belittle Lenin, but Leninism was not destroyed and continued to influence ideology and social consciousness both at home and abroad. Stalin did great harm to the nation's defense capacity, but the Soviet people overcame all difficulties to defend their native land and defeat fascism. Stalinism had a great influence on the psychology and morality of Soviet people, but it could not stop the spread of a truly socialist morality and a new socialist psychology. Some elements of national hostility reappeared under Stalin, but friendship among the peoples and the republics continued to gain ground. Stalin weakened the alliance between the workers and the peasants but he did not destroy its foundation. Stalin perverted the methods of leadership; even so he was obliged to reckon with the opinions and wills of Soviet people. Thus, if only indirectly, the people exerted considerable influence on the direction of state affairs. Stalin held back science and literature, but he could not repress them altogether. He slowed down but did not halt the development of the world socialist revolution.

Inevitably one must ask whether or to what degree the dictatorship of the proletariat was preserved in the years of the cult. Various historians and sociologists, Marxists included, give various answers. Some Marxists maintain that there was in fact no dictatorship of the workers but only the dictatorship of a single individual, of single chiefs. But such an approach would lead to the conclusion that the Egyptian pharaohs, the Chinese emperors, and the Russian tsars were not representatives of certain classes. That cannot be. There is no such thing as an individual standing outside of a class and not carrying out the policy of a class. The dictatorship of Napoleon, for example, was a dictatorship of the big bourgeoisie, though not all of Napoleon's actions corresponded to the interests of that class.

Most Soviet historians believe that Stalin's personal dictatorship did not completely abolish the dictatorship of the proletariat. In this view, which the author shares, Stalin introduced many bureaucratic distortions into the system of the proletarian dictatorship, but he could not completely destroy the system. He received his mandate from the proletarian Leninist Party, after the victory of a socialist revolution. He did a poor job of carrying out the historical mission assigned to him by the Party and the proletariat, but he did carry it out to some extent, not only in the twenties, as G. Pomerants writes, but also in the thirties and forties—in the struggle against imperialism, for example. Lenin said that the Soviet Union is a workers' state with bureaucratic distortions. Under Stalin those distortions became more dangerous, but the whole political system cannot be reduced to them. Unlimited personal power was a form, the worst possible form, of the proletarian dictatorship; it was clearly inconsistent with the nature of the regime and severely checked progress toward communism.

Some historians suggest that a peculiar dual power[39] existed under Stalin. On the one hand there was the dictatorship of the proletariat, on the other the petty-bourgeois dictatorship of Stalin's clique. In other words, power was shared by proletarian activists and by careerists and degenerates.

Finally, there are historians who recognize the essentially socialist nature of the economic base but believe that the state lost the character of a dictatorship of the proletariat. They draw such analogies as a society that is completely capitalist in its socioeconomic make-up but has a monarchical government reflecting primarily the interests of the nobility and landowners. In particular one can point to post-Napoleonic France or to Germany in the 1860's. A socialist economic formation, unlike capitalism, can arise only as a result of a socialist revolution and the dictatorship of the proletariat. However, once it has arisen, the socialist economic base becomes stable and can exist even when the nature of the state has changed. If, for example, state power falls into the hands of nonproletarian elements, it does not automatically follow that the economy will cease to be socialist. It may happen that these nonproletarian—e.g., petty-bourgeois and bureaucratic—elements will have to accept the major social changes and try to adapt to them. Lenin noted the possibility of such a course of events when he told the XIth Party Congress in 1922 that "the machine of power may go in the wrong direction." Some historians believe that something of this sort happened in the years of the cult.

These theories need to be investigated by historians, economists, and sociologists. In any event, the dangerous consequences of Stalin's arbitrary rule must neither be exaggerated nor understated. In the last years of the cult the nation looked like a fairly healthy organism only externally. The disease that was eating away society and the state was skillfully hidden. Only a determined exposé of Stalin's cult, only bold if painful surgical intervention, enabled the Soviet people to see how mortally dangerous that disease really was.

[39] *Ed.: Dvoevlastie,* the word that Lenin used to describe the coexistence of the Provisional Government and the Soviets in 1917.

Conclusion

1

DECREPITUDE MARKED the last years of Stalin's life, following his seventieth birthday in 1949. The old despot became more and more suspicious. Few were allowed to know where he would be at any given moment, in the Kremlin or at one of his dachas. The woods surrounding the dachas were filled with traps and mines. The corps of guards, under his direct command, grew larger. Everyone who was summoned to a reception was carefully searched. None of them, even a Politburo member, ever knew how such a reception would end: with his arrest or his return home. For the most part Stalin lived in complete isolation, both in his Kremlin apartment and in his dachas. Isolation gave rise to strange habits. He began, for example, to cut pictures out of magazines and newspapers and make them into montages that he stuck to the walls of his rooms and office. To argue with Stalin, to dispute any of his opinions, was equivalent to suicide. One could only agree with him, since it was known a priori that Stalin never made wrong decisions. Officials called in to play chess with him were warned not to win.

In these years, Stalin even became suspicious of such devoted aides as Molotov, Kaganovich, Voroshilov, and Poskrebyshev. Molotov's wife was arrested and exiled, Poskrebyshev's wife was arrested, and Kaganovich's brother was driven to suicide. More and more these chief aides were excluded from important decision making. They were no longer summoned to Politburo meetings. Shortly before the XIXth Party Congress of 1952, Stalin publicly called Molotov and Voroshilov British spies and Mikoian a Turkish spy. At a dinner with literary people Stalin called Alexis Tolstoy, Ilya Ehrenburg, and Peter Pavlenko international spies.[1] None of these people was arrested. At the XIXth Congress Molotov, Kaganovich, Voroshilov, and Mikoian were

---

[1] A. Fadeev, who was at the dinner, reported the comment to his friend N. K. Iliukhov. *Ed.:* Tolstoy, Ehrenburg, and Pavlenko were very successful writers in the Stalin era. So was Fadeev, who became an alcoholic and committed suicide in 1956.

re-elected to the Politburo, which was renamed the Presidium and
swamped with new members. For the moment Stalin was probably
concerned not so much with destroying these former aides as with
scaring them. Similarly, his personal secretary Poskrebyshev, who had
attended him for over fifteen years, was barred from the Kremlin. He
spent the last months before Stalin's death at his dacha awaiting arrest.

The "doctors' case" and the so-called Mingrelian case, which led
to the arrest of many of Beria's creatures—and many honorable
officials as well—in Georgia,[2] caused Beria himself to be banished
from Stalin's presence. The press began to stress once again the thesis
of intensified class struggle as the country moved forward. On January
13, 1953, *Pravda* denounced "right opportunists . . . who take the
anti-Marxist position that the class struggle is dying out. . . . The more
we progress, the more intense will be the struggle of enemies of the
people." On January 31 and February 6 *Pravda* repeated the charge,
this time describing the people who were allegedly creating new,
widespread counterrevolutionary organizations:

> Fragments of the shattered exploiting classes, . . . masked epigones
> of defeated anti-Soviet groups—Mensheviks, S-R's, Trotskyites,
> Bukharinites, bourgeois nationalists . . . all sorts of degenerate ele-
> ments—people who kowtow to all things foreign, pilferers of social-
> ist property. . . . The Anglo-American imperialists are now placing
> their bets on such people.[3]

All the signs pointed to another 1937. Only Stalin's death at the beginning of March, 1953, prevented a renewal of mass repression.

Stalin died of a brain hemorrhage in one of his dachas near
Moscow. Many of the circumstances are still unclear. The story goes
that Stalin, who spent his evenings in complete isolation, did not ask
for his dinner on time. His guards were worried, but could not bring
themselves to open the iron-bound door to his room. Only a few hours
later, after they called the Presidium and some members arrived, was
the door opened. And only at that point were the doctors finally called.
Stalin died hard. Among the few truthful pages in his daughter's insincere, highly distorted book is the description of his death.

> My father died a difficult and terrible death. . . . For the last twelve
> hours the lack of oxygen was acute. His face altered and became
> dark. His lips turned black and the features grew unrecognizable.
> The last hours were nothing but a slow strangulation. The death
> agony was horrible. He literally choked to death as we watched. At
> what seemed like the very last moment he suddenly opened his eyes

[2] See *Ocherki po istorii KP Gruzii* (Tbilisi, 1963), p. 248. *Ed.:* For the doctors' case, see
above, pp. 494–95. The Mingrelians, a subgroup of the Georgian nationality, were
charged with nationalism in 1951.
[3] *Pravda,* Feb. 6, 1953.

and cast a glance over everyone in the room. It was a terrible glance, insane or perhaps angry and full of the fear of death and the unfamiliar faces of the doctors bent over him. The glance swept over everyone in a second. Then something incomprehensible and awesome happened that to this day I can't forget and don't understand. He suddenly lifted his left hand as though he were pointing to something above and bringing down a curse on us all. The gesture was incomprehensible and full of menace, and no one could say to whom or at what it might be directed. The next moment, after a final effort, the spirit wrenched itself free of the flesh.[4]

Stalin's death was indirectly the cause of one more tragedy. During the time he lay in state millions of people crowded into central Moscow to pay their last respects to this man whom they knew so little, whom they had trusted so long. Because of the authorities' incompetent organization, the crowd got out of hand. Hundreds, perhaps thousands, of Soviet people perished, trampled to death by other Soviet people, blinded by the cult of Stalin's person. In those same days the NKVD arrested hundreds of people in Moscow alone, as part of the "mobilization plan" of preventive arrests, designed for war or any serious domestic or foreign complications. This plan was put into partial effect while Stalin lay in state. But those were probably the last tragedies connected with Stalin's name. A new era began, which requires special study and analysis.

2

THE EVALUATION of Stalin's activity has attracted many bourgeois as well as Soviet historians. Bourgeois historians typically see Stalin as the greatest leader of the world Communist movement after Lenin, whose actions changed not only the face of Russia but of the whole world. While acknowledging and to some degree condemning Stalin's crimes, the typical bourgeois historian tries to prove that socialism could not have been built in the USSR without such crimes, without a barbarous totalitarian state. Stalin's activity is seen as the logical continuation of Lenin's, of the program and methods of socialism in general. Isaac Deutscher, one of Stalin's best-known biographers, propounded this view.[5] Telling the story of industrialization and collectivi-

---

[4] Svetlana Alliluyeva, *Twenty Letters to a Friend,* trans. P. J. McMillan (New York, 1967), p. 10.

[5] *Ed.:* Medvedev cites a 1962 Stuttgart edition of Deutscher's *Stalin: A Political Biography.* He seems unaware of Deutscher's ideological position, which places him among the "socialists and revisionists of various persuasions." He was a Polish Jewish Communist, expelled in 1932 for Trotskyism, who kept the faith that democratic socialism would someday triumph over Stalinism in the Soviet Union.

zation, Deutscher called Stalin the greatest reformer of all times and nations. Lenin and Trotsky led the October Revolution and gave the Soviet people the ideas of socialism, but only Stalin put these ideas into effect. The price was very high, but Deutscher saw in that fact merely proof of the difficulty of the task. Similarly the West German bourgeois newspaper *Die Welt* declared that Stalin transformed Russia from a backward agrarian country into a mighty industrial power capable of resisting the Germans, as tsarist Russia could never have done. To the question whether the misery and destruction of millions were really necessary in order for Russia to keep her independence, *Die Welt* has no answer. This is allegedly one of the great enigmas of history.[6]

Marxist historiography should reject such reasoning. It was not Stalin who inspired the people with the ideas of socialism or taught them to read and write, as the article in *Die Welt* claims. The door to education and culture was opened by the October Revolution. The great transformation would have been effected much more quickly if Stalin had not destroyed hundreds of thousands of the intelligentsia, both old and new. Prisoners in Stalin's concentration camps accomplished a great deal, building almost all the canals and hydroelectric stations, many railways, industrial plants, oil pipelines, even tall buildings in Moscow. But industry would have developed faster if these millions of innocent people had worked as free men. Likewise, the use of force against the peasantry slowed down the growth rate of agriculture, with painful effects on the whole Soviet economy to the present day. It is an incontrovertible, arithmetically demonstrable fact that Stalin did not choose the shortest path; he did not speed up, he slowed down the movement toward socialism and communism.

Many socialists and revisionists of various persuasions take a view of Stalin that is essentially similar to that of the bourgeois historians. Pietro Nenni, for example, asks what enabled Stalin to win and hold power, and answers: "More than any other Bolshevik leader he had absorbed 'Russian reality.' "[7] Intent on escaping from the notion that one man was responsible for the multitude of events and processes associated with Stalin's name, Nenni simply identifies Stalinism with "the Communism of three decades, from the death of Lenin to the death of Stalin."[8] Djilas expands on this theme. He calls Stalin "the greatest criminal in history," yet warns against injustice in the final appraisal:

---

[6] *Die Welt,* Mar. 5, 1963.
[7] Nenni, *Le prospettive dei socialismo dopo la destalinizzazione* (Turin, 1962). Medvedev quotes a Russian translation, *Perspektivy sotsializma posle destalinizatsil* (Moscow?, 1963), p. 16.
[8] *Ibid.,* p. 5.

What he wished to accomplish, and even that which he did accomplish, could not be accomplished in any other way. The forces that swept him forward and that he led, with their absolute ideals, could have no other kind of leader but him, given that level of Russian and world relations, nor could they have been served by different methods. The creator of a closed social system, he was at the same time its instrument and, in changed circumstances and all too late, he became its victim. Unsurpassed in violence and crime, Stalin was no less the leader and organizer of a certain social system.[9]

The main point of such arguments is clear: if the socialist system created in the USSR could not have been created in any other way than by monstrous crimes, it follows that in the future the Soviet Union should refrain from making any more such experiments and renounce the dictatorship of the proletariat. By maintaining that Stalin's lawlessness derived from the very essence of socialism, from Marxism-Leninism, from the proletarian revolution, the revisionists try to compromise the ideas of socialism, Marxism-Leninism, and the proletarian revolution in the eyes of the masses. They try to transfer to the whole social system the disillusionment and anger that rise in people when they learn of Stalinist crimes.

Dogmatists and Stalinists of various persuasions take a different point of view. They depict Stalin's crimes as *mistakes*, serious ones, to be sure, but still limited. "We know," wrote Molotov, "that particular mistakes, sometimes serious mistakes, are inevitable in carrying out such great and important historical tasks. No one has or can have any guarantees on this score."[10] The Chinese newspaper *People's Daily*, in 1956 and 1957 articles on Stalin, was equally lenient.[11] Another series of articles between 1963 and 1965 was even more lenient. "The Communist Party of China," said an editorial on September 13, 1963,

has always believed that Stalin did make certain mistakes. These mistakes had both epistemological and sociohistorical roots. . . . Some of these were mistakes of a principled character, others were connected with concrete work; some mistakes could have been avoided, but others were hard to avoid in the absence of any precedent for a dictatorship of the proletariat. . . . In the course of the struggle inside and outside of the Party, Stalin sometimes confused the two different kinds of contradictions, those between enemies and ourselves and those within the people, and he therefore confused the different methods of resolving these two kinds of contradictions. In the course of the struggle to root out counterrevolution,

---

[9] Milovan Djilas, *Conversations with Stalin*, trans. M. B. Petrovich (New York, 1962), pp. 187, 190, 191.

[10] *Pravda*, Apr. 22, 1957. See also *Stenograficheskii otchet XXII s'ezda KPSS*, II, p. 224.

[11] See *Narodnyi Kitai*, 1957, No. 2, prilozhenie, p. 7.

which was carried out under Stalin's leadership, many counterrevolutionaries who needed to be punished were justly punished,
but innocent people were also mistakenly condemned. Thus, in
1937 and 1938, there were errors and excesses in the struggle with
the counterrevolution.

The editorial goes on to an amazingly "dialectical" conclusion:
Stalin's mistakes were useful, for they provided a lesson to other
Communists. Stalin is compared to August Bebel and Rosa Luxemburg,
whom Lenin respected as revolutionaries though they too made mistakes, and the Chinese paper sums up with a Russian saying: "Eagles
occasionally drop down lower than chickens, but chickens can never
rise like eagles."

The authors of such "dialectical reasoning," who are themselves
committing monstrous crimes both against their own Party and people
and against the whole international Communist movement, are also
completely ignorant of the historical facts. In 1936–38 Stalin was not
engaged in a real struggle with counterrevolutionaries. On the contrary, it was Stalin whose actions in those years were objectively like
a counterrevolutionary's. The main tendency of the mass repression of
1936–38 was an assault on the Party, on old Bolshevik cadres, on
proletarian revolutionaries, on the intelligentsia that were honorably
serving the interests of the masses. Of course real counterrevolutionaries were occasionally caught up in the vast flood of arrests. But they
were rare cases. "In the seventeen years I spent in Stalinist prisons
and camps," A. V. Snegov writes in his "Open Letter to Mao Tse-
tung," "I saw no counterrevolutionaries." The memoirs of Ia. I.
Drobinskii, former *gorkom* secretary from Belorussia, tell a bitterly
ironic episode. A real Polish spy, an officer in the intelligence section
of the Polish General Staff, was suddenly put in a cell in Minsk Prison
full of Party activists and Soviet officers. The Pole was utterly astonished, and the Communists, especially the army men, were hostile to
him. At one point the Pole got angry and asked a Major Notman:
"What do you want from me? I am a Polish citizen, a Polish nationalist, an officer and a patriot, in a Soviet prison. That is normal,
that is absolutely normal. But why are you, a Soviet patriot and a
Communist, in a Soviet prison? That is completely incomprehensible
to me, and not at all normal. Can you explain it to me?" Naturally no
one could. Subsequently the Pole was exchanged for a Soviet intelligence agent, while most of the Soviet officers from the same cell
were shot.

Unfortunately, many articles, speeches, and books on Party history
are beginning to revive the story of Stalin's "particular mistakes,"
though the XXIInd Party Congress rejected it. *Essays in the History
of the CPSU* (*Ocherki istorii KPSS*), published in 1966 as a textbook

for schools on the fundamentals of Marxism-Leninism, is a typical example of such writing.

The second thesis advocated today by many dogmatists and Stalinists could be called balancing. They concede that Stalin committed some mistakes and even crimes or, as it is usually said, "violations of revolutionary legality," which were not necessary for the building of socialism. But Stalin also accomplished a great deal, they say. He was a great Marxist-Leninist and Communist, a great theorist and practical leader. If we put all his crimes and mistakes on one side of the scales and his achievements on the other, the second side far outweighs the first. One dogmatist has even declared that Stalin's record is 30 per cent crime and 70 per cent accomplishment. The Peking *People's Daily* urged this view in 1956 and again in 1963:

> All of Stalin's activity is closely connected with the struggle of the great Communist Party of the Soviet Union and the great people and is inseparable from the revolutionary struggle of the peoples of the whole world. Stalin's life and activity are the life and activity of a great Marxist-Leninist, a great proletarian revolutionary. . . . If Stalin's merits are compared with his mistakes, his merits are greater than his mistakes.

Many such evaluations appeared in the Soviet press, especially in the period before the XXIInd Party Congress of 1961. The article on Stalin in the *Great Soviet Encyclopedia,* which went to press in November, 1960, declared: "His name is inseparable from Marxism-Leninism. It would be a very gross distortion of historical truth to extend the mistakes Stalin made in the last years of his life to the entire period of his leadership." Even today there are people who are beginning to revive, if not in the press then by word of mouth, the old myth of Stalin as a great leader, whose name is inseparable from the Party, from Marxism-Leninism.

Genuine Communists cannot pose the question in such a way: "Which were greater, Stalin's accomplishments or crimes?" Such a formulation contains a hidden suggestion, that great merits give someone the right to commit certain crimes. It would be immoral to suggest that a man who has saved a thousand people from death can receive an indulgence from history and then with impunity can kill one or two hundred innocent people. While the Soviet Union made progress in the years of Stalin's rule, it does not follow that Stalin was a staunch Communist and a great Marxist-Leninist. A good army can win even under a poor commander. And in the given case, as we have shown, the great achievements of the Party and the people in the thirties and the forties were achieved by them in spite of Stalin's mistakes and crimes.

Stalin was a leader in hard times. He did enjoy the confidence of a majority of the Party and the people. That confidence, that faith of the common people in Stalin, to some degree helped them endure the hardships of economic construction and the war with fascism. But would not the solidarity between the people and the government have been stronger had there been no mass repression? Would not the people have shown the Central Committee more confidence if the best people in the Party, government, economic, and military *apparat* had not been destroyed in the mid-thirties? Would not economic and cultural progress have been much greater if Stalin had not destroyed thousands upon thousands of scientists, engineers, teachers, doctors, writers? Would not the war have ended much faster and with fewer losses if our finest officers had not perished before the war and if Stalin had conducted a more sensible foreign and military policy? Would not agriculture have achieved greater progress if Stalin had not grossly and constantly violated Lenin's plan for agricultural co-operatives? And the bureaucracy and rule by fiat, the multitude of mistakes in nationality policy, the inhumanity and willfulness of Stalinist administration—could all this in any measure strengthen the solidarity of the Soviet people, the friendship among the peoples of the Soviet Union? What then do we have to thank Stalin for? For the fact that his thirty-year rule did not completely ruin the Party, the army, Soviet democracy, agriculture, and industry? For the fact that he did not completely pervert Leninism and the proletarian character of the October Revolution, that he did not destroy all honorable Soviet people, did not bring the country to catastrophe?

Stalin was for thirty years the helmsman of the ship of state, clutching its steering wheel with a grip of death. Dozens of times he steered it onto reefs and shoals and far off course. Shall we be grateful to him because he did not manage to sink it altogether?

Of course, Stalin made some correct decisions and expressed some correct ideas. But it would be wrong to lay special stress on these relatively insignificant merits, which—if we are to use the theory of balancing—are far fewer than his crimes and mistakes. For Stalin was no hereditary monarch whom the people, in obedience to tradition, were supposed to endure, accepting him and his faults as something coming from god. The Party is a political organization of like-minded people; its leader is supposed to be its most worthy member. That is the sole criterion that should guide the people in electing a Party leader and in making an historical evaluation of one. And Stalin does not begin to meet this criterion.

In the past many people valued Stalin highly, not knowing of his crimes. But today his crimes have been exposed by the Party. Thus it is impossible to understand how there can still be those who try to place him on a pedestal. Any rehabilitation of Stalin would be a grave crime against the Party, a cynical outrage to its basic principles. "To restore respect for Stalin, knowing what he did," the philosopher G. Pomerants wrote not long ago,

> is to establish something new, to establish respect for denunciations, tortures, executions. Even Stalin did not try to do that. He preferred to play the hypocrite. To restore respect for Stalin is to set up a moral monstrosity near our banner. This has never happened before. Loathsome things have been done, but our banner has remained unsullied. On it was written: "An association in which the free development of each is the condition for the free development of all." Near the banner are Marx, Engels, Lenin—people who had human weaknesses, but people . . . Stalin can no longer be placed alongside of them. To do so is to rub filth on our own banner.[12]

In 1917 there was no one who could have taken the place of Lenin. But in the twenties and thirties there were several leaders who could have headed the Party and led it forward much faster and better than Stalin. This must be taken into consideration when we evaluate Stalin's role in history. The job he did so poorly could have been done far more effectively by others. Stalinism cannot be regarded as the Marxism-Leninism or the Communism of three decades. It is the perversions that Stalin introduced into the theory and practice of the Communist movement. It is a phenomenon profoundly alien to Marxism-Leninism, it is pseudocommunism and pseudosocialism.

Many great men have had shortcomings and weaknesses. To contemporaries at times the faults seemed considerable, but subsequently they were forgotten in favor of the essential merits. That cannot be the case with Stalin. His lawlessness will never be forgotten. Humanity can never take pride in him.

Stalin himself was sensitive to the opinion of history. Like many tyrants, he wanted to rule over the future as he did over his own times. He had monuments erected to himself in every conceivable place; he renamed cities and factories for himself; he destroyed people whose accomplishments might overshadow his own in the eyes of posterity. But no one can rule over the court of history. It has severely condemned Stalin, as it condemns all those who promote lawlessness. "Evil rulers," says an Eastern proverb, "find no refuge even in the grave. Posterity pursues their memory, and twenty centuries cannot wipe the disgrace from them."

History cannot hide the truth if it wants to remain a science. And many more bitter truths must be told about the times of the cult of

---

[12] *Ed.:* Pomerants, *op. cit.* on p. 429.

personality. We must also discuss what must be done in order not to repeat the mistakes of the past. Socialism does not generate lawlessness, as its enemies maintain. But we know now that socialism in itself is no guarantee against lawlessness and the abuse of power.

Some may wonder whether the tragedy of 1937 was not inevitable even if Stalin had not headed the Party. I think not. The tragedy certainly could have been avoided. In this respect the epoch of which I have written is still more evidence that the individual plays a great role in history. Of course various sociopolitical tendencies existed in Soviet society and the Party from the beginning. But the triumph of one or another was to a large extent determined by the personality that led the Party at one or another moment. That epoch also offers evidence of the decisive role played by the masses in history. For it was the masses, aroused by the socialist revolution, who managed to check and later to overcome many of the harmful consequences of the cult of Stalin's personality.

The Soviet Union passed through a serious disease and lost many of its finest sons. When the cult of Stalin's personality was exposed a great step was made to recovery. But not everything connected with Stalinism is behind us, by no means everything. The process of purifying the Communist movement, of washing out all the layers of Stalinist filth, is not yet finished. It must be carried through to the end.

August, 1962–August, 1968

INDEX

INDEX

iii

A NOTE ABOUT THE EDITORS

David Joravsky is professor of history at Northwestern University. Born in Chicago in 1925, he received his B.A. from the University of Pennsylvania and his Ph.D. from Columbia University. He has also taught at the University of Connecticut and Brown University. Mr. Joravsky is the author of *Soviet Marxism and Natural Science, 1917–32* (1961) and *The Lysenko Affair* (1970). He has contributed articles and reviews to the *New York Review of Books, The Nation, Scientific American, Science, Slavic Review,* and *The American Historical Review.* Mr. Joravsky lives in Evanston, Illinois, with his wife and two children.

Georges Haupt is professor of history at the École Pratique des Hautes Études in Paris. He was born in Satu Mare, Romania, in 1928 and was awarded graduate degrees in history from the University of Leningrad and the University of Paris. From 1968 to 1970 he was a visiting professor at the University of Wisconsin. He is married and resides in Paris.

A NOTE ON THE TYPE

The text of this book was set on the Linotype in a type face called LIFE. Brought out by the German type foundry of Ludwig and Mayer in 1964, Life is an adaptation by Francisco Simoncini of Times Roman, the popular British type face. Designed especially for use in a newspaper, Times Roman is widely appreciated for its legibility. Life, with its angular points exaggerated to compensate for loss of detail in reproduction, seems ideally suited for both text and newspaper settings.

This book was composed by
Cherry Hill Composition, Pennsauken, New Jersey,
and printed and bound by
Haddon Craftsmen, Scranton, Pennsylvania.
Typography and binding design by
CHRISTINE AULICINO.